P9-EDY-116

CRIME AND CRIMINOLOGY

CRIME AND CRIMINOLOGY

SIXTH EDITION

Sue Titus Reid, J.D., Ph.D.

PROFESSOR OF PUBLIC ADMINISTRATION AND
DIRECTOR OF DEVELOPMENT, COLLEGE OF SOCIAL SCIENCES
FLORIDA STATE UNIVERSITY

Holt, Rinehart and Winston, Inc.
Fort Worth   Chicago   San Francisco   Philadelphia
Montreal   Toronto   London   Sydney   Tokyo

Publisher: Ted Buchholz
Aquisitions Editor: Chris Klein
Project Editor: Mike Hinshaw
Production Manager: Ken Dunaway
Art & Design Supervisor: Serena Barnett

Credits and permissions acknowledgment are on page 687.
Library of Congress Cataloging-in-Publication Data

Reid, Sue Titus.
  Crime and criminology / Sue Titus Reid.—6th ed.
    p.   cm.
  Includes index.
  ISBN 0-03-035302-5
    1. Criminology.   2. Crime—United States.   3. Criminal justice,
Administration of—United States.   I. Title.
HV6025.R515 1991
364—dc20   90-5168
                                                        CIP

Copyright © 1991, 1988, 1985, 1979, 1976 by Holt, Rinehart and Winston, Inc.

All rights reserved. No part of this publication may be reproduced or transmitted in any form or by any means, electronic or mechanical, including photocopy, recording, or any information storage and retrieval system, without permission in writing from the publisher.

Requests for permission to make copies of any part of the work should be mailed to the Copyrights and Permissions Department, Eighth Floor, Holt, Rinehart and Winston, Inc., 6277 Sea Harbor Drive, Orlando, Florida 32887.

Address for editorial correspondence: Holt, Rinehart and Winston, Inc., 301 Commerce Street, Suite 3700, Fort Worth, TX 76102

Address for orders: Holt, Rinehart and Winston, Inc., 6277 Sea Harbor Drive, Orlando, Florida 32887. 1-800-782-4479, or 1-800-433-0001 (in Florida)

PRINTED IN THE UNITED STATES OF AMERICA
1 2 3 4   049   9 8 7 6 5 4 3 2

Holt, Rinehart and Winston, Inc.
The Dryden Press
Saunders College Publishing

DEDICATION
To
Donald M. Dewey, M.D.
Fredrick A. Koehler, M.D.
and
Charles H. Wingo, M.D.
with my appreciation for your excellent medical care

Preface to the Sixth Edition

As a discipline, criminology must be concerned with the causes of crime—the traditional emphasis of sociologists—but also with the criminal justice system and corrections. Therefore, this text reflects my training in both sociology and law.

During my years of teaching criminology to undergraduates, I have been impressed with their eagerness to learn how law relates to the traditional topics covered in the course, even to the point of their enjoying reading judicial opinions. Thus, excerpts from appellate opinions have been used to illustrate some concepts and to demonstrate the role of the courts in the reformation of the criminal justice system. To minimize the need for supplementary materials, the text also provides the results of sociological research—both historical and contemporary— on the criminal justice system. Summaries and critiques of classic works in criminology, analyses of recent sociological research, and attention to major sociological theorists who have contributed significantly to the study of crime are also included.

The response to the five previous editions of this text indicates that students and faculty find the integration of law and social science to be a viable approach to the study of criminal behavior. No less important to users of earlier editions has been the assessment of society's response to criminal behavior. Therefore the basic format has been retained, but with some significant changes.

The organization of the text remains essentially the same, although the coverage is changed. In addition to updating all social science discussions and legal cases, the inserts have all been carefully checked for relevance. Some classic examples and illustrations are retained, but many of the inserts are new, reflecting recent changes in the criminal justice system and in criminology. Special attempts were made to include current news items that illustrate a concept or idea discussed in the text.

Part I, "Introduction to the Study of Crime and Criminology," introduces the study of criminology, with Chapter 1, "Crime, Criminal Law, and Criminology," explaining and analyzing the concept of crime. This chapter includes expanded coverage of criminology and the nature of criminal law and criminal defenses.

Chapter 2, "The Measurement of Crime and Its Impact," focuses on the accumulation of crime data through both official and unofficial methods, utilizing the most recent data available during the final stages of production of the manuscript. A new section on the National Incident-Based Reporting System (NABRS) was added, along with a brief description of the National Youth Survey (NYS).

Part II, "Explanations of Criminal Behavior," follows the same organization as in the previous edition, including four chapters on causation. Chapter 3, "Early Explanations of Criminal Behavior and Their Modern Counterparts," opens with a brief introduction to the methods of studying crime and then explores the historical explanations of criminal behavior that have strongly influenced modern developments. The influence of the classical and positive schools of thought are explained, contrasted, and related to current philosophies of punishment and sentencing. In this chapter, some modern implications of the impact of drugs on criminal behavior is discussed in relationship to deterrence, but the importance of drugs in studying crime has resulted in including a discussion in other chapters as well.

Chapter 4, "Biological and Psychological Theories," covers topics that appeared in earlier editions, such as the historical development of biology and psychology as explanations of criminal behavior, along with the more recent emphasis on the effect of alcohol and other drugs on criminal behavior. Biological and psychological-based issues such as the use of the battered woman's syndrome as a defense in criminal cases are also discussed. Another new feature is a brief discussion of the economic cost of substance abuse and crime.

Part II concludes with two chapters on sociological explanations of criminal behavior. Chapter 5, "Sociological Theories of Criminal Behavior I: Social-Structural Approach," focuses on the relationship between social structure and criminal behavior. Chapter 6, "Sociological Theories of Criminal Behavior II: Social-Process Theories," focuses on the processes by which criminal behavior may be acquired. These two chapters follow the same format as the previous edition, but the material has been updated. Social scientists continue to contribute to our understanding of criminal behavior through their careful research and data analyses, and their contributions since the publication of the fifth edition of this text have been included. Chapter 5 also contains new sections on gangs and on family structure and crime. The discussion of critical criminology has been completely rewritten and simplified. Chapter 6 contains new material on most sociological process theories as well as on females and crime and the relationship of pornography to crime. The latter issue gained national attention when Ted Bundy, just prior to his January, 1989 execution, attributed his acts of violence to pornography.

Part III, "Typologies of Crime," retains the same basic organization as that of the fifth edition, which represented significant changes from previous editions. Chapter 7, "Crimes of Violence," has been illustrated with numerous recent examples of violence, such as the Lisa Steinberg murder and the Central Park gang rape and battering of a bright female who was working her way up the ladder of success on Wall Street. A new section on incest between mothers and sons has been added, thus questioning the traditional stereotype that views incest as a problem only between male aggressors and female victims. Additional information is also given on female battering of males, and a new discussion on gun control reflects the growing concern with that issue in society today.

Chapter 8, "Property Crimes," contains updated coverage of all major and minor property crimes. Particular attention is given to such crimes as credit card theft as well as the problems of repeat offenders. Chapter 9, "Crimes of the Business World," was new to the fifth edition and coverage of the subject has been expanded in this edition, along with the use of recent incidents, such as the Alaska oil spill, to illustrate such crimes as environmental pollution. A new section on fraud is also included, as well as recent sociological theory developments on crimes in the business world.

Chapter 10, "Organized Crime and Terrorism," was a new chapter in the fifth edition, featuring an expanded discussion of organized crime and an added section on terrorism. This edition updates the data on terroristic acts (such as sentences of the convicted defendants) and adds discussions of terrorist acts that have occurred since the publication of the fifth edition of this text, such as the bombing of Pan Am Flight 103. The terrorism section also features new information on treason and sedition, including recent trials, and more information on political crimes and radical theory. The first successful prosecution on product tampering, a terroristic act that has gained world-wide attention in recent years, is also discussed. New information on organized crime updates previous discussions and adds such topics as hate groups, organized crime among Asians in the U.S., and recent prosecutions of organized criminals.

Part IV, "The Criminal Justice System," was reduced from five chapters to three in the fifth edition because many departments offer separate courses in criminal justice and corrections. That change was widely accepted and has been retained in this edition. Part IV retains coverage of the important elements of the criminal justice system but offers briefer discussions. Chapter 11, "The American System of Criminal Justice," introduces the reader to the procedures, stages, and steps of the criminal justice system. This chapter, with its overall discussion of the constitutional rights of defendants, sets the stage for the subsequent chapters in Part IV. This discussion is enhanced with a brief section on the concept of equal protection. The importance of defendants' rights is highlighted by a discussion of the case of a man who served 21 years in prison (including time on death row) for murders that later evidence indicates he did not commit. Discussions on search and seizure and other defendants' rights, along with victims' rights, have been updated and illustrated with recent court decisions.

Chapter 12, "The Police," retains the same outline with the addition of historical background and an emphasis on the importance of discretion in policing. In addition to significant updating, this chapter contains a new section on community-oriented policing and expanded discussions on police stress, stop and search, race and arrests, and police violence. The exclusionary rule discussion is updated with the Supreme Court's most recent cases in this area.

Chapter 13, "The Court System," contains an overview of the criminal justice processes that occur in the courts, from pretrial to posttrial. This chapter is extremely important despite the fact that its discussions of necessity must be condensed. Significant changes in the court system, especially in sentencing, are an important part of this chapter. The Supreme Court's recent cases on capital punishment, including those relating to juveniles and the mentally retarded, are featured, along with the Court's recent holding regarding the new federal sentencing guidelines. The chapter also features expanded discussions of defense and prosecution and updated bail release data.

Part V, "Social Reaction to Crime: Corrections," was changed from three to two chapters in the fifth edition. The two chapters on prisons were combined, along with the discussion of jails, to form Chapter 14, "The Confinement of Offenders." The chapter contains a brief historical account of the emergence of prisons and jails for punishment; discusses the U.S. contribution to this movement; and distinguishes jails, prisons, and community corrections. Jail and prison overcrowding is one focus of this chapter; the discussion includes an analysis of the attempted solutions to this serious problem. The inmate's social world within prison is discussed, as are prison violence and control within prisons. A new feature is a discussion of prison gangs. The chapter concludes with a brief overview of prisoners' legal rights.

Chapter 15, "Corrections in the Community," covers probation, parole, and community corrections, with almost all inserts featuring new material and all cases updated. New features on AIDS, and new material on furloughs, house arrest, and electronic monitoring include such recent examples as the case of Willie Horton, who became a campaign issue when George Bush ran against and defeated Michael Dukakis in the 1988 presidential election.

As in the previous edition, each chapter of the sixth edition begins with a brief outline, an abstract, and a list of key terms. At a glance readers will be alerted to the chapter's coverage and will have useful tools for review. Key terms are also boldface within the text and defined in a comprehensive glossary at the end of the book. Endnotes are at the end of each chapter rather than at the end of the text.

Highlights and exhibits, two other features of the previous edition, are also retained. Highlights, generally taken from popular sources, illustrate how the media depicts crime. Exhibits focus on more scholarly materials. These features, along with the continued use of tables, figures, and photographs, provide the text with textual and visual variety. The text also includes a subject index, a name index, a case index, and a guide indicating how to read court cases. An Instructor's Manual that includes test questions is available upon adoption of the text.

Acknowledgments

During the writing of all of my previous books, including five editions of this text, I have been a full-time faculty member, with all the time control that that position involves. Finding time to write a revision while serving as a full-time dean was a problem I was not certain I could solve. The work had to be confined to nights and weekends, for the dean's office features far too many interruptions to permit the time and concentrated effort required for writing a text. The problem was solved, however, by doctors who eased my medical problems (and to them this text is dedicated), and by family, friends, and professional associates who provided support and technical expertise.

Of greatest significance is my sister, Jill Pickett, who has always been a dear friend and supportive family member, and has now become a valuable assistant. Her efficiency and hard work made it possible for us to get this manuscript to the publisher on time. In addition to correcting the drafts on the computer, Jill edited the entire manuscript, put all the footnotes in order, proofread, and compiled the index. To her the publisher and I owe a big thanks, for her efficiency, technical expertise, and her dependability enabled us to produce the text on schedule. Perhaps to me Jill's greatest contribution is her continued emotional support and friendship. Her family (husband Roger, son Clint, and daughter Rhonda) all helped at various stages and provided us all with entertainment when we needed to relax. Our mother, Martha L. Titus, was also a source of support and encouragement, and to her we are both grateful.

Our work was facilitated by the research assistance of Lenny Krzycki, Ph.D. candidate at the Florida State University School of Criminology, who learned legal research skills while sharpening his skills at social science research. Lenny's prompt attention to details and his enthusiasm for the project were a source of comfort when the schedule got tough.

This edition was written during my first year as Dean of the School of Criminology at Florida State University. Provost Augustus Turnbull III and Dean of the Faculties Steve Edwards provided support and encouragement for the project. They, along with our President, Bernard Sliger, provide an atmosphere in which research and writing are encouraged and supported. My appreciation also goes to Michael J. Lynch, Assistant Professor in the School of Criminology, who assisted with the redrafting of the discussion on critical criminology. Laura Nagy, Internship Director in the School of Criminology, provided some of the photographs for the text and accompanied me on several visits to correctional facilities and law enforcement agencies. She has also provided needed support for this project.

Writing can be very confining, and the need to "get away" is critical. My special thanks to the FSU basketball head coach Pat Kennedy, the assistant coaches and the players who permit me to travel with them to their away games, thus providing an excellent opportunity to relax while watching my favorite sport as well as to meet criminal justice practitioners and professors in other parts of the United States. I have thoroughly enjoyed my position of "team dean"!

Many of my colleagues in criminology and criminal justice have continued their support by assisting with the reviewing process. I am grateful to the following professors for their ideas and their constructive criticisms:

Howard Standish Bergman
Manchester Community College

Mitchell Chamlin
University of Oklahoma

Lynne A. Douglass
Northern Illinois University

Will C. Kennedy
San Diego State University

Jud Landis
California State University

Manju Sheth
Glassboro State College

Leslie Sue
Vincennes University

Sol Tannenbaum
University of Houston

The staff at Holt, Rinehart and Winston provided the needed editorial and production assistance, and I very much appreciate their efforts. Shortly before we began work on this edition, the New York office of Holt moved to Fort Worth, Texas, a convenience for my sister (who lives in Dallas) and me, but a problem for many of my editors and friends at Holt, who were firmly settled in the New York area. My fear was that the move and a new staff would result in delays and the inevitable problems that can occur when new people work on a project. This was not the case, and to my new editor, Christopher P. Klein, I am most grateful for your assistance in a smooth transition. The revision moved smoothly and in a timely fashion, and I did not encounter any of those horrible fears that had initially arisen when I was informed of the move. Chris was ably assisted by Molly Shepard, Permissions Editor. My special thanks to Project Editor Mike Hinshaw for his meticulous attention to detail.

Finally, I would like to express my appreciation to all of you who have used this text over the years. This sixth edition represents a major accomplishment for a solo author, and your help and support over the previous five editions have made this book a success. I particularly appreciate those of you who have served as reviewers, either formally or informally, and assisted me in my efforts to keep the book informative, up-to-date, and challenging to generations of students.

Contents

CRIME AND CRIMINOLOGY

PART I

Introduction to the Study of Crime and Criminology

CHAPTER 1

This first chapter provides an introduction to the study of crime and the criminal. The legal and nonlegal definitions of crime are defined and analyzed. The concept of criminal law is examined, followed by a discussion of the purpose of criminal law as an agency of social control. Laws regulating substance abuse and private consensual sexual behavior are used to illustrate the growing controversy over whether the criminal law should be used to control morality. This controversy has existed for centuries but was brought back to center stage in the United States as the result of a 1986 Supreme Court decision and the increasing concern with the spread of AIDS.

OUTLINE

Crime, Criminal Law, and Criminology

Attempts to explain and control criminal behavior involve many disciplines. Although other disciplines are mentioned, this text focuses on sociology and criminology and their interaction with criminal law, the legal mechanism by which society reacts to crime and through which society attempts to prevent criminal behavior. This chapter establishes the foundation for all subsequent discussions in the text. It begins with the critical concept of crime.

THE CONCEPT OF CRIME AND CRIMINAL LAW

Though the word *crime* is difficult to define because of the lack of a general agreement on its meaning, legal and nonlegal definitions of crime are examined after a brief historical overview of the concept of crime.

Historical Meaning of Crime

Originally crimes were not defined. They involved no official action because they were private matters. Individuals who were wronged would take action against the wrongdoer or the wrongdoer's family. The system broke down when the family structure changed, societies became more complex, and people became more mobile.

Later the concept of crime developed but was confined to acts committed against the king. Private revenge remained the only punishment for acts against private citizens. Eventually the king, representing the state, realized that the peace of the community was at stake and decreed that the act of wronging a person should be reported to him. Anyone who injured one of the king's subjects was considered to have injured the king, and the phrase "keeping the peace of the king" developed.

Gradually the payment of compensation to the victim by the offender replaced family feuding and other forms of private revenge. Later the fine system developed, with the fine being paid to the king (now to the state). Out of this approach emerged a dual system: **criminal law** and **civil law.**

Criminal Law Distinguished from Civil Law

Although there is considerable overlap between criminal and civil law, there are also important distinctions. When a criminal wrong has been committed, the state or federal government initiates action against the person accused of the crime. The state initiates action because a crime is considered to be so serious that it threatens the welfare of the entire society, not just of the immediate victim.

A noncriminal wrong, on the other hand, is considered to be a wrong against a particular individual. In such cases the person wronged initiates action against the accused. Noncriminal law generally refers to laws that regulate the rights between individuals or organizations—divorce laws, contract laws, laws regulating property rights, torts, and others. **Torts** are civil acts for which the law gives redress, such as personal injuries, both physical and mental; assault and battery; defamation of character; invasion of privacy; and illegal interference with the possession of land. Some acts may be both criminal and noncriminal and can give rise to criminal and noncriminal actions.

Civil wrongs and crimes may also be distinguished in terms of remedies. In a criminal case, the state may seek any of the following: probation, work (such as community service), imprisonment, capital punishment, or a fine payable to the state. In a torts action, the court may order the wrongdoer to pay monetary damages to the victim. The difference between noncriminal and criminal law may also determine in which court the case will be heard, and different procedural rules are applicable.

DEFINITION OF CRIME

The definition of crime must be precise, unambiguous, and usable. The definition must clarify who is and who is not a criminal. Various approaches have been used to define and study crime. This text emphasizes the legal approach, for our system of criminal justice is based on a legal definition of crime.

Legal Definition of Crime

 Crime is an act defined by law; unless the elements specified by criminal law are present and proved beyond a reasonable doubt, a person should not be convicted of a crime. The following legal definition serves as our reference point:

> Crime is an intentional act or omission in violation of criminal law (statutory and case law), committed without defense or justification and sanctioned by the state as a felony or misdemeanor.[1]

An Act or Omission

The first part of the definition embodies some philosophies central to the American system of law. A person may not be punished for his or her thoughts; action must be taken. In some cases, words may be considered acts, as in **treason** or in assisting another to commit a crime. In those cases it is argued that some action has been taken, but an individual cannot be punished under the American system of law for thinking about committing a crime if no elements are put into action toward the commission of that crime. To consider murdering a spouse but to do nothing toward the commission of that act is not a crime. However, hiring someone to murder the spouse is a crime.

The failure to act may also be a crime, or a tort, but not unless there is a legal duty to act in a particular case. Moral duty will not suffice. The following dramatically illustrates this point. An eight-year-old boy illegally entered a mill where weaving machinery was in operation. The foreman told the boy to leave; but the boy did not understand English, and the foreman did not remove him although it was obvious that the machine was dangerous. The boy stuck his hand in the machine and was badly injured. The court held that since the foreman had no legal duty toward this child, because the child was trespassing, the child could not recover in a tort suit. According to the court, a tort is based on the concept of legal duty. "With purely moral obligations the law does not deal."[2]

The same principle applies to criminal law. We do not have general affirmative duties to prevent people from being injured or killed. We may watch while people are brutalized by others; we may watch while a child is drowning. Unless there is a legal duty to aid, the law may not be invoked even though it would have been easy for us to prevent the injury or death. We may be moral monsters, but we have not violated the civil or criminal law in these situations.

A legal duty may exist, however, if we are the parent, spouse, or other close relative, or if we have assumed a duty through a contractual relationship such as operating a licensed day-care center. Legal duties may also be imposed in other special relationships. Acts or omissions, in order to be criminal, must also be voluntary, and the actor must have control over his or her actions. If a person has a heart attack while driving a car and kills another human being, he or she should not be charged with a crime since the heart attack was an involuntary act over which the person had no control. The case might be different, however, if the individual had had a series of heart attacks and therefore knew it might be dangerous to drive an automobile.

Requirement of Intent

An act or the omission of an act alone is not sufficient to constitute a crime. The law requires criminal **intent,** or *mens rea,* the mental element required to establish culpability. This element is extremely important, for in many cases it will be the critical factor in determining whether an act was or was not a crime. It may also determine the degree of crime committed (for example, whether a killing is first- or second-degree murder). Despite the importance of *mens rea,* historically the term has not been clearly defined or developed.

The American Law Institute, in its **Model Penal Code,** divides culpability into four mental states: "A person is not guilty of an offense unless he acted <u>purposely</u>, <u>knowingly</u>, <u>recklessly</u> or <u>negligently</u>, as the law may require, with respect to each material element of the offense."[3] Each mental state is defined in Exhibit 1.1. The interpretation of these four tiers of culpability has been the subject of considerable dispute. It is clear, however, that one may be held criminally liable for the unintended consequences of an intended act. One may also be held criminally liable for injury or death to a victim other than the intended victim or for a more serious degree of harm than that intended. Consider the following examples.

In the first case, Jones shot at Anders with the intent of killing him, but being a bad shot, he missed Anders and killed Williams instead. Jones could be held for the death of the victim. In the second case, an unhappy husband wanted to scare his wife to convince her that they should move to another neighborhood. The husband hired a man to fire several shots into the air while his wife was out walking the dog, but he was a bad shot and killed the woman. Even though there was no specific intent to kill the woman, both men were charged with murder. They had plotted an act, and one did carry out an act that a reasonable person should have known could have resulted in serious injury or death. It is possible, of course, that in such a case the charge would be reduced to reckless or negligent homicide. But the point is that the actors could be tried for murder.

Exceptions to the Requirement of Intent—There are exceptions to the requirement of a criminal intent. In some situations employers may be liable for acts of their employees, even if the employers do not know their employees are committing the acts. For example, in the following case, the president of a drug company was found guilty of violating a provision of the Pure Food and Drug Act that required the proper labeling of drugs. He personally did not know that the drugs had been mislabeled by those of his employees responsible for repackaging and labeling the drugs received from the manufacturer, but the U.S. Supreme Court upheld the conviction.[4]

Another exception to the requirement of intent is the **felony-murder doctrine** under which a person may be held criminally responsible for the death of another when the death is the result of the commission of another felony. For example, a person who commits arson by setting fire to a house in which several children die as a result may be charged with murder and arson. The felony-murder doctrine is usually limited to deaths that follow the commission of inherently dangerous felonies such as forcible rape, robbery, arson, and burglary.

Violation of the Elements of Criminal Law

To be convicted of a crime, a person must violate the criminal law. Criminal law comes from three sources: <u>constitutions</u>, <u>statutes</u>, and <u>court decisions</u>. Congress and the state legislatures enact constitutions that include

EXHIBIT 1.1

General Requirements of Culpability: The Model Penal Code

Section 2.02

(1) *Minimum Requirements of Culpability.*

Except as provided in Section 2.05, a person is not guilty of an offense unless he acted purposely, knowingly, recklessly or negligently, as the law may require, with respect to each material element of the offense.

(2) *Kinds of Culpability Defined.*

  (a) *Purposely.*

   A person acts purposely with respect to a material element of an offense when:

   (i) if the element involves the nature of his conduct or a result thereof, it is his conscious object to engage in conduct of that nature or to cause such a result; and

   (ii) if the element involves the attendant circumstances, he is aware of the existence of such circumstances or he believes or hopes that they exist.

  (b) *Knowingly.*

   A person acts knowingly with respect to a material element of an offense when:

   (i) if the element involves the nature of his conduct or the attendant circumstances, he is aware that his conduct is of that nature or that such circumstances exist; and

   (ii) if the element involves the result of his conduct, he is aware that it is practically certain that his conduct will cause such a result.

  (c) *Recklessly.*

   A person acts recklessly with respect to a material element of an offense when he consciously disregards a substantial and unjustifiable risk that the material element exists or will result from his conduct. The risk must be of such a nature and degree that, considering the nature and purpose of the actor's conduct and the circumstances known to him, its disregard involves a gross deviation from the standard of conduct that a law-abiding person would observe in the actor's situation.

  (d) *Negligently.*

   A person acts negligently with respect to a material element of an offense when he should be aware of a substantial and unjustifiable risk that the material element exists or will result from his conduct. The risk must be of such a nature and degree that the actor's failure to perceive it, considering the nature and purpose of his conduct and the circumstances known to him, involves a gross deviation from the standard of care that a reasonable person would observe in the actor's situation.

SOURCE: Copyright 1985 by the American Law Institute. Reprinted with the permission of the American Law Institute.

criminal laws. Congress passes statutes that apply to the commission of federal crimes (such as treason, kidnapping, assassination of the President, and bank robbery). These statutes constitute **statutory law** and are frequently a codification of laws that have evolved through custom and prior judicial decisions known as the **common law.** This term comes from the English system that developed after the Norman Conquest in 1066. Before that time there was no distinction among law, custom, religion, and morality. Decisions might be different in different communities. The Normans, however, wanted to establish some unity. To do so the king employed representatives to travel to the various villages and towns to inform the people about happenings in different areas. The body of law that emerged was called the *common law*.

Because the common law was developed on a case-by-case basis, the term **case law** is often used synonymously with *common law* and is contrasted with written, or statutory, law. Case law is just as important as statutory law, and the English common law has had a significant influence on the development of both statutory and case law in the United States.

Common law offenses have been kept alive and interpreted by judicial decisions, which are also an important part of American law today. Even when state legislatures enact laws to cover common law offenses, the interpretation of those statutes is often left to common law decisions.

It is also important to understand that all elements of a crime must be proved in each case, and doing so is often difficult. For example, in the 50 to 100 cases of criminal prosecutions for spreading the AIDS virus (acquired immunity deficiency syndrome, a deadly disease first discovered in 1979), most prosecutions have not been successful in proving the elements of **causation** and intent. Causation is difficult to prove because of the long period that may elapse between sexual intercourse and detection of the AIDS virus. It is also difficult to prove that an infected person intended to infect his or her sexual partner. "Usually you do not find a premeditated killer; usually you find a pathetic, sick, vulnerable person."[5]

Administrative Law

One further type of law should be noted—**administrative law.** The legislatures of the states and the Congress of the United States often delegate to administrative agencies—the Federal Trade Commission, the Internal Revenue Service, public universities, human rights commissions, and others—the power to make rules that regulate the governing of those institutions. The rules must be made following certain specified guidelines.

When actions, even if they involve violations of the criminal law, are handled by administrative agencies instead of the courts, such actions are not technically criminal law violations. The administrative agency, upon report of a violation, will conduct a hearing that does not involve all the procedural protections required in a criminal trial. The agency may issue orders such as a cease and desist order in the case of a restaurant owner who violates food and drug laws. If the restaurant owner refuses to obey, the agency may get a court order, which, if violated, may constitute **contempt of court,** a criminal act. Even in that case, the offender is not looked on by society in the same negative light as persons who are convicted in criminal courts.

Without Justification or Defense

Individuals are not responsible for all acts that cause harm or injury to others; the law recognizes some extenuating circumstances. An act or omission of an act is not a crime if the individual has a legally recognized justification or defense for the act.

    <u>Justification</u>—A person faced with the possibility of being killed might use the defense of *justifiable homicide.* A police officer in pursuit of an armed robbery suspect who fires at the officer may be justified in killing that suspect. People may also be excused from criminal liability for inflicting serious bodily harm on others if they are in danger of being injured by these persons, but they may use only the extent of force necessary for that protection.

    <u>Defenses</u>—An individual charged with a crime may offer evidence to defeat the criminal charge. A variety of defenses are recognized; the extent and complexity of legal defenses are beyond the scope of this discussion, but a few are summarized. Chapter 4 explores the insanity defense, one of the more publicized although infrequently used defenses.

    Entrapment is a defense that may be used successfully when a police officer or someone acting as the agent of a law enforcement officer entraps a person to commit a crime. The defense is generally limited to less serious crimes. The entrapment defense frequently arises in cases involving alleged illegal sales of drugs.

    Providing an *opportunity* for someone to commit a crime does not constitute entrapment. "To determine whether entrapment has been established, a line must be drawn between the trap for the unwary innocent and the trap for the unwary criminal." That line is hard to draw. But the U.S. Supreme Court recognized the defense in a case involving a government informer who first met the defendant in a doctor's office where both were undergoing treatment for narcotics addiction. Several accidental meetings followed, either at the doctor's office or at the pharmacy where the two men had their prescriptions filled. Eventually the informer asked the defendant if he knew of a good source for purchasing illegal narcotics. The defendant at first ignored the questions. Only after repeated requests in which the informer proclaimed that he was really suffering from lack of drugs did the defendant finally acquiesce. After several occasions on which the defendant sold drugs to the agent, he was arrested. The Supreme Court overturned the conviction, ruling that the defendant was induced by the agent. The following brief excerpt from the case explains why the Court considered this a case of entrapment.[6]

Sherman v. United States

The case at bar illustrates an evil which the defense of entrapment is designed to overcome. The government informer entices someone attempting to avoid narcotics not only into carrying out an illegal sale but also into returning to the habit of use. Selecting the proper time, the informer then tells the government agent. The set-up is accepted by the agent without even a question as to the manner in which the informer encountered the seller. Thus the Government plays on the weaknesses of an innocent party and beguiles him into committing crimes which he otherwise would not have attempted. Law enforcement does not require methods such as this.

It is also permissible to use force to protect other persons or yourself when threatened by serious bodily harm or death. **Self-defense** is technically a legal defense only when force is used by a person who faces circumstances that would lead a reasonable person to think that he or she was in danger of *imminent* bodily harm or death. This defense has, however, been raised lately in numerous cases in which a woman, previously battered by her husband or other significant male, seriously wounds or kills that individual although she is not in danger of *imminent* danger. Popularized by the movie, *The Burning Bed*, the variation on self-defense is usually called the *battered woman's syndrome* defense.

Jurisdictions have differed in their treatment of the battered woman's defense. In 1988, the Kansas Supreme Court held that the defense was not proper in the case of a woman who, after enduring 12 years of abuse from her spouse, killed him while he slept.[7] Such cases do, however, frequently elicit sympathy that results in a refusal to prosecute. Thus, in Tallahassee, Florida, in late 1988, a woman who had been abused for years by her husband, shot and killed him in a parking lot when he was not armed and was not threatening her. No criminal charges were filed against her.

Highlight 1.1 focuses on other recent defenses that, some argue, have gone too far. Unsuccessful defenses in early 1989 were illustrated by Lt. Col. Oliver North's conviction of three criminal charges in the Iran-Contra Affair. Using the *patriotism defense*, North argued that whatever he did he did "for his country" and under orders of his superiors. A Tampa, Florida, mother was convicted of first-degree murder for beating and drowning her five-year-old daughter despite her defense that "years of sexual abuse" led her to commit the crime.[8]

Felony or Misdemeanor

Historically, a **felony** was a crime for which a person could be required to forfeit all property. That was the main distinction between a felony and

HIGHLIGHT 1.1

THE ROUGH-SEX DEFENSE: WHEN KILLERS BLAME EROTIC IMPULSES, DOES ROUGH JUSTICE RESULT?

Before he was charged with second-degree murder in the 1986 death of Kathleen Holland, 17, Joseph Porto calmly confessed on videotape that he had strangled his girlfriend till "my hands got tired," then used his high school graduation tassel to finish the job. Porto, now 19, gave a similar account to a prosecution psychiatrist, explaining that he had exploded in jealous anger when Holland told him she wanted to date other boys.

But when Porto took the witness stand at his trial on Long Island last month, he made a stunning recantation. He had invented the murder story, he tearfully claimed, because he was ashamed to tell the truth: Holland had begged him to wrap a rope around her neck to produce a state of near suffocation, called sexual asphyxia, that is said to heighten erotic pleasure. In his excitement, he said, he pulled too hard. Nassau County Prosecutor Kenneth Littman derided the new story as the "oops defense." But the jury found Porto guilty on only the lesser charge of criminally negligent homicide, a crime punishable by no more than four years in prison.

Holland's family was outraged. Last week her brother made public a 6,000-signature petition demanding that Porto get the maximum penalty. "Rough sex?" scoffs her father

Denis, a retired policeman. "That phrase wasn't even part of my daughter's vocabulary." It had, however, become part of the public's vocabulary earlier this year during the "preppie murder" trial of Robert Chambers, who claimed to have killed Jennifer Levin accidentally during an unbridled sexual episode in Manhattan's Central Park. Last week Levin's father Steven held a press conference to protest such defense tactics. "It's become open season on women," he said. Porto Prosecutor Littman agrees: "Rough sex is the defense du jour."

Some are calling it a new twist on the old trial strategy of blaming the victim. "The she-asked-for-it defense doesn't work anymore," says Harvard University Law Professor Alan Dershowitz. "So now we're hearing she demanded it." The first use of that argument may have been in the trial last year in St. Louis County, Mo., of Dennis Bulloch, who faced murder charges in the death of his wife. Julia Bulloch's body, bound to a chair with adhesive tape, had been found in the burned remains of the couple's garage, which Bulloch admitted torching. He claimed that his wife had choked to death accidentally during an episode of sexual bondage. Though he faced the death penalty for murder, he drew only a seven-year prison term on the lesser charge

of manslaughter. Frustrated prosecutors have now moved to try him for arson.

Much of the controversy surrounding the Porto trial hinged upon whether sexual asphyxia would have been part of a teenage girl's erotic habits. Porto Attorney Barry Slotnick, who defended Subway Gunman Bernhard Goetz, put an expert on the stand who testified that the practice was far more common than people realize, though deaths occur mostly among males engaged in solitary sex.

Ironically, the rough-sex defense may require an attractive defendant to succeed. It will work only if the accused is "sympathetic, not a hardened type of character," says New York Attorney Thomas Puccio. It may also require a certain kind of jury to accept the premise that young women might pursue the ultimate in unsafe sex. During jury selection in the Chambers trial, recalls Defense Jury Consultant Andrea Longpre, "we were looking for people who had grown up in the '60s and '70s. Young people who were experimenting with life." Whatever the truth about her death, Kathleen Holland's experiments with life are now over.

SOURCE: Time, 23 May, 1988 p. 55. Copyright 1988 by Time Inc. Reprinted by permission.

HIGHLIGHT 1.1 (Continued)

Judges preside over criminal trials as well as impose sentences and, in some cases, determine the ultimate question of fact: guilt or innocence.

a **misdemeanor.** Today the distinction is made primarily in terms of the sentence that may be imposed. Usually, a felony is a crime for which a person may be sentenced to death or a long prison term, while a misdemeanor is a less serious offense for which a fine or short prison term may be imposed. Most criminology texts and even many criminal law texts cover only felonies.[9] But misdemeanors are very important in that many are committed, and in many instances, the lines drawn between felonies and misdemeanors are very fine legal lines.[10]

Judge or Jury as Final Decision Makers

Crimes are defined as acts or omissions of acts that violate criminal statutory or case law and for which the state has provided a penalty. Acts may meet these criteria, however, and still not result in conviction. In cases that are tried before a jury, the jury may refuse to return a verdict of guilty even when the defendant is clearly guilty. In cases tried without a jury, the judge may do the same.

HIGHLIGHT 1.2

PULLING THE PLUG: MERCY KILLING OR MURDER?

Rudy Linares and his wife Tamara arrive for a preliminary hearing in Chicago in April, 1989. Linares was charged with removing his son's life-support system.

On April 26, 1989, Rudy Linares held the hospital staff and police at bay with a gun for 45 minutes while he pulled the plug on his 16-month-old son's life support machine and held the baby in his arms until he died. Said Linares, "I am not here to hurt anyone. I will harm you only if you try to plug in my son's machine." The child had been in a coma since August 1988, when he was rushed to the hospital after swallowing an object thought to be a balloon or a small piece of aluminum foil. He had been deprived of oxygen long enough to become partially brain-dead.

Linares unhooked his son's machine in December 1988, but hospital staff rehooked the machine in time. Dr. Robert Stein, the Chicago medical examiner, said that although termination of mechanical life support was a fact that contributed to the youngster's death, it was not the immmediate cause of death. Stein said he would later list the official cause of death after thoroughly reviewing the child's entire medical history. Linares was charged with murder but the grand jury refused to indict.

The issue has arisen recently in cases of *euthanasia* (mercy killing), which is legally premeditated murder. But in many of these cases criminal charges are not filed, and when they are filed, juries often refuse to convict defendants of first degree murder or for a lesser crime (see Highlight 1.2). In other cases, the defendant may be convicted of a crime by the jury, but the judge may grant the defendant's motion for acquittal because he or she does not think the evidence was sufficient to show guilt beyond a reasonable doubt. The judge may allow the conviction to stand but reduce the sentence.

Analysis of the Legal Approach

Social scientists argue that restricting studies of crime and of criminals to persons who are convicted of violating the criminal law is too limiting. If we are interested in knowing why people engage in behavior that is detrimental to society, we should go beyond the strict legal definitions. We should also include behavior that is defined as crime but for which no arrests have been made. Accused persons who are not prosecuted because of a legal technicality should also be included. The focus is on the behavior: Why do people do what they do? This approach claims that the legal technicalities are not relevant to a study of the behavior.

According to this approach, an example of behavior that should be considered criminal and thus studied as such occurred in May 1989 when a man convicted of raping a disabled thirteen-year-old was freed on a legal technicality. Lee Curtis Davis was ordered released from prison by a Florida court which held that Davis had been charged and convicted under the wrong statute. Davis was convicted of the rape of a physically helpless person, but the victim did not meet the law's definition of a physically helpless person. Although she was in a wheelchair, suffering from muscular dystrophy, she was able to scream and push Davis during the attack. Davis could have been convicted under the general rape statute, but to do so now would violate the U.S. constitutional provision that prohibits trying a person twice for the same offense.[11]

There are a variety of nonlegal approaches to the study of criminal behavior. One of the best known proponents of this approach historically was criminologist Thorsten Sellin. Sellin did not claim that there is no place for the legal definition in criminology but "that if a science of human conduct is to develop, the investigator in this field of research must rid himself of shackles which have been forged by the criminal law." Sellin discussed the development of *conduct norms*, ways of doing things that are developed by a group through social interaction. "For every person . . . there is from the point of view of a given group of which he is a member, a normal (right) and an abnormal (wrong) way of reacting, the norm depending upon the social values of the group which formulated it." These conduct norms are socially defined, differ from group to group, and are not necessarily codified into law. But Sellin believed that those who engaged in such abnormal conduct should be included in studies of criminals.[12]

Others have argued that nonlegal definitions of crime are too loose and too ambiguous, leaving too much room to the definer to determine what is crime.[13] The term crime should be used in its strict legal definition and the term criminal used only to refer to those who have been convicted in the criminal courts. The terms crime and criminal have severe implications and repercussions. They should be used only after proper procedures for establishing which acts are criminal, as in the case of defining *crime,* or in the case of *criminal,* after a guilty plea or the determination of guilt by a judge or jury. This is not to suggest that nonlegal definitions are unimportant. From the point of view of the causes of human behavior, it is important for social scientists to study the behavior of persons who have committed criminal acts but who have not been processed through the criminal justice system to the point of conviction.

THE CONCEPT OF LAW

An understanding of crime, the criminal, and the criminal law must rest on an understanding of the nature and purpose of law. Law is important because it touches virtually every area of human interaction. Law is used to protect ownership, to define the parameters of private and public property, to regulate business, to raise revenue, and to provide compensation when agreements are broken. Laws define the nature of institutions such as the family. Laws regulate marriage and divorce or dissolution, the handling of dependent and neglected children, and the inheritance of property.

Laws are also designed to protect the legal and political systems. Laws organize power relationships. They establish who is superordinate and who is subordinate in given situations. Laws maintain the status quo but also permit flexibility when times change. Laws, particularly criminal laws, not only protect private and public interests but also preserve order. Society determines that some interests are so important that a formal system of control is necessary to preserve them; therefore, laws must be passed to give the state the power of enforcement. Law thus becomes a formal system of social control that may be exercised when other forms of control are not effective. Always an issue to criminologists then is to determine how a formal system of control can protect society without jeopardizing its constitutional rights.

The Source and Nature of Law

Earlier discussion of criminal law pointed out that laws may come from constitutions, statutes (statutory law), or from court decisions (case law).

But historically philosophers and other scholars have argued over the source of law, some contending that laws derived from rulers, referred to as *positive law*, are not the only laws. *Natural law*, referred to as *higher law*, comes from a source higher than the rulers and is understood to be binding on people even in the absence of, or in conflict with, laws of the sovereigns.

The concept of natural law is seen in the first known written legal document, the Code of Hammurabi, dated approximately 1900 B.C. This code, the embodiment of existing rules and customs of Babylonia, was named in honor of King Hammurabi. The code incorporates the religious habits of the people and emphasizes the importance of religious beliefs. For example, the penalty provided that a priestess who entered a tavern be burned alive. The code also reflects the economic problems of Babylonian society, giving specific regulations about how commodities were to be priced and marketed. The "eye for an eye, tooth for a tooth" philosophy was ingrained in the code. If a physician performed a careless operation, his hand would be removed; if he were responsible for the death of a woman through a miscarriage, the life of one of his daughters would be taken. The code "presented the idea that justice was man's inherent right, derived from supernatural forces rather than by royally bestowed favor."[14]

The late civil rights leader Martin Luther King, Jr., appealed to higher law, or natural law, in his "Letter from the Birmingham Jail," in which he wrote that there are two types of laws, just and unjust, and that it is permissible for people to disobey unjust laws. Just as people have a moral responsibility to obey just laws, they also have a moral responsibility to disobey unjust laws. A just law is in accordance with God's moral law, but an unjust law is in conflict with that law. An unjust law is not "rooted in eternal law and natural law. Any law that uplifts human personality is just. Any law that degrades human personality is unjust."[15]

King's position was the basis of the civil rights movement of the 1960s and later; it is also used by many people to protest laws they perceive as unfair. It is important to understand this concept, for it is one of the reasons why some people who violate statutory law and case law do not believe that they are committing wrongful acts. Another rationalization for violating law is the belief that laws are enforced in an arbitrary and discriminatory manner. These positions raise issues about the use of law as a method of social control.

Law as Social Control

Law is used as an agency of social control. Prior to the emergence of law, social control was achieved in less formal ways, which are not sufficient in today's complex societies. Every society has certain functions that must be performed in order for the society to continue. Some provision must be made for replacing members; providing food and other needed resources such as housing and clothing; maintaining a sense of belonging sufficient to maintain the group; and deciding how much deviation from the **norms,** or rules, of the group will be permitted and what sanctions will be imposed on those who deviate. Societies must also teach these norms to new members, a process sociologists call **socialization.**[16]

Human societies may be described and studied by analyzing the **social systems** that make up those societies. By a social system, sociologists mean the interrelationship of acts of the system's members. Because all people in a complex society cannot do everything necessary for the continuance of society, or even for their own personal needs, a division of labor develops. Individuals occupy different positions within the society. These positions involve social roles, the obligations of which are defined by the social norms of that group.

Informal Social Control

An early sociologist William Graham Sumner distinguished between two types of norms, **folkways** and **mores.** According to Sumner, behavior begins with acts, not thoughts. The first reason for acts is need, and needs are satisfied by a trial-and-error method in an attempt to find the best solution. Gradually these ways of acting become habit or routine. They are "not creations of human purpose and wit." They are the folkways, and they are the correct way of doing things because they are tradition.

When the folkways are "developed into doctrines of welfare," they are called mores. That is, folkways contain elements of what is right and wrong, but when that distinction is extended to the public welfare, the result is mores. The mores are not questions; they are answers. They tell people how to behave. "They coerce and restrict the newborn generation. They do not stimulate thought, but the contrary. The thinking is already done and is embodied in the mores." Folkways make life easier and more predictable. "The great mass of the folkways give us discipline and the support of routine and habit."[17]

Out of mores come laws, but laws do not emerge until people are capable of verification, reflection, and criticism. Until then, customs and taboos regulate civilization. Among primitive societies there is little differentiation in positions or statuses. With limited or no technology, there are fewer kinds of jobs than in more complex societies. Most people take care of their own needs and live at subsistence level. They grow or capture their own food and make their own clothing and housing; they therefore have no need for exchanging goods and services. They have some kind of a normative structure, but it is not codified law. It is not civil or criminal law either but submission to custom that controls most of their behavior.[18] Nuclear and extended families predominate over any other social group. Because such a society does not need many rules to regulate activities outside the group, it can have informal methods of social control.

One of the reasons that codified law is not necessary among primitive tribes and other small human groups is the visibility of offenses and the power of the community to deal with transgressors. Among primitive people there are few conflicting and competing interests. Formal law is therefore not needed to protect individuals' interests. Those who deviate from the norms of the group are easily spotted; the community can react with sanctions other than laws. These informal sanctions, which are often more effective than laws, may be a disapproving glance, an embarrassed silence following an action, a smile, a nod, a frown, a social invitation, or social ostracism. The threat of being banished from society can be a serious deterrent to deviant behavior among such groups. The key to the success of these informal methods of social control is that the groups are closely knit. Within close-knit groups of humans it is relatively easy to know the norms and the general will of the group.[19]

Evolution of Formal Social Control

Why did it become necessary for human societies to move beyond the informal methods of social control and develop law? Sociologist Émile Durkheim believed that as societies grew more complex, they developed a division of labor; as that occurred, they moved from mechanical (the less complex type of society in which members are highly integrated through their cultural and functional similarities) to organic solidarity (the more complex type of society in which members are integrated because they are functionally interdependent). Along with these developments, repressive sanctions were replaced by restitutive sanctions, leading to a more formal system of social control.[20]

Sociologists have also argued that the development of a formal system of social control was necessary for society to progress. Max Weber, for example, studied modern capitalism and reasoned that a precondition of its growth was the development of formal legal rationality. As societies became more complex and economically advanced, there was an increasing rationality.[21] Not everyone agrees, however, on how and why laws evolved. We examine this controversy in chapters 5 and 6.

Comparison of Law and Other Social Controls

Although there are similarities between law and other methods of social control, there are also significant differences. Law is, at least in theory, more specific. In criminal law, the law defines the nature of the offense and the punishment to be administered for conviction of that offense. Laws cannot, of course, define every possible situation that would constitute a violation, but the law will be declared unconstitutional if vague. The law must be clear enough to give adequate notice to potential transgressors that they are in danger of violating the law. An example of a city ordinance declared void for vagueness is seen in Exhibit 1.2.

A second distinction between law and other forms of social control is that law arises from a more rational procedure. It is a formal enactment

EXHIBIT 1.2

Statutes Will Be Declared Void If They Are Vague: The Case of *State v. Metzger*

The case involves Douglas E. Metzger, who was convicted of violating a city code that provided in part, "It shall be unlawful for any person within the City of Lincoln . . . to commit any indecent, immodest or filthy act in the presence of any person, or in such a situation that persons passing might ordinarily see the same."

According to the evidence, Metzger lived in a garden-level apartment located in Lincoln, Nebraska. A large window in the apartment faces a parking lot which is situated on the north side of the apartment building. At about 7:45 A.M. on April 30, 1981, another resident of the apartment, while parking his automobile in a space directly in front of Metzger's apartment window, observed Metzger standing naked with his arms at his sides in his apartment window for a period of five seconds.

The resident testisifed that he saw Metzger's body from his thighs on up. The resident called the police depart-ment and two officers arrived at the apartment at about 8 A.M. The officers tes-tified that they observed Metzger stand-ing in front of the window eating a bowl of cereal. They testified that Metzger was standing within a foot of the window and his nude body, from the mid-thigh on up, was visible.

. . . The more basic issue presented to us by this appeal is whether the ordi-nance, as drafted, is so vague as to be un-constitutional. We believe that it is. . . .

A criminal statute cannot rest upon an uncertain foundation. The crime and the elements constituting it must be so clearly expressed that the ordinary per-son can intelligently choose in advance what course it is lawful for him to pur-sue. Penal statutes prohibiting the doing of certain things and providing a punish-ment for their violation should not admit of such a double meaning that the citizen may act upon one conception of its re-quirements and the courts upon an-other. A statute which forbids the doing

by a legislative body or a court that presumably occurs after discussion and reflection. The law is to be applied to all who transgress its provisions, unless there are justifications or defenses for the otherwise illegal acts. Law also specifies sanctions, and only those sanctions specified may be applied. Law differs from other types of social control in that its sanctions are applied exclusively by organized political agencies. Physical coercion may be involved in enforcing the sanctions of law, although the force will be limited to reasonable force applied by an official party.

Law is also characterized by regularity, which does not mean abso-

of an act in terms so vague that men of common intelligence must necessarily guess as to its meaning and differ as to its application violates the first essential elements of due process of law. It is not permissible to enact a law which in effect spreads an all-inclusive net for the feet of everybody upon the chance that, while the innocent will surely be entangled in its meshes, some wrongdoers may also be caught.

The ordinance in question makes it unlawful for anyone to commit any "indecent, immodest or filthy act." We know of no way in which the standards required of a criminal act can be met in those broad, general terms. There may be those few who believe persons of opposite sex holding hands in public are immodest, and certainly more who might believe that kissing in public is immodest. Such acts cannot constitute a crime. Certainly one could find many who would conclude that today's swimming attire found on many beaches or beside many pools is immodest. Yet, the fact that it is immodest does not thereby make it illegal, absent some requirement related to the health, safety, or welfare of the community. The dividing line between what is lawful and what is unlawful in terms of "indecent," "immodest," or "filthy" is simply too broad to satisfy the constitutional requirements of due process. Both lawful and unlawful acts can be embraced within such broad definitions. That cannot be permitted. One is not able to determine in advance what is lawful and what is unlawful. . . .

BOSLAUGH, Justice, dissenting. The ordinance in question prohibits indecent acts, immodest acts, *or* filthy acts in the presence of any person. . . . The exhibition of his genitals under the circumstances of this case was, clearly, an indecent act.

SOURCE: State v. Metzger, 319 N.W.2d 459, 460–463 (Neb.1982), citations omitted.

lute certainty. Law adheres to the principle of *stare decisis*, which means to abide by or adhere to settled cases. It is the doctrine that once a court has established a principle of law pertaining to certain facts, it will pertain to those same facts, or substantially those same facts, in the future. It is based on the assumption that security and certainty are important in the law. Decided cases establish precedent for the future. Courts may, however, overrule their prior decisions in light of new facts, reasoning, or changing social conditions.

Unlike other social controls, law usually does not reward conforming behavior. Law is concerned mainly with negative sanctions. Also, unlike other forms of social control, the legal system provides, in most cases, the right of appeal from its decision when the strict provisions of the rules of procedure established by legislation, constitutions, and the courts have been violated.

The Limits of Law

Law, however, cannot control the behavior of all people in a complex mass society. We should not expect to regulate all behavior by law if to do so means the loss of individual freedom and liberty. Furthermore, some disputes, by their very nature, should not be regulated by laws. Courts, for example, will not regulate how parents train their children unless there is abuse. There are also some injuries that the law cannot restore, and therefore the legal machinery emphasizes monetary damages. The law can force one party to convey property to another, but it cannot restore the reputation of an individual who has been defamed. It can force one party to pay the hospital bills of another, but it cannot alleviate the pain and suffering caused by an automobile accident.

If the law cannot regulate all behavior, what then is its basic purpose? The law should provide some standards, goals, and guidelines—a statement of what conduct is so important that is must be sanctioned. The law should also provide some moral guidance, but controversy arises over the extent to which the law should be used to provide moral guidance.

THE PURPOSE OF CRIMINAL LAW

The seriousness of the impact of criminal law should lead us to question what kinds of behavior ought to be covered by its reach. In 1983, in New Bedford, Massachusetts, a woman was gang-raped in a bar by four men while a crowd of drinkers stood by watching. No one made any effort to stop the crime. Should the observers be criminally responsible for the crime, or should criminal liability be limited only to the perpetrators? This case raises the issue of whether the criminal law should impose an affirmative duty to act to prevent a crime. In the United States, the legal answer is no, although there may be an ethical duty to act.

In 1982 an interesting situation arose in Los Angeles when public health officials began throwing Peking ducks found in restaurants into garbage cans. The Chinese, who have been preparing these ducks for 4000 years, were violating a health regulation concerning refrigeration of food. According to the state code, the duck had to be chilled to 45 degrees or less or heated to at least 140 degrees at all times. According to the Chinese, "If we put it in the refrigerator, the skin won't be crispy. If we put it in the heat too long, the meat will be tough and dry. . . . If we cooked it according to the health department, no one would come to buy our duck."

Some health experts said that the method of preparing Peking duck did not pose a health problem although it did violate health codes. "This is an old traditional method of preparation . . . and it has never been implicated in any cases of food poisoning."[22]

Both these cases raise the question of how extensive the law should be. Clearly we need to protect public health, but do we need to do so in a case that violates the technical law but creates no health problem? Clearly we should try to prevent rape, but should we do that by imposing on all people who witness a crime an affirmative duty to help prevent it? Must they do so at risk to themselves? And if we decide to regulate any or all of the above, should we do so by civil or criminal law or both? How should the law respond to activities such as homosexuality, prostitution, the use of alcohol or other drugs, and suicide? These activities involve what some people call **victimless crimes,** actions that relate only to the person involved. On the other hand, it is argued that we all are harmed by such actions. In short, we are faced with the critical question of whether the criminal law should be used to regulate activities that may be considered religious or moral but not *legal* issues.

The Control of Crime

Clearly the criminal law should be used to regulate criminal activity. The problem, of course, is to define what is a crime. We have looked at the legal definition of crime and explored its elements. But that explanation does not solve the problem of what behavior should be included within those elements. First, we look at the distinction between acts that are criminal within themselves and those that are criminal because they are so defined.

Distinction Between Mala in Se and Mala Prohibita Crimes

Crimes that are *__mala in se__* are those that are evil in themselves—rape, murder, robbery, arson, and aggravated assault. There is general agreement that such acts are criminal. In contrast, *__mala prohibita__* crimes, such as traffic offenses, are considered evil because they are forbidden. Until recently in some states the prescription, sale, or use of contraceptives was illegal. These acts were criminal because they were prohibited, but there was not general agreement they were criminal per se. Historically there was little difference between *mala in se* and *mala prohibita* crimes, because in primitive societies, morality, sin, and law are usually not distinguished. Many of the early criminal statutes in the American colonies included sins and were identical in wording to the Scriptures.

The Control of Morality

It is argued that in addition to regulating criminal behavior, a purpose of the criminal law is to regulate moral behavior; but this position has led others to conclude that our law overreaches or overcriminalizes.[23] The position is that crimes such as the illegal use of alcohol and other drugs and consensual sexual behavior are actions that harm only the people involved. In other words, they are victimless crimes.

Edwin Schur has defined victimless crimes as "the willing exchange, among adults, of strongly demanded but legally proscribed goods or services." Schur points out that there is clearly a lack of public consensus on laws that govern behavior such as gambling, prostitution, and the use of narcotics. Schur distinguishes these laws from other laws characterized by a lack of consensus, such as income tax laws, by indicating the difference in the exchange of elements of transaction: "Crimes without victims may be limited to those situations in which one person obtains from another, in a fairly direct exchange, a commodity or personal service which is socially disapproved and legally proscribed." Such crimes are also distinguished by the lack of apparent harm to others and by the difficulty in enforcing the laws against them because of low visibility and the absence of a complainant.[24]

Substance Abuse

The use and abuse of alcohol and other drugs and the legal reaction in this country to such abuse clearly illustrate the successes and problems associated with attempting to control moral behavior by law. It is impossible to separate these two kinds of substance abuse in terms of effect, as most people who abuse drugs abuse a variety of different kinds of drugs. For our purposes of analysis, however, there are some differences both historically and currently; so we look first at alcohol and then at other drug abuse before discussing the overall impact of substance abuse on criminal behavior.

Alcohol—December 5, 1983, marked the fiftieth anniversary of the repeal of Prohibition, a celebration that could be marked by the fact that Americans that year spent $59 billion on alcohol with an estimated additional $49 billion consumed by alcohol in related work loss, accidents, sickness, and death.[25] Alcohol is also blamed for thousands of deaths each year, constituting the number one cause of death among persons ages fifteen to twenty-one. Alcohol is also responsible for enormous personal and societal costs caused by illness and absenteeism from work.[26] Thus, the effects of alcohol create more than personal problems; they create problems for society as well. There have been numerous attempts to legislate alcohol abuse.

In 1919 the Eighteenth Amendment to the U.S. Constitution, prohibiting the manufacture, sale, and transportation of intoxicating liquors, was enacted. According to a columnist writing fifty years after that experiment ended,

> It made life both better and worse. With 170,000 saloons closed, alcohol consumption was cut by as much as half, as were arrests for disorderly conduct and drunkenness. The death rate for cirrhosis of the liver was cut two-thirds . . . [but it also] lessened faith in government, made it adventurous and profitable to dare the law, and human to admire those who did it.[27]

The Eighteenth Amendment did not prohibit drinking liquor; it attempted to make liquor more difficult to obtain. But violations of the law were rampant, and bootlegging became acceptable to most people. The experiment failed and national Prohibition was repealed in 1933. The result is that we can legally make, sell, and use liquor; but the criminal law is still used to regulate driving under the influence of alcohol and the age at which consumers may legally buy liquor. These uses of the criminal law may be considered appropriate, but they must be distinguished from defining as criminal all manufacture and sales of alcohol (as during Prohibition) or public drunkenness. Many persons arrested for public drunkenness are poor, unemployed, and suffering from acute personal problems. Most are arrested more than once, and many spend so much time in jail that they have been described as serving a life sentence on the installment plan. Such persons are not aided by being placed in jail, and as a result of enforcing criminal laws in this area, the police are diverted from other, more important functions.

Today, the trend in some jurisdictions is toward treatment and rehabilitation, not prosecution for criminal behavior for alcoholics. A Georgia statute illustrates this trend:

> It is the policy of this State that alcoholics may not be subject to criminal prosecution because of their consumption of alcoholic beverages but rather should be afforded a continuum of treatment in order that they may lead normal lives as productive members of society.[28]

On the other hand, in 1988 the U.S. Supreme Court, in a civil case involving health benefits, refused to rule that alcoholism is a disease over which the victim has no control. The Court held that alcoholism is a condition over which the individual has control.[29]

Drugs—Criminal law is used even more extensively to regulate drug abuse. However, in the latter half of the 1800s and in the early part of the 1900s, drugs could be purchased in this country by anyone without penalty. Gradually laws were passed to regulate the sale and the use of drugs. Former President Reagan and his administration declared "war" on drugs, aimed mainly at the sale of drugs, especially drug trafficking by pushers associated with organized crime. In early 1982 the FBI was assigned jurisdiction in drug offenses. According to Attorney General William French Smith, "For the first time since its establishment over fifty

EXHIBIT 1.3

President Reagan Reacts to the Drug Problem

On September 15, 1986, President Ronald Reagan issued Executive Order No. 12564, which authorizes federal agencies to establish programs for drug testing of employees. That order in part provides the following:

Section 1. Drug-Free Workplace

(a) Federal employees are required to refrain from the use of illegal drugs.

(b) The use of illegal drugs by federal employees, whether on duty or off duty, is contrary to the efficiency of the service.

(c) Persons who use illegal drugs are not suitable for federal employment.

---

years ago, the full resources of the FBI will be added to our fight against the most serious crime problem facing our nation—drug trafficking." The FBI's efforts are coordinated with those of the Drug Enforcement Administration, U.S. attorneys, other agencies in the Department of Justice, and other general agencies.[30]

The use of drugs became a big issue in 1986, with President Reagan's wife, Nancy, urging people to "Just say no" to drugs. She headed the campaign to draw attention to the problems created for individuals and for society by the illegal use of drugs. A CBS news poll in August of that year reported that concern with drugs had probably reached its highest point in history, with many people viewing illegal drugs as the most serious problem in our society. President Reagan successfully urged Congress to pass a comprehensive law aimed at the control of drugs. Despite the controversy over including the death penalty for deaths relating to the illegal sale of drugs (this provision was deleted from the final bill), Congress quickly passed a statute, backed with a promise of $1.7 billion in financing.

Americans reacted to the campaign to combat illegal drugs. Some children reported their parents to police. Employers began devising drug-testing programs for employees, and attorneys began preparing briefs about the constitutionality of such procedures. As Exhibit 1.3 indicates, President Reagan issued an executive order authorizing federal agencies to establish programs for drug testing of employees.

President Bush continued the administrative war against drugs. In September 1989 Bush announced his drug war plan that includes a 7.9 billion dollar price tag, much of which would come from state, not federal budgets. Bush's drug policy director, William J. Bennett, emphasized that there is "no one Sugar Daddy" to finance the war against drugs. Critics

quickly branded the Bush plan as totally inadequate to make significant progress in combatting illegal drug sales.[31]

Many agree that some aspects of substance abuse should be included in criminal law. The production and sale of dangerous narcotics are examples. There is not, however, much agreement on the criminalization of the possession of small amounts of drugs such as marijuana, the use of which is considered by many people to be a private matter. That issue is clearly debatable, but the critical issue still remains concerning whether criminal law should be used to control this behavior. Is this an effective use of criminal law? The chief of the Justice Department's organized crime section stated, in emphasizing lack of success in controlling the general drug problem, "You can't take a problem that is a medical, social and law enforcement problem, and hold law enforcement responsible for solving the whole problem by itself."[32] Highlight 1.3 also emphasizes the problem of trying to reduce drug use.

The legalization of drugs argument has recently gained ground, with

HIGHLIGHT 1.3

ALMOST ALL OF AMERICA IS ON DRUGS

The patriotic indignation against the use of illegal drugs and in favor of President Bush's resorting to extreme methods to combat drug traffic leaves the armchair detective puzzled.

The sales figures for legal drugs tell us that Americans are in love with drugs—that they need them desperately and spend their hard earned money to buy them.

Take, for example, legal drugs. Most adults begin their day with caffeine-laden coffee or tea. The amount of prescription "speed"—drugs that give millions energy to suffer through the day at work—totals hundreds of millions of dollars. In addition, Americans use downers—tranquilizers—which doctors (the legal drug pushers) prescribe.

Then, too, Americans drink caffeine-laden Coca-Cola or diet Pepsi throughout the day. They smoke billions of dollars of cigarettes a year, and, of course, cigar and pipe smoking have not disappeared.

The average adult also drinks beer or wine. In addition, many take one, two, three or more drinks of hard liquor. At night, millions use sleeping pills, Valium or some variety of legal drug in order to get their eight hours' sleep.

Some of these people obviously also use cocaine, marijuana and some exotic designer drugs. Ice, a super-"speed," is spreading through California. "Ecstasy" remains high on the list of middle class excitement experiences. And few scientists doubt that a synthetic variety of crack will appear even if the Medellín cartel doesn't survive President Bush's war.

If, as the Drug Enforcement Administration says, up to $150 billion worth of illegal drugs is consumed in the United States each year, who exactly is using them?

Clearly, cocaine consumption extends far beyond the ghettos. Indeed, middle- and upper-class use of illegal drugs is considerable.

Are those who tell pollsters that drugs must be stopped hypocrites or self-haters who cannot stop?

Why do the opinion polls reflect such anger, such desperation, on the part of a public, that, according to Government statistics, uses drugs, legal and illegal, regularly?

The users apparently do not

---

the mayors of Washington D.C., Baltimore, and Minneapolis, along with some members of Congress, calling upon the federal government to look carefully at the issue of legalizing drugs.[33]

Sexual Behavior

Sexual behavior between consenting adults is another area in which the law attempts to regulate private behavior. Norval Morris and Gordon Hawkins, who have written extensively on using the law to regulate moral behavior, emphasized that with the possible exception of John Calvin's sixteenth-century Geneva, the United States has the most moralistic criminal law in history. They refer to sex offense laws as possibly designed "to provide an enormous legislative chastity belt encompassing the whole population and proscribing everything but solitary and joyless masturbation and 'normal coitus' inside wedlock."[34]

HIGHLIGHT 1.3 (Continued)

offer the pollsters any positive feedback on the drugs that they take to make them happy or enable them to function.

Clearly, one reason for the mad rush to do something about illegal drugs is the crime wave that has resulted from trafficking. Drug-related murders and robberies grab headlines, and those who must bear the pain and anxiety of living under such conditions—or who fear that they may one day be affected by them—must rightly feel desperate.

Oddly, the market logic of legalizing drugs now deemed illegal—and thus diminishing the violence—seems to be something the majority does not want.

Since no politician would declare that we work at unhealthy levels of pressure and anxiety and thus need relief, drugs may

continue to be necessary to maintain the American way of life. For people in the ghetto, this way of life means crime, poor housing, bad health care and rotten education—all reasons why . . . crack is so widespread.

In light of the failure of President Bush and the Congress to deal with the public's need for drugs, the President's response is seen by users as both militant enough to maintain the facade of real action and sufficiently irrational to make possible the displacement of emotion and action.

If the angry messages from the White House and Capitol Hill reflect public thinking, then users do not blame themselves for drug use.

Instead, they displace that blame onto foreigners—Colom-

bians, Bolivians and Peruvians—who grow coca and manufacture the evil powder, and Mexicans, Panamanians and Cubans who allow it to be transported into the U.S. Somehow these wily Latins lure and tempt us innocent gringos into cocaine addiction.

For all the attention and money going into stopping the illegal traffic and maybe even usage, there is precious little being spent on answering this central question: Why so many Americans continue to use the stuff? Unless this question is answered, the prevention measures will amount to little.

SOURCE: Saul Landau, *New York Times,* 23 September, 1989 p. 15, col. 1.; © 1988/89 the New York Times Company. Reprinted by permission.

Fornication—"Prostitution may be our oldest profession; fornication is surely among our oldest crimes."[35] The word **fornication** comes from the Latin word for brothel *(fornix)* and legally means "unlawful sexual intercourse between two unmarried persons."[36]

With the greater acceptance of cohabitation, defined legally as "living together as man and wife," many states have changed their statutes and now permit sexual relations in private between consenting adults even though they are not married. Some jurisdictions have retained the statutes regarding fornication. The Idaho statute is an example:

> Any unmarried person who shall have sexual intercourse with an unmarried person of the opposite sex shall be deemed guilty of fornication, and, upon conviction thereof, shall be punished by a fine of not more than $300 or by imprisonment for not more than six months or both such fine and imprisonment; provided that the sentence imposed or any part thereof may be suspended with or without probation in the discretion of the court.[37]

Sodomy—Typical of the statutes regulating sexual behavior are those prohibiting deviant sexual acts, usually **sodomy** statutes. Historically, sodomy has referred to both bestiality (intercourse between a human and an animal) and buggery (anal intercourse between a man and another man or a woman). In most jurisdictions in the United States, however, this crime has been interpreted to include other sexual acts considered by some to be deviant—for example, oral stimulation of the sexual organs.

Historically, the reason for criminalizing sodomy has been that the act is "unnatural." Some statutes refer to sodomy as a "crime against nature." An example is the Idaho statute: "Every person who is guilty of the infamous crime against nature, committed with mankind or with any animal," which has been interpreted to include not only "the common-law crime of sodomy . . . but all unnatural carnal copulations, whether with man or beast, committed per os [mouth] or per anum [anus]."[38]

Another traditional argument for criminalizing sodomy is to prevent the spread of disease. The recent focus on AIDS has called attention to homosexuality as a health problem because the incidence of the disease is higher among male homosexuals than among any other group. The public argues that it must be protected from the possibility of contracting the deadly disease and that this can be done only by controlling homosexuality. More recent evidence, however, indicates that the disease is also communicated through blood transfusions and unsterile needles as well as by heterosexual contacts. In fact, recent evidence points to a future crisis in the spread of AIDS among extremely sexually active teenagers engaging in heterosexual intercourse. "And some studies indicate that as many as one percent of teenagers in cities like New York are already infected."[39]

Some of the sodomy statutes are written to apply only to male homosexuals; some are sex neutral and thus could also apply to females; others apply to heterosexual behavior between persons not married to each other; still others extend to sexual behavior between married persons. Sodomy statutes are not usually enforced except in cases involving male homosexuals or an adult engaging in sodomy with a minor of either sex. This development has led to allegations of discrimination in the enforcement of the statutes, along with allegations of the violation of the right to privacy. Some states have changed their statutes to permit any sexual behavior between consenting adults in private; others have revised statutes to permit the behavior between consenting married persons acting in private.

In 1986 the Supreme Court decided a case involving the Georgia sodomy statute. *Bowers v. Hardwick*, decided with a five-to-four vote, has created considerable controversy over the role of the government in the regulation of sexual behavior.[40] The case involved two male homosexuals engaging in oral sex in their bedroom, where they were seen by a police officer coming to the house with a warrant for the arrest of Hardwick, who had not paid a fine owed for conviction of drinking on a public street in Atlanta. The case thus raises the issue of state regulation of private, consensual sexual behavior between consenting homosexual adults in the privacy of a home. The case must be limited to its facts, consensual homosexual sodomy, but the Georgia statute in question is not limited to homosexual conduct. In 1985, the statute was held to apply to a husband who forced his wife to engage in sodomy.[41]

Excerpts from the majority and the dissenting opinions of *Bowers v. Hardwick* indicate the reasoning of the Supreme Court justices in this controversial case.[42]

Bowers v. Hardwick

. . . It is obvious to us that neither of these formulations of prior cases would extend a fundamental right to homosexuals to engage in acts of consensual sodomy. Proscriptions against that conduct have ancient roots. Sodomy was a criminal offense at common law and was forbidden by the laws of the original thirteen States when they ratified the Bill of Rights. . . . [U]ntil 1961, all 50 States outlawed sodomy, and today, 24 States and the District of Columbia continue to provide criminal penalties for sodomy performed in private and between consenting adults. Against this background, to claim that a right to engage in such conduct is "deeply rooted in this Nation's history and tradition" or "implicit in the concept of ordered liberty" is, at best, facetious. . . .

Respondent, however, asserts that the result should be different where the homosexual conduct occurs in the privacy of the home. . . . Plainly enough, otherwise illegal conduct is not always immunized whenever it occurs in the home. Victimless crimes, such as the possession and use of illegal drugs, do not escape the law when they are committed at home. . . . And if respondent's submission is limited to the voluntary sexual conduct between consenting adults, it would be difficult, except by fiat, to limit the claimed right to homosexual conduct while leaving exposed to prosecution adultery, incest, and other sexual crimes even though they are committed in the home. We are unwilling to start down that road. . . .

The law . . . is constantly based on notions of morality, and if all laws representing essentially moral choices are to be invalidated . . . the courts will be very busy indeed. Even respondent makes no such claim but insists that majority sentiments about the morality of homosexuality should be declared inadequate. We do not agree, and are unpersuaded that the sodomy laws of some twenty-five States should be invalidated on this basis.

Justice Blackmun wrote a dissenting opinion, in which three other justices joined. Blackmun emphasized that the case involved the "right to be let alone." Two years later, Justice Marshall, in a news report, commented on the case as follows:

> Well, a couple of more decisions like the Georgia sodomy case and we won't have any privacy left. But I will raise my voice against it as long as I've got breath. You've got Big Brother in the bedroom. I don't know any place else that you can keep Big Brother out of.
>
> I think a man's home is his castle, and goodness knows if his home is his castle, the bedroom is in the middle of it. I don't want anybody snooping around my bedroom. I don't have a gun, but I might be tempted.[43]

In Maryland the sodomy statute was upheld, with the court reasoning that the statute does not violate the right to privacy when applied to consenting, unmarried, heterosexual adults.[44]

Analysis of the Purpose of Criminal Law

This brief discussion of the use of criminal law to regulate morality raises the question of whether law is the best method of social control in this area of behavior. Highlight 1.4 raises the issue whether even the church is the appropriate institution to regulate moral behavior. Whether the law serves its purpose of deterrence is a serious question that is discussed in a subsequent chapter. Whether the law serves as an adequate symbol of morality can be questioned when the law is enforced infrequently. Whether the law is used to discriminate against particular groups, such as the poor, minorities, foreigners, or homosexuals, is also an important issue.

Other examples could also be raised. Should the law be used to protect people against themselves, for example, requiring motorcyclists to wear helmets? Some states now require the wearing of seatbelts and shoulder straps in automobiles. Failure to do so results in a fine. Should the criminal law be employed to regulate this behavior? If this concept were carried further, it could be argued that the state should regulate the diet of its citizens and prohibit cigarette smoking and excessive drinking. The state might also prevent overweight persons from shoveling snow because they are apparently more susceptible to heart attacks. There are limits to how far the law should go in protecting people against themselves, but there is little consensus on what those limits should be.

Attempts to legislate morality have not been successful when the laws lacked substantial support by the American people, as illustrated by the widespread violation of prohibition laws in earlier days and of drug laws today.

The state does have an interest in preserving the morals of its people. Clearly the law must be concerned with some moral principles and cannot permit people to abuse one another. The law should provide moral guidance. But can that happen if the law creates disrespect because it is

HIGHLIGHT 1.4

THE CONTROL OF MORALITY—THE CHURCH OR THE STATE?

"What we did for Marian" was out of love, so said the elders of the Church of Christ in Collinsville, a small community near Tulsa, Oklahoma. The elders were reacting to the $390,000 damage award—"The Will of the Lord"—decided in favor of Marian Guinn, who sued the elders and the members of the church for invading her privacy and causing her "extreme emotional distress."

Guinn, a young divorced mother of four, had joined the church but was not attending regularly when an elder informed her that she should not be dating the former mayor, a divorced man. "He is not suitable for you," she was told. When the former mayor called one of the elders about another matter, the mayor was asked about his relationship with Guinn and admitted to intimacy. When the elder confronted Guinn, she admitted that she was having an affair. She was told that she must end the relationship, come back into the church, and repent before all the

members. Guinn refused and personally delivered a handwritten letter to the elders. In this letter she indicated that she wished to resign from the church and that the information she gave to the elders about her personal life should be kept confidential. She was assured that it would be, but the letter was later read to the congregation. She was told that she could not resign because "We have to withdraw from you."

The elders claim it was their duty to inform Marian that her fornication was a sin, that she must stop, and that she must repent. If they did not attempt to "save" her, they too would be guilty for her sin. But Guinn, her attorney, and the jury took the view that the elders had violated Guinn's personal rights.

The Oklahoma case gained national attention; it was the subject of television's "60 Minutes" and will become a movie. Shortly after the award was announced, a similar suit was filed in San Jose, California, by a man

who confided in a counselor in his church, giving him details of his marital and sexual problems. "That material that I gave to him in confidence, six weeks later, was publicly read before six hundred members of the church."

Although criminal law may not be the best form of social control of morality, these cases illustrate that the church may not be, either. In exercising what church members consider to be their responsibility, they are violating the rights of their members. Our courts recognize as torts the violation of the right of privacy, as well as the subjecting of others to "extreme emotional distress," for which the individuals who have suffered the civil wrong may sue in civil court. In Guinn's case the jury awarded actual damages—a measure of money that is to compensate the victim for the injury. The jury also awarded punitive damages to deter this kind of activity.

SOURCE: Compiled by the author from various media.

---

applied unfairly or because it encompasses those kinds of conduct that are acceptable to many but difficult or impossible to enforce? Some laws cannot be enforced—those regulating sexual behavior, for example—without violating some of the basic freedoms, such as the right to privacy. Therefore in many cases no attempt is made to enforce the laws, which creates disrespect for the law. If these criminal laws do not deter the behavior at which they are aimed, do they serve any function in society?

Laws regulating moral behavior are, to some extent, functional. Edwin Schur suggested that attaching the label of deviant or criminal to some persons who violate these laws may serve a positive function for the conformists in that the process may increase their group cohesion.[45] Selective enforcement of the laws also serves to preserve the power of the majority—the weaker, unimportant members of society are kept in their places. In that sense, unequal administration of the law is functional because it keeps the status arrangements of society from being disrupted. When, for example, drunks appear in public, police may often react differently depending on the drunks' social status. If they are lower class, they may have a greater chance of being arrested. If they are upper or middle class, they may more likely be driven home. Laws regulating morality may also serve the function of making the majority feel that something is being done to preserve the morals of society. That is, these laws may create the impression that certain questionable behavior is officially disapproved. To abolish the laws, it is argued, would condone the behavior and would not be a politically wise move for politicians.

On the other hand, some of the statutes that regulate victimless crimes or morality may have negative repercussions. Violation of privacy to obtain evidence of criminal conduct, use of police decoys to catch people violating sexual laws, driving demanded services underground, and many other problems might result. Laws may give the impression that something is being done when actually nothing is being done. For example, passing laws to criminalize the act of spreading AIDS may look good on the books and have little effect on sexual behavior because of the difficulties in getting convictions in these cases. Throughout the discussions in the text, we question why we have criminal laws, why we do or do not enforce those laws, and what the consequences are of our decisions.

THE STUDY OF CRIME

The study of crime, criminals, and criminal law is of ancient origin. Historically the primary focus has been on attempts to explain the behavior of criminals. The causes of crime are explored through discussions of biological, psychological, economic, and sociological theories. But the modern study of crime involves more than an attempt to understand why people violate the law. The discipline of criminology also includes the sociology of law (which analyzes why some acts and not others are defined as crimes) and a study of the social responses to crime (which examines why some people and not others are processed through the system after committing the same acts). These areas of focus are not, however, always separable. There is considerable overlap. Nor is there agreement on which areas should receive research priorities. This text includes material on all three areas.

ORGANIZATION OF THE TEXT

Chapter 2 introduces the data on crime and victims and concludes the introductory section. Part II focuses on explanations of criminal behavior, consisting of four chapters that cover early explanations of crime before discussing biological, psychological, economic, and sociological theories.

Part III contains four chapters on typologies of criminal behavior. These chapters illustrate how sociologists attempt to understand crime and reactions to crime by focusing their studies on types of crime. The chapters cover violent crimes, property crimes, crimes of the business world, and organized crime and terrorism.

In Part IV, "The Criminal Justice System," the focus shifts to the sociology of law and an analysis of the social responses to crimes, two other interests of criminologists. The three chapters of Part IV explore the role of police, explain the system of criminal justice, and discuss the criminal court system. Part V contains two chapters on social reaction to crime: "The Confinement of Offenders," which discusses jails and prisons, and "The Supervision of Offenders in the Community," which explores the ways in which inmates are released from prison and the problems they encounter upon their return to the community.

Throughout the discussions, materials are used from law and from criminology and sociology in addition to some references to other disciplines where pertinent. The text material is illustrated by charts, graphs, highlights, exhibits, and figures.

 ## *CONCLUSION*

This chapter has explored the meaning of crime and the nature and purpose of criminal law. Because criminal law defines criminal behavior, thus formulating the basis for the kinds of behavior on which this study of criminology focuses, this discussion is important in setting the stage for the text. Many of the issues raised throughout the text are in some way related to the central issue of this chapter—the purpose of criminal law and the kinds of behavior that should be included within its reach. The answers to these questions largely determine who is and who is not a criminal and therefore who does and who does not constitute a basis for the study of criminology.

The inclusion or exclusion of morality within the reach of criminal law will affect all elements of the criminal justice system. The rights of defendants versus the rights of victims and the right of society to be protected from criminal behavior will be affected. Crackdowns on drinking, especially while driving, have aggravated the already serious problems of jail and prison overcrowding. Removal of substance abuse from criminal law requires the provision of other kinds of institutions and facilities for handling such problems. Central to the entire discussion is the underlying theme of deterrence, that sanctions are imposed to deter people from engaging in the proscribed behavior. Sociological contributions to our understanding of whether or not laws deter is crucial in our analysis of this issue.

What, then, should be the purpose of law? It has been argued that the main purpose of criminal law is to protect persons and property from the abuse of others. "When the criminal law invades the spheres of private morality . . . it exceeds its proper limits at the cost of neglecting its primary tasks. This unwarranted extension is expensive, ineffective, and criminogenic."[46]

What should be included within the province of criminal law? Certainly criminal law should be used to protect individuals from being forced to engage in certain behaviors. For example, no person, adult or juvenile, should be forced to engage in any sexual behavior. Criminal law should penalize those who participate in sexual behavior with persons under the age of consent; that is, immature persons should be protected from sexual exploitation. The sexism of laws should be removed, and males as well as females should be protected from the unwilling viewing of sexual behavior. When consenting behavior is permitted, it should be restricted to places where one can reasonably expect privacy.

The law cannot, however, control the behavior of all people in a complex society. The law should provide some standards, goals, and guidelines—a statement of what conduct is so important that it must be formally sanctioned. The law should also provide some moral guidance; but it should not be used to regulate behavior that is more properly regulated by other agencies or by individuals.

Nor should the law interfere with our rights of privacy: "Any attempt to criminalize all wrongful conduct would involve intolerable intrusions into citizens' lives and choices. Much wrongdoing in people's private and working lives should not be legally punishable because it involves areas of behavior which a free society should keep clear of the drastic intervention of the criminal law."[47]

Finally, law is inherently social. Sociological perspectives and inquiries are necessary if we are to appreciate the social nature of law.[48]

ENDNOTES

1. Paul Tappan, *Crime, Justice and Correction* (New York: McGraw-Hill, 1960), p. 10.
2. Buch v. Amory Manufacturing Co., 69 N.H. 257 (1897).
3. American Law Institute, *Model Penal Code*, Section 2.02.
4. U.S. v. Dotterweich, 320 U.S. 277 (1943).

5. L. Gostin, executive director of the American Society of Law and Medicine, quoted in *Criminal Justice Newsletter* 20 (April 17, 1989), p. 2.

6. Sherman v. United States, 356 U.S. 369 (1958).

7. State v. Stewart, 763 P.2d 572 (Kan. 1988).

8. "Mother who Killed Child is Convicted," *Tallahassee Democrat*, 4 September 1988, p. 3D, col. 1.

9. For an exception in criminal law texts, see Sue Titus Reid, *Criminal Law* (New York: Macmillan, 1989).

10. For a discussion of misdemeanors, see John H. Lindquist, *Misdemeanor Crime: Trivial Criminal Pursuit* (Beverly Hills, CA.: Sage Publishers, 1988).

11. "Technicality to Free Man Convicted of Raping Girl," *Tallahassee Democrat*, 6 May 1989, p. 1, col. 3.

12. Thorsten Sellin, "A Sociological Approach," in Marvin E. Wolfgang et al., eds., *The Sociology of Crime and Delinquency*, 2d ed. (New York: John Wiley, 1970), p. 6.

13. Paul W. Tappan, "Who Is the Criminal?" *American Sociological Review* 21 (February 1947): 99.

14. Henry J. Abraham, *The Judicial Process* (New York: Oxford University Press, 1968), p. 5.

15. Martin Luther King, Jr., *Why We Can't Wait* (New York: Harper & Row, 1963), pp. 84–85.

16. Paul W. Tappan, "Who Is the Criminal?" *American Sociological Review* 21 (February 1947): 99.

17. William Graham Sumner, *Folkways* (New York: Dover, 1906), pp. 1–79.

18. See William Seagle, *The Quest for Law* (New York: Knopf, 1941).

19. See, for example, Richard D. Schwartz, "Social Factors in the Development of Legal Control: A Case Study of Two Israeli Settlements," *Yale Law Journal* 63 (February 1954): 471–491.

20. Émile Durkheim, *The Division of Labor in Society*, trans. George Simpson (New York: Free Press, 1947).

21. Max Weber, *Law in Economy and Society*, Max Rheinstein, ed. (Cambridge, Mass.: Harvard University Press, 1954). Weber's work on legal evolution is discussed in Talcott Parsons, "Evolutionary Universals in Society," *American Sociological Review* 26 (June 1964): 350–353. For a more recent article that discusses the various theories used to analyze the origins of laws and reviews empirical studies of the laws of delinquency and probation, alcohol and drug abuse, and prostitution and sexual deviance, see John Hagan, "The Legislation of Crime and Delinquency: A Review of Theory, Method, and Research," *Law & Society Review* 14 (Spring 1980): 603–628.

22. "Battle in Chinatown Over Peking Duck Heating Up," *Los Angeles Times*, 3 March 1982, p. 1, col. 5.

23. See Norval Morris and Gordon P. Hawkins, *The Honest Politician's Guide to Crime Control* (Chicago: University of Chicago Press, 1969).

24. Edwin M. Schur, *Crimes Without Victims: Deviant Behavior and Public Policy* (Englewood Cliffs, N.J.: Prentice-Hall, 1965), pp. 169, 170–171.

25. These figures and most of the historical account come from an editorial by John Barbour of the Associated Press, reprinted in the *Tulsa World*, "50 Years Ago, America Opened the Bottle Again," 4 December 1983, p. D3, col. 1.

26. See the report by Joseph A. Califano, former secretary of Health, Education and Welfare, reported in *The 1982 Report on Drug Abuse and Alcoholism* (New

York: Warner). For an excellent discussion of the various theories used to analyze the origins of laws regulating alcohol and drugs and for a review of empirical studies, see John Hagan, "The Legislation of Crime and Delinquency: A Review of Theory, Method, and Research," *Law & Society Review* 14 (Spring 1980): 603–628.

27. Barbour, "50 Years Ago. . . ."
28. Ga. Code Ann. Section 99–3901 (1982).
29. Traynor v. Turnage, 485 U.S. 535 (1988).
30. *Justice Assistance News* 3 (March 1982).
31. See "Drug Plan Would Shift Burden to Local Level, Critics Say," *Criminal Justice Newsletter* 20 (15 September, 1989), p. 1. For a general overview of drug abuse see Howard Abadinsky, *Drug Abuse: An Introduction* (Nelson-Hall Publishers: Chicago, 1989), p. 335.
32. David Margolis, quoted in "President's Antidrug Task Forces Are Falling Behind in Organizing," *New York Times*, 1 May 1983, p. 1, col. 5.
33. For a scholarly discussion on the pros and cons of legalizing drugs, see Part 4, Richard C. Monk, ed., *Taking Sides: Clashing Views on Controversial Issues in Crime and Criminology* (Guilford, Conn.: The Dushkin Publishing Group, Inc., 1989), pp. 290–307. The Washington, D.C. mayor was arrested in 1990 for illegal possession of drugs. After a six-week trial, Barry was convicted of one drug charge, acquitted of another, and a mistrial was declared when the jury indicated that it was deadlocked on all other—including more serious—charges.
34. Morris and Hawkins, *The Honest Politician's Guide*, p. 15.
35. "Note: Fornication, Cohabitation, and the Constitution," *Michigan Law Review* 77 (December 1978): 253.
36. *Black's Law Dictionary*, 5th ed. Delux (St. Paul: West Publishing, 1979), p. 588.
37. Idaho Criminal Code, Section 18–6603.
38. Idaho Criminal Code, Section 18–6605; State v. Altwater, 157 P. 256, 257 (Idaho 1916).
39. "Experts Alarmed by Rise in AIDS Among Teen-Agers," *New York Times*, 8 October 1989, p. 1, col. 1.
40. Bowers v. Hardwick, 478 U.S. 186 (1986), *reh. den.* 478 U.S. 1039 (1986).
41. Warren v. State, 336 S.E.2d 221 (Ga. 1985).
42. Bowers v. Hardwick, 478 U.S. 186 (1986), *reh. den.* 478 U.S. 1039 (1986).
43. "Marshalling His Views: Justice's Controversial Comments Break 20-year Silence," *ABA Journal* (March 1988): 36.
44. Schochet v. State, 541 A.2d 183 (Md. App. 1988), *cert. granted*, 547 A.2d 201 (1988).
45. Schur, *Crimes Without Victims*, p. 4. See also Durkheim, *Division of Labor in Society*, pp. 96–110.
46. Morris and Hawkins, *The Honest Politician's Guide*, p. 2.
47. Andrew von Hirsch, "Desert and Previous Convictions in Sentencing," *Minnesota Law Review* 65 (April 1981): 607.
48. Edwin M. Schur, *Law and Society: A Sociological View* (New York: Random House, 1968.)

CHAPTER 2

The focus of this chapter is on crime data. We examine the official and unofficial ways in which data are collected on crimes, criminals, and victims of crime. The variables, such as police discretion, methods of reporting, victims' cooperation or refusal to cooperate, and administrative and bureaucratic changes that may affect the accuracy of data, are discussed. Following this background on the problems of collecting data, we analyze the most recent data on crime and crime victims in terms of the variables of age, race, and sex. Finally, we consider whether a new perspective on crime data is needed.

OUTLINE

The Measurement of Crime and Its Impact

KEY TERMS

Bureau of Justice Statistics (BJS)
cartographic school
computer crime
Crime Classification System
  (CCS)
crime rate
crimes known to the police
discretion
index offense
National Crime Survey (NCS)
National Incident-Based
  Reporting System (NABRS)
National Youth Survey (NYS)
organized crime
property crime
self-report data (SRD)
Uniform Crime Reports (UCR)
violent crimes
white-collar crime

In 1968 for the first time in three decades of public opinion polling, Americans listed crime as the most serious national problem. At that time crime rates were rising almost nine times as fast as the population. Crime did not become an important political issue until the 1964 presidential campaign, although in 1960 the Democratic party platform had cursorily mentioned rising crime rates.[1] In 1965 Congress passed the Law Enforcement Assistance Act, and the President's Commission on Law Enforcement and Administration of Justice was established. That commission issued its volumes of reports in 1967. Since that time the National Advisory Commission on Criminal Justice Standards and Goals (appointed in 1971 and the first commission in this country appointed for the purpose of formulating national criminal justice standards and goals for reducing and preventing crime) has also issued several reports, including one on disorders and terrorism.

In the early 1980s Americans viewed inflation, the recession, and other domestic problems as more serious than crime. By 1986 many people once again listed crime or illegal drugs as the number one domestic problem. These views continued through the 1980s. A perception of increasing violence among juveniles and violence against the elderly has led many Americans to fear being on the streets in the daytime as well as at night. Others are terrified even behind the locks and bars of their own homes. This fear of violent crime has led to a boom in the sales of locks, bars, and sophisticated crime-prevention alarm systems. To add to the fear, each year, with few exceptions, the annual official data on crime have indicated increases in crime rates.[2]

This chapter more carefully examines official and unofficial crime data. The importance of this discussion cannot be overemphasized. The reader should realize that in many respects the nature of all other discussions of crime hinges on such data. How we count crime and criminals influences to a great extent the theories we advance for causation. It also influences the allocation of resources in the criminal justice system.

THE PERCEPTION OF CRIME

The 1980s began with many popular articles on crime depicting America as being in a crisis concerning the incidence and fear of crime. According to a dramatic presentation by *Newsweek* in 1981, "Defying any cure, [violent crime] overwhelms the police, the courts and the prisons—and warps U.S. life."[3]

In 1989 popular news magazines have carried such headlines as the following:

> Dead Zones: Whole Sections of Urban America are Being Written off as Anarchic Badlands, Places Where Cops Fear to Go and Acknowledge: "This is Beirut, U.S.A."[4]

The Other Arms Race: America's Streets Become Free-fire Zones as Police, Criminals, and Terrified Citizens Wield More and Ever Deadlier Guns.[5]

Sociologists know that public perceptions are important in determining how the public will react. If we believe that crime is more extensive and more violent than it is, we may change our lifestyles unnecessarily. There is evidence that this change occurs among the elderly. As an early sociologist W. I. Thomas said, "If men believe situations are real, they are real in their consequences." It is important to have an accurate measure of crime and to convey that accuracy to the public. This need raises two issues: that of measuring crime and that of altering the public perception. We will look at the latter first and then devote the remainder of the chapter to the issues surrounding the measurement of crime and its impact.

Some earlier studies showed general agreement in public perception of the seriousness of crime,[6] while more recent ones question this conclusion,[7] but some researchers have concluded that public perception is inaccurate because of distorted presentations by the media. One investigator, after reviewing the research conducted by psychologists, political scientists, and sociologists, concluded, "In general, the available research shows that crime is a relatively staple topic in the media's news and entertainment presentations. The amount of crime depicted has little relationship to the amount of crime occurring, and violent crimes are highly overrepresented by the media." The research differs in conclusions regarding the impact of this distortion. "On the other hand, the research strongly supports the notion that the viewing of violence increases the probability of behaving aggressively."[8]

Media distortion of crime was evident in the 1988 presidential election with Vice-President George Bush, in the latter days of the campaign, focusing heavily on the prison furlough policy of Massachusetts. Bush's opponent, Massachusetts Governor Michael Dukakis, was portrayed as "soft on crime" after Willie Horton, murderer and rapist, committed atrocious violent crimes while on a prison furlough. Highlight 2.1 contains more details on the Willie Horton ads. The implication was that Dukakis was responsible for these atrocities and that Bush, if elected president, could eliminate them. The reality is that most people on prison furloughs do not commit violent crimes and that the president has little, if any, power to change state laws and procedures such as those that permitted the temporary release of Willie Horton.

Others have questioned the conclusion that the media present a distorted picture of crime. They argue that this conclusion is not based on empirical evidence, that there is no evidence that the public bases its perceptions of crime totally on media presentations, or that the public accepts media presentations without critical analysis.[9] Empirical investigations have questioned these assumptions, finding, for example, that although people who most often watch television tend to be the most afraid of crime, "When the effect of neighborhood is removed, the 'effect' of television is reduced to almost nothing."[10] There is also some evidence that the

HIGHLIGHT 2.1

THE 1988 PRESIDENTIAL CAMPAIGN AGAINST CRIME: THE CASE OF WILLIE HORTON

Willie Horton, a convicted murderer, became nationally known during the 1988 presidential campaign because of its emphasis on crime. While on furlough in Massachusetts (home state of unsuccessful candidate Michael Dukakis), Horton committed additional violent crimes.

HIGHLIGHT 2.1 (Continued)

Willie Horton. Black. Murderer. Rapist. Most valuable player in George Bush's no-holds-barred bid for the White House.

Of all the tactics used by Bush's strategists to brand Michael Dukakis a gooey liberal out of touch with mainstream values, none worked better than the relentless pounding of Horton's horrible tale. By the end of the campaign, scarcely a voter had not been exposed to the lurid details of the rapacious spree Horton committed while on weekend furlough from the Massachusetts prison to which he had been sentenced to life without parole for a brutal 1974 homicide.

Like most attack ploys, there was a grain of truth to be exploited: the prison-furlough policy used by Massachusetts went beyond the boundaries of common sense. Unlike other states and the Federal Government, which usually employ furloughs to gradually acclimate prisoners near the end of their sentences to living outside the walls, Massachusetts granted weekend leaves to convicts whom judges had condemned to remain behind bars until they died. Horton is precisely the sort of criminal that people have in mind when they say someone should lock him up and throw away the key.

It was one of Dukakis' rivals for the Democratic nomination, Tennessee Senator Al Gore, who first unearthed the furlough policy as a campaign issue. The fact that it was inaugurated by Dukakis' Republican predecessor is irrelevant. As Governor, Dukakis stubbornly resisted attempts to rescind furloughs for first-degree murderers until a drive to ban such leaves through a state referendum gathered steam. By then, the presidential-primary season was under way.

If the Republican assault on Dukakis' furlough policy had stopped with making these valid points, Democrats and blacks would have no just cause for complaint. But the Republican attack did not stop there. Instead, Bush's handlers tapped into the rich lode of white fear and resentment of blacks that the G.O.P. staked out more than 20 years ago, when the party of Lincoln recast itself as the embodiment of the white backlash. It started with Barry Goldwater railing against Earl Warren's Supreme Court and civil rights legislation. Then, as the long hot summers blazed, Richard Nixon courted voters with a "law-and-order" harangue. Ronald Reagan kept it up with his allusions to "welfare queens" and the "strapping young buck" using food stamps to buy a T-bone steak.

The fear of crime is, to be sure, deeply implanted among Americans of all races. No group is more victimized by street thugs than the law-abiding citizens of the ghetto. Doubtless the G.O.P. would have exploited Dukakis' furlough policy if Horton were white. Yet the glee with which Bush's campaign team leaped upon the Horton affair belies its denials that it intended to tweak white prejudices. In Horton, Bush's staff found a potent symbolic twofer: a means by which to appeal to the legitimate issue of crime while simultaneously stirring racial fears.

How else to explain Bush campaign manager Lee Atwater's remark to Republican activists gathered in Atlanta last July? Observing that Jesse Jackson, then pressing his demand to be selected as Dukakis' vice-presidential running mate, had visited Dukakis' home on July 4, Atwater suggested that "maybe he will put this Willie Horton on the ticket after all is said and done." Or the relish with which Bush press secretary Mark Goodin pasted a mug shot of Horton on the wall above his desk. Or the ardor with which Bush's media guru Roger Ailes declared, "The only question is whether we depict Willie Horton with a knife in his hand or without it." In the end, the Bush campaign re-

HIGHLIGHT 2.1 (Continued)

frained from using Horton's likeness in its campaign spots, leaving an independent political-action committee to saturate the airwaves with the rapist's glaring visage while a few state Republican parties stuffed mailboxes with flyers banging home the same message.

Dukakis, of course, might have spiked the Horton offensive early on by pointing to its racist implications. But the Massachusetts Governor was pursuing his own racially callous strategy, ignoring black supporters in an attempt to reach out to fickle Reagan Democrats, who abandoned their traditional political home at least in part because it is seen as the party of minorities. Only after his suit was rebuffed did Dukakis, in desperation, mend fences with Jackson, visit black churches and reassure the party's most reliable supporters that he was, after all, "on your side."

In 1964, in his first attempt at elected office as a Senate candidate from Texas, George Bush came out against the civil rights law that desegregated hotels, restaurants and water fountains—a stance he later admitted he regretted. Four years later, as a Congressman, he cast a courageous vote for open housing. In this year's race for the White House, Bush, alas, came closer to the 1964 model, a politician who will do whatever it takes to win an election, even when his instincts tell him it's wrong.

SOURCE: Jack E. White, "Bush's Most Valuable Player," *Time,* 14 November 1988, pp. 20–21. Copyright 1988 by Time, Inc. Reprinted by permission.

---

public is fairly accurate in its perceptions of actual crime.[11] That, of course, assumes that actual crime can be measured.

THE MEASUREMENT OF CRIME

For a science of criminal behavior to have developed, it was necessary to have empirical data on criminals and to be able to analyze those data. The next chapter will analyze early theories of criminal behavior, but first, we will discuss the origin of the scientific study of crime.

The Emergence of Scientific Criminology: The Cartographic School

The **cartographic school** views crime as a necessary expression of social conditions. Geographic phenomena—including climate (temperature, humidity, and barometric pressure), topography, natural resources, and geographic location—are thought to influence criminal behavior. Cartographic studies were made possible only when data became available on population distribution, births, and deaths. The systematic collection of such data did not begin until the nineteenth century in France with the work of André Michel Guerry and in Belgium with the work of Adolphe Quételet. Guerry's work is considered by many to be the "first work in 'scientific criminology,'" and Quételet has been called the "first social criminologist."[12]

Guerry analyzed crime data by districts within France. He made charts, tables, and maps and looked at the variables of age, sex, and education. He also classified crimes as those against property and those against persons. He attempted to identify the factors that *predispose* one to criminal behavior rather than those factors that *cause* the behavior. He rejected the simplistic explanations that poverty or increases in population density cause an increase in crime and that education will prevent criminal behavior. Guerry's work appears to have been the first to use crime data to test assumptions about the relationship of certain variables to criminal behavior. He also questioned the belief that crime is the result of the moral turpitude of the offender.

Like Guerry, Quételet was also concerned with patterns and regularity found in the analysis of social data. A statistician, Quételet is sometimes called "the father of modern statistics." Trying to measure social phenomena with statistics, he published detailed analyses of crime and moral social conditions in Holland, Belgium, and France.[13] Both Guerry and Quételet were important in influencing other researchers in Europe. Some related crime to such factors as density and poverty. They saw the densely populated areas as collecting rather then breeding crime. Others looked at the relationships between crime and broken homes, poverty, and lack of education.[14]

Although these early scholars are not often mentioned by sociologists and criminologists who are studying crime today, they were responsible for the beginning of scientific criminology. Their contributions should be accorded an important place in the development of criminological thought. Although they were naive about statistics and the principles of causation, their great value lies in the fact that they did use quantitative techniques with some skill. They believed that crime cannot be understood merely in terms of the characteristics of individual offenders; the total environment in which that crime occurs must also be studied. These early scholars thus paved the way for measuring and analyzing crime according to relevant variables such as geography and climate in addition to the more frequently used variables of age, sex, socioeconomic class, and race and ethnicity.[15]

SOURCES OF CRIME DATA

Measurement of crime today is more sophisticated and more extensive than the work of the earlier scholars, but there is serious disagreement over how crime should be measured. Methods used for collecting official crime data vary according to their source; unofficial sources differ from official sources. This section examines each type. But we must keep in mind that they do differ; that they are not always comparable; and that conclusions about how much crime exists, the nature of the crime, who committed the crime, and who was victimized will differ according to the sources used.

Most media reports and most analyses of crime data are based on official data. Two major sources of official data are the *Uniform Crime Reports (UCR)* and the National Crime Survey (NCS). Official compilers of crime data are government agencies that collect crime data for a variety of different purposes. The most common source is agency reports. At the state level, data about the criminal justice system are maintained routinely, but the systems differ in scope, definition, and quality. As a result, comparison of crime data obtained from the various states is difficult.

The situation is not much better at the federal level. Many agencies have independent data systems; the usefulness of the data is reduced because of different definitions, reporting periods, and classification schemes. The sources of federal crime data cover many agencies, such as the Federal Bureau of Investigation; the National Criminal Justice Information and Statistics Service; the Drug Enforcement Administration; the National Institute on Drug Abuse; the Federal Aviation Administration; the Secret Service; the Administrative Office of the United States Courts; the Federal Prison System; the Bureau of Alcohol, Tobacco, and Firearms; the Customs Service; the Census Bureau; the National Council on Crime and Delinquency; the Institute for Law and Social Research; the National Institute for Juvenile Justice and Delinquency Prevention; the National Center for Juvenile Justice; and the National Center for Health Statistics.

Partly as a response to this fragmentation, in 1981 Congress authorized the creation of the **Bureau of Justice Statistics (BJS).** Its main goal is to furnish an objective, independent, and competent source of police-relevant data to the government and to criminal justice and academic communities.[16] Goals of BJS are the unification of data, development of a program to follow an offender from the time of entering the criminal justice process until release from the correctional system, and provision of services to states and local communities to aid in comprehensive data gathering. The bureau is not, however, to be involved in policy decisions.[17]

Although BJS data are useful, the most frequently cited and most comprehensive source of crime data is the *Uniform Crime Reports (UCR)* under the jurisdiction of the FBI.

The Uniform Crime Reports (UCR)

In the 1920s the International Association of Chiefs of Police (IACP) appointed a committee to develop a system for securing crime data on a national scale. By 1929 the committee had developed a plan that became the basis for the *UCR*. In 1930 Congress passed a law requiring the U.S.

Attorney General to report annually on the amount of crime in the United States. That same year the FBI began issuing its publication on national crime data, the *Uniform Crime Reports*. At first the *UCR* was issued monthly; later it was issued quarterly. From 1942 until 1957 the reports were semiannual; in 1958 the present format of one annual publication was started.

Standardized definitions of crime were developed for all offenses to provide uniformity in reporting data. Local agencies compile data and submit it to the *UCR* through state *UCR* agencies. Although the FBI has the responsibility for administering the *UCR* program, the organization has no authority to compel reporting by state and local jurisdictions. Even though it is voluntary, the national *UCR* program currently covers 98 percent of the U.S. population.

UCR Coverage

Seven crimes were originally selected because of their seriousness and frequency to constitute the *UCR* Crime Index; arson, the eighth, was added in 1978. These are known as Part I Offenses. They are the serious **violent crimes**—murder and nonnegligent manslaughter, forcible rape, robbery, and aggravated assault—and the serious **property crimes**—burglary, larceny-theft, motor vehicle theft, and arson. Each month law enforcement agencies report the number of **crimes known to the police,** the number of Part I Offenses verified as having been committed after police investigation of the complaint. The number of actual crimes in the index category is reported whether or not there is any further action in the case; that is, a crime known to police is counted even if no suspect is arrested and no prosecution ever occurs.

If a criminal activity involves several different crimes, only the most serious is reported as an **index offense.** For example, if a victim is raped, robbed, and murdered, only the murder is counted in the *UCR*. Offenses known to police do not indicate how many persons were involved in a particular reported crime. The *UCR* reports total Part I Offenses and a **crime rate,** which is calculated by dividing the number of reported crimes by the number of people in the country. The result is expressed as as rate of crime per 100,000 people. The *UCR* also reports trends in offenses and crime rates.

The number of Part I Offenses that are cleared by arrest is also reported. Offenses are cleared in two ways. They may be cleared by arrest when a suspect is arrested, charged, and turned over to the judicial system for prosecution; or they may be cleared by circumstances beyond the control of the police. The death of a suspect or a victim's refusal to press charges normally ends police involvement. Crimes are considered cleared whether or not the person arrested is convicted.

Several persons may be arrested and one crime cleared, or one person may be arrested and many crimes cleared. The *clearance rate* is the

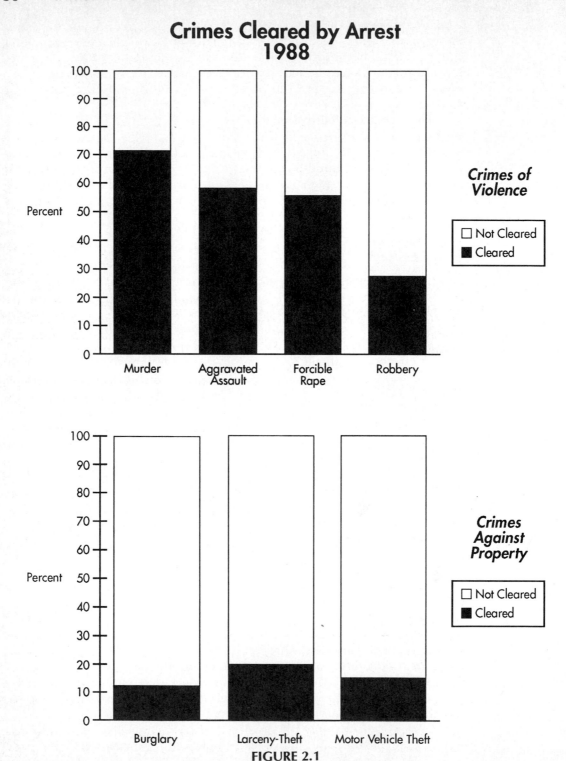

FIGURE 2.1

number of crimes solved expressed as a percentage of the total number of crimes reported to the police. The clearance rate is critical in policy decisions because it is one measure used to evaluate police departments. The higher the number of crimes solved by arrest, the better the police force looks in the eyes of the public. As Figure 2.1 indicates, the clearance rate is higher for violent than for property crimes.

The *UCR* records and publishes arrest data for Part II Offenses, the less serious crimes. The *UCR* also lists the number of arrests made during one year for each of the serious offenses per 100,000 population. The *UCR* does not report the number of persons arrested each year because some individuals are arrested more than once during the year. The actual number of arrested persons is likely to be smaller than the number of arrests.[18]

Limitations of the *UCR*

It has been argued that the number of crimes known to police seriously underestimates actual crime in society. Police do not know about all criminal incidents, as many crimes are never reported by victims or witnesses. Moreover, police departments do not use uniform procedures for coding a complaint. For example, sexual offense may be coded as rape, indecent assault, assault with intent to harm, or another sex offense.[19]

Police Discretion—Police **discretion,** used in deciding whether a complaint is actually a crime, affects the number of crimes known to police. Several variables may influence police decision making, as indicated by the classic study of Donald J. Black, summarized in Exhibit 2.1. In Chicago, an internal investigation by the police department disclosed that the police were throwing out fourteen times more crime reports than other city police departments. At least 40 percent of the crimes called unfounded were labeled in error. Chicago police blamed part of the problem on poor guidelines in classification and a belief that superior officers wanted the cases dropped. After procedures for classifying crime reports changed, Chicago's crime figures rose by 25 percent, a direct result, said Chicago police, of paperwork changes.[20]

Victim's Cooperation—Reporting of crimes may also be affected by the climate surrounding them and the belief that something will be done. Some individuals do not report crimes because they do not think the police will do anything. In the case of rape, the feelings of the victim that nothing will be done and that the victim will be suspected of having encouraged the crime have probably led to underreporting. Therefore, an increase in reported rapes might not reflect an actual increase in incidents of rape but rather an increase in the willingness of victims to report the crime. Many cities have developed rape relief centers that provide counseling for rape victims. In addition, some jurisdictions have given police special training in the handling of these cases; these and other changes may result in increased reporting by rape victims.[21]

Police and citizen interaction is important in crime prevention. This police officer is on foot patrol, talking to children in a neighborhood school

Rape is not the only crime many victims do not report to the police. Victim-survey data indicate that approximately two-thirds of all personal and household crimes were not reported by victims. As Exhibit 2.2 indicates, only 37 percent of all crimes were reported to the police in 1987, with the reporting rates higher for violent than for property crimes. Why do people not report crimes? The most frequent reason given was that the crime was a personal or private matter. The most frequent reason for not reporting household crimes or personal thefts was that the offender was not successful in the attempted theft or that stolen items were recovered after a successful theft. Race or income of victims did not appear to be related to the decision not to report the crime.[22]

Even when victims or witnesses do decide to report a crime, there will be some delay, the length of which depends on such factors as the

EXHIBIT 2.1

Variables in Police-Citizen Interaction That Affect Whether Police Will Take Official Action on Complaint of a Crime

1. Police-citizen encounters on crime result in official data much more often in cases of felonies than in cases of misdemeanors.

2. The wish of the complainant is associated with police action. In no cases in which the complainant wanted an informal disposition of the case did police write an official report. In most cases where the complainant wanted official disposition of the case, the police did so; the incidence was higher for the more serious offenses.

3. The greater the relational distance between the complainant and the alleged offender, the more likely the police are to file an official report. When friends or family are involved in an alleged offense, the police are less likely to record the crime.

4. The more deference the complainant showed to the police, the more likely an official report would be made.

5. There was no evidence that the race of the complainant was related to official reporting.

6. There was some evidence the socioeconomic status was related to official reporting. Police gave preferential treatment to white-collar complainants but only in felony situations. There appeared to be no relationship between social class and the reaction of the police to a complainant in cases of misdemeanors.

SOURCE: Donald J. Black, "Production of Crime Rates," *American Sociological Review* 35 (August 1970): 746, reprinted with permission.

time it may take to notice or discover the crime, the decision to report, the search for a phone, the call to the police, and actual police arrival on the scene.[23] These delays may be decisive in determining whether the police will arrest a suspect.

The victims' decisions whether to report a crime may also be determined by their experiences with police, judges, and attorneys. One study disclosed that fewer than 33 percent of crime victims think the court system cares about their needs, although 32 percent indicated a belief that courts do about as good a job as they can, and 63 percent responded that judges generally make fair decisions. Respondents suggested ways in which the criminal justice system could make a more positive reponse to victims: keep victims better informed, improve social services for victims, require restitution more frequently, and treat the offender more

EXHIBIT 2.2

Reporting Crimes to the Police

Rates of reporting

● In 1987 only 37% of all crimes were reported to the police. Almost half of all violent crime victimizations, 28% of personal theft victimizations, and 41% of household crimes were reported to the police.

● The more serious or costly crimes were more likely to have been reported to the police. Violent crimes had the highest reporting rate, followed by household crimes and crimes of theft. Generally, completed crimes and victimizations resulting in injury were more likely to be reported than attempted crimes and those victimizations not resulting in injury.

● The crimes most frequently reported to the police included completed motor vehicle thefts, forcible entry burglaries, completed robberies, and aggravated assaults. The most infrequently reported crimes were personal and household larcenies under $50. An 89% reporting rate was associated with completed motor vehicle thefts, whereas less than 15% of personal and household larceny victimizations under $50 were reported to the police.

● Female victims reported violent crimes to the police at higher rates than male victims. There were no significant differences between the reporting rates for white and black victims and for Hispanic and non-Hispanic victims.

● Rates of reporting violent crimes to the police by victims of crimes by strangers were higher than by non-strangers.

● Teenage victims of personal crimes were least likely to report crimes to the police, compared with other age groups.

● Among victims of household crimes, homeowners were more likely to report crimes to the police than renters.

● Frequency of reporting household crimes to the police tended to increase as the level of family income increased; the households with a family income of less than $10,000 had a lower reporting rate than the households in higher income categories. However, not all the differences among other income categories were statistically significant.

● The greater the value of cash or property loss, the more likely the police were notified of a household crime.

Reasons for reporting and not reporting

● In 1987 the most frequently cited specific reasons for reporting a violent crime to the police were to keep the incident from happening again or to others and to intervene in the current incident.

● For both personal theft and household crimes, the most frequent reason for reporting the offense to the police was the desire to recover property.

● The most frequent specific reason given by victims for not reporting violent crimes to the police was that the event was a private or personal matter. The most common reason cited for not reporting personal theft or household crimes to the police was that the objects were recovered or the offender was unsuccessful.

● Reasons for not reporting crimes to the police did not vary markedly for victims from different race or income groups.

● Thirty-five percent of victims of a violent crime by a nonstranger did not call the police because they felt the crime was a private or personal matter, compared with 15% of victims of that crime by a stranger.

● The rate of nonreporting for incidents in which stolen objects were recovered or the offender was unsuccessful was higher for crimes involving strangers than nonstrangers. Fear of reprisal was greater in crimes by nonstrangers than in crimes by strangers.

● Of household crime victims sustaining losses valued at less than $50, 46% did not report the crime to the police because the object was recovered or the offender was unsuccessful. Of victims with losses valued at $250 or more, the most frequently cited reasons for not reporting the offense to the police were lack of proof or "other" reasons. Of those who gave specific responses, that it was a private or personal matter was cited as the most frequent reason by victims with losses valued at more than $1,000.

SOURCE: *Criminal Victimization in the United States, 1987* (Washington, D.C.: U.S. Department of Justice, June 1989), p. 10.

harshly.[24] Improvement in victims' attitudes would increase crime reporting and enhance police ability to clear crimes by arrest.

Administrative and Bureaucratic Changes—Another variable that might influence official crime data is a change in the administration or organization of police departments. A reduction in the size or location of the police force might affect data; methods of reporting may also be changed, resulting in an apparent increase or decrease in the data. This change may occur as the police force becomes more professionalized.

A study by David Seidman and Michael Couzens of the crimes of larceny, burglary, and robbery in Washington, D.C., where such crimes constituted 73 percent of the index offenses, indicated some of the ways the analysis of the act determines the number of crimes in a given category. For example, the criminal act of stealing might be classified as burglary or larceny, depending on the circumstances. Burglary requires an unlawful entry into premises for the purpose of stealing. The investigators found, however, that in some cases police would ignore the unlawful entry, especially if the premises were not locked, and would classify as larceny an act that had all the elements of burglary.[25]

A program of crime control was begun. It included a significant increase in police staff, which gave the District of Columbia the country's largest number of police per resident; more cars and other equipment; use of a computer to provide quick information on arrests and stolen cars; younger, better educated police and more black police, many of whom had participated in police-community sensitivity programs. Although a cause-and-effect relationship cannot be assumed because all other variables that might affect crime rates could not be controlled, the data did indicate "a decline in crime in the District, roughly coincident with at least some features of the Adminstration's program." It was also possible, however, that a change in administration caused the change in crime rates. In 1969 a new police chief indicated that police who could not reduce crime in their jurisdictions would be replaced.

After examining the data on larcenies and burglaries, Seidman and Couzens concluded that "the political importance of crime apparently caused pressures, subtle or otherwise, to be felt by those who record crime—pressures which have led to the downgrading of crimes." They also analyzed data for twenty-nine other cities and concluded that crime data are misleading. Because they are used as offical data and there is pressure to have those data show certain things, they can be and are manipulated to show higher or lower crime rates.

Method of Counting Crime—Crime data will also be affected by such decisions as whether a series of criminal acts by one perpetrator will be counted as one crime or as several. If a person appears before a group of people, pulls a gun, and asks each of the group for money, has the individual committed one act of armed robbery or several? If a perpetrator twice engages in sexual intercourse with force and without the consent of the woman, have two rapes been committed or only one? England and Wales follow the one-victim, one-crime rule although the English rule with regard to property crime is not clear. The one-operation, one-crime rule is followed in the U.S. and Canada. Official reports record crimes as single events, but victim surveys may record each victim separately.[26] The two sources are not comparable in this regard.

The method of counting crimes also has implications for sentencing, as illustrated by the recent case of *People v. Harrison*, decided in 1989 by the California Supreme Court. The case involved a defendant who was convicted of burglary and of three counts of violating a statute prohibiting sexual intercourse by instrumentation. The defendant argued that it was improper to convict him of three counts because his acts occurred during a brief period. The court held that it was proper to convict the defendant of three counts, and gives its reasons in the following excerpt, which begins with a summary of the facts.[27]

People v. Harrison

[The defendant broke into the home of the victim, who lived alone and was legally blind. He sexually attacked her by reaching inside her underwear and inserting his finger into her vagina. The victim struggled and screamed, pulled away, and eventually dislodged his finger, which had been inserted for approximately four seconds. Defendant managed to insert his finger a second time for approximately five seconds, and after another struggle and another dislodging, managed to do so a third time for approximately five seconds. The victim estimated that the entire attack lasted from seven to ten minutes. The statute prohibited "any penetration, however slight."]

It follows logically that a *new and separate* violation of [the statute] is "completed" each time a *new and separate* "penetration, however slight" occurs. Here, defendant does not dispute that his finger actually penetrated the victim's vagina against her will three *separate* times; that *each* penetration was accomplished with the statutorily prescribed intent; that the requisite degree of force or fear preceded, and was used to accomplish *each* penetration; or that a finger is a foreign object within the meaning of the statute. . . .

Obviously, *one* purpose of the "slight penetration" language used throughout this family of sex-offense statutes is to make clear that prolonged or deep insertion, or emission or orgasm, is unnecessary to "complete" the crime. . . . [T]he "essential guilt" of sex offenses lies in the "outrage to the person and feelings of the victim. . . ." The "slight penetration" language confirms that this peculiar "outrage" is deemed to occur each time the victim endures a new, unconsented sexual insertion. The Legislature, by devising a distinctly harsh sentencing scheme, has emphasized the seriousness with which society views each separate unconsented sexual act, even when all are committed on a single occasion.

The above crimes would not have been recorded within the serious violent crimes of the *UCR*, which defines *forcible rape* as "the carnal knowledge of a female forcibly and against her will."[28] The term *carnal knowledge* has traditionally been defined to include sexual penetration (however slight) of a male sexual organ with a female sexual organ. It has been only in recent years that some states have enacted statutes to cover sexual penetration by instrumentation or "by a foreign object." These sex crimes, considered violent and serious by most people, would not be included in the *UCR*'s data on violent crimes.

The *UCR* method of counting crimes also does not take into account the differing degrees of seriousness of crimes that have the same legal label. Even serious crimes such as rape or robbery will differ in circumstances and severity. Some investigators measure crime by using an index that takes into account the components of the criminal act and the aggravating factors accompanying it. For example, greater weight would be given to a rape aggravated by use of a dangerous weapon compared to one in which no weapon was used. The index would thus list all the events involved, not merely the crime or delinquency.[29]

Crimes Not Included in the Official Reports—Official reports have been criticized for excluding some crimes. The *UCR* does not include federal offenses. The index crimes, on which crime rates are based, do not include **computer crime, organized crime,** and **white-collar crime,** all discussed in subsequent chapters. Some of these offenses, although they are violations of criminal law, are handled by administrative agencies rather than by criminal courts. Since these crimes of the middle and upper classes are not included in the crime index, by looking only at official data on crime, we can conclude that there is a high correlation between crime and socioeconomic status, with the greatest proportions of crimes being committed by the lower class.

National Incident-Based Reporting System (NABRS)

Because of the deficiencies in the *UCR*, a new method of collecting crime data has been approved by the FBI and will be implemented in the near future. The new system, the **National Incident-Based Reporting System (NABRS),** views crimes as involving numerous elements, such as the relationship between the offender and the victim, the use of alcohol and/or

EXHIBIT 2.3

Current Part I, or Index, Offenses of the *Uniform Crime Reports*

Serious Violent Crimes	Serious Property Crimes
Murder and nonnegligent manslaughter	Burglary
Forcible rape	Larceny-theft
Robbery	Motor vehicle theft
Aggravated assault	Arson

Crime Categories in the New FBI Approach to Categorization

Following is a list of offenses that will be included in the new FBI reporting system utilizing the Incident-Based Reporting System. These categories will be used instead of the more limited list of eight offenses in the current Index or Part I Offenses of the FBI's *Uniform Crime Reports.*

Arson	Drug Offenses	Larceny	Sex Offenses
Assault	Embezzlement	Motor Vehicle	Forcible
Bribery	Extortion	Theft	Sex Offenses
Burglary	Fraud	Pornography	Nonforcible
Counterfeiting	Gambling	Prostitution	Stolen Property
Destruction of	Homicide	Robbery	Weapons
Property	Kidnaping		Violation

drugs by one or both, the type of weapon used and the type of victims.[30] Twenty-two crimes will be categorized. Those crimes are listed in the second portion of Exhibit 2.3, and may be compared with the current Part I Offenses listed in the first portion of Exhibit 2.3.

National Crime Survey Data (NCS)

Victimization surveys were developed in response to criticisms of the FBI's *Uniform Crime Reports*, which do not record all crimes since many are not reported to the police. To determine actual crime trends and to ascertain the true level of crime in society, it is important to know the dark figure of crime, the amount of crime that is not reported to police. One purpose of victimization surveys is to determine why citizens do not report crime. We have already mentioned some of the reasons, but victims' cooperation is critical. Victims are still the most important link in the system. "In the overwhelming majority of cases, if the victim does not report the crime to the police, the event will not be dealt with by the criminal justice system." The more serious the crime, the more likely the victim will bring it to the attention of authorities. Similarly, if a weapon is used, or if the victim sustains serious physical or financial injury, the crime is more likely to be reported. In fact, the seriousness of the crime is the most important factor in the decision to report.[31]

The major source of victimization data is the **National Crime Survey (NCS),** which comes from the Bureau of Justice Statistics. The NCS measures six crimes: rape, robbery, assault, household burglary, personal and household larceny, and motor vehicle theft. As Exhibit 2.4 indicates, two crimes included in the Index Offenses of the *UCR* are omitted: murder and arson. Murder obviously cannot be measured by survey since the victim is dead. Arson is excluded because of the difficulty of determining whether the property owner was also the perpetrator of the crime. The NCS, based on interviews with persons in 60,000 households, is conducted every six months. The survey also includes research on large samples in twenty of the largest cities in the country along with eight "impact cities." Business and personal victimizations are included in the survey.

In January 1989 the BJS published an overview of responses given by crime victims to the new version of the NCS questionnaire introduced in July 1986. Included in the new version are questions on victims' perception of drug and alcohol abuse, protective actions taken by observers to an apparent crime, and responses made by police and other criminal justice authorities when crimes were reported. Key findings of this first report are reported in Exhibit 2.5.[32]

The NCS should be considered a valuable addition to, not a substitute for, the *UCR*. The NCS includes data on crimes that victims did not report to the police and the reasons for not reporting, data not available in the *UCR*. The NCS has been criticized, however, because it depends on the willingness and ability of alleged victims to report data accurately. A comparison of *UCR* and NCS data indicates that despite the differences in crimes recorded for each offense, the rank order of offenses in terms of frequency of commission is similar.[33]

Although improvements can be made in the collection of victimization data and efforts are being made in that direction, BJS data have been praised as "a storehouse of information on who is being victimized under what conditions." Its design principles have been adopted by numerous foreign countries as well as by the United Nations.[34]

Comparison of the *UCR* and the *NCS*

Officially reported crimes and citizen-defined victimization incidents are both imperfect measures of crime. However, if they are analyzed together, information about the actual level of crime in society, the limitations of each crime measurement method, or the possibility of a new

EXHIBIT 2.4

Comparison of the *Uniform Crime Reports* and the *National Crime Survey*

How do UCR and NCS compare?

	Uniform Crime Reports	National Crime Survey
Offenses measured:	Homicide	
	Rape	Rape
	Robbery (personal and commercial)	Robbery (personal)
	Assault (aggravated)	Assault (aggravated and simple)
	Burglary (commercial and household)	Household burglary
	Larceny (commercial and household)	Larceny (personal and household)
	Motor vehicle theft	Motor vehicle theft
	Arson	
Scope:	Crimes reported to the police in most jurisdictions; considerable flexibility in developing small-area data	Crimes both reported and not reported to police; all data are available for a few large geographic areas
Collection method:	Police department reports to FBI or to centralized State agencies that then report to FBI	Survey interviews; periodically measures the total number of crimes committed by asking a national sample of 49,000 households encompassing 101,000 persons age 12 and over about their experiences as victims of crime during a specified period
Kinds of information:	In addition to offense counts, provides information on crime clearances, persons arrested, persons charged, law enforcement officers killed and assaulted, and characteristics of homicide victims	Provides details about victims (such as age, race, sex, education, income, and whether the victim and offender were related to each other) and about crimes (such as time and place of occurrence, whether or not reported to police, use of weapons, occurrence of injury, and economic consequences)
Sponsor:	Department of Justice Federal Bureau of Investigation	Department of Justice Bureau of Justice Statistics

SOURCE: Bureau of Justice Statistics, *Report to the Nation on Crime and Justice: The Data*, 2nd ed. (Washington, D.C.: U.S. Government Printing Office, 1988), p. 11.

EXHIBIT 2.5

Key Findings of the Redesigned NCS Survey

- Victims reported that they believed their assailants were under the influence of drugs or alcohol in about 36% of violent crime incidents (rapes, robberies, and assaults), including 46% of rapes. In 43% of violent crimes the victims reported that they did not know whether the offender was under the influence of drugs or alcohol.

- Seventy-three percent of violent crime victims reported taking some self-protective measure. The most common measures were resisting or trying to capture the offender (32% of cases where at least one self-protective measure was taken), running away or hiding (26%), and persuading or appeasing the offender (26%).

- About three-fifths of the victims who took self-protective measures stated that their actions had a positive effect on the outcome of the crime. About 7% of the victims taking self-protective measures reported that their actions hurt the situation, and 6% reported both positive and negative effects.

- When notified of a crime, the police came to see the victim in 76% of violent crimes, in 71% of household crimes (burglary, household theft, and motor vehicle theft), and in 54% of personal thefts.

- According to the crime victims, in about 56% of the violent crimes, 38% of personal thefts, and 35% of household crimes where the police came to see the victim, the police arrived within 10 minutes after being notified. Police arrived within an hour in 95% of violent crimes, 84% of personal thefts, and 85% of household crimes.

- Police had later contact with victims in 37% of the violent crimes reported to the police (including 62% of rapes), 35% of reported household crimes (including 58% of motor vehicle thefts), and 25% of reported personal thefts.

- In those cases where the crime was reported to the police, victims were aware that an arrest was made in 25% of violent crimes (including 34% of aggravated assaults and 15% of robberies), 7% of household crimes, and 4% of personal thefts.

- In about 1 in 9 violent crimes reported to the police, the victim received help or advice from a victim assistance office or agency other than the police.

SOURCE: Bureau of Justice Statistics, *The Redesigned National Crime Survey: Selected New Data* (Washington, D.C.: U.S. Department of Justice, January 1989), p. 1.

way to count crime may be discovered.[35] Comparisons of the two sources of data must be made carefully, with consideration given to the different methods and different time periods.

It is hoped that some of the methodological problems in comparing data from the NCS and the *UCR* can be solved. Additional research may result in using one source to test or predict the other or to measure criminal activity in areas not measured effectively by either approach.[36]

One limitation common to both the NCS and the *UCR* is that neither can estimate the extent to which a few offenders are responsible for large numbers of crimes. These reports only tell us how many crimes occurred (not how many can be traced to the same offenders) and how many arrests were made (not how many times a particular person was arrested).[37]

Self-Report Data (SRD)

Official crime data report the number of crimes that come to the attention of law enforcement officials. Victimization surveys report the number of crimes that occur regardless of whether they are reported to the police. Another way to measure crime is to survey people about their own criminal activity.

Earlier **self-report data (SRD)** disclosed that much criminal activity is not reported to officials. In 1947 two investigators reported the results of their sample of upper-income persons, 99 percent of whom answered that they had committed one or more acts for which they could have been arrested.[38] Such results were also reported in a study of college students and institutionalized delinquents. College students reported types of delinquency similar to those of youths who had been judged to be delinquent. That is, although probably with less frequency of commission, college students admitted having committed delinquent and criminal acts as serious as those for which delinquents had been officially adjudicated. Some of these students were leaders of school organizations and honor students.[39] These studies were, however, somewhat unsystematic. The actual systematic use of the self-report method of measuring delinquency was introduced by James F. Short and F. Ivan Nye in 1957 and since that time has been improved and used extensively.[40]

Self-report data are secured through interviews or anonymous questionnaires. Although originally the SRD approach was used mainly with juveniles, the method is also used today to measure adult criminality. Several studies by the Rand Corporation, which conducts extensive research in many areas of criminal justice, have used the SRD to obtain data on the past criminal behavior of incarcerated persons. These studies, discussed later in the text, indicate interesting facts about career criminals, those few who commit most of the crimes. They also indicate that individuals who are serving time after conviction of a crime were not arrested for most of the crimes they reported having committed.[41] The SRD method has also been used to measure the extent of rule breaking of incarcerated offenders by comparing self-reports of inmates to self-reports of guards concerning their observations of rule breaking.[42]

The SRD method provides data on criminal behavior that do not come to the attention of official authorities. Perhaps even more important, this measure provides information on unapprehended law violators. The approach has, however, been criticized because of the possibility that respondents may overreport their criminal activities. At the other extreme, some may purposely underreport; others may forget. This problem may be reduced by comparing SRD responses with official data when available.

Crime data secured by the SRD method have been criticized for excluding serious crimes and for the fact that too few blacks have been included in the samples surveyed. These criticisms raise serious questions since research indicates that black respondents tend to report illegal acts that are less frequent but more serious, whereas white respondents tend to report greater involvement in less serious crimes that occur more frequently. According to one study, black males are three times more likely than white males to report known offenses.[43]

National Youth Survey (NYS)

Self-report studies may yield more useful data in the future. A new program, the **National Youth Survey (NYS),** has been structured to overcome many of the criticisms of older self-report studies. The NYS, using interviews with adolescents over a five-year period, includes all *UCR* offenses except homicide and includes crimes that are likely to be relevant to a "delinquent lifestyle or culture," such as gang fights, sexual activity, and misdemeanors. The NYS may be more useful for comparison because it measures criminal activity "from Christmas a year ago to the Christmas just past." This period is close to the *UCR* calendar period and coincides with the more recent victimization surveys. The NYS allows researchers to pinpoint more types and levels of delinquent behavior and shows promise for gathering more accurate data.[44]

Crime Classification System (CCS)

The Police Executive Research Foundation is testing the **Crime Classification System (CCS)** as an alternative to the *UCR* and the NCS. The focus of the CCS is the harm suffered by the victim and the context in which the criminal activity occurs. Unlike the *UCR*, the CCS has the capacity to measure the degree of severity, giving more refined measures of the harm suffered by victims and the type of circumstances in which that harm occurred. This system might provide a more useful data base for criminal justice agencies and a better understanding of the risk of victimization.[45]

Sources of Data: A Conclusion

This discussion of sources should be kept in mind as we look at particular data. When analyzing data, we must consider the source and the time period covered. For example, the media may report what appears to be conflicting crime data, but the conflict comes from reporting two different sources at two different time periods. Some examples of this problem are provided in the following discussion. We should not conclude that the situation is hopeless because no source is totally accurate. The secret nature of crime, the shame and fear with which some victims react, and many other factors may contribute to the inaccuracy of crime data; but our sources are better today than ever before and continue to improve.[46]

It is also important to analyze the different sources in terms of trends. For example, in a recent analysis of short-term crime trends of *UCR* Part

Crime in this country cannot be prevented by police; citizen cooperation is important. These citizens are patrolling the gang and drug infested Garfield Park in Chicago in an effort to prevent crime.

I, or more serious offenses, Professor Scott Menard found that the *UCR* data, compared to other data sources, more frequently indicated increasing crime rates. Menard suggested that these varying results may suggest "that rates of actual criminal behavior may generally be stable or may fluctuate randomly over time, but rates of discovery of crime by the police and rates of arrest are increasing, with few exceptions."[47]

CRIME IN THE UNITED STATES: AN OVERVIEW

Following is a brief look at the most recent official data on crime as reported by the Bureau of Justice Statistics and the *Uniform Crime Reports*. Data on all serious crimes and on some less serious ones are analyzed more carefully in later chapters as we discuss the nature and elements of those crimes.

National Crime Survey Data

In September 1983 BJS issued a special report containing a brief analysis of the 1982 victimization data, the tenth in its annual series. The 1982 data, compared to 1981, with a general downturn of 1.7 million victimizations, represented "one of the most sweeping, single direction changes to have taken place since the program's inception. Virtually all categories of crime contributed to the reduction, and there were no statistically significant increases."[48]

The decline in reported victimizations continued through 1983, 1984, 1985, 1986, and 1987. Between 1975, when BSJ began publishing data, and 1988, the latest available data, the decrease in households touched by any crime was 23 percent. Personal theft without contact decreased by 32 percent; household burglary by 30 percent; rape, robbery, and assault by 17 percent; and motor vehicle theft by 12 percent as indicated in Figure 2.2. During that period, however, there were some increases in victimizations of blacks and others in contrast to whites, with households headed by blacks showing greater vulnerability to crime than those headed by whites. Furthermore, the recent years showed increases in overall victimization, with an increase of 1.8 percent between 1986 and 1987 and another 1.8 percent increase between 1987 and 1988. Between 1985 and 1987 one in four households was touched by a violent crime or theft.[49]

Uniform Crime Report Data

In the Foreword to the *Uniform Crime Reports* for 1982, William H. Webster, then director of the FBI, with cautious optimism, announced that the

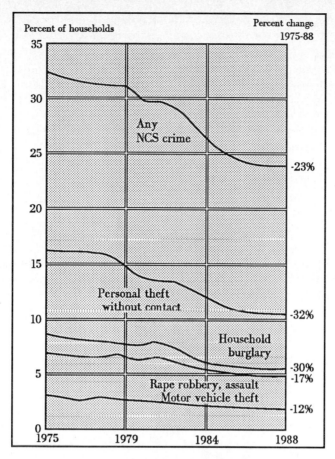

Source: Bureau of Justice Statistics, **Households Touched by Crime,**
1988 (Washington, D.C.: U.S. Department of Justice, June 1989), p. 1.

FIGURE 2.2 Households Touched by Crime

rate of serious crimes or Index Offenses was down 3 percent from 1981.
The cautiousness of his optimism stemmed from the fact that in the 1970s
the crime rates dropped twice, only to turn upward again shortly thereafter. The estimated 12.9 million Crime Index Offenses of 1982, although
up 47 percent from 1973 and 15 percent from 1978, represented the first
significant decline in Index Offenses since 1977. The figures were down in
both violent and property crimes.[50]

Both the number of offenses and the rate per 100,000 inhabitants continued their downward trends in 1983 and 1984 but started back up in
1985, although the 1985 figures were still below those of 1981. Nevertheless, there was cause for concern after three consecutive years of declines
in serious offenses. All property and violent crimes comprising Index
Offenses increased in number in 1985. In reaction to these data, Webster

emphasized that data must be analyzed over time, that data do not represent all the human suffering that results from crime, and that data do not indicate the tremendous economic losses from crime. Declines in offenses and crime rates are welcome; they may be due to any number of factors and "their accuracy is often questionable and certainly controversial." With regard to the increases in 1985, Webster commented, "There are few social statements more tragic than these."[51]

The upward trend continued through 1988, as indicated in Figure 2.3, with dramatic rises shown in some cities. Miami Beach, Florida, for example, led the nation in serious crime, with a 27 percent increase over its 1987 figures. Miami Beach had never previously been in the top ten! Property crimes also rose in Miami Beach, with police estimating that 70 percent of the larcenies and burglaries were committed by cocaine addicts. Washington, D.C., ranked No. 1 in homicides, a position that had been held by Detroit, Michigan, for the previous four years. Officials in the District of Columbia blamed drugs for the large number of homicides in the nation's capital.[52] By October 31, 1989, the number of 1989 homicides in Washington, D.C., had already matched the number for *all* of 1988, "with

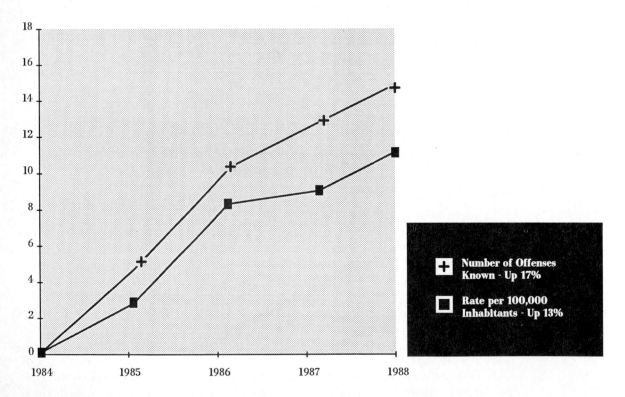

Source : Federal Bureau of Investigation, **Uniform Crime Reports: Crime in the United States,**
1988 (Washington, D.C.: U.S. Government Printing Office, 1989), p. 48.

FIGURE 2.3 Crime Index Total

more than half blamed on drug-related violence—and officials say they see no end in sight."[53]

A November 12, 1989, news release from the FBI indicated that during the first six months of 1989 crimes known to the police increased by 3 percent over the same period in 1988. Robbery rose 7 percent, murder 5 percent, and aggravated assault 4 percent, while forcible rape declined by 2 percent. Among property crimes there was a 1 percent decrease in burglary and a 4 percent decrease in arson, while motor vehicle thefts rose 11 percent and larceny thefts rose 3 percent. By April 1990, the FBI reported that U.S. crime rose to an all-time high in 1989, with violent crime increasing by 5 percent.[54]

CHARACTERISTICS OF OFFENDERS

A thorough study of crime includes not only an analysis of the number and type of crimes but also information on the characteristics of those who commit crimes. Data on offenders are discussed by the variables of age, race, and sex after a general overview of sources.

In the *UCR* arrest data, the variables of age, race, sex, and ethnic status are considered. Before the collection of self-report data, most studies of criminals were based on the *UCR* data, which indicated that a higher percentage of the arrestees were young blacks from a low social class. Thus, many people concluded that persons with these characteristics were more likely to commit crimes. Others concluded that the data represented discrimination against persons with these characteristics.

When looking at the data here, we should understand that the differences between the crime rates of men and women and of blacks and whites do not mean that sex or race *causes* the criminal activity or the reaction to that activity. Indeed, there is evidence that it is not race or age or sex that influences the official reaction to the alleged offender but, rather, the seriousness of the offense committed and the degree of involvement in that offense.[55] There is also evidence that the differences in crime rates between the SRD and *UCR* data may be explained by such factors as a small number of blacks in the self-report studies. The studies also indicate that blacks and whites differ in their tendencies to report certain crimes.[56]

There are also scholars who contend that the differences in crime rates by race are too great to be explained in any way other than discrimination. Daniel E. Georges-Abeyie, a social scientist who has written extensively in this area, emphasizes that the variables of race and crime are complex and all the elements of each must be considered, along with the entire criminal justice system.[57]

Age

Of the 13.8 million arrests in 1988, 47 percent were of persons under the age of twenty-five; 30 percent were under twenty-one; 16 percent were under eighteen; and 5 percent were under fifteen. When only serious offenses are included, persons under twenty-five accounted for 57 percent of all arrests, and 43 percent of arrestees were under twenty-one.[58]

There is also more crime among the elderly, although the figure is insignificant when compared with the total number of arrests. Crimes of the elderly could, however, become critical in view of their increasing percentage in the population. By far the greatest number of arrests of the elderly are for larceny-theft. These arrests are mainly for shoplifting, a crime among the elderly described as alarming and "reaching epidemic proportions."[59]

A recent study emphasizes the increasing problems of deviance among the elderly, increases that may be associated with criminal activity. One example is alcoholism. "Alcohol-related offenses such as public drunkenness make up a large portion of the arrests of older persons. . . . This kind of offender has been treated more often as a curiosity than as a serious social problem." Today, however, more attention is being given to these and to other problems of the elderly.[60]

Race

The National Commission on the Causes and Prevention of Violence reported in 1969 that black crime rates were four times higher than white crime rates for the four major violent crimes of homicide, rape, robbery, and aggravated assault. In 1967 the black arrest rate for homicide was about seventeen times higher than the rate for whites, and for forcible rape, twelve times higher. Among juveniles, the homicide rate for blacks was seventeen times higher than for whites. The commission also found that the rate for crimes of violence among blacks had increased more rapidly than had the rate for whites during the previous decade.[61]

Recent data on crime and race indicate that although 68.6 percent of all arrests in 1988 were of white persons, compared with 29.6 percent for blacks, the percentages were much closer in the serious crimes, the greater differences occurring in arrests for less serious offenses. For example, 82.3 percent of arrests for runaways were white, and 88 percent of arrests for driving under the influence and 87.8 percent of arrests for violating liquor laws were white. Arrests for sex offenses (except forcible rape and prostitution) also more often involved whites than blacks, 76.9 percent compared with 21.4 percent. For serious violent crimes, 51.7 percent of all arrestees were white, compared with 46.8 percent black.[62]

While analyzing these data, we must realize that even in cases in which the arrest rates are higher for whites than for blacks, they may still be disproportionate, as blacks constitute only approximately 11 percent of the total population. Second, we must consider not only arrest data but also the fact that official and unofficial crime data show differences between blacks and whites at all levels of the criminal justice system.

Sex

Historically, crime rates for males have been higher than those for females, with the exception of those crimes that are by definition predominantly female, such as prostitution. Males accounted for 82 percent of all arrests in 1988. However, when the arrests of males and females in this country are examined, some interesting trends emerge. Between 1979 and 1988 the percent change in total arrests of females increased by 37.4 percent compared to an increase of 18.9 percent for males. The crime for which the greatest increase between 1979 and 1988 in arrests of females occurred was embezzlement, representing an increase of 138.6 percent in 1988 arrests compared to 1979. Arrests of males for that crime increased 29.3 percent during the same period.

Women also registered high percentage changes in arrests between 1979 and 1988 in offenses against family and children (106.0 percent increase compared to a decrease of 2.1 percent for males), violation of liquor laws (80.5 percent increase compared to 41.6 percent for males), and weapons carrying, possessions (31.1 percent increase compared to a 20.7 percent increase for males). Arrests of women for prostitution and commercialized vice increased by 7.8 percent between 1979 and 1988, compared to a 1.6 percent decrease in arrests of males for that crime. Yet of the total 1988 arrests for prostitution and commercialized vice, 68.4 percent were female and 31.6 percent were male.[63]

CRIME VICTIMS

Earlier we noted that surveys of victims have produced significant insights into the nature and extent of crime. Such studies have also given us information on the characteristics of victims, who for years were ignored by scholars, researchers, and institutions.[64] In the past decade or so, this situation has changed. Professional societies have been formed, workshops on victims have been held, journals have been established, and a national organization has been actively pursuing the rights of victims. Changes have also been made in the court system, a greater emphasis being placed on the needs and rights of victims. These changes are discussed in Chapter 11. Victims of violence are discussed in Chapter 7.

An analysis of victimization data indicates differences in the rates of victimization of specific groups in the population. The most common victims of violent crime are young people, males, blacks, Hispanics, divorced or separated persons, unemployed persons, and those with an annual income of less than $3,000.

Race

Blacks are far more frequently the victims of crime than are whites. According to the NCS data, between 1975 and 1988, blacks were more often the victims of personal theft with contact, but whites were more likely to be victimized by personal larceny without contact. When the variables of race and sex are compared, the highest rates of victimization for violent crimes are among black males, followed by white males, black females, and white females. Blacks, compared with whites and with other minorities, are more often the victims of serious crimes, and they are most often victimized by other blacks. Black-on-black homicide, for example, is a major cause of death among black Americans, particularly among black males.[65] Black women may be particularly victimized by rape, both in terms of the crime itself as well as the way in which the criminal justice system reacts to the crime.[66]

Various explanations have been given for the high rates of violent crime against blacks. One study emphasized the importance not only of race but also of variables in the social structure. For example, as urbanization increases, crime rates also increase. Violent crimes in particular are "committed in heavily populated areas which have larger proportions of blacks in the population. The view that crime is committed more frequently in the black community should be restricted to violent crime."[67]

The rates of victimization are also higher among the unemployed and the poor than among the employed and the higher-income population; blacks, compared with whites, represent a higher proportion of these groups.

Many blacks believe that they are more often the victims of crime because of *systemic racism:* the differential impact of unemployment; poor schools, resulting in a lower quality of education; the greater likelihood of police to arrest blacks; and the other injustices of the criminal justice system.[68] Blacks also contend, and there is some evidence to support this position, that when they are victimized by crime, they are less likely than whites to receive assistance from others.[69]

Sex

Even though males are much more likely than females to be victims of violent crime, many studies indicate that the fear of violent crime is greater among females, mainly because of the crime of forcible rape.[70] Female victims of violent crimes may be further victimized by the reaction (or lack thereof) of the criminal justice system to the types of violent crimes that victimize women more often than men. In addition to rape, women are more often the victims of family violence, a crime that is gaining more attention and will be discussed in a later chapter.

Age

Age is also an important variable in the study of victims. Although it is often suggested that the elderly are most often victimized by crime, the data do not support this position. For crimes of violence or theft, the elderly are least frequently the victims, and those persons aged twelve to twenty-four are most frequently the victims. The rates of victimization decrease with each age group after the age of twenty-four and this pattern holds when sex is also considered as a variable. Males aged twelve to twenty-four were particulary vulnerable to the crimes of assault, robbery, or personal larceny.[71]

Most of the crimes against the elderly are not violent. The rates of assaults, robberies, or rapes committed against elderly persons are only one-fifth of those for similar crimes against younger persons.[72] The incidence of crimes against the elderly may not be as important, however, as their perception of the probability of such crimes. According to some authorities, the fear of crime is the number one fear among the elderly.[73] This fear may be unrealistic, but its impact on the elderly is dramatic. Many change their life-styles as a result, moving if possible. If they cannot move, many will become prisoners in their dwellings, afraid to venture out even in the daylight hours.

For many elderly people, it is not the *probability* of becoming a victim that is crucial; it is the *possibility*. A purse snatching can have a far more serious effect on the elderly than it would have on younger victims. The elderly are more likely to be seriously injured if there is any altercation between the assailant and the victim, and such direct contact may also be much more frightening to an elderly person. The loss of money may also be more harmful to the elderly, many of whom live on fixed incomes. A recent study in Florida, which has a large elderly population, indicates that not only have crimes against the elderly increased, but insufficient attention and assistance is being given to assist the elderly in coping with crime. The Attorney General's Task Force on Crime and the Elderly had numerous suggestions to combat the problems and concluded that the elderly who most need help are those who are least likely to get it—"the low-income residents of crime-ridden inner cities."[74]

Just as the elderly may be peculiarly susceptible to some kinds of crime because they are so defenseless, the very young may also be easy prey. Children as victims of sexual abuse, child abuse, and other forms of family violence are also discussed later in the text. The young are also often victimized by the growing incidence of violence in our schools, such as that which occurred in January 1989 when Patrick Purdy, 24, allegedly walked into the school yard where he had played during his childhood and started firing on the students. Five children died; 30 children and a teacher were wounded.[75]

Relationship of Victim and Offender

One final issue regarding victims is important—the relationship between the victim and the offender. Violence in the form of assault or murder is usually preceded by social interaction. Physical violence is more likely if both the offender and the victim define the situation as one calling for such violence. If only one is prone toward physical violence, the altercation will probably not become physical. In this sense, the victim may contribute to his or her own injury or death. Often the social interactions have been preceded by numerous other interactions, some of these recent. In a study of homicide victims, Marvin Wolfgang found that one in every four of the victims of homicide precipitated the event that led to their deaths. The victim was the first to strike a blow, show force with a deadly weapon, or use that weapon.[76]

Recent victimization data indicate that 46 percent of the violent crimes of rape, robbery, and assault were perpetrated by strangers, with another 11 percent "committed by persons known to the victim by sight only." There is reason to suspect, however, that domestic violence is seriously underreported. If that is true, it is possible that a large majority of violent crimes are committed by friends, family members, or acquaintances. Males are more likely than females to be attacked by strangers, and whites are slightly more likely than blacks to be attacked by strangers.[77]

CONCLUSION

This chapter examined the official and unofficial sources of data on criminal activity. After a brief look at Americans' perceptions of crime, it considered early attempts to measure crime. The cartographic school, despite its lack of sophistication in statistical analysis, at least began to emphasize the need for a scientific study of crime, which set the stage for the development of criminology.

The official source of data on crime in this country, the *UCR*, was examined in terms of its coverage and its limitations. Recognition of those limitations led to the use of other sources of data, such as victimization surveys and self-report surveys. An overview of the extent of crime and the demographic characteristics of criminals and their victims established the background for a later study of particular types of crime and particular types of criminals.

We saw that the data from official and unofficial sources do not always agree, and we considered the pros and cons for using the different methods of measuring crime. In the final analysis, the debate has been over which method is most accurate—that is, which most successfully minimizes the dark figures of unreported crime.

One sociologist concluded that in trying to understand crime data, the important concern is not the accuracy with which data describe the extent of criminal behavior or illuminate the dark figures of unreported crime. Instead, the main concern is the way in which the data reflect the complex relationship between society and criminal behavior, providing a barometer of society's attitudes toward deviant behavior.[78] Others emphasize that official crime data are the product of decisions to classify some behavior as criminal. Therefore crime rates "can be viewed as indices of organizational processes rather than as indices of the incidence of certain forms of behavior."[79] The official data represent decisions by those in authority, and the decision to detain is based on a whole network of social action.[80] Such positions have led some sociologists to argue that new approaches should be taken toward official crime data. Instead of being criticized for not including all crimes, the data should be recognized for what they are—data concerning the social control of crime. The data should also be considered an end in themselves rather than a means to an end. Crime rates are phenomena that are part of the natural world; they therefore cannot be evaluated as inaccurate or unreliable. As an aspect of social organization, they cannot, from a sociological point of view, be wrong.[81] Thus, official crime rates may be viewed as rates of socially recognized deviant behavior. Any social system has rates of deviance that are not socially or officially recognized, but deviance should be regarded in terms of the reaction of legal and social control systems.

It is sociologically relevant to determine from the official data what behavior is defined as deviant and how society organizes, classifies, and treats those forms of behavior. Official data do indicate that deviants are distinguished from nondeviants. It is sociologically relevant to analyze the difference between a convicted person and one whose crime stops at the crimes-known-to-the-police stage. That both persons may have committed the same deviant act is sociologically important, as is the fact that they have been officially treated differently. Thus, official crime data may be viewed as the structural response to crime rather than as indicators of the actual incidence of deviancy.[82] They also provide important information about crime victims, changing policies of the courts (increases or decreases in the number of offenders placed on probation or fined) or trends in the length of sentencing; that is, they can be viewed as an *index of official action.*

Stanton Wheeler suggested that the concept of crime data should be reformulated and considered as the interrelationship of three elements: (1) the person who commits the crime, (2) the victim or other citizens who may report the crime, and (3) the official agents of the state who are charged with controlling crime. Wheeler recommends this reformulation because there is increasing recognition that deviance depends on a social definition. Therefore any analysis of crime data should recognize not only those who commit crimes but also those who define the behavior as criminal. He compares crime data to admission to and release from mental hospitals, arguing that neither can be understood by referring only to the characteristics of the subjects. Patients referred to child guidance clinics by doctors are more quickly admitted than those referred by members of their families; people with a higher socioeconomic status can more quickly get their family members into mental hospitals than can people from lower classes. In these cases the reaction of others is important in determining who is labeled deviant.

Wheeler discussed three practical consequences of this reformulation: First, police forces could be analyzed; perhaps the crime rates are high because the police are efficient. The police organizations of high-rate and low-rate areas could then be compared; the crime rates might, for example, reflect the relationship of the number of police cars to the number of people in an area. Differences among individual police could also be analyzed.

A second consequence would be an improved understanding of citizens and social control. Citizens who observe crimes being committed or who are victims affect the crime rate by their decision on whether to report the crimes. Third, Wheeler's approach would lead to the development of consumer-oriented crime data. Crime data indicate who commits the crimes by age, sex, and race. But more relevant to consumers is the *probability* that a crime will be committed against them. It is important to know that the crime rate went up because of an increase of people in the age bracket that typically commits crimes, but it is more important to citizens to know the increase or decrease of their chances of being victimized. Empirical data could be used to describe the victims, not just the criminals.

Wheeler concluded that the result of this approach would be an improved understanding of criminals and criminal acts. Currently, comparisons of crime rates of one community with another have little meaning because of all the variables that make such comparisons of data unreliable. But within a community, crime could be better understood if the relevant variables were examined. Wheeler suggested that his new orientation toward crime data begin by collecting data on (1) the complaining witnesses, (2) the social characteristics of the community, (3) the reporting or arresting officer, and (4) the nature of the police system as a whole.[83]

In addition to deciding how to collect data and what kind of data should be collected, we have the problem of analyzing the data and explaining the meaning of the variables. In the next chapter, we examine the emergence of the scientific analysis of crime data and the subsequent development of theories to explain criminal behavior.

ENDNOTES

1. For a more detailed discussion, see James O. Finckenauer, "Crime as a National Political Issue: 1964–76: From Law and Order to Domestic Tranquility," *Crime and Delinquency* 24 (January 1978): 13–27.

2. For a recent, brief discussion on the relationship between fear of crime and policing, see Mark H. Moore and Robert C. Trojanowicz, National Institute of Justice, *Policing and the Fear of Crime* (Washington, D.C.: U.S. Department of Justice, June 1988.

3. *Newsweek*, 23 March 1981, p. 46.

4. *U.S. News & World Report*, 10 April 1989, p. 20.

5. *Time*, 6 February 1989, p. 20.

6. See, for example, Terance D. Miethe, "Public Consensus on Crime Seriousness: Normative Structure or Methodological Artifact?" *Criminology* 20 (November 1982): 515–526.

7. Francis T. Cullen et al., "Consensus in Crime Seriousness: Empirical Reality or Methodological Artifact?" *Criminology* 23 (February 1985): 99–118; Mark A. Cohen, "Some New Evidence on the Seriousness of Crime," *Criminology* 26 (May 1988): 343–353; and Mark Warr, "What is the Perceived Seriousness of Crimes?" *Criminology* 27 (November 1989): 795–820.

8. James Garofalo, "Crime and the Mass Media: A Selective Review of Research," *Journal of Research in Crime and Delinquency* 18 (July 1981): 319–350. See also Drew Humphries, "Serious Crime, News Coverage, and Ideology: A Content Analysis of Crime Coverage in a Metropolitan Paper," *Crime & Delinquency* 27 (April 1981): 191–205.

9. See D. A. Graber, *Crime News and the Public* (New York: Praeger, 1980).

10. Anthony N. Doob and Glenn E. MacDonald, "Television Viewing and Fear of Victimization: Is the Relationship Causal?" *Journal of Personality and Social Psychology* 37 (February 1979): 175.

11. Mark Warr, "The Accuracy of Public Beliefs About Crime: Further Evidence," *Criminology* 20 (August 1982): 185–204.

12. George B. Vold and Thomas J. Bernard, *Theoretical Criminology*, 3d ed. (New York: Oxford University Press, 1986), p. 131.

13. Terence Morris, "Some Ecological Studies of the 19th Century," reprinted as chap. 2 in Harwin L. Voss and David M. Petersen, eds., *Ecology, Crime and Delinquency* (New York: Appleton-Century-Crofts, 1971).

14. Yale Levin and Alfred Lindesmith, "English Ecology and Criminology of the Past Century," chap. 1 in Voss and Petersen, eds., *ibid.*, pp. 59–61.

15. Morris, "Some Ecological Studies," p. 66. See also Gregory S. Kowalski et al., "Spatial Distribution of Criminal Offenses by States, 197–76," *Journal of Research in Crime and Delinquency* 17 (January 1980): 4–25.

16. "BJS Announces Five-Year Program Plan," *Justice Assistance News*, October 1982, p. 3. For the legislative history of the creation of the BJS, see Roland Chilton, "Criminal Statistics in the United States," *The Journal of Criminal Law and Criminology* 71 (Spring 1980): 56–67.

17. *Criminal Justice Newsletter*, 6 June 1983, pp. 1–2.

18. See Hans Zeisel, "The Disposition of Felony Arrests," *American Bar Foundation Research Journal*, 1981 (Spring 1981): 409–462. For additional information on arrest rates, see David F. Greenberg, "A Panel Model of Crime Rates and Arrest Rates," *American Sociological Review* 44 (October 1979): 843–850.

19. See, for example, Michael J. Hindelang, "Variations in Sex-Race-Age-Specific Incidence Rates of Offending," *American Sociological Review* 46 (August 1981): 461–474; Wesley G. Skogan, "The Validity of Official Crime Statistics: An Empirical Investigation," *Social Science Quarterly* 55 (June 1974): 25–38; Donald J. Black, "Production of Crime Rates," *American Sociological Review* 35 (August 1970): 1–16; Yale Kamisar, "How to Use, Abuse—and Fight Back with—Crime Statistics," *Oklahoma Law Review* 25 (May 1972): 239–255; and Robert A. Silverman, "Measuring Crime: More Problems," *Journal of Police Science and Administration* 8 (September 1980): 265–274.

20. "Burying Crime in Chicago," *Newsweek*, 16 May 1983, p. 63, and "Chicago Police Audit Finds Many Crimes Passed Over," *New York Times*, 2 May 1983, p. 11, col. 5. For an analysis of the factors that influence police behavior in detection and arrest of suspects, see Lawrence W. Sherman, "Causes of Police Behavior: The Current State of Quantitative Research," *Journal of Research in Crime and Delinquency* 16 (January 1980): 69–100.

21. For a recent analysis of crime reporting among rape victims, see James D. Orcutt and Rebecca Faison, "Sex-Role Attitude Change and Reporting of Rape Victimization, 1973–1985," *Sociological Quarterly* 29 (No. 4 1988): 589–604.

22. Bureau of Justice Statistics, *Households Touched by Crime*, 1988 (Washington, D.C.: U.S. Department of Justice, June 1989), p. 1.

23. See William Spelman and Dale K. Brown, *Calling the Police: Citizen Reporting of Serious Crime* (Washington, D.C.: National Institute of Justice, October 1984), p. 82.

24. National Institute of Justice, *The Criminal Justice Response to Victim Harm* (Washington, D.C.: U.S. Department of Justice, June 1985), p. 5.

25. David Seidman and Michael Couzens, "Getting the Crime Rate Down: Political Pressure and Crime Reporting," *Law and Society Review* 8 (Spring 1974): 475–493.

26. Gwynn Nettler, *Explaining Crime*, 3d ed. (New York: McGraw-Hill, 1984), p. 41.

27. People v. Harrison, 768 P.2d 1078, 1082 (Cal. 1989), citations omitted; emphasis in the original.

28. Federal Bureau of Investigation, *Uniform Crime Reports: Crime in the United States*, 1987 (Washington, D.C.: U.S. Government Printing Office, 1988), p. 13.

29. Thorsten Sellin and Marvin E. Wolfgang, *The Measurement of Delinquency* (New York: John Wiley, 1964), p. 294.

30. For details, see Federal Bureau of Investigation, *Uniform Crime Reporting: National Incident-Based Reporting System*, Vol. 1. *Data Collection Guidelines* (Washington, D.C.: U.S. Department of Justice, July 1, 1988).

31. Michael R. Gottfredson and Don M. Gottfredson, *Decisionmaking in Criminal Justice: Toward the Rational Exercise of Discretion* (Cambridge, Mass.: Ballinger, 1980), pp. 21–59.

32. For a description of the new NCS survey design, see Bureau of Justice Statistics, *New Directions for the National Crime Survey* (Washington, D.C.: U.S. Department of Justice, March 1989).

33. Nettler, *Explaining Crime*, pp. 71–73.

34. National Institute of Justice and Bureau of Justice Statistics, *Supplementing the National Crime Survey: Research Solicitation* (Washington, D.C.: U.S. Department of Justice, 1987).

35. See Larry J. Cohen and Mark I. Lichback, "Alternative Measures of Crime: A Statistical Evaluation," *The Sociological Quarterly* 23 (Spring 1982): 253–266.

36. See Edwin W. Zedlewski, "Deterrence Findings and Data Sources: A Comparison of the Uniform Crime Reports and the National Crime Surveys," *Journal of Research on Crime & Delinquency* 20 (July 1983): 262–276.

37. Bureau of Justice Statistics, *Examining Recidivism* (Washington, D.C.: U.S. Department of Justice, 1985).

38. James S. Wallerstein and C. J. Wyle, "Our Law-Abiding Lawbreakers," *Probation* 25 (April 1947): 107–112.

39. See Austin Porterfield, "Delinquency and Its Outcome in Courts and College," *American Journal of Sociology* 49 (November 1943): 199–208; Maynard L. Erikson and Lamar T. Empey, "Court Records, Undetected Delinquency, and Decision Making," *Journal of Criminal Law, Criminology, and Police Science* 54 (December 1963): 456–469; and Jay R. Williams and Martin Gold, "From Delinquent Behavior to Official Delinquency," *Social Problems* 20 (Fall 1962): 209–213.

40. James F. Short and F. Ivan Nye, "Extent of Unrecorded Juvenile Delinquency: Tentative Conclusions," *Journal of Criminal Law, Criminology, and Police Science* 49 (November-December 1957): 296–302. For an analysis, see Michael J. Hindelang, Travis Hirschi, and Joseph G. Weis, *Measuring Delinquency* (Beverly Hills, Calif.: Sage Publications, 1981).

41. See "Career Criminals and Criminal Careers," *Criminal Justice Research at Rand* (Santa Monica, Calif.: Rand Corp., 1985), pp. 3–7.

42. John D. Hewitt, Eric D. Poole, and Robert M. Regoli, "Self-Reported and Observed Rule-Breaking in Prison: A Look at Disciplinary Response," *The Justice Quarterly* 1 (No. 3, 1983): 437–447.

43. Michael J. Hindelang, Travis Hirschi and Joseph G. Weis, "Correlates of Delinquency: The Illusion of Discrepancy Between Self-Report and Official Measures," *American Sociological Review* 44 (December 1979): 995–1014. For a review of these and other criticisms of self-report studies, see Wesley G. Skogan, "The Validity of Official Crime Statistics: An Empirical Investigation," *Social Science Quarterly* 55 (June 1974): 25–38; Delbert S. Elliott and Suzanne S. Ageton, "Reconciling Race and Class Differences in Self-Reported and Official Estimates of Delinquency," *American Sociological Review* 45 (February 1980): 95–110; and Charles R. Tittle et al., "The Myth of Social Class and Criminality," *American Sociological Review* 43 (October 1978): 643–656.

44. For an extensive discussion of the new structure of the NYS, see Elliott and Ageton, "Reconciling Race," 95–110.

45. David H. Konstantin, "CCS: The Crime-Data Frontier," *Law Enforcement News* 11 (11 February 1985): 1, 5.

46. For a recent discussion of the pros and cons of crime data, see Part 2, "Measuring Crime: Its Extent and Distribution," in Richard C. Monk, ed., *Taking Sides: Clashing Views on Controversial Issues in Crime and Criminology* (Guilford, Connecticut: The Dushkin Publishing Group, Inc., 1989), pp. 83–101.

47. Scott Menard, "Short-Term Trends in Crime and Delinquency: A Comparison on UCR, NCS, and Self-report Data," *Justice Quarterly* 4 (September 1987): 468, 470.

48. Bureau of Justice Statistics Special Report, *Criminal Victimization in the United States: 1973–82 Trends* (Washington, D.C.: U.S. Department of Justice, September 1983), p. 1.

49. Bureau of Justice Statistics, *Households Touched by Crime, 1988* (Washington, D.C.: U.S. Department of Justice, June 1989), p. 1.

50. Federal Bureau of Investigation, *Uniform Crime Reports: Crime in the United States,* 1982 (Washington, D.C.: U.S. Government Printing Office, 1983), p. iii.

51. Federal Bureau of Investigation, *Uniform Crime Reports: Crime in the United States:* 1985 (Washington, D.C.: U.S. Government Printing Office, 1986), p. iii.

52. Federal Bureau of Investigation, Newsrelease, 24 April 1989.

53. "'89 D.C. Homicides Match Record '88 Toll—With 2 Months to Go," *Atlanta Journal and Constitution,* 31 October 1989, p. A–3, Col. 1.

54. "Crime up 3%, FBI Reports," *Crime Control Digest,* 13 November 1989, p. 7; FBI newsrelease, April, 1990.

55. See Charles R. Tittle, "Labelling and Crime: An Empirical Evaluation," in Walter Gove, ed., *The Labelling of Deviance: Evaluating a Perspective,* 2d ed. (Beverly Hills, Calif.: Sage Publications, 1980), pp. 241–270.

56. Hindelang, "Variations in Sex-Race-Age-Specific Incidence Rates," 462. See also Hindelang, Hirschi, and Weis, "Correlates of Delinquency"; and Delbert S. Elliott and David Huizinga, "Social Class and Delinquent Behavior in a National Youth Panel: 1976–1980," *Criminology* 21 (May 1983): 149–177.

57. Daniel E. Georges-Abeyie, "Race, Ethnicity, and the Spatial Dynamic: Toward a Realistic Study of Black Crime, Crime Victimization, and Criminal Justice Processing of Blacks," *Social Justice.* 16 (No. 4, 1989): 35–54. See also Georges-Abeyie, "Studying Black Crime: A Realistic Approach," in Paul J. Brantingham and Patricia L. Brantingham, eds., *Environmental Criminology* (Beverly Hills, CA.: Sage Publications, 1981), pp. 97–109. For further discussion on the issue, see William Wilbanks, *The Myth of a Racist Criminal Justice System* (Monterey, CA.: Brooks/Cole, 1987), and Joan Petersilia et al., *Racial Equity in Sentencing* (Santa Monica, Calif.: Rand Corporation, February 1988).

58. Federal Bureau of Investigation, *Uniform Crime Reports: Crime in the United States:* 1988 (Washington D.C.: U.S. Government Printing Office), p. 163.

59. "Old Enough to Know Better: A Stunning Rise in Crime by Senior Citizens Creates a Quandary," *Time,* 20 September 1982, p. 77.

60. Letitia T. Alson, *Crime and Older Americans* (Springfield, Ill: Chas. C Thomas, 1986), pp. 123, 124. See also Neal Shover, *Aging Criminals* (Beverly Hills, CA.: Sage Publications, 1985).

61. U.S. National Commission on the Causes and Prevention of Violence, *Violent Crime: Homicide, Assault, Rape, Robbery,* introduction by Daniel Patrick Moynihan (New York: Braziller, 1969).

62. Federal Bureau of Investigation, *Uniform Crime Reports: Crime in the United States:* 1988 (Washington, D.C.: U.S. Government Printing Office, 1989), p. 186.

63. *Ibid.,* pp. 173, 185.

64. See Hans von Hentig, *The Criminal and His Victim* (New Haven, Conn: Yale University Press, 1948); Stephen Schafer, *The Victim and His Criminal* (New York: Random House, 1968); and Stephen Schafer, *Compensation and Restitution to Victims of Crime and Victimology: The Victim and His Criminal* (Reston, Va.: Reston, 1977).

65. For an analysis of this phenomenon, see H. M. Rose, *Black Homicide and the Urban Environment,* Final Report, U.S. Department of Health and Human Services, National Institute of Mental Health/Center for Minority Group Mental Health Programs, 1981. For an account of the 1988 data, see Bureau of Justice Statistics, *Households Touched by Crime, 1988* (Washington, D.C.: U.S. Department of Justice, June 1989).

66. For a detailed discussion of the history of rape, along with an analysis of

racism as it relates to the crime, see Jennifer Wiggins, "Rape, Racism, and the Law," *Harvard Women's Law Journal* 6 (Spring 1983): 103–141.

67. Paul E. Joubert et al., "U.S. Social Structure, Crime, and Imprisonment," *Criminology* 19 (November 1981): 354–355. See also Georges-Abeyie, "Race, Ethnicity, and the Spacial Dynamic."

68. All the quotations in the preceding two paragraphs are from Lee A. Daniels, "Black Crime, Black Victims," *New York Times Magazine*, 16 May 1982, p. 92.

69. See Samuel L. Gaertner et al., "Race of Victim, Nonresponsive Bystanders, and Helping Behavior," *Journal of Social Psychology* 117 (June 1982): 69–77.

70. Other studies question this conclusion and maintain that the apparent differences are the result of measurement problems in the research. See, for example, Randy L. LaGrange and Kenneth F. Ferraro, "Assessing Age and Gender Differences in Perceived Risk and Fear of Crime," *Criminology* 27 (November 1989): 697–715.

71. Bureau of Justice Statistics, *Criminal Victimization in the United States*, 1987 (Washington, D.C.: U.S. Department of Justice, June 1989), p. 3.

72. Bureau of Justice Statistics, *Crime and the Elderly* (Washington, D.C.: U.S. Department of Justice, 1985).

73. See John H. Lindquist and Janice M. Duke, "The Elderly Victim at Risk," *Criminology* 20 (May 1982): 115–126.

74. "Crime Overtaking the Elderly, Panel Told," *St. Petersburg Times*, 23 February 1989, p. B3, col. 2.

75. "Death on the Playground: Why do Mass Murderers Kill Children?" *Newsweek*, 30 January 1989, p. 35.

76. See Marvin Wolfgang, *Patterns in Criminal Homicide* (Philadelphia: University of Pennsylvania Press, 1958).

77. Bureau of Justice Statistics, *Violent Crime by Strangers and Nonstrangers* (Washington, D.C.: U.S. Department of Justice, January 1987), p. 1.

78. Keith Bottomley, *Decisions in the Penal Process* (South Hackensack, N.J.: Fred B. Rothman, 1973), p. 21.

79. John I. Kitsuse and Aaron V. Cicourel, "A Note on the Uses of Official Statistics," *Social Problems* 11 (Fall 1963): 137.

80. Aaron V. Cicourel, *The Social Organization of Juvenile Justice* (New York: John Wiley, 1968), p. 37.

81. See Donald J. Black, "Production of Crime Rates," *American Sociological Review* 35 (August 1970): 733–748. See also Kitsuse and Cicourel, "A Note on the Uses of Official Statistics," 131–139.

82. Kitsuse and Cicourel, *ibid.*

83. Stanton Wheeler, "Criminal Statistics: A Reformulation of the Problem," *Journal of Criminal Law: Criminology and Police Science* 58 (September 1967): 317–324.

PART II

Explanations of Criminal Behavior

CHAPTER 3

This chapter begins with a brief discussion of the nature and purpose of research in criminology and then analyzes the contributions of the classical, neoclassical, and positive schools to its development. The impact of these schools on our modern philosophies of punishment is examined. The classical position of "letting the punishment fit the crime," with its emphasis on the belief that we are rational in our thoughts and that we rationally choose to seek pleasure and avoid pain, argued that sufficient punishment would be a deterrent to criminal behavior: If the punishment is a little worse than the pleasure of committing the crime, we will not commit the crime. Empirical research on this issue is analyzed. The current emphasis on deterrence and retribution or, in the perhaps more palatable terms of today, just deserts, is contrasted with the former emphasis on the need to reform or rehabilitate the criminal.

OUTLINE

Early Explanations of Criminal Behavior and Their Modern Counterparts

The preceding chapter discusses the measurement of crime and its evaluation. It also considers some of the variables, such as age, sex, and race, that are related to crime data. However, collecting data on crime is only the first step toward the eventual goal of controlling or preventing criminal behavior. In order to do so, we must develop ways to evaluate the data. Why do males have a higher crime rate than females? What are the reasons, the explanations? If we can understand why people engage in criminal behavior, we may be able to predict and control that behavior.

Simple explanations are not sufficient; for example, it is not very helpful to know only that there are more arrests of males than of females. We need to know what the patterns and the variables are that might explain these differences. To answer these questions, social scientists, like physical scientists, engage in research, developing and testing ideas. This research can be very complex, so we will not go into a detailed analysis of research methods; rather, we will look at the process of research with the view of understanding its overall purpose.

This chapter sets the stage for our discussions of theory. What happens in research also influences the decisions that are made regarding the processing of offenders. If we believe, for example, that stiff penalties are greater deterrents to criminal activity than are lighter sentences, we probably will institute harsher penalties. Unfortunately, such policy decisions are often made on the basis of intuition or "common sense," without any reference to existing social science findings or an attempt to conduct research if such is needed.

RESEARCH IN CRIMINOLOGY

Research in criminology is conducted to understand criminal behavior. If we can understand the behavior, we will have a better chance of predicting when it will occur and will be able to take policy steps to control, eliminate, or prevent it. All these purposes are, however, controversial.

Basing Policy Decisions on Research

Although it might seem obvious to the casual observer that the purpose of research is to control, there has traditionally been disagreement within the social sciences over the role of the social scientist in the decision making process. In a provocative book entitled *Can Science Save Us?*, sociologist George Lundberg stated the problem succinctly: "If we want results in improved human relations we must direct our research to the solution of these problems."[1] Early sociologists were more interested in social reform; later sociologists argued that they should not take positions on issues of value. That is, they should not be involved in decision making on the basis of the results of their research; scientists should be value-free. They should conduct their research rigorously but leave the policy-making decisions to others.

Others have taken the position that the whole process of the criminal justice system is political and, furthermore, that the system is used to discriminate against those people who are not in positions of power in the society, for example, minorities. More recently, because of the widespread belief that nothing works in the criminal justice field, there is a tendency to avoid research findings and to use common sense in making policy decisions. Sociologist Daniel Glaser contends that public officials and many criminologists have abandoned crime-causation theory. But, says Glaser, "Explanatory theory cannot disappear, for it is inherent in human thinking, even in that of persons who disavow it." Glaser emphasizes that any time we explain, we theorize, "and we theorize scientifically whenever we offer explanations that observation could prove erroneous." It is therefore important to recognize these processes, for unless "it is made explicit, it cannot have cumulative growth and improvement." Most important, says Glaser, "The foundations of any science are the basic statements of its theory—its principles."[2]

The Search for Explanations

The need for adequate research on criminal behavior has long been emphasized by social scientists and recently gained the attention of the President's Task Force on Violent Crime. When the task force made its preliminary report in 1981, it stated, "It is imperative that we discover what works—what does not."[3] If we are to discover the answer to that question—what works?—we must conduct scientific research. Such research is complicated, and adequate understanding requires, at the minimum, a course in research methods. Accordingly, our discussion here will be limited to analyzing the pitfalls and problems that we need to keep in mind as we review the results of empirical research throughout this text.

In scientific research, both in the physical and the social sciences, many different types of errors may occur. Some may be avoidable, and others may be due to the nature of the material being studied. Social scientists study human beings who are capable of thinking, reflecting, forgetting, misrepresenting, and even refusing to tell the truth. Given this practical reality, no research is without problems for the social scientist studying criminal behavior.

Selection of a Research Method

Several methods are used to gather data. In the previous chapter we looked at official data gathered by the FBI, by the Bureau of Justice Statistics (BJS), and by social scientists using self-report data (SRD). Data may be secured by asking agencies to report data from their files, by asking individuals to complete questionnaires about their own behavior or the behavior of others, or by interviewing people about their involvement in crime or about their perceptions of the behavior of other people.

There are advantages and disadvantages to selecting a particular method of securing data; some of these are discussed in Chapter 2. Before selecting a method, the researcher should consider the nature of the study to be conducted. For example, although an in-depth study or a case study of a few inmates convicted of murder may give detailed information on the history of those criminals, such information is not sufficient to allow us to generalize to the whole population of murderers. Such case studies are, however, very helpful in identifying variables that we might study in larger populations. In other situations, it might be more valuable to survey a large number of murderers even though we would not find out as much about each individual murderer as we would if we conducted an intensive case study.

Research might also take place over a period of time, with data gathered more than once. For example, if we wanted to know whether persons released from prison commit further crimes, we might want to gather information six months or a year after their release. We could also continue the research further into the future. But if we did not want the time variable to be considered, we might select samples of subjects (for example, male inmates and female inmates) at the same time and collect data for comparative purposes. The method of gathering data will depend not only on the nature of the study but also on the cost of the project. Following a sample over a period of years is expensive, and research funds are not always available for such studies. Also, selecting a large sample for an in-depth study is costly in the short run, particularly if the subjects are located in different cities and numerous researchers are needed to conduct the study.

The selection of a research method might also be influenced by the fact that the activities the researcher wishes to study have already taken place and cannot be repeated. In that case, an *ex post facto* method would be appropriate. A sample of people already convicted of murder might be selected and studied to find out whether any past events or characteristics of these persons could explain why they murdered. In contrast, when researchers want to study ongoing activities, they might go into the field to study behavior as it occurs. But the researchers must be careful not to get so involved in the behavior under study that they lose their objectivity.[4]

Errors in Interpreting Data

Extreme care must be taken in analyzing empirical data, for facts do not always speak for themselves. They must be interpreted. Researchers must also be careful not to go beyond the data—that is, to use the data to explain something that was never measured and to generalize the findings beyond the scope of the study. For example, if all members of the sample are male, we cannot conclude that the research findings also apply to females, as gender might be an important variable in explaining the delinquent or criminal behavior under study.

The Dualistic Fallacy

One of the most common errors in interpreting crime data is the **dualistic fallacy,** the assumption that there is a distinct difference between two groups: criminals and noncriminals. The assumption is that these groups are homogeneous and that studies can therefore compare them on a given trait and conclude that the findings represent the differences between the two groups. That is, the assumption is that criminals violate the law and noncriminals do not. However, research indicates that this assumption is not true. The dualistic fallacy is so serious that all empirical studies of criminal behavior involving the error must be assumed to have limited scientific validity in distinguishing between those who commit crimes and those who do not. But this does not mean that the studies are useless. The key question is whether the conclusions are limited to the subject matter that is actually being studied.

Science assumes that a phenomenon can be measured empirically with valid and reliable tools. Further, it assumes that this phenomenon can be clearly distinguished from something that is similar but not of the same classification. Even if the phenomenon cannot be measured with the senses, science presumes that it has consistent indicators of its existence and that those indicators can be measured.

When these assumptions are applied to the study of crime, the critical issue is what phenomenon is assumed to exist. Is there something called crime that is unique behavior? Can it be distinguished from all other behavior? The answer to that question must be no. There is nothing intrinsically unique or distinguishable about crime. A crime is defined not in terms of the properties or attributes of an act but in terms of the social situation in which it occurs. Sexual intercourse may be a lawful relationship between a husband and wife. It is a physical act that can be described. However, the same act may also be **incest, adultery, rape, statutory rape,** or **fornication,** all of which are crimes in some jurisdictions. Furthermore, even though certain acts are defined as crimes, many violators are not prosecuted, in which case they should not be considered criminals.

Crime, then, is clearly a definitional term. It exists because certain acts are defined as such. But those acts cannot be clearly distinguished from similar acts, or even from identical acts, except by social reaction because intrinsically crime is just like noncrime. The behavior in question is a crime when committed by some people in some situations and not a crime when committed by others in other situations. In trying to understand criminal behavior, then, we must not only understand why people commit acts that are defined as crimes, the approach taken by many sociological theorists, but we must also understand the *process* by which some but not all people who engage in the acts are labeled criminal.

We could conclude that social science research is inherently suspect and that it will never be sufficiently free of methodological problems to explain crime. But many of the problems can be resolved with adequate planning. As one noted methodologist observed, "Many of the fruits of science . . . can be used to advantage while still in the process of development. Science is at best a growth, not a sudden revelation." Research in the social sciences can be used "imperfectly and in part while it is developing."[5]

We have come a long way from the writings and thinking of the people whose ideas dominated the nineteenth century, but those ideas were important in establishing the foundation for our success today.

NINETEENTH-CENTURY EXPLANATIONS

The formal development of criminology as a discipline is very recent, but the ideas of people who might be called early **criminologists** can be traced historically. Most of these people were lawyers, doctors, philosophers, or sociologists, whose primary interest was in reforming the criminal law, not in creating a science of criminal behavior. Nevertheless, their contributions to criminology are immense, and for an adequate understanding of current criminological theories, some familiarity with these earlier approaches is important.

The Classical Beginnings

Ideas and philosophies do not exist within the vacuum of a human mind; they must be understood in the light of the social context in which they appear. To understand the classical writers and their contributions to criminology, we must know something about the social conditions that existed at that time.

The **classical theorists** were rebelling against a very arbitrary and corrupt system of law in which the judges held an absolute and almost tyrannical power over those who came before them. The law was applied unequally; corruption was widespread. Confessions were obtained by means of torture, and the death penalty was used for many offenses.

Cesare Beccaria

The leader of the classical school was Cesare Beccaria, born in Milan, Italy, on March 15, 1738. He published only one major book, not entirely original, for many of the ideas were merely syntheses of those already expressed by others.[6] But it was widely received because many people in Europe were ready to hear and to implement the kinds of changes Beccaria proposed.[7]

Beccaria's work is extremely important today. His short essay contains almost all modern penal reforms, but its greatest contribution was "the foundation it laid for subsequent changes in criminal legislation."[8] His underlying philosophy was **free will.** He maintained that behavior is purposive and is based on **hedonism,** the pleasure-pain principle: human

Cesare Beccaria, leader of the classical school, believed that punishment should fit the crime.

beings choose those actions that will give pleasure and avoid those that will bring pain. Therefore, punishment should be assigned to each crime in a degree that will result in more pain than pleasure for those who commit the forbidden acts. The *punishment should fit the crime.* This hedonistic view of conduct implies that the laws must be clearly written and not open to interpretation by the judges. Only the legislature can specify punishment. The law must apply equally to all citizens; no defenses for criminal acts are permitted. The issue in court is whether a person committed the act; if so, the particular penalty prescribed by law for that act should be imposed. Judges are mere instruments of the law, allowed only to determine innocence or guilt and thereafter to prescribe punishment. Under this system the law is rigid, structured, and theoretically impartial.

The impact of Beccaria's arguments on modern American criminal law can be seen in this statement: "Our substantive criminal law is based upon a theory of punishing the vicious will. It postulates a free moral agent, confronted with a choice between doing right and doing wrong, and choosing freely to do wrong."[9] The person who chooses to do wrong *deserves* to be punished. Beccaria's position may be seen as a forerunner to the modern justice model of punishment discussed later in the chapter.

Beccaria has also been praised for helping to make the law impartial. Contemporary American philosophy holds that all people should be equal under the law and that all cases must be weighed on an impartial, blind scale of justice. Athough that ideal has never been fully implemented, Beccaria should be recognized for his contributions to the concept of justice. Others, however, argue that Beccaria's attacks on the criminal justice system of his day were misplaced. Graeme Newman is perhaps the most critical of Beccaria, referring to him as a "pampered intellectual who had no firsthand knowledge of the criminal justice system."[10]

The major weaknesses of Beccaria's ideas were the rigidity of his concepts and the lack of provision for justifiable criminal acts. These problems were acknowledged by the neoclassical school, discussed later.

Jeremy Bentham

Jeremy Bentham, born in 1748 and therefore a contemporary of Beccaria, was a British philosopher trained in law. His impact on legal thinking led one critic to admit that he was tempted to "proclaim Bentham the greatest legal philosopher and reformer the world has ever seen."[11]

Bentham's philosophy can be summed up in the phrase "let the punishment fit the crime," for he believed that people act rationally. We choose certain acts because they bring us pleasure; likewise, we avoid acts that result in pain. Our choice is a rational one. Therefore, if we perceive that an act will bring pain—that is, the punishment for the crime is sufficiently severe—we will choose to avoid that act because engaging in it would result in pain that would outweigh any pleasure we might have in committing the crime.

Bentham referred to his philosophy of social control as **utilitarianism:** "An act is not to be judged by an irrational system of absolutes but by a supposedly verifiable principle . . . [which is] 'the greatest happiness for the greatest number' or simply 'the greatest happiness.'" Despite his belief in utilitarianism and the free will of individuals, Bentham also hinted at the theory of learned behavior in contrast to a deterministic explanation of criminal behavior.[12]

The Neoclassical School

The **neoclassical school** of criminology, which flourished during the nineteenth century, had the same basis as the classical school—a belief in free will. But the neoclassical criminologists, who were mainly British, began complaining about the need for individualized reaction to offenders, as they believed the classical approach was far too harsh and, in reality, unjust.

Perhaps the most shocking aspect of these harsh penal codes was that they did not provide for the separate treatment of children. One of the changes of the neoclassical period was that children under seven years of age were exempted from the law on the basis that they could not understand the difference between right and wrong. Mental disease also became a reason to exempt a would-be criminal from conviction. Mental disease was seen as a sufficient cause of impaired responsibility; thus, defense by reason of insanity crept into the law. Indeed, any situation or circumstance that made it impossible to exercise free will was seen as reason to exempt a person from legal responsibility for what might otherwise be a criminal act.

Although the neoclassical school was not a scientific school of criminology, unlike the classical school it did begin to explore the causation issue. The neoclassical theorists made exceptions to the law and thus implied multiple causation. The doctrine of free will could no longer stand alone as an explanation for criminal behavior. Even today, much modern law is based on the neoclassical philosophy of free will tempered by certain exceptions.

The classical and neoclassical schools were based on philosophy and armchair thinking, not on actual research. But they have influenced the thinking and policies of Europeans as well as Americans, as illustrated in Exhibit 3.1. But before a science of criminal data could emerge, it was necessary to gather and analyze empirical data on criminals. The use of data to explain criminal behavior is characteristic of the positive school of thought.

The Positive School

The **positive school** of criminology was composed of several Italians whose approaches differed to some extent, but they all agreed that the

EXHIBIT 3.1

Classical Influence in Other Countries

Thinking about criminal sentencing has undergone a remarkable transformation in Scandinavia during the last decade. There has been a movement away from positivist sentencing ideology—that is, away from indeterminacy of sentence, and from rehabilitation and prediction of future criminality as the basis for sentencing. There has been growing support for a "neoclassical" sentencing rationale that would emphasize penalties proportionate to the gravity of the criminal conduct. This movement has had its greatest impact in Finland, where "neoclassicism" has come to be official policy. Article 6 of the Finnish criminal code, as amended in 1976, declares that sentences should be in "just proportion" to the harmfulness of the criminal conduct and the culpability of the offender.

SOURCE: Andrew von Hirsch, "Neoclassicism, Proportionality, and the Rationale for Punishment: Thoughts on the Scandinavia Debate," *Crime & Delinquency*, (January 1983): 52, reprinted with permission.

emphasis in the study of crime should be on the scientific treatment of the criminal, not on the penalties to be imposed after conviction.[13]

The classical school, defining crime in legal terms, emphasized the concept of free will and the position that punishment gauged to fit the crime would be a deterrent. The positivists rejected the harsh legalism of the classical school and substituted the doctrine of **determinism** for that of free will. They focused on the **constitutional,** not the legal, approach to crime, and they emphasized a philosophy of individualized, scientific treatment of criminals, based on the findings of the physical and social sciences. As Stephen Schafer said, "Their emergence [in the late eighteenth century] symbolized clearly that the era of faith was over and the scientific age had begun."[14]

Cesare Lombroso

Cesare Lombroso (1835–1909), the leader of the positive school, has been called "the father of modern criminology."[15] Lombroso rejected the classical doctrine of free will, but he was strongly influenced by the contemporary writings on positivism by early influential sociologists. He was most famous for his biological theory of crime, which is discussed in the next chapter.

Lombroso described himself as a "slave to facts." Indeed, he should

Cesare Lombroso, leader of the positive school, believed that punishment should fit the criminal.

be recognized for his emphasis on careful measurement in securing data. Despite his conscientiousness, Lombroso may be criticized for his failure to interpret his data in light of his theory. It was his belief that the data, even if they appeared unrelated at the moment, would subsequently evolve into a theory of universal applicability. His method was largely one of analogy and anecdote from which he drew his conclusions.

The reaction to Lombroso ranges from severe criticism to high praise. Edwin H. Sutherland and Donald R. Cressey, in an early edition of their text, *Criminology,* asserted that Lombroso and his school "delayed for fifty years the work which was in progress at the time of its origin and in addition made no lasting contribution of its own." In an edition published nineteen years later, the authors were milder in their criticism, stating only that the Lombrosian school "fell into disrepute."[16] Criminologist Marvin Wolfgang disagreed and concluded that "Lombroso served to redirect emphasis from the crime to the criminal, not from social to individual factors."[17] Wolfgang acknowledged the serious methodological problems in Lombroso's research, as evaluated by modern techniques and knowledge, but concluded that Lombroso "also manifested imaginative insight, good intuitive judgment, intellectual honesty, awareness of some of his limitations, attempts to use control groups and a desire to have his theories tested impartially. Many researchers of today fare little better than this."[18]

Contributions of the Positive School

The contributions of the positive school to the development of a scientific approach to the study of criminal behavior and to the reform of criminal law were extensive. The positivists emphasized the importance of empirical research in their work. They believed that punishment should fit the criminal, not the crime, as recommended by the classical school. The positivists substituted the doctrine of determinism, some arguing that it was physical, others that it was psychic, social, or economic, thus introducing the concept of environment into the study of crime.

The positive school and the classical approach had an important impact on the emergence and development of criminology. The basic differences between these schools of thought are listed in the following table. This visual summary will facilitate our discussion of the impact the two schools had on modern criminology. In fact, the basic premises on which our policies of punishment, treatment, and sentencing have been based for the past quarter of a century may be traced to these schools of thought.

Classical School	Positive School
1. legal definition of crime	1. rejection of legal definition
2. let the punishment fit the crime	2. let the punishment fit the criminal
3. doctrine of free will	3. doctrine of determinism
4. death penalty for some offenses	4. abolition of the death penalty
5. anecdotal method—no empirical research	5. empirical research, inductive method
6. definitive sentence	6. indeterminate sentence

THE CLASSICAL AND POSITIVE SCHOOLS AND PHILOSOPHY OF PUNISHMENT

The writings of the classical and positive schools illustrate the basic philosophies of punishment: retribution or revenge, deterrence of the individual and of others, and reform or rehabilitation.

Retribution or Revenge

Historically, victims (or their families) were permitted to take measures to avenge crime. This practice is referred to as revenge, retaliation, or retribution. But the terms are not synonymous. **Retribution,** which focuses on the conduct of the wrongdoer, is the concept in vogue today and will be discussed in detail later. **Revenge,** or retaliation, more accurately reflects the practices of earlier days when victims could, within the law, inflict on their attackers the same or similar kind of offense as that suffered by the victim. The practice may be traced back for centuries and is referred to as the "eye for an eye, tooth for a tooth" doctrine.

In modern times some jurisdictions have recognized the doctrine of revenge, even permitting crime victims to take extreme measures against those who wronged them. In Texas, until relatively recently, a husband who found his wife engaged in sexual relations with another man was permitted to kill the man, provided he did so before the couple separated. The killing was justifiable homicide, meaning the husband was not legally responsible for the act; it was, in essence, not a crime.

Some countries still permit victims to take revenge or retaliate against criminals, but more frequently, this behavior is not legally acceptable. Thus, in 1989 when a Lisbon, Portugal, man found his wife in bed with another man and cut off the right ear of each, he was arrested.[19]

The classical thinkers did not accept the "eye for an eye" extreme philosophy of punishment. They rejected punishments that were too harsh, believing that criminal law should not be used as vengeance against the criminal. The punishment should "fit the crime." Beccaria, for example, insisted that the state had no right to impose a punishment greater than was necessary. "Any law or punishment in excess of this limit is an abuse of power, not justice, and no unjust punishment may be tolerated, however useful it seems."[20]

Deterrence

In addition to emphasizing a philosophy of punishment based on what the criminal deserves, the classical thinkers believed that a major purpose of punishment was **deterrence.** There are two types of deterrence, individual and general.

Individual (or **specific**) **deterrence** refers to the effect of punishment in preventing a particular individual from committing additional crimes. In the past, this form of deterrence often became **incapacitation,** making it impossible for a particular offender to repeat the crime. For example, the hands of the thief were amputated; rapists were castrated; and prostitutes would be disfigured in ways that would repel potential customers.

The second type, **general deterrence,** is based on the assumption

The government of the People's Republic of China advocates deterrence theory by severe punishments. Some of the Chinese students who demonstrated for democracy in 1989 were later executed.

that punishing individuals who are convicted of crimes will set an example to potential violators, who, being rational beings and wishing to avoid such pain, will not violate the law. Again, we can see the influence of the classical thinkers with their emphasis on free will and rational choice. People will seek pleasure and avoid pain; thus, if the punishment is perceived as too painful, people will avoid the criminal activity that might result in that punishment.

Reform or Rehabilitation

Retribution and deterrence were the philosophies of the classical and neoclassical schools, with their emphasis on "let the punishment fit the crime." The positive school, on the other hand, emphasized the importance of the "punishment fitting the criminal." It was the individual criminal, not the crime, that was the focal point in positive thinking. Positivists believed that to prevent crime changes must be made in the social environment. They favored **indeterminate sentences,** tailored to meet the needs of individual criminals. They also set the stage for further developing the philosophy of **rehabilitation,** a philosophy that dominated our criminal justice system until recently.

Rehabilitation—A Modern Ideal?

A *Time* magazine article in late 1982 phrased this key question and then answered it in the subtitle of the article: "What Are Prisons For? No longer rehabilitation, but to punish—and to lock the worst away." The article referred briefly to the original purpose of prisons in this country, not only to punish but also to transform criminals "from idlers and hooligans into good, industrious citizens." The article concluded, however, that "no other country was so seduced for so long by that ambitious charter. The language, ever malleable, conformed to the ideal: when a monkish salvation was expected of inmates, prisons became penitentiaries, then reformatories, correctional centers and rehabilitation facilities." The simple fact is that prisons did not work as intended.[21]

The philosophy of rehabilitation nonetheless continued and even gained momentum during this century, becoming the modern philosophy of incarceration. It was described by one authority as the rehabilitative ideal, based on the premise that human behavior is the result of antecedent causes that may be known by objective analysis and that permit scientific control. The assumption was, therefore, that the offender should be *treated*, not punished.[22]

Social scientists strongly endorsed the rehabilitative ideal and began developing treatment programs for institutionalized inmates. The ideal was even incorporated into some statutes, proclaimed by courts, and supported by the President's Crime Commission.

The Indeterminate Sentence

The backbone of the philosophy of rehabilitation was the *indeterminate sentence.* No longer would a court, at the time of sentencing, give an offender a definite term, as a judge could not possibly predict in advance how much time would be needed for treatment and rehabilitation. Consequently, in most jurisdictions the legislature established minimum and maximum terms for each offense. In its purest form, the indeterminate sentence meant that a person would be sentenced to prison for one day to life. Treatment personnel would then evaluate the person, recommend and implement treatment, and decide when that individual had been rehabilitated and could be safely released. The punishment was fitted to the criminal, not to the crime. In short, the basic philosophy was that we should incarcerate people until they were cured, or rehabilitated.[23]

HIGHLIGHT 3.1

DO WE BELIEVE IN REHABILITATION?

I don't mourn for John Mack, the congressional aide who has lost his well-paid and powerful job because of something he did 16 years ago.

The "something he did" was so awful, so crazy, so brutish that I wouldn't have objected if he had been sentenced to die for his crime. By my imperfect lights, he should at the very least still be in prison.

What worries me about the Mack case is the public reaction—my reaction—to it when we learned, years later, that (1) he had been dealt an absurdly lenient sentence, and (2) that he had risen to power and prominence, while his victim still struggles to keep her mind intact.

You know the details. Mack, a 19-year-old manager of a suburban Virginia store at the time, lured a young woman to a backroom of the shop and, for reasons that make no sense what-

soever, bludgeoned her with a hammer, stabbed her several times, put her in her own car and drove her off to a secluded spot, leaving her to die.

That Pamela Small didn't die is nothing short of a miracle. She regained consciousness, drove herself to a service station to summon help and, with the help of surgeons, was restored at least to physical health.

You also know what happened to Mack. He served 27 months in the Fairfax County (Va.) Jail, won an early release on his 15-year "malicious wounding" sentence when he was offered a clerical job on the staff of House Speaker Jim Wright, whose daughter was married at the time to Mack's brother, and made good.

By the time we learned about the case, through a gut-wrenching Washington Post interview with Pamela Small, Mack was

Wright's top aide: competent, respected on the Hill and earning $89,500 a year.

And we went crazy. How could this man, whose public utterances are devoid of any show of remorse, be prospering as though nothing had happened? How could Small's painful physical and emotional recovery be left to the resources of her family, with no help from the public, while her attacker led the good life on the public payroll? Twenty-seven months in the county jail? What kind of justice is that?

These were my questions, too. But even now, weeks after the interview was published (and after Mack, yielding to our outrage, resigned his post), I still don't have any answers that make sense.

Were we outraged by the shortness of the sentence? (Should Mack have said: "Look,

---

The Decline of the Rehabilitative Ideal

The philosophy of rehabilitation was based on a belief that we could predict when offenders had been rehabilitated and were ready for release. Prediction is not that accurate in the social sciences, however, although individuals trained in the behavioral sciences would be in a better position to make that decision after working with an offender than would a judge at the time of sentencing. But, it is alleged, treatment has not been very effective in prisons.

Perhaps an even greater problem has been the administrative abuse of the power to release. Under the indeterminate system in California, offenders served longer terms than they would have served under definite sentences, and there was no evidence that these longer terms were necessary for rehabilitation. Another criticism of the indeterminate sen-

HIGHLIGHT 3.1 (Continued)

your honor, I think I ought to do more time, and in the state prison"?) Was it his rise to prominence and power that upset us? (Would we have been happier if he were earning $15,000 a year as ditch-digger, or if he had remained in the clerical job Wright originally gave him at $9,000 a year?) Was it his apparent lack of remorse? (What revelation of sleepless nights or psychiatric treatment or thoughts of suicide would have altered our reaction?)

Pamela Small touched on a part of our frustration when she said that Mack had risen to power and middle-class affluence "because he tried to kill me." It's true. Mack, a high-school graduate who had evinced no interest in government, might still have been an ordinary working-class stiff if his crime had not led to the intervention of a powerful sponsor.

Still it seems to me that a part of our outrage stems not from the fact that Wright found him a job but that the did so incredibly well at it.

This is no holier-than-thou put down or societal vengeance. I was outraged, too. I still am.

But my outrage worries me. I try to picture Mack as a black man who, apparently an ordinarily decent guy before his unexplained savagery, and unarguably an exemplary worker afterwards, had made a success of his life. Would I still be outraged? Or would I be wondering at the ethics and motivation of a newspaper story seemingly calculated to destroy him?

"John Mack's crime was undeniably savage," I might have written, "and his punishment too light. But his rehabilitation is undeniable. Since we cannot undo his crime, or, at this stage, lengthen his sentence, doesn't it

make sense to let this man, no doubt haunted by the savagery of what he did, get on with his life?"

Would I have written any such thing? Would I have thought it even if I didn't have the courage to say it? I honestly don't know.

What I do know is that as awful as I feel for Pamela Small, I don't feel good about my share of the vengeance that led to the derailing of Mack's life. It's one thing to wish that the courts had done their job when it was their's to do; quite another for the rest of us to transform their laxity into an after-the-fact sentence of life without parole.

SOURCE: William Raspberry, a Washington Post Writers Group columnist, "Do We Believe in Rehabilitation?" reprinted in the *Tallahassee Democrat,* 25 May 1989. Reprinted with permission.

---

tence was that it caused feelings of hostility toward the criminal justice system. Offenders never knew when they would be released. According to one report, inmates referred to the indeterminate sentence as the "never-knowing system," and it created psychological problems for them.[24]

Another serious problem was the lack of guidelines, rules, or standards for release from prison. This lack and the general unwillingness of the appellate courts to review the trial judges' sentencing decisions led to serious attacks on this form of sentencing. These problems, combined with increasing dissatisfaction with the rehabilitative ideal and concern about the extent of crime, especially violent crime, led many to favor a get-tough policy in sentencing. The argument is that treatment did not work; so let us try incarceration for longer periods of time. "Lock 'em up and throw away the key! Crudely put, that increasingly is the rallying cry in an America fed up with violent crime."[25]

The trend toward harsher punishments, including greater use of the death penalty, is based on two philosophies. First, harsh punishment is what the criminal deserves; second, by imposing harsh penalties on deserving individuals, they and others will be deterred from committing crimes. Thus the two philosophies of justice and of deterrence are merged. These two philosophies have virtually replaced the former emphasis on rehabilitation. Yet, some writers still question whether we should consider rehabilitation as a viable punishment philosophy. Consider the comments of columnist William Raspberry in Highlight 3.1.[26]

"Let the punishment fit the crime" has been heard once again, with Beccaria and the classical school of thought ringing in the ears of those who follow cycles in history. This time, however, the philosophy of retribution carries a different name. We now talk about **just deserts,** or justice, but the underlying philosophy of retribution remains. We will examine the modern use of that philosophy as a prelude to our discussion of the justice approach and its companion philosophy of deterrence.

MODERN PUNISHMENT PHILOSOPHIES

The concept of retribution, severely criticized in much of the scholarly social science literature and in judicial opinions in the first two-thirds of this century, was recognized in 1972 by the U.S. Supreme Court as an appropriate reason for capital punishment.[27] In a 1976 opinion, the Court again discussed retribution as a justification for capital punishment. It indicated that although retribution is no longer the dominant philosophy,

> neither is it a forbidden objective nor one inconsistent with our respect for the dignity of men. . . . Indeed, the decision that capital punishment may be the appropriate sanction in extreme cases is an expression of the community's belief that certain crimes are themselves so grievous an affront to humanity that the only adequate response may be the penalty of death.[28]

The Court noted that the instinct for retribution is a part of human nature and that if the courts do not handle these situations, private individuals might take the law into their own hands. Regarding retribution, the Court concluded:

> In part, capital punishment is an expression of society's moral outrage at particularly offensive conduct. This function may be unappealing to many, but it is essential in an ordered society that asks its citizens to rely on legal processes rather than self-help to vindicate their wrongs.[29]

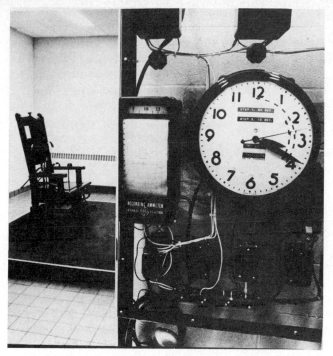

The electric chair at Ohio Penitentiary, Columbus. The state electrocuted 312 men and 3 women, the latest in 1963.

It has been argued that the Supreme Court justices have recently given more support to the doctrine of retribution as a justification for capital punishment because they realize the evidence on deterrence is not strong and the public has become disillusioned with the doctrine of rehabilitation. Retribution is the only doctrine supporting punishment in general and the death penalty in particular in which there need be no question of effectiveness. Effectiveness is not an issue. The argument under retribution is that people are incarcerated because they deserve to be. Retribution is not *utilitarian*. Because its goal is "'doing justice' rather than the prevention of crimes, it makes no instrumental claims," and that is its principal merit.[30]

Another current justification for retribution is that it serves the important social function of legitimizing punishment. The argument is that society desires to see crime punished because "the criminal has pursued his interests, or gratified his desires, by means noncriminals have restrained themselves from using for the sake of the law and in fear of its punishments." Therefore, the offender's act must be punished to justify the self-restraint of noncriminals. It is also argued that society punishes because it feels it wants to or it ought to; the sole purpose of retribution is to express moral outrage.[31]

The Justice Model of Punishment

Retribution also provides the rationale for the modern **justice model** of punishment and sentencing, illustrated by the writings of Andrew von Hirsch, representing the position of the Committee for the Study of Incarceration in his book *Doing Justice: The Choice of Punishments*. Indicating their basic mistrust of the power of the state, the committee members rejected rehabilitation and the indeterminate sentence and turned to deterrence and just deserts as reasons for punishment. In its rejection of rehabilitation, however, the committee advocated shorter sentences and a sparing use of incarceration.[32]

The person most often cited as responsible for the current popularity of the justice model is David Fogel, who expressed his views in detail in his book *We Are the Living Proof: The Justice Model for Corrections*. Fogel formulates twelve propositions on which he believes the justice model can be based. He argues that punishment is necessary to implement the criminal law, a law based on the belief that people act as a result of their own free will and must be held responsible for their actions. Prisoners should be considered and treated as "responsible, volitional and aspiring human beings." All the processes of the agencies of the criminal justice system should be carried out "in a milieu of justice." This requirement precludes a correctional system that "becomes mired in the dismal swamp of preaching, exhorting, and treatment." According to Fogel, discretion cannot be eliminated, but under the justice model it can be controlled, narrowed, and subjected to review.[33]

In the justice model, the emphasis is shifted away from the processor (the public, the administration, and others) to the consumer of the criminal justice system. And according to Fogel, justice for the offender must not stop with the process of sentencing but continue throughout the correctional process. *"Properly understood, the justice perspective is not so much concerned with administration of justice as it is with the justice of administration."*[34]

Under Fogel's justice model, an incarcerated person should retain all the rights "accorded free citizens consistent with mass living and the execution of a sentence restricting the freedom of movement." Inmates should be allowed to choose whether they wish to participate in rehabilitation programs. The purpose of the prison becomes solely to confine for a specified period of time, not to rehabilitate the criminal. Offenders receive only the sentences they deserve, and those sentences are implemented according to fair principles.

The influence of the classical school may be seen in this return to a theory of just deserts or retribution. Bentham and Beccaria argued that the punishment should fit the crime. The just and humane approach is to punish the criminal for what he or she has done, not to follow the treatment-rehabilitation approach.

The justice model, with its emphasis on retribution and just deserts, sounds fair and simple. Offenders get the punishment they deserve—no more, no less. The problem, however, is in determining what is fair and just punishment for a particular offense. The justice model thus does not answer the important question: *How much* punishment is deserved? That question must be answered by legislators, judges, or administrators, and the argument is made that those in power will use it to discriminate against certain groups, such as minorities. When that happens, we do not have a just and fair system, and the justice model is a farce.[35]

Modern Deterrence Theory

The classical position that the punishment should fit the crime, not the criminal, and the belief in free will and rational thought led to the conclusion that appropriate punishments could deter criminal activity because rational humans would not choose behavior that would bring more pain than pleasure. Again, we see the modern counterparts illustrated by a *Time* article on capital punishment, stating the position quite simply: *"If I know I will be punished so severely, I will not commit the crime."*[36] But the author quickly noted that because capital punishment in this country is not swift or sure, the deterrent effect is reduced. Nonetheless, the philosophy is clear: Punishment will deter. Today's reaction to the criminal is based on this philosophy; it is therefore important not only to see the connection between this emphasis of today and the writings of the classical thinkers but also to examine whether the philosophy has merit.

Empirical Evidence Regarding Deterrence

Pro and con reactions to the question of whether punishment deters are often based on conjecture, faith, or emotion, with little or no empirical data. Advocates simply "know" that punishment does or does not deter, and this is particularly so in the death penalty debate. Policies in the People's Republic of China, featured in Highlight 3.2, illustrate this point. Such dogmatic statements cloud the issues and, therefore, it is important to analyze the empirical evidence.[37]

Sociologist Jack P. Gibbs has addressed the issue of deterrence in an insightful and provocative book, *Crime, Punishment, and Deterrence*, in which he reviews the empirical findings on punishment and deterrence. Noting that much of the earlier sociological research on deterrence was concerned solely with the relationship of crime rates and the statutory existence of the death penalty, Gibbs points out that more recently sociologists have turned to an "examinaton of the relation between actual legal punishments (imprisonment in particular) and crime rates." According to Gibbs, the findings of the earlier studies cannot be generalized to other types of punishment. They are even limited in their application to our understanding of the deterrent effect of capital punishment, as most

HIGHLIGHT 3.2

CHINA USES CAPITAL PUNISHMENT—CLAIMS CRIME RATE DROPS DRAMATICALLY AS A RESULT

Belief in the effectiveness of capital punishment as a deterrent led the government of the People's Republic of China to announce in the spring of 1982 that corrupt government and Communist Party officials would be executed. According to the party newspaper *People's Daily,* "It is necessary to kill one to warn a hundred . . . the seriousness of a few economic offenses has reached such an extent that the death penalty may have to be employed to beat down the offenders' arrogance and to educate and save others."*

The current wave of execu-

tions began in August of 1983, with reports of thousands of people being executed for the crimes of murder, rape, arson, and robbery as well as gansterism and even less violent crimes. Some of those executed were driven through the streets, accompanied by placards proclaiming to the masses the crimes for which the offenders would be executed.

The list of capital crimes in China, expanded in 1983, now includes gang leaders, organizers of prostitution, and embezzlers. Furthermore, there is no longer a requirement that capital sentences have to be reviewed by the Supreme People's Court. Execution for violent crimes may be carried out swiftly after the sentence is imposed by a lower

court. The processes of arrest, indictment, trial, sentence, and execution may take place in four days. In China, the usual method of execution is a single shot in the back of the head.†

In the spring of 1984, the Chinese claimed that as a result of increased executions (estimated by some to be as high as ten thousand since August of 1983), the crime rate had dropped 42 percent.‡

In 1990 the Chinese executed some individuals who participated in the Beijing riots.

*"Peking to Execute Corrupt Officials, Paper Indicates," *Los Angeles Times,* 11 March 1982, pt I, p. 10, col. 1.

†"China Suddenly Taking a Tougher Line on Crime," *New York Times,* 13 September 1983, p. 10Y, col. 1.
‡National news broadcast, Spring 1984.

ignore the variable of certainty of actual execution. In addition, studies of the deterrent effect of punishment, argues Gibbs, must allow for the differences between general and individual deterrence and take into account properties of punishment such as the perceived certainty that one would actually suffer a punishment. If a potential criminal thinks the law will not be enforced, he or she might not be deterred from criminal activity merely because the law provides a severe penalty for violation.[38]

There is some evidence that convicted inmates believe they will get away with committing additional crimes when they are released. In a study of inmates in three states, the percentage of inmates who said they thought they could commit the same crime again without getting caught was as follows:

- 50 percent of the California inmates
- 34 percent of the Michigan inmates
- 23 percent of the Texas inmates[39]

Some social scientists have agreed that we cannot actually test deterrence until we can refine our research models and specify the variables determining whether or not punishment deters.[40] There is, for example, some evidence that punishment may have a quick but not a long-term deterrent effect.[41] Some studies of the deterrent effect of jailing drunk drivers support this position.[42] And there is some evidence that mandatory jail sentences for convicted DWI offenders are not significant deterrence for future convictions.[43]

Even if increased arrests and more severe penalties for conviction have a deterrent effect, we also have to consider the effect that stiffer penalties for crimes have on the total criminal justice system. Many jurisdictions have faced severe problems of overcrowding in their jails and prisons, caused in large measure by the increased penalties and more extensive imposition of penalties on drug offenders. For example, Connecticut, whose prisons are overcrowded mainly because of an increase in individuals convicted for drug-related crimes, began releasing inmates early to make room for new inmates. The Connecticut Corrections Commissioner described his overcrowded prisons as follows:

> This is the everyday world for us. . . . It's a world where people have no place to keep their belongings, where sewage systems back up, where everything is fast-tracked to deal with numbers, not quality. We just can't absorb the growth.[44]

Prisons are not the only aspects of the criminal justice system that are overcrowded because of drug-related arrests. In New York City, for example, the entire criminal justice system is in a crisis state. Judges and lawyers report that the system is barely able to take care of the increased number of police arrests for drug-related offenses. "So desperate is the situation . . . that without a major new infusion of money, manpower, new courtrooms and more jail space, the system will be swamped." A judge warned that "what is being lost is the certainty of punishment, which is even more important as a deterrent to crime than the severity."[45]

The American Bar Association alleged that it is the war on drugs, not the recognition of offenders' constitutional rights, that is overwhelming the criminal justice system. "The entire system is starved." Meanwhile, drug problems increase, and law enforcement officials seem powerless to do anything about them.[46] This is not to suggest that we should retreat from our attempts to control drug-related offenses, but it does mean that the total effect of any action should be considered before the proposed reform is implemented. Highlight 3.3 focuses on the drug problem and its impact on the criminal justice system while questioning the deterrent effect of the current war on drugs.

Deterrence of Types of Crime and Types of People

The debate over deterrence should be narrowed to types of crime and types of people, a point often overlooked. Perhaps punishment (or the

HIGHLIGHT 3.3

DRUG OFFENSES AND THE CRIMINAL JUSTICE SYSTEM

It's late on a sunny spring afternoon at the Bronx Criminal Court, and the latest POW's in the drug war move steadily through Judge Max Sayah's dingy basement courtroom. The attorney for Raymond Maldonado, a teenage defendant, huddles briefly with Sayah and a prosecutor, finalizing a plea bargain that will send his client to prison for eight months on a string of charges, including possession of crack, violating parole and assaulting a police officer. "Do you have anything to say?" the judge asks. "I want to know if I get eight months," Maldonado replies. "You should worry about the rest of your life, not eight months," Sayah angrily snaps. "You've got to get your life together."

The exchange was a flicker of the deep frustration that judges, lawyers and corrections officials feel with a criminal-justice system overwhelmed by an unprecedented surge in drug arrests. Under pressure from angry citizens and panicked politicians, police in a number of cities have mounted dramatic crackdowns on narcotics sales and drug-re-

lated violence. But the new hard line on the street has not been matched by an investment in additional jails and courts. The $1 billion in new federal prison construction announced last week by President George Bush will do little to improve the immediate situation: clogged court dockets, overcrowded prisons and a message to many young drug entrepreneurs that time behind bars is no more than a cost of doing business. "Ask a politician what to do about crime, and he'll say, 'Hire more cops.' It's totally irrelevant," says Mark Kleiman, former drug-policy analyst for the Department of Justice and now a lecturer at Harvard University. "What cops produce are more arrests. We've already got more arrests than we can deal with."

Court systems have been hard hit by political shortsightedness. New York City laid out $110 million last year for new Tactical Narcotics Teams to sweep crack-infested neighborhoods, but only $9.5 million for legal-aid lawyers and prosecutors. While a proposal to provide additional judges is pending in the state leg-

islature, the city currently has just 75 criminal judges to hear a projected 110,000 drug cases this year—a 30 percent increase over 1988. Ninety-seven percent will be disposed of through plea bargaining; such arrangements are often harder on small offenders, who lack the higher-priced legal counsel of serious criminals. "The public and politicians always talk in terms of more police and more jails. The middle part [the courts] is the invisible part," says New York state Chief Judge Sol Wachtler. "The mouth of the funnel is being made wider, but the neck is just as narrow."

Tent jails: Drug-spawned prison congestion is growing worse. More arrests and tougher sentencing swelled state and federal inmate population 7.4 percent in 1988 to 627,000; in 1978 it was 284,000. Should the trend continue, says the American Correctional Association, an organization of prison professionals, a million Americans could be in custody by the mid-1990s, placing enormous pressures on the correctional system. In gang-plagued south central

threat of punishment) is effective in deterring people from shoplifting but not necessarily from killing their spouses. Perhaps certain types of people are deterred by laws, but others are not. Or perhaps "perceptions of certain punishment may have a deterrent effect on some form of common, nonserious delinquency" but not on other types of crime.[47]

In the case of murder and other violent crimes, offenders are often under the influence of drugs or alcohol or are consumed by passion, as in

HIGHLIGHT 3.3 (Continued)

Los Angeles, the word on the street is to turn yourself in if you're wanted for anything but a serious crime: L.A. County's jail system is bursting at the seams and the prospect of a long stretch behind bars is remote. Broward County, Fla., Sheriff Nick Navarro wants to erect tent jails again this summer for the overflow from a planned crackdown on drug sales, even though prisoner advocates forced the dismantling of the makeshift detention centers last year. "I know every jail is overcrowded, but I couldn't care less. These people should be separated from the community."

The overcrowding has forced prison officials into increasing reliance on controversial early-release programs. In 1977, according to a recent Justice Department study, seven out of 10 inmates paroled from prison were released by parole boards. By 1987 that number had declined to four out of 10; many others get their tickets back to the street through court-mandated programs to ease prison populations.

Florida's auditor general reported last year that state inmates were serving less and less of their sentences due to "gain time" programs aimed at alleviating overcrowding. Between 1982 and 1987 the percentage of inmates serving six months or less went from 8 to 44 percent. Floridians were outraged last November when a 34-year-old man charged with killing two Dade County police officers with their own guns had been released from prison after serving just eight years of a 15-year sentence for attempted manslaughter. Plea bargaining spared him the 30-year maximum. In Washington, D.C., Mayor Marion Barry has had the city's prisons on "emergency" status since 1987 because of overcrowding, allowing 3,100 inmates to leave early. "The system is being driven by the goal of not overloading the prisons rather than putting away people who are a danger to the community," complains D.C. police-union chief Gary Hankins.

Clear choice: The situation lends a hollow ring to the stiff sentences public officials threaten on the evening news. "The penalties are the last thing [young drug dealers] think about," says 20-year-old Joseph, a Washington cocaine dealer just back from his first one-year sentence. "The kids don't watch the news. When you're locked up you watch the news."

Experts say the choice is clear for elected officials: roll back on tougher enforcement and sentencing or ante up the tax dollars for more prisons and rehabilitative programs. Just putting more cops on the beat may be good politics, but not good policy. "This isn't a criminal-justice problem," says Florida circuit court Judge Arthur Franza. "Criminal justice is working fine. It is the legislative and executive branches that are not doing their jobs."

SOURCE: "Why Justice Can't Be Done: America's Courts and Prisons are Overwhelmed," *Newsweek,* 29 May 1989, pp. 37–38, reprinted with permission.

domestic crimes. Thus, most of these people are probably not thinking very rationally when they commit crimes. Irrational thinking may also characterize those who violate traffic laws, particularly laws prohibiting driving while under the influence of alcohol or other drugs.

Sociologist H. Laurence Ross has studied this issue in other countries and in the United States, analyzing the effect that drunk-driving laws have had on the incidence of drunk driving. Ross concludes that there is an immediate deterrent effect when such laws are passed or there is a crack-down on enforcement, but the deterrent effect is short-lived. Ross believes that social learning is the key variable. Over time, individuals learn that despite the crackdown, their chances of being caught are slim; and if caught, the chances of significant punishment are also slim—and so the deterrent effect is minimal.[48]

What the Ross study does not show, however, is what the deterrent effect of severe punishment might be or what is considered *severe* punishment. In an effort to measure the effect of severe punishment on general deterrence of drunk driving, three social scientists selected a sample of American and Norwegian citizens for comparison. Norway was selected because, of all Western democracies, it has the toughest sanctions for drunk driving. A first offender faces a three-week jail term and a two-year suspension of his or her driver's license. These sentences are usually imposed.[49] The investigators found that a higher percentage of Americans than Norwegians reported driving under the influence of alcohol to some degree. We must, however, be careful about drawing conclusions from such data. Scholars continue to debate whether the tougher laws in Norway are effective as general deterrents. Norwegian scholar Johannes Andenaes has long maintained that the tough statutes are an effective deterrent; Ross has questioned that conclusion based on his studies in Scandanavia, but Andenaes and others have questioned Ross' methodology.[50]

The cultural characteristics of Norway must be considered when we analyze the effect of its strict laws. Norwegians, compared to Americans, are more likely to disapprove of driving after drinking; they are more likely to have accurate technical information about the drinking laws; they are more likely to use public transportation to get to a party; they are more likely to stay overnight with the host after drinking at a party; and they have stronger peer pressure not to drink and drive.[51]

Evidence also indicates that although Norwegians do not drink as frequently as Americans, they drink more when they do drink, and alcoholism and public drunkenness (not a crime) are serious problems. The stiff penalties for drunk driving have also led to a problem that might decrease the potential deterrent effect of the law. Prisons are full; Norwegians do not overcrowd their prisons as Americans often do. The result is a waiting list to get into prison, and the list consists mainly of persons convicted of drunk driving. In 1990, police officers told this author that the waiting list was two years long, and they were concerned that this situation would lead some Norwegians to think they would never have to serve a prison term; thus, the statutes would lose their deterrent effect. One might also argue, however, that having to wait and not knowing when the term will be served would be an even greater deterrent, for it decreases a person's ability to plan.

One final question should be considered: What type of people need stiff penalties compared to those who are more likely to be deterred by publicity or lesser penalties? For an executive who must drive for business and entertainment of clients, the revocation of a driver's license and publication in the paper of the arrest and type of punishment might be sufficient deterrence. It might also be sufficient to deter other professionals from driving while intoxicated. But even if those sanctions are sufficient deterrents, their effect may be short-lived. The effect might be lost entirely if people perceive that they will not be caught and/or if caught, the probability of actually receiving these or other punishments is slim.

Corporate crime should also be mentioned when we are considering whether the threat of legal sanctions deters criminal behavior. Two social scientists, John Braithwaite and Gilbert Geis, argued that although the traditional reasons for punishment may not be effective with those who commit traditional crimes, they will deter corporate criminals. Corporate crimes are not crimes of passion or emotion; rather, they are usually rationally calculated and consequently more amenable to deterrence.[52] Sociologists Marshall Clinard and Robert Meier agreed that punishment may be a greater deterrent for future-oriented persons who are status conscious than for people who are less concerned with social status and more concerned with immediate gratification.[53]

Recent news articles suggest support of this position. The Executive Director of the National Collegiate Athletic Association (NCAA) has suggested that severe penalties, such as the "death penalty," which forbids one or more athletic programs to operate for a specified period of time at an institution in which certain NCAA rules have been violated, are a deterrent effect.[54] After Michael Deaver, a deputy White House chief of staff under former President Ronald Reagan, was convicted of perjury (for lying to Congress and a Federal grand jury) and given a light penalty (a suspended prison sentence, a $100,000 fine, and 1500 hours of community service), the *New York Times* editorial blasted the sentence and the sentencing judge's comment that these were "crimes of circumstance and opportunity" and not likely to be repeated. Implying the deterrent effect of stiff penalties, the editorial continued:

> Lying isn't inconsequential and white collar criminals are the very ones most deterred by the fear of prison. Judge Jackson squandered the opportunity to send those important messages.[55]

Perceived Deterrence

What we are considering, say some researchers, is perceived deterrence—what people actually think will happen will determine whether they are deterred. The perception of the certainty and severity of punishment may be the key variable in explaining deterrence. It is said that the *actual* certainty of punishment influences people's perceptions of certainty. If they believe that punishment is certain, they will be afraid to violate the law. This proposition has not, however, been examined explicitly,[56] although the conclusions of two studies question its validity.[57]

The relationship between the actual certainty of punishment and the perceived certainty of punishment is difficult to test empirically, although there have been some suggestions of ways in which it might be done.[58] But until this relationship is measured empirically, it would be difficult, if not impossible, to measure the deterrent effect of certainty of punishment.[59]

Empirical evidence is not necessary, however, for many people to conclude that deterrence works. In a recent article on our nation's crime problems, *Time* noted that under recent changes in the law, it is now easier to charge some drug offenders under federal law. Furthermore, administrative policies have reduced the power of prosecuting and defense attorneys to reach bargains that in effect reduce penalties, a process called **plea bargaining** and discussed in more detail in a subsequent chapter. The result is that prison sentences are more likely than ever for those who are convicted of drug offenses. Will this deter? "Of course," says a White House aide and one of the architects of President Bush's latest proposals to fight the war against crime.

> The people who are committing these crimes are not dumb. They know what the chances are of getting caught and getting sent to prison, and as we increase those odds, we can change their behavior.[60]

Furthermore, perceptual deterrence may involve more variables than just perceived legal punishment. Two investigators studied the deterrent effect of three variables: moral commitment (internalization of legal norms), fear of social disapproval, and fear of legal punishment. They found that all three forms of social control were important as inhibitors of illegal behavior.[61] They note that according to some deterrence theorists, many people who internalize norms behave in legal ways, not because they fear punishment but because this is the proper way to behave. For these people, internalization of norms is thus a more effective form of social control than is fear of legal apprehension and punishment.[62] The researchers conclude, however, that the perceived threat of punishment is somewhat effective at all levels of moral commitment.[63]

The relationship between your perception of what will happen if you violate the law and whether you decide to take that course may thus be far more complex than the classical theorists envisioned when they argued that all behavior is rational and that people will choose to avoid behavior that might result in pain. Irving Piliavin and his colleagues question the validity of the classical approach. They found that persons in high-risk groups for imposition of criminal sanctions (for example, drug addicts) were not significantly deterred from criminal acts because of their perception of a risk of being caught and formally sanctioned. They were, however, influenced by their perceptions of their opportunities to commit crime and by their respect for criminal activities. Piliavin and his colleagues emphasize the need to refine our research on the deterrent effect of the law.[64]

Punishment Theory: An Analysis

Where does this discussion leave us? The classical thinkers argued that punishment should fit the crime; some modern thinkers have taken that statement to mean that criminals should get the punishment they deserve. Others have interpreted classical thinking in terms of its utilitarian principle of deterrence—that people behave rationally and will seek pleasure and avoid pain. Therefore, for the criminal law to deter, it must be swift and sure. It must provide penalties that are considered just a little worse than the pleasure that would be gained from engaging in the criminal behavior. Others argue that people do not always behave rationally; they may indeed choose criminal behavior even when they know the chances of getting caught are high and that the penalty is severe.

Other problems arise from the justice model based on the classical position. If we assume that criminals should get what they deserve but that punishment should also be severe enough to deter others from committing crimes, what do we do when these two are in conflict? We might assume that the degree of punishment deserved by a particular criminal is not sufficient for deterrence of others. Under the justice model, a criminal must not be punished more than he or she deserves; that would be as unfair as too little punishment. Thus, if this criminal gets what is deserved, the result may be punishment that has little or no deterrent effect on others.

What might happen if the only punishment that is a sufficient deterrent is one considered to be unfair or unjust? **Castration** may be the only effective punishment to deter some men from committing rape. Is that a just punishment? Our courts today say that it is not because it violates the Eighth Amendment prohibition against imposing cruel and unusual punishments. Furthermore, castration does not necessarily prevent rape, particularly **rape by instrumentation,** now defined as illegal in some jurisdictions that reject the traditional definition of rape and recognize that many rapes are committed not because of a desire for sexual release but as a statement of power over a female.

How do the principles of just deserts, utilitarianism, and deterrence apply to the punishment of corporate offenders? Should the corporation be punished perhaps by fine or by a withdrawal of its charter, or should its individual executives be punished? If so, how? Would it ever be just to punish the corporation for the criminal behavior of its employees? Would it be just to punish the employees if they were acting as directed? Which would be the greater deterrent?[65]

CONCLUSION

This chapter began with a brief overview of the importance of research and a glance at the methods of social science research and its problems.

This background was necessary for understanding the modern empirical studies on which the chapter focused—the relationship between the modern views of punishment and sentencing and the view of the thinkers of the classical, neoclassical, and positivist periods. We discussed the debate over how much punishment we should have in order to deter criminal behavior.

We briefly considered retribution as a philosophy for punishment, noting that it was the dominant basis for punishment before the recent return to deterrence and just deserts. Unfortunately, when these philosophies of deterrence, retribution, and just deserts overtook rehabilitation as the dominant themes of our approach to criminals, the goal of rehabilitation was mostly abandoned. As one judge said, "The guiding faith of corrections—rehabilitation—has been declared a false god." The problem with rehabilitation as a justification for punishment is that it "should never have been sold on the promise that it would reduce crime. Recidivism rates cannot be the only measure of what is valuable in corrections. Simple decency must count, too."[66]

Others, in recognizing and even approving of the demise of the rehabilitative ideal as the primary purpose of punishment, have emphasized the importance of maintaining the *opportunity* for treatment. Fogel's justice model does not preclude treatment; it only precludes *coercive* treatment. As he said in 1975, "What I suggest we do is give up this nonsense [coerced treatment] and return to a very open system . . . where we don't try to screw people's heads on right." In reporting those comments from his speech, the *Seattle Times* ran the headline "Ex-prison Director Mocks Rehabilitation."[67] But that headline is not correct. It is only the *coerced* treatment, the attempt to *force* rehabilitation, that is being shunned.

Norval Morris, a noted authority on criminal justice and a professor and former dean of the University of Chicago College of Law, also argues for salvaging something of the rehabilitative ideal: "Rehabilitative programs in prisons have been characterized more by false rhetoric than by solid achievement. They have been corrupted to punitive purposes. But it does not follow that they should be discarded." According to Morris, we should not send people to prison for *treatment.* We should keep treatment programs but distinguish between the purposes of incarceration and the opportunities that might be provided to the incarcerated person. "Rehabilitation can be given only to a volunteer." Morris is not arguing that treatment does not work and therefore should be abolished. Rather, he is saying that the treatment model should be liberated and not coercive. He is referring to the *"substitution of facilitated change for coerced cure."*[68]

The rehabilitative ideal retains some support with the author of the terminology, who is not only writing a history of the concept but also expressing his hope that it will still have a role in punishment.[69]

ENDNOTES

1. George A. Lundberg, *Can Science Save Us?* (New York: Longman, 1961), p. 134.
2. Daniel Glaser, "A Review of Crime-Causation Theory and Its Application," in Norval Morris and Michael Tonry, eds., *Crime and Justice: An Annual Review of Research*, vol. 1 (Chicago: University of Chicago Press, 1979), pp. 204–205.
3. Attorney General William French Smith, "Federal, State, and Local Law Enforcement Must Cooperate to Fight Crime in America," *Justice Assistance News*, August 1981, p. 2.
4. See Hans Toch, "Cast the First Stone: Ethics as a Weapon," *Criminology* 19 (August 1981): 185–194; and Marvin E. Wolfgang, "Confidentiality in Criminological Research and Other Ethical Issues," *Journal of Criminal Law & Criminology* 71 (Spring 1981): 345–361.
5. Lundberg, *Can Science Save Us?*, pp. 143–144.
6. Cesare Beccaria, *On Crimes and Punishments*, trans. Henry Paolucci (Indianapolis: Bobbs-Merrill, 1963), pp. ix–xxxiii.
7. Eliott Monochese, "Cesare Beccaria," in Herman Mannheim, ed., *Pioneers in Criminology* (Montclair, N.J.: Patterson Smith, 1973), p. 48.
8. Stephen Schafer, *Theories in Criminology* (New York: Random House, 1969), p. 106.
9. Roscoe Pound, quoted in Frank Tannenbaum, *Crime and the Community* (New York: Ginn, 1938), p. 4.
10. Graeme Newman, *Just and Painful: A Case for the Corporal Punishment of Criminals* (New York: Free Press, 1983), p. 71.
11. Coleman Phillipson, *Three Criminal Law Reformers: Beccaria, Bentham, and Romilly* (New York: Dutton, 1923), p. 234.
12. Gilbert Geis, "Jeremy Bentham," in Mannheim, ed., *Pioneers*, p. 57.
13. See Raffaele Garofalo, *Criminology*, trans. Robert W. Millar (Boston: Little, Brown, 1914); Francis Allen, "Raffaele Garofalo," in Mannheim, ed., *Pioneers*, pp. 318 340; Enrico Ferri, *The Positive School of Criminology* (Chicago: Kerr, 1913); and Enrico Ferri, *Criminal Sociology*, trans. Joseph Killey and John Lisle (Boston: Little, Brown, 1917). For a discussion and an evaluation of Ferri's contributions, see Thorsten Sellin, "Enrico Ferri," in Mannhein, ed., *Pioneers*, pp. 316–384.
14. Schafer, *Theories in Criminology*, p. 123.
15. Marvin E. Wolfgang, "Cesare Lombroso," in Mannheim, ed., *Pioneers*, pp. 232–291. See also Cesare Lombroso, *Crime, Its Causes and Remedies*, trans. H. P. Horton (Boston: Little, Brown, 1911), p. 33.
16. Edwin H. Sutherland and Donald Cressey, *Criminology*, 10th ed. (Philadelphia: Lippincott, 1978), p. 59.
17. Wolfgang, "Cesare Lombroso," p. 288. For a discussion of the attempts of the Englishman George Buckman Goring (1870–1910) to test Lombroso's theories, see Charles Goring, *The English Convict* (London: H. M. Stationery Office, 1913).
18. Wolfgang, "Cesare Lombroso," p. 271.
19. "Wife and Lover Lose Their Ears," *Miami Herald*, 24 May 1989, p. 10, col. 1.
20. Francis Edward Devine, "Cesare Beccaria and the Theoretical Foundation of Modern Penal Jurisprudence," *New England Journal of Prison Law* 7 (Winter 1981): 13. See also Beccaria, *On Crimes and Punishments*, pp. 10–13, 53–54, 66–67.

21. *Time*, 13 September 1982, p. 38.

22. Francis Allen, "Criminal Justice, Legal Values and the Rehabilitative Ideal," *Journal of Criminal Law, Criminology, and Police Science* 50 (September–October 1959): 226–232.

23. For a more detailed discussion of the indeterminate sentence, see Sue Titus Reid, "A Rebuttal to the Attack on the Indeterminate Sentence," *Washington Law Review* 51 (July 1976): 565–606.

24. David A. Ward, "Evaluation Research for Corrections," in Lloyd E. Ohlin, ed., *Prisoners in America* (Englewood Cliffs, N.J.: Prentice-Hall, 1973), pp. 196, 198.

25. *Time*, 13 September 1982, p. 38.

26. See also an article by Kenneth Polk and Don C. Gibbons, "The Uses of Criminology, the Rehabilitative Ideal, and Justice," in the July 1988 issue of *Crime and Delinquency*. The entire issue is devoted to a collection of original essays written about noted criminologist, Donald Cressey, shortly after Cressey's death.

27. Furman v. Georgia, 408 U.S. 238 (1972).

28. Gregg v. Georgia, 428 U.S. 153, 184–185 (1976).

29. Gregg v. Georgia, 428 U.S. 153, 183 (1976).

30. Jack P. Gibbs, "The Death Penalty, Retribution and Penal Policy," *Journal of Criminal Law & Criminology* 69 (Fall 1978): 294.

31. Ernest van den Haag, "Punishment as a Device for Controlling the Crime Rate," *Rutgers Law Review* 33 (Spring 1981): 719–730.

32. Andrew von Hirsch, *Doing Justice: The Choice of Punishments* (New York: Hill & Wang, 1976).

33. David Fogel, *We Are the Living Proof: The Justice Model for Corrections*, 2d ed. (Cincinnati: W. H. Anderson, 1979), pp. 183–184.

34. Fogel, *Ibid.*, p. 192; emphasis in the original.

35. See, for example, Richard Quinney, *Criminology*, 2d. ed. (Boston: Little, Brown, 1979).

36. "An Eye for an Eye," *Time*, 24 January 1983, p. 32.

37. See Scott H. Decker and Carol W. Kohfeld, "Capital Punishment and Executions in the Lone Star State: A Deterrence Study." *Criminal Justice Research Bulletin* (Huntsville, Texas: Sam Houston State University Criminal Justice Center, 1988). For a brief overview of the literature on deterrence, along with details of his own recent research, see Raymond Paternoster, "Examining Three-Wave Deterrence Models: A Question of Temporal Order and Specification," *Journal of Criminal Law & Criminology* 79 (Spring, 1988): 135–179 and Paternoster, "The Deterrent Effect of the Perceived Certainty and Severity of Punishment: A Review of the Evidence and Issues," *Justice Quarterly* 4 (June 1987): 173–217.

38. Jack P. Gibbs, *Crime, Punishment and Deterrence* (New York: Elsevier, 1975), pp. ix, 11. See also John Hagan, ed., *Deterrence Reconsidered: Methodological Innovations* (Bevery Hills, CA: Sage Publications, 1982); Douglas A. Smith and Patrick R. Gartin, "Specifying Specific Deterrence: The Influence of Arrest on Future Criminal Activity," *American Sociological Review* 54 (February 1989): 94–106; and Paternoster, "The Deterrent Effect of the Perceived Certainty and Severity of Punishment."

39. A study by the Rand Corporation, reported in Bureau of Justice Statistics, *Report to the Nation on Crime and Justice*, 2d ed. (Washington, D.C.: U.S. Department of Justice, March, 1988), p. 45.

40. See Robert F. Meier, "Correlates of Deterrence: Problems of Theory and Method," *Journal of Criminal Justice* 7 (Spring 1979): 18–19.

41. See Robert F. Meier et al., "Sanctions, Peers, and Deviance: Preliminary Models of a Social Control Process," *Sociological Quarterly* 25 (Winter 1984): 67–82, and Meier, "Perspectives on the Concept of Social Control," *Annual Review of Sociology* 8 (1982): 35–55.

42. See, for example, National Institute of Justice, *Jailing Drunk Drivers: Impact on the Criminal Justice System* (Washington, D.C.: U.S. Government Printing Office, May 1985).

43. See Gerald R. Wheeler and Rodney V. Hissong, "Effects of Criminal Sanctions on Drunk Drivers: Beyond Incarceration," *Crime & Delinquency* 34 (January 1988): 29–42.

44. "Swamped by Drug-Related Arrests, Connecticut Releases Inmates Early," *New York Times*, 2 January 1989, p. 10, col. 1.

45. "Drug Cases Clog New York City Courts," *New York Times*, 4 April 1989, p. 24, col. 1.

46. "War on Drugs Overwhelming Legal System, Bar Study Says," *New York Times*, 5 December 1988, p. 11, col. 1.

47. Paternoster, "Examining Three-Wave Deterrence Models," p. 177.

48. See H. Laurence Ross, *Deterring the Drinking Driver: Legal Policy and Social Control* (Lexington, Mass.: Lexington Books, 1982).

49. John H. Snortum et al., "Deterring Alcohol-Impaired Driving: A Comparative Analysis of Compliance in Norway and the United States," *Justice Quarterly* 3 (June 1986): 139–165.

50. For a brief summary of this debate, see Snortum et al., *ibid.*

51. *Ibid.*

52. John Braithwaite and Gilbert Geis, "On Theory and Action for Corporate Crime Control," *Crime & Delinquency* 28 (April 1982): 305.

53. Marshall B. Clinard and Robert F. Meier, *Sociology of Deviant Behavior*, 5th ed. (New York: Holt, Rinehart and Winston, 1979).

54. "For the first time in collegiate history, the NCAA is winning the war against illegal recruiting." "NCAA Chief Says Illegal Recruiting is Becoming Scarce," *Tallahassee Democrat*, 9 January 1988, p. D1, col. 1.

55. "Justice Blinked for Michael Deaver," *New York Times*, 28 September 1988, p. 26, col. 1.

56. See the discussions of Gibbs, *Crime, Punishment, and Deterrence;* and Johannes Andenaes, "General Prevention Revisited: Research and Policy Implications," *Journal of Criminal Law, Criminology, and Police Science* 66 (September 1975): 338–365.

57. See Assembly Committee (1968) *Deterrent Effects of Criminal Sanctions*, Progress Report of the Assembly Committee on Criminal Procedure. California legislature, and Nigel Walker, *Sentencing in a Rational Society* (Hammondsworth, Eng.: Penguin Books, 1969).

58. See Gibbs, *Crime, Punishment, and Deterrence;* and Andenaes, "General Prevention Revisited." For a critique of these proposals, see Jerry Parker and Harold G. Grasmick, "Linking Actual and Perceived Certainty of Punishment," *Criminology* 17 (November 1979): 366–379.

59. For an example of early studies attempting to measure this relationship, see Gibbs, *Crime, Punishment, and Deterrence;* and Charles R. Tittle, "Crime Rates and Legal Sanctions," *Social Problems* 16 (Spring 1969): 409–423.

60. Richard Lacayo, "Our Bulging Prisons," *Time*, 29 May 1989, p. 29.

61. Harold G. Grasmick and Donald E. Green, "Legal Punishment, Social Disapproval and Internalization as Inhibitors of Illegal Behavior," *Journal of Criminal Law & Criminology* 71 (Fall 1980): 325–335. See also Grasmick and Green, "Deterrence and the Morally Committed," *Sociological Quarterly* 22 (Winter 1981): 1–14.

62. See, for example, the works of Johannes Andenaes, "The General Preventive Effects of Punishment," *University of Pennsylvania Law Review* 114 (May 1966): 949–983; Charles Tittle, "Sanction Fear and the Maintenance of Social Order," *Social Forces* 55 (1977): 569–596; and Franklin Zimring, "Perspective on Deterrence," Public Health Science Publication No. 2056 (Washington, D.C.: U.S. Government Printing Office, 1971).

63. Grasmick and Green, "Deterrence and the Morally Committed," 2, 13. For similar findings, see Ronald Akers et al., "Social Learning and Deviant Behavior: A Specific Test of a General Theory," *American Sociological Review* 44 (August 1979): 636–655; Gary F. Jensen, Maynard L. Erikson, and Jack P. Gibbs, "Perceived Risk of Punishment and Self-Reported Delinquency," *Social Forces* 57 (September 1978): 57–78.

64. Irving Piliavin et al., "Crime, Deterrence, and Rational Choice," *American Sociological Review* 51 (February 1986): 101–119. See also Raymond Paternoster et al., "Estimating Perceptual Stability and Deterrent Effects: The Role of Perceived Legal Punishments in the Inhibition of Criminal Involvement," *Journal of Criminal Law & Criminology* 74 (Spring 1983): 270–297.

65. For a debate on this issue, see John Braithwaite, "Challenging Just Deserts: Punishing White-Collar Criminals," *Journal of Criminal Law & Criminology* 73 (Summer 1982): 723–763; and Andrew von Hirsch, "Desert and White-Collar Criminality: A Response to Dr. Braithwaite," *Journal of Criminal Law & Criminology* 73 (Fall 1982): 1164–1175.

66. David L. Bazelon, "Street Crime and Correctional Potholes," *Federal Probation* 41 (March 1977): 3.

67. *Seattle Times*, 18 June 1975, p. A10, col. 1.

68. Norval Morris, *The Future of Imprisonment* (Chicago: University of Chicago Press, 1974), pp. 13, 15, 27; emphasis in the original.

69. Francis A. Allen, *The Decline of the Rehabilitative Ideal: Penal Policy and Social Purpose* (New Haven, Conn.: Yale University Press, 1981). See also Francis T. Cullen and Karen E. Gilbert, *Reaffirming Rehabilitation* (Cincinnati: Anderson Publishing, 1982).

CHAPTER 4

This chapter brings together a wide variety of approaches to understanding criminal behavior, many of which were popular in the past, lost favor, and are now being revived, but with more sophisticated research. The current developments in biology and psychology are discussed against the background of the earlier contributions of the positive school, the constitutional approach, and the body-type theories. We also consider the importance of genetic background as well as the possible relationship of the nervous system, endocrinology and body chemistry, and criminal behavior. We also study the practical and legal implications of the developments in biology and psychology.

OUTLINE

Biological and Psychological Theories

Efforts to curb substance abuse through arrests and convictions have led to such problems as overcrowded prisons and jails, thus illustrating the negative impact of what are thought to be positive efforts.

The fashions and fads in human thought are interesting, and the field of criminology is no exception. We have already seen that the major emphasis regarding criminals in the eighteenth century was a philosophy of punishment and sentencing that lost favor in the following century. During the nineteenth century the influence of biology was strong, stemming from the theory of evolution of Charles Darwin, who in 1859 published his *Origin of the Species*, a work hailed by some as one of the most important books ever written. The immense controversy that immediately surrounded the theory of evolution is still present today as some people continue to debate whether the theory should be taught in the public schools.

In criminology, biological and psychological explanations of behavior have been out of style for some time, but recently there has been a resurgence of interest in these theories. Both became important in the 1980s in the analysis of such criminals as Richard Speck with the attention given in 1986 to the twentieth anniversary of his 1966 mass murders of

HIGHLIGHT 4.1

RAPE AND BEATING IN CENTRAL PARK: A SOCIETY SEEKS CAUSES

As many as thirty members of a black youth gang in New York City went on a rampage of theft and violence, described as *wilding,* terrorizing numerous people in New York City's Central Park before attacking a twenty-eight-year-old jogger on April 19, 1989. The white victim, an investment banker with a bright future, was sodomized, raped, brutally beaten, and left for dead in a wooded area of the park. Later found near death, she remained in a coma for two weeks but miraculously recovered. After months of hospitalization and treatment, she was able to go home for Thanksgiving dinner and shortly thereafter returned to work on a restricted schedule.

Several youths were arrested and charged with attempted murder, rape, and assault. Some are only fourteen and fifteen; they were tried as adults. When asked why he beat the woman, one youth replied, "Because it was fun." Investigations into the backgrounds of the accused revealed that some were from average families, who, along with their friends, were shocked at the news of these crimes. They and others look for clues to an understanding of the behavior of these men. Some argue that the attack was racially motivated; others say the youths were angry, suffering from severe psychological problems that have caused deep-seated anger. The police ruled out drugs as a cause for the evening of wilding. Greed was also dismissed, for only a sandwich was stolen by the gang that night.

Such brutal acts of violence demonstrate our lack of understanding about the causes of crime and our inability to predict and control such behavior. Biological, psychological, and sociological theories have been advanced to explain the acts of these youths, and allegations of racism have been raised not only to explain the crimes but also the extensive interest the media and the rest of us have shown in this case while paying little or no attention to many other acts of violence in New York and other cities. These and other violent as well as property crimes challenge social scientists in their continuing efforts to understand criminal behavior.

In August, 1990, three defendants were found guilty of rape but acquitted of sodomy and attempted murder.

---

eight Chicago nurses and with the 1989 gang rape and beating of a New York Wall Street investment banker, summarized in Highlight 4.1.

Psychological theories have received considerable attention in the context of the hotly debated insanity defense. But other, recent controversial defenses to criminal behavior have also involved biological explanations. Law and scientists have given increasingly more recognition to biological and psychological explanations of behavior. This chapter will present some of the most recent studies of the alleged relationship between our bodies and our behavior. Taken together, research on the relationship between biology and crime leaves no doubt that social and biological variables and their interactions are important to our understanding of the origins of antisocial behavior.[1]

BIOLOGICAL FACTORS AND CRIME

Although the major theories of biological explanations of criminal behavior were developed in the nineteenth century, biological explanations can be found much earlier. One criminologist has traced back to Aristotle the belief that personality is determined by the shape of the skull. The relationship between criminal behavior and body type has been traced back to the 1500s and the study of facial features and their relationships to crime, to the 1700s. In the latter part of the 1700s **phrenology** emerged as a discipline. Its development is associated mainly with the work of Franz Joseph Gall (1758–1828), who investigated the bumps and other irregularities of the skulls of the inmates of penal institutions and asylums for the insane. Gall also studied the heads and head casts of persons who were not institutionalized and compared those findings to data on criminals. Phrenology is based on the proposition that the exterior of the skull corresponds to the interior and to the brain's conformation. The brain can be divided into functions; those functions, or faculties, are related to the shape of the skull. By measuring the shape of the skull, therefore, we can measure behavior.

The Positive School

If the study of phrenology is considered applicable, we are placing the beginning of scientific criminology about 70 years before the contributions of Lombroso and the positivists. With historical perspective, this may become a more commonly accepted conclusion; but today, most scholars begin that study with Lombroso and his colleagues.

Cesare Lombroso (1835–1909) is "rarely discussed in a neutral tone; he is either adulated or condemned. 'In the history of criminology probably no name has been eulogized or attacked so much as [his].'"[2] Lombroso developed several categories of criminals, but he was best known for his concept of the biological, or born, criminal. He believed that he saw in criminals some of the same characteristics of savages. He called this phenomenon an *atavism*, a throwback or a reversion to prehuman creatures.[3]

Theories of evolution introduced during Lombroso's time argued that as humans evolved, their physical constitution changed, becoming more complex as it developed to a higher stage. Lombroso used these theories of evolution to support his belief that criminals were not only physically different from noncriminals but also physically inferior, as they had not evolved as far as noncriminals. Lombroso also said that he had found biological characteristics that distinguished criminals according to the *kind* of crime they committed.

Other writers in the positive school supported Lombroso's biological explanations of criminal behavior but also emphasized the possibility of environmental or psychic factors. The belief that criminal behavior is inherited was tempered with the suggestion that inherited traits were not sufficient to *cause* criminal behavior. Psychological and environmental or social factors might also be necessary. If that were true, crime could be prevented only by making changes in society.[4]

Much criticism has been hurled at the positivists, especially at Lombroso, because of an *overemphasis* on biological causes of criminal behavior to the neglect of environmental factors. Nevertheless, these writers are important because they brought attention to the need to study the criminal from a scientific point of view. They thus laid the foundation for a scientific and biological analysis of criminal behavior; some of the writers also foresaw the need for changing the social structure and environment if crime prevention is to be effective. The framework for the study of the psychological aspects of animal behavior was also established during this period.

Physique and Crime

Constitutional or physical-type explanations rest on the assumption that function is determined by structure. Applied to crime, this approach advocates that behavior is determined by the body's build, which may be the body type, the endocrine system, some other physical characteristic—or the mind. The belief that criminal behavior is related to body type can be formally traced back to a 1926 book,[5] but the first real development of this approach began in the 1940s with the work of William Sheldon, who measured physique and compared body type with temperament. Sheldon defined three body types: ectomorph, endomorph, and mesomorph. The *ectomorph* is the tall, skinny body; the *endomorph*, the short, fat body; and the *mesomorph*, the athletic body. Sheldon also identified three types of temperament that he claimed were associated with body types. His purpose was to lay a foundation for a systematic study of human behavior and human personality.[6]

Sheldon has been criticized for the selection of his samples, the implication being that he selected only persons who would best support his theory,[7] and for not defining his three body types precisely enough so that they could be sufficiently distinguishable.[8] He is also alleged to have overemphasized constitutional factors to the exclusion of environmental causes of crime. Sheldon reacted to this criticism by saying that he was not excluding environmental factors but only emphasizing constitutional factors because their importance had been neglected.

Sheldon and Eleanor Glueck also conducted many studies on the relationship of body type and criminal behavior, although they concentrated most of their research on juvenile delinquents. The Gluecks were two of the most prolific and most controversial writers in the field of constitutional criminology. They claimed that their research was of high quality, skillfully utilizing the precision control of matched samples of 500 delinquents and 500 nondelinquents. The two groups were matched on age, general intelligence, ethnic-racial origins, and residence in underprivileged neighborhoods. Physicians, psychiatrists, anthropologists, and others were involved in gathering the data from the samples. Delinquency was found to be most often associated with the mesomorphic body type.[9]

Critics point out that the Gluecks' finding is not surprising, as many delinquent activities require a strong body build. Other critics, after examining the researchers' data, concluded that the information was complicated and not significant because there was no specific combination of character, physique, and temperament that would permit a prediction about whether or not a young person would become delinquent.[10] Critics also argued that since the delinquent sample was taken from "persistently delinquent" boys, the data could not be generalized to the total population of delinquents. The Gluecks' concepts and measuring techniques have also been criticized as vague.[11]

Criticisms of the body type studies of Sheldon and of the Gluecks led many to discredit the entire approach of explaining crime in terms of physique. Juan B. Cortés and others, however, thought the approach had merit. In 1972 Cortés published the results of his ten years of research in which he reported finding a high correlation between mesomorphy and delinquency. Cortés warned, however, that his research did not show that body type *causes* delinquency, only that the two often occur together.[12]

Cortés' work has also been criticized because it was based on small samples that were not randomly selected; because he did not precisely define his terms for measurement; and because he, too, neglected the importance of the environment. His work is important, however, in establishing the *foundation* for a return to some concern with the genetic factor in criminal behavior. He emphasized that constitution (which he said was a term used almost synonymously with physique and body build) was not fixed and unalterable but was a result of genetics and environment: "It is not, therefore, and should not be, heredity or environment, nor heredity versus environment nor heredity under or over environment, but only and always heredity *and* environment."[13] Therefore, it is necessary to look at heredity and examine what, if any, role genetic factors play in human behavior.

Genetic Factors

It was perhaps not too difficult for some of the early students of criminal behavior, upon seeing the differences between criminals and noncriminals, to conclude that these differences *caused* the criminal behavior and, furthermore, were inherited. The criminal was seen as one who was predisposed or predetermined by biological factors to commit crimes. The next step was to look at the family background to see whether the family had a history of criminal behavior. If so, then criminality must be inherited.

Family Studies

Most of the early studies of family histories, conducted in an effort to show the relationship between heredity and crime as well as other forms of deviant behavior, have been discredited as lacking sufficient methodological sophistication to permit significant conclusions.[14] Two exceptions, however, deserve brief attention.

Sheldon and Eleanor Glueck included family histories in their comparisons of delinquents and nondelinquents. They found that delinquent boys, as compared with nondelinquent boys, more often came from families characterized by a history of delinquency and crime. The criminality of the father was the best predictor.[15]

There is also the work of Charles Goring, an English psychiatrist and philosopher, who, in his pursuit of evidence to disprove Lombroso's theory of the born criminal, used some of the newly developed statistical techniques to measure the degree of correlation, or resemblance, of members within a family line. He compared brothers as well as fathers and sons, attempting to show that the correlations for general criminality, as measured by imprisonment, were as high as for two other categories he measured: (1) ordinary physical traits and features and (2) inherited defects, insanity, and mental disease. He then attempted to show that the correlations were the *result* of heredity, not environment. He used several arguments to support his position, such as the discovery that boys who were taken out of the home early in life became criminals as frequently as did those who remained longer in the home with their fathers. Also, he found the correlations as high for sex crimes (in which the fathers would presumably try to conceal their sons' activities) as for stealing (in which the fathers might set an example for their sons).[16]

Goring's findings may be criticized on several grounds. He did not adequately measure environmental influences; indeed, it is questionable whether all environmental variables can be satisfactorily isolated. He did not consider criminality among sisters. He assumed that mental ability is inherited but offered no proof. He assumed that removing a boy from his criminal father's home and placing him in some other environment at an early age was automatically putting him in a noncriminal environment.

Although the earlier studies of families have been strongly criticized, they were influential in terms of policy. The belief that criminality was inherited led to the passage of laws that permitted the compulsory sterilization of persons thought to be capable of passing on to their children bad genes that would result in criminal behavior. These statutes were upheld by earlier courts.[17]

The basic problem, however, with these early family studies was that they could not control for environment. The parents who produced the children, thereby determining their genetic background, were also those who helped socialize them; thus, genetics and environment were inseparable. This problem led to two other methods of studying genetic factors and criminality: the study of twins and adoptees.[18]

Studies of Twins

If behavior is inherited, we would expect to find the same behavior among people with identical genes. Thus, identical twins should behave alike. Fraternal twins (nonidentical) of the same sex have about 50 percent identical genes; their behavior should be quite similar.

Early studies of twins led researchers to conclude that heredity does play a major role in explaining behavior, but these studies were usually based on very small samples.[19] Until recently, the most recognized studies of twins were those conducted by Karl O. Christiansen, who avoided most of the sampling problems of the earlier studies. Christiansen studied the incidence of criminal behavior among 3586 twins in one region of Denmark between 1881 and 1910. He reported that if one twin engaged in criminal behavior, the probability that his or her identical twin would also be a criminal was 35 percent, compared with only 12 percent if the twins were not identical.

Sarnoff A. Mednick and his associates have updated the Christiansen study to include more than 5000 twins and are now working on a study of more than 13,000. Thus far, these biologists have concluded "that genetic factors account for some of the variables associated with anti-social behavior."[20] Researchers at the University of Minnesota Center for Twin and Adoption Research conclude that about one-half of personality characteristics of twins is due to heredity. More information on the Minnesota study is contained in Highlight 4.2.

Adoption Studies

Concern with the problem of separating the influence of environment and of heredity, even in the study of twins, has led some researchers to select samples of adoptees for study. Most adoptees are adopted at birth and do not know their biological parents. Indeed, many do not even know they are adopted, at least not during their formative years. Thus, it is possible to separate the factor of genetic characteristics from the study of environmental influences.

Mednick and his associates have already completed some adoption studies on the basis of the adoption register in Denmark, using a sample of about 72,000 persons. These and other studies of adoptees, says Mednick, indicate that we cannot ignore the genetic factor in explaining criminal behavior.[21] Mednick's studies have come under fire from others, and he and his associates have also raised some pertinent questions about the research. In Denmark, where the studies were conducted, efforts are made to place adoptable children in homogeneous environments; the evidence is that the efforts are successful. Babies born to lower-class parents are usually adopted by lower-class parents. It is also important to consider that Denmark is a rather homogeneous society. These and other factors indicating that the environment may play a part in criminal behavior have been studied by Mednick and his associates, who remain firm in their belief that there is some association between genetic factors and criminal behavior.

Chromosomal Abnormality

The possible relationship between chromosomal abnormality and criminal behavior has also been the subject of research. The most common area of investigation has been the **XYY chromosome abnormality.** The X chromosome is female; the Y, male. Males are XY and females, XX. The XYY is a male with an extra Y chromosome. The abnormality was first discovered in 1961, but it did not receive much attention until papers were published in the mid-1960s by Scottish researchers who studied 197 inmates and found that a significant number of them were XYY.[22]

Later studies have not consistently found that XYY males are more likely to be criminals than are males without the chromosomal abnormality, but the studies were based on very small and nonrandom samples that prohibit generalization. They did indicate that the XYY male is more introverted and has more asocial attitudes than does the rest of the population and that he has a tendency toward homosexuality and aggressiveness.[23]

What was needed was a larger study using a **control group** of noncriminals. In 1977, several investigators reported the results of a study conducted in Denmark on all of the 31,436 men who were born in Copenhagen during a four-year period and who were over a certain height. Their blood was then checked for chromosome composition; only twelve XYY men were found. The investigators discovered the XYY men had engaged in "significantly more criminal behavior than did the XY men of their age, height, intelligence, and social class," but they had not engaged in violent behavior. The small number of XYY men in the sample, however, limits the conclusions that can be drawn.[24]

Genetics: A Brief Modern View

The early criminologists did not have sophisticated research tools; their studies were often based on small samples, and their analysis of data was unsophisticated. During this century, with the development of modern tools of analysis and the increased sophistication of the study of genetics, the conclusions of the early studies have been seriously questioned and, in many cases, rejected. For the past several decades, little attention has been paid to genetic explanations of criminal behavior; many criminologists have thought it unnecessary to tell their students about these earlier approaches.

Recently, however, the study of genetics has again gained attention as a possible explanation of criminal behavior. This resurgence of interest in the possible genetic basis of criminal behavior parallels the more exten-

HIGHLIGHT 4.2

EXPLORING THE TRAITS OF TWINS: IS BEHAVIOR INHERITED?

Like many identical twins reared apart, Jim Lewis and Jim Springer found they had been leading eerily similar lives. Separated four weeks after birth in 1940, the Jim twins grew up 45 miles apart in Ohio and were reunited in 1979. Eventually they discovered that both drove the same model blue Chevrolet, chain-smoked Salems, chewed their fingernails and owned dogs named Toy. Each had spent a good deal of time vacationing at the same three-block strip of beach in Florida. More important, when tested for such personality traits as flexibility, self-control and sociability, the twins responded almost exactly alike.

The two Jims were the first of 348 pairs of twins studied at the University of Minnesota, home of the Minnesota Center for Twin and Adoption Research. Much of the investigation concerns the obvious question raised by siblings like Springer and Lewis: How much of any individual's personality is due to heredity? The center's answer: about half.

The project, summed up in a scholarly paper that has been submitted to the *Journal of Personality and Social Psychology,* is considered the most comprehensive of its kind. The Minnesota researchers report the results of six-day tests of their subjects, including 44 pairs of identical twins who were brought up apart. Well-being, alienation, aggression and the shunning of risk or danger were found to owe as much or more to nature as to nurture. Of eleven key traits or clusters of traits analyzed in the study, researchers estimated that a high of 61% of what they call "social potency" (a tendency toward leadership or dominance) is inherited, while "social closeness" (the need for intimacy, comfort and help) was lowest, at 33%.

The study finds that even a penchant for conservatism seems to have a genetic base. One of the eleven traits, traditionalism (respect for authority, rules, standards and high morals), was discovered to be 60% inherited. Among other traits

listed at more than 50% were vulnerability or resistance to stress, dedication to hard work and achievement and the capacity for being caught up in imaginative experiences.

The director of the study, Thomas Bouchard, cautions that the numbers so far may not be strictly accurate. "In general," he says, "the degree of genetic influence tends to be around 50%." Attributing the 28-point gap between potency and closeness to possible sampling errors, he predicted that "social potency will drop and social closeness will creep up."

All the twins took several personality tests, answering more than 15,000 questions on subjects ranging from personal interests and values to phobias, aesthetic judgment and television and reading habits. Twins reared separately also took medical exams and intelligence tests and were queried on life history and stresses. Not all pairs matched up as well as the two Jims. California Twins Ann Blandin and Barbara Parker, 40, showed only

---

sive understanding that physical and biological scientists have made in the study of genetics. In January 1989 a molecular biologist who chairs the Human Genome Advisory Committee, which is in charge of a $3 billion National Institutes of Health-sponsored project, declared, "We are initiating an unending study of human biology." The goal of the project is to gain a complete understanding of the human *genome,* described by a biochemist as "the complete set of instructions for making a human being."[25]

A complete understanding of human genes may not only explain

HIGHLIGHT 4.2 (Continued)

minor similarities. Said Blandin: "Bouchard said we were the most different set of twins in the study."

Psychologist David Lykken, one of the Minnesota researchers, thinks the study will shove the pendulum further away from the "radical environmentalism" of those who believe the characters of children are more or less created by their parents and environment. Lykken says Test Pilot Chuck Yeager is daring because he was "genetically endowed with a low scale of fearlessness," a trait that might have been redirected or tamped down but not eradicated. Says Psychologist Nancy Segal, a member of the project: "Parents can work to make a child less fearful, but they can't make that child brave."

Adam Matheny of the Louisville Twin Study, the oldest of U.S. twin study groups, says the "mechanism for change is laid down the moment a child is conceived" and that the genes provide a "rough sketch of life."

Some psychologists who stress the influence of genes on behavior often speak as if nurture were a by-product of nature. "All of us make our own environment," says Developmental Psychologist Sandra Scarr of the University of Virginia. Lykken makes the same point: "The environment molds your personality, but your genes determine what kind of environment you have, seek and attend to." Since the early 1960s, several twin studies have reported that identical twins reared apart are actually more alike than those raised in the same home. Scarr thinks the reason is that parents faced with identical twins try hard to stress differences between siblings. Says she: "Living with the same family seems to increase intellectual similarity and decrease resemblance in personality."

Some scholars, such as Princeton Psychologist Leon Kamin, fear that the Minnesota results will be used to blame the poor and downtrodden for their own condition. Political liberals

have long believed that crime and poverty are largely by-products of destructive environments. As a result, they are usually suspicious of biological or genetic explanations for behavior. "These are very ambiguous data that can be interpreted any way you want to," says Kamin. "I'm not saying that anyone is falsifying facts or anything, just that we really know very, very little." For the Minnesota researchers and their allies, however, their study is just one more proof that parenting has its limits. Says Psychologist and Twin Researcher David Rowe of the University of Oklahoma: "Parents should be blamed less for kids who have problems and take less credit for kids who turn out well."

SOURCE: "Exploring the Traits of twins: A New Study Shows that Key Characteristics May be Inherited," *Time,* 12 January 1987, p. 63. Copyright 1987, Time, Inc. Reprinted by permission.

more about the physical and chemical make-up of humans and permit genetic control, but it may also explain human *behavior*, both noncriminal and criminal.

Evaluation of Genetic Studies and Crime

Despite the renewed interest in the relationship between genetics and criminal behavior, the findings still draw the skepticism of many, and the studies should be interpreted carefully. The small samples are obviously a problem and seriously limit the generalizations that may be drawn. The problems in separating genetics from environment are also serious. It may also be true that the role of genetics in criminal behavior cannot be separated from the role of the autonomic and central nervous systems of the body. Thus, the findings relating genetics to criminal behavior may be important mainly in the fact that they point toward the importance of studying biological factors in general.[26]

Neurological Factors

All the nervous systems enclosed within the body portions of the skull and spine are part of the *central nervous system* (CNS). Complex sensory information is processed in the CNS, which also controls voluntary muscle movement. Two basic tests of the CNS's functioning are the electroencephalogram (EEG) and various forms of neuropsychological testing.[27] The EEG has been the most common tool for research on the relationship between the CNS and criminal behavior, with some findings that "incarcerated individuals tend to have higher proportions of abnormal EEGs than do individuals in the general population."[28] The relationship between epilepsy and criminal behavior has also been tested, but the results have not yet resolved the issue of whether epilepsy is significantly related to crime.[29]

The second way to examine the CNS's functioning is by tests such as X-rays, CAT scans, and spinal taps, which determine whether the brain has been damaged. The results may then be used to analyze the relationship between brain damage and criminal behavior. "Results of neuropsychological tests administered to criminals suggest that violent, impulsive individuals suffer from damage to specific brain areas." Studies also indicate that criminals suffer injury with resulting unconsciousness earlier in life than noncriminals do. Brain injury may also occur during pregnancy or delivery and may be related to subsequent criminal behavior.[30]

Neuroendocrinology

Criminal behavior has also been attributed to an imbalance of the body's chemicals. The endocrine or glandular system and its relationship to criminal behavior were the focus of a 1928 book entitled *The New Criminology*. At that time, it was alleged that "the glandular theory of crime accounts for all the discrepancies, errors, oversights and inadequacies of the earlier explanations," a conclusion that in 1941 was cited and seriously criticized by a well-known anthropologist.[31]

More recent research has disclosed, in both animals and humans, a relationship between male hormones and behavior, with lower levels of certain hormones occurring in males who are more dominant, aggressive, and hostile than the normal male.[32] Research indicating a relationship between female hormones and the reduction of the male sex drive and potency has led to **chemical castration** as a method of treating sex offenders. Such findings should be considered tentative, claim some researchers, pointing to other research that does not show a significant relationship between hormones and male behavior.[33]

Among women, premenstrual tension, which is common in about 25 percent of the female population, appears to be associated with the imbalance of the two female hormones, estrogen and progesterone. There also appears to be a relationship between the presence of premenstrual and menstrual tension and the number of suicides, suicide attempts, admissions for psychiatric illness or acute medical and surgical reasons, and criminal acts. "It would appear that, for a number of women, hormonal changes resulting in irritability, tension, nervousness, and related symptoms markedly increase the probability of committing crimes." The researchers are quick to point out, however, that a cause-and-effect relationship between endocrine factors and behavior cannot be assumed because endocrine factors do not work independently of other factors. One researcher found, for example, that women who complained that they were irritable during premenstrual and menstrual periods were more likely to be irritable at other times than were women who did not so complain.[34]

Obesity has also been linked to biochemical causes. Although researchers do not fully understand obesity, they are gaining greater insights into the relationship between body chemistry and body weight. One researcher who has studied obesity for more than twenty-five years, questions the traditional explanation of obesity: that fat people are lazy and do not exercise, that they overeat because of psychological problems, or that they are pleasure seeking and do not even try to control what they eat. "Ever since I've been in the field, I've been looking for some biochemical or cellular abnormality that makes people fat." The researcher suggests that overweight people will not find long-range benefits in faddish diets. Rather, they must increase their exercise and decrease their diets. "I don't want to discourage people from losing weight, but they will have to pay for it."[35]

Neurochemistry

Although obesity may be associated with behavior, it is important to understand that changes in body chemistry that have been linked to criminal behavior do not necessarily involve obesity. Recently scientists have been looking at a possible relationship between criminal behavior and diet.

In October 1983 the National Conference on Nutrition and Behavior focused on an issue of growing recognition—the effect on human behavior of nutrition (or its lack) and of chemicals, food additives, or preservatives. A 1988 publication supported by the Robert J. Kutak Foundation and the National Institute of Corrections briefly summarizes the complex information now available on the relationship between behavior and diet and the implications that has for understanding criminal behavior. Diana Fishbein and Susan Pease begin their publication with a brief review of the study of **biocriminology,** which is the introduction of biological variables into modern criminology.[36]

After their extensive review of the literature, Fishbein and Pease conclude that the evidence is not yet sufficient to support a causal relationship between diet and criminal behavior. "Nevertheless, we do feel that current findings justify further attention to the possibility of a diet/behavior link that is relevant to the criminal justice system." They emphasized the need for further research.[37]

Autonomic Nervous System Studies

Another area of biological studies involves the Autonomic Nervous System (ANS), which "mediates physiological activity associated with emotions. . . . Examples of peripheral manifestations of ANS activity include changes in heart rate, blood pressure, respiration, muscle tension, pupillary size, and electrical activity of the skin," the last being the most frequently used measure of the psychophysiological characteristics of antisocial persons.[38]

Psychologists have for a long time studied criminals classified as psychopaths or, more recently, **sociopaths.** These people are aggressive, highly impulsive, antisocial persons who appear to have little or no concern for society's values. This lack of concern contributes to their extreme difficulty in establishing meaningful relationships. Recent studies of **serial murderers** have refocused attention on the sociopath, for people who continue to murder over a period of time frequently show sociopathic tendencies.

The problem lies in identifying the causes of sociopathy. In recent years, several books and a movie about Ted Bundy have refocused attention on the sociopath. Bundy, a handsome, bright, and personable young man, was convicted of murders in Florida and linked to over thirty murders in several states. Most of these cases involved women who voluntarily accompanied the man who later allegedly killed them. Bundy's arrest shocked virtually everyone who knew him, for his antisocial tendencies did not always rise to the surface, and he had an uncanny ability to fool most people about his intentions and his nature. Bundy's execution was postponed several times, but he was executed in Florida's electric chair in January 1989. Just before his execution he confessed to some of the murders with which he had been linked but for which he had not been tried and convicted.

Concern with the increasing incidents of antisocial behavior and serious violent crimes has led psychologists to consider whether the sociopathic personality is accompanied by changes in physiology. We might consider a simple example. In order to learn not to steal, a child must be taught—socialized—that it is wrong to take the property of others without their permission. This socialization usually occurs within the family, acting as a censuring agent. The appropriate fear response is developed. Children learn to fear punishment if they steal, and that fear enables them to inhibit their stealing impulses. Antisocial children, however, do not learn adequate initial fear responses; thus, they are not usually able to anticipate negative reactions if they steal. The fear inhibitor does not work to repress their stealing impulses.

How does this factor relate to ANS? The ANS largely controls the fear response. If children have quick ANS responses, they will learn to react to stimuli with fear, and that fear will generally inhibit their desire to steal. Children who have slow ANS responses, however, will learn slowly to inhibit stealing, if at all. A number of research studies have indicated that those who exhibit criminal behavior do tend to have slower ANS responses.[39]

Substance Abuse: A Special Case?

The focus within recent years on the relationship between substance abuse, including alcohol and other drugs, and criminal behavior deserves special and more extensive attention. Americans rank alcohol and other drugs and crime among their highest concerns, giving all high priority for government funding, and the National Institute of Justice "as part of our Nation's team contributing to the fight against these scourges . . . places research in support of our war against drugs as its highest priority."[40]

Studies indicate that a high percentage of individuals who are arrested, convicted, and incarcerated have abused alcohol and other drugs. Figure 4.1 graphs the percentages of male arrestees in 10 large cities

Cities listed:

Los Angeles
San Diego
Portland
Phoenix
Houston
New Orleans
Chicago
Indianapolis
Detroit
Fort Lauderdale
District of Columbia
New York City

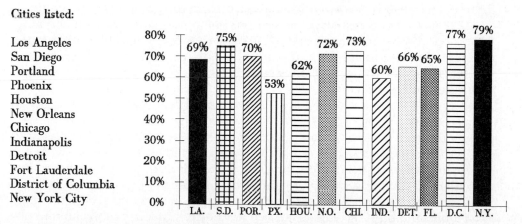

FIGURE 4.1 Percentage of Male Arrestees Testing Positive for any Drug, Including Marijuana (June-November 1987) *SOURCE:* National Institute of Justice, *Research in Action* 208 (Washington, D.C.: U.S. Department of Justice, March-April, 1988), p.9

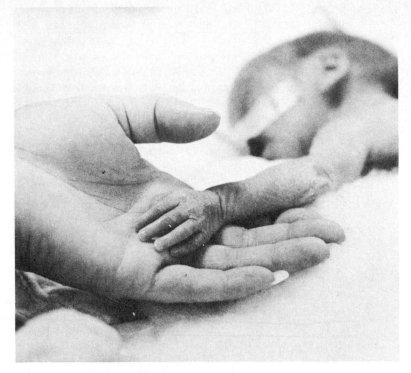

Substance abuse by pregnant women may result in birth defects or deformities among their young. Although such problems may not *cause* subsequent criminal behavior, they have been linked to such behavior.

who tested positive for any drug in 1987. The National Institute of Justice reported in July 1989 that its analysis of data for the last three months of 1988 indicated that a large majority of persons arrested in 14 major cities tested positive for illegal drugs.[41] Recent data on federal (Exhibit 4.1) and state offenders (Exhibit 4.2) also indicate a high extent of substance abuse.[42] Specific studies of alcohol abuse also indicate an association between substance abuse and crime.

The National Council on Alcoholism reports that approximately 64 percent of murders, 41 percent of assaults, 34 percent of rapes, 29 percent of other sex crimes, 30 percent of suicides, 56 percent of fights or assaults in the home, and 60 percent of the cases of child abuse may be attributed to alcohol misuse. Furthermore, "when alcoholism is treated, associated violent behavior is known to decrease."[43] Alcoholism is not the only problem, however, for social drinkers also engage in criminal acts, cause automobile and other accidents, and contribute to other social problems such as domestic violence.[44] Up to 40 percent of industrial fatalities and 47 percent of industrial injuries are associated with alcohol abuse. Typical drug users are 3.6 times more likely than non drug users to injure themselves

EXHIBIT 4.1

Federal Drug Law Violators, 1980–86

- During 1986, 12,285 defendants charged with Federal drug law violations were convicted in Federal courts—an increase of 134% over the number of convictions in 1980. By contrast, convictions of persons charged with other types of offenses increased 27%.

- Criminal charges were filed in Federal District Court against 80% of all suspected drug offenders in matters referred to U.S. attorneys during the 12 months preceding September 30, 1986. This was a higher filing rate than for all other categories of crime.

- Among suspected drug offenders referred to U.S. attorneys, 87% were alleged to have distributed or manufactured drugs illegally, 9% were suspected of importing drugs into the country, and 4% were suspected of illegal possession without intent to distribute.

- The increase in convictions for people charged with drug offenses accounted for 51% of the increase in all Federal convictions during the 1980–86 period.

- More than three-fifths of all Federal drug law offenders convicted in 1986 were charged with offenses involving heroin or cocaine. Convictions of persons charged with heroin or cocaine violations increased 190% during the 1980–86 period.

SOURCE: Bureau of Justice Statistics, *Drug Law Violators, 1980–86* (Washington, D.C.: U.S. Department of Justice, June 1988), p. 1.

on the job.[45] Excessive consumption of alcohol and drugs among pregnant women lowers the IQ of their unborn babies.[46] Alcohol is the third leading cause of birth defects and the only cause that is totally preventable.[47] The fact that substance abuse also results in babies born with a dependency on drugs, causing some to die, leads to legal implications discussed later in this chapter.

The economic cost to society of substance abuse is also immense although impossible to measure. Experts estimate that alcohol abuse is costing U.S. businesses $130 billion a year in absenteeism, additional health benefits, and faulty products produced by workers under the influence of alcohol.[48] In May 1989 New York City mayor Edward J. Koch proposed an additional $1.2 billion for drug treatment, while noting that the city spent $500 million a year for law enforcement activities related to combatting drug offenses.[49]

EXHIBIT 4.2

Drug Use and Crime Among State Inmates

- In 1986, 35% of State prison inmates reported that they were under the influence of drugs at the time they committed their current offense, compared with 32% in the 1979 survey.

- Almost 80% of inmates had used drugs at some time in their lives; 52% had used a major drug.

- White inmates and female inmates were somewhat more likely than others to have been regular users of major drugs at some time in the past.

- Among State prison inmates who had used drugs, about half began their use by age 15.

- A large majority of inmates (81%) were not daily users of a major drug in the month before the offense for which they were sentenced to prison. About one-seventh (13%) of inmates seem to fit the pattern of drug addicts who committed crimes for gain.

- Of State prisoners who were sentenced for robbery, burglary, larceny, or a drug offense, half were daily drug users, and about 40% were under the influence of an illegal drug at the time they committed the crime. These proportions were higher than those reported by inmates convicted of other crimes.

- The greater an offender's use of major drugs, the more prior convictions the inmate reported: Less than 13% of those who had never used a major drug had six or more prior convictions, compared to nearly 30% of daily users of major drugs.

- Users of major drugs were substantially more likely than nonusers to report that they received income from illegal activities during the time they were last free (48% vs. 10%).

- Twenty-eight percent of inmates reported a past drug dependency. The drugs most frequently mentioned were heroin (14%), cocaine (10%), and marijuana or hashish (9%).

SOURCE: Bureau of Justice Statistics, *Drug Use and Crime: State Prison Inmate Survey, 1986* (Washington, D.C.: U.S. Department of Justice, July 1988), p. 1.

It is important to understand that an association between substance abuse and criminal behavior does not prove **causation**. In the case of alcohol, for example, data are based on reports of alcohol use rather than on actual tests of use. Furthermore, they do not isolate how many others were drinking at the time the criminal behavior occurred; indeed, a large percentage of the population drinks but does not engage in criminal behavior, at least as far as the official data indicate. Thus, alcohol use or abuse "may be an effect of the same social or other environmental factors which cause the individual to engage in criminal activity. The question unanswered by the existing literature is whether alcohol ingestion accounts for a portion of variance of criminal behavior independently of environmental factors."[50]

All we can conclude now is that the presence of crime and substance abuse does not necessarily mean that there is a direct cause-and-effect relationship. On the other hand, it is unreasonable to ignore the possible effect of substance abuse, present in so many instances when crimes are committed.[51]

PSYCHOLOGICAL EXPLANATIONS OF CRIMINAL BEHAVIOR

Biologists and chemists were not the only professionals to link behavior to physical characteristics. Some early psychologists attempted to explain criminal behavior by means of the inherited trait we now call *intelligence*. The influence of the positivists can also be seen in these early attempts to link criminal and other forms of antisocial behavior with mental retardation. Family studies were their sources of data. As the researchers traced criminality through generations of the same family, they concluded that mental retardation was the cause of crime. It was not important to them what happened in the mind of the criminal: "It never occurred to positivists to ask *how* feeblemindedness could affect an individual, causing him to rob a stagecoach or habitually drink to excess."[52]

The Mind and Its Relationship to Crime: The Beginnings

Today we often hear comments about the criminal mind, and the literature devoted to explaining it is extensive. Before the development of more scientific theories of criminal behavior of mental illness, one of the most popular explanations was **demonology.** Individuals were thought to be possessed by good or evil spirits, which caused good or evil behavior. Modern counterparts are discussed in Highlight 4.3. The behavior could not be changed unless the spirits were changed. An early method of treating criminal behavior was to use a crude stone to cut a hole in the skull of a person thought to be possessed by devils. The process, called *trephining,* was thought to permit the evil spirit to escape; there is evidence that some people survived the surgery. But the usual treatment for evil spirits was *exorcism,* which included the drinking of horrible concoctions, praying, and making strange noises. Later it was assumed that the only way to drive out the devils was to insult them or to make the body an unpleasant

HIGHLIGHT 4.3

SATANISM, OCCULTISM, AND CRIMINAL BEHAVIOR

Cauldrons with voodoo ritual objects were found at a ranch near Matamoros, Mexico, where the bodies of twelve victims were found, including the body of University of Texas student Mark Kilroy.

place for them to inhabit, such as by flogging and other forms of corporal punishment. During the latter part of the fifteenth century, the belief arose that some possessed people were actively and deliberately working with the devil of their own free will, and society reacted to this alleged witchcraft by imposing the death penalty.

In the eighteenth century, scholars began developing knowledge about human anatomy, physiology, neurology, general medicine, and chemistry. The discovery of an organic basis for many physical illnesses led to the discovery of an organic basis for some mental illnesses. This organic view replaced the demonological theory of causation and domi-

HIGHLIGHT 4.3 (Continued)

A large cauldron in which human blood, human brains, and other body parts were mixed with goats' feet and heads, roosters' feet, horseshoes, turtles, and large sticks was part of the alleged ritualistic killings uncovered at a ranch in Matamoros, Mexico, near the Texas border. Adolfo de Jesus Constanzo was said to be the leader of the cult that dismembered and killed at least fifteen people whose remains were found in the spring of 1989. Constanzo was a powerful leader who convinced his followers that human sacrifices would protect them against police; bullets could not enter their bodies! Said one of the followers: "Of course we believed. We were afraid not to believe."

This satanic drug cult with its powerful leader, who is said to have ordered his own death when police were closing in on him, is reminiscent of the earlier crimes of Charles Manson and

his followers. Manson convinced his followers that their killings, which involved a pregnant actress, Sharon Tate, 26, and six other people, would lead to a race riot that would eventually lead to his rulership. Manson, who along with some of his followers was convicted of these murders, is incarcerated in a California prison.

In March 1989 Anthony Allan Hall, 25, was convicted of first-degree murder in the death of a Vietnamese immigrant on whose chest Hall had carved an inverted cross to indicate that he was a human sacrifice before shooting the victim seven times in the head and neck. Hall claimed a devil-worshipping friend, Bunny Dixon, nineteen, and a high-school dropout, had forced him to shoot. Hall testified that Dixon used an Ouija Board to communicate with the spirit of a dead boy after which she suggested the criminal plan

in which they and two other friends kidnapped the victim, robbed him of $120, threw him in the trunk of the car, and drove to a wooded area before carving and killing him. Hall was sentenced to death; Dixon was sentenced to fifty years. A third offender was sentenced to seventeen years and another to life in prison.

What causes such crimes is still a subject of debate, but defense attorneys who argue for lesser penalities because of the cult influence are generally unsuccessful. Meanwhile, local citizens react with fear, rage, and religion. In Matamoros, priests reported that frightened residents flocked to churches, and participation in communion and confessions increased significantly as people tried to cope with their fear of satanism.

Summarized by the author from media sources.

---

nated the fields of psychology and psychiatry until 1915. But by the turn of the twentieth century, it was argued that psychological problems could *cause* mental illness, and a new viewpoint in psychiatry was created.

Psychiatric Approach

Psychiatry is a field of medicine that specializes in the understanding, diagnosis, treatment, and prevention of mental problems. **Psychoanalysis** is a branch of psychiatry based on the theories of Sigmund Freud and employing a particular personality theory and a particular method of

Dr. Sigmund Freud of Vienna, Austria, had an impact on the study of crime through his development of psychoanalytic theories of behavior.

treatment, usually individual case study. Psychiatry holds that each person is a unique personality and that the only way that person can be understood is through a thorough case study.

The use of the case study in psychiatry characterized the work of William Healy, who is credited with shifting the positivists' emphasis in studying anatomical characteristics to one on the psychological and social elements. Healy and his colleagues believed that the only way to find the roots or causes of delinquent behavior was to delve deeply into the individual's background, especially the emotional development. But they also measured personality disorders and environmental pathologies, theorizing that delinquency was purposive behavior resulting when children were frustrated in their attempts to fulfill some of their basic needs. Healy and his associates found that delinquents had a higher frequency of personality defects and disorders than did nondelinquents.[53] Despite their popularization of the case study method, Healy and his colleagues have been criticized for basing their studies on vaguely defined terms, giving little information on how they measured the concepts and characteristics and using samples too small to permit generalization to the total population of delinquents.

Sigmund Freud (1856–1939), who is credited with having made the greatest contribution to the development of psychoanalytic theory, did not advance a theory of criminality per se. His theories attempted to explain all behavior and, in so doing, have implications for criminology. The psychoanalytic theories of Freud and his colleagues introduced the concept of the *unconscious*, along with techniques for probing that element of the personality, and emphasized that all human behavior is motivated and purposive.

According to Freud, humans have mental conflict because of desires and energies that are repressed into the unconscious. These urges, ideas, desires, and instincts are basic, but they are repressed because of society's morality. People are constantly trying, however, to express these natural drives in some way, often indirect, to avoid the reactions of others. Dreams are one example of indirect expression.

Freud saw original human nature as assertive and aggressive. It is not learned but is deeply rooted in early childhood experiences. We all have criminal tendencies; but during the socialization process, most of us learn to control them by developing strong and effective inner controls. The improperly socialized child does not develop an ability to control impulses and acts them out or projects them inward. In the case of the latter, the child may become neurotic; in the case of the former, delinquent.[54]

The psychiatric approach has been criticized for several reasons.[55] The terms are vague; no operational definitions for most concepts are given; and most of the data are open to the analyst's subjective interpretation. Moreover, the research has been based on samples that are too small and have usually been selected from psychiatric patients and often from institutionalized patients. The use of control groups has not been adequate. The individual is the focus of the psychiatric approach, and that focus does not permit generalizations on *patterns* of behavior and therefore limits generalization. Finally, the emphasis on early childhood experiences has been seriously questioned by social scientists, who de-emphasize the deterministic nature of such experiences, arguing that their impact can be decreased or even eliminated through proper training.[56]

Personality Theory

Emotional conflict and personality deviation characterize many criminals, especially habitual offenders. But the critical questions are whether these factors distinguish criminals from law-abiding persons and, if so, whether the traits *cause* the illegal behavior. A number of early researchers found such differences,[57] but others found evidence that questioned the relationship between personality traits and criminal behavior.[58]

The earlier studies emphasized the frequency of an association between mental disorders and crime. The belief that mental disorders *cause* criminal behavior led to confinement of the mentally ill in jails and prisons rather than in public hospitals. A report from the National Institute of Justice indicates that although mental disorders are higher among criminals than among noncriminals, the explanation lies not in the fact that mental disorders *cause* crime but in the fact that mental disorders and crime are both highly associated with some of the same demographic factors, such as age, gender, and race.[59]

Intelligence and Crime

Closely associated with the mental disorder approach is the linking of crime and intelligence. It is argued that low intelligence causes crime. This approach also has long historical roots; early studies of family histories that found many people of lower intelligence in a family line of criminals concluded that the criminal behavior was caused by the low intelligence. These studies were discredited when researchers found few differences between the intelligence of criminals and that of World War I army draftees. In the 1960s, however, attention once again turned to intelligence and crime.

The relationship between crime and intelligence got a boost with the publication in 1985 of *Crime & Human Nature* by James K. Wilson and Richard J. Herrnstein, who take the position that there is a "clear and consistent link between criminality and low intelligence" and criticize text writers for ignoring the research in this area.[60] Once again, however, the authors have shown only that low intelligence and crime often appear together in the same groups; they have not demonstrated that low intelligence is the *cause* of crime.

Cognitive Development Theory

Another type of psychological theory that has been used to explain criminal behavior is **cognitive development.** This approach is based on the belief that the way in which people organize their thoughts about rules and laws results in either criminal or noncriminal behavior. Psychologists refer to this organization of thoughts as *moral reasoning*. When that reasoning is applied to law, it is termed *legal reasoning*, although that term has quite a different meaning to persons trained in law. The approach stems from the early works of Jean Piaget, who believed that there are two stages in moral reasoning: (1) the belief that rules are sacred and immutable, and (2) the belief that rules are the products of humans.

According to Piaget, we leave the first stage at about the age of thirteen, and the second stage leads to more moral behavior than the first.[61]

In 1958, Lawrence Kohlberg made some changes in this approach. He called the first stage *preconventional* and the second *conventional*, and he added a third and higher stage, *postconventional reasoning*. According to Kohlberg, between the ages of ten and thirteen, a person usually moves from preconventional to conventional reasoning or thinking; those who do not make this transition may be considered arrested in their development of moral reasoning, and they may become delinquents.[62] He and others later refined this position, with a development of stages of moral judgment that are applicable to all kinds of behavior. The progression to higher stages should preclude criminal behavior, but most criminals do not progress beyond the earlier stages.[63]

Other modern scholars have developed the thesis that both criminal and noncriminal behavior are related to cognitive development and that people choose the behavior in which they wish to engage, just as the classical writers proclaimed in the eighteenth century. For example, psychologists at the United States Penitentiary at Leavenworth, Kansas emphasize that although environmental factors such as family background, peer relationships, and poverty may limit one's choices, they do not *determine* those choices. Criminal behavior exists because of the way people think and the choices they choose to make. Thus, either criminals must be confined forever, or they must be taught how to change their ways of thinking. "The root causes of crime . . . are thought and choice."[64]

Behavior Theory

Behavior theory originated in the late 1800s but gained more attention in this century through the work of B. F. Skinner. Behavior theory is the basis for behavior modification, one approach used in institutionalized and noninstitutionalized settings for changing behavior. The primary thesis is that all behavior is learned and can be unlearned. The approach is concerned with observable behavior in contrast to the traditional psychoanalytic emphasis on deep, underlying personality problems that must be uncovered and treated.

Behavior theory is thus based on the belief that it is not the unconscious that is important but, rather, the behavior, which can be observed and manipulated. It is assumed that neurotic symptoms and some deviant behavior are acquired through an unfortunate quirk of learning and are rewarding to the patient. The undesirable behavior can be eliminated, modified, or replaced by taking away the reward value or by rewarding a more appropriate behavior that is incompatible with the deviant one. Behavior, it is argued, is controlled by its consequences. In dealing directly with behaviors that are undesirable, behavioral therapy attempts to change the person's long-established patterns of response to himself or herself and to others.

Social-Learning Theory

Social-learning theory acknowledges that individuals have physiological mechanisms that enable them to behave aggressively, but whether they will do so or not and the nature of their aggressive behavior are learned. This theory may be contrasted with behavior theory in that the latter emphasizes performance and reinforcement, whereas social-learning theory emphasizes that learning may be accomplished by using other people as models; it is not necessary to engage in all the behavior that we learn. We engage in the behavior only if we have incentives and motivations to do so. Motivations may come from biological factors or from mental factors, the latter giving us the ability to imagine the behavior's consequences.[65]

Under social-learning theory, behavior is seen as maintained by consequences, of which there are three types: (1) *external reinforcement*, such as goods, money, social status, and punishment (effective in restraining behavior); (2) *vicarious reinforcement*, for example, observing the status of others whom one observes being reinforced for their behavior; and (3) *self-regulatory mechanisms*, such as people responding to their own actions in ways that bring self-rewards or self-punishment. Social-learning theorists emphasize the importance of the family, the subculture, and the media.

Social-learning theories have also been combined with biological approaches to explain criminal behavior. An English scholar and psychologist, H. J. Eysenck, in his work *Crime and Personality*, emphasized the interrelationship between psychology and biology in explaining how humans learn to behave. Unlike most psychologists, he related his approach directly to criminal behavior.[66]

Eysenck's approach was based on the principle of *conditioning*. We learn appropriate and inappropriate behavior through a process of training that involves rewards for appropriate behavior, punishment for inappropriate behavior, and the establishment of models of appropriate behavior. Through these processes, we learn moral preferences as well as behavior. The process is slow and subtle. We often do not realize how we obtained our moral preferences, but in the process of learning, most of us develop a conscience. This conscience provides us with feelings of responsibility and duty, shame and guilt, of the need to do the right thing. If we do the wrong thing, we will feel guilty, assuming, of course, that our conscience incorporates the moral preferences that define that activity as wrong.[67]

The process of training uses three tools: classical conditioning, operant conditioning, and modeling. Most of us have heard about classical conditioning in terms of Pavlov's dogs, who were trained to salivate when a bell rang because they knew from conditioning that they would be fed. *Classical conditioning*, then, is a learned response to a stimulus.

Operant conditioning is based on a reaction after we have acted. It is argued that this is the most powerful form of training. We are rewarded, or reinforced, when we behave appropriately, and we are punished when we misbehave. We also learn by *models;* social learning occurs through the observation of others and from the media. In many languages, the verb "to teach" is synonymous with the verb "to show."[68]

Eysenck's approach was based almost entirely on classical conditioning and took the position that "criminality can be understood in terms of conditioning principles." Criminals do not condition adequately to stimuli that society deems should be incorporated in a conscience.[69] Eysenck believed that conditioning depends on the sensitivity of the inherited autonomic nervous system as well as the quality of conditioning that is received during the process of socialization. In the third edition of his book, Eysenck emphasized that his original plan in 1964 was to outline a theory of antisocial behavior, relate that theory to personality, "and indicate some of the biological factors underlying both personality and criminality." Biological and psychological approaches were not given much credit at the time; but by 1977, Eysenck argued that we had much more evidence of the relationship between genetic factors and criminality, more evidence that personality traits are strongly determined by genetic factors, and much more empirical work "on the biological causes of personality differences, and by implication, of psychopathic and criminal conduct." Eysenck also took the position that some of the sociological theories that had previously overshadowed biological and psychological theories were now less acceptable in explaining criminal behavior. He cited particularly the variables of poverty, poor housing, and social inequality. However, Eysenck has been criticized for his overemphasis on classical conditioning to the exclusion of operant conditioning and modeling.[70]

IMPLICATIONS OF BIOLOGICAL AND PSYCHOLOGICAL RESEARCH

The implication of our discussion thus far is the possibility of integrating the social, physical, and psychological sciences in our attempt to understand criminal behavior.

Attention given to biological and psychological explanations of human behavior and its implications for studying crime was fueled in 1985 by *Crime & Human Nature,* the work of Harvard University professors James Q. Wilson, a political scientist, and Richard J. Herrnstein, a psychologist. The comprehensive book, replete with pages of summaries of criminological literature, received national attention through television talk shows, popular magazines, and newspapers. The authors, who refocused attention on genetic and biological components of criminal behavior, have been well received by some but criticized by others. Sociologist Jack P. Gibbs wrote that the book "may startle numerous sociologists, and those who suffer from high blood pressure should be cautious in reading it. Sociologists are accustomed to occasional forays by economists into criminology, but many will be unprepared for a flank attack by formidable scholars from political science . . . and psychology."[71]

In 1976 we were warned that we should not ignore biology and psychology: "Contrary to the beliefs of many American criminologists, the constitutional school is not dead. Research continues in this area, and it behooves the skeptic whether he be sociologist, psychiatrist or psychologist to at least keep an open mind toward it."[72] That declaration had little effect; among criminologists, the biological or constitutional school of thought lost its importance as a reasonable explanation for criminal behavior. More recently, however, psychologists and biologists have gained more attention. Much of the work has been done by Sarnoff A. Mednick and his associates. Their conclusion is this:

> A half century of research and common sense leaves no doubt that social and cultural factors play a considerable role in the etiology of crime. The biological factors . . . must be seen as another set of variables involved in the etiology of crime. Both social and biological variables *and their interactions* are important for our complete understanding of the origins of antisocial behavior.[73]

The key in this statement is *interaction*. Many scholars today argue that the issue is no longer nature *or* nurture but nature *and* nurture. It is not a question of whether human behavior is the result of biology *or* environment, but what effect each has on the other.

One of the manifestations of using both the physical and social sciences to explain behavior is seen in the work of sociobiologists. Edward O. Wilson, who introduced the concept of **sociobiology**, defines the term as "the systematic study of the biological basis of all social behavior."[74] The concept has been denounced by some as just another deterministic approach,[75] but others view the work of Wilson and his colleagues as providing the framework for the future unification of the social and natural sciences.[76]

That claim may not be accurate, but there are important policy implications in integrating the social and physical sciences. One has been analyzed by sociologist C. Ray Jeffery. The progress of the sciences, he believes, "will be developed to the point where the major behavioral disorders can be brought under control." According to Jeffery, we must explain criminal behavior "directly in terms of the consequences of the behavior, and not indirectly in terms of noncriminal variables such as poverty, race, or social class." If we are to change criminal behavior, we must work directly on the factors in our environment that reinforce that kind of behavior.[77]

Like other theorists, Jeffery has his critics. Conflict criminologists

Tony Platt and Paul Takagi acknowledge that Jeffery has had a significant impact on the "new impetus and respectability" of biosocial criminology, but they argue that he has failed to assess the true picture of crime. To Jeffery, they argue, crime is really street crime, and he avoids discussing white-collar crimes and proceeds as if those crimes by the middle- and upper-classes are not proper subjects of discussion for criminologists. They are more properly the subject matter of politics and economics. In addition, claim Platt and Takagi, Jeffery has an "inaccurate understanding of genetics, biology and social psychology" and "like other scientists who have ventured outside their fields of expertise . . . Jeffery demonstrates that a little knowledge can be irresponsible as well as dangerous." They characterize Jeffery's scholarship as shoddy, referring to its lack of an empirical or scientific basis. They also question his conservative ideology with its lack of attention to history, politics, and economics.[78]

The debate between Jeffery and Platt and Takagi illustrates the degree to which scholars differ in their reactions to biocriminology. Both have their points and their followers, and the critical student will carefully analyze each position, along with those of other scholars, before drawing his or her own conclusions on this and other important subjects in criminology.[79]

BIOLOGY, PSYCHOLOGY, AND THE LAW

The final implication of the renewed emphasis on biological and psychological research is a legal one and concerns the use of such information in court, particularly to support defenses to criminal acts. These implications are serious. Our system of criminal law is based on the premise that people are legally responsible only for criminal acts over which they have control; they are not responsible if they cannot control their behavior. Thus, if someone forces you to shoot at another person, you may have a defense of duress. The problem is that we do not fully understand the effect of psychological and biological factors on behavior. We do, however, know that many people have biological and/or mental problems. A lengthy discussion of the legal implications of the discussions in this chapter is beyond the scope of this book, but the following overview is worthwhile.

Insanity Defense

The most controversial defense related to biological and psychological factors is the **insanity defense.** The current movement is away from its use. The public was apparently incensed at the successful application of this defense in the case of John W. Hinckley, Jr., who on March 30, 1980, attempted to assassinate President Ronald Reagan. That case appeared to be an easy one for the prosecutor to win, for many of us watched on television as Hinckley fired shots at the President and his party, wounding the President; his press secretary, James Brady; and a security officer.

Because it was obvious that Hinckley had pulled the trigger, his attorneys indicated that he would plead not guilty by reason of insanity. Hinckley was then ordered to undergo nearly four months of psychiatric testing. Nearly fourteen months after the shooting, Hinckley's trial finally began. According to defense psychiatrists, Hinckley was psychotic, was consumed by paradoxical thoughts, was severely depressed, had hypochondriacal tendencies, hated himself, suffered from schizophrenia spectrum disorder, had a totally abnormal thought process, thought of himself as a little boy who had done something terrible, and was torn between childish love and dependence on his father and subconscious fantasies about killing him.

During the closing arguments, the prosecution contended that Hinckley was completely rational when he shot the President and emphasized the months of planning that went into his scheme to attract the attention of Jodie Foster, an actress with whom he had become obsessed. The defense attorney reviewed Hinckley's life from childhood to adulthood and tried to convince the jury that anyone who thinks that he or she can shoot the President in order to gain attention from a woman has to be suffering from delusions.

The jury deliberated for twenty-five hours over four days and found Hinckley not guilty by reason of insanity. The public's reaction was immediate outrage. A Texas district attorney commented, "Only in the U.S. can a man try to assassinate the leader of the country in front of 125 million people and be found not guilty." The next day's headline in the *Indianapolis News* stated, "Hinckley Insane, Public Mad."[80]

The Meaning of Insanity

Insanity is a legal, not a medical, term, and there is no agreement on its meaning. It is a legal conclusion that the defendant was not responsible for his or her actions. The basic test for determining whether a defendant was insane at the time the crime was committed is called the **M'Naghten rule**. This test arose from the celebrated case of Daniel M'Naghten, who committed a murder in 1843. M'Naghten intended to kill British Prime Minister Robert Peel because he was under the delusion that Peel was persecuting him. He shot Edward Drummond instead, believing that Drummond was Peel. At his trial, M'Naghten claimed that he was insane and that he should not be held responsible for his actions because his delusions caused him to murder Drummond.[81]

The M'Naghten rule became the majority rule in most of the United States; it provides that a mental disability must produce one of two conditions to be valid as a defense. The accused must have suffered from a defect of reason or from a disease of the mind so that at the time of the act the accused did not know the nature and quality of the act or that the act was wrong. Some states use the M'Naghten test plus the **irresistible impulse** test, which allows a defendant to use the insanity defense if a mental disease has rendered the defendant incapable of choosing between right and wrong, even though he or she can recognize the difference. This is sometimes called *temporary insanity* and means that a defendant cannot control his or her behavior and conform it to the law.

A third insanity test that was never widely adopted was the **Durham rule,** also known as the *product rule.* This rule was based on an assessment of whether the offender's behavior was the product of mental disease or defect. The test was first articulated in the District of Columbia in 1954 in *Durham v. U. S.,*[82] and abandoned in that jurisdiction in 1972 in *U. S. v. Brawner.*[83] In its place the court adopted the **substantial capacity test** or the **ALI rule,** named after the American Law Institute, which proposes model laws. This test, a modified version of the rule stated in *Brawner,* essentially asks the question of whether the offender had the substantial capacity to appreciate the criminality of his or her conduct or if so, to control that conduct. It thus substitutes the requirement of *appreciate* for that of *knowledge* in the M'Naghten test. These rules, along with the current federal insanity rule, are summarized in Exhibit 4.3.[84]

EXHIBIT 4.3

Insanity Tests Used in the U.S.

Test	Legal Standard
M'Naghten	"didn't know what he was doing or didn't know it was wrong"
Irresistible Impulse	"could not control his conduct"
Durham	"the criminal act was caused by his mental illness"
Brawner-ALI	"lacks substantial capacity to appreciate the wrongfulness of his conduct or to control it"
Present Federal Law	"lacks capacity to appreciate the wrongfulness of his conduct"

SOURCE: National Institute of Justice, Norval Morris, *Insanity Defense* (Washington, D.C.: U.S. Department of Justice, no date or page number given).

Public Attacks on the Insanity Defense

The results of the Hinckley trial created intense public reaction to the use of the insanity plea. An ABC news poll showed that 75 percent of respondents disapproved of laws allowing defendants to be found not guilty by reason of insanity. An Associated Press/NBC poll reported that 87 percent of the public believed too many killers were using the insanity defense to avoid incarceration.[85] These conclusions are, however, factually inaccurate. Although it is difficult to gather accurate data on the frequency of insanity pleas nationwide, the estimates range from 1 to 2 percent. In other words, only 1 to 2 percent of defendants plead insanity, and only one in four of those is successful in obtaining a verdict of not guilty by reason of insanity.[86]

Despite the relative infrequency with which the insanity plea is used successfully, when it is used in a highly publicized case, it arouses great public indignation that the defense permits heinous criminals to go free. That conclusion is also inaccurate in that the small percentage of persons found not guilty by reason of insanity are not necessarily turned loose in society. Hinckley, for example, is confined in a mental hospital. The public fear, however, rests on the realization that Hinckley and others *could* be released. Apparently, the public feels that a lengthy prison term is necessary to protect society from such persons.

Guilty but Mentally Ill

One of the suggestions for dealing with the insanity defense comes from Michigan, a state that in 1975 adopted the defense of guilty but mentally ill (GBMI), a statute that has become the model for other states and that was upheld by the Michigan Supreme Court in 1985.[87] Approximately 20 percent of the states have adopted this defense.

Under the Michigan statute, insanity and mental illness are two distinct concepts. To return a verdict of guilty but mentally ill, the jury must find (1) that the defendant is guilty of the offense charge, (2) that the defendant was mentally ill when the offense was committed, but (3) the defendant was not insane at the time of the offense. The court may then impose any sentence that could be imposed on a defendant found guilty of the same offense. Psychiatric treatment will be provided for the offender, and the time spent in treatment will be applied toward the sentence to be served in a correctional facility provided the offender completes treatment before the end of the specified sentence. If, after the length of the sentence is completed, the offender still needs treatment, civil commitment procedures must be followed.[88]

Expansion of the Insanity Defense

There is concern that the insanity defense may be extended beyond reasonable limits. Despite sociological findings that gambling is a compulsive social problem and the conclusions of some that it is also an illness,[89] a federal court refused to accept compulsive gambling as an indication of mental disease or defect required by the jurisdiction's insanity test. The court followed the ALI test for insanity and concluded that there is not sufficient evidence "to lead us to conclude that there is substantial acceptance in the relevant discipline that compulsive gambling disorder causes some persons to be unable to resist buying cars with bad checks and then transporting the cars and the paper over state lines."[90]

Some defendants have, however, successfully raised the defense of **posttraumatic stress disorder (PTSD),** a debilitating brain dysfunction first generally recognized about 1980. The defense has been raised by Vietnam veterans, who argue that they suffer nightmares, flashbacks, depression, and survivor guilt.[91] Veterans afflicted with PTSD often lose their orientation and believe that they are back in the jungles of Vietnam, taking action to protect themselves and their combat buddies by shooting, attacking, or maiming the people around them—people they believe are dangerous Viet Cong or North Vietnamese. Defense lawyers have argued that these trances or flashbacks are so severe that the veterans are not responsible for their acts and that reliving combat so intensely has destroyed their ability to distinguish right from wrong. The defense has been used to acquit not only veterans accused of murder but also those who have committed armed robberies and violated drug laws.[92]

Another area related to the insanity defense is the **premenstrual tension syndrome (PMS),** which is characterized by both physical and psychological symptoms: abdominal bloating, backaches, weight gain, tenderness in the breasts, headaches, skin disorders, cravings for sweet or salty food, irritability, fatigue, insomnia, tension, depression, lethargy, and clumsiness. "In its most extreme form [PMS] can spark uncontrollable rages that vent in violent acts."[93]

This syndrome is recognized as a form of legal insanity in France and has been used to mitigate or reduce sentences in England. The English debate over PMS began when Sandie Smith, a barmaid with thirty previous offenses, was put on probation for threatening to kill a police officer and for carrying a knife. Her attorney argued that PMS had turned her into "a raging animal each month" and had forced her to act out of character. The second English case involved a woman charged with murder: Christine English had run over her lover with a car. She was given twelve months of jail-free supervison after a medical expert witness testified that she suffered from "an extremely aggravated form of premenstrual physical condition."[94]

Arguments have also been made for recognizing the PMS defense in the U. S., as the following quotation indicates:

> It is unfortunate that many PMS sufferers may have been imprisoned because the law does not recognize PMS as a valid defense. This injustice must be corrected. Premenstrual syndrome is real. Its effects on many

women can be catastrophic and must be taken into account by the criminal justice system.[95]

Another extension of the insanity defense (although in some cases actually a matter of self-defense, not temporary insanity) is the **battered woman syndrome defense.** Women who have physically attacked or killed their husbands and who had previously been beaten by them, have been permitted in some courts to introduce expert testimony that they were suffering from severe physical and psychological abuse at the time they committed what would otherwise be a criminal act. Although American courts have allowed testimony on this syndrome, they have not been consistent in establishing rules for its use. The defense is in its infancy, and we can expect varying rulings as judges consider what, if any, weight should be given to the syndrome when it is raised as a defense to murder.[96]

Another attempt to expand the insanity defense is to use the presence of the XYY chromosome abnormality, discussed earlier in the chapter. The defense has been used somewhat successfully in other countries. An example is the French case of Daniel Hugon, who in 1968 was accused of murdering a sixty-five-year-old prostitute. But the XYY chromosome defense has not yet become an acceptable extension of the insanity plea in this country. When it was raised in a criminal case in Los Angeles in 1969, the judge ruled that there was "no clear link between the chromosomal abnormality and behavior." He stated that the "field of genetics is 30 years behind the point where it can be used in the courts."[97] In fact, general attempts to introduce at trial expert testimony on genetics have been rebuffed by judges. An attorney who sought to introduce evidence of chromosome variants on the issue of whether a child born of an alleged rape was fathered by the defendant received a negative response from the trial judge. The judge indicated that there is no significant agreement in the medical community on whether such analysis does in fact prove paternity.[98]

One final area concerning criminal liability and biology has been raised. A study of death row inmates links criminal behavior to childhood head injuries. In reaction to this study, the American Bar Association published an article entitled "From Victim to Victimizer?" in which it raised the issue of whether such studies provide data that can be used by defense attorneys in murder cases. The Supreme Court requires that before capital punishment can be imposed on a defendant convicted of murder, mitigating and aggravating circumstances must be considered. It is now being argued that head injuries may constitute mitigating factors that must be considered in death penalty cases. "If lawyers can show a history of head trauma, which might have been the cause of defective mental responses, then they could show that the defendant acted under extreme emotional disturbance."[99] In some jurisdictions, that evidence would permit a reduction of a murder charge to first degree manslaughter, for which the death penalty could not be imposed.

CONCLUSION

In this chapter we have continued our inquiry into the explanations of criminal behavior by concentrating on the contributions of biologists and psychologists. Once again, we have seen the impact of the positive school, how its constitutional approach to criminal behavior influenced the body type theories of Sheldon and the Gluecks. But these researchers, along with Cortés, also saw the importance of environmental factors.

From a discussion of genetic factors, including family studies, studies of twins and adoptees, and chromosomal abnormalities, we considered the importance of the central nervous system, neuroendocrinology and neurochemistry, and the autonomic nervous system.

We then turned to psychiatry and psychology, beginning with a brief glance at demonology before exploring the psychiatric approach and personality theory. We also studied intelligence and crime, cognitive development theory, behavior theory, social-learning theory, and the relationship between psychological conditioning and biology. We considered the implications of the current research in biology and psychology as well as the impact of these findings on criminology in understanding criminal behavior.

In the final section, we looked at the legal implications, particularly the insanity defense, as well as related defenses based on biology. It may be that biological implications of criminal behavior will have a greater impact in the courtroom than in the social science journals. To date, however, social science theories of criminal behavior continue to dominate the literature; the next two chapters are devoted to their explanation and analysis.

ENDNOTES

1. Sarnoff A. Mednick and Jan Volavka, "Biology and Crime," in Norval Morris and Michael Tonry, eds., *Crime and Justice: An Annual Review of Research*, vol. 2 (Chicago: University of Chicago Press, 1980), p. 86.
2. Stephen Schafer, *Theories in Criminology* (New York: Random House, 1969), p. 24, quoting Marvin E. Wolfgang, "Cesare Lombroso," in Herman Mannheim, ed., *Pioneers in Criminology*, 2d ed. (Montclair, N.J.: Patterson Smith, 1973), pp. 232–291. See also "Cesare Lombroso," Chapter 2 in Randy Martin et al., *Criminological Thought: Pioneers Past and Present* (New York: Macmillan, 1990), pp. 31–44.
3. Cesare Lombroso, *Crime, Its Causes and Remedies*, trans. H. P. Horton (Boston: Little, Brown, 1911), p. 365.
4. See Raffaele Garofalo, *Criminology*, trans. Robert W. Millar (Boston: Little, Brown, 1914); Francis Allen, "Rafaele Garofalo," in Mannheim, ed., *Pioneers,*

pp. 318–340; Thorsten Sellin, "Enrico Ferri," in Mannheim, ed., *Pioneers,* pp. 370–371; Enrico Ferri, *The Positive School of Criminology* (Chicago: Kerr, 1913); and Enrico Ferri, *Criminal Sociology,* trans. Joseph Killey and John Lisle (Boston: Little, Brown, 1917).

5. Ernst Kretschmer, *Physique and Character,* trans. W. J. H. Sprott (New York: Harcourt, Brace, 1926).

6. W. H. Sheldon, *The Varieties of Human Physique: An Introduction to Constitutional Psychology* (New York: Harper & Row, 1940); *The Varieties of Temperament* (New York: Harper & Row, 1942); *Varieties of Delinquent Youth: An Introduction to Constitutional Psychiatry* (New York: Harper & Row, 1949); and *Atlas of Men* (New York: Harper & Row, 1954). See also "William Herbert Sheldon," Chapter 6 in Martin et al., *Criminological Thought,* pp. 119–136.

7. Juan B. Cortés with Florence M. Gatti, *Delinquency and Crime: A Biopsychosocial Approach* (New York: Seminar Press, 1972), p. 8.

8. Albert K. Cohen, Alfred Lindesmith, and Karl Schuessler, *The Sutherland Papers* (Bloomington: Indiana University Press, 1956), p. 289.

9. See Sheldon Glueck and Eleanor Glueck, *Physique and Delinquency* (New York: Harper & Row, 1956); *Five Hundred Criminal Careers* (New York: Knopf, 1930); *Later Criminal Careers* (New York: Commonwealth Fund, 1937); *Criminal Careers in Retrospect* (New York: Commonwealth Fund, 1943); and *Unraveling Juvenile Delinquency* (New York: Commonwealth Fund, 1950).

10. Hermann Mannheim, *Comparative Criminology* (Boston: Houghton Mifflin, 1965), p. 241.

11. Cortés, *Delinquency and Crime,* p. 19.

12. *Ibid.,* p. 19.

13. *Ibid.,* p. 158.

14. See Richard L. Dugdale, *The Jukes: A Study in Crime, Pauperism, Disease, and Heredity,* 4th ed. (New York: Putnam, 1942), and Henry H. Goddard, *Feeblemindedness, Its Causes and Consequences* (New York: Macmillan, 1914).

15. Sheldon Glueck and Eleanor Glueck, *Of Delinquency and Crime* (Springfield, Ill: Chas. C Thomas, 1974). The same conclusion was reached in the classic study by Lee N. Robins, *Deviant Children Grown Up* (Baltimore: Williams & Wilkins, 1966). For a recent assessment of the Glueck's work, see John H. Lamb and Robert J. Sampson, "Unraveling Families and Delinquency: A Reanalysis of the Glueck's Data," *Criminology* 26 (August 1988): 355–380.

16. Charles Goring, *The English Convict* (London: H. M. Stationery Office, 1913).

17. Buck v. Bell, 274 U.S. 200 (1927). For a recent compilation of articles on the family, see Frank E. Hagan and Marvin B. Sussman, eds., *Deviance and the Family* (Binghamton, N.Y.: The Howorth Press, Inc. 1988).

18. See Nicholas F. Hahn, "Too Dumb to Know Better: Cacogenic Family Studies and the Criminology of Women," *Criminology* 18 (May 1980): 3–25. For a brief recent discussion of the studies of twins and of adoptees, see C. R. Cloninger and I. I. Gottesman, "Genetic and Environmental Factors in Antisocial Behavior Disorders," in Sarnoff A. Mednick et al., *The Causes of Crime: New Biological Aproaches* (New York: Cambridge University Press, 1987), pp. 96–107.

19. See, for example, the works of J. Lange, *Crime as Destiny,* trans. C. Haldane (London: Allen & Unwin, 1931). For a detailed review of these early studies, see Karl O. Christiansen, "A Review of Studies of Criminality Among Twins" and "A Preliminary Study of Criminality Among Twins," in Sarnoff A. Mednick and Karl O. Christiansen, eds., *Biosocial Bases of Criminal Behavior* (New York:

Gardner Press, 1977), pp. 89–108. See also Luke Tellegen et al., "Personality Similarity in Twins Reared Apart and Together," *Journal of Personality and Social Psychology* 54 (June 1988): 1031–1039. For recent information on other studies of twins, see Richard J. Rose, "Shared Genes, Shared Experiences, and Similarity of Personality: Data from 14,288 Adult Finnish Co-Twins," *Journal of Personality and Social Psychology* 54 (January 1988): 161–171; and David C. Rowe, "Sibling Interaction and Self-Reported Delinquent Behavior: A Study of 265 Twin Pairs," *Criminology* 23 (May 1985): 223–240.

20. Mednick and Volavka, "Biology and Crime," p. 97.
21. See Sarnoff A. Mednick et al., "Genetic Factors in Criminal Behavior: A Review," in Dan Olweus et al., eds., *Development of Antisocial and Prosocial Behavior: Research, Theories, and Issues* (New York: Academic Press, 1986), pp. 33–50.
22. P. A. Jacobs et al., "Aggressive Behavior, Mental Subnormality, and the XYY Male," *Nature* 208 (December 1965): 1351.
23. See, for example, T. R. Sarbin and J. E. Miller, "Demonism Revisited: The XYY Chromosomal Anomaly," *Issues in Criminology* 5 (1970): 195–207.
24. Mednick and Volavka, "Biology and Crime," p. 93.
25. "The Gene Hunt," *Time*, 20 March 1989, p. 62.
26. Vicki Pollock et al., "Crime Causation: Biological Theories," in Sanford H. Kadish, ed., *Encyclopedia of Crime and Justice*, vol. 1 (New York: Macmillan, 1983), p. 311. For a discussion of genetic theories and crime, see Sarnoff A. Mednick et al., "Genetic Factors in the Etiology of Criminal Behavior," in Mednick et al., *The Causes of Crime*, pp. 74–91; and C. R. Cloninger and I. I. Gottesman, "Genetic and Environmental Factors in Antisocial Behavior Disorders," in Mednick et al., *The Causes of Crime*, pp. 92–109.
27. Unless otherwise indicated, the information in this and the following sections on neuroendocrinology and neurochemistry and the autonomic nervous system are taken from Pollock et al., "Crime Causation," pp. 311–315.
28. *Ibid.*, p. 311, referring to the study of Sarnoff A. Mednick et al., "EEG as a Predictor of Antisocial Behavior," *Criminology* 19 (August 1981): 219–229.
29. Mednick and Volavka, "Biology and Crime," pp. 130–132, 143.
30. Pollock et al., "Crime Causation," p. 312. For a discussion of neurological factors and human behavior, see the following articles in Mednick et al., *The Causes of Crime:* W. Buikhuisen, "Cerebral Dysfunctions and Persistent Juvenile Delinquency," pp. 168–184; Israel Nachshon and Deborah Denno, "Violent Behavior and Cerebral Hemisphere Function," pp. 185–217; and Robert D. Hare and John F. Connolly, "Perceptual Asymmetries and Information Processing in Psychopaths," pp. 218–238.
31. Quoted in Ashley Montagu, "The Biologist Looks at Crime," *Annals of the American Academy of Social and Political Science* 217 (September 1941): 55–56.
32. Saleem A. Shah and Loren H. Roth, "Biological and Psychophysiological Factors in Criminality," in Daniel Glaser, ed., *Handbook of Criminology* (Chicago: Rand McNally, 1974), pp. 101, 123.
33. See Dan Olweus, "Aggression and Hormones: Behavioral Relationship with Testosterone and Adrenaline," in Olweus et al., eds., *Development of Antisocial and Prosocial Behavior*, pp. 51–74. See also the following essays in Mednick, *The Causes of Crime:* Robert T. Rubin, "The Neuroendocrinology and Neurochemistry of Antisocial Behavior," pp. 239–262; Dan Olweus, "Testosterone and Adrenaline: Aggressive Antisocial Behavior in Normal Adolescent Males," pp.

263–282; Daisy Schalling, "Personality Correlates of Plasma Testosterone Levels in Young Delinquents: An Example of Person-situation Interaction?" pp. 283–291.

34. Shah and Roth, "Biological and Psychophysiological Factors in Criminality," pp. 124–125.

35. "Vindication for a Leading Proponent of Theory 'People are Born to Be Fat.'" *New York Times*, 25 February 1988, p. 17, col. 1.

36. Diana Fishbein and Susan Pease, *The Effects of Diet on Behavior: Implications for Criminology and Corrections* (Boulder, Colorado: National Institute of Corrections, June 1988), pp. 2–3. For textbook discussions of many of these subjects, see Katharine Blick Hoyenga and Kermit T. Hoyenga, *Psychobiology: The Neuron and Behavior* (Pacific Grove, CA.: Brooks/Cole Publishing Co., 1988).

37. Fishbein and Pease, *ibid.*, p. 32.

38. Mednick and Volavka, "Biology and Crime," p. 106. See also Peter H. Venables, "Autonomic Nervous System Factors in Criminal Behavior," in Mednick, *The Causes of Crime*, pp. 110–137.

39. Pollock et al., "Crime Causation," p. 315. See also Sarnoff A. Mednick et al., "Biology and Violence," in Marvin E. Wolfgang and Neil A. Weiner, eds., *Criminal Violence* (Beverly Hills, Calif.: Sage Publications, 1982), pp. 21–81.

40. National Institute of Justice Program Announcement, *Research Program Plan Fiscal Year 1989* (Washington, D.C.: U.S. Department of Justice, November 1989), p. 52.

41. "Many Felony Suspects on Drugs, Study Says," *Miami Herald*, 31 July 1989, p. 8A., col. 5.

42. See, for example, Marcia R. Chaiken and Bruce D. Johnson, *Characteristics of Different Types of Drug-Involved Offenders*, National Institute of Justice (Washington, D.C.: U.S. Department of Justice, February 1988).

43. *Facts on Alcoholism*, National Council on Alcoholism, Inc., 2 Park Avenue, New York, N.Y. 10016.

44. See James B. Jacobs, *Drinking and Crime*, National Institute of Justice (Washington, D.C.: U.S. Department of Justice, 1988).

45. *Workers at Risk: Drugs and Alcohol on the Job*, The National Clearinghouse for Alcohol and Drug Information, P.O. Box 2345, Rockville, Md. 20852.

46. See *Substance Abuse Report* 20 (1 May 1989): 2.

47. "Alcohol-Related Birth Defects: Current Trends in Research," *Alcohol Health and Research World* 10 (Fall 1985): 4–5.

48. "Alcohol Abuse Costs U.S. Companies Billions, Expert Says," *Florida Times-Union*, 29 October 1988, p. A.11, col. 1.

49. "Koch Outlines a $1.2 Billion Drug Plan," *New York Times*, 18 May 1989, p. 12, col. 1.

50. Mednick and Volavka, "Biology and Crime," p. 138. See also James J. Collins, "Alcohol and Interpersonal Violence: Less Than Meets the Eye," in Neil Alan Weiner and Marvin E. Wolfgang, eds. *Pathways to Criminal Violence* (Beverly Hills, CA.: Sage Publications, 1989), pp. 49–67.

51. Paul J. Goldstein, "Drugs and Violent Crime," in Weiner and Wolfgang, eds. *Pathways to Criminal Violence*, pp. 16–48.

52. Hans Toch, "Perspectives on the Offender," in Hans Toch, ed., *Psychology of Crime and Criminal Justice* (New York: Holt, Rinehart and Winston, 1979), p. 157.

53. See William Healy, *The Individual Delinquent* (Boston: Little, Brown, 1915);

Franz Alexander and William Healy, *Roots of Crime* (New York: Knopf, 1935); and William Healy and Augusta Bronner, *New Light on Delinquency and Its Treatment* (New Haven, Conn.: Yale University Press, 1931).

54. See Sigmund Freud, *New Introductory Lectures on Psychoanalysis*, ed. and trans. James Strachey (New York: Norton, 1933). See also "Sigmund Freud," Chapter 4 in Martin et al., *Criminological Thought*, pp. 67–91.

55. For an extensive analysis, see Gerry Johnstone, "The Psychiatric Approach to Crime: a Sociological Analysis," *Economy and Society* 17 (August 1988): 317–373.

56. Herbert C. Quay, "Crime Causation: Psychological Theories," in Kadish, ed., *Encyclopedia of Crime and Justice*, vol. 1, p. 332.

57. See, for example, Cyril Burt, *The Young Delinquent* (New York: D. Appleton, 1925); Sheldon Glueck and Eleanor Glueck, *One Thousand Juvenile Delinquents: Their Treatment by Court and Clinic* (Cambridge, Mass.: Harvard University Press, 1934); and Healy and Bronner, *New Light on Delinquency and Its Treatment.*

58. See, for example, Karl F. Schuessler and Donald R. Cressey, "Personality Characteristics of Criminals," *American Journal of Sociology* 55 (March 1950): 476–486. One of the earlier researchers, Cyril Burt, was later accused of altering the data he reported. See *Psychology Today* 10 (February 1977): 33.

59. John Monahan and Henry J. Steadman, *Crime and Mental Disorder*, National Institute of Justice (Washington, D.C.: U.S. Department of Justice, September 1984). See also Robert J. Menzies and Christopher D. Webster, "Mental Disorder and Violent Crime," in Weiner and Wolfgang, eds. *Pathways to Criminal Violence*, pp. 109–136.

60. James Q. Wilson and Richard J. Herrnstein, *Crime & Human Nature*, (New York: Simon & Schuster, 1985), pp. 148–172.

61. See Jean Piaget, *The Moral Judgment of the Child* (New York: Harcourt Brace Jovanovich, 1932).

62. Lawrence Kohlberg, "The Development of Modes of Moral Thinking and Choice in Years 10 to 16," Ph.D. diss., Harvard University, 1958.

63. Lawrence Kohlberg et al., *The Just Community Approach to Corrections: A Manual* (Niantic: Connecticut Department of Corrections, 1973). For a more recent report on the experiments in this area, see Joseph E. Hickey and Peter Scharf, *Towards a Just Correctional System* (New York: Jossey-Bass, 1980); and Merry Ann Morash, "Cognitive Developmental Theory: A Basis for Juvenile Correctional Reform?" *Criminology* 19 (November 1981): 362–363.

64. Glenn D. Walters and Thomas W. White, "The Thinking Criminal: A Cognitive Model of Lifestyle Criminality," Sam Houston State University Criminal Justice Center, *Criminal Justice Research Bulletin* 4 (No. 4, 1989): 8.

65. See Albert Bandura, "The Social Learning Perspective: Mechanisms of Aggression," in Toch, ed., *Psychology of Crime and Criminal Justice.*

66. H. J. Eysenck, *Crime and Personality* (London: Routledge & Kegan Paul, 1977). For a later account, see Hans J. Eysenck and Gisli H. Gudjonsson, *The Causes and Cures of Criminality* (N.Y.: Plenum, 1989); and Peter B. Krasha, "The Sophistication of Hans Jurgen Eysenck: An Analysis and Critique of Contemporary Biological Criminology," *Criminal Justice Research Bulletin* 4 (Huntsville, Tx.: Sam Houston State University, 1989).

67. Gwynn Nettler, *Explaining Crime*, 3d ed. (New York: McGraw-Hill, 1984), p. 207.

68. Eysenck, *Crime and Personality*, p. 13.

69. Nettler, *Explaining Crime*, p. 297.

70. *Ibid.*

71. Wilson and Herrnstein, *Crime & Human Nature;* Jack P. Gibbs, "Review Essay," *Criminology* 23 (May 1985): 381.

72. Julian B. Roebuck, *Criminology Typology* (Springfield, Ill.: Chas. C Thomas, 1967), p. 39.

73. Mednick and Volavka, "Biology and Crime," pp. 143–144; emphasis in the original.

74. Edward O. Wilson, *Sociobiology: The New Synthesis* (Cambridge, Mass.: Harvard University Press, 1975), p. 4. See also Edward O. Wilson, *On Human Nature* (Cambridge, Mass.: Harvard University Press, 1978).

75. See, for example, Sociobiology Study Group of Science for the People, "Sociobiology–Another Biological Determinism," in Arthur L. Caplan, ed., *The Sociobiology Debate: Readings on the Ethical and Scientific Issues Concerning Sociobiology* (New York: Harper & Row, 1978), pp. 280–290.

76. Boyce Rensberger, "The Nature-Nurture Debate I: On Becoming Human," *Science* 83 (April 1983): 41.

77. C. Ray Jeffery, *Crime Prevention Through Environmental Design* (Beverly Hills, CA.: Sage Publications, 1971), pp. 184–185. See also Jeffery, *Criminology: An Interdisciplinary Approach* (Englewood Cliffs, N.J.: Prentice Hall, 1989).

78. Tony Platt and Paul Takagi, "Biosocial Criminology: A Critique," in Richard C. Monk, ed., *Taking Sides: Clashing Views on Controversial Issues in Crime and Criminology* (Guilford, Conn.: The Dushkin Publishing Group, Inc., 1989), p. 43.

79. For a proposal to join biology, psychology, and sociology into an interdisciplinary theory of criminal behavior, see William S. Laufer and Freda Adler, eds., *Advances in Criminological Theory: Volume I* (New Brunswick, N.J.: Transaction Books, 1989). See also Diana H. Fishbein, "Biological Perspectives in Criminology," *Criminology* 28 (February 1990): 27–72.

80. *Time,* 5 July 1982, p. 22.

81. M'Naghten's case, 8 Eng. Rep. 718 (1843). For an analysis and historical account of the insanity defense, see Norman J. Finkel, *Insanity on Trial* (N.Y.: Plenum, 1988).

82. Durham v. U.S., 214 F.2d 862 (D.C.Cir. 1954).

83. U.S. v. Brawner, 471 F. 2d 969 (D.C.Cir. 1972).

84. For a discussion of insanity tests, see Robert F. Schopp, "Returning to *M'Naughten* to Avoid Moral Mistakes: One Step Forward, or Two Steps Backward for the Insanity Defense," *Arizona Law Review* 30 (No 1, 1988): 135–153.

85. *National Law Journal,* 3 (May 1982): 11. See also Valerie P. Hans, "An Analysis of Public Attitudes Toward the Insanity Defense," *Criminology* 24 (1986): 393–414.

86. See, for example, the estimated figures in *Time,* 5 July 1982, p. 27; and *New York Times,* 27 June 1982, p. E4, col. 3.

87. People v. Ramsey, 375 N.W.2d 297 (Michigan, 1985); Mich. Comp. Laws, Section 768.36.

88. For discussions of GBMI, see "Alaska's Insanity Defense and the 'Guilty But Mentally Ill' Verdict," *Alaska Law Review* 4 (June 1987): 171–196; and Ira Michenberg, "A Pleasant Surprise: The Guilty But Mentally Ill Verdict has both Succeeded in its Own Right and Successfully Preserved the Traditional Role of the Insanity Defense," *University of Cincinnati Law Review* 55 (No. 4, 1987): 943–996.

89. See John Rosecrance, "Compulsive Gambling and the Medicalization of Deviance," *Social Problems* 32 (February 1985): 275–284.

90. U.S. v. Gillis, 773 F.2d 549, 558 (5th Cir. 1985).

91. See P. G. Bourne, *Men, Stress, and Vietnam* (Boston: Little, Brown, and Company, 1981); and Ari Kiev, "Post-Traumatic Stress Disorder: The Unrecognized Syndrome," *Trial* 24 (March 1988): 62–65.

92. See *Newsweek*, 23 November 1981, p. 103. See also "Post-Traumatic Stress Disorder–Opening Pandora's Box?" *New England Law Review* 17 (1 November 1981): 91–117.

93. *National Law Journal*, 15 (February 1982): 12.

94. *Ibid.*

95. Thomas L. Riley, "Premenstrual Syndrome as a Legal Defense," *Hamline Law Review* 9 (February 1986): 193–202. Quote is on pp. 201–202.

96. For an analysis of the battered woman syndrome as a defense in criminal cases, see Victoria Mikesell Mather, "The Skeleton in the Closet: The Battered Woman Syndrome, Self-Defense, and Expert Testimony," *Mercer Law Review* 39 (Winter 1988): 545–589. For a recent case in which the defense has been attempted, see State v. Stewart, 763 P.2d 572 (Kan. 1988). See also State v. Hennum, 441 N. W. 2d 793 (Minn. 1989).

97. For a more thorough discussion of these and other cases, see Note, "The XYY Syndrome: A Challenge to Our System of Criminal Responsibility," *New York Law Forum* 16 (Spring 1970): 232. For a more recent analysis, see Lawrence E. Taylor, "Genetically Influenced Antisocial Conduct and the Criminal Justice System," *Cleveland State Law Review* 31 (1982): 61–75. See also People v. Yukl, 372 N.Y.S.2d 313 (Sup.Ct.N.Y. 1975).

98. Cobey v. State, 533 A. 2d 944 (Md.Ct.Spec. App. 1987), *cert. denied*, State v. Cobey, 538 A. 2d 778 (1988).

99. "From Victim to Victimizer? Study Ties Criminal Behavior to Childhood Head Injuries," *American Bar Association Journal*, 1 (September 1986): 17.

CHAPTER 5

This chapter analyzes sociological theories of criminal behavior, especially structural theories, which consider society's social structure or organization. The two basic approaches are consensus and conflict. In the first, folkways, mores, and laws are seen as reflecting society's values. Some crime is seen as inevitable, even functional. In the conflict approach, however, criminal behavior is seen as emerging from conflicts within society. The consensus approach is illustrated by the ecological school, the contributions of Durkheim and Merton, and the subculture theories. Discussion of these early theories will be followed by a look at some of their modern counterparts. Examination of the conflict approach will distinguish the pluralist model (which sees conflict as emerging from multiple sources) from the critical view, which is based on the Marxist position of conflict created by capitalism.

OUTLINE

Sociological Theories of Criminal Behavior I: The Social-Structural Approach

KEY TERMS

anomie
concentric circle
conflict
consensus
culture conflict theory
differential association
differential opportunity
ecological school
functional consequences
labeling theory
norms
routine activity approach
social system
status offenses
subculture

Most of the explanations of criminal behavior examined thus far have focused on the *characteristics* of criminals and how they differ from non-criminals. The emphasis has been on individual characteristics, although the cartographic school attempted to relate crime to characteristics outside the individual. Climate, topography, natural resources, and geographic location were studied in relation to criminal behavior; and that school of thought, although a very early one, was a forerunner of the approaches discussed in this chapter.

Contemporary sociologists have approached the study of the etiology of crime from two perspectives: structure and process. The first views crime in relation to the social organization or structure of society and asks how crime is related to the **social system.** What are the characteristics of the situation or social *structure* in which crime takes place? Do crime rates vary as these situations or structures change? The second approach looks at the *process* by which criminals are produced, but it is not an individualistic approach. Sociologists look for *patterns* of variables and relationships that might explain how people become criminals.

Although sociological theories may be classified abstractly as structural or process theories, most theories do not fall exclusively into either category. Likewise, it is not possible to isolate sociological from nonsociological theories. However, for analysis, some categorizations may be made. Chapters 5 and 6 examine the explanations and theories that illustrate the *sociological* approach to criminal behavior.

EARLY SOCIAL-STRUCTURAL APPROACHES

Early sociologists studied crime through a variety of approaches, some of which influenced modern sociological theory.

Ecological Theories

The study of ecology concerns the distribution of phenomena and their relationship to their environment. The **ecological school** attempts to explain crime as a function of social change that occurs along with environmental change. Discussion of the cartographic school in Europe noted some nineteenth-century studies of the geographic and spatial distribution of crime, but in the United States the ecological approach began much later.

The early ecological school in the United States was centered during the 1920s and 1930s at the University of Chicago, where it was strongly influenced by the works of Ernest Burgess and Robert Park.[1] Burgess and Park developed their ecological approach to explain the growth of Chicago. They saw the city as a living, growing, organic whole, and the various areas of the city as organs that served different functions.

Studies of the city's areas of high crime rates and other forms of deviance indicated to researchers that even the deviant's world was characterized by differentiated social roles, which were both ordered and stratified with rules that were enforced. They also had rewards and satisfactions, not all of which were deviant.[2] Some researchers found evidence of this approach in their studies of hobos and homeless men, who were found to have a stratified society, defined social roles, regulations, and traditions.[3]

The city's characteristics, social change, and distribution of people and their behavior have been studied by means of the **concentric circle**, an approach developed to study Chicago but thought to be equally applicable to other cities. The concentric circle theory divides the city into five zones. At the center of the city is Zone 1, the *central business district.* This zone is characterized by light manufacturing, retail trade, and commercialized recreation. Zone 2, surrounding the central business district, is the *zone of transition* from residential to business. This zone is heavily populated by low-income people, although it also typically has an area of high-cost luxury housing. Zone 3 is the *zone of working-class homes*, which is less deteriorated than the zone of transition and populated largely by

Although the area of the city has been associated with crime, there is no evidence that the area *causes* crime.

"workers whose economic status enables them to have many of the comforts and even some of the luxuries the city has to offer." Zone 4, the *area of middle-class dwellers*, is populated largely by professional people, clerical forces, owners of small businesses, and the managerial class. On the outer edge of the city is Zone 5, *the commuters' zone*. This zone includes satellite towns and suburbs. Many of the occupants vacate the area during the day and commute to the city for their employment.[4]

To explain crime, delinquency, and other vices, Burgess and Park stated that the key zone is Zone 2, transition. Because of the movement of businesses into this zone, it becomes an undesirable place to live even though it previously claimed some of the most desirable housing in the city. Houses deteriorate. Zoning laws change. People who can afford to move out do so, and there is no prospect of improving the housing in the area without public subsidy. "The general effect of this process has been the gradual evacuation of the central areas in all large American cities, leading to the expression frequently heard: The city is dying at its heart."[5]

The population in the city is segregated by economic and occupational forces. The poor live in Zone 2, and they represent mainly unskilled workers. This economic and occupational segregation often leads to racial and ethnic segregation. Zone 2 is characterized by warehouses, pawn shops, cheap theaters, restaurants, and a breakdown in the usual institutional methods of social control. The investigators hypothesized that crime and vice would flourish there.

Clifford Shaw, often with other associates, conducted several research projects to determine the relationship between crime (especially juvenile delinquency) and the Chicago zones. Shaw and Henry McKay plotted the residences of delinquent youths on transparent maps. They marked off the city in square-mile areas and computed a delinquency rate for each area. Then they looked at the distribution of other community problems in Chicago—rates of school truancy, young adult offenders, infant mortality, tuberculosis, and mental disorder—and compared them with rates of delinquency and adult crime. "It will be noted that there is not a single instance in which they do not vary together. . . . On the basis of the facts presented, it is clear that delinquency is not an isolated phenomenon."[6] Some of the conclusions of the ecological school are featured in Exhibit 5.1.

Evaluation

Numerous criticisms have been directed at the ecological studies, but these must be analyzed in light of the investigator's actual claim. Shaw and McKay did not argue that the area *causes* crime, as some have suggested. In fact, they specifically warned that cause-and-effect relationships should not be assumed because high correlations between variables exist. Although Zone 2 may attract or collect criminals, another explanation of the higher rates may be differential law enforcement. Police may be more likely to make arrests in Zone 2 than in other zones.

EXHIBIT 5.1

Conclusions of the Ecological School

1. There are marked variations in the rate of school truants, juvenile delinquents, and adult criminals between areas in Chicago. Some areas are characterized by very high rates, while others show very low rates. . . .

2. Rates of truancy, delinquency, and adult crime tend to vary inversely in proportion to the distance from the center of the city. In general the nearer to the center of the city a given locality is, the higher will be its rates of delinquency and crime. . . .

3. Another striking finding in this study is the marked similarity in the distribution of truants, juvenile delinquents, and adult criminals in the city. Those communities which show the highest rates of juvenile delinquency also show, as a rule, the highest rates of truancy and adult crime. . . .

4. The difference in rates of truancy, delinquency, and crime reflect differences in community backgrounds. High rates occur in the areas which are characterized by physical deterioration and declining populations. . . .

In this study . . . we have indicated in a general way that there are characteristic social conditions which accompany crime and delinquency. . . .

5. The main high rate areas of the city—those near the Loop, around the Stock Yards and the South Chicago steel mills—have been characterized by high rates over a long period. . . . Relatively high rates persisted in certain areas notwithstanding the fact that the composition of population has changed markedly. . . .

6. The rate of recidivism varies directly with the rate of individual delinquents and inversely with the distance from the center of the city. . . . Delinquents living in areas of high delinquent rates are more likely to become recidivists, and . . . the recidivists from these areas are more likely to appear in court three or more times than are recidivists from areas with low rates of delinquents.

SOURCE: Clifford R. Shaw et al., *Delinquency Areas* (Chicago: University of Chicago Press, 1929), pp. 198–204; footnotes deleted.

The ecologists have also been criticized on the grounds that ecology does not explain all types of deviant behavior. Their response is that it was never intended to do so. It was intended to explain mainly those offenses involving groups and social organizations that usually engage in crimes against property. Those crimes account for a large proportion of the crimes committed by young boys.

The Chicago studies found that areas with high rates and those with low rates of crime and delinquency were distinguished on the basis of physical status, economic status, and population composition, as well as social values. Data from other cities supported these findings. Furthermore, despite changes in the population, rates of crime and delinquency remained highest in the zone of transition. Shaw and McKay concluded that the social and economic crime-producing factors were inherent in the community and constituted a normal reaction to living in a disorganized area.

In contrast with children who live in the zone of transition are those who live in the zones with better physical and economic conditions. These children are not exposed to contrasting values; their values are relatively consistent. Shaw and McKay found few cases of delinquency among these children.

In the revised edition of Shaw and McKay's *Juvenile Delinquency and Urban Areas*, an introduction by contemporary sociologist James F. Short, Jr., pointed out that although much has been learned about delinquency in the years since the original publication, the book has not only stood the test of time but also remains a stimulus for research and for programs of delinquency and crime control. The revised edition also presents new data showing that rates of delinquency and crime are highest in the zone of transition.

Several sociologists have written critical analyses of Shaw and McKay's theory and research. They have questioned the methodology of the studies, the representativeness of the data, and the logic of the research. They have also noted that the ecological approach does not explain varying rates of crime when ethnic groups are compared.[7] Many modern scholars approach ecology by a careful analysis of the geography of crime.

In an attempt to refocus the study of criminal behavior on sociology rather than social psychology, Rodney Stark has emphasized the need to look at "kinds of places" rather than "kinds of people." He examined the literature on ecology and attempted to codify the theories and empirical research. His 30 propositions are stated in Exhibit 5.2.[8]

Durkheim's Contributions

Émile Durkheim (1858–1917), a noted French sociologist, made significant contributions to the study of all human behavior. But his greatest contribution to the study of crime was his idea that crime is both normal and has **functional consequences** and that no society can be completely exempt from it: "There is . . . no phenomenon that presents more indisputably all the symptoms of normality, since it appears closely connected with the conditions of all collective life."[9]

According to Durkheim, it is impossible for all people to be alike and to hold the same moral consciousness that would prevent any dissent. Because there will always be some individuals who differ from the collective type, inevitably some of these divergences will include criminal behavior—not because the act is intrinsically criminal but because the collectivity will define the act as criminal.

Durkheim saw crime as the product of norms. The concept of wrong is necessary to give meaning to right and is inherent in that concept. Even a community of saints will create sinners. According to Durkheim, crime is also functional and is a necessary prerequisite for social change. For a society to be flexible enough to permit positive deviation, it must also permit negative deviation. If no deviation is permitted, society will become stagnant. Consequently,

> nothing is good indefinitely and to an unlimited extent. . . . To make progress, individual originality must be able to express itself. In order that the originality of the idealist whose dreams transcend his century may find expression, it is necessary that the originality of the criminal, who is below the level of his time, shall also be possible. One does not occur without the other.[10]

Crime helps prepare society for such changes. The criminal, says Durkheim, should no longer be viewed as a completely unacceptable human being. Crime is one of the prices we pay for freedom.

In 1893 Durkheim introduced his version of the concept of **anomie**, which derives from a Greek word meaning "lawlessness." Durkheim was not the first to use the term, nor did he develop the concept as extensively as did the American sociologist Robert Merton. But Durkheim was responsible for making the concept an integral part of sociology and criminology.

Durkheim believed that one of society's most important elements is its social cohesion, or *social solidarity*, which represents a *collective conscience*. As Highlight 5.1 indicates, the absence of a sense of community is viewed by some as a major problem in our society. In explaining this phenomenon, Durkheim defined two types of solidarity, mechanical and organic. Primitive societies are characterized by *mechanical solidarity*, which is dominated by the collective conscience. The type of law manifests this dominance—the reason for law is to repress individuals from acting in a way that would threaten the collective conscience. As societies become larger and more complex, the emphasis in law shifts from the collective conscience to the individual wronged, and law thus becomes *restitutive*. This shift from mechanical to *organic solidarity* is characterized by an increased need for a division of labor, a division that is often forced and therefore abnormal, leading to the creation of unnatural differences in class and status. People are then less homogeneous; and the traditional forms of social control, appropriate to a simple homogeneous society, are no longer very effective in controlling behavior. Greater loneliness, more social isolation, and a loss of identity result, with a consequent state of anomie, or normlessness, replacing the former state of solidarity and providing an atmosphere in which crimes and other antisocial acts may develop and flourish.[11]

EXHIBIT 5.2

A Theory of "Kinds of Places": Propositions Derived from 30 Years of Ecological Research

1. The greater the density of a neighborhood, the more association between those most and least predisposed to deviance.

2. The greater the density of a neighborhood, the higher the level of moral cynicism.

3. To the extent that neighborhoods are dense and poor, homes will be crowded.

4. Where homes are more crowded, there will be a greater tendency to congregate outside the home in places and circumstances that raise levels of temptation and opportunity to deviate.

5. Where homes are more crowded, there will be lower levels of supervision of children.

6. Reduced levels of child supervision will result in poor school achievement, with a consequent reduction in stakes in conformity and an increase in deviant behavior.

7. Where homes are more crowded, there will be higher levels of conflict within families weakening attach-

ments and thereby stakes in conformity.

8. Where homes are crowded, members will be much less able to shield discreditable acts and information from one another, further increasing moral cynicism.

9. Poor, dense neighborhoods tend to be mixed-use neighborhoods.

10. Mixed use increases familiarity with and easy access to places offering the opportunity for deviance.

11. Mixed-use neighborhoods offer increased opportunity for congregating outside the home in places conducive to deviance.

12. Poor, dense, mixed-use neighborhoods have high transience rates.

13. Transience weakens extra-familial attachments.

14. Transience weakens voluntary organizations, thereby directly reducing both informal and formal sources of social control (see Proposition 25).

15. Transience reduces levels of community surveillance.

16. Dense, poor, mixed-use, transient neighborhoods will also tend to be dilapidated.

17. Dilapidation is a social stigma for residents.

18. High rates of neighborhood deviance are a social stigma for residents.

19. Living in stigmatized neighborhoods causes a reduction in an individual's stake in conformity.

20. The more successful and potentially best role models will flee stigmatized neighborhoods whenever possible.

21. More successful and conventional people will resist moving into a stigmatized neighborhood.

22. Stigmatized neighborhoods will tend to be overpopulated by the most demoralized kinds of people.

23. The larger the relative number of demoralized residents, the greater the number of available "victims."

24. The larger the relative number of demoralized residents, the lower will be residents' perception of chances for success, and hence they will have lower perceived stakes in conformity.

25. Stigmatized neighborhoods will suffer from more lenient law enforcement.

26. More lenient law enforcement increases moral cynicism.

27. More lenient law enforcement increases the incidence of crime and deviance.

28. More lenient law enforcement draws people to a neighborhood on the basis of their involvement in crime and deviance.

29. When people are drawn to a neighborhood on the basis of their participation in crime and deviance, the visibility of such activities and the opportunity to engage in them increases.

30. The higher the visibility of crime and deviance, the more it will appear to others that these activities are safe and rewarding.

SOURCE: Rodney Stark, "Deviant Places: A Theory of the Ecology of Crime," *Criminology* 25 (November 1987): 893–909, emphasis deleted.

HIGHLIGHT 5.1

THE POWER OF MYTH: A DIALOGUE

MOYERS:

What happens when a society no longer embraces a powerful mythology?

CAMPBELL:

What we've got on our hands. If you want to find out what it means to have a society without any rituals, read the *New York Times*.

MOYERS:

And you'd find?

CAMPBELL:

The news of the day including destructive and violent acts by young people who don't know how to behave in a civilized society.

MOYERS:

Society has provided them no rituals by which they become members of the tribe, of the community. All children need to be twice born, to learn to function rationally in the present world, leaving childhood behind. I think of that passage in the first book of Corinthians: "When I was a child, I spake as a child, I understood as a child, I thought as a child: but when I became a man, I put away childish things."

CAMPBELL:

That's exactly it. That's the significance of the puberty rites. In primal societies, there are teeth knocked out, there are scarifications, there are circumcisions, there are all kinds of things done. So you don't have your little baby body anymore, you're something else entirely.

When I was a kid, we wore short trousers, you know, knee pants. And then there was a great moment when you put on long pants. Boys now don't get that. I see even five-year-olds walking around with long trousers. When are they going to know that they're now men and must put aside childish things?

MOYERS:

Where do the kids growing up in the city—on 125th and Broadway, for example—where do these kids get their myths today?

CAMPBELL:

They make them up themselves. This is why we have graffiti all over the city. These kids have their own gangs and their own initiations and their own morality, and they're doing the best they can. But they're dangerous because their own laws are not those of the city. They have not been initiated into our society.

MOYERS:

Rollo May says there is so much violence in American society today because there are no more great myths to help young men and women relate to the world or to understand that world beyond what is seen.

CAMPBELL:

Yes, but another reason for the high level of violence here is that America has no ethos.

SOURCE: Joseph Campbell with Bill Moyers, *The Power of Myth* (New York: Doubleday, 1988), p. 8.

Evaluation

Durkheim had a strong impact on other theorists discussed in this chapter. His theory of the relationship between social integration or anomie and suicide is still important today, with a recent study of suicide and other causes of death finding support for his approach. Events such as presidential elections result in increased social integration in the society, and during those periods, rates of suicide and other causes of death decrease. Such findings "suggest the importance of increasing the social integration of societies and of encouraging social participation by individual members of those societies."[12]

Robert Merton's Theory of Anomie

Durkheim's belief that crime is normal and his theory of anomie form the basis of Robert Merton's contributions toward an understanding of criminal behavior. Whereas Durkheim's theory of anomie is very abstract, Merton, a contemporary sociologist, develops a paradigm and relates the theory to real cases in American life.[13]

Merton was reacting against biological theories—which suggest that behavior is the result of inherited traits—and psychiatric, especially Freudian, theories—which state that humans are characterized by the inevitable struggle between biological desires and social restraints. The problem, said Merton, is to answer the question of "why it is that the frequency of deviant behavior varies within different social structures and how it happens that the deviations have different shapes and patterns in different social structures."[14] Merton's thesis is that *social structures* exert pressure on some persons to behave in nonconforming rather than conforming ways. His approach is therefore sociological, with an emphasis on the social structure. If evidence is found for this thesis, it will follow that nonconforming behavior is as normal as conforming behavior.

Merton begins by suggesting that all social and cultural structures are characterized by two elements that are not always separable in reality but that may be categorized that way for analysis. First are the *goals*, which are to be the aspirations of all individuals in the society. These goals are those things that are worth striving for. Second are the *means* by which those goals may be obtained. The means are socially approved methods, and that involves the element of norms, which are culturally defined. A society's norms define not only the goals but also the methods by which those goals may be obtained. According to Merton, when there is a focus on the goals to the virtual exclusion of the norms and when the socially approved means for obtaining those goals are not equally available to all, many people will turn to unapproved and unacceptable means to achieve those goals. For example, if there is a great emphasis on winning a football game, with no significant emphasis on doing so by means of the game's acceptable rules, the players may resort to slugging one another or even bribing other players. The result is a situation of normlessness, or anomie.

Merton suggests that in contemporary American culture the emphasis is primarily on goals, not means, and that the main goal is a monetary one. Noting that money is "well adapted to become a symbol of prestige," Merton argues that to many, money is a value in itself. Americans are also faced with the pressure to be highly ambitious. It is assumed that high goals are open to all and that all should aspire to those goals, that what may appear to be failure now is but a steppingstone to success, and that real failure consists only in quitting or lessening one's ambition.[15]

Modes of Adaptation

After examining these American cultural patterns, Merton designed a typology to describe the methods, or *modes*, of adaptation that were available to those who react to society's goals and means. He identified five modes: conformity, innovation, ritualism, retreatism, and rebellion. Table 5.1 summarizes Merton's typology. It is important to remember that these are *modes of adaptation*, not personality types. Merton is not suggesting that individuals may be categorized as personalities that fit the typologies but that in a given situation one of the modes of adapting to the social structure may be adopted. Merton is talking about socially or culturally *approved* means and goals, and he argues that the modes of adaptation are ways of adapting to the tensions of goal attainment in a competitive society.

Conformity Conformity describes the acceptance of a society's goals and also of its means. It is the most frequently used adaptation.

TABLE 5.1   A Typology of Modes of Individual Adaptation

Modes of Adaptation	Culture Goals	Institutionalized Means
Conformity	+	+
Innovation	+	−
Ritualism	−	+
Retreatism	−	−
Rebellion	±	±

+ signifies acceptance.

− signifies rejection.

± signifies rejection of prevailing values and substitution of new values.

SOURCE: Reprinted with permission of the Free Press, a Division of Macmillan, Inc., from *Social Theory and Social Structure* by Robert K. Merton, p. 194. Copyright 1968, 1967, by Robert K. Merton.

Innovation—Innovation represents acceptance of the goals but rejection of the means for obtaining them. For example, if a college degree is the goal, the student who adopts that goal but who chooses to reject the acceptable means for attaining it may cheat.

Merton illustrates the innovative adaptation as it leads to deviant and criminal behavior. He draws attention to criminal behavior engaged in by many people but which is not reacted to officially by society. Merton refers to studies that indicate that the social class structure, which imposes the goals, also prevents some people from attaining them by socially approved means. The low status and income of unskilled labor and the basic occupational opportunities open to members of the lower class do not often permit them to achieve high status in terms of power and income, and they may therefore turn to deviant behavior.

Merton says that the social-structural pressure to attain the goals, along with the social-structural limitations of the availability of legitimate means, produces the pressure toward deviant behavior. The social structure places incompatible demands on persons of the lower socioeconomic class. The key to widespread deviant behavior is that the social structure is proclaiming that *all* should achieve these goals but is blocking the legitimate efforts of large numbers of persons to do so: "In this setting, a cardinal American virtue, 'ambition,' promotes a cardinal American vice, 'deviant behavior.'"[16]

This situation helps explain the high rate of crime in poverty areas. Merton is quick to point out that poverty does not *cause* crime but that when goals are stressed for all and when social structure places limits on attaining those goals, high rates of criminal behavior should be expected.

Ritualism—Ritualism is rejection of the goals but acceptance of the means. People lose sight of the reasons for doing things, such as going to church, but continue the socially approved methods, thus making a ritual out of the method. Merton says this adaptation is more characteristic of the lower-middle class than of any other social class, whereas innovation is more characteristic of the lower class. The middle class stresses the socially approved means of obtaining goals, thus making it more difficult for its members to deviate from those means. Often this adaptation is characteristic of the people who lower their ambitions to avoid the frustrations that come with failure: "Don't aim high and you won't be disappointed."

Retreatism—Retreatism, the least common of the five adaptations, refers to the rejection of both the goals and the means. This adaptation occurs after a person has accepted both the goals and means but has repeatedly failed to achieve the goals by legitimate means. At the same time, because of prior socialization, the individual is not able to adopt illegitimate means. Thus, in terms of the social structure, he or she is cut off from both legitimate *and* illegitimate methods of obtaining society's goals. Both the goals and the means are rejected. "The escape is complete, the conflict is eliminated and the individual is asocialized.''[17] Conventional society is more critical of the adaptor than of the innovator, who is at least smart; the conformist, who keeps society running as it was intended; and the ritualist, who at least accepts the means. The retreatist mode of adaptation represents a nonproductive liability to conventional society and is characterized by psychotics, autists, outcasts, tramps, chronic drunkards, drug addicts, vagrants, and vagabonds. People who follow this form of adaptation do so mainly as isolates, although they may gravitate toward other, similar deviants. But it is not a collective form of adaptation.

Rebellion Rebellion is characterized by a rejection of the goals and means of society and an attempt to establish a new social order. Merton says this adaptation is clearly different from the others, as it represents an attempt to change the social structure rather than to make an individual adaptation within that structure. It is therefore an attempt to *institutionalize new goals and means* for the rest of society.

Evaluation

Merton has raised some criticisms of his own theory. The theory does not take into account social-psychological variables that might explain the adoption of one adaptation over the other. It only briefly examines rebellious behavior, and it does not consider the social-structural elements that might predispose an individual toward one adaptation over another. Merton, acknowledging that it might not be possible to explain *all* types of behavior, defined his theory as a prelude to a full explanation of deviant behavior.[18]

Others have argued that Merton's theory of anomie does not explain the nonutilitarian element of much juvenile delinquency, which appears to be engaged in for fun and not to meet society's specific goals. It has also been argued that the theory does not explain the destructive nature of some delinquent and criminal acts, that it does not explain crime in societies where esteem goals are not seen as available to everyone, and that it has not been sufficiently tested empirically.[19]

Some have advocated abandoning Merton's approach,[20] while others have proposed revisions of the theory.[21] More recently, Margaret Farnworth and Michael J. Leiber have analyzed criticisms of the theory and concluded as follows:

> Merton's theory of strain and crime has withstood half a century of theoretical controversy, but recent disillusionment with its empirical verification has led many to reject it as a viable explanation for delinquency. We question that the theory has been falsified by evidence to this date on the grounds that conceptual reinterpretations have differed from Merton's original statement.[22] But even those who have tested Merton's theory and not found full support for his conclusions have emphasized the practical aspects of his approach. Merton's theory has gained wide support, and its influence can be seen in some of the subculture theories.

Subculture Theories

The theory of anomie, as developed by Durkheim and Merton, established a framework for the development of **subculture** theories of delinquent and criminal behavior. Modern subculture theories were preceded by the classic study of Frederic M. Thrasher, who saw the juvenile gang developing in Chicago as a result of social disorganization in the zone of transition.[23] For the past couple of decades little attention has been paid to Thrasher's study of gangs or, for that matter, any studies of gangs. Recent gang-related crimes, especially those associated with substance abuse, have resulted in a refocusing of attention on gangs. The gang rape and beating of a young female financial adviser in New York's Central Park in the spring of 1989 drew front page headlines for weeks as the public eagerly awaited news of the victim's fight for life. After two weeks she came out of a coma, and as noted earlier, she was back at work on a limited schedule by the end of 1989.

In late May 1989 a group of forty youths, ranging in age from twelve to eighteen, roamed through New York's Greenwich Village, using ice picks and razors to threaten pedestrians as they grabbed gold chains and other valuables. Gangs are linked to the spread of drugs and violence throughout the U.S.,[24] and as Highlight 5.2 indicates, some school administrators have taken measures to decrease gang activities. Although most of the gang members are males, there is increasing evidence of female gangs.[25]

Although Thrasher did not specifically talk about subcultures, his work is a forerunner to these theories. The subculture theorists do not agree on why certain norms exist within the subcultures, but all their studies may be characterized by their attempt to understand delinquent behavior as sanctioned by the subculture and influenced by its status requirements.

Lower-Class Boy and Middle-Class Measuring Rod

The publication in 1955 of Albert Cohen's *Delinquent Boys* set the stage for a new look at subculture theories as an explanation for delinquency. Cohen says the lower-class child is constantly measured by a middle-class measuring rod and suggests that the lower-class boy accepts the goals of the middle class but is unable to meet those goals by the socially approved means. The lower-class boy must function within institutions that are run by middle-class people who judge him according to their standards. All are expected to strive for accomplishments and all are expected to succeed.

The lower-class boy, however, does not have the prior socialization that the middle-class boy has had and is therefore unprepared for aspiring to and achieving middle-class goals. He has been socialized to live for today and to place more value on physical aggression than does the middle class. He is also less likely as a child to have played with educational toys, and

HIGHLIGHT 5.2

ON GUARD AGAINST GANGS AT A LOS ANGELES SCHOOL

At Jordan High School, in the heart of Watts, it is forbidden to wear brown or green or purple, to sport colored belts or sneakers or a hat of any kind, to display a bandanna or wear braided hair or more than one stud earring.

In a setting in which gang colors and insignia like these can quickly start a confrontation, 13 security guards, two police officers, one parole officer and several administrators go on patrols with walkie-talkies. A painter checks the walls each morning to remove any graffiti that might touch off a battle; a student making a hand signal associated with gangs can be suspended.

Here at David Starr Jordan High School, where students from troubled housing projects mingle, where the territories of at least six gangs intersect, the security concerns of inner-city schools come out in high relief.

For some students at highest risk, particularly on their dangerous walk to school, the city school department is opening a separate group of classrooms in the housing project where they live.

As the use of crack has spread in the cities and gangs' activity has intensified, tensions have intensified in high school hallways, particularly in New York and Los Angeles. Extra guards and metal detectors have helped New York

reduce violence in schools, but officials there have not imposed strict restrictions on dress and insignia because the threat to students on their way to and from school comes more from random groups of youths than from organized gangs.

Peter Blauvelt, president of the National Association of School Security Directors, said Jordan's security measures were "probably more stringent than any other place I've heard of." But he also said that Jordan was only an extreme example of what is going on all over the country.

To varying degrees, the security measures have proved effective, but they exact their own costs.

Priority on safety and order

"It takes a very high toll on burnout as far as teachers and administrators are concerned," Mr. Blauvelt said. "You can never, never relax your vigilance."

At Jordan High, the tension of potential violence commingles with the rhythms of high school life, with English tests, with art class, with cheerleading practice. Teachers and administrators say they must make safety and order their first concern before trying to focus their students' attention on schoolwork. This is a school

where just showing up each day is as much a measure of success as an achievement test score.

"I tip my hat to any student who comes here and graduates from here," said Joseph P. Santana, the assistant principal. "What they have to work with in this school—making it through shows me they have guts, they have pride, they have integrity. When these kids come to school they've got to be watching their backs all the way. You see the environment: it's not conducive to peace of mind. Over the past weekend, 8 people were killed and 12 were wounded in gang-related problems in this area."

Of the 1,800 students, he said, 300 to 400 are absent each day. To counter that, one teacher says he asks half the class to stand up at the start of the year and tells his students, perhaps with a bit of exaggeration, "If you don't get it together, at the current dropout rate, that's how many will be left at the end of the year."

There are no comprehensive figures on violence in and around the school. Yet teachers and students alike describe Jordan, with its strict security, as a sanctuary from the violence and hopelessness of the neighborhoods outside. For many students it is the walk to school, through the projects and across

HIGHLIGHT 5.2 (Continued)

gang boundaries, that poses the day's most difficult test.

"Coming to school, you've just got to be cool," said Luz Maria Hernandez, a ninth grader. "If you see gang members, you just smile or you don't look at them. For the kids who have to go through the projects, I mean it's dangerous. A lot of things go on in those projects."

Wesley Mitchell, chief of the Los Angeles schools' police department, said the spread of crack had intensified violence tenfold in the communities around the schools and had increased tensions, if not violence, in the schools themselves. What we have seen, more than an increase in violence in the schools, is increased jeopardy to children trying to get to and from schools," he said.

For many students who live in the Imperial Courts housing project, 12 blocks south, the daily confrontation at school with students from the Jordan Downs project and the walk through the territory of the Grape Street gang have been too much. The school is taking an extraordinary step to accommodate them.

Work is under way to open small classrooms in the next few weeks for up to 60 students in housing units of the Imperial Courts project, said Sidney A. Thompson, Deputy Superinten-

dent for operations in the Los Angeles Unified School District.

"They're not coming to school, so we'll take the school to the youngsters," he said. "We've never done that before."

Santiago James Tomlinson, the dean of students, points out that no one has been killed at Jordan. But in his job as one of the school's disciplinarians, he sees a daily traffic of hardened teenagers.

The body language of clothes

As the bell rang for lunch one recent day, the situation at Jordan was under control.

"You see that group just chilling-out over there?" Mr. Santana said. "Does everything look normal to you? It's not. There's a guy over there with a hat on."

A hat is part of the gang uniform, along with low-slung trousers and, for the Hispanic youths, a shirt buttoned at the throat. Violation of the rule against wearing hats could be a signal that gang violence is brewing, Mr. Santana said.

Miss Hernandez, whose parents brought her from Mexico in infancy, stood at the edge of the playing field as the cheerleaders practiced near the wall that

keeps out intruders from the Jordan Downs project.

The gang as a family

Peer pressure leads many young people to join gangs, the ninth grader said. "You don't want to walk around with everybody saying you're a dork or something. You want to be with the right crowd. The gang is like their family. There's the feeling that they'll be there for you."

Harvey Boulton, a running back with the football team, was practicing nearby for the next night's game, with Roosevelt High School. He said gangs have tried to recruit him, but he is hoping a college football team will recruit him.

"We have some excellent athletes in the projects, but they don't care, and some guys in other areas are afraid to come here," he said. "So we just work with what we've got."

Then he and his teammates held up their index fingers in what looked at first like a forbidden gang signal. Then they grinned, saying, "We're No. 1."

SOURCE: Seth Mydans, "On Guard Against Gangs at a Los Angeles School," *New York Times,* 19 November 1989, p. 1, col. 2., Copyright © 1989/by The New York Times Company. Reprinted by permission.

he has restricted aspirations. He thus finds himself deprived of status, as compared with middle-class norms. His problem is further complicated because he accepts the middle-class standards. He learns this acceptance from his parents (who want him to achieve at a higher level than they did), from the mass media, from the realization that some people do move up in the social hierarchy, and from the cultural emphasis on competition. The lower-class boy learns that the way to status and success is to adopt middle-class values, but he is not able to do so. The result is low self-esteem and major adjustment problems. To meet these problems, says Cohen, lower-class boys develop a subculture that inverts middle-class values.[26]

The basic difference between Merton's adaptations and Cohen's subculture theory lies in Cohen's explanation of the subculture's emergence. According to Cohen, the "crucial condition for the emergence of new cultural forms is the existence, *in effective interaction with one another, of a number of actors with similar problems of adjustment.*" The emphasis is on *interaction.* The boys look for signs or gestures of agreement from their peers. As those signs gradually appear, the boys as a group become progressively committed to the new behavior, a process Cohen calls *mutual conversion.* Again, the process of interaction is crucial: ". . . we do not first convert ourselves and then others. The acceptability of an idea to oneself depends upon its acceptability to others."[27] As these new group standards emerge, the new subculture is formed. The characteristics of the adolescent subculture according to Cohen are featured in Exhibit 5.3.

Evaluation—The reviews of Cohen's book have been generally positive, and his theory has been given considerable recognition in sociological literature.[28] Nevertheless, some criticisms have been raised. Cohen's statement that the working-class boy measures himself by middle-class norms has been questioned.[29] Cohen was ambivalent about this point, noting that some working-class boys may not be concerned about middle-class values. But he argues that most children do seek the approval of adults with whom they have significant contacts. Critics have responded that Cohen is not convincing; and that if there are class differences in socialization, it is reasonable to expect that they will affect the working-class boy's perspective of how he is perceived by middle-class people.[30]

Cohen's use of the psychological concept of *reaction formation* to describe the culture of the delinquent gang has also been questioned. His development of this concept is based on the assumption that the lower-class boy wants to improve himself in terms of middle-class status. But Cohen also suggests that the lower-class boy is constantly confronted by middle-class standards of the people who are in charge of the agencies within his community, "which he does not share. . . . [In order] to win favor of the people in charge he must change his habits, his values, his ambitions, his speech and his associates. . . . Having sampled what they have to offer, he turns to the street or to his 'clubhouse' in a cellar where

EXHIBIT 5.3

?

Characteristics of the Adolescent Subculture

1. *Nonutilitarian.* The delinquents do not steal things for which they have a need or a desire. They steal "for the hell of it."

2. *Malicious.* Delinquent activities are characterized by "an enjoyment in the discomfiture of others, a delight in the defiance of taboos itself."

3. *Negativistic.* The norms of the delinquent subculture appear to be the polar opposites of those of adult society.

4. *Versatility.* They steal a variety of different things.

5. *Short-run hedonism.* The boys are interested in momentary pleasures, giving no thought to planning activities or budgeting time and money for the future. The gang usually congregates with no specific activity in mind.

6. *Group autonomy.* The gang is intolerant of restraint except from the informal pressures within the group itself. The members resist efforts of social institutions, such as the family, school, or church, to regulate their lives.

SOURCE: Adapted with permission of the Free Press, a Division of Macmillan, Inc., from Albert K. Cohen, *Delinquent Boys: The Culture of the Gang.* Copyright 1955 by the Free Press, copyright renewed 1983 by Albert K. Cohen.

'facilities' are meager but human relations more satisfying."[31] Critics argue that this statement does not support the concept of reaction formation as Cohen wanted but, on the contrary, suggests that the lower-class boy does not want to strive for middle-class standards and resents the intrusion into his community of those who hold such values and try to impose them on him.

Cohen's description of the delinquent subculture as nonutilitarian, malicious, and negativistic has also been criticized. Some of the activities attributed to the lower-class gang are not characteristic of those gangs today but do characterize some middle-class delinquent activities, which are excluded from Cohen's theories. In contrast, many of the lower-class gangs' activities are much more serious than Cohen indicates. The critics thus question what Cohen considers to be the facts supporting his theory.[32]

Techniques of Neutralization

The theory of *techniques of neutralization*, developed by Gresham Sykes and David Matza, and Matza's theory of delinquency and drift are in one sense social-process theories. But we consider them here because of their relationship to the subculture theories, which do involve an analysis of the social structure.

In developing their theory, Sykes and Matza attack Cohen's assumption that delinquents are responding to values that differ from those of the adult society as a reaction to the failures they experienced in their initial acceptance of those values. First, they argue, if delinquents had established a subculture with different norms and had accepted those norms in place of the society's norms, they would not exhibit shame or guilt when violating them. Such feelings are, however, evident. Second, the juvenile delinquent often admires the law-abiding citizen. He often resents the attribution of criminal or immoral behavior to those who are important to him, for example, his mother. He therefore appears to be recognizing the "moral validity of the dominant normative system in many instances." Third, juvenile delinquents distinguish between appropriate victims and persons or groups considered inappropriate targets for their activities. Finally, the delinquent has internalized and accepted some of society's norms. For these reasons, Sykes and Matza argue that the delinquent is "at least partially committed to the dominant social order."[33]

Sykes and Matza contend that the delinquent may become committed to the dominant norms but may rationalize his deviance from those norms. They describe the delinquent's reaction not as a rejection of society's values, as Cohen indicates, but as an "apologetic failure. . . . We call these justifications of deviant behavior techniques of neutralization." Sykes and Matza list five major types of neutralization: (1) denial of responsibility, (2) denial of injury (3) denial of the victim (the delinquents choose a person who *deserves* to be a victim), (4) condemnation of the condemners, and (5) appeal to higher loyalties. Sykes and Matza argue that these techniques of neutralization may not be strong enough to shield the individual from his or her own values and those of others, but they help reduce the impact of social-control forces.[34]

Evaluation—Two sociologists developed a scale for measuring the concept of neutralization as articulated by Sykes and Matza,[35] but problems of testing the theory have led some to conclude that the theory has neither been substantiated or empirically questioned.[36] In a recent analysis, the importance of neutralization theory in "bridging the gulf that exists between social-structural analysis and social-psychological analysis" was emphasized.[37]

Others have questioned the theory. For example, Sykes and Matza proposed that certain types of offenders would favor certain types of neutralizing excuses, but tests of that proposition have not shown a significant relationship between the two factors.[38]

Cohen responded to Sykes and Matza in an article with James F. Short, Jr.; Cohen and Short agree that the failure of Cohen's theory to consider techniques of neutralization was a serious omission. They then tried to incorporate it into their theory, suggesting that their discussion of reaction formation is really a technique of neutralization in which the subculture itself is a neutralizing factor.[39]

Delinquency and Drift

Similar to neutralization theory is David Matza's theory of delinquency and drift. Matza's studies of delinquency adopted an approach that he called *soft determinism.* It is a middle-of-the-road position between the extremes of the classicists—who believed that crime was the product of free will and the positivists—who argued that crime was the result of forces beyond the criminal's control. Matza argued that although modern-day criminologists' theories incorporate different elements of determinism compared with those of the positivists of Lombroso's day, they have gone to an extreme. Although Matza did not adopt the doctrine of free will, he did argue that some movement should be made back in that direction; hence his "soft determinism." He suggested that the delinquent *drifts* into delinquency: The delinquent drifts between conventional and criminal behavior, "responding in turn to the demands of each, flirting now with one, now with the other, but postponing commitment, evading decision."[40]

Differential Opportunity

When Richard Cloward and Lloyd Ohlin introduced their theory of **differential opportunity,** they said that their work was influenced by two schools of thought: Durkheim's and Merton's concepts of anomie, which focus on the pressures associated with deviance, and Sutherland's **differential association** theory, discussed in the next chapter.[41]

Cloward and Ohlin maintain that sociological and psychological factors limit a person's access to both illegitimate *and* legitimate roles. The theory of anomie looks at the person from the legitimate opportunity structure, and it asks questions about the differentials in access to legitimate means. It assumes that either illegitimate routes to success goals are freely available or "differentials in their availability are of little significance." Sutherland's theory of differential association "assumes that access to illegitimate means is variable, but it does not recognize the significance of comparable differentials in access to legitimate means."

Cloward and Ohlin's theory of differential opportunity structures unites the theories of anomie and differential association and considers the individual, not in terms of either the legitimate or the illegitimate systems, but in terms of both. The theory of differential opportunity contains three types of subcultures, defined in Exhibit 5.4.

Evaluation—Differential opportunity theory has led to extensive research and provided the basis for numerous programs aimed at crime

EXHIBIT 5.4

) Basic Types of Subculture

CRIMINAL SUBCULTURE

The criminal subculture develops mainly in lower-class neighborhoods where the successful criminal is not only visible to juveniles but often willing to associate with them. The juveniles in this social class do not have the conventional role models of successful people who have achieved their success through legitimate channels. But they do have access to criminal success models. Consequently, they have an opportunity structure that permits and facilitates illegitimate instead of legitimate activities.

CONFLICT SUBCULTURE

The conflict subculture features a manipulation of violence as a method of getting status. Although slums are not always disorganized, some are characterized by disorganization resulting from transiency and instability. Such unorganized communities cannot provide the criminal subculture that is based on an integration of different age levels and on an integration of conventional and criminal values. The youth are thus left without access to legitimate or illegitimate opportunities, and social controls are weak. The area is populated by failures from conventional society as well as failures from the criminal world. With no organized way in which to solve their frustrations, the youth in these areas "seize upon the manipulation of violence as a route to status not only because it provides a way of expressing pent-up angers and frustrations but also because they are not cut off from access to violent means by vicissitudes of birth."

RETREATIST SUBCULTURE

Finally, youths who fail in both the criminal and the conflict subcultures tend to retreatism, which is manifested by the use of drugs. Again, the social-structural emphasis can be seen. Cloward and Ohlin contend that "whether the sequence of adaptations is from criminal to retreatist or from conflict to retreatist . . . limitations on legitimate and illegitimate opportunity combine to produce intense pressures toward retreatist behavior."

SOURCE: Adapted with permission of the Free Press, a Division of Macmillan, Inc., from Richard A. Cloward and Lloyd E. Ohlin, *Delinquency and Opportunity: A Theory of Delinquent Gangs.* Copyright 1960 by the Free Press.

prevention.[42] More recently, Francis T. Cullen has argued that the theory is really more than a variation of Merton's strain theory. It is a theory rooted in the Chicago School of ecology, and because of that, some have relegated differential opportunity theory to historical status only. Rather, says Cullen, the theory should be carefully re-examined for its potential contributions in our analysis of crime causation. "Therefore I would invite students of crime and deviance to 'revisit' *Delinquency and Opportunity*; it may prove an enlightening adventure."[43]

One of the problems with the differential opportunity theory is the lack of precise, measurable definitions of the relevant concepts. In addition, Cloward and Ohlin do not specify what degree of organization is required for a gang to fall within their theoretical framework. The empirical validity of the theory has also been questioned. Despite these criticisms, the theory does identify an important element in the development of deviant behavior: the differences in the deviant's perceptions of the availability of illegitimate as compared to legitimate opportunities and the belief in a greater chance of success through illegitimate sources.[44]

Social Class and Delinquency

In a study of delinquency and school dropouts, Delbert S. Elliott and Harwin L. Voss attempted to modify and expand the differential opportunity theory of Cloward and Ohlin. Although the latter theory was limited to gang delinquency among lower-class urban males, Elliott and Voss studied both sexes and all social classes.

The guiding principle for this extension of opportunity theory was that "both delinquent behavior and dropping out are alternative responses to failure, alienation, and selective exposure to these forms of behavior" and that of the three contexts in which the investigators studied delinquency and dropout—the home, the school, and the community—the school would be the most important. For male and female dropouts, the strongest predictors are academic failure, school normlessness and social isolation, exposure to dropout in the home, and commitment to peers. School "dropout is related to class while delinquency is not," and "a strong commitment to one's peers was conducive to delinquency, regardless of the extent of delinquency in that group." The investigators concluded that "peer culture itself is conducive to delinquency."[45]

The relevance of this study to other subculture studies of delinquency is important, for the results challenge some of the latter's conclusions.

1. There appeared to be no relationship between delinquent behavior and social class or ethnic origins.

2. The degree to which students participated in extracurricular activities was not predictive of delinquency.

3. Delinquency among females compared to that of males was more frequently a response to alienation and rejection.

4. For males and females the school context was more important socially than home or community.

5. Associations with delinquent friends, along with alienation and normlessness, were both causes and results of delinquency in both males and females.[46]

Lower-Class Boy and Lower-Class Culture

A final subculture theory links social class and delinquent behavior. Walter Miller developed his class theory of delinquent subcultures around the thesis that lower-class delinquents respond to a lower-class subculture. First, the lower class has a *female-based household;* the family is organized around a woman, not a man. Men may be present but not in the stable form of marriage known in the middle and upper classes. When present, the male in the lower class does not participate as fully in the rearing of children and in the economic support of the family, as is characteristic of other social classes. Second, the *one-sex peer unit* is the most significant unit for males and females, in contrast to the two-parent unit that is the focus of other social classes.[47]

The lower class is characterized by six *focal concerns*, which Miller defines as "area or issues which command widespread and persistent attention and a high degree of emotional involvement." He labels them *trouble, toughness, smartness, excitement, fate,* and *autonomy*, resulting in a *cultural system* that distinguishes the lower class from the middle and upper classes. According to Miller, there is an indication that this cultural system is growing more distinctive and that the size of the group that shares the tradition is also growing larger.

In contrast with Cohen's theory that the lower-class boy is engaging in reaction formation against the middle-class values that he cannot attain, Miller is suggesting that the lower-class values come from the inherent characteristics of the lower class itself. When lower-class males act according to the focal concerns that dominate the socialization within their social class, they conflict with middle-class values.

Evaluation—The author of an ecological study in Portland, Oregon, concluded that Miller's theory, although relevant as a tool for understanding the black lower class, is not applicable to all lower-class areas.[48] A study in Seattle, Washington, reported that social class was not a significant factor in predicting delinquency.[49]

Evaluation of the Early Subculture Theories

The subculture theories of Cohen, Cloward and Ohlin, and Miller seek to explain the high rates of delinquency in the lower class. Despite their focus on delinquency rather than on crime, we included them in this text because of their importance to criminological theory and their emphasis on social class. These researchers and their critics have assumed a significant place in criminology, and they cannot be ignored. On the other hand, their approaches do have limitations. Tests of these theories, which have often been based on samples from institutionalized populations, have been questioned by studies based on noninstitutionalized populations, such as questionnaires administered anonymously to the general population. These studies indicate that most people commit acts for which they could be adjudicated delinquent or criminal (although the extent and severity of the delinquent and criminal activity vary) and that social class is not significantly related to criminal behavior among the general population.[50]

Other researchers have suggested that the differences between the findings of the earlier and those of the later studies may be due to differences in the *types* of communities from which the samples were taken. The subculture studies usually select samples from metropolitan areas, and the anonymous questionnaires given to the general population of young people have usually been administered in rural areas and small urban but not metropolitan cities.

This analysis suggests the possibility that social class per se may not be the important element that some researchers have concluded. One problem is that social class is usually measured in terms of parental income. Francis T. Cullen and his colleagues reviewed the literature on delinquency and class and found that the results varied according to how delinquency was measured. In their study of adolescents in a small midwestern town, these investigators "did not find class differences in reported delinquency" on either of two scales used for the research, but they did find that "having money enhances rather than diminishes delinquency." Delinquency may be a pleasurable pursuit, not a desperate move to acquire status. The more money adolescents have, the more likely they are to engage in status, alcohol/drug, and property violations, although the amount of money to which they have access does not seem to increase their involvement in violent crimes.[51] In short, the relationship between social class and delinquent or criminal behavior is complex, and "depending mainly on the measure of social class used, the relationship between class and violence is nonexistent, moderate, or relatively strong."[52]

Family Structure and Crime

Just as social class per se may not be a cause of delinquency or crime, any other variable thought to be related must be considered along with other factors. For example, a traditional approach is to argue that delinquency and broken homes are related variables. In the previous chapter brief attention was given to the early studies associating crime and family structure.[53] Recent research indicates that the relationship between these variables is much more complex than originally thought. For example, there is evidence that school and justice officials "discriminate on the basis of family structure alone." They are more likely to intervene in families of adolescents when the adolescent in question is a female with a mother but no father. Another family structure that is predictive of delinquency is that of an adolescent boy with a stepfather in the home. Some research indicates that some family structures are not closely related to delinquency,[54] while other research, both earlier and recent, has found some relationship between adult criminality and family structure,[55] family size (with delinquent and criminal behavior more frequent among those from large families),[56] and the absence of one parent, although that relationship is not a strong one, and exists mainly in cases of status offenses.[57]

In a recent analysis of adult women who continued their criminal careers after being committed to the California Youth Authority when they were teens, Jill Leslie Rosenbaum looked at the variables of family violence, parent-child conflict, family size, structure, and stability. She reports that none of these individual variables explains the women's crimes, but that all of the women came from families with problems. Rosenbaum suggests that since most of the earlier offenses of these women were **status offenses,** such as running away from home, for which they are more frequently apprehended than are young males, her findings may indicate that "females have more difficulty than males in handling the stress of dysfunctional homes, which may account for their higher runaway rate."[58]

Figure 5.1 indicates that numerous factors may be associated with delinquency among urban males, but as the next chapter points out, association may not be the same as *explanation* or *causation*. Many young people who are associated with any or many of these factors do not become delinquent. The *process* of acquiring delinquent and criminal behavior is the subject of the next chapter.

RECENT DEVELOPMENTS IN THE SOCIAL-STRUCTURAL APPROACH

The theme of our discussion thus far is that the environment's structure is related to behavior, specifically criminal behavior. The early ecologists were concerned with the distribution in space of people and their institutions; Durkheim and Merton studied social integration or anomie; and the subculture approach examined the norms that groups, usually adolescents, developed in response to the social structure. Family structure was also considered.

Although the primary emphasis is on the social structure, the approaches in this chapter also provide a basis from which process theories, sociological or otherwise, may be considered. For example, an environmental explanation of criminal behavior might include not only the ecology of the area in which the criminal behavior occurs but also the

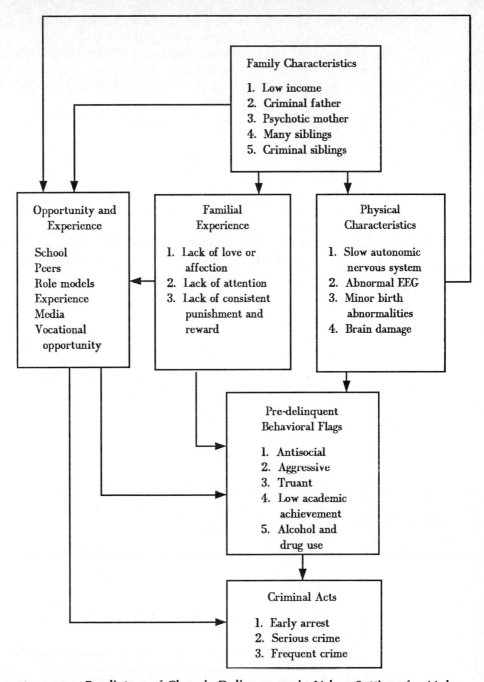

Figure 5.1 Predictors of Chronic Delinquency in Urban Settings for Males

SOURCE: Peter W. Greenwood and Franklin E. Zimring, *One More Chance: The Pursuit Promising Intervention Strategies for Chronic Juvenile Offenders* (R-3214-0JJ5DP) (Santa Monica, CA.: Rand Corporation, May 1985), p. 10.

impact that the environment has on a person's decision to engage in criminal behavior. Thus, the process of becoming a criminal might be intertwined with the structure in which the behavior takes place. These social-structural explanations are therefore important not only for their own merit in explaining criminal behavior but also for the framework they establish for process theories.

Location of Crime

The Chicago ecologists found that crimes are most frequently committed in the zone of transition. A study of land use in Washington, D.C., confirmed this finding. The investigators computed the commuting distance of criminals and found that criminals generally victimize people who live in transitional areas—areas with a high proportion of construction, demolition, and temporary lodgings; the correlation is highest for robbery and burglary but also significant for rape. Business areas are also heavily hit by criminal activity. The areas of high crime rates are characterized by multiple-family dwellings, as contrasted with single-family homes.[59]

Research also shows that most offenders live in or near the area where they commit their crimes. That does not mean that offenders never travel to commit their crimes; some commuting does take place. But when it does, it appears to be related to the characteristics of the offenders, where they live, the type of crime they intend to commit, the attractiveness of the area, and the location of potential targets. Commuting to commit a crime is an investment; it takes time and expense and will probably increase the risk. By traveling outside their own environments to commit the crime, the offenders may be indicating that they see the crime as worth the increased risk.[60] If that is the case, opportunity theory and economic theory may be combined. That is, the economic motivation to commit a crime may be related to the existing opportunities or the need to expand the opportunities for successful criminal behavior.

Density and Crime

In 1972 Oscar Newman published a book called *Defensible Space*.[61] Although other writers had recently introduced the concept of environmental impact on crime, he is credited with popularizing it among the public as well as among professional architects, city planners, and social science researchers.[62]

Newman introduced the concept of *defensible space*. He believed that crime could be reduced by modifying the environment's physical features to the point that crime would be more difficult to commit because the area gave the impression that the residents were in control of it.

The approach may be illustrated by a simple example. Assume that a potential burglar makes decisions concerning the probability of successfully getting into and out of the place to be burglarized. Any increase in the probability of failure will increase the probability that the person will not commit the crime. The judgment involves a particular street, a particular house site or lot, and a residence. A series of cues are used by the potential offender in making the decisions regarding potential success or failure, and the potential for intrusion will be greater if the person perceives the area to be public rather than private—the assumption being that private areas, such as houses, are more likely to be occupied for longer periods of time than are public places. The latter, therefore, are more accessible and risk-free.

Environmental factors may also affect the defensible space of houses. For example, houses in certain neighborhoods may be considered too risky in the summer because people are often outside, and neighbors might have a better watch on the potential target. But the fact that people go on vacation during the summer can make the house more attractive as a target. Lighting is also important—a well-lighted area is less likely to become a target because of the increased possibility of detection.[63]

Evaluation

Newman's approach has been criticized as difficult to test empirically because many of his concepts are not clearly articulated and defined. Yet numerous researchers, many in Great Britain, have conducted research on his concepts, with strong support for his position coming from studies of burglary that show that the "border blocks in city housing areas are much more vulnerable to burglary offenses than the interior blocks."[64]

Another criticism is that changing the environment does not reduce crime; it just displaces it—the potential criminals go elsewhere. This may be desirable for a potential victim, but it will not reduce the crime rate in the community. It also raises serious problems for research, for it will be difficult, if not impossible, to measure this process of displacement.

Physical Environment and Social Integration

It is quite possible that it is not the physical environment that is relevant in explaining criminal behavior but the social integration or anomie that the physical environment facilitates or perhaps produces. Durkheim, in his analysis of suicide, spoke of anomie, the feeling of normlessness, and of a lack of integration within society as being characteristic of people who commit suicide.

Similarly, the design of a building—or its location—may affect the social integration of the people who live in that area and in turn affect the potential for crime. The physical environment may impair the informal social controls that help inhibit criminal behavior. The physical environment might also influence formal controls, such as the police, who, according to research, expect to find criminal activity in high-density areas. Thus, it is possible that the research does not reflect a higher crime rate in dense areas but, rather, a higher rate of apprehension.[65]

Anomie and Environment

We must look then not only at the characteristics of the area but also at the reaction of the police and the characteristics of the people who live in the area. The crime rates will be higher in areas in which there are greater opportunities for crime. Density and overcrowding are not the only relevant variables; the interactions among social and environmental variables are also important. Limited interaction among residents will result in limited knowledge about the area and increase the anonymity of the people—thus increasing the opportunities for successful criminal activity. In a neighborhood characterized by a lack of social integration, or anomie, residents are not as likely to be concerned about what is happening in other homes.[66]

This anomie may be increased where there are high rates of mobility or fast rates of industrialization. On the other hand, urbanism may not create alienation and anomie. There is some indication that we need to distinguish between public and private life when examining the effects of urbanization on social integration, for it has been found that "urbanism does not produce estrangement from close associates or from familiar groups such as neighbors. It does seem to produce estrangement from, and even conflict with, the unknown, socially dissimilar, and potentially threatening people and subcultures who make up the city—the inhabitants of the 'world of strangers.'"[67]

Routine Activity Approach

Lawrence Cohen and Marcus Felson have taken the position that crime may be explained as the convergence of three elements: (1) likely offenders (people who are motivated to commit crimes), (2) suitable targets (the presence of things that are valued and that can be transported fairly easily), and (3) absence of capable guardians (people to prevent the criminal activity). They developed an explanation called the **routine activity approach,** in which human ecology may be used to explain how legal activities increase the probability of illegal activities. For example, the movement of women into the work force reduces the number of women at home during the day and increases the "absence of capable guardians." The family's larger income as a result of the woman's working may also increase the number of desirable goods or suitable targets. If these two elements converge in time and space with likely offenders, the crime rate will increase. The absence of any of these elements may inhibit or prevent crime. Furthermore, "the convergence in time and space of suitable targets and the absence of capable guardians can lead to large increases in crime rates without any increase or change in the structural conditions that motivate individuals to engage in crime."[68]

In a private letter to this author, Felson explained his approach more fully as follows:

> The idea of the routine activity approach is to *bypass* traditional socio-logical theories, including those dealing with motivation and those of Clo-ward and Ohlin. Indeed, I selected the term "routine activity" to *distinguish* this approach from differential opportunity, which means something entirely different from what I mean. I also deliberately avoided the word "theory," calling it instead an "approach," hoping that this might exempt it from the usual muddle.[69]

Evaluation

The routine activity approach was tested in Sweden and found to be as effective in explaining increasing crime rates there as in the United States, despite the differences in welfare expenditures and the resulting income redistribution between the two nations. The researcher emphasized that this is not the finding we would expect from a theory emphasizing that income redistribution would be an effective crime preventive, as some have suggested. He concluded: "The results suggest that opportunity fac-tors may be more important in generating blue-collar crime than the pres-ence of social welfare institutions."[70] The routine activity approach has also been found useful in explaining urban homicides,[71] differences between violence among males and females,[72] and victimization in prop-erty crimes.[73]

The routine activity approach may be called a *crime of places* rather than a *crime of persons*. It has some of the same problems as a crime of persons: it cannot explain all crime, and changes in high-crime places will not eliminate all crime just as changes in high-risk persons will not do so. "But since the routine activities of places may be regulated far more easily than the routine activities of persons, a criminology of place would seem to offer substantial promise for public policy as well as theory."[74]

The routine activity approach, however, has been questioned by sociologists in this country. Leo Carroll and Pamela Irving Jackson raise the possibility that the dispersal of routine activities away from the home does not have a direct effect on the crime rate. Rather, it "is itself a process influencing the structural factors that motivate offenders to commit direct contact predatory crimes." It influences income inequality at both ends of the income distribution scale. As more married women enter the work force, there are more two-income families with a higher total income than before. On the other hand, as the number of families headed by females increases, the number of families at the lower-income level also rises since the incomes of working women remain considerably lower, on the average, than those of working men. And this income inequality is directly related to crime rates.

Carroll and Jackson stress, however, that their study is limited and is not an exact test of the routine activity explanation. They emphasize the need for additional research to consider the impact of income inequality on crime, particularly considering the passage-of-time factor. "Indeed, the whole question of the impact of income inequality on crime seems to be a central one that for some unknown reason has been largely overlooked by criminologists."[75]

SOCIAL-STRUCTURAL THEORIES AND VICTIMIZATION

Social-structual theories have also been used to explain victimization. For example, women are warned not to leave their purses in shopping carts at the grocery store and not to walk in crowds with their purses open and easily accessible to others. Someone might steal the purse because of the opportunity to do so easily, quickly, and probably without apprehension. Women are told not to walk alone at night in isolated areas or to leave a bar with someone they do not know.

An analysis of burglaries also indicates the importance of considering the victims' characteristics. One study disclosed that the types of people who are most likely to be burglarized are central-city residents, the young, persons with income higher or lower than average, nonwhites, and persons whose homes are relatively often unoccupied. "[T]hese data suggest that the key to a reduction in burglary rates may be tighter social organization of neighborhoods, whereby residents pool their resources to increase guardianship of their own property and that of their neighbors."[76]

The opportunity, or life-style concept, approach suggests that if we understand offenders, we may also understand victims and vice versa. "The processes that reduce the restraints to offend are similar to the processes in lifestyle terms that affect the probability that persons will be in places at times and around people where the risk of victimization is high."[77]

SOCIAL-STRUCTURAL THEORIES AND FEMALE CRIMINALITY

Social-structural theories, especially opportunity theory, have been utilized to explain both the victimization and the criminal behavior of women. This approach has also been rejected as an explanation of why women engage in criminal behavior. In fact, scholars do not even agree on the nature of female criminality, and like other issues, the data are questionable in terms of the behavior's extent. It is therefore important to examine the various approaches to female criminality.

The Study of Female Criminality

Until recently females were seldom studied either as offenders or as victims in the criminal justice system. Various reasons have been given for this neglect. As offenders, women have constituted a much smaller percentage than their proportion in the population. Their crimes have generally been ones that do not seriously threaten society, except perhaps its moral fiber, as in the case of prostitution. Arrested females are usually first offenders. Female offenders have not been seen as a serious social problem and have not presented the serious problems of violence in prison that

Female criminality traditionally has been associated mainly with prostitution; here two members of New York City's police department have arrested an alleged prostitute. However, some evidence indicates that females are entering other areas of criminal activity.

have been characteristic of men's prisons. Because female inmates have been easier to manage than male inmates, the female institutions have less security, and some are seen as country clubs compared to men's prisons. Some of these widely held beliefs, however, have been challenged, as scholars have begun to take a serious look at females in the criminal justice system.

The Extent and Nature of Female Criminality

A 1975 article in a popular news magazine indicated that some people thought female criminality was increasing and that women were becoming more violent in their criminal activity. In effect, they were becoming more like male criminals. The headline was "Crimes by women are on the rise all over the world," and the subhead, "In one country after another the story is the same: Female criminals are growing in numbers— and becoming more violent, as well. Why?"[78] In the past decade, especially in the past five years, scholars have debated that conclusion.

In 1975 in *Sisters in Crime*, criminologist Freda Adler set the stage for the debate on the amount and nature of female criminality. According to Adler, the data indicated that not only was crime among women increasing but also women were more frequently engaging in crimes considered to be male rather than female crimes. Women, she said, were becoming murderers, muggers, bank robbers, and even penetrating organized crime (although they have not attained much success in doing so).[79]

Others have supported Adler's position that female crime is increasing and becoming more violent, although not all agree on why this is occurring.[80] But some scholars argue that the differences in the extent and nature of female, as compared with male, criminality may be due to the source of data used, official data generally indicating that males are more involved in property and violent offenses and females in sex and home-related offenses. Studies based on self-report data, however, more often show similarities than differences in male and female criminality.[81] It is also argued that female crimes today are quite similar to the crimes women have always committed and that these crimes are closely associated with sex roles and opportunities.

Opportunity Theory and Female Criminality

Sociologist Rita Simon has taken the position that female crime rates have been increasing only in certain property crimes, such as larceny/theft and fraud/embezzlement, and that the increase in these crimes can be explained by opportunity theory. More women are in the labor force, and they are working in a larger variety of jobs, leading to greater opportunities to commit crimes. The propensies of men and women to commit crimes are not basically different; the difference has been in opportunities. Simon's position is that women are more involved in economic crimes because they have more opportunities to commit these crimes, and they are less involved in violent crimes because the frustrations that lead to the latter are decreased as women become liberated.[82]

Darrell J. Steffensmeier, who has written extensively on female criminality, agrees that there has been an increase in some kinds of crime among females, but he takes the position that women are still primarily involved in traditional female crimes. Shoplifting, for example, is a crime for which traditionally most arrests have been of women. Increases in shoplifting are reflected in the higher rates of larceny. According to Steffensmeier, "Women may be a little more active in the kinds of crime they have always committed," but they are "still typically nonviolent, petty property offenders."[83] Steffensmeier also notes the lack of success of females in organized crime.[84] Regarding female criminality, Steffensmeier concludes that women are still principally regarded as sex objects, wives, and mothers. Female delinquency continues to reflect traditional female sex roles; the women's movement has had little effect on this phenomenon.[85]

Other scholars have supported Steffensmeier's argument that women are still engaging in traditional female sex roles even when they commit crimes generally considered to be masculine, as illustrated by Highlight 5.3. Lee H. Bowker, in his provocative book on female criminality, also raised this issue. He referred to one study that found that:

> [t]he criminal roles played by female robbers and burglars were more consistent with general female sex-role behavior than with the behavior of male robbers and burglars. In the majority of cases, the women were partners rather than sole perpetrators of the acts, and there were also a number of cases in which they were only accessories (who played secondary roles) or conspirators (who did not participate at all in the criminal acts). In only one case out of every seven did a woman carry out a robbery or burglary on her own.[86]

Joseph W. Weis has taken the position that the new female criminal is a myth based on pop criminology and too much reliance on official crime data. After studying self-reports of middle-class delinquency, Weis concluded that these data reflect sex-role opportunities and that the alleged relationship between female liberation and the emergence of a new type of female criminal is a social invention, not reality: "Women are no more violent today than a decade ago and the increase in property offenses suggests that the sexism which still pervades the straight world also functions in the illegal marketplace."[87]

The Need for Research and Analysis of Female Criminality

The studies and analyses of female criminality, compared and contrasted with those of males, present a confusing picture. Some of the differences clearly stem from the differences in the data base used for analysis, as

HIGHLIGHT 5.3

JUDGE: BOYFRIEND PRESSURED THIEF TO ROB BANKS: SHE GETS OFF EASY

A bank robber dubbed the "Miss America" bandit because of her glamorous disguises received two years in prison from a judge who said he was giving her a light sentence because she had been under the influence of a Svengali-like boyfriend.

"It's a fact of life that men can exercise a Svengali influence over women," U.S. District Judge Andrew Hauk, 76, said in sentencing Dannielle Tyece Mast, 24, of Reedsport, Ore.

"It's happened all through the centuries, but the sentencing guidelines don't take it into consideration. Women are a soft touch, particularly if sex is involved."

Mast, a former cheerleader and bank teller who favored fashionable wigs and sunglasses as disguises, was convicted of taking $13,000 in five holdups last summer. She could have received up to five years in prison.

Assistant U.S. Attorney Gregory Alarcon asked for a stiff sentence, but Hauk, one of the most experienced judges on the federal bench, agreed with Mast's lawyer that she acted under the spell of her live-in boyfriend.

The prosecutor complained that Mast had shown no remorse, and he argued that the boyfriend wasn't present during any of the robberies and hasn't been charged.

In the Tuesday sentencing, Hauk said men historically have exercised control over women.

"I'm not going to ignore that no matter how much flak I get from women's libbers," the judge said.

Feminist attorney Gloria Allred said Hauk's remarks were unfortunate.

"That is an untrue stereotype, that men are able to control women," she said. "Unscientific generalizations such as this one have no place in the courtroom or in the decision-making process."

Hauk, 76, was appointed to the federal court by President Lyndon Johnson in 1966. His off-the-cuff remarks from the bench have frequently made headlines during his 23 years as a judge.

Mast's attorney, David E. Wood, argued that she should be given a light sentence because her boyfriend, Lonnie Jackson, pressured her to commit the bank robberies.

SOURCE: Miami Herald, 11 May 1989, p. 14A, col. 1. Reprinted with the permission of Herald Wire Services.

---

noted in the discussion in Chapter 2 of the differences between official and self-report data. Part of the problem also comes from a too-narrow focus in some studies; it is entirely possible that if there are significant differences between actual male and female delinquency and criminality, those differences cannot be explained by one variable, such as women's liberation, or one theory, such as opportunity theory.

After considering the studies of female criminality, Stephen Norland and Neal Shover warned against premature conclusions, arguing that "no clear-cut pattern of change in the criminality of women can be observed. . . . The inconsistent picture presented by these different types of data appears to require a more complex explanation than the relatively simple one suggested in the argument that crime is a function of aggressiveness or masculinity."[88] Among other considerations, we must consider the possible sexist assumptions on which some studies are based. It is also important to consider female victimization. Female children are more likely than males to be sexually abused, and that abuse may be related to some of their subsequent juvenile and criminal activities. This subject is explored in greater detail in a subsequent chapter.[89]

THE CONFLICT APPROACH

Earlier in the text we noted that the **consensus** approach views the emerging norms and laws of society as representative of the common feeling about what is right and proper; that is, they represent a consensus of views. They also represent a mechanism for maintaining social order, but that order is maintained through consensus.

In the **conflict** perspective, on the other hand, values, norms, and laws are viewed as creating dissension, clash, and conflict. Conflict thinkers do not agree on the nature of this process; in fact, they do not agree on what to call it. Nor have the thinkers in this field agreed with one another over time; for some, the process has been an evolving one, and their positions today differ from their earlier ones. It is therefore quite difficult for the student who wants a quick perspective of this area of thinking in criminology to get an accurate view. We will not be able to go into great detail on any one approach, but we do compare and contrast the ideas of the most frequently cited authorities in the field.[90]

The Pluralist Model

The pluralist approach was briefly described by a sociologist in his analysis of the critical perspective: "Until recently . . . conflict theory has gone beyond class conflict to interest-group conflict of all kinds and has had more similarity to political-interest-group theory, or a *pluralistic* model of society."[91] Unlike Marxism, with its focus only on the class struggle, the pluralistic approach sees conflict emerging from several sources.

Culture and Group Conflict

Conflict may exist between cultures, between subcultures within cultures, and between interest groups. The first, **culture conflict theory,** is illustrated by the work of sociologist Thorsten Sellin. Sellin argued that crime must be analyzed as conflicts among norms. For every person, he said, there is a right (normal) and wrong (abnormal) way of acting in specific situations, and these conduct norms are defined by the groups to which the individual belongs. In the normal process of social differentiation, these norms clash with other norms; culture conflict is thus the inevitable result of conflict between conduct norms.

HIGHLIGHT 5.4

LIGHT SENTENCE IN HUSBAND'S SLAYING OF WIFE STIRS OUTRAGE

A judge's decision to give probation to a Chinese immigrant convicted of killing his wife has angered some Asian-American groups, who objected to the judge's statement that Chinese attitudes about adultery helped explain the crime.

The case has also raised questions about the legal argument that cultural factors can relieve people of responsibility for violent behavior, and today, the Brooklyn District Attorney said she may appeal the decision.

"There should be one standard of justice, not one that depends on one's culture," said the District Attorney, Elizabeth Holtzman. "I am deeply concerned by the statement that a man's cultural background should excuse him from serving a jail sentence."

His meek behavior

The judge, Justice Edward K. Pincus of State Supreme Court in Brooklyn, said today that he considered several factors—including cultural background—in giving Dong Lu Chen, 51 years old, five years' probation, which is the minimum sentence on a manslaughter conviction. Other considerations were his lack of a record, his remorse, his meek behavior during the year and a half he spent in jail awaiting trial and the unlikelihood that he would commit another crime.

But Ms. Holtzman said sentencing should reflect "the seriousness of the crime, and the deterrent impact of the sentence."

Several Asian-American groups declined comment on the case, saying they intended to study the court record first, but others expressed outrage because they said it cast a shadow on Chinese culture.

"We have always wanted a more culturally informed judicial system, but this case completely crosses the line—to the point of excusing a murder," said Monona Yin, from the Committee against Anti-Asian Violence. "The judge is using very archaic, academic interpretation."

In a nonjury trial last December, Justice Pincus found Mr. Chen guilty of second-degree

Sellin distinguished between *primary conflict*—which refers to the conflict of culture norms when two different cultures clash—and *secondary conflict*—which occurs within the evolution of a single culture. The first is exemplified by the man from Sicily, who, while living in New Jersey, killed the man who seduced his sixteen-year-old daughter. The father was surprised to be arrested for committing a crime. In his country, such an act by a father would be expected behavior for defending the family's honor. But in the United States it was a crime. Here is a clear case of conflict between the norms of two different cultures. But, said Sellin, because the volume of crime is higher among the native born than among the foreign born, it is secondary conflict that is most important in explaining crime in the United States. Such conflicts "grow out of the process of social differentiation which characterizes the evolution of our own culture."[92] In the normal growth of cultures from homogeneous to heterogeneous, social differentiation occurs. This in turn produces different social groupings, each with its own values and its lack of understanding of the values

HIGHLIGHT 5.4 (Continued)

manslaughter, after reducing a charge of second-degree murder. Mr. Chen had confessed to killing his wife, Jian Wan Chen, 40, after she had admitted to him she was having an affair.

On Sept. 7, 1987, after confronting her in their Brooklyn bedroom about their own sexual relations, he went to the next room, collected a hammer and then beat her eight times in the head, causing five skull fractures.

Legally, the lesser manslaughter charge means that Mr. Chen did not intentionally kill his wife. His court-appointed lawyer, Steward Orden, argued that the overwhelming sense of shame and humiliation brought on by his wife's adultery had put Mr. Chen, who had emigrated from Canton, China, in 1986 in a frame of mind where he was no longer in control of his actions.

To buttress his point, Mr. Orden used an expert witness, Burton Pasternak, an anthropology professor at Hunter College, who testified that in China, adultery is an "enormous stain," which reflects not only on the aggrieved husband, but "is a reflection on his ancestors and his progeny."

Dooming his chances

The defense argued that given the close-knit Chinese community, such private matters would have inevitably become public, marking Mr. Chen a pariah.

Justice Pincus said today that he had been "very impressed" by the testimony on Mr. Chen's background. "I was convinced that what happened at that time was because he had become temporarily, totally deranged," said Justice Pincus. "I didn't feel that he had formed an intent to murder."

"He was the product of his culture," he said. "The culture was never an excuse, but it is something that made him crack more easily. That was the factor, the cracking factor."

SOURCE: New York Times, 5 April 1989, p. 17, col. 3. Copyright © 1989 by the New York Times Company. Reprinted by permission.

of other groups. The result is an increase in social conflict. Highlight 5.4 gives a modern version of Sellin's primary conflict approach.

Sellin's theory has been attacked by those who disagree with his thesis that criminals and delinquents are responding to different norms. They argue that such people are responding to the same norms but that there is a scarcity of rewards associated with them. For example, data indicate that in areas with high rates of delinquency, there is more often a duality of conduct norms than a dominance of conventional or criminal norms.[93]

Perhaps the way to resolve these differences is to recognize that culture conflicts may account for some types of crime, especially among subculture groups, such as gangs, and among the foreign born, but that they do not explain all types of crime. An example of this approach is Miller's subculture analysis, discussed earlier in the chapter. Miller's approach focuses on subcultures but is also a conflict theory in that he sees the lower class's values as conflicting with the middle class's values and laws.

Conflict may also exist between interest groups within the same society, an approach developed by George Vold. Vold did not believe that the conflicts between groups were caused by any abnormality but were normal, natural responses made by "natural human beings struggling in understandably normal and natural situations for the maintenance of the way of life to which they stand committed."[94] Examples are racial conflicts that involve violence between interest groups and the violent behavior accompanying conflict between the interest groups of management and labor. The focus is on conflicts between interest groups, not subcultures or cultures.

Austin Turk views society's social structure as organized into weak and powerful groups, the powerful dictating the norms that are proper for all and establishing the sanctions if those norms are violated. But Turk then begins to sound like a labeling theorist (**labeling theory** is discussed in the next chapter), thereby taking a social-process approach, for he suggests that the persons most likely to be designated criminal because of their law violations are members of the least powerful groups in society.[95] His is also a social-structural approach, in that he sees the structure of social institutions as relevant to the labeling process.

Turk emphasizes that criminology must study the differences between the status and role of legal *authorities* and *subjects.* He argues that these two statuses will be differentiated in all societies and that authority-subject relationships are accepted because it is felt that they are necessary for the preservation of a social order that permits individuals to coexist. He speaks, then, for the *norms of domination* and the *norms of deference,* which he says exist in all social arrangements: "*Lawbreaking* is taken to be an indicator of the failure or lack of authority; it is a measure of the extent to which rulers and ruled, decision-makers and decision-acceptors, are not bound together in a stable authority relationship."[96] Thus Turk does not view conflict over social norms in the traditional sense that some have internalized the norms and others have not. Instead, he contends that people relate differently to different norms, according to "their own individual bio-social experience—some of which norms are institutionalized as norms of domination, others of which are assigned the status of deference. Conflict, and the assignation of a criminal status to various kinds of behavior, will depend on the congruence or lack of congruence between social norms and the cultural evaluation of the norms."[97]

Turk, then, is a modern conflict theorist who views political organization as the result of, and characterized by, conflicts. Those in power have some control over the goods and services that might be available to people in social relationships. That control is exercised through the use of power.[98] Turk's conflict theory has been criticized for dismissing, as do most conflict theorists, research indicating that there is considerable consensus regarding crime. However, Turk's approach—viewing crime as a status that is conferred on those who do not follow the laws of society— indicates the conflict between those in power and those not in power. "As such, this perspective may be applied to a wide range of 'criminal behavior' occurring in various types of social structures and diverse political and economic systems."[99]

Critical Criminology

According to a young critical theorist, Michael J. Lynch, "critical theory is the most significant and sustained theoretical movement to emerge within criminology in recent years."[100] Since the mid-1970s a variety of critical theories have emerged. These include radical theory, Marxist theory, the new criminology, and realist criminology.

The New Criminology was the first noted publication that challenged traditional criminology and invited a new critical look at the American criminal justice system. This work was closely followed by *Critical Criminology* by the same authors.[101] These classic works were followed by numerous other critiques of criminal justice utilizing a Marxist perspective. The interest continues today, although as noted by Michael J. Lynch and W. Byron Groves, "[T]here is no firm consensus or precise definition of radical criminology, either with respect to its key concepts or its primary theoretical emphasis."[102] Consequently this school of thought cannot be characterized as a wholly unified tradition.

Critical theory emerged following the social turbulence that rocked the U.S. in the 1960s. Social conflict between different groups affected virtually every American. The Vietnam War began to be viewed as a way to enhance the economic gains of corporate America, and many insisted that it end. Women insisted that rights granted to their male counterparts be granted equally to women. The U.S. witnessed the most dramatic social movement of the century, led by Dr. Martin Luther King. Existing racial and economic class discrimination was exposed openly to the nation and to the world. Other black leaders such as Malcolm X, George Jackson, and Eldridge Cleaver utilized a Marxist perspective to expose social and economic inequality and to insist on change.

These events caused many to admit that social and economic inequality were so widespread that new theories were required to address the nation's problems. During this time, some American scholars turned to the teachings of Marx to analyze social conflicts. As Lynch and Groves note, "It was a time of change and challenge, and even the sheltered were forced to examine issues of fairness, equality, and justice."[103]

Despite its recency as an approach to the study and explanation of crime and its lack of a unified approach, there are several basic premises that unite critical theorists. These concerns include 1) their reliance on economic explanations of behavior, and 2) their belief that crime cannot be solved within the existing confines of capitalism. They are also united in their conviction that street crime, those crimes included in the FBI's *Uniform Crime Reports* as the eight index crimes, are not the most serious criminal threat to an organized society. Critical criminologists assert that corporate, political, and environmental crimes pose a greater danger. Critical criminologists are united in directing attention to how structural conditions and social inequality in class societies affect criminal behavior and response to crime. The emphasis is on social and economic conditions rather than the characteristics of individual criminals. Finally, critical theorists draw upon a Marxist orientation of society to analyze social relations and processes.

A redefinition of crime proposed by critical theorists based on a Marxist perspective would result in emphasis being placed on violations of human rights denied because of racism and sexism, on unsafe and exploited working conditions, substandard housing, political and military crimes, unaccessible medical care, violations against the environment by pollution and disregard, and on blocked opportunity for every person to be able to excel to his or her greatest potential because of policy dictated by the powerful. In general Marxism promotes an equitable distribution of wealth and decision-making power.[104]

According to critical theory, capitalism is an economic system that creates a class system which greatly benefits some members of society at the cost of other members of that same society. Class membership determines how individuals relate to one another both economically and politically since economic ownership is also related to political power. According to critical criminologists, the class bias contained in laws is also reflected in social control. For example, individuals belonging to the lower classes are more likely to be arrested, convicted, and given harsh sentences than persons from the upper class. Self report studies (unofficial data) show that crime is more evenly distributed among all classes than official figures indicate. Critical criminologists contend that the social control of criminals is biased because criminal law focuses on behaviors in which the powerless are most likely to engage. Examples of this include laws concerned with public loitering and public drunkenness. The class bias in law is also evident in the fact that harmful social behaviors of the upper classes are treated by civil and administrative procedures and not criminally.

Critical criminologists focus on existing social and economic conditions in society and examine how these conditions affect individuals and classes, and how these conditions affect criminal activity. This is in direct contrast to conventional criminology which concentrates on the actions of the individual.

Evaluation

The most serious criticism of critical criminology is that it is not a theory of empirically tested propositions but, rather, a "viewpoint, a perspective, or an orientation."[105] The terms that are crucial to the theory, such as social class, are not clearly defined in terminology that enables empirical testing. Consequently, little testing has been done. Others disagree. For example, critical criminologist Michael J. Lynch maintains that a Marxist approach to the explanation of crime can be quantitatively assessed.[106]

Critical criminology has produced a large body of literature in criminology, not all of which is Marxist. But it is the Marxist, or radical, approach that has drawn the greatest criticism. In a review and critique of a series of original papers written by conflict criminologists, some of whom were Marxists, Ronald L. Akers, a sociologist and criminologist, commented on Marxist criminology. Akers, who first acknowledged that he was personally and professionally acquainted with all the authors whose papers he reviewed, indicated that he found little empirical support for Marxist theory in criminology and that he disagreed with Marxism. Despite his criticism of critical criminology, Akers concludes that "however much I disagree with Marxist criminology, I believe we should continue to hear about it and respond to it."[107]

Others have pointed out that critical criminology "holds out the promise of having a profound impact on our thinking about crime and society." Conflict or critical criminology forces a reexamination of notions of equality before the law and a consideration of whether such really exists, or whether "there is ample evidence that our ideals of equality before the law are being compromised by the facts of income and race in an industrial, highly bureaucratized social order. If a 'critical criminology' can help us solve that issue, while still confronting the need to control crime, it will contribute a great deal."[108]

CONCLUSION AND ANALYSIS OF SOCIAL-STRUCTURAL THEORIES

In the previous two chapters we studied explanations of criminal behavior that focused on the individual criminal and his or her characteristics. In this chapter we have examined explanations that focus on crime as a function of social structure. During the past several decades, this approach has been the most popular one of liberals, many of whom concentrated on such characteristics as unemployment and other forms of economic deprivation. They viewed the entire society as being to blame for crime. Even violent crime was seen as the result of the social structure—the oppressed will kill and steal to get even with a society that had wronged them.

Although some writers saw crime as a reflection of the family and other social institutions, and some even offered psychological and psychiatric causes, the consensus of the liberal writings was that whatever or whomever was blamed, severe punishment based on a concept of personal evil and wickedness was not appropriate. The principal problem in dealing with crime was to curb poverty and racism. Conflict and critical criminology explanations particularly stressed the role of poverty in explaining crime rates.[109]

The social-structural emphasis has lost popularity in this country.

The swing now is toward the criminal, who is presumed to think rationally and who, it is assumed, can be deterred from criminal activity if the correct disincentives are imposed. The contributions of social-structural theories must not, however, be overlooked. In identifying social institutions and political institutions as possible causes of crime, we have made some significant changes, some that may be questioned and some that have obviously been functional for individuals and for society. One hopes that we have also learned that "neither the patterns of criminal areas nor the putative causes for them will yield to simplistic explanations. The motivations to crime are not just economic, nor social nor yet psychological but a complex and ever-changing amalgam."[110] Thus it is important to consider crime from many perspectives.

In developing an understanding of crime that will reduce it, we also need to assess sociological theories that are concerned with the *process* of becoming a criminal. The contributions of sociologists in this area are significant, and to those developments we devote the next chapter.

ENDNOTES

1. For a recent discussion of Park's contributions, see Randy Martin et al., *Criminological Thought: Pioneers Past and Present* (N.Y.: Macmillan Publishers, 1989), pp. 93–116.
2. David Matza, *Becoming Deviant* (Englewood Cliffs, N.J.: Prentice-Hall, 1969), p. 31.
3. Nels Anderson, *The Hobo* (Chicago: University of Chicago Press, 1923). See also Harvey Zorbaugh, *The Gold Coast and the Slum* (Chicago: University of Chicago Press, 1929); and Paul Cressey, *The Taxi-Dance Hall* (Chicago: University of Chicago Press, 1932).
4. Noel P. Gist and Sylvia Fleis Fava, *Urban Society*, 5th ed. (New York: Thomas Y. Crowell, 1964), pp. 108–109. For a recent analysis of the Chicago school, see Francis T. Cullen, *Rethinking Crime and Deviance Theory* (Totowa, N.J.: Rowman & Allanheld, 1984), pp. 102–122.
5. Clifford R. Shaw and Henry D. McKay, *Juvenile Delinquency and Urban Areas*, rev. ed. (Chicago: University of Chicago Press, 1972), p. 21; first published in 1942.
6. *Ibid.*, p. 106.
7. See, for example, Solomon Kobrin, "The Formal Logical Properties of the Shaw-McKay Delinquency Theory," chap. 5 in Harwin L. Voss and David M. Petersen, eds., *Ecology, Crime and Delinquency* (New York: Appleton-Century-Crofts, 1971), pp. 101–131; and Christen T. Jonassen, "A Re-evaluation and Critique of the Logic and Some Methods of Shaw and McKay," chap. 6 in Voss and Petersen, eds., *Ecology, Crime and Delinquency*. For information on earlier attempts to test the theory of ecology in Baltimore, see Bernard Lander, *Towards an Understanding of Juvenile Delinquency* (New York: Columbia University Press, 1954). For a recent analysis of the criticisms, see Robert J. Bursik, Jr., "Social Disorganization and Theories of Crime and Delinquency: Problems and Prospects," *Criminology* 26 (November 1988): 519–551.

8. See Douglas A. Smith and C. Roger Jorjoura, "Social Structure and Criminal Victimization," *Journal of Research in Crime and Delinquency* 25 (February 1988): 27–52, for recent data supporting Shaw and McKay's social disorganization approach.

9. Émile Durkheim, *The Rules of Sociological Method* (New York: Free Press, 1964), p. 66; first published in 1938. For a modern analysis of functionalism, see Gary F. Jensen, "Functional Research on Deviance: A Critical Analysis and Guide for the Future," *Deviant Behavior* 9 (No. 1, 1988): 1–17. For a discussion of Durkheim's life and works, see Martin et al., *Criminological Thought*, pp. 47–64.

10. Durkheim, *The Rules of Sociological Method*, p. 71.

11. Émile Durkheim, *The Division of Labour in Society*, paper ed. (New York: Free Press, 1964), pp. 374–388.

12. See Myron Boor, "Effects of United States Presidential Elections on Suicide and Other Causes of Death," *American Sociological Review* 46 (October 1981): 616–618, for the results of his studies and citations to related research; the quotation is on page 618. For a recent discussion and reformulation of Durkheim's analysis of suicide and religion, see Bernice A. Pescosolido and Sharon Georgianna, "Durkheim, Suicide, and Religion: Toward A Network Theory of Suicide," *American Sociological Review* 54 (February 1989): 33–48.

13. Robert K. Merton, *Social Theory and Social Structure*, enlarged ed. (New York: Free Press, 1968). For more information on Merton, see Piotr Sztompka, *Robert K. Merton: An Intellectual Profile* (New York: St. Martin's Press, 1986); and Martin et al., *Criminological Thought*, pp. 207–235.

14. Merton, *Social Theory and Social Structure*, p. 185.

15. *Ibid.*, pp. 189, 190, 192–193.

16. *Ibid.*, p. 200.

17. *Ibid.*, p. 208.

18. *Ibid.*, p. 241.

19. Edward Sagarin, *Deviants and Deviance: An Introduction to the Study of Disvalued People and Behavior* (New York: Holt, Rinehart and Winston, 1975), pp. 108–109. For a recent analysis of Merton's theory, see Steven F. Messner, "Merton's 'Social Structure and Anomie': The Road Not Taken," *Deviant Behavior* 9 (No. 1, 1988): 33–53.

20. See Ruth Kornhauser, *Social Sources of Delinquency* (Chicago: University of Chicago Press, 1978).

21. See, for example, Robert Agnew, "A Revised Strain Theory of Delinquency," *Social Forces* 64 (1985): 151–66.

22. Margaret Farnworth and Michael J. Leiber, "Strain Theory Revisited: Economic Goals, Educational Means, and Delinquency," *American Sociological Review* 54 (April 1989): 263.

23. Frederic M. Thrasher, *The Gang*, abbrev. ed. (Chicago: University of Chicago Press, 1927, 1963). William F. Whyte, in his classic study, *Street Corner Society* (Chicago: University of Chicago Press, 1943), disputed the social disorganization theory.

24. For an analysis of social organization of gangs and drug use, see Jeffrey Fagan, "The Social Organization of Drug Use and Drug Dealing Among Urban Gangs," *Criminology* 27 (November 1989): 633–670. For an analysis of gangs and homicide, see G. David Curry and Irving A. Spergel, "Gang Homicide, Delinquency, and Community," *Criminology* 26 (August 1988): 381–405; and Paul E. Tracy,

"Subcultural Delinquency: A Comparison of the Incidence of Gang and Non-gang Member Offenses," in Marvin E. Wolfgang, Terrence P. Thornberry, and Robert M. Figlio, eds., *From Boy to Man, From Delinquency to Crime* (Chicago: University of Chicago Press, 1988).

25. See Anne Campbell, "Self Definition by Rejection: The Case of Gang Girls," *Social Problems* 34 (December 1987): 451–466; and Campbell, *Girls in the Gang* (N.Y.: Basil Blackwell, 1984). For a discussion of public policy and gangs, see C. Ronald Huff, "Youth Gangs and Public Policy," *Crime & Delinquency* 35: (October 1989): 524–537.

26. Albert K. Cohen, *Delinquent Boys: The Culture of the Gang* (New York: Free Press, 1955). For more information on Cohen, see Martin et al., *Criminological Thought*, pp. 239–258.

27. Cohen, *Delinquent Boys*, pp. 59–65; emphasis in the original.

28. See, for example, Frank E. Hartung, *American Sociological Review* 20 (December 1955): 751–752; Donnell M. Poppenfort, *American Journal of Sociology* 62 (July 1956): 125–126; and Hermann Mannheim, *British Journal of Sociology* 7 (July 1956): 147–152.

29. John I. Kitsuse and David C. Dietrick, "Delinquent Boys: A Critique," in Harwin L. Voss, ed., *Society, Delinquency, and Delinquent Behavior* (Boston: Little, Brown, 1979), pp. 238–245.

30. *Ibid.*, p. 240.

31. Cohen, *Delinquent Boys*, p. 117.

32. Kitsuse and Dietrick, "Delinquent Boys," pp. 244–245.

33. Gresham Sykes and David Matza, "Techniques of Neutralization: A Theory of Delinquency," in Marvin E. Wolfgang et al., eds., *The Sociology of Crime and Delinquency*, 2d ed. (New York: John Wiley, 1970), pp. 292–299. For information on the contributions of Sykes, see Martin et al., *Criminological Thought*, pp. 299–318.

34. Sykes and Matza, "Techniques of Neutralization," pp. 295–298.

35. See Joseph W. Rogers and M. D. Buffalo, "Neutralization Techniques: Toward a Simplified Measurement Scale," *Pacific Sociological Review* 17 (July 1974): 313–331.

36. See William W. Minor, "The Neutralization of Criminal Offense," *Criminology* 18 (May 1980): 103–120. In a later work, Minor reported finding some support for neutralization theory. See Minor, "Techniques of Neutraliztion: A Reconceptualization and Empirical Examination," *Journal of Research in Crime and Delinquency* 18 (July 1981): 295–318.

37. John E. Hamlin, "The Misplaced Role of Rational Choice in Neutralization Theory," *Criminology* 26 (August 1988): 425–438.

38. Sykes and Matza, "Techniques of Neutraliztion."

39. Albert K. Cohen and James F. Short, Jr., "Research in Delinquent Subcultures," *Journal of Social Issues* 14 (1958): 20–37.

40. David Matza, *Delinquency and Drift* (New York: John Wiley, 1964), p. 28.

41. Richard A. Cloward and Lloyd E. Ohlin, *Delinquency and Opportunity: A Theory of Delinquent Gangs* (New York: Free Press, 1960). See also Cullen, *Rethinking Crime*, pp. 39–54. For more information on Ohlin, see Martin et al., *Criminological Thought*, pp. 260–297.

42. See James F. Short, Jr. et al., "Perceived Opportunities, Gang Membership, and Delinquency," *American Sociological Review* 30 (February 1956): 56–67.

43. Francis T. Cullen, "Were Cloward and Ohlin Strain Theorists? Delinquency

and Opportunity Revisited," *Journal of Research in Crime and Delinquency* 25 (August 1988): 236.

44. Clarence Schrag, "Delinquency and Opportunity: Analysis of a Theory," in Voss, ed., *Society, Delinquency, and Delinquent Behavior,* pp. 259–261.

45. Delbert S. Elliott and Harwin L. Voss, *Delinquency and Dropout* (Lexington, Mass.: D. C. Heath, 1974), pp. 5, 204–205.

46. *Ibid.,* pp. 206–207.

47. Walter B. Miller, "Lower Class Culture as a Generating Milieu of Gang Delinquency," in Wolfgang et al., ed., *Sociology of Crime and Delinquency,* pp. 351–363.

48. Kenneth Polk, "Urban Social Areas and Delinquency," *Social Problems* 14 (Winter 1967): 320–325; reprinted in Voss and Petersen, eds., *Ecology, Crime, and Delinquency,* pp. 273–281.

49. Richard E. Johnson, "Social Class and Delinquent Behavior: A New Test," *Criminology* 18 (May 1980): 91.

50. See, for example, James F. Short, Jr., "Differential Association and Delinquency," *Social Problems* 4 (January 1957): 233–239; F. Ivan Nye, *Family Relationships and Delinquent Behavior* (New York: John Wiley, 1958).

51. Francis T. Cullen et al., "Having Money and Delinquent Involvement: The Neglect of Power in Delinquency Theory," *Criminal Justice and Behavior* 12 (June 1985): 171–192.

52. David Brownfield, "Social Class and Violent Behavior," *Criminology* 24 (August 1986): 435.

53. See Sheldon and Eleanor Glueck, *Unravelling Juvenile Delinquency* (Cambridge, MA.: Harvard University Press, 1950); John H. Laub and Robert J. Sampson, "Unraveling Families and Delinquency: A reanalysis of the Gluecks' Data," *Criminology* 26 (August 1988): 355–380.

54. Richard E. Johnson, "Family Structure and Delinquency: General Patterns and Gender Differences," *Criminology* 24 (February 1986): 65–84.

55. See, for example, Joan McCord, "Some Child-Rearing Antecedents of Criminal Behavior in Adult Men," *Journal of Personality and Social Psychology* 37 (1979): 1477–1486.

56. See F. Nye, *Family Relationships and Delinquent Behavior* (New York: John Wiley, 1958).

57. See L. Rosen, "Family and Delinquency: Structure or Function?" *Criminology* 23 (1985): 553–573; and Patricia Van Voorhis et al., "The Impact of Family Structure and Quality on Delinquency: A Comparative Assessment of Structural and Functional Factors," *Criminology* 26 (May 1988): 235–261.

58. Jill Leslie Rosenbaum, "Family Dysfunction and Female Delinquency," *Crime & Delinquency* 35 (January 1989): 31–44, with quotation on p. 43. See also P. Van Voorhis et al., "The Impact of Family Structure and Quality on Delinquency: A Comparative Assessment of Structural and Functional Factors," *Criminology* 26 (May 1988): 235–261.

59. William M. Rhodes and Catherine Conly, "Crime and Mobility: An Empirical Study," in Paul L. Brantingham and Patricia L. Brantingham, eds., *Environmental Criminology* (Beverly Hills, CA.: Sage Publications, 1981), pp. 182–183.

60. *Ibid.,* p. 172.

61. Oscar Newman, *Defensible Space* (London: Architectural Press, 1972).

62. John Baldwin, "Ecological and Area Studies in Great Britain and the United

States," in Norval Morris and Michael Tonry, eds., *Crime and Justice: An Annual Review of Research,* vol. 1 (Chicago: University of Chicago Press, 1979), p. 54.

63. Barbara B. Brown and Irwin Altman, "Territoriality and Residential Crime: A Conceptual Framework," in Brantingham and Brantingham, eds., *Environmental Criminology,* p. 66.

64. Baldwin, "Ecological and Area Studies," p. 57, referring to the research of Brantingham and Brantingham.

65. See A. R. Gillis and John Hagan, "Density, Delinquency, and Design: Formal and Informal Control and the Built Environment," *Criminology* 19 (February 1982): 514–529.

66. Dennis W. Roncek, "Dangerous Places: Crime and Residential Environment," *Social Forces* 60 (September 1980): 74–96.

67. Claude S. Fischer, "The Public and Private Worlds of City Life," *American Sociological Review* 46 (June 1981): 315.

68. Lawrence E. Cohen and Marcus Felson, "Social Change and Crime Rate Trends: A Routine Activity Approach," *American Sociological Review* 44 (August 1979): 604.

69. Private letter from Marcus Felson to the author, 25 January 1988. For further development of this theory, see Marcus Felson, "Routine Activities and Crime Prevention in the Developing Metropolis," *Criminology* 25 (November 1987): 911–931.

70. Steven Stack, "Social Structure and Swedish Crime Rates: A Time-Series Analysis, 1950–1979," *Criminology* 20 (November 1982): 510.

71. Steven F. Messner and Kenneth Tardiff, "The Social Ecology of Urban Homicide: An Application of the 'Routine Activities' Approach." *Criminology* 23 (May 1985): 241–267.

72. See Robert M. O'Brien, "Exploring the Intersexual Nature of Violent Crimes," *Criminology* 26 (February 1988): 151–170.

73. See James L. Massey et al., "Property Crime and the Routine Activities of Individuals," *Journal of Research in Crime and Delinquency* 26: (November 1989): 378–400.

74. Lawrence W. Sherman et al., "Hot Spots of Predatory Crime: Routine Activities and the Criminology of Place," *Criminology* 27 (February 1989): 27–55. For an analysis of victimization, see Leslie W. Kennedy and David R. Forde, "Routine Activities and Crime: An Analysis of Victimization in Canada," *Criminology* 28 (February 1990): 137–152.

75. Leo Carroll and Pamela Irving Jackson, "Inequality, Opportunity, and Crime Rates in Central Cities," *Criminology* 21 (May 1983): 181, 192. Jackson later found some support for the theory. Pamela Irving Jackson, "Opportunity and Crime: A Function of City Size," *Sociology and Social Research* 68 (January 1984): 172–193.

76. Lawrence E. Cohen and David Cantor, "Residential Burglary in the United States: Life-Style and Demographic Factors Associated with the Probablilty of Victimization," *Journal of Research in Crime and Delinquency* 18 (January 1981): 125.

77. Michael R. Gottfredson, "On the Etiology of Criminal Victimization," *Journal of Criminal Law & Criminology* 72 (Summer 1981): 725–726.

78. *U.S. News & World Report,* 22 December 1975, p. 49.

79. Freda Adler, *Sisters in Crime* (Prospect Heights, Ill.: Waveland Press, 1975; reprinted 1985), pp. 19–20.

80. See, for example, Richard Deming, *Women: The New Criminals* (Nashville, Tenn.: Thomas Nelson, 1977), and Nanci Koser Wilson, "The Masculinity of Violent Crime—Some Second Thoughts," *Journal of Criminal Justice* 9 (1981): 111–123. For a critique, see Darrell Steffensmeier, "Flawed Arrest 'Rates' and Overlooked Reliability Problems in UCR Arrest Statistics: A Comment on Wilson's 'The Masculinity of Violent Crime—Some Second Thoughts,'" *Journal of Criminal Justice* 11 (1983): 167–171.

81. These studies are reviewed briefly in Rachelle J. Canter, "Sex Differences in Self-Report Delinquency," *Criminology* 20 (November 1982): 373–393. For a recent review of feminist criminology, see Kathleen Daly and Meda Chesney-Lind, "Feminism and Criminology," *Justice Quarterly* 5 (December 1988): 497–538. See also Sally S. Simpson, "Feminist Theory, Crime, and Justice," *Criminology* 27 (November 1989): 605–631.

82. Rita J. Simon, *Women and Crime* (Lexington, Mass.: D. C. Heath, 1975). See also Freda Adler and Rita James Simon, *The Criminology of Deviant Women* (Boston: Houghton Mifflin, 1979).

83. Darrell J. Steffensmeier, "Crime and the Contemporary Woman: An Analysis of Changing Levels of Female Property Crime, 1960–75," *Social Forces* 57 (December 1978): 566–584.

84. Darrell J. Steffensmeier, "Organization Properties and Sex-Segregation in the Underworld: Building a Sociological Theory of Sex Differences in Crime," *Social Forces* 61 (June 1983): 1010–1032.

85. Darrell J. Steffensmeier and Renee Hoffman Steffensmeier, "Trends in Female Delinquency: An Examination of Arrest, Juvenile Court, Self-Report, and Field Data," *Criminology* 18 (May 1980): 62–85.

86. Cited in Lee H. Bowker, *Women, Crime, and the Criminal Justice System* (Lexington, Mass.: D. C. Heath, 1978), p. 277.

87. Joseph G. Weis, "Liberation and Crime: The Invention of the Female Criminal," *Crime and Social Justice* 6 (Fall–Winter 1976), p. 24.

88. Stephen Norland and Neal Shover, "Gender Roles and Female Criminality," *Criminology* 15 (May 1977): 95.

89. See Meda Chesney-Lind, "Girls' Crime and Woman's Place: Toward a Feminist Model of Female Delinquency," *Crime & Delinquency* 35 (January 1989): 5–29.

90. See C. Ronald Huff, "Conflict Theory in Criminology," in James A. Inciardi, ed., *Radical Criminology: The Coming Crises* (Beverly Hills, CA.: Sage Publications, 1980), pp. 61–77, for a brief but excellent overview of conflict theory.

91. Ronald L. Akers, *Deviant Behavior: A Social Learning Approach*, 2d ed. (Belmont, Calif.: Wadsworth, 1977), p. 15; 3rd ed., 1985.

92. Thorsten Sellin, *Culture, Conflict, and Crime*, Bulletin no. 41, (New York: Social Science Research Council, 1938), p. 105.

93. Solomon Kobrin, "The Conflict of Values in Delinquency Areas," *American Sociological Review* 467 (January 1962): 167–175.

94. George B. Vold, *Theoretical Criminology* (New York: Oxford University Press, 1958), p. 208. See also George B. Vold with T. J. Bernard, *Theoretical Criminology*, 3d ed. (New York: Oxford University Press, 1986).

95. Austin T. Turk, "Law as a Weapon in Social Conflict," *Social Problems* 23 (February 1976): 288.

96. See Austin T. Turk, *Criminality and the Legal Order* (Chicago: Rand McNally, 1971), p. 48.

97. Ian Taylor et al., *The New Criminality: For a Social Theory of Deviance* (London: Routledge & Kegan Paul, 1973), p. 243.

98. See Austin T. Turk, *Political Criminality: The Defiance and Defense of Authority* (Beverly Hills, CA.: Sage Publications, 1982).

99. Ronald L. Akers, "Theory and Ideology in Marxist Criminology: Comments on Turk, Quinney, Toby, and Klockers," *Criminology* 16 (February 1979): 537.

100. Michael J. Lynch, private communication, June 1989.

101. I. Taylor, P. Walton, and J. Young, *The New Criminology: For a Social Theory of Deviance* (N.Y.: Harper and Row, 1973), and Taylor, Walton, and Young, *Critical Criminology* (London: Routledge and Kegan Paul, 1975).

102. Michael J. Lynch and W. Bryon Groves, *A Primer in Radical Criminology* 2nd ed. (New York: Harrow and Heston, 1989), p. 4.

103. *Ibid.*, p. 2.

104. See Karl Marx, *Critique of Political Economy* (New York: International Library, 1904; originally published 1859).

105. Gresham M. Sykes, "The Rise of Critical Criminology," *Journal of Criminal Law and Criminology* 65 (June 1974): 212–213. See also the critique of critical criminology by Jackson Toby, "The New Criminology Is the Old Baloney," in Inciardi, ed., *Radical Criminology,*, pp. 124–132; and Dorio Melossi, "Overcoming the Crisis in Critical Criminology: Toward a Grounded Labeling Theory," *Criminology* 23 (No. 2, 1985): 193–208.

106. Michael J. Lynch, "The Extraction of Surplus Value, Crime and Punishment: A Preliminary Examination," *Contemporary Crisis* 12 (1988): 329–344.

107. Akers, "Theory and Ideology," pp. 528, 543.

108. Sykes, "The Rise of Critical Criminology," p. 213.

109. For a recent analysis of unemployment and crime, see Emile Anderson Allan and Darrell J. Steffensmeier, "Youth, Underemployment, and Property Crime," *American Sociological Review* 54 (February 1989): 107–123.

110. R. N. Davidson, *Crime and Environment* (New York: St. Martin's Press, 1981), p. 93.

CHAPTER 6

This chapter is concerned with the process by which people become criminals. Do they learn this behavior and, if so, how and under what types of circumstances? The chapter begins with a discussion of the social-learning theory called differential association. The influence of that theory is assessed in light of the recent reformulations of social-learning theory by sociologists and criminologists. A second major focus is on the relationship between pornography and criminal behavior. The third section examines social-control theories, which are based on the assumption that criminal behavior occurs when society's normal methods of controlling people break down. A fourth section discusses labeling theory, which focuses on the process by which people who engage in certain acts come to be called (or labeled) criminal whereas others who engage in those same kinds of behavior are not so labeled. The chapter closes with an analysis of theories of criminality.

OUTLINE

Sociological Theories of Criminal Behavior II: Social-Process Theories

KEY TERMS

containment theory
differential anticipation theory
differential association-
  reinforcement theory
differential association theory
differential identification theory
differential opportunity theory
labeling theory
norms
plea bargaining
self-concept
self-report
social-control theory
social-learning theory

Chapter 5 discusses sociological theories that emphasize the relationship of criminal behavior to the social structure, or organization, of society. Whether the environment is seen as a determining or a facilitating factor in the causation of crime, the emphasis is on the environment's structure, not on individual characteristics as in the constitutional theories. The social-structural theories, however, do not explain how individuals become criminals. This chapter focuses on an analysis of *social-process* theories, which attempt to explain *how* people become criminals.

It is, of course, not possible to separate all sociological theories neatly into the categories of social structure and social process. Some theories could easily be considered in both categories. For example, the techniques-of-neutralization theory of Sykes and Matza might be considered a social-process as well as a social-structural approach because of its emphasis on motivation. That theory explains the *process* by which a person neutralizes any inhibitions he or she might have against violating laws. On the other hand, the theory is related to subcultures, an aspect of the social structure. Likewise, in this chapter labeling theory is discussed because it explains the *process* by which a person becomes a criminal— the person is labeled by those in a position to make that determination. Labeling theory has also been characterized as a social-structural theory, with some similarities to conflict theory, although it can also be seen as the *process* by which the structure of conflict is applied.

Social-process theories developed as sociologists began to analyze the obvious fact that not all people exposed to the same social-structural conditions respond in the same way. Some become law-abiding citizens, and others become criminals. Not all criminals always respond in criminal ways; likewise, not all noncriminals always respond by observing the law. There must be some process that explains the differential reaction to the environment. Sociologists began to hypothesize that human behavior is learned and that criminal behavior may be acquired in the same way that noncriminal behavior is acquired. This approach has also been taken by other disciplines.

DIFFERENTIAL ASSOCIATION THEORY

Differential association theory as an explanation of criminal behavior is based on the premise that criminal behavior is learned in the same way that any other behavior is learned. The key figure in the development of this theory was Edwin H. Sutherland.

Sutherland's Contributions

Edwin H. Sutherland, sometimes referred to as the dean of American criminology, had a tremendous impact on sociologists and criminologists

EXHIBIT 6.1

DEAN of Amer. Criminologists

Sutherland's Theory of Differential Association

1. Criminal behavior is learned.

2. Criminal behavior is learned in interaction with other persons in a process of communication.

3. The principal part of the learning of criminal behavior occurs within intimate personal groups.

4. When criminal behavior is learned, the learning includes (a) techniques of committing the crime, which are sometimes very complicated, sometimes very simple; (b) the specific direction of motives, drives, rationalizations, and attitudes.

5. The specific direction of motives and drives is learned from definitions of the legal codes as favorable or unfavorable.

6. A person becomes delinquent because of an excess of definitions favorable to violation of law over definitions unfavorable to violation of law.

7. Differential associations may vary in frequency, duration, priority, and intensity.

8. The process of learning criminal behavior by association with criminal and anticriminal patterns involves all the mechanisms that are involved in any other learning.

9. While criminal behavior is an explanation of general needs and values, it is not explained by those general needs and values, since noncriminal behavior is an expression of the same needs and values.

SOURCE: Edwin H. Sutherland and Donald R. Cressey, *Principles of Criminology*, 10th ed. (Philadelphia: Lippincott, 1978), pp. 80–82; emphasis deleted.

in the United States. He is best known in criminology for his theory of differential association, a theory of crime causation he introduced in 1939.

When Sutherland was asked to write a criminology text in 1921, his primary interest was in the controversy that was raging between theories of environment and theories of heredity. Sutherland wanted to analyze criminal behavior by utilizing some of the prevailing sociological concepts. He was also interested in finding concrete causes of crime. But as he examined the concepts, he decided that no concrete explanation could explain crime. For example, the concrete condition most frequently associated with crime is gender; most people apprehended for crimes were male. But Sutherland said that it was obvious that gender was not the *cause* of crime. So he turned to abstract explanations and finally decided that a learning process involving communication and interaction must be the principle that would explain all types of crime.[2]

In the 1939 edition of his book, Sutherland introduced the concept of differential association, although he was reluctant to do so. His concern about the hypothesis was expressed in his reference to it as "an hypothesis which might quickly be murdered or commit suicide."[3] The hypothesis was, however, developed into a theory. The 1947 version of the theory, containing nine statements, was Sutherland's final version. It is reproduced in Exhibit 6.1.

Evaluation

In one of his efforts to test a portion of Sutherland's theory, James F. Short, Jr., called the theory "the most truly sociological of all theories which have been advanced to explain criminal and delinquent behavior."[4] Short also pointed out some of the problems with the theory, which he said was not testable in its general terms; some reformulations were necessary. Short did attempt to measure the theory's frequency, duration, priority, and intensity. Within the limitations of his study he found strong support for the theory, although in a later study he again concluded that a reformulation might be necessary before the theory's concepts could be measured.[5]

Others have attempted to test differential association by measuring actual delinquency as reported by best friends. They concluded, "We are led to question the postulate that differential association is a necessary and sufficient condition explaining delinquency."[6] Sutherland considered this and other criticisms in a paper that was not published until after his death: "The Swan Song of Differential Association," written in 1944. He acknowledged that some of the criticisms were valid, and he concluded that criminal associations alone do not explain criminal behavior. Rather, it is those

> associations plus tendencies toward alternate ways of satisfying whatever needs happen to be involved in a particular situation. Consequently, it is improper to view criminal behavior as a closed system, and participation in criminal behavior is not to be regarded as something that is determined exclusively by association with criminal patterns. . . . For the reasons that I have outlined and doubtless for additional reasons differential association as a sufficient explanation of criminal behavior is invalid.[7]

In that 1944 article, Sutherland considered returning to multiple causation and abandoning the attempt to explain all criminal behavior by means of one theory. But in the 1947 edition of his text, he did not try to incorporate these ideas, and the theory of differential association has remained as he stated it in that edition.

Cressey's Defense of Differential Association

The late Donald Cressey, who wrote the editions of the Sutherland text after Sutherland's death in 1950, acknowledged the criticisms. He agreed with some. The theory of differential association "is neither precise nor clear. . . . Most significantly, the published statement gives the incorrect impression that there is little concern for accounting for variations in crime and delinquent rates. This is a serious error in communication on Sutherland's part."[8] Cressey believed that the theory needed reformulation, but he made no attempt to do so in subsequent editions of the text. He stated his reasons: "The theory is presently in a period of great popularity. . . . It would be inappropriate to modify the statement in such a way that research work now in progress would be undermined."[9]

Cressey did, however, analyze the criticisms and defend the theory against some of the attacks. He stated that one result of the theory's ambiguity and the critics' failure to read the theory carefully was the assumption that people become criminals because of their association with either criminals or criminal patterns of behavior and attitudes. But, observed Cressey, the theory is that people become criminals because of an *overabundance* of associations with criminal, as compared with anticriminal, behavior patterns.[10]

Some critics argued that a person can become a criminal without associating with criminals; therefore, differential association does not apply. That, said Cressey, was not the point. One may be exposed to criminal attitudes and behavior without being exposed to criminals. For example, parents who teach their children not to steal may indicate that it is permissible to steal a loaf of bread if they are starving. "One can learn criminal behavior patterns from persons who are not criminals, and one can learn anti-criminal behavior from hoods, professional crooks, habitual offenders, and gangsters."[11]

Critics have reasoned that certain types of criminal behavior are not covered by the theory of differential association. Cressey's reaction to this criticism was that in all but five of the cases no research was conducted. Thus, the criticisms are research proposals, not valid criticisms. He did agree that if research were conducted to test the theory, and if it were found that a type of crime was not covered, the theory should be revised.

According to Cressey, Sutherland was aware of the criticisms of his theory by social psychologists, who believed that the theory did not explain why some people responded to opportunities for crime by committing crimes and why others did not. But differential association was perceived by Sutherland to account for such differential response patterns. Whether or not a person took money from an open cash register would be related to his or her previous associations. More damaging criticisms, asserted Cressey, are those that point out the difficulties of operationalizing some of the theory's terms: it is impossible to measure the precise mechanism by which people learn criminal behavior, a limitation of differential association as a *theory* from which testable hypotheses may be derived. Cressey noted that the theory of differential association was developed by Sutherland primarily to interpret crime data. Sutherland was probably not trying to devise a theory that would explain individual criminal behavior but, rather, one that would bring some order to the understanding of crime rates. Cressey argued that differential association is really a principle, not a "precise statement of the process by which one becomes a criminal."[12]

Even after Cressey's defense, criticisms of the theory have remained and have led to modifications; however, the influence of Sutherland continues to be strong, although the criticisms continue. The 1986 statement of two theorists that the differential association theory has "virtually no importance whatsoever" has been challenged by sociologist James Orcutt, who calls such allegations exaggerations and concludes that "clearly, Sutherland's work is still worth a close look."[13] Modifications of differential association theory have also been offered.

Differential Association and Set Theory

Melvin L. DeFleur and Richard Quinney attempted to express differential association in the language of set theory. They developed a formal model of the theory and tested it, concluding that differential association theory is "internally consistent and consistent with more general behavioral theory."[14] Cressey's reaction was that the set theory formulation "states the theory of differential association more beautifully and more efficiently than it has ever been stated before."[15]

Differential Association-Reinforcement Theory

In an effort to provide a "more adequate specification of the learning process" required in the theory of differential association, Robert L. Burgess and Ronald L. Akers created **differential association-reinforcement theory.** Their purpose was to integrate Sutherland's theory with the more general behavior theory associated with the work of psychologist B. F. Skinner. Their assumption was that in so doing, the theory would be made more testable, while at the same time the learning processes would be indicated more clearly.[16]

Social-learning theory is based on the assumption that the "primary learning mechanism in social behavior is operant (instrumental) conditioning in which behavior is shaped by the stimuli which follow, or are consequences of the behavior." Direct conditioning and imitation of others are important in determining this behavior. Rewards, or positive reinforcement, as well as avoidance of punishment, or negative reinforcement, strengthen it. The behavior may be weakened by aversive stimuli, or positive punishment, as well as by loss of reward, or negative punishment. The determination of whether the behavior is deviant or conforming depends on *differential reinforcement*, defined as "past and present rewards or punishments for the behavior and the rewards and punishments attached to alternative behavior." Furthermore, from others who are important to them, people learn norms, attitudes, and orientations that define certain behaviors as good or bad. Such definitions help reinforce behavior and serve as cues for behavior. The more positive definitions people have of the behavior, the more likely they will be to engage in it. These definitions are learned from peer groups and from family but also may come from schools, churches, and other groups.[17]

This social learning first occurs in a process of differential association. The person interacts and identifies with groups that provide models for social reinforcements and behavior. The person first learns definitions of behavior through imitation within these groups; the definitions are then reinforced by the group and eventually serve as reinforcers for the person's behavior. Akers and his colleagues tested their social-learning theory in the context of drug and alcohol use and abuse. They found that the theory explained 55 percent of the variance in drinking behavior and 68 percent of the variance in the use of marijuana.[18]

The social-learning theory of Burgess and Akers has been widely cited. Cressey, the major proponent of Sutherland's theory of differential association, included their work in a group of works he described as "the major theories of criminologists."[19] But the theory has also been criticized. One critic concluded that the Burgess and Akers effort contained major oversights and that these might have misled sociologists and criminologists who were not familiar with the principles of operant conditioning.[20]

Differential Association and Peer Group Influence

Many of the empirical tests of differential association theory have found strong relationships among the variables of criminal associations, criminal definitions, and criminal behavior. Many of the studies do not, however, examine the complete causal structure that the theory implies. What is the order of cause? Do the criminal associations cause the criminal definitions, which in turn lead to criminal behavior? Or does the criminal behavior occur for some other reason, followed by a need to develop criminal associations and then criminal definitions? Is it possible that people who have criminal friends are pressured into criminal acts *before* they develop "an excess of definitions favorable to violation of the law?" Or is this conclusion based on a simplistic view of "excess of definitions," which fails to consider the concepts of frequency, priority, duration, and intensity that are also important to Sutherland's theory of differential association?[21]

Research has also emphasized the need to consider the type of primary group influences on behavior when testing differential association. It may be that during adolescence, peer groups have a very strong influence on the development of attitudes favorable or unfavorable to violating the law but that the impact decreases significantly with age, when other primary groups, such as the family or work groups, take on a greater significance. It may also be true that the impact of any of these groups will differ according to the type of criminal behavior.[22]

Several investigators have found a relationship between the seriousness of delinquency and the orientation of the peer group to which the delinquents belonged. A 1986 report on the relationship among gender, peer group experiences, and the seriousness of delinquency concluded that the major effect of gender appeared to be on the type of peer group to which a delinquent belonged. Lower rates of female compared to male delinquency were related to the fact that females were less likely than males to belong to delinquent groups. Research should be conducted on why this is true, a shift in focus from a social-structural approach (the peer group itself) to the process by which a male or female becomes a member of a particular peer group.[23]

Differential Identification and Differential Anticipation

Daniel Glaser studied differential association theory in relation to other theories of criminal behavior. He outlined all the facts that such a theory must explain, such as why the frequency, duration, and intensity of criminal or delinquent associations is predictive of criminal behavior. He concluded that differential association theory is more successful than other sociological theories as an explanation of such predictors but that the theory is deficient in other ways. Glaser therefore developed his own approach, first with **differential identification theory** and later with **differential anticipation theory.**

In his earlier development of differential identification, Glaser related his approach to role theory. Criminal behavior is seen basically as role playing; the theorist must explain why *criminal* roles are selected. Glaser defined identification as "the choice of another, from whose perspective we view our own behavior." The selected choices may come from direct association with criminals through identification with persons heard or viewed through the mass media or "as a negative reaction to forces opposed to crime." In essence, according to Glaser, the theory of differential identification is that "a person pursues criminal behavior to the extent that he identifies himself with real or imaginary persons from whose perspective his criminal behavior seems acceptable." It focuses on persons' interactions with the situation or environment and their interactions with themselves in rationalizing their conduct. In this sense, the theory is an integrative one, for it permits analysis of the relevance in each case of criminality of "economic conditions, prior frustrations, learned moral creeds, group participation, or other features of an individual's life."[24] Any or all of these may be important in that they may affect the person's choice of behavior.

Later, in an attempt to account for the successes and failures of inmates after they are released from prison, Glaser created the theory of differential anticipation. This theory relies on differential association but also on **differential opportunity theory.** The theory postulates that when people consider the legitimate and illegitimate behaviors available, they select the alternative that is perceived or anticipated to be the best. It makes no difference which actually is the best alternative; the anticipation of what is best is what counts.

Glaser's theory of differential anticipation draws on opportunity, differential association, social-learning, and self-concept theories. This approach, along with differential association, also has implications for the impact of the mass media on criminal behavior.

Differential Association and the Mass Media

Glaser stressed that identification with criminal behavior may be the result of contact with the media and is therefore not dependent on association with actual criminals. Whether the process is one of identification or imitation, the result is the same: What the media portray may influence how the viewers behave. Some of that impact may be seen in the current concern over whether television has an effect on behavior, a concern that raises the possibility of both psychological and sociological explanations of the process by which a person becomes deviant or law abiding. Before looking at research on behavior and mass media, we must take a brief look at an early theorist, Gabriel Tarde, who can be considered a forerunner of modern imitation theory.

Tarde and Imitation Theory

Gabriel Tarde (1843–1904) was born in southern France. After studying law, he was a magistrate for many years. As a judge, he showed extreme interest in social problems and proved himself a deep thinker and profound philosopher. Reacting against Lombroso and the positive school, Tarde argued that people are not born criminal; they become criminals. He saw criminal behavior as primarily the result of social factors, a belief that constitutes one of his greatest contributions to criminology:

> The majority of murderers and notorious thieves began as children who have been abandoned, and the true seminary of crime must be sought for upon each public square or each crossroad of our towns, whether they be small or large, in those flocks of pillaging street urchins who like bands of sparrows associate together, at first for marauding, and then for theft because of a lack of education and food in their homes.[25]

Tarde rejected the biological and physical theories of criminal behavior, but he did not become a social determinist. He thought people had some choice in their behavior, although he did believe that when that ability to choose is impaired, people should not be held responsible for their criminal acts.[26]

The second outstanding contribution of Tarde, which has had great influence on subsequent criminologists, is his analysis of the professional criminal. "He saw murderers, pickpockets, swindlers and thieves as individuals who had gone through a long period of apprenticeship, just as doctors, lawyers, farmers or skilled workmen. It was that the accident of birth placed them in an atmosphere of crime."[27]

Tarde's social-process theory of criminal behavior is reflected in his belief that all of the "important acts of social life are carried out under the domination of example."[28] Upon this belief he formulated his *theory of imitation*, through which he explained the process of acquiring criminal as well as noncriminal behavior. In developing his theory, Tarde distinguished between fashion and custom, which are both forms of imitation. *Fashion* is characteristic of the imitation that takes place in crowds or cities where contact is close and frequent. *Custom* refers to the phenomenon that occurs in small towns and rural areas where contact is less frequent and change occurs less often. Since fashion and custom are both forms of imitation, each occurs to a degree within a society; fashion may uproot and create a new custom. Since fashion and custom are related to the degree of social contact, Tarde formulated his first law of imitation: "Men imitate one another in proportion as they are in close contact."[29]

Tarde's second law of imitation is that the *inferior imitates the superior*. Peasants imitate royalty; small town and rural residents imitate the acts of city residents. He gave several examples: mutilations of women, the woman's practice of disfiguring her lover's face, the crimes of Jack the Ripper. "Infectious epidemics spread with the air or the wind; epidemics of crime follow the line of the telegraph."[30]

The third law of imitation is the *law of insertion:* "When two mutually exclusive fashions come together, one can be substituted for the other. When this happens, there is a decline in the older method and an increase in the newer method."[31] Tarde gives the example of using the gun rather than the knife for murder.

Tarde's neglect of the physical, psychological, and economic influences in behavior and his oversimplification of causation have led most sociologists to reject his theories of imitation.[32] But his "emphasis on the social origins of crime had a lasting impact on criminological thought in both Europe and America."[33]

Television and Imitation

According to psychological learning theorist Albert Bandura, research has shown that television, the most influential of the media for adolescents, has four types of effects on their social behavior:

1. The teaching of aggressive styles of conduct

2. The lessening of restraints on aggression

3. Desensitization and habituation to violence

4. The shaping of images of reality on which people base their actions

Bandura claims that television can distort people's perceptions of the real world. "Heavy viewers see the society at large as more dangerous regardless of their educational level, sex, age, and amount of newspaper reading."[34]

EXHIBIT 6.2

Mass Media Violence and Crime

Children spend more time watching television than in pursuing any other single activity. Even children at the lower end of the TV-use spectrum (2.5 hours of viewing per day) will have spent more time in front of a television set by the time they are 18 years of age than in the classroom. Adults spend about 40 percent of their leisure time watching television; television viewing thus ranks third behind sleep and work as occupier of adults' time.

The content of television programs is replete with depictions of violence. By the age of 18, the average person has witnessed over 18,000 murders on television. Sixty percent of prime-time television story-programs contain violent solutions to conflict situations. Cartoons are among the most violent television programs.

Most research findings to date are based on small-scale, experimental studies. While there is a need for further validation based on large-scale longitudinal field surveys, accumulating data clearly suggest that a relationship between televised and "real world" violence exists. (The exact extent to which televised violence contributes to other cultural and interpersonal violence will probably remain unknown since such an estimate depends on knowledge of a myriad of individual and situational predispositions.)

Children who watch violence on television are much less likely, than those who do not, to stop other children from hurting one another. Labeled the DESENSITIZATION EFFECT, this phenomenon may have considerable long-range anti-social consequences, extending, perhaps, even to a tolerance for war and other types of cultural violence.

Although once a widely accepted theory, the notion that television violence has a CATHARTIC EFFECT on the viewer, whereby his or her violent energy is drained off via empathetic experience with the screen actor, is not supported by research findings.

The theory most accepted by the scientific community as an explanation for the apparent link between televised violence and "real world" violence, and one with considerable empirical support, is SOCIAL LEARNING THEORY. According to this theory, depictions of violence on television teach people that violence is an acceptable means to an end or an appropriate response to frustration. Televised violence can also teach the "how-to's" of specific violent behaviors.

SOURCE: Preliminary Report, State of California Commission on Crime Control and Violence Prevention, *An Ounce of Prevention: Toward an Understanding of the Causes of Violence* (Sacramento, CA.: 1982), pp. 7–8.

Recently, attention has been given to the effect that violence on television might have on the behavior of adults and children. Exhibit 6.2 contains some of the conclusions of a California study of this issue, suggesting that children learn not only about violence but also exactly "how to do it." In 1989, after a thirteen-year-old male confessed to participating with a friend in a killing that involved beating their victim with a fireplace poker and kicking and stabbing him before choking him to death with a dog chain, when asked why he committed the act, said, "Oh, I don't know. I just seen it on TV."[35]

Researchers warn, however, that watching television does not occur in a vacuum. Although most of the surveys of reactions to a particular show occur right after the show in question, we cannot assume a direct cause-and-effect relationship. The behavior must be examined in the total context in which it occurs. By what process do some people react to television viewing with fear, with deviant behavior, or with no negative reactions? Psychological and sociological theories of behavior must be considered.[36]

The simplistic approach continues, however, and is given even greater strength by mass media reports. For example, in April 1984, a twelve-year-old boy was charged with the sexual assault of a ten-year-old girl, whom he forced to perform oral sex and then forced onto a pool table and further assaulted while other children watched. Officials claim that he might have gotten the idea from watching the television account of the rape trial in New Bedford, Massachusetts, in which several defendants were tried for raping a woman on a pool table in a bar while other people watched and did nothing to prevent the attack. That case resulted in two acquittals and two convictions.[37] Again, however, the process is important. Probably other children viewed the trial on television and did not copy the behavior at issue. A recent study of the effect of television on behavior emphasized this point.

> The empirical and theoretical evidence suggests that . . . the effects of television's content depend in part on the extent to which contradictory messages are available, understood, and consistent. In the case of sex-role attitudes, messages from television are consistent and either absent or reinforced in real life, whereas in the case of aggressive behavior, most viewers receive contradictory messages from both sources. All viewers may learn aggression from television, but whether they act agressively will depend on a variety of factors.[38]

PORNOGRAPHY AND CRIMINAL BEHAVIOR

The 1986 publication of the final report of the Commission on Pornography, appointed by Attorney General Edwin Meese, focused nationwide attention on the relationship between pornography and aggressive behavior. The commission concluded that there is a causal relationship between some forms of aggressive behavior and pornography. Some of the commission's conclusions and twelve of its ninety-two recommendations are contained in Exhibit 6.3.

Two members of the commission issued a strong dissent from the commission's finding that hard-core pornography may cause violent behavior. According to one of the dissenters, "The idea that 11 individuals studying in their spare time could complete a comprehensive report on so complex a matter in so constricted a time frame is simply unrealistic. . . . No self-respecting investigator would accept conclusions based on such a study." Many social scientists have agreed with this criticism. Others have pointed out that the commission's conclusions contradict those of a 1970 presidential panel "which found no link between violence and sexually explicit material."[39]

In defense of its conclusions, some members of the commission argued that since 1970 the nature of sexually explicit material has changed; today it is more violent and more explicit. This conclusion is

There is no agreement on what constitutes pornography in this country; nor is there agreement on what impact, if any, pornography has on crime.

EXHIBIT 6.3

Meese Commission on Pornography: Selected Conclusions and Recommendations

CONCLUSIONS

1. Some forms of sexually explicit material bear a causal relationship both to sexual violence and to sex discrimination, but we are hardly so naive as to suppose that were these forms of pornography to disappear the problems of sex discrimination and sexual violence would come to an end. . . .

2. When clinical and experimental research has focused particularly on sexually violent material, the conclusions have been virtually unanimous. In both clinical and experimental settings, exposure to sexually violent materials has indicated an increase in the likelihood of aggression. More specifically, the research . . . shows a causal relationship between exposure to material of this type and aggressive behavior towards women. . . .

3. With respect to sexually violent materials the evidence is strongest, societal consensus is greatest, and the consequent harms of rape and other forms of sexual violence are hardly ones that this or any other society can take lightly. In light of this, we would urge that the prosecution of legally obscene material that contains violence be placed at the top of both state and federal priorities in enforcing the obscenity laws.

RECOMMENDATIONS

1. [The commission had several recommendations concerning federal and state laws.]

2. The attorney general should direct the United States attorneys to examine the obscenity problem in their respective districts.

3. The attorney general should appoint a high-ranking official from the Department of Justice to oversee the creation and operation of an obscenity task force. . . .

4. Judges should impose substantial periods of incarceration for persons

questioned by social scientists who argue that neither the commission's report nor current scientific evidence supports a causal relationship between pornography and violence.

The relationship between pornography and violence, especially sexual violence against women, received widespread media attention in January 1989 after the execution in Florida of Ted Bundy, convicted killer who was accused of multiple murders in addition to the one for which he was executed. Shortly before his execution Bundy confessed to other murders and attributed his problems to stimulation by pornography. His state-

who are repeatedly convicted of obscenity law violations and when appropriate should order payment of restitution to identified victims as part of the sentence.

5. Congress should enact legislation to make the acts of child selling or child purchasing, for the production of sexually explicit visual depictions, a felony.

6. State legislatures should amend laws, where necessary, to make the knowing possession of child pornography a felony.

7. Judges should impose appropriate periods of incarceration for convicted child pornographers and related offenders.

8. Judges should use, when appropriate, a sentence of lifetime probation for convicted child pornographers.

9. State and federal correctional facilities should recognize the unique problems of child pornographers

and related offenders and designate appropriate programs regarding their incarceration.

10. A multi-media educational campaign should be developed which increases family and community awareness regarding child sexual exploitation through the production and use of child pornography.

11. "Adults Only" pornographic outlet peep show facilities which provide individual booths for viewing should not be equipped with doors. The occupant of the booth should be clearly visible to eliminate a haven for sexual activity.

12. Holes enabling interbooth sexual contact between patrons should be prohibited in the peep show booths.

SOURCE: *Attorney General's Commission on Pornography: Final Report* (Washington, D.C.: U.S. Department of Justice, July 1986), pp. 309, 324, 326–327. The recommendations are on pp. 433–458.

ments were questioned by many, as indicated in the media report in Highlight 6.1.

Many who believe pornography causes violence have called for stricter laws. Congress has responded with the Child Protection Act of 1984, a statute that was first enacted in 1978 and amended in 1984. This act cited the following findings:

1. Child pornography has developed into a highly organized, multimillion-dollar industry which operates on a nationwide scale;

HIGHLIGHT 6.1

DID PORNOGRAPHY INFLUENCE BUNDY?

Ted Bundy's dramatic confession that pornography "guided and shaped" him into a serial killer has touched off a debate over how much of it was drama and how much confession.

In a videotaped interview released to reporters after he was electrocuted Tuesday morning, Bundy told California-based religious broadcaster James C. Dobson that hard-core pornography fueled his fantasies and ultimately led to his violent sexual crimes.

"What interests me is why there would be so much interest in this kind of off-the-wall, wacko commentary," said Jack Moore, chairman of American studies at the University of South Florida. Moore, a long-standing member of the American Civil Liberties Union, has a special interest in issues such as pornography.

Alluding to the Bundy-Dobson interview as a performance, Moore said: "Here is a condemned man in the last moments of his life, of questionable mental state, talking to an evangelical huckster, and people are suddenly concerned with what the man has said. In a way this is baffling.

"It's certainly possible to oppose pornography, but no serious scholar would use Bundy's testimony as containing any substance," Moore said. "The man has been thoroughly discredited as a human being, so on what subject is he an expert?"

Dobson, a psychologist and antipornography crusader was a vocal member of former Attorney General Edwin Meese's federal Commission on Pornography. The commission's conclusion in 1986 that most pornography can lead to violence was ridiculed by two members of the panel and by many social scientists as not being based on firm scientific evidence.

One of the panelists who dissented, Judith V. Becker, a professor of psychology at Columbia University, said by telephone Thursday: "Why people develop the type of sexual interest patterns they do and why they commit sexual crimes is a rather complex issue, and we don't have any evidence that there's just one factor involved."

She advised taking Bundy's words with a lot of caution.

Even though she is concerned about sexually violent material and has seen more than 1,000 sex offenders, Becker said: "We really don't have data to say that (pornography) causes something or that it doesn't."

But many people do make that connection, adamantly.

Jerry Kirk, head of the National Coalition Against Pornography and chairman of the Religious Alliance Against Pornography, compares it to the link between smoking and lung cancer.

"The evidence was overwhelming for years before we said there really is a causal rela-

tionship," he said in an interview Thursday. "Why should (the pornography-violence connection) surprise us? If good books can educate us to good qualities and thoughts and behavior—which is the premise of all education—then why in the world would we be surprised that books that promote bad, violent, degrading, humiliating behavior produce those kinds of thoughts and that kind of behavior?"

"I was not at all surprised with what Ted Bundy said," added Kirk, who is co-pastor of a Presbyterian church in Cincinnati.

"It's not only people who are predisposed to violence that hard-core pornography is impacting," he said. "A significant percentage of the men of America are being taught by hard-core pornography that women enjoy being raped . . . that they say no but mean yes (and) will yield to you and enjoy it so much that they will plead for more."

In his interview with Dobson, Bundy said his exposure to pornography began with magazines found in trash cans, then progressed to "more potent, more explicit, more graphic kinds of material," until he reached "that jumping off point where you begin to wonder if maybe actually doing it would give you that which is beyond just reading it or looking at it." He also said that "alcohol reduced my inhibitions at the same time the fantasy life that was fueled by pornography eroded them further."

HIGHLIGHT 6.1 (Continued)

Bundy, suspected of killing as many as 50 women in several states, was executed for the death of 12-year-old Kimberly Leach of Lake City.

At another point in the interview he said that in his many years in prison he had met a lot of men who "were motivated to violence just like me. And without exception, every one of them was deeply involved in pornography, without question; without exception, deeply influenced and consumed by an addiction."

To Sarah Bradley, a Clearwater counselor who treats compulsive behaviors, Bundy's statements show the progression of an addiction to sex. She said his behavior mirrors the three levels of sexual addiction outlined by Patrick Carnes in his book, *Out of the Shadows:* A first level that may include the use of written and visual pornography or masturbation for sexual stimulation; a second level in which the addict starts involving other people, by way of exhibitionism or voyeurism, for example; and a third level in which the addict moves to rape or incest or, in some cases, murder.

Of course not every sex addict becomes a Ted Bundy. "Some are prominent people," Bradley said. "They are not just scum bags."

Many are angry people who may have been rejected or may have been a victim of incest, and they try to use sex as medication for their psychic or emotional pain. Like a drug, their anger soothes the pain only to a point.

As their addiction progresses, they become trapped in a cycle of obsessive-compulsive behavior that is very hard to stop.

Because of what she sees as pornography's role in this addiction, Bradley said, "I'd just like to burn it all."

"If you look at the Romans, all of this stuff has been there, probably from the beginning of time, in some form," she said. "But society has changed, and more people have started to act out, and in more destructive ways."

Some people say that banning pornography would erode the Constitution's protection of free speech, but Bradley compares it to efforts to restrict advertising for cigarettes and beer.

"This is just as detrimental," she said. "People die from alcoholism, and they die from smoking, and they could die from sex addiction. . . . They are destroying their body, mentally and physically."

She said the growing awareness of sexual addiction has led to the formation of self-help groups like Sex and Love Addicts Anonymous and, for spouses, Codependents of Sex Addicts.

A Detroit psychiatrist who interviewed Bundy before his trial for the murders of two Florida State University students said Bundy's remarks about pornography were just another effort to manipulate.

Emanuel Tanay, an expert witness in the cases of other serial killers, was quoted Thursday by the *Orlando Sentinel* as saying:

"Pornography doesn't have the power to cause the severe deformity of personality that he had. Whatever he was like, it was laid down as a young boy before he was old enough to set eyes on pornography. Whatever would attract him to pornography would attract him to his other behavior. It's one more ramification of his twisted mind, if you will."

Moore, the USF professor, marveled at the "whole circus" surrounding Bundy's execution, calling it "social hysteria" and a "mob reaction" for people to publicly urge that Bundy "fry" or "broil" for his crimes and for disc jockeys to play records with anti-Bundy sentiment "expressive of barbarism."

To Moore, this was more than speaking out for capital punishment. Bundy became "the focal point for all psychological needs that other people have in terms of hatred and vituperation," he said. "The issue for these people is something other than the death penalty—some kind of kink in their own lives perhaps. They're calling him a savage and themselves acting in a savage manner."

SOURCE: Kris Wells, "Did Pornography Influence Bundy?" *St. Petersburg Times,* 27 January 1989, p. D1, col. 4. Reprinted with permission from the St. Petersburg Times.

2. Thousands of children including large numbers of runaway and homeless youth are exploited in the production and distribution of pornographic materials;

3. The use of children as subjects of pornographic materials is harmful to the physiological, emotional, and mental health of the individual child and to society.[40]

One problem with pornography statutes, however, is that they are often unconstitutionally vague by not describing the prohibited activity with sufficient specificity, or too broad, thus including behavior that is not prohibited. Such statutes may also be declared unconstitutional if they unreasonably inhibit a citizen's First Amendment right to free speech. Each case must thus be examined individually to see whether the statute in question is constitutional.[41]

In addition to calling for stricter laws, pornography opponents have also called for greater surveillance techniques and stricter penalties for persons convicted of statutory violations. But these actions might infringe on the right to free speech and the right to be free of unreasonable searches and seizures. Civil libertarians have expressed great concern over the repercussions of attempts to enforce laws regulating pornography.[42] The controversy over pornography has also led to a debate on feminism, with some taking the position that although the sexually explicit material may be offensive to feminists, it has not been shown to be "sufficiently harmful to justify state intrusion."[43]

The recent emphasis on the possible causal relationship between criminal behavior and violence on television, in magazines, and in movies (many of which can be purchased or rented for home viewing) may result in even greater attention being paid by social scientists to the theory of differential association. A study of these issues might also be important in the next major category of social-process theories, the social-control theories.

SOCIAL-CONTROL THEORY

Earlier discussions of the classical approach and modern deterrence theory examined the proposition that criminal behavior is rational, that it is the response of people who have decided what they want and calculated the costs. Crime is more attractive than achieving the goods or services by legitimate means. If so, the economic approach is to control such behavior by increasing the cost or the punishment.

Sociologists and psychologists have developed other explanations of how behavior can be controlled. According to control theorists, deviance results when social controls are either weakened or broken down. When controls are strong, deviance does not occur. The problem is to try to explain what can be done in a positive way to elicit appropriate behavior. The question is not how to prevent criminal behavior but how to train people to engage in law-abiding behavior. This training is done through control theory, which begins with the assumption that all persons have to be trained to behave properly.

Like many other explanations of criminal behavior, **social-control theory** is really not a theory in the sense of rigorous scientific procedures of developing and testing hypotheses; rather, it is an approach or an explanation. There are three types. In one, training is basically a psychological approach, considered in Chapter 4. In this section we will examine the other two types: containment, illustrated by the work of Walter C. Reckless, and attachment and commitment, illustrated by the work of Travis Hirschi. It is important, however, to begin by pointing out that all three approaches have some common assumptions, articulated by one sociologist as follows:

1. That the human animal requires nurturing.

2. That differences in nurturing account for variations in attachment to others and commitment to an ordered way of living.

3. That attachment and commitment may be described as "internal controls," commonly called "conscience" and recognized in *guilt*, and "external controls," usually tested by the production of *shame*.

4. That evidence from experimental studies, longitudinal research, comparative studies, and cross-cultural investigation tells us *how* attachment and commitment are developed. Conversely, such evidence describes the situations that loosen the moral bond with others and that are, therefore, productive of crime.[44]

Containment Theory

One version of social-control theory is **containment theory,** which stresses that we live in a society that provides a variety of opportunities for conformity or nonconformity. Clearly not everyone chooses the illegal opportunities; thus social-structural theories that stress the availability of illegal and legal opportunities, the existence of a subculture, the location of goods and services within the city, density, and other variables cannot adequately explain criminal behavior. What we need to know is why those phenomena affect some people and not others. That is, why are some of us apparently immune to such influences in that our exposure is not followed by criminal behavior? Reckless suggested that the answer lies in containment theory, which he defined as follows:

The assumption is that there is a containing external social structure which holds individuals in line and that there is also an internal buffer which protects people against deviation of the social and legal norms. The two containments act as a defense against deviation from the legal and social norms, as an insulation against pressures and pulls, as a protection against demoralization and seduction. If there are "causes" which lead to deviant behavior, they are negated, neutralized, rendered impotent, or are paired by the two containing buffers.[45]

There are two types of containment: *outer containment* and *inner containment*. Outer containment might also be called social pressure, and in simple societies, this kind of social control works quite well. The community's social **norms** are taught to new members, who internalize them but who are also restrained by the community's reaction to their violation. Social ostracism may be the most effective social control in such societies or communities, but as societies become more complex, outer containment is not so effective. It is therefore important that people develop inner containment mechanisms by which they can control their own behavior.

Inner containment refers to our ability to direct ourselves, which is related to our **self-concept**. "One of the components of capability of self is a favorable self-image, self-concept, self-perception. The person who conceives of himself as a responsible person is apt to act responsibly."[46] A high goal level, especially regarding societal goals, and a high aspiration level geared to society's expectations are also essential components of the self. Frustration tolerance and identification with society's values and laws are important. The opposite of this is alienation—the release of inner containment.

Reckless emphasized that the components of external and internal containment are buffers, not causes. They operate to help the individual refrain from succumbing to pressures to violate laws. If the buffers are strong, the person will be law abiding. But if they are weak, he or she will commit a crime.

One way that these buffers operate is in helping to neutralize the norms. Recent research on self-concept has given us more insight into the process of neutralization. A sample of white, working-class males was examined in sixth grade and then again in ninth grade. When the boys were in the sixth grade, their behavior appeared to be more strongly controlled by the norms they attributed to their peers than by their own internalized norms. But by the time they were in the ninth grade, internalized norms were a stronger factor. This suggests that inner containment theory does not have the same influence at all stages of adolescent development. The study also found that the boys' self-concept "is especially important as an explanation of such behavior and as an intervening variable that affects the relationship between other attitudes and possible behavioral outcomes."[47]

Evaluation

Despite the claims of Reckless and his associates that containment theory can explain most delinquency and crime; that the theory might bring psychologists and sociologists together in the study of crime because it involves both disciplines; and that the theory, unlike many others, can be used in an individual case history,[48] the theory has also been severely criticized. It cannot explain why people who do the same things are differentially labeled; it is limited in its predictive ability; and its measure of self-concept has been questioned, along with the lack of control groups in some of the early works. The difficulty of measuring the strength or weakness of external and internal containment is a problem. Nor does the theory explain why some children with bad self-concepts are not delinquent.[49]

Containment theory may be most useful when combined with other approaches. In a comparison of containment theory with differential association theory, one sociologist concluded that they are similar, except that differential association emphasizes the *process* of differential association, whereas containment theory emphasizes the *product* of socialization—the self-concept. Both of these theories can account for delinquency more fully than either can separately.[50]

It has also been argued that containment theory is too general. Its concepts are too vague and its theory too broad to produce testable hypotheses for rigorous empirical research.[51] Travis Hirschi attempted to eliminate these criticisms by refining the elements of control theory.

Hirschi's Social-Control Theory

Hirschi emphasizes that it is not deviance that we need to explain but, rather, conforming behavior. The real question, says Hirschi, is why, with so many opportunities and pressures to commit crimes, most of us are law-abiding citizens most of the time. The basic concept of control theory, asserts Hirschi, is "the bond of the individual to society." That bond has four components: attachment, commitment, involvement, and belief, which are defined in Exhibit 6.4. Hirschi believes that delinquency becomes more likely as this social bond is weakened.

> In every case, the conclusion is the same: the absence of control increases the likelihood of delinquency regardless of the presence of group traditions of delinquency. Although social support increases the likelihood that delinquent acts will be committed, the view that the child must somehow be taught crime in intimate, personal groups greatly overstates the case.[52]

Hirschi tested his theory on a sample of California youths, using the self-report method (discussed and analyzed in Chapter 2) of collecting data. The four thousand junior and senior high school students were given questionnaires designed to measure their attitudes toward friends, neighborhood, parents, school, teachers, and human relations. They were asked to respond to the following six questions, indicating whether they had (1) never committed the offense, (2) committed the offense more than

EXHIBIT 6.4

Hirschi's Social-Control Theory: Elements of the Social Bond

1. *Attachment* refers to our affective ties to people who are important to us and to our sensitivity to their opinions. Our feelings of obligations to others help control our behavior.

2. *Commitment* refers to the time and energy that we invest in our way of living. According to Hirschi, commitment "is the rational component in conformity." Youngsters who are involved in smoking, drinking, and wasting time, for example, are not investing time and energy in conventional behavior. They are therefore risking the chances of attaining sufficient education and a high-paying job. Without this commitment to conventional values, they are more likely to become delinquent.

3. *Involvement* refers to engrossment or immersion in conventional values. Involvement is a consequence of commitment. The person who chooses to pursue nonconventional behavior because of a lack of commitment will thereby exclude some opportunities, as will the person who chooses involvement in conventional behavior. Thus, the student who is committed to and involved in academic work excludes some possibilities for "fun and games." Likewise, the person who is committed to and involved mainly in living the "good life" will thereby exclude some opportunities for development in the academic world.

4. *Belief* means that a person attributes moral validity to conventional norms. The laws and rules of society are seen as "right" and "moral." Youngsters with intense belief are less likely to become delinquent.

SOURCE: Paraphrased from Travis Hirschi, *Causes of Delinquency* (Berkeley and Los Angeles: University of California Press, 1969), pp. 16–34; copyright 1969 The Regents of the University of California.

one year ago, (3) committed the offense during the past year, or (4) committed the offense during the past year as well as more than a year ago:

1. Have you ever taken little things (worth less than $2) that did not belong to you?

2. Have you ever taken things of some value (between $2 and $50) that did not belong to you?

3. Have you ever taken things of large value (worth over $50) that did not belong to you?

4. Have you ever taken a car for a ride without the owner's permission?

5. Have you ever banged up something that did not belong to you on purpose?

6. Not counting fights you may have had with a brother or sister, have you ever beaten up on anyone or hurt anyone on purpose?[53]

The responses to these questions were used as an index of self-reported delinquency. In addition, questions were asked about work, money, expectations, aspirations, participation in school activities, and use of leisure time. School records, including grades, and police records were also utilized as sources of data for the study.

The high association between low socioeconomic class and crime, found in the earlier studies using official crime data, has been questioned by self-report studies. Hirschi also found strong evidence that this traditional association does not exist. Indeed, he found very little association between social class as measured by the father's occupation, and admitted or official delinquency, with the exception of a low incidence, by both measures, of delinquency among the sons of professionals. He did find, however, that boys "whose fathers have been unemployed and/or whose families are on welfare are more likely than children from fully employed, self-sufficient families to commit delinquent acts." The study also indicated that positive attitudes toward teachers and school were related to nondelinquent behavior. Hirschi also found that the closer the ties to the parents, the less likely it was that the youths would engage in delinquent acts. It was not the parent's status that was important but, rather, the child's *attachment* to the parent.[54]

Hirschi concluded that young people who are not very attached to their parents and to school are more likely to be delinquent than are those with these kinds of attachments. He also found that youths who have positive attitudes toward their own accomplishments are more likely to believe in the validity and appropriateness of conventional laws and moral rules of society than are youths who are negative about their own accomplishments.

Evaluation

Although Hirschi's study in California was based on a sample of urban respondents, a study of a rural sample in New York State, conducted by Michael Hindelang, found support for Hirschi's social control theory.[55] However, Hindelang "failed to replicate a positive relationship between attachment to parents and attachment to friends . . . he failed to show that attachment to friends increases the likelihood of delinquent behavior." In fact, claimed a critic, Hindelang "found a slight positive relationship between identification with peers and delinquency which is unexplainable in terms of control theory." This does not mean, however, that the theory is incorrect—only that it is incomplete. We need to go beyond attachment to peers and discover the type of peer to whom the individual

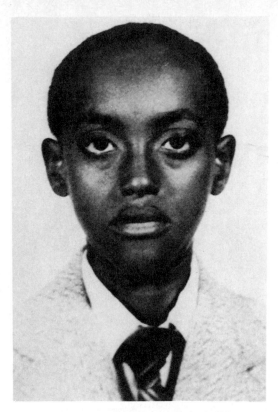

Various theories of criminal and delinquent behavior have been advanced, but it is difficult to explain the behavior of the 13-year-old who set afire David Aupont, 12, in New York. Prior to immolating Aupont, the other boy beat and bound him, trying to force him to smoke crack against his will. Aupont was hospitalized in critical condition with burns on more than half his body.

is attached before the analysis has validity for the prediction of delinquent behavior.[56]

Others have found that the type of peer does not matter[57] or that the likelihood of delinquent behavior seems to be decreased by attachment to conventional peers but increased by attachment to delinquent peers.[58] Hirschi recognized that his theory of social control "does not escape unscathed." In the first place, his theory "underestimated the importance of delinquent friends; it overestimated the significance of involvement in conventional activities." He also decided that one should probably look at the relationship between delinquent activities and the person's self-concept or self-esteem. That relationship might be important in explaining "the potency of the adult-status items, such as smoking, drinking, dating, and driving a car." Although social-control theory can help us understand these relations, Hirschi noted, it leaves a lot unexplained. However, he concludes on an optimistic note with regard to his theory: "I am confident that when the processes through which these variables affect delinquency are spelled out, they will supplement rather than seriously modify the control theory, but that remains to be seen."[59]

Perhaps a more serious challenge to Hirschi's theory has been raised by those who emphasize that most tests of the theory have used cross-sectional data at a particular time rather than measuring the relationship of variables over time. A sample of males at the beginning of their sophomore year in high school and then again near the end of their junior year indicated that Hirschi's social-control theory is more limited than he claims. This study showed that the theory does not accurately predict delinquency among middle to older adolescents, although it might very well be important in predicting delinquency among younger adolescents.[60] Similar findings were reported by other investigators, who concluded that adolescence should not be viewed as a unitary period but should be further refined by age.[61]

Another criticism of Hirschi's social control theory, discussed here as a social process theory, comes from one of Hirschi's doctoral students, Thomas J. Bernard, who argues that the four elements of the theory are not all social psychological variables as Hirschi suggests. According to Bernard, *commitment* is a social structural variable that differs from the other three variables of Hirschi's theory: attachment, involvement, and belief which are social psychological variables. Commitment, says Bernard, "confuses the definition and the explanation of conformity" and "is properly conceived as an antecedent variable that measures the role of social structure in the origin of delinquency."[62]

Bernard argues that viewing commitment as a social structural rather than a social process variable would eliminate the current perception in Hirschi's theory that "the individual's bonding to society is independent of social structural characteristics, and therefore can be enhanced without broader societal changes."[63]

Despite Bernard's suggestions for revision of Hirschi's social control theory, he emphasizes that none of his suggestions should challenge

> the substantial contribution of Hirschi's theory to criminology {which has} generated a host of studies that have advanced criminology as a science, whether or not they support Hirschi's conclusions.[64]

Hirschi's contributions have also been cited by others. His 1969 work, *Causes of Delinquency*, in which he stated his theory, has been described as "a benchmark for theory construction and research in the delinquency field."[65] As Bernard indicated, Hirschi's theory has generated considerable research, some of which has resulted in additional suggestions for modification or extension.

According to some critics, Hirschi's social-control theory is more complete than subcultural or differential association theory, but it does not give a complete explanation. The theory does not show how the four elements of attachment, commitment, involvement, and belief might operate simultaneously to discourage delinquent behavior. Furthermore, Hirschi does not empirically test the relationships among the social bond's four elements. Consequently, the theory raises three issues:

1. Are the four elements "empirically distinct components of socialization?"

2. Why are only four elements identified?

3. Although Hirschi talks about educational and occupational aspirations, he does not incorporate into the theory elements such as family socioeconomic level, ability, and the influence of significant others, and research has found that all of them are important.[66]

Investigators who attempted to replicate Hirschi's theory and incorporate these additional elements found general support for the social-bond theory's four elements, but they found that the theory needed reformulation and expansion:

> In the context of statistical controls for ability, social class, and grades in school, the bond elements which emerge as important explanatory variables are attachment to parents, dating, attachment to school, belief, and involvement. A model incorporating these bond elements appears more isomorphic with theories of adolescent socialization which treat education as important in the integration of the youth into adult social life.[67]

Social-Control Theory and Female Criminality

Social-control theory also has implications for explaining female criminality. Numerous studies have delved into the problem of whether crime is the result of masculinity; the results of those studies are not consistent.[68] Others have suggested that the explanation lies in social-control theory; that is, people with weaker bonds to conventional society are more likely than those with closer bonds to engage in criminal behavior. Thus, "males may be more involved than females in delinquency because they have weaker bonds to conventional society."[69]

Social bonding might also be used to explain why women murder. One study, which examined the rare form of murder among women (killing other females), although based on a small sample (fifteen women arrested for killing females in the predominantly black city of Detroit, Michigan, during 1982 and 1983) reported that nearly one-half of the victims were children or stepchildren of the offenders. Women who kill other women (or female children) are characterized by social isolation from mainstream culture.

> These are minority mothers who, for the most part, are living in loosely structured relationships with men, and are poorly equipped to overcome the daily mundane struggles to just get by. They are drastically limited in the educational and occupational resources and in the social skills required to maintain a life of comfort and dignity in the United States today. Though their knowledge of the street scene is particularly keen, they are shrouded in ignorance in other areas critical to their sense of well-

being. . . . In-depth accounts describing the interpersonal dynamics of these women's lives would shed light on the antecedents to their violence—those rooted in personality as well as role structures.[70]

Self-Help and Social Control

The first chapter discussed the purpose of law, noting that prior to the emergence of law, many problems were solved on an individual basis. People were not only permitted—but also were expected—to take action for revenge when they had been victimized by the acts of others. Such self-help was not seen as criminal; it was appropriate behavior. Many kinds of behavior that are criminal today are criminal because they are so defined. Thus, some of the crimes today are acts that in the past were considered appropriate measures of self-help.

Donald Black, who has written extensively on the purposes of criminal law, has also advanced a social-control theory that incorporates self-help. He defines self-help as "the expression of a grievance by unilateral aggression. It is thus distinguishable from social control through third parties such as police officers or judges and from avoidance behavior such as desertion and divorce." According to Black,

Crime often expresses a grievance. This implies that many crimes belong to the same family as gossip, ridicule, vengeance, punishment, and law itself. It also implies that to a significant degree we may predict and explain crime with a sociological theory of social control, specifically a theory of self-help.[71]

Social Control: A Conclusion

Social-control theory has produced extensive and significant research that is helpful in understanding and explaining delinquent and criminal behavior. It has the advantage of an individualized approach in that it recognizes that we all do not respond in the same way to the same environment. For that reason, the theory may be popular with the public, but it does not provide blueprints for the kinds of changes that can be implemented by politicians. In that sense, it may be less attractive, despite its empirical basis, than social-structural approaches that do give a basis for political change. If unemployment is seen as the cause of crime, plans can be implemented to change employment opportunities. But if commitment to an involvement with family are significant elements, change will be more difficult. As one expert concluded, "The truth sometimes tells us more clearly what we can*not* have and what will *not* work."[72]

LABELING THEORY

A final approach to explaining crime is quite different from the others discussed. Most theories and explanations of criminal behavior look for its *cause.* Why did the individual commit the crime, and what can be done to prevent such actions in the future? The answer may be found in the individual physique, body build, chemical imbalance, hormones, or chromosomes; it may be found in the environment; or it may be the result of some type of social process. The emphasis is on finding out why the person engaged in the behavior.

Labeling theory, in contrast, asks why the person was *designated* deviant and thus applies to all kinds of deviant and nondeviant behavior. The critical issue is not the behavior but why the behavior is labeled deviant. This theory is not interested in what was done, but, rather, in how people reacted to what was done. Not all who engage in certain kinds of behavior are labeled deviant, but some are. What is the reason for this distinction? One sociologist has described this approach as follows:

> Some men who drink heavily are called alcoholics and others are not, some men who behave oddly are committed to hospitals and others are not . . . and the difference between those who earn a deviant title in society and those who go their own way in peace is largely determined by the way in which the community filters out and codes the many details of behavior which come to its attention.[73]

If criminal behavior is to be explained according to the response of others rather than the characteristics of the offender, the appropriate subject matter will be the *audience*, not the individual; for it is the existence of the behavior, not why it occurred, that is significant. Only the audience's response determines whether that behavior will be defined as deviant.

This final section of the chapters on theory will consider the history and development of the labeling perspective along with a critique of this approach. In some respects it is a social-structural approach, like conflict theory, but it is primarily a social-process theory because it attempts to explain labeling as a process by which some people who commit deviant acts come to be known as deviants whereas others are not.

Emergence and Development of Labeling Theory

A 1938 statement reprinted in Exhibit 6.5 describes the labeling concept. This concept was further developed by Edwin Lemert, who distinguished primary and secondary deviance as follows:

> Primary deviation is assumed to arise in a wide variety of social, cultural, and psychological contexts, and at best has only marginal implication for the psychic structure of the individual; it does not lead to symbolic reorganization at the level of self-regarding attitudes and social roles. Secondary deviation is deviant behavior or social roles based upon it, which becomes a means of defense, attack or adaptation to the overt and covert problems created by the societal reaction to primary deviation.[74]

EXHIBIT 6.5

The Process of Labeling Behavior

The process of making the criminal is a process of tagging, defining, identifying, segregating, describing, emphasizing, making conscious and self-conscious; it becomes a way of stimulating, suggesting, emphasizing, and evoking the very traits that are complained of.

The person becomes the thing he is described as being. Nor does it seem to matter whether the valuation is made by those who would punish or by those who would reform. In either case the emphasis is upon conduct that is disapproved of. The parents or the policeman, the older brother or the court, the probation officer or the juvenile institution, insofar as they rest on the thing complained of, rest upon a false ground. Their very enthusiasm defeats their aim. The harder they work to reform the evil, the greater the evil grows under their hands. The persistent suggestion, with whatever good intentions, works mischief because it leads to bring out the bad behavior it would suppress. The way out is through a refusal to dramatize the evil. The less said about it the better.

SOURCE: Reprinted with permission of Columbia University Press from Frank Tannenbaum, *Crime and the Community* (1983), pp. 19–20.

To labeling theorists, primary deviance is relatively unimportant; it is secondary deviance that is most important, for it is the interaction between the person labeled deviant and the labeler that counts. This approach is often called *interaction theory*.

Another contributor to the early development of labeling theory was Howard S. Becker who pointed out that because many people who break rules are not considered deviant and others are, we must distinguish between rule breaking and deviance. Rule breaking describes the behavior, but deviance describes the other's reaction to that behavior; rule breaking is thus defined as deviant when engaged in by *some* people. It is important to find out who is and who is not labeled deviant. According to labeling theorists, the people who will most often be labeled deviant for their rule-breaking behavior are those on the margin of society, and once they are labeled deviant, they usually cannot escape the designation. According to Becker, "Social groups create deviance by making rules whose infractions constitute deviance, and by applying those rules to particular people and labeling them as outsiders. From this point of view, deviance is not a quality of the act a person commits, but rather a consequence of the application by others of rules and sanctions to an 'offender.' The deviant is one to whom the label has successfully been applied; deviant behavior is behavior that people so label."[75]

The effect of the deviant label also extends to the self-concept of the labeled person who, according to labeling theory, has experienced a socialization process that is virtually irreversible, not only from the point of view of the labeler, but also from that of the person labeled. That person develops a self-concept consistent with the deviant label and also acquires the knowledge and skills of the labeled status. Whether or not labeling occurs depends on (1) the time the act is committed, (2) who commits the act and who is the victim, and (3) society's perception of the consequences of the act.[76]

The Labeling Process

Another labeling theorist, Edwin Schur, has identified the key processes in labeling as stereotyping, retrospective interpretation, and negotiation.[77]

Stereotyping is most often associated with racial prejudice, but, says Schur, the process also applies in criminal justice to situations that do not necessarily involve race. For example, research has shown that police reaction to juveniles is often related to the cues police perceive and their reactions to those cues, with greater deference on the part of the juvenile resulting in a lower chance of apprehension by the police.[78]

By *retrospective interpretation*, Schur means that once a person is "identified as deviant, he is seen in a totally 'new light.'" In addition to distinguishing personal characteristics, the person is given a new personal identity by the labelers. Through the process of a degradation ceremony, the deviant person "becomes in the eyes of his condemners literally a different and *new* person. It is not that the new attributes are added to the old 'nucleus.' He is not changed; he is reconstituted. . . . The former identity stands as accidental; the new identity is the 'basic reality.' What he is now is what 'after all,' he was all along."[79]

The third identifiable process in labeling is *negotiating*. This is seen more clearly in cases of adults, often involving the **plea-bargaining** process in which the attorney for the accused will try to make a deal with the prosecutor, such as agreeing to plead guilty and thus avoiding a trial, in exchange for a promise that the prosecutor will drop other charges or recommend a light penalty.

Effects of Labeling

What are the effects of labeling on the individual? Labeling theory is based on the assumption that people respond to other people in an informal and unorganized way until these others are placed in categories that lead to stereotyping, which then causes corresponding responses. The response may become what sociologists call the self-fulfilling prophecy. Labeling is particularly important in the area of delinquent behavior because of the discretion police and other authorities have when a juvenile commits a delinquent act. Most youths commit some delinquent acts; only a few are labeled delinquent. "The evidence suggests that official response to the behavior in question may initiate processes that push the misbehaving juveniles toward further delinquent conduct, and, at least, make it more difficult for them to reenter the conventional world."[80] If, on the other hand, the juvenile does not experience official response to the delinquent acts, he or she may continue committing them while receiving no help in changing behavior.

Once labeled, the labelee has an almost impossible task shedding that status. The effects of labeling may also snowball in that once a person is stigmatized by the label, new restrictions are placed on legitimate opportunities and the labelee's probabilities of further deviance are increased. Such a vicious circle is reinforced by the tendency of the public to believe that one who commits a crime will always be a criminal.

In assessing these processes, Schur reminds us that one act may not be enough to result in the negative label, but that whether or not a person is labeled brings into play the differentials of power. Certain types of groups may be more likely to be labeled deviant than others: groups that do not have political power and therefore cannot put pressure on officials for not enforcing the law, groups that are seen to threaten the persons in power, and groups that have low social status. The last is particularly important. Even when middle- and upper-class persons are suspected of committing conventional types of crimes, they are less likely to be labeled criminal than are lower-class persons.

The upper classes have greater access to attorneys and are more likely to know their legal rights. They are more sophisticated and are less likely to negotiate a plea or admit guilt. They also have the symbols of the middle and upper classes, and those symbols are not associated with criminal status. For example, they are more likely to have strong family ties, to have a job, to have sufficient income, to speak fluently and knowledgeably, to be poised, to be able to rationalize their behavior, to have a record of continuous employment, and to have the respect not only of the community but also of law officials. They are more likely to have friends who may intervene at any stage in the legal process. They live in areas that are unlikely to be the target of raids for drugs. They are more likely to get probation if a condition of probation is that they obtain psychiatric or other professional services.[81]

Visibility of crime may also be a factor in determining whether a person is labeled criminal. People who live in ghettos are more likely to be visible in committing a crime. They are also more likely to be visible after crimes are committed because of their greater contact with public services. For example, *statutory rape* cases are usually brought to the attention of the police through referrals from public welfare agencies. Thus, statutory rape is punished mainly among the poor, who become visible by applying for maternity aid from welfare authorities.

Early Empirical Evidence

Attempts have been made to test labeling theory empirically. In an earlier classic study, Richard Schwartz and Jerome Skolnick measured the reaction of employers to a potential employee with a criminal record. The one hundred employers were divided into four groups, and each group was shown a different folder on the prospective employee. Stated simply, the conclusion was that employers would not offer a job to a person with a criminal record. In the second phase of this study, Schwartz and Skolnick studied fifty-eight doctors who had been sued for medical malpractice (a tort not a crime) in Connecticut. They did not find that these doctors had lost patients because of the malpractice suits. Most reported no change; five specialists reported an increase in the number of patients.[82]

Schwartz and Skolnick warn of the problems of comparing these two phases of their study. The doctors had a *protective institutional environment* that did not exist for the prospective employee. The doctors were permitted to continue using the facilities of the hospital and had no difficulty getting malpractice insurance, although often at a higher rate. This protective institutional environment perhaps eliminated the negative labeling process that normally occurs after one loses in a court battle. Possibly another reason is that physicians were in short supply, and unskilled laborers were not. But most probably the difference in reaction was due to the doctors' occupational status and the protection they got from their profession. An interesting question unanswered by this study, however, is how the doctor would be labeled if he or she had been acquitted of a charge of assault and battery or some other *criminal* offense.

Another example of the effect of labeling gained national attention in the 1970s. Eight persons of varied backgrounds but all sane sought admission to the psychiatric wards of twelve hospitals in various parts of the United States. The hospitals were also of different types, some with excellent treatment facilities and others with poor ones. The researchers called the hospitals for appointments, and upon their arrival for the initial interview, they each feigned mental illness, all stating that they heard voices. When asked about the significant events in their backgrounds, all related the events accurately; none had a history of pathological experiences. After admission to the hospital, all the pseudopatients acted like sane persons. All except one had been labeled schizophrenic, and none of the doctors or staff suspected the researchers' pseudopatient status. Once labeled insane, they were presumed insane by the staff, who interacted with them daily. Their behavior did not identify them as insane; the identity came from a label given to them upon admission. Thus, they differed from sane persons only in the label.[83]

Another study involved the simulation of prison life, with student volunteers assigned to the roles of guards and prisoners. The experiment had to be terminated because of serious problems. In short, "conferring of differential power on the status of 'guard' and 'prisoner' constituted, in effect, the institutional validation of those roles. . . . Within a surprisingly short period of time, we witnessed a sample of normal, healthy American college students fractionate into a group of prison guards who seemed to derive pleasure from insulting, threatening, humiliating and dehumanizing their peers—those who by chance selection had been assigned to the 'prisoner' role. The typical prisoner syndrome was one of passivity, dependency, depression, helplessness and self-deprecation."[84]

Many of the early empirical studies on the effects of labeling focused on juveniles. These studies have been categorized as measuring (1) the effect of labeling on subsequent delinquent behavior, (2) the effect of the family's and community's reaction to a youth who has contact with the juvenile justice system, and (3) the effect that labeling a juvenile has on his or her self-concept. In summary, the studies report some evidence that white youths are more affected than minority youths by the juvenile delinquency label, that the community's reaction to the labeled youth is negative, but that the little evidence available on family reaction indicates that the labeled youths found little change in their parents' perceived attitudes toward them after the label had been attached. Juveniles do not feel that the experience is highly stigmatizing, although there is some evidence that some youths, especially whites, do change their self-definitions after a juvenile court experience. But "there is a hint in two of the studies . . . that the labeling effects of court contact may erode over time. In summary, we don't know much about the effects of court labeling on juveniles."[85] The research raises interesting questions but provides few answers.

Recent Research

Much of the recent research of labeling theory has focused on juvenile delinquency. This research calls for refining the approach. For example, sex roles should be considered. Males and females do not necessarily respond in the same way to labels.[86] Other characteristics of the juvenile may also be related to the effect of the label; research indicates that in addition to females, those in the higher socioeconomic classes, whites, or first-time offenders are "more susceptible to the labeling processes" than others.[87] The differences between negative and positive labeling also continue to be important.[88] All these findings have practical applications for policymakers who must decide whether to impose formal negative sanctions on juvenile offenders.

Two University of Maryland researchers have recently analyzed labeling theory as it applies to juvenile delinquency. After giving an overview of the theory and its critics, Raymond Paternoster and Leeann

Iovanni "suggest that labeling theory is not as invalid as its critics have claimed, and that what is needed is a restatement and revitalization of a labeling theory of delinquency."[89]

Evaluation

Labeling theory has been described as "one of the most influential in the field of deviance over the past two decades."[90] Not all agree with that statement, however, and the criticisms have been extensive.

One of the most serious criticisms of labeling theory is that it is not a theory—it is a perspective. That is, no systematic theory has been developed. The empirical assessment of a theory requires that it produce testable propositions. Not only is that difficult with labeling theory, but some of the theorists "unashamedly claim to eschew precise propositional statements in favor of 'sensitizing observations' which 'jostle the imagination,' to create a crisis of consciousness which will lead to new visions of reality." From this perspective, "empirical tests of labeling theory are both impossible and ridiculous."[91]

A systematic theory cannot be created unless it has precisely defined terms that can be measured. Characteristic of the empirical research on labeling is the assumption "that the imposition of any sanction or any official act of negative classification constitutes labeling" without systematically defining that term. Critics have contended that the theory's major propositions have not been supported empirically but that that is no reason for rejecting it. The methodological problems of the empirical efforts are crippling, and the data are poor. The research therefore cannot be used to support the theory, but neither can it be used to reject it. For adequate testing, it is imperative that specific hypotheses be derived and tested after precise, operational definitions have been articulated.[92]

One of the common criticisms of labeling theory is that it avoids the question of causation. Even if labeling is the key to continued criminal behavior, it is still important to know why a person committed the first criminal act, especially when the act is a serious violation of the law. Another criticism of labeling theory is that it views the actor, or labelee, as too passive and that greater acknowledgment should be given to the reciprocal relationship between the actor and the reactor. Thus, most labeling theorists overemphasize the action of society and deemphasize the action of the subject being labeled. Social interaction should receive greater attention.

Labeling theory has also been criticized for its lack of attention to the personality characteristics of those who engage in deviant behavior. To the labeling theorists, characteristics of the individual, such as personality traits, are just not important in explaining behavior. It is the *reaction* to the person that is critical. Yet labeling theory does not really explain differential law enforcement. Why do police arrest some and not others for the same offense?

A final category of criticisms is the assumption that labeling produces only negative results. It is argued that labeling a person deviant might deter that person from further deviant behavior rather than plunge him or her into further deviance. It is suggested that whether or not the labeling process produces negative or positive results depends on a number of factors that have been overlooked by labeling theorists.[93]

First, it seems that labeling has different effects on the deviant at various stages in his or her career. Labeling thus might thrust a delinquent into a career but deter a female shoplifter. Perhaps the key element is peer support, not labeling. On the other hand, labeling may create a subculture, thereby establishing the peer support.

A second factor concerns the confidentiality of the labeling. If the label is confidential and given to a nonprofessional deviant, that person may be more likely to abandon his or her deviant behavior than if the label is public and the individual is a professional. Third, the result is more often positive than negative when the subject has some commitment and is sensitive to the person who is doing the labeling. For example, there is some evidence that former alcoholics and drug addicts are more successful than are nonpeers, counselors, or psychiatrists in the rehabilitation of fellow deviants. Fourth, a person is more likely to abandon deviant behavior if the label of deviant, once given, can easily be removed.

Fifth, the reaction of friends and society is important to whether the label results in positive or negative behavior. If friends and others are supportive in assisting the individual to improve, the results are more likely to be positive. Sixth, labeling theorists have generally overlooked the possibility that positive labeling can increase positive behavior. In one study, public school teachers were told that certain students, because of tests given at the end of the previous school year, could be expected to be fast learners. At the end of the school year, these students scored considerably higher scholastically than other students did. They were described by their teachers as happier, more affectionate, more interesting, more appealing, better adjusted, and having less need for social approval.[94]

EVALUATION OF SOCIAL-PROCESS THEORIES

This chapter examined theories that emphasize the *process* by which a person becomes a criminal. The social-process theories have been instrumental in achieving a better understanding of criminal behavior. As a group, social-process theories are probably more acceptable to sociologists and criminologists today than are any other approaches. The theories attempt to explain differential reaction to the social structure; they are based on the sociological proposition that behavior of humans is acquired through the process of social interaction, just as noncriminal behavior is acquired. In addition, the research faces fewer methodological problems than do any of the other approaches. Some theorists—for example, Sutherland—tried to avoid the class bias in criminological studies created by selecting samples of convicted criminals, who are mainly lower-class individuals, by also analyzing the crimes of the upper classes. The use of random samples has helped in this effort. The studies of self-concept had follow-up studies, although more research on that procedure is needed.

Despite these factors, the social-process theories still face some methodological problems, most of which have already been noted. In summary, the concepts are often not precisely defined, and the samples used in empirical research are often not properly selected to avoid bias. Some of the theoretical approaches do not go beyond theory to empirical research.

CONCLUSION TO THEORIES OF CRIMINALITY

We have looked at the various theories of criminal behavior: the economic, biological, physiological, psychological, psychiatric, and sociological approaches. All have methodological problems: Crime is difficult to define in operational terms; samples are often limited; and follow-up studies are expensive and time consuming. All the research today is plagued with an increasing lack of public interest in what caused the behavior; rather, the hue and cry is "Let the punishment fit the crime." Thus, understanding the reasons for the behavior does not command a high priority in research funding.

These problems do not mean that the theories of causation should be abandoned. But they do mean that we must be careful in our interpretations of such studies. As we saw in earlier chapters, conclusions must be analyzed according to the type of sample and the source of data; thus, official data must be compared with the self-report survey data collected from large samples of crime victims.

We need more extensive research, watching and controlling for as many methodological problems as possible and integrating the approaches of the various disciplines. Most important, we should not conclude that research on criminal behavior is hopeless: "Many of the fruits of science . . . can be used to advantage while still in the process of development. Science is at best a growth, not a sudden revelation. . . . We do not abandon cancer research because the patients of today may not be saved by it." Research in the social and physical sciences can be used "imperfectly and in part while it is developing."[95]

ENDNOTES

1. For a recent discussion of social learning theory see L. Thomas Winfree, Jr. et al., "Social Learning Theory, Drug Use, and American Indian Youths: A Cross-Cultural Test," *Justice Quarterly* 6 (September 1989): 395–417.

2. Albert K. Cohen et al., *The Sutherland Papers* (Bloomington: Indiana University Press, 1956), p. 19.

3. *Ibid.*, p. 18.

4. James F. Short, Jr., "Differential Association and Delinquency," *Social Problems* 4 (January 1957): 233.

5. James F. Short, Jr., "Differential Association as a Hypothesis: Problems of Empirical Testing," *Social Problems* 8 (Summer 1960): 14–25. See also Ross L. Matsueda, "Testing Control Theory and Differential Association," *American Sociological Review* 47 (August 1982): 489–504.

6. Albert J. Reiss, Jr., and A. Lewis Rhodes, "An Empirical Test of Differential Association Theory," *Journal of Research in Crime and Delinquency* 1 (January 1964): 12.

7. Cohen et al., *Sutherland Papers*, p. 37. For a more recent collection of these papers with a new introduction, a short autobiographical statement by Sutherland, and a bibliographic update, see Edwin H. Sutherland, *On Analyzing Crime*, ed. and with an introduction by Karl Schuessler (Chicago: University of Chicago Press, 1973).

8. Donald R. Cressey, "The Theory of Differential Association: An Introduction," *Social Problems* 8 (Summer 1960): 3.

9. Edwin H. Sutherland and Donald R. Cressey, *Criminology*, 9th ed. (Philadelphia: Lippincott, 1974), p. 78. This position was retained in the 10th edition, published in 1978. See also Mark S. Gaylord, *The Criminology of Edwin Sutherland* (New Brunswick, N.J.: Transaction, 1988).

10. Sutherland and Cressey, *Criminology*, p. 84.

11. *Ibid.*, p. 85.

12. *Ibid.*, p. 90.

13. James Orcutt, "Differential Association and Marijuana Use: A Closer Look at Sutherland (With a Little Help from Becker)," *Criminology* 25 (May 1987): 355, 356, referring to George B. Vold and Thomas J. Bernard, *Theoretical Criminology*, 3d ed. (N.Y.: Oxford, 1986). For other recent analyses of differential association theory, see Elton F. Jackson et al., "Offense-specific Models of the Differential Association Process," *Social Problems* 33: (1986): 335–356; Anastasios Marcos et al., "Test of a Bonding/Association Theory of Adolescent Drug Use," *Social Forces* 65 (1986): 135–161; and James L. Massey and Marvin D. Krohn, "A Longitudinal Examination of an Integrated Social Process Model of Deviant Behavior," *Social Forces* 65 (1986): 106–134.

14. Melvin L. DeFleur and Richard Quinney, "A Reformulation of Sutherland's Differential Association Theory and a Strategy for Empirical Verification," *Journal of Research in Crime and Delinquency* 3 (January 1966): 1–22.

15. Donald R. Cressey, "The Language of Set Theory and Differential Association," *Journal of Research in Crime and Delinquency* 3 (January 1966): 23.

16. Robert L. Burgess and Ronald L. Akers, "A Differential Association-Reinforcement Theory of Criminal Behavior," *Social Problems* 14 (Fall 1966): 128–147. See also Akers' discussion in Ronald L. Akers, *Deviant Behavior: A Social Learning Approach*, 3d ed. (Belmond, Calif.: Wadsworth, 1985), pp. 39–61.

17. Ronald L. Akers et al., "Social Learning and Deviant Behavior: A Specific Test of a General Theory," *American Sociological Review* 44 (August 1979): 637–638.

18. *Ibid.*, pp. 638–639, 651.

19. Donald R. Cressey and David A. Ward, *Delinquency, Crime and Social Process* (New York: Harper & Row, 1969), p. xi.

20. Reed Adams, "Differential Association and Learning Principles Revisited," *Social Problems* 20 (Spring 1973): 458–470.

21. See, for example, Ronald L. Akers et al., "Social Learning and Deviant Behavior," and Kenneth H. Andrews and Denise B. Kandel, "Attitude and Behavior: A Specification of the Contingent Consistency Hypothesis," *American Sociological Review* 44 (April 1979): 298–310.

22. Susan M. Jaquith, "Adolescent Marijuana and Alcohol Use: An Empirical Test of Differential Association Theory," *Criminology* 19 (August 1981): 277–278.

23. Merry Morash, "Gender, Peer Group Experiences, and Seriousness of Delinquency," *Journal of Research in Crime and Delinquency* 23 (February 1986): 43–67.

24. Daniel Glaser, "Differential Association and Criminological Prediction," *Social Problems* 8 (Summer 1960): 13. See also Daniel Glaser, *The Effectiveness of a Prison and Parole System* (Indianapolis: Bobbs-Merrill, 1964).

25. Gabriel Tarde, *Penal Philosophy*, in Sawyer F. Sylvester, Jr., ed., *The Heritage of Modern Criminology* (Cambridge, Mass.: Schenkman, 1972), p. 84. For a recent analysis of Tarde's work in comparison to the early positivist and classical approach, see Piers Berne, "Between Classicism and Positivism: Crime and Penalty in the Writings of Gabriel Tarde," *Criminology* 25 (November 1987): 785–819.

26. See Margaret S. Wilson Vine, "Gabriel Tarde," in Hermann Mannheim, ed., *Pioneers in Criminology*, 2d ed. (Montclair, N.J.: Patterson Smith, 1973), p. 292, for further details on Tarde's theories.

27. *Ibid.*, p. 294.

28. Tarde, *Penal Philosophy*, p. 90.

29. Vine, "Gabriel Tarde," p. 295 (emphasis added).

30. Tarde, *Penal Philosophy*, p. 94.

31. Vine, "Gabriel Tarde," p. 295.

32. See Michael Davis, *Psychological Interpretations of Society*, Columbia University Studies in History, Economics, and Public Law, vol. 33, no. 2, (New York: Columbia University Press, 1909), pp. 132–137, for a critique. This source is summarized in Vine, "Gabriel Tarde," pp. 301–302.

33. Stephen Schafer, *Theories in Criminology* (New York: Random House, 1969), p. 239.

34. Albert Bandura, "The Social Learning Perspective: Mechanisms of Aggression," in Hans Toch, ed., *Psychology of Crime and Criminal Justice* (New York: Holt, Rinehart and Winston, 1979), pp. 204–205. See also David P. Phillip's, "The Impact of Mass Media Violence on U.S. Homicides," *American Sociological Review* 48 (August, 1983): 560–568.

35. Carl M. Cannon, "TV Violence Linked to Kids' Cruelty," *Miami Herald*, 28 May 1989, p. 7, col. 1.

36. See David Pearl et al., *Television and Behavior: Ten Years of Scientific Progress and Implications for Eighties* (Washington, D.C.: U.S. Government Printing Office, 1982). For the full report see J. Ronald Milavsky et al., *Television and Aggression: A Panel Study* (New York: Academic Press, 1983). For a brief over-

view of studies, particularly government studies on the relationship between television violence and behavior, see J. Ronald Milavsky, *TV and Violence*, National Institute of Justice (Washington, D.C.: U.S. Department of Justice, 1988).

37. "Boy Accused of Sex Assault: Barroom Rape Case Cited," *Tulsa World*, 18 April 1984, p. 1A, col. 3.

38. Tannis MacBeth Williams, "Summary, Conclusions, and Implications," in Tannis MacBeth Williams, ed., *The Impact of Television: A Natural Experiment in Three Communities* (New York: Academic Press, 1986), p. 411.

39. "2 on U.S. Panel Dissent on Pornography's Impact," *New York Times*, 19 May 1986, p. 13, col. 1.

40. S.R.Rep. No. 438, 95th Cong., 2d Sess. (1978), *reprinted* in 1978 U.S. Code Cong. &. Ad. News 40, 41–54, and in United States v. Reedy, 632 F.Supp. 1415, 1417 (W.D.Okl.1986), *aff'd.* 845 F.2d 239 (10th Cir. 1988), *cert. den.*, 109 S.Ct. 1318 (1989).

41. See, for example, FW/PBS, Inc. v. City of Dallas, 110 S.Ct. 596 (1990).

42. See, for example, Part V, "Legal Implications of Research on Pornography and Sexual Aggression," in Neil M. Malamuth and Edward Donnerstein, eds., *Pornography and Sexual Aggression* (New York: Academic Press, 1984), pp. 245–304.

43. Alexis M. Durham III, "Pornography, Social Harm, and Legal Control: Observations on Bart," *Justice Quarterly* 3 (March 1986): 94–102; quotation is on p. 102. Durham is responding to an article by Pauline B. Bart, "Pornography: Hating Women and Institutionalizing Dominance and Submission for Fun and Profit: Response to Alexis M. Durham III," in the same journal, pp. 102–105.

44. Gwynn Nettler, *Explaining Crime*, 3d ed. (New York: McGraw-Hill, 1984), p. 290; emphasis in the original.

45. Walter C. Reckless, "Containment Theory," in Marvin E. Wolfgang et al., eds., *The Sociology of Crime and Delinquency*, 2d ed. (New York: John Wiley, 1970), p. 402.

46. *Ibid.*, p. 402.

47. Richard A. Ball, "Development of Basic Norm Violation: Neutralization and Self-Concept Within a Male Cohort," *Criminology* 21 (February 1983): 90.

48. Walter C. Reckless, *The Crime Problem*, 5th ed. (Englewood Cliffs, N.J.: Prentice-Hall, 1973), pp. 55–57; reprint of article from *Federal Probation* 25 (December 1961): 42–46.

49. For a discussion of these and other criticisms, see Jim Orcutt, "Self-Concept and Insulation Against Delinquency: Some Critical Notes," *Sociological Quarterly* 11 (Summer 1970): 381–390.

50. Harwin L. Voss, "Differential Association and Containment Theory: A Theoretical Convergence," in Harwin L. Voss, ed., *Society, Delinquency and Delinquent Behavior* (Boston: Little, Brown, 1970), pp. 198, 206. For examples of more recent research, see Arnold Meadow et al., "Self-Concept, Negative Family Affect, and Delinquency: A Comparison Across Mexican Social Classes," *Criminology* 19 (November 1981): 434–448; and L. Edward Wells and Joseph H. Rankin, "Self-Concept as a Mediating Factor in Delinquency," *Social Psychology Quarterly* 46 (March 1983): 11–22.

51. See Nettler, *Explaining Crime*, p. 293.

52. Travis Hirschi, *Causes of Delinquency* (Berkeley and Los Angeles: University of California Press, 1969), pp. 16–34.

53. *Ibid.*, pp. 54, 56.

54. *Ibid.*, 72, 108, 132, 134.

55. *Ibid.*, pp. 16–34. For a discussion, see Michael J. Hindelang, "Causes of Delinquency: A Partial Replication and Extension," *Social Problems* 20 (Spring 1973): 471–487.

56. Rand D. Conger, "Social Control and Social Learning Models of Delinquent Behavior: A Synthesis," *Criminology* 14 (May 1976): 19, 35.

57. See Delbert S. Elliott and Harwin L. Voss, *Delinquency and Dropout* (Lexington, Mass.: Lexington Books, 1974). See also Roger C. Mills, Roger G. Dunham and Geoffrey P. Alpert, "Working with High-Risk Youth in Prevention and Early Intervention Programs: Toward A Comprehensive Wellness Model," *Adolescence* 23 (Fall 1988): 643–660.

58. Eric Linden and James C. Hackler, "Affective Ties and Delinquency," *Pacific Sociological Review* 16 (January 1973): 27–46.

59. Hirschi, *Causes of Delinquency*, pp. 230–231.

60. Robert Agnew, "Social Control Theory and Delinquency: A Longitudinal Test," *Criminology* 23 (February 1985): 58, 59.

61. Randy L. LaGrange and Helene Raskin White, "Age Differences in Delinquency: A Test of Theory," *Criminology* 23 (February 1985): 36.

62. Thomas J. Bernard, "Structure and Control: Reconsidering Hirschi's Concept of Commitment," *Justice Quarterly* 4 (September 1987): 409.

63. *Ibid.*, p. 422.

64. *Ibid.*, p. 423.

65. Michael D. Wiatrowski et al., "Social Control Theory and Delinquency," *American Sociological Review* 46 (October 1981): 525. See also Richard E. Johnson, *Juvenile Delinquency and Its Origins: An Integrated Theoretical Approach* (Cambridge, England: Cambridge University Press, 1979).

66. Wiatrowski et al., "Social Control Theory and Delinquency."

67. Wiatrowski, p. 537. See also Jill Leslie Rosenbaum, "Social Control, Gender, and Delinquency: An Analysis of Drug, Property and Violent Offenders," *Justice Quarterly* 4 (March 1987): 117–132.

68. See, for example, the research of F. T. Cullen et al., "Sex and Delinquency: A Partial Test of the Masculinity Hypothesis," *Criminology* 17 (November 1970): 301–310.

69. Stephen Norland, Randall C. Wessell, and Neal Shover, "Masculinity and Delinquency," *Criminology* 19 (November 1981): 424.

70. Ann Goetting, "When Females Kill One Another: The Exceptional Case," *Criminal Justice and Behavior* 15 (June 1988): 186, 187. See also Goetting, "Patterns of Homicide Among Women," *Journal of Interpersonal Violence* 2 (1988): 3–20.

71. Donald Black, "Crime as Social Control," *American Sociological Review* 48 (February 1983): 34, 42. See also Donald Black, ed., *Toward a General Theory of Social Control* (New York: Academic Press, 1983).

72. Nettler, *Explaining Crime*, p. 314; emphasis in the original.

73. Kai T. Erikson, "Notes on the Sociology of Deviance," *Social Problems* 9 (Spring 1962): 308. See also Kai T. Erikson, *Wayward Puritans* (New York: John Wiley, 1966).

74. Edwin M. Lemert, *Human Deviance, Social Problems, and Social Control* (Englewood Cliffs, N.J.: Prentice-Hall, (1967), p. 17. See also Edwin Lemert, *Social Pathology* (New York: McGraw-Hill, 1951).

75. Howard S. Becker, *Outsiders: Studies in the Sociology of Deviance*, (N.Y.: Free Press, 1963), p. 9.

76. For a summary of the development of labeling theory, see Walter R. Gove, ed., *The Labelling of Deviance: Evaluating a Perspective*, 2d ed. (Beverly Hills, Calif.:

Sage Publications, 1980). For a discussion and analysis of the major assumptions of labeling theory, see Charles Wellford, "Labelling Theory and Criminology: An Assessment," *Social Problems* 22 (February 1975): 332–345.

77. See Edwin M. Schur, *Radical Nonintervention: Rethinking the Delinquency Problem* (Englewood Cliffs, N.J.: Prentice-Hall, 1973), pp. 120–126.

78. See the research of Irving Piliavin and Scott Briar, "Police Encounters with Juveniles," *American Journal of Sociology* 70 (September 1964): 206–214. For a contrasting position, however, see Donald J. Black and Albert J. Reiss, Jr., "Police Control of Juveniles," *American Sociological Review* 35 (February 1970): 63–77.

79. Harold Garfinkel, "Conditions of Successful Degradation Ceremonies, *American Journal of Sociology* 61 (March 1956): 421–422.

80. Stanton Wheeler and Leonard S. Cottrell, Jr., *Juvenile Delinquency: Its Prevention and Control* (New York: Russell Sage, 1966), pp. 22–27.

81. Stuart L. Hills, *Crime, Power and Morality* (Scranton, Pa.: Chandler, 1971), pp. 19–21.

82. Richard D. Schwartz and Jerome H. Skolnick, "Two Studies of Legal Stigma," *Social Problems* 10 (Fall 1962): 136–141.

83. D. L. Rosenhan, "On Being Sane in Insane Places," *Science* 179 (January 1973): 250.

84. Craig Haney et al., "Interpersonal Dynamics in a Simulated Prison," *International Journal of Criminology and Penology* 1 (1973): 69–97; reprinted in Darrell J. Steffensmeier and Robert M. Terry, eds., *Examining Deviance Experimentally* (Port Washington, N.Y.: Alfred Publishing Co., 1975), p. 223.

85. Anne Rankin Mahoney, "The Effect of Labeling Upon Youths in the Juvenile Justice System: A Review of the Evidence," *Law & Society Review* 8 (Summer 1974): 583–614. Quotation is on page 609. See this article for a listing and discussion of the empirical studies.

86. Melvin C. Ray and William R. Down, "An Empirical Test of Labeling Theory Using Longitudinal Data," *Journal of Research in Crime and Delinquency* 23 (May 1986): 169–194.

87. Malcolm W. Klein, "Labeling Theory and Delinquency Policy," *Criminal Justice and Behavior* 13 (March 1986): 47–79.

88. Gordon Bazemore, "Delinquent Reform and the Labeling Perspective," *Criminal Justice and Behavior* 12 (June 1985): 131–169.

89. Raymond Paternoster and Leeann Iovanni, "The Labeling Perspective and Delinquency: An Elaboration of the Theory and An Assessment of the Evidence," *Justice Quarterly* 6 (September 1989): 359.

90. Danial L. Dotter and Julian B. Roebuck, "The Labeling Approach Re-Examined: Interactionism and the Components of Deviance," *Deviant Behavior* 9 (No. 1., 1988): 19.

91. Charles T. Tittle, "Labelling and Crime: An Empirical Evaluation," in Walter R. Gove, ed., *The Labelling of Deviance* (New York: Halsted Press, 1975), pp. 157–179; quotation is on p. 158; citations omitted.

92. *Ibid.*, p. 176.

93. Bernard A. Thorsell and Lloyd D. Klemke, "The Labeling Process: Reinforcement and Deterrent?" *Law & Society Review* 6 (February 1972): 393–403.

94. Robert Rosenthal and Lenore Jacobson, "Teacher Expectations for the Disadvantaged," *Scientific American* 218 (1968): 19.

95. George A. Lundberg, *Can Science Save Us?* (New York: Longman, 1961), pp. 143–144.

PART III

Typologies of Crime

CHAPTER 7

This is the first of four chapters on criminal typologies or the study of criminals according to the type of crime they commit. This chapter discusses two types of violent crime: serious violent crimes as recorded by the FBI's official data on crime (aggravated assault, murder and nonnegligent manslaughter, robbery, and forcible rape) and domestic violence (child abuse, abuse of elderly parents, female battering, marital rape, and male battering). These discussions are followed by an analysis of reactions to violence.

OUTLINE

Crimes of Violence

KEY TERMS

aggravated assault
child abuse
date rape
forcible rape
granny bashing
incest
larceny
marital rape
murder
nonnegligent manslaughter
rape
robbery
serial murderer
statutory rape
voluntary manslaughter

In 1980 the murder rate in the United States was the highest in this century. *Newsweek* labeled the year 1981 as the "year that mainstream America rediscovered violent crime" and concluded, "Defying any cure, it overwhelms the police, the courts and the prisons—and warps U.S. life."[1] By 1989 violence had escalated to the point that one national news magazine headlined an article as follows: "Dead Zones: Whole Sections of Urban American Are Being Written Off as Anarchic Badlands, Places Where Cops Fear to Go and Acknowledge: 'This is Beirut, U.S.A.'" Focusing on the impact of drugs, especially crack-cocaine, and on violence, the article continued:

> The image that overrides all others is that of urban war zone. However complex the causes and dynamics, however remote any chance of soon resolving this new civil war, one truth is inescapable: From Gangland Los Angeles to Murder Capital Washington, D.C., city after city now tolerates its own Beirut, a no man's land where drug dealers hoot it out to command street corners, where children grow up under a reign of "narcoterror" and civil authority has basically broken down.[2]

Increasing emphasis on violence, particularly random violence, has led to some distortions and misconceptions about the nature and extent of violent crime. It has also led to an increase in the fear of violent crime, which results in changes in life-styles. The purpose of this chapter is to place in proper perspective the violence in the United States. It looks at data on violence and analyzes the risk of violent crime and the reasonableness of the fear of crime.

The legal approach is used to define each crime discussed in this and the following chapter. Official crime data are based on the legal definition; many sociological studies of criminals are based on samples of inmates who have been categorized as robbers, rapists, murderers, or burglars because these labels are the appropriate legal ones to categorize the behavior for which the criminals have been convicted. This is not to suggest that other perspectives are not important. In fact, we also look at data secured from victims.

Attaching the label of a particular crime to a person does not necessarily mean that that was the crime actually committed. For a variety of reasons, defendants might not be charged with the crime they are thought to have committed, or they may be charged with that crime but allowed to plead guilty to a lesser one. A man who rapes, for example, may be permitted to plead guilty to assault and battery. In official data, therefore, he would be classified by the latter, not the former, category.

SERIOUS CRIMES: AN OVERVIEW

For official crime data, the FBI's *Uniform Crime Reports (UCR)* originally selected seven crimes (because of their seriousness and frequency) as the

Index Offenses. These crimes, known as Part I Offenses, are murder and nonnegligent manslaughter, forcible rape, robbery, aggravated assault, burglary, larceny-theft, and motor vehicle theft. In 1978 Congress added arson. Murder and nonnegligent manslaughter, forcible rape, robbery, and aggravated assault are considered by the FBI to be violent crimes and will be discussed in this chapter. They are defined in Table 7.1. The rest are property crimes and are discussed in Chapter 8. All are serious crimes, but the category of violent crimes designates those that might result in injury to a person. The rates of property crimes over the years have been much higher and fluctuated more dramatically than the rates of violent crimes, but it is the possibility of violent crimes that seems to engender the most fear.

Data on Serious Violent Crimes: An Overview

We must consider the data on violent crimes in historical perspective. According to the *UCR*, violent crime rates were high in the 1920s but decreased during the Depression and World War II. The rates began climbing again in the 1960s. The *amount* of violent crime increased more than 16 percent each year between 1965 and 1970, although during this period the *rates* of increase were much lower, only 6 percent a year. In 1976 and 1977 the violent crime rate decreased for the first time since 1961, but by 1978 the rates began climbing again. By the time the 1980 data were analyzed, the Department of Justice proclaimed, "Since the early 1960's, the United States has been in the grip of a crime wave of epic proportions."[3]

In 1982, although the volume of violent crime dropped 2.7 percent from that of the previous year, the first significant decline since 1977, it still represented a 21.2 percent increase since 1977.[4] The volume of violent crimes recorded in official data for 1984 indicated a 1 percent increase over 1983 and a 22 percent increase over 1975.[5] In 1985, overall violent crime increased 4 percent over the previous year. This increase followed three consecutive years of decline.[6]

In 1988, the latest year for which FBI data were available at the time of this writing, violent crime increased by 6 percent over 1987 and by 23 percent over 1984. Aggravated assault increased 6 percent; robbery increased 5 percent (after a 5 percent decrease between 1986 and 1987); murder was up 3 percent; and forcible rape increased by 2 percent.[7]

In June of 1989, William Sessions, Director of the FBI, announced that the FBI will be making the investigation of violent crime a national priority, along with foreign counterintelligence, terrorism, drugs, organized crime, and white collar crime. According to Sessions, if Congress approves President Bush's request for $19.5 million to hire 300 new FBI agents, those agents will be assigned to violent crime.[8]

What do the data on violent crime mean? The FBI, in issuing its official data on crime, warns that we must be careful in interpreting the data. Many factors may affect the reporting of official data, and all of them must

TABLE 7.1   Characteristics of the Most Common Serious Violent Crimes

Crime	Definition	Facts
Homicide	Causing the death of another person without legal justification or excuse, including UCR crimes of murder and nonnegligent manslaughter and negligent manslaugher.	● Murder and nonnegligent manslaughter occur less often than other violent UCR Index crimes. ● 58% of the known murderers were relatives or acquaintances of the victim. ● 20% of all murders in 1985 occurred or were suspected to have occurred as the result of some felonious activity.
Rape	Unlawful sexual intercourse with a female, by force or without legal or factual consent.	● Most rapes involve a lone offender and a lone victim. ● About 32% of the rapes recorded by NCS in 1985 were committed in or near the victim's home. ● 73% of the rapes occurred at night, between 6 p.m. and 6 a.m. ● 58% of the victims of rape in 1985 were under 25 years old.
Robbery	The unlawful taking or attempted taking of property that is in the immediate possession of another, by force or threat of force.	● Robbery is the violent crime that most often involves more than one offender (in almost half of all cases in 1985). ● About half of all robberies reported by NCS in 1985 involved the use of a weapon.
Assault	Unlawful intentional inflicting, or attempted inflicting, of injury upon the person of another. Aggravated assault is the unlawful intentional inflicting of serious bodily injury or unlawful threat or attempt to inflict bodily injury or death by means of a deadly or dangerous weapon with or without actual infliction of injury. Simple assault is the unlawful intentional inflicting of less than serious bodily injury without a deadly or dangerous weapon or an attempt or threat to inflict bodily injury without a deadly or dangerous weapon.	● Simple assault occurs more frequently than aggravated assault. ● Most assaults involve one victim and one offender.

SOURCE: Bureau of Justice Statistics, *Report to the Nation on Crime and Justice: The Data,* 2d ed. (Washington, D.C.: U.S. Government Printing Office, 1988), p. 2.

EXHIBIT 7.1

The Nature and Impact of Violent Crime

Violent criminal behavior is one of the most frightening experiences in the evolution of human communities. It can destroy the future. Our social responsibility is to control these despicable acts.

The National Institute of Justice has demonstrated some policies that can reduce future violence. However, more research is needed. According to the 1987 Uniform Crime Report a violent crime—a murder, a rape, a robbery, or an aggravated assault—occurred on average every 21 seconds. The rate of violent crimes per 100,000 population has increased sharply in the last quarter century: 159.0 (1960) and 609.7 (1987). A recent report by Langan and Innes estimated that 6 million Americans are targets of violent crime annually. Recently, the influence of illegal drugs upon the origin of violent criminal behavior has become of concern as well as the effect of such drugs in escalating less serious crimes into violent crimes. Violent crimes not only bring suffering and hardship to victims and their families, but also impact upon the quality of life of everyone in our society.

According to the FBI, 47 percent of all homicides are caused by arguments; 55 percent of all homicides involve people who know each other and 25 percent involve family members. The evidence on rape and assault from victim surveys indicates a similar pattern: 40 percent of all rapes and assaults involve acquaintances or family members. Of great concern is violence directed at children. According to one study, over 1 million children have been beaten by a parent during childhood. There is even evidence that there is a significant amount of violence being directed at elderly parents by their adult children.

Domestic violence may be the most common violent crime and the most difficult to control. Courts are unable to do much to protect family member victims from future victimizations. While statistics show that violence occurs most often among persons acquainted with one another, one of the most significant fears is of being attacked by a stranger, either at home or elsewhere. This pervasiveness and fear of violent crime make it one of the most important priorities within the criminal justice system.

SOURCE: National Institute of Justice, *Research Program Plan: Fiscal Year 1989* (Washington, D.C.: U.S. Department of Justice, November 1989), p. 68, footnotes omitted.

be taken into consideration. But as Exhibit 7.1 indicates, violent crime affects many people in various ways. Its impact is enormous.

One way to analyze crime data from a personal point of view is to consider the probability that you will become the victim of a violent crime.

The first two photos show 52-year-old Ernest Mitchell of Baltimore after being thrown to the ground and attacked by two black youths while a group of bystanders casually watch. Mitchell had just cashed a welfare check and is struggling to keep possession of it and a six-inch knife. In the ensuing struggle, Mitchell manages to regain possession of his knife and chases one of his two assailants. Neither youth was captured. Mitchell later said only one older man from the surrounding crowd tried to offer assistance.

Photo by Irving H. Phillips, **Baltimore Sun**

The Risk of Violent Crime

The most frequent victims of serious violent crimes are young people, males, blacks, Hispanics, divorced or separated people, unemployed people, and those with an annual income of less than $3,000. The rates of robbery and assault, for example, are approximately twice as high for men as for women. Males aged twelve to twenty-four are particularly vulnerable to the crimes of assault and robbery. When both race and sex are considered, the highest rates of victimization for violent crimes are among black males, followed by white males, black females, and white females.

Unemployed persons are victims of violent crime about twice as often as employed persons, with unemployed men being victimized by crime more frequently than women. Crimes of violence are higher in the central cities than in the suburbs or rural and semirural areas.[9] Yet despite an increase in rural crime in recent years, many people still consider the country a relatively safe place to live.

Men who live alone and people who live together but are not related are more frequently victimized by robbery. Men are more frequently robbed by strangers than are women. People who spend a lot of time in public places are more likely to be victims of personal violence than those who do not frequent such places. People who are convenient and who appear vulnerable and desirable are more likely to be victims of violent crime.[10]

The Bureau of Justice Statistics (BJS), using a newly developed measure of the probability of becoming a victim of violent crime, reported in 1985 that each year Americans have a 3 percent chance of becoming the victims of manslaughter by drunk drivers, kidnapping, child abuse, or other violent crimes that are not measured by the official data. The 3 percent figure, however, applies only to a given year. Over a lifetime the chances of becoming a victim of violent crime would be much higher.[11]

In fact, the Bureau of Justice Statistics estimates that over a lifetime, four-fifths of us will be the victims of attempted or completed violent crimes, with blacks and males being more likely victims than females and whites. Many of us will be victimized more than once by violent crimes; most of us will be larceny victims three or more times. Among other predictions are the following:

- Over a span of twenty years, most households will be victimized by burglary or larceny.
- More than a third of all households and almost half of all urban households will be victims of two or more burglaries.
- Almost two-thirds of all households will be victims of two or more household larcenies.[12]

TYPES OF SERIOUS VIOLENT CRIMES: OFFICIAL DATA

The *UCR* includes aggravated assault, murder and nonnegligent manslaughter, robbery, and forcible rape as serious violent crimes. Each is considered before a discussion of violent crimes not included in this listing.

Aggravated Assault

Aggravated assault is an unlawful attack by one person on another for the purpose of inflicting severe or aggravated bodily injury. This type of assault usually involves a weapon. Attempts at aggravated assault are included in the official data for this category. It is not necessary that an injury result if a gun, knife, or other weapon is used that could and probably would result in serious personal injury if the crime were carried out.

Aggravated assault is the most common serious violent crime according to official FBI data. For each 100,000 people in 1988, an average of 370.2 were victims of aggravated assault. The number of offenses increased by 5.4 percent between 1987 and 1988. The region with the largest percentage of aggravated assaults was the South, with 36 percent; followed by the West, with 25 percent; the Midwest with 20 percent; and the remainder in the Northeast. Aggravated assault is the most frequently reported violent crime; it also has the largest percentage of arrests, constituting 67 percent of all arrests for violent crime. Fifty-eight percent of the arrestees were white, and 41 percent were black.[13] There are few empirical studies of persons convicted of aggravated assault. The main reason is probably the expected similarity between these offenders and those convicted of murder.

Murder and Nonnegligent Manslaughter

The *UCR* combines **murder** and **nonnegligent manslaughter** and defines the crime as "the willful (nonnegligent) killing of one human being by another." This definition may appear simple, but not all willful killings are included. For example, the killing of another person might be *justifiable homicide,* as when a police officer kills in the line of duty. This killing is not considered murder or nonnegligent manslaughter. A homicide may also be excusable. If a small child discharges a firearm and kills another, the child, because of his or her tender years, will usually not be held criminally responsible. There are other kinds of excusable and justifiable homicides, and as with any crime, the definitional lines are often thin.

Some statutes separate murder and nonnegligent (or voluntary) manslaughter and provide different penalties. The definitional problem remains, however, as the English case of *Bedder v. Director of Public Prosecutions* illustrates. The defendant, convicted of murder, argued on appeal that the circumstances of his case required the trial judge to instruct the jury that he could be convicted of a lesser offense, **voluntary manslaughter.**[14]

Bedder v. Director of Public Prosecutions

. . . The relevant facts as far as they bear on the question of provocation can be shortly stated. The appellant has the misfortune to be sexually impotent, a fact which he naturally well knew and, according to his own evidence, had allowed to prey upon his mind. On the night of the crime he saw the prostitute . . . and spoke to her and was led by her to a quiet court off a street in Leicester. There he attempted in vain to have intercourse with her, whereupon . . . she jeered at him and attempted to get away. He tried still to hold her, and then she slapped him in the face and punched him in the stomach: he grabbed her shoulders and pushed her back from him whereupon (I use his words), "She kicked me in the privates. Whether it was her knee or her foot, I do not know. After that I do not know what happened till she fell." She fell, because he had taken a knife from his pocket and stabbed her with it twice, the second blow inflicting a mortal injury.

It was in these circumstances that the appellant pleaded that there had been such provocation by the deceased as to reduce the crime from murder to manslaughter. . . . [The appellate judge then indicated his belief that the instruction to the jury on the issue of reasonableness had been proper.] "Provocation would arise if the conduct . . . of the deceased woman . . . was such as would cause a reasonable person, and actually caused the person, to lose his self-control suddenly and to drive him into such passion and lack of self-control that he might use violence of the degree and nature which the prisoner used here. The provocation must be such as would reasonably justify the violence used, the use of a knife . . . an unusually excitable or pugnacious individual, or a drunken one or a man who is sexually impotent is not entitled to rely on provocation which would not have led an ordinary person to have acted in the way which was in fact carried out."

Voluntary manslaughter usually means an intentional killing that takes place while the defendant is in the heat of passion, provoked by the victim—a situation that mitigates but does not excuse the killing. The nature of the heat of passion and the surrounding circumstances must be examined to determine whether the crime is a form of murder or manslaughter. The provocation must be such that it would cause a reasonable person to kill.

The judge in the *Bedder* case obviously did not agree with the defendant, so the conviction for murder was upheld. The court refused to rule that the jury should have been instructed to judge the defendant's conduct by a standard of the reasonable impotent male rather than the reasonable man. Had the jury been so instructed, the act that resulted in the killing of another human being might have been considered manslaughter rather than murder.

Data on Murder and Nonnegligent Manslaughter

In 1988 the FBI reported 20,675 acts of murder and nonnegligent manslaughter, up 2.9 percent from 1987, representing a rate of 8.4 per 100,000 people. The most populous region, the South, accounted for 42 percent of the offenses. More murders occurred in August (December in 1987) than in any other month, while February (April in 1987) was the month with the fewest of these crimes.[15] Seventy-five percent of the murder victims were males. Of each 100 victims, 50 were white, 49 were black, and the rest were of other races. Eighty-six percent of murdered whites were killed by whites; 94 percent of black murder victims were killed by other blacks. Most male victims were killed by male offenders, but 9 of every 10 female victims were killed by male offenders.[16] Nearly 3 out of 5 victims were killed by family members or by other persons known to the victim. Thirty-one percent of female victims were killed by their husbands or lovers, while only 5 percent of male victims were killed by their wives or girl friends. Thirty-four percent of the murders were preceded by arguments between the victim and his or her assailant. Forty-five percent of those arrested for murder were white; 53 percent were black. Forty-five percent of the arrestees were under twenty-five.[17]

Murder is a more serious problem in some cities than the above overall data indicate. As earlier discussions in this text have indicated, in some of our larger cities the drug wars are involving increasing acts of violence, including death through murder and nonnegligent manslaughter.

Analysis of Murderers

Murderers have often been the focus of sociological and psychological studies, and several types of offenders have been identified. According to researchers, most murders are committed by people who may be categorized as the *normal* or *typical murderer*, meaning that the offender is not characterized by marked psychopathology.[18] Most of the early studies of murderers were based on this type of offender. Marvin Wolfgang, a noted criminologist who has conducted extensive research on murder and other forms of violence, summarized his findings as follows:

> The typical criminal slayer is a young man in his 20s who kills another man only slightly older. Both are of the same race; if Negro, the slaying is commonly with a knife, if white it is a beating with fists and feet on a public street. Men kill and are killed between four and five times more frequently than women, but when a woman kills she most likely has a man as her victim and does it with a butcher knife in the kitchen. A woman killing a woman is extremely rare, for she is most commonly slain by her husband or other close friend by a beating in the bedroom.[19]

Another type of murderer is the *hit man*, or *professional murderer*, the person who is hired to murder. Although we might understand the process by which someone drifts into a career of crime, kills during a fit of passion, or associates with deviants and learns to accept their way of life, is it possible for us to accept murder as a profession?

Mass and *serial murderers* are the atypical types, but they are the most feared. Recently, the media and social scientists have focused on the

serial murderer. What do serial murderers have in common? Authorities say sexual problems are a shared characteristic. Many of the violent, torture-type murders have involved homosexual males. John Wayne Gacy, convicted in Illinois in 1980 of the slaying of thirty-three boys and young men, apparently had sexually molested most of them before they were strangled. Their bodies were found in the crawl space of Gacy's home in Des Plaines, Illinois. Gacy awaits execution for those murders; his appeal was rejected in May 1989.[20]

Henry Lee Lucas, a serial murderer, a drifter who claims to have murdered 165 women since he was thirteen (investigators and scholars debate that figure), said the reason was sex. He said he killed them because they refused to have sexual relations with him; he then had sex with the deceased victims—a practice known as necrophilia. Theodore Ted Bundy, executed in January 1989 for the murder of a Florida child and confessed killer of others, also sexually abused his victims. Bundy also drifted from state to state and was accused of numerous murders throughout the U.S.

In contrast, James Oliver Huberty, who opened fire in a McDonald's restaurant on July 18, 1984, killing twenty-one people and injuring twenty others, had been earning $25,000 to $30,000 as a security guard until he was fired the previous week. Seven months before the mass murders, he had lost his job as a welder after the closing of a plant in Massillon, Ohio. Workers say that at that time he vowed to kill people if he could not work to support his family. July 18 is believed to be the worst one-day massacre by one person in U.S. history.

The FBI has focused on serial murders in its National Center for the Analysis of Violent Crime, located at the FBI training headquarters in Quantico, Virginia. In March 1989 the Center held its first national conference on serial murderers, discussing data on Ted Bundy and others who had been interviewed by the FBI. Preliminary results of the FBI's study of serial killers indicates the following:

> The organized killer was of average or above-average intelligence, was socially and sexually competent, generally was employed in a skilled position, lived with a wife or girlfriend, drove a car in good condition, controlled both his emotions and those of his victim during the crime, and followed accounts of the crime in the news media, among other things.[21]

The organized killer carefully planned his crimes, picking a stranger as his victim. Restraints were used on the victim, and evidence was carefully destroyed. The large number of murders committed by some serial killers before they were apprehended is evidence of their success.

The disorganized killer, on the other hand, was sloppy in his work, often committing a spontaneous crime on someone he knew. "The crime scene was random and sloppy and sudden violence immobilized the victim. The body was left in plain sight, the murder weapon often found, and, generally, the body sexually violated." Both the organized and the disorganized killers were "consumed with a desire or need to kill, but the organized serial killer tries to perfect his craft." According to the FBI after the crime the organized killer "critiques his behavior, and thinks about how he did it, and how he could have done it better. Gradually he becomes better and better at what he does."[22]

Robbery

Robbery, a form of theft, is usually distinguished from the less serious crime of **larceny,** discussed in Chapter 8, by two elements. First, in robbery, possessions are taken from a person by the use or threat of force. The FBI defines robbery as "the taking or attempting to take anything of value from the care, custody, or control of a person or persons by force or threat of force or violence and/or by putting the victim in fear."[23]

Robbery is thus not just a property crime but also a crime against the person, a crime that might result in personal violence. The use or threat of force must be such that it would make a reasonable person fearful. In that sense, the line between theft and robbery is sometimes thin. For example, if an offender grabs a purse, billfold, or other piece of property from the victim so quickly that he or she cannot offer any resistance, in some jurisdictions the crime will be classified as larceny, not robbery. In others it will be considered robbery because of the possibility of force. If there is a struggle between the victim and the offender, it will more likely be classified as a crime of robbery. Second, robbery may be further classified according to the *degree* of force used or threatened; thus, a state might consider armed robbery a more serious crime than robbery without a weapon.

Data on Robbery

Official data indicate a 2.7 percent increase in the number of robberies between 1984 and 1985, a 4.6 percent decrease between 1986 and 1987, and a 4.9 percent increase between 1987 and 1988. Figure 7.1 is a graph of the changes in the number of offenses and in robbery rates between 1984 and 1988.

Robbery comprised 35 percent of serious violent crimes in 1988. The highest robbery rates were in the larger cities. The area with the highest robbery rates was the South, with 33 percent of all robberies, followed by the Northeast with 28 percent, the West with 21 percent, and the Midwest with the rest. Between 1987 and 1988 bank robberies were up by 16 percent, convenience store robberies by 36 percent, robbery of commercial houses by 25 percent, robbery of gas stations by 2 percent, and robbery of residences by 1 percent. Forty-three percent of the 1988 robberies involved strong-arm tactics, 33 percent involved firearms, and 14 percent involved knives or other cutting instruments. Of the robberies reported, 26 percent were cleared by arrest. Of the persons arrested in 1988 for robbery, 92 percent were male, 59 percent were under twenty-five, 63 percent were black; and 36 percent were white.[24]

Robbery, one of the most frightening violent offenses, occurs more

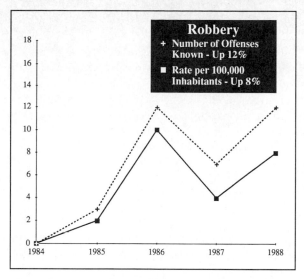

Figure 7.1 Trends in Robberies, 1984—1988

SOURCE: Federal Bureau of Investigation, *Uniform Crime Reports*, 1988 (Washington, D.C.: U.S. Government Printing Office, 1989), p. 20.

frequently than rape or homicide. A special report, published in 1987 and covering the previous twelve years of National Crime Survey (NCS) data on robbery, indicated that one-third of the victims of robbery are injured and nearly one-fourth suffer property loss and personal injury. Robbery victims were much more likely than rape or assault victims to be victimized by two or more offenders at the same time. Further, "robbery victims generally did not know their assailants or knew them only by sight, while victims of other violent crimes were victimized by strangers only about half the time." Other data from this study of robbery victims are contained in Exhibit 7.2.[25]

Empirical Research on Robbery

An in-depth study of forty-nine inmates serving time for armed robbery in a medium-security facility in California indicated that all the men had served at least one prison term before the one being served at the time of the study. The inmates had committed a total of 10,500 crimes, ranging from 6 rapes to the largest number of offenses, drug sales, at 3620. They averaged 20 crimes per person per year. The level of criminal activity diminished with age. Most of the inmates had started their criminal careers with auto theft in their juvenile years, then moved to burglary, and, as they got older, to robbery. They shifted to robbery because they could do it alone and therefore did not run the risk of being implicated by a partner. Robbery has the additional advantage of requiring few tools;

EXHIBIT 7.2

Characteristics of Robbery Victims and Their Offenders

● About 1 in 12 robbery victims experienced serious injuries such as rape, knife or gunshot wounds, broken bones, or being knocked unconscious.

● About half of all completed robberies involved losses of $82 or less; 10% involved losses of $800 or more. Most theft losses were never recovered.

● Offenders displayed weapons in almost half of all robberies; they had guns in about 1 in 5. Offenders with weapons were more likely to threaten than attack their victims.

● In almost 9 out of 10 robbery victimizations, robbers were male; in about half, they were black or worked in groups of 2 or more.

● Blacks experienced robberies at 2½ times the rate for whites; the rate for male victims was twice the rate for female victims.

● Over half of all robbery victims were attacked. Female robbery victims were more likely to be attacked than were male victims; victims 65 and older were more likely to be attacked than victims under 65.

● Victims who were attacked were more likely to be injured if they were female, if the incident occurred at night, if there was more than one offender, or if a weapon was present.

● Robbery rates declined by 15% from 1973 to 1984, largely because of a decline in attempted robberies.

● Robbery victims were more likely than rape or assault victims to encounter multiple offenders, strangers, or offenders with weapons.

SOURCE: Caroline Wolf Harlow, Bureau of Justice Statistics, *Robbery Victims* (Washington, D.C.: U.S. Department of Justice, April 1987): 1.

there are unlimited targets, and usually the crime does not require that the offender hurt anyone.

Most of the career robbers did not earn much money from their crimes. Drugs and alcohol were frequently involved. The investigators had expected the data to show a consistent pattern from juvenile delinquency to career criminal, but they found that the presumed pattern was too simplistic. The major overall finding was diversity, both in personality and in the career offenders' conduct. The investigators concluded that "many of the traditional assumptions about the development of criminal careers need to be reconsidered." They also concluded that rehabilitative efforts had not been successful. The best approach probably would be to help the offenders decrease their dependence on drugs and alcohol and to provide more help in finding employment upon release.[26]

Empirical studies of robberies also indicate that people differ significantly in the probability that they will be victimized by robbery. Chances of becoming a robbery victim decrease with age and substantially increase with unemployment. As income increases, chances of being victimized by robbery decrease, but chances increase for those living alone.[27]

Forcible Rape

The crime many women most fear is rape. As Highlight 7.1 indicates, the crime can be and is especially heinous in some cases involving multiple offenders inflicting severe injuries on their victims. The FBI's official data on **rape** as an Index Offense include only the crime of **forcible rape,** unlawful sexual intercourse involving force. The FBI defines the crime as "the carnal knowledge of a female forcibly and against her will. Assaults or attempts to commit rape by force or threat of force are also included."[28] The FBI definition thus excludes **statutory rape,** which is unlawful intercourse with a willing female who is under the age of consent. Today state statutes define forcible rape in different ways. Some include only rape of women; others include homosexual rape. Some require actual penetration of the vagina by the penis; others encompass rape by instrumentation, including the penetration of any bodily cavity by a foreign object. Some exclude sexual acts between husband and wife; other statutes include those acts in which force is involved. In comparing data on rape, therefore, we must look carefully at the definitions.[29]

Data on Rape

The FBI recorded 91,111 rapes in 1987, down 4 percent overall from 1986, although the number of offenses increased by up to 7 percent in some cities. Between 1987 and 1988, however, the number of rapes increased by 2 percent nationwide. When the volume of forcible rape in 1988 is compared with 1984, the increase in volume is 10 percent.[30]

Although, according to FBI data, rape victims are women of all ages, races, and income, victims are more likely to be young, unmarried, and from low-income families. They usually do not know the sex offender; women are twice as likely to be raped by a stranger as by someone they know. Most victims are raped at night; most are attempted rather than completed rapes. Only about one-half of the victims report the crime to police.[31]

Such data on victims of forcible rape, however, may be very misleading because of the reluctance of women to report this crime. A psychiatrist reported to the January 1989 meeting of the American Association for the Advancement of Science that the acutal incidence of rape may be as much as ten times higher than the National Crime Survey data. As

HIGHLIGHT 7.1

FORCIBLE RAPE: A VIEW OF RECENT CASES

Central Park, New York City, May 1989.

She is a bright investment banker who, until a tragic night in May 1989, had a promising career on Wall Street. Today she is a victim of gang rape, aggravated assault, and attempted murder, who after two weeks in a coma near death, fights to recover her physical, emotional, and psychological health. While jogging in New York City's Central Park one evening, she was attacked by a gang of young males who reportedly had victimized others during their rampage that evening. She has made a remarkable recovery physically and went to work part-time in November 1989, but her physical and emotional wounds may never be completely healed.

Although this crime was in the news for weeks, it was not extraordinary, according to the president of the New York City Chapter of the National Organization for Women. During the week of the above gang rape and attempted murder, twenty-eight other females in New York City, one as young as eight, were the victims of rape or attempted rape, along with robbery and other crimes. And those crimes represent only the one out of

two rapes that are actually reported to police.

Glen Ridge, New Jersey, March 1989

"I thought I could trust them," said an eighteen-year-old woman of her acquaintances who invited her into the home of one where she was allegedly sexually assaulted with a miniature baseball bat and a broomstick by three eighteen-year-olds and two juveniles while eight others, including the son of a police lieutenant, watched. The young woman said some of the activity was voluntary on her part since she feared they would not like her if she did not comply with their requests. But some was by force. The alleged incident occurred March 1. It was reported to the swimming coach on March 4 by one of the on-lookers but was not reported to the police until March 22.

San Diego, Texas, 1988

Late one spring evening in 1988 in the small Texas town of San Diego, a nineteen-year-old mother of two left a party, which was also attended by her husband, to walk home to check on her children who were staying

with their grandmother. She was approached by several men she knew, abducted, taken to an isolated area where a cockfight was in progress, and raped by fifteen or more men while others watched.

Lawyers for the defense argued that the woman voluntarily accompanied the men and engaged in sex with them but fabricated the story because she feared her jealous husband. The woman refused to testify until threatened by the judge with a contempt of court citation and jail time. Several defendants have already been convicted; one has received a thirty-year sentence after being convicted of aggravated kidnapping. Two twelve-year-olds testified that this particular defendant, referred to as the "head dog" of a group of defendants who "acted like dogs" at the scene of the rape, held the victim down while others raped her. The victim testified that during her four-hour ordeal on-lookers, both men and women, were laughing and shining lights on her to get a better view of the crimes.

SOURCE: Summarized by the author from media sources.

---

we discussed in an earlier chapter, the NCS was begun in an attempt to discover the extent of crime victimizations that were not officially reported. The psychiatrist believes that as many as one in five women are rape victims at some time during their lives.[32] Women who are raped by their husbands may not report the crime even when forcible sex is defined as forcible rape. **Marital rape** is discussed under domestic violence, but it should be understood that exclusion of marital rape from the definition of forcible rape or the refusal of victims to report the crime will affect the data on forcible rape. There is, however, some evidence that during the 1970s and 1980s, "broader definitions of rape have contributed to increased reporting of certain forms of sexual assault to police."[33]

Date Rape

Another kind of forcible rape that is infrequently reported is date rape. **Date rape,** or acquaintance rape, refers to forcible sex when the victim is known to the offender. The victim has agreed to some social interaction but not to sexual intercourse. Victims may be less likely to report these rapes than to report forcible rape by a stranger. There is also evidence that some people do not consider these to be actual rapes even though the acts fall within the legal definition of forcible rape. A 1988 survey of seventh, eighth, and ninth grade students indicated among other findings, the following:

> 24 percent of the boys and 16 percent of the girls . . . said it is acceptable for a man to force a woman to have sex with him if he has spent money on her.
> 50 percent of the students said a woman who walks alone at night and dresses seductively is asking to be raped.
> 51 percent of the boys and 41 percent of the girls said a man has a right to force a woman to kiss him if he has spent a "lot of money" on her. "A lot of money" was defined by twelve-year-olds as $10 to $15.
> 65 percent of the boys and 47 percent of the girls . . . said it is acceptable for a man to force a woman to have sex if they have been dating for more than six months.
> 87 percent of the boys and 79 percent of the girls said rape is OK if a couple is married.[34]

Studies indicate that from 11 to 25 percent of college women (depending on the study) reported they had been in stituations in which their boyfriends forced them to have sexual intercourse; other studies revealed that as many as 23 to 35 percent of male college students reported they had become so sexually aroused on dates that they forced themselves on unwilling females or believed they were capable of doing so.[35]

Recent reports indicate that date rape is widespread (see Highlight 7.2). Many of the victims of date rape report more than one occurrence of victimization. The crime is most pervasive during the female's high school years; after the first year in college, few women report that they are victims of date rape.[36] Other studies indicate that date rape on college and university campuses may take the form of gang rape, the rape of college

HIGHLIGHT 7.2

THE NEW REALITIES OF "DATE RAPE"

She met him two years ago at a fraternity party on a neighboring campus. His dashing good looks, she recalls now, coupled with his shy grin and friendly manner made him appear "sweet, but not macho." They talked and danced for hours, and later that evening, he took her in his arms and they kissed.

When he asked if she would like to get something to eat, she agreed. But instead of heading toward a nearby restaurant, he swerved onto a side street, pulled over to the curb and stopped the car. Then he raped her . . .

Similar incidents have cropped up at Yale, Stanford, Cornell and Columbia, among other schools. And several universities, including the University of Wisconsin, are conducting special training sessions designed to make students and faculty members aware of the problem . . .

"Women are hesitant to think that someone they met in an English class or at a fraternity party might assault them," said Anne Saddler, a legal advocate at the Pittsburgh Action Against Rape crisis center. "We tend to visu-

alize rapists as wearing stocking masks and jumping out at women from dark alleys."

Several recent studies contradict that image. The most comprehensive is a three-year survey of 6,500 students at thirty-five universities nationwide, sponsored by *Ms.* magazine and coordinated by Dr. Mary Koss, a psychology professor at Kent State University. Preliminary results show that of the first 1,000 respondents, one out of eight women said she had been raped. Of that group, 47 percent said the rapists were either first dates, casual dates or romantic acquaintances. . . .

At Brown University, a survey of 500 students conducted last year found that 16 percent of the women had been forced to have sexual intercourse by men whom they either knew or were dating, and 11 percent of the men surveyed said they had forced a woman to have intercourse.

The problem extends beyond the traditional boy-meets-girl dating scenario, said Toby Simon, director of health education in the health services department at Brown.

"A woman does not necessarily have to be on a formal 'date' for this to happen," she said. "We have had cases where students come in and say that their boyfriends, whom they had known for months or even years, had forced them to have sexual intercourse."

This situation is quite different from other instances when a woman consents to have sexual intercourse with an acquaintance or a lover, Mrs. Simon said, because of the element of coercion involved. . . .

In cases of date rape, they say, victims are even more reluctant to press charges. . . .

"Many times, the assailant and the victim share the same friends," said Ellen Doherty, coordinator of the Rape Intervention Program at Roosevelt Hospital in New York, where Columbia University students are sent for counseling: "Women are afraid that they will not be believed, that they will alienate the people who are closest to them."

The fear is understandable. Rape crisis counselors maintain that victims of date rape are often subjected to grueling

women by groups of college men, usually at parties. Most of these incidents follow heavy drinking and/or the use of other drugs.

In 1987, the director and legal counsel of the Santa Monica Rape Treatment Center began noticing an increase in the number of females who came to them to report rape on campus. Many of these alleged rapes

HIGHLIGHT 7.2 (Continued)

cross-examinations by lawyers and police officers attempting to discredit their accounts. In some instances, they may have difficulties convincing their friends and family that a rape has occurred.

"The situation is not as clear-cut as when the rapist is a stranger," said Nkenge Touré, director of community education at the D.C. Rape Crisis Center in Washington. Of the 500 rape victims who were treated at the center last year, she said, 60 percent knew their attackers.

"Instead of focusing on the rape itself," Miss Touré said, "the issue shifts to whether or not the woman gave her consent. Usually she has not been beaten. There are no bruises. It is basically his word against hers."

At the same time, some men are shocked to discover that they have been accused of date rape. These men, counselors say, are more likely to perceive themselves as the dominant aggressor when dating, while viewing women as passive and compliant.

"Some men have the capacity to fool themselves into thinking that date rape is normal behavior," said Dr. Mark Stevens, a clinical psychologist at Ohio State University. "They believe the myth that when a woman says no, she really means yes."

In an attempt to dispel this and other notions, the university began implementing a series of educational programs focusing on rape prevention. Since they were begun two years ago, more than 1,000 students have participated in the sessions.

Similar programs have been developed at colleges throughout the country. . . .

At Auburn University, a series of studies on sexual violence prompted students to make a videotape based on an actual experience. The film, titled "It Still I Iurts," depicts an interview with a woman raped by two acquaintances who gave her a ride to school. With her face in stark silhouette, she softly describes the anger and self-loathing she felt in the aftermath of the attack.

Such feelings are not uncommon. In addition to the disorders often experienced by rape victims—such as nightmares, depression, insomnia and nervousness—women who have been raped by a date or an acquaintance may suffer additional psychological trauma. Perhaps the most disturbing emotion, counselors say, is a profound sense of guilt.

"Women tend to blame themselves," said Miss Saddler of the Pittsburgh rape crisis center. "By leaving a party with someone or getting into someone's car, they feel they are partially responsible for what happened because they didn't exercise good judgment."

The young woman who was raped after the fraternity party, for instance, berated herself initially for not picking out some flaw in her assailant's character. She recalls wondering whether her blouse was too low-cut, or whether she had said or done anything to provoke the assault.

"It took me a long time," she says ruefully, "to realize that it wasn't my fault."

SOURCE: Beth Sherman, *New York Times,* 23 October 1985, p. 17, col. 1. Copyright © 1985 by the New York Times Company. Reprinted by permission.

were date rapes. According to these officials, the women were from all over the country and from small colleges and major universities. "There were instances of fraternity-party gang rapes, dormitory rape, date rape, stranger rape. The single factor that stood out in all of these cases is that universities were totally unprepared to respond to these cases."[37]

Males as Rape Victims

Although most victims of heterosexual rape (with the exception of inside prisons) are female, a growing body of literature is devoted to the study of males who are victims of heterosexual rape. Although earlier court cases often exonerated women accused of sexually assaulting men, on the grounds that a female cannot rape an unwilling male, scholarly research questions that position, noting that men are capable of sexual performance under adverse circumstances, such as fear and anger.[38] Furthermore, modern rape statutes are broader than traditional ones, as noted earlier.

Several scholars, interested in societal perceptions of male as compared to female rape victims, questioned students at the University of Washington. The students were given a hypothetical case involving either a female (or a male) victim forced to participate in oral sex with the male (or female) assailants. Students were then asked to decide whether the evidence presented would be sufficient for a conviction. They were also asked to decide whether the victim encouraged the act, experienced pleasure from the act, was stressed by the act, or was "personally responsible" for the sexual acts.

The results indicated that male victims were more likely to be perceived as having suffered less stress, encouraged the acts, and derived more pleasure from the sexual acts than female victims. Male respondents were particularly inclined to view male victims of sexual assault as less traumatized than female victims, even to the point of this response from one: "Some guys have all the luck!" The researchers suggested that male respondents focused on the sexual, rather than the violent nature of the sex acts. It must be emphasized, however, that this study was not of actual rape victims but rather of perceptions young people had of a hypothetical fact pattern that could be viewed as rape. Nevertheless, the study is important because it raises the issue of whether as a society we might still consider sexual assault as a violent act as existing only when a female is victimized by a male. More awareness is needed of the victimization of males as well as females.[39]

The results might be different when the respondents are males who have been sexually victimized by females, especially when a male child is sexually abused by a female adult. Consider the case of a St. Petersburg, Florida, woman, age fifty, who has been charged with rape after she was accused of having sexual relations with the thirteen-year-old son of her lover who was at the time in prison. After seeing a television program on sexual abuse, the child reported the abuse, indicating that he thought it was wrong, asked his father, and was told the behavior was all right. The father and the defendant deny that the alleged sexual acts ever occurred. Experts consulted about the case, however, indicated that an increasing number of males are reporting sexual abuse by women, especially their mothers.

A University of Michigan study indicates that approximately 14 percent of the sexual abusers referred to in its "Project on Child Abuse and Neglect" were women. Others say the figures are higher and that males are frequently sexual abuse victims. The result may be more difficult for men raised in a society that tells them that to be masculine is to be strong and powerful and certainly not to be overpowered sexually by a female. A Boston-area sex therapist notes that "when an abuser is female, it's much more likely not to be treated as abuse, but treated as an initiation to adult." Yet, the effects of sexual abuse on male victims may be long-term; in some cases those abused as children never recover. They become emotionally crippled adults, unable to give and receive love. They may become promiscuous and excessively occupied with pornography. And even those who attain success in a career may have a low self-esteem, which may lead to substance abuse or an extreme focus on athletics. Some will later abuse others sexually.[40]

Analysis of Rapists

It is particularly important to analyze carefully the empirical studies of rapists, since these studies rarely, if ever, include date rape offenders. Furthermore, the studies are not comparable in their sources of data. Some involve studies of convicted rapists; others secure data about rapists from victims. Some include only rapists; others include rape and other sexual offenses. Furthermore, the development of theory in this field of study has been sparse. In short, "criminal justice research related to rape has suffered from insufficient theoretical development, inadequate data, and poorly developed methodology."[41] With these reservations in mind, we will consider some of the empirical studies.

Most studies of rapists do not separate the violent rapist thought to account for only a small percentage of rapes. Thus, it is not surprising that these studies indicate that those convicted of rape are not generally psychologically deviant. In fact, an earlier study showed that men who rape adult women are generally not distinguishable except for their sexual conduct, although those who are convicted of statutory rape are rather impulsive individuals.[42] Further insight into rapists has come from the work of Menachem Amir, who studied a sample of 646 forcible rape cases in Philadelphia. Amir found that rapes were primarily intraracial, with the rate much higher among blacks than among whites; the offenders and victims were young, usually under twenty-five, and were unmarried. Most of the offenders were unemployed and from the lower socioeconomic class. About one-half of the victims had had a previous relationship, often a primary one, with the offenders. The majority of the victims were found to be submissive (although that could be because of fear), and the majority of the incidents did not involve repeated intercourse, fellatio, cunnilingus, or brutality.[43]

Myths about rapists were discussed by A. Nicholas Groth and H. Jean Birnbaum, who conducted clinical studies of five hundred rapists and reported that rape is more often an expression of nonsexual than of sexual needs. One-third of the sample were married men who had an active sex life with their wives, and the majority of the unmarried offenders had an active sex life with a consenting woman. According to Groth and Birnbaum, rape is not the result of sexual arousal but rather of an emotional problem. Most rapists are persons who lack secure and close emotional relationships with others.[44]

Sex is a motivating factor in some rapes, usually those occurring between persons who had a previous acquaintance, but sex is not the primary motivation for rape; and in many cases, sex is not even a relevant variable. Motivation for rape has been analyzed according to three categories: anger, power, and sadism.

The *anger rapist* is expressing hostility, anger, rage, contempt, hatred, and other negative emotions, usually toward a significant woman in his life. The rape victim is insignificant; she could be any woman. The rape is often impulsive, not planned, and the victim is brutalized far beyond what is necessary to cause her submission.

In the *power rape*, the perpetrator uses his power to force a woman into submission. This control is necessary for the male to cope with his own feelings of insecurity and inadequacy. For him, the act is full of anxiety, excitement, and anticipation. It is planned and preceded by sexual fantasies. The power rapist experiences little sexual satisfaction during the attack; rather, his gratification comes from the power of committing the act.

The *sadistic rapist* stalks his victim; he plans carefully and waits for the right moment to attack. He then brutalizes and tortures his victim. He may not have sexual intercourse with her; rather, the rape occurs with the use of an instrument such as a stick or a bottle. The victim suffers severe injury and may die. This type of rape is usually committed by a person who is mentally ill or under the influence of drugs.[45]

DOMESTIC VIOLENCE

Some types of interpersonal violence have not historically been considered as serious violent crimes. An example is domestic violence, which occurs within the setting where people can and should expect warmth, reinforcement, support, trust, and love. Domestic violence has been considered a personal, domestic problem, not an act of violence. In early Roman and English law parents had almost exclusive rights to discipline their children, and these rights permitted physical punishment and death. The Bible said that a stubborn and rebellious child could be taken by the parents into the city and there stoned to death by the elders. The death sentence was permitted for children who cursed or killed their parents. Historically wives were the property of their fathers and then their husbands, who were allowed to discipline them virtually without penalty.

Even after the abuse of family members was no longer sanctioned as proper, little attention was paid to such actions. They were considered to be domestic matters and of little or no concern to the rest of society. Thus, although we have known about family violence for a long time, it has been only recently that these long-known facts have been pulled together into a general analysis of violence in the home.

The seriousness of domestic violence was emphasized by the Task Force on Victims in its 1982 report to President Ronald Reagan. Domestic violence, the commission reported, is far more complex than is violence against strangers. The task force recommended that the government appoint a new task force specifically to study the problem of family violence. On September 19, 1983, the attorney general of the United States announced the formation of the Task Force on Family Violence.[46]

Definition of Domestic Violence

The seriousness of domestic violence is beyond question, but its definition is difficult. In this chapter we will use the broad concept of domestic violence in the Oklahoma statute.

Protection from Domestic Abuse Act

60.1 Definitions

As used in this act:

1. "Domestic abuse" means the occurrence of one or more of the following acts between family or household members:
   a. causing or attempting to cause serious physical harm, or
   b. threatening another with imminent serious physical harm; and
2. "Family or household members" means spouses, ex-spouses, parents, children, persons otherwise related by blood or marriage, or persons living in the same household or who formerly lived in the same household. This shall include the elderly and handicapped.[47]

This definition incorporates all the victims of domestic violence that we will include: children, elderly parents, spouses, ex-spouses, and people who live together but who are not related by blood or marriage. Even so, the definition is ambiguous, and the courts will still have to determine the meaning of such terms as "serious physical harm" and "threatening another with imminent serious physical harm."

Domestic Violence Data

For several reasons domestic violence data vary according to the source. The first reason is the lack of a clear definition of what constitutes domestic violence. Second, most of the surveys on domestic violence have utilized small samples and have been highly localized, and are thus not representative of the total population. Third, funds for research in this area have been limited. Perhaps most important, these crimes are underreported. According to the Bureau of Justice Statistics, an estimated 3.8 million domestic crimes occur annually. Richard Gelles, a sociologist who has studied family violence, estimates that figure to be much higher.[48]

A recent government document, although not giving a figure estimate of the extent of domestic violence, notes that approximately one-fourth of all serious assaults and homicides are cases of domestic violence and that minor domestic violence is even more pervasive. The report continues:

> While it is hard to measure, "family" violence is probably the most widespread form of violence in the country and can occur in all social classes and income groups. The recent resignation of a high Federal official under pressure of publicity about his admitted wife beating illustrates both the presence of the problem among the well-to-do and the new morality that refuses to tolerate such conduct.

The report also notes, however, that most of the cases in which police are called to scenes of domestic violence involve poor people. That fact is not taken to mean that most of the cases of domestic violence involve poor people but only that they are more likely to find it necessary to rely on the police for hope in solving the problem.[49]

Child Abuse

In recent years considerable media attention has focused on child abuse. **Child abuse** is a broad term used to include neglect as well as physical and sexual abuse. Sexual abuse includes sexual activities that are voluntary in the sense that no force is used, but the child is coerced by the parent or other relative into engaging in sexual activities. Child abuse may also include child stealing or parental kidnapping, in which the parent who does not have legal custody of the child takes the child without permission and refuses to return the child to his or her legal guardian or parent. Child abuse may also include the involvement of children in pornography.[50]

Recent examples of child abuse illustrate the serious nature of the problem. In 1989, former attorney Joel B. Steinberg was sentenced to from 8⅓ to 25 years, the maximum sentence in New York, for killing six-year-old Lisa Steinberg. This case gained national publicity for months.

> Although the District Attorney's office reported that more than 100 children were killed in New York City by their parents or other adults who

Hedda Nussbaum, 45, and her common-law husband, Joel Steinberg, 46, are escorted to Central Booking following their arrests in connection with the death of six-year-old Lisa Steinberg.

were caring for them, the fatal beating of Lisa Steinberg and the physical and mental abuse inflicted by Mr. Steinberg on her and on Hedda Nussbaum, his companion, raised the city's consciousness about child abuse and battered women, reminding citizens that abuse was not confined to the poor but occurred among well-educated middle-class professionals.

In the 16 months since she died from a beating that the jury found was inflicted by Mr. Steinberg, Lisa has become a national symbol of the horrors of child abuse.[51]

Also in 1989 the nation responded with shock and sympathy to the plight of Carmina Salcido, age three, whose father allegedly killed seven others, including her mother and two sisters. Carmina's throat was slit, nearly from ear to ear, and she was left to die. She received over 15,000 cards from across the country. After surgery and several weeks in the hospital, Carmina was able to go home to live with relatives, and in April, 1990, it was announced that Carmina would probably be adopted by a

HIGHLIGHT 7.3

MOTHER SENTENCED TO LIFE FOR DROWNING CHILD

The judge spared her from the death sentence but declared that her act of drowning her son in a septic tank was the "saddest and most despicable and horrible crime I've heard of in my life." Julie Noe, a twenty-four-year-old who could no longer tolerate her child's crying, placed him in a septic tank and then put the lid on when he continued to cry, stood quietly and impassively as the judge sentenced her. The judge then commented on Julie's husband, who according to his own sister, left his wife and children without food and adequate shelter while he spent his money on drugs and liquor.

"Frankly, I think your husband is a disgrace to this community and a disgrace to humankind because of the infliction of abuse he imposed on you and Jonathan.

As far as I'm concerned, he should banish himself to another part of the world or dedicate his body to science so they can study his brain and soul to see if either exist in his body."

Although the defense introduced evidence of Julie Noe's mental illness, they were not able to prevail on an insanity defense. The evidence, however, perhaps swayed the jury in its recommendation for a life sentence rather than capital punishment in Florida's electric chair.

SOURCE: Paraphrased from media sources. Quotations are from "Judge Blasts Husband at Noe's Sentencing," *Tallahassee Democrat,* 13 December 1989, p. 1, col. 1.

---

wealthy Missouri family. In late 1989 a mother who drowned her son in a septic tank was sentenced to life. (See Highlight 7.3).

At the other extreme from child abuse, the year 1989 saw what some consider a case of extreme love for a child, although others call it murder. Rudy Linares, father of a comatose toddler who was left partially brain dead after swallowing an object that blocked his wind pipe, held hospital officials away with a gun while he disconnected his son's respirator and waited for him to die. He was charged with murder, but a grand jury refused to indict him on that charge. He was called a hero by many, but the emotional impact of the case was perhaps the cause of his subsequent substance abuse problems. (See Highlight 1.2.)

Data on Child Abuse

Accurate data on child abuse are impossible to obtain because of the varying definitions of the term, the refusal of many children to report the crime, and the unwillingness of parents to report the act to authorities when it is brought to their attention. Reports of data may also vary because of the different methods of collection. For example, some researchers collect data by asking adults to indicate whether they were ever the victims of child abuse, but this method suffers from the possible lack of accurate recall.[52]

The only firm fact is that we do not have accurate data and that we must be extremely careful in our interpretation of published reports. The lack of accurate data has also hindered the development and testing of causation theories. Indications that incidents of abuse are rising may reflect a growing awareness of the problem and the consequent willingness to report, rather than an actual increase.

With these reservations in mind, we should consider some data. A survey of all states indicated that in 1982 reported child abuse had increased by 10 percent and that deaths resulting from child abuse increased by over 40 percent in many states and by 100 percent in New Jersey.[53] Other studies reported dramatic rises in sexual abuse of children both in the United States and in other countries.[54] One study reported a 35 percent increase in child sexual abuse cases in one year but concluded that the data represented only "the tip of the iceberg."[55]

Reports indicate that the sexual exploitation of children is not always passive; about 50 percent of the cases involve violence. The largest group of offenders are "caretakers—parents, babysitters and those to whom we entrust children." Very small children are sometimes victims of sexual abuse. Some reports indicate that children have been stimulated to the extent that they go through withdrawal when stimulation is withdrawn.[56]

Prosecution of Child Abuse Cases

Prosecution of child abuse cases is very complicated, especially in charges of sexual abuse.[57] The complications of such cases are illustrated by the McMartin Preschool case in a Los Angeles suburb where the owner and six other members of the staff were charged with 115 counts of sexual molestation of children. The alleged molestation involved rape, sodomy, and the taking of pornographic pictures. Some of the victims were as young as two years of age. The children were kept quiet for years because of threats from staff members, who, among other alleged acts, physically tortured animals in the presence of the children and told them, "This will happen to you if you tell." In January 1986, after an eighteen-month investigation and preliminary hearing, charges were dropped against all but two of the defendants. Prosecutors cited insufficient evidence as the reason. Many parents refused to permit their children to testify, thereby illustrating one of the most difficult problems with the prosecution of child abuse cases.

In the spring of 1989, the Los Angeles day care center trial against Peggy McMartin Buckey and her son Raymond Buckey, entered its second year, with jurors in the case marking the time with a cake. By that time testimony had been heard from ninety-nine witnesses, and the evidence had filled 50,000 pages of transcript. To that point the case had cost taxpayers $15 million.[58] In late November 1989 the jury returned their first verdict, which has remained sealed, and said they were deadlocked on another of the sixty-five charges in the nation's longest criminal trial in history. In December they turned in a second sealed verdict and rejected suggestions that they cancel their scheduled two-week Christmas holiday. In January 1990, the nation's longest and most expensive trial ended in acquittals on fifty-two counts of molesting young children, but the jury was deadlocked on one count of conspiracy against both defendants and twelve molestation charges against Raymond Buckey, who had spent five years in jail before he posted bond. The second trial of Mr. Buckey, who was retried on the molestation charges on which the jury deadlocked, opened in April 1990 and ended in mistrial.[59]

Empirical Studies of Child Abuse

With the problems of data collection in mind, we take a cautious look at some of the studies of child abuse. One study that did not focus on sexual abuse found that parents abuse their male children as frequently as they abuse their female children and that in approximately 60 percent of these cases, the mother is the offender. This study also found that although there are more cases of child abuse among low-income families, there were also cases of child abuse among high-income families. Children of all ages are affected, but half were under six, a particularly important finding "because the younger the child the more serious the physical consequences of abuse and neglect." Of those who die from child abuse, 60 percent are under two.[60]

A survey of 521 parents in Boston reported some interesting information on the problem of sexual abuse. First, most parents think that the perpetrators of such crimes are strangers, a myth that may indicate why many parents do not warn their children about the possibility of sexual abuse by friends, siblings, parents, or other relatives. Nearly one person in ten indicated that his or her own child had been the victim of sexual abuse or attempted abuse, and nearly one-half of the parents indicated that they knew a child who had been victimized sexually. Of those children, 37 percent were six or younger. Fifteen percent of the mothers and 6 percent of the fathers indicated that they had been sexually abused as children, and in one-third of those cases, the abuse occurred before the child was nine. A higher percentage of the cases occurred in families in which one or both parents had remarried. Children of both sexes were abused, but the abuser was most often male.[61]

Incest

The increased attention given nationally to the sexual abuse of children has created a greater awareness of the crime of **incest.** Children often cooperate with the abusing parent or siblings because they are eager to please and they do not understand what is going on. They also usually cooperate in the warning not to tell anyone about the sexual behavior. Because many cases of incest are not reported, the data on this crime are not accurate.

Incest usually involves father and daughter; cases of incest between mother and son are rare but do exist. Father-son incest is also a problem, but less is known about this type of sexual abuse.[62] Most of the studies of incest are about father-daughter relationships, indicating that the sexual abuse usually does not begin with sexual intercourse; other forms of activity may take place for years before sexual penetration. The activity usually begins with exhibitionism, then masturbation, mutual masturbation and other fondling, digital penetration of the vagina or anus, and finally sexual intercourse. Daughters who are involved usually have poor relationships with their mothers and therefore do not feel they can turn to them when their fathers initiate sexual activity. Fathers who have sexual relations with their daughters are usually having problems, often sexual, with their wives, and they see their wives as threatening and rejecting.[63]

Fathers usually deny the incestuous relationship or, if it is admitted, attribute it to overindulgence in alcohol or drugs. The father often begins the relationship with his daughter when she is quite young. When confronted, the father rationalizes the behavior in terms of "teaching his daughter the facts of life" or "she seduced me." The mother is often passive and possesses other traits characteristic of battered wives: extreme dependence on her husband, poor self-image, hostility, and jealousy of her spouse. "By exploiting her jealousy, her husband conditions her to accept the incest." In some cases, the mother even becomes an accomplice.[64]

Very little has been written about brother-sister incest, thought to be the least damaging of all types of incest and usually transitory. Mother-son sexual relationships are rarely reported. "Masters and Johnson state that the most traumatic form of incest is mother-son contact. The boy's social relationships with peers of both sexes are badly damaged."[65]

Sociological Theories of Child Abuse

The literature on theories of family violence and child abuse is extensive, but the approach has moved from an emphasis on the individual offender's pathology to sociological analyses, such as the social organization of the family and the culture in which family violence occurs.[66]

Both social-process and social-structure theories are used to explain child abuse. For example, the lack of social integration is used to explain why the mother is the most frequent family child abuser in those situations not involving sexual abuse. The female offender in child abuse cases is generally a socially isolated person who probably came from a background of inadequate nurturing. These are parents who are not able to sublimate or redirect their anger; yet they constantly face strains and stresses that contribute to feelings of anger. Such parents have a low threshold for children's typical activities, such as crying, soiling, and periodically rejecting food. One study found that battering parents "yearned for a mature response from their babies, for a show of love that would bolster their sagging egos and lack of self-esteem."[67]

Lack of self-esteem was cited frequently in early attempts to explain the abuse of children. In times of crisis, we all need some reassurances from others; but for the parent who abuses his or her children, this need is severe. It is suggested that the reason mothers are more often involved in nonsexual child abuse than are fathers is that the child interferes to a greater extent with the self-esteem of the mother than with that of the father.[68]

Social-structural variables were the focus of a national study of family violence, including child abuse, conducted by sociologist Richard Gelles. Gelles emphasized that the causes of child abuse are complex. Clearly they are not solely attributed to mental illness or psychiatric disorder. A number of variables are involved, including "stress, unemployment and underemployment, number of children, and social isolation." Gelles examined the social characteristics of the abusing parents, the social characteristics of the abused children, and finally the situational or contextual properties of the child abuse itself. Gelles concluded that if we are to treat and prevent the abuse of children, we must stop thinking of the abuser as a "sick" person who can be "cured" and begin working on social-structural variables, such as unemployment and child-rearing techniques.[69]

Consequences of Violence Against Children

Victims of child abuse not only often become child abusers when they have children but also often become violent against other children and other adults while they are children. Studies of juvenile offenders indicate that many were victims of child abuse or were witnesses to the abuse of other children. The same is true of adult offenders.

> A study of inmates at the California Institution for Men at San Quentin found that many inmates had been abused extensively as children. Although data are limited, some studies suggest that adolescents subjected to extreme abuse and violence at home may develop psychotic symptoms, neurological abnormalities, and violent behavior.[70]

A psychiatrist at Columbia University's New York State Psychiatric Center notes that many of the children who are committing sex crimes against other children do so after being the victims of sexual abuse. One example she cited was the case of a young male who at nine was sodomized by his step-father who threatened him with greater harm if he told anyone. When the victim reached twelve, he sodomized his nine-year-old brother who was also afraid to report the act. He then sodomized a five-year-old neighbor who told his mother who reported the incident.[71]

It is important to understand, however, that sexual (or for that matter nonsexual) abuse of children does not necessarily cause them to engage in the same kind of behavior against others.

> [Although] experiencing child abuse may increase the odds of subsequent antisocial behavior . . . it does not predetermine criminality. . . . the pres-

ence or absence of emotional neglect, family criminality, and a support system within and outside of the home, as well as the sex of the abusing parent and how parents resolve conflicts are all important for understanding the relationship between child abuse and subsequent violent criminal behavior.[72]

Abused and neglected children also suffer physical reactions such as impairment of neurological function, retardation, or impairment of intelligence, and many have personality disorders. Even when the child does not manifest obvious problems, sexual abuse may be considered a time bomb that will go off later in the victim's adult sexual experiences.

Abuse of Elderly Parents

One type of violence against the elderly that has recently gained attention is the abuse of elderly parents by members of their own families. This form of violence has been referred to as the King Lear syndrome (after the aging character in Shakespeare's play who was mistreated by his two daughters), **granny bashing,** and parental abuse. Abuse of the elderly includes not only violent attacks but also such acts as withholding food, stealing savings and social security checks, and verbal abuse and threats of being sent to a nursing home.

Accurate data on domestic abuse of the elderly are not available. Some victims will not report the abuse because of their fear of losing financial support or of being placed in a nursing home. Abuse of the elderly is also difficult to prove. The fact that elderly people bruise easily and fall often accounts for three-fourths of all home accidents. Because doctors are not trained to detect abuse, many incidents do not come to the attention of those who collect the data. Thus, despite the estimates that range from 500,000 to a million incidents of such abuse annually, we really have no idea of the extent of the problem.

Because social scientists have only recently begun to study family abuse of the elderly, we do not know much about its causes. The roots of the problem may lie in child abuse. Abuse of elderly family members may also be the result of an attempt to do the right thing but an inability to cope with the problems of an aging parent or grandparent, coupled with the inability, because of guilt, to place that parent in a nursing home. Transferring the responsibility for the person is difficult.[73]

Female Battering

Despite the seriousness of child abuse and the apparently growing incidence of parental abuse of elderly parents, the wife is the one who is most often the victim of domestic violence. Our definition of domestic violence stated that physical violence against a woman who lives with but is not married to the male batterer is also a type of domestic violence. Thus, we include former spouses, estranged spouses, and persons who are not married to each other but who live together. One study found that instances of violence are greater among cohabiting couples than among married couples, although it was also found that cohabitation without marriage is not the only critical variable. For example, persons over thirty, divorced women, persons with high incomes, and couples who had cohabited for over ten years had very low rates of domestic violence in their relationships. The same variables that are related to low (or high) rates of violence among married couples are also related to low (or high) rates of violence among the unmarried who live together. The one exception was that married couples were more successful in coping with their problems.[74]

Historically, by law and by social convention, husbands had the authority to control their wives, considered to be their property. Much of our law comes from English common law, which gave men the authority to chastise their wives. The rule-of-thumb measure apparently referred to the specification that a husband could discipline his wife by beating her as long as he used a stick no longer than his thumb. Medieval practices permitted beating, even killing, a wife or a serf if done for the purpose of disciplining. In this country, wife beating was permitted by statute. This historical recognition of a husband's legal right to discipline his wife with physical brutality has changed, as the following excerpt from a 1913 case illustrates.[75]

Bailey v. People

This assertion of the right of a husband to control the acts and will of his wife by physical force cannot be tolerated. . . .

To say that a court of law will recognize in the husband the power to compel his wife to obey his wishes, by force if necessary, is a relic of barbarism that has no place in an enlightened civilization.

Data on Female Battering

The data on abuse of female companions are probably less accurate than those on any other crime, including rape. The attorney general, in his appearance before the Task Force on Domestic Violence in the spring of 1984, estimated "conservatively" that two million wives are beaten each year by their husbands.[76] Popular magazines report that as many as six million women are physically abused each year by their spouses or other males with whom they currently have (or have had) an intimate relationship.[77] Sociologists have reported that one out of every six couples in this country engages in at least one act of violence each year and that during the years of their marriages the chances are greater than one in four that a couple will engage in physical violence.[78]

Approximately 2000 to 4000 women are beaten to death each year by their spouses; battery is the "single major cause of injury to women, more significant than auto accidents, rapes, or muggings." According to a study in a major metropolitan hospital, "25% of all women's suicide attempts are preceded by a prior history of battering."[79]

The Male Batterer

Despite the stereotype of the male batterer as a lower-class, pathological male, researchers have found that all races and social classes are involved. Statistically, wife battering may occur more often in the lower than in the upper classes, but that may be due to variations in reporting. There appear to be three major variables associated with wife beating: frustration or stress, sex roles or learned behavior, and alcohol.[80] Stress in the male spouse may occur for many reasons. Frustration and stress may result from the man's deep sense of inadequacy as a male, as a provider, and as a father or a husband. Insecurities may result from his extreme dependency on his wife, coupled with his fear of losing her.

Sex roles, learned through the process of socialization, may also be related to wife battering. Men learn to be aggressive and dominant and to expect women to be feminine and passive. Any show of superiority by the wife, for example, if she is employed and he is unemployed or if both are employed and she earns more money, may trigger a violent response. Of course, many men and women adjust to changing sex roles without violence; the point is that those who continue to hold traditional sex-role differentiations may be more likely to explode when the situation gets out of hand. This desire to maintain traditional sex-role stereotypes may also explain the willingness of the female spouse to tolerate the physical abuse.

The socialization process may also trigger a violent reaction in the male. If he comes from a home in which his mother was battered, a characteristic of many batterers, he may have accepted violence as an appropriate way to handle the problems between men and women. If he were a battered child, he may have decided that it is acceptable for the one who loves you to beat you as a method of control.[81]

Another factor in abusive behavior may be alcohol. Because of the frequent association of alcohol with violence, many battered wives have assumed that drinking causes the violence, but the relationship is much more complex. In some situations, both spouses are under the influence of alcohol when violence occurs. There is a tendency of both the abuser and the abused to blame alcohol. The abuser uses it as an excuse for his behavior, and the wife assumes that if she can get her husband to stop drinking, the physical abuse will end.

Battered Women: Myths, Stereotypes, and a Research Profile

There are many myths about domestic violence, especially wife battering, as indicated in Exhibit 7.3. Investigations have examined the prevalent public attitudes toward the victims, who are thought to be weak, sick,

EXHIBIT 7.3

Myths about Domestic Violence

1. Domestic violence is a private "family matter." Officials are acting "in the best interest of the family" if they don't interfere.

2. Domestic violence is usually precipitated by the victim's provoking statements or actions.

3. Battered women must be masochistic. If they wanted the abuse to end, they would seek outside help, or would leave or prosecute their abusers.

4. Batterers are "sick," poor, or alcoholic.

5. Battering is caused by an inability to express anger or handle stress.

SOURCE: Gail A. Gooklasian, *Confronting Domestic Violence: A Guide for Criminal Justice Agencies* (Washington, D.C.: U.S. Government Printing Office, May 1986), pp. 3–4; emphasis deleted.

guilty (she nagged him until he beat her), lower class, and willing to take physical abuse for a meal ticket.[82]

Although research on the battered woman is just as limited in scope and depth as is research on the battering male spouse, the available studies indicate similarities between them. One writer has described the battered women in these terms:

> The profile of the battered woman looks almost identical to that of her batterer: she is all ages, all ethnicities, from all socioeconomic groups, has a low level of self-esteem, and for the most part has very traditional notions of male and female behavior. She may feel that her husband is supposed to be in charge of the family, even if that means beating her; she must be supportive of him, even if that means allowing herself to be abused repeatedly. Her role as a woman includes marriage, even a bad marriage, and to leave the home would be to admit that she is a failure as a woman.[83]

Perhaps the battered woman is best understood by analyzing why she remains in the marriage. The pioneer work on this approach was conducted by Gelles, who explored the three main reasons why battered women do not leave their husbands. First, women are less likely to leave if the violence is not frequent or severe. Second, wives who were abused by their own parents are more likely to remain with abusive husbands than are wives who were not abused. Third, the more resources and options a wife has, the more likely she is to leave an abusive spouse.[84]

Marital Rape

Marital rape has received even less attention than wife battering. Historically a husband had unlimited sexual access to his wife; she was expected, and in most cases she herself expected, to comply with his sexual desires. He could be charged with rape only if he forced her to have sexual intercourse with a third person. No amount of force on his part would classify sexual intercourse with his wife as rape even if the couple had legally separated. This common law provision became a part of most of our rape statutes. Recently some legislatures and courts have rejected the common law approach and eliminated the marital exemption from rape statutes. In 1985 the Supreme Court of Georgia held that when a woman says "I do," she does not give up the right to say, "I won't."[85]

Diana E. H. Russell, an authority on women as both offenders and victims, marked the beginning of scholarly interest in marital rape in 1975 with a chapter entitled "Fathers, Husbands, and Other Rapists" in her book *The Politics of Rape: The Victim's Perspective.*[86] But in 1983 she noted that most of the "research on marital rape is so new that it is not yet in print, but is contained in papers presented at recent professional meetings," with the exception of two books, one on marital rape and one on wife beating.[87] According to Russell, women reported being raped by their husbands twice as often as they reported rape by strangers. Twelve percent of a sample of 644 married women over eighteen reported being raped by their husbands.[88]

Research papers indicate that the incidents of marital rape are much higher than previously thought and probably exceed all other kinds of rape; possibly as many as one of every ten wives is victimized. David Kinkelhor and Kersti Yllo, who interviewed victims of marital rape, found that

> There is increasing evidence that forced sex in marriage is a widespread social problem . . . such incidents seem to occur both in generally violent and in violence-free relationships, often near their end. The offender's goal, in many instances, appears to be to humiliate and retaliate against his wife and the abuse may often include anal intercourse.[89]

Prosecutions for marital rape are becoming more frequent. In 1977 Oregon became the first state to repeal the marital rape exemption. The state, upon complaint by Greta Rideout, filed criminal charges against her husband, John, and he was tried under this statute. This was the first trial on marital rape in the country, but on December 27, 1979, John Rideout was acquitted.[90] Shortly thereafter, the Rideouts were reconciled, although the reconciliation did not last very long.

Approximately one-half of the states have repealed the marital rape exemption. In 1979 a defendant in Massachusetts, convicted of raping his estranged wife, was believed to be the first person in this country to be convicted of that offense. On appeal, his conviction was upheld, and he was sentenced to three to five years in prison and to three years on probation after release.[91]

We must be cautious in analyzing the studies of marital rape. The concept is new, as are the statutory provisions, and the research to date has been based on small samples. Projections to the general population are therefore risky. The research is valuable, however, in giving us more insight into family problems and into the abusive behavior of spouses.

Male Battering

Although data indicate that most of the acts of domestic violence are committed against females by their spouses, ex-spouses, or lovers, there is evidence that women also batter their spouses, ex-spouses, or lovers. Data are not available on the extent of domestic violence by women, but it is argued that when women do strike men, they usually do so for retaliatory reasons. Gelles found that although women kill their husbands about as frequently as men kill their wives, the reasons are quite different. Women are seven times more likely to commit this violent act in self-defense, either to avoid physical attacks or physical violence in the form of rape.[92] Even if that is not the case, says sociologist Mildred Daley Pagelow, an expert in domestic violence, the man who lives with a habitually violent woman, unlike women who live with such men, "is not tied economically or through fear. He mostly needs psychological help."[93] Female victims of *reported* domestic abuse are more often economically tied to the men who abuse them. Furthermore, data indicate that once a female spouse is victimized by her spouse, she is very likely to be victimized again.[94]

REACTIONS TO VIOLENCE: AN ANALYSIS OF FEAR

Many people believe it is necessary to change their life-styles because of their fear of crime. As Exhibit 7.4 indicates, that fear has been increasing. The greatest fear is probably caused by the randomness of some violence, the belief that "random mayhem has spilled out of bounds and that a sanctuary can become a killing ground almost at whim."[95] This fear of violent crime by strangers who often pick their victims randomly led former Supreme Court Chief Justice Warren E. Burger to refer to the "reign of terror in American cities" and one privately funded study of crime to conclude, "The fear of crime is slowly paralyzing American society."[96]

The fear of crime has changed our lives in many ways. We must have exact change for buses and small bills for taxi drivers, who will not change large bills. We must lock our doors, bar our windows, and maybe install burglar alarms, paying a high price for security. Many people refuse to go out alone at night. Elderly people have suffered or even died from heat strokes in their apartments, not leaving their homes during hot weather for fear they would be burglarized or attacked. On Halloween, our children might be given candy or other treats that have been laced with poison or injected with razor blades.

Some of these fears are realistic; others are not. Earlier in the chapter we discussed the probability of violent crime. Americans are more likely to die from natural causes than from violent crime,[97] but people do not necessarily respond in terms of probabilities. Research indicates that women and the elderly have the greatest fears of violent crime, but they are less likely than the young and males to become victims.[98] Furthermore, the most fearful are frequently those who have not been attacked recently or at all, although there is also evidence of an *indirect* effect of actual victimization on creating fear of crime, resulting in even greater fear by some groups, such as women and the elderly, than had been previously reported.[99]

Women and the elderly may perceive that they are more vulnerable to crime and that they are less able to protect themselves from violent predators than are men and the young. Research indicates that compared with men, women take far more precautions to protect themselves. They are more likely to avoid being on the streets at night and, if on the streets, to use what has been called "street savvy," meaning the use of "tactics intended to reduce risks when exposed to danger, such as wearing shoes that permit one to run, or choosing a seat on a bus with an eye to who is sitting nearby." They are also less likely to go to a public place alone at night.[100]

The nature of crimes against women is also important in understanding their fear of violent crime. Men are rarely raped outside prison. Although rape is, according to official data, not a common crime, women are almost always the victims. Rape usually takes longer to commit than other crimes, so there is increased contact with the offender and an increased probability of personal injury. Studies of the effects of rape indicate that it is one of the most traumatic of all personal crimes. In addition, the victim is often blamed for the rape. Rape may also be greatly feared because of the inaccurate belief that it is usually coupled with violence beyond that of the rape itself.

The elderly are also more vulnerable to crime and thus to fear, for they are less likely to be able to change residences to protect themselves, to be able to afford locks and other protective measures for their homes, and to be able to defend themselves should they be attacked on the streets.

In addition to altering their life-styles because of a fear of crime, some people join neighborhood organizations such as "Crime Watch," whereas others move to what they think is a safer neighborhood. Rather than joining with others to prevent crime, some people develop a distrust of others and an unwillingness to participate in crime-prevention measures. Others have alarm systems installed in their homes and/or busi-

EXHIBIT 7.4

The Fear of Crime

Society does not yet systematically collect data on fear. Consequently, our map of fear—its levels, trends, and social location—is sketchy. Nonetheless, its main features are easily identified.

First, fear is widespread. The broadest impact was registered by "The Figgie Report on Fear of Crime" released in 1980. Two-fifths of Americans surveyed reported that they were "highly fearful" they would become victims of violent crime. Similar results were reported by the Harris poll of 1975, which found that 55 percent of all adults said they felt "uneasy" walking their own streets. The Gallup poll of 1977 found that about 45 percent of the population (61 percent of the women and 28 percent of the men) were afraid to walk alone at night. An eight-city victimization survey published in 1977 found that 45 percent of all respondents limited their activities because of fear of crime. A statewide study in Michigan reported that 66 percent of respondents avoided certain places because of fear of crime. Interviews with a random sample of Texans in 1978 found that more than half said that they feared becoming a serious crime victim within a year.

Second, fear of crime increased from the late 1960's to the mid-1970's, then began decreasing during the mid-1970's.

According to the 1968 Gallup poll, 44 percent of the women and 16 percent of the men said that they were afraid to walk alone at night. In 1977, when a similar question was asked, 61 percent of the women and 28 percent of the men reported they were afraid to walk alone at night—an increase of 17 percent for women and 12 percent for men. In 1975, a Harris poll found that 55 percent of all adults felt "uneasy" walking their own streets. In 1985, this number had fallen to 32 percent—a significant decline.

Third, fear is not evenly distributed across the population. Predictably, those who feel themselves most vulnerable are also the most fearful. Looking at the distribution of fear across age and sex categories, the greatest levels of fear are reported by elderly women. The next most frightened group seems to be all other women. The least afraid are young men. Looking at race, class, and residence variables, blacks are more afraid of crime than whites, the poor more afraid than the middle class or wealthy, and inner-city dwellers more afraid than suburbanites.

Indeed, while the current national trend may show a decline in fear, anecdotal evidence suggests that this trend has not yet reached America's ghettos. There, fear has become a condition of life. Claude Brown describes Harlem's problem in 1985:

> . . . In any Harlem building, . . . every door has at least three locks on it. Nobody opens a door without first finding out who's there. In the early evening, . . . you see people . . . lingering outside nice apartment houses, peeking in the lobbies. They seem to be casing the joint. They are actually trying to figure out who is in the lobby of *their* building. "Is this someone waiting to mug me? Should I risk going in, or should I wait for someone else to come?"
>
> If you live in Harlem, USA, you don't park your automobile two blocks from your apartment house because that gives potential muggers an opportunity to get a fix on you. You'd better find a parking space within a block of your house, because if you have to walk two blocks you're not going to make it. . . .
>
> In Harlem, elderly people walking their dogs in the morning cross the street when they see some young people coming. . . . And what those elderly men and women have in the paper bags they're carrying is not just a pooper scooper— it's a gun. And if those youngsters cross the street, somebody's going to get hurt.

These findings suggest that one of the most important privileges one acquires as one gains wealth and status in American society is the opportunity to leave the fear of crime behind. The unjust irony is that "criminals walk city streets, while fear virtually imprisons groups like women and the elderly in their homes." James K. Stewart, Director of the National Institute of Justice, traces the important long-run consequence of this uneven distribution of fear for the economic development of our cities: if the inner-city populations are afraid of crime, then commerce and investment essentially disappear, and with them, the chance for upward social mobility. If Hobbes is correct in asserting that the most fundamental purpose of civil government is to establish order and protect citizens from the fear of criminal attack that made life "nasty, brutish and short" in the "state of nature," then the current level and distribution of fear indicate an important governmental failure.

SOURCE: National Institute of Justice, Mark H. Moore and Robert C. Trojanowicz, *Policing and the Fear of Crime* (Washington, D.C.: U.S. Department of Justice, 1988), p. 2, footnotes omitted.

nesses or turn to weapons to protect themselves, their families, and their property.[101] Regulations concerning the legal use of weapons for such protection varies from state to state, but all states permit the use of weapons in situations in which it is reasonable to believe that deadly force is necessary to protect *human* life. This has led to problems with gun control.

GUN CONTROL

Sociologists have found that the decision to use self-help to prevent or control crime, specifically by purchasing guns, involves many dimensions. Included in those dimensions is a perception that that is the only way for effective protection.[102] Some empirical studies question the deterrent effect of civilian gun ownership on criminals.[103] Yet, carrying weapons, especially guns, is characteristic of many offenders.

Guns account for 30,000 deaths each year, some of which are accidental; some are suicides; others are the result of offenders killing their victims. Thousands more are injured by firearms, leading to the call for gun control.[104] In 1989, after a series of accidental killings involving children, the Florida legislature enacted a statute providing that a negligent parent whose child is killed by a loaded gun within reach of a child in the home could be imprisoned for five years. Florida is the first state to enact such a statute. The immediate result was that many gun owners purchased trigger and other protective devices for the guns they keep at home.

 *CONCLUSION*

This chapter covers a wide range of criminal activity, moving from a discussion of the violent crimes considered serious by the FBI to the less physically violent but perhaps more emotionally damaging sexual crimes committed by family members against their own children, spouses, parents, or siblings. The chapter begins by looking at types of crimes and types of criminals. The contents of this chapter, more than any of the following, illustrate the difficulty of studying crime by typologies: Many categories of people commit the crimes discussed.

The chapter begins with a brief discussion of criminal typologies and an overview of serious crimes, contrasting violent and property crimes. After a look at the risk of violent crime, the chapter turns to an analysis of individual serious violent crimes. The major crimes as categorized by the FBI's *Uniform Crime Reports* are featured: aggravated assault, murder and nonnegligent manslaughter, robbery, and forcible rape. The discussion of each includes the legal definition of the crime, data, and an overview of research.

The second half of the chapter focuses on domestic violence, beginning with a definition of the subject and a brief overview of the problems of collecting and analyzing data. This section then discusses the major types of domestic violence: child abuse, abuse of elderly parents, female battering, marital rape, and male battering. The discussion of each crime includes a definition of the crime, data, and a brief analysis of research.

Explanations of reactions to violence enumerate some of the methods people use to alter or protect their environments. The fact that the fear of crime and the reactions to that fear may be more important than the prevalence of crime reminds us of the often-quoted statement by the early sociologist W. I. Thomas: "If men believe situations are real, they are real in their consequence." But the fears appear to be out of proportion to the data, especially in the case of women and the elderly. If our fears of being victimized by crime are unrealistic, we should concentrate on programs for reducing that fear. We also need to conduct more research on how people respond to their fears of violent crime; much of the current evidence on this issue is anecdotal, not empirical. Last, we need to continue to assess more accurately the extent and nature of crime in this country and to try to prevent it. A brief discussion of private gun ownership and gun control highlights the need to analyze more carefully the issue of deterrence. It also illustrates the need to consider all results of social action—for example, accidental deaths of children caused by *legal* gun possession and negligence on the part of those parents in securing those guns.

ENDNOTES

1. "The Plague of Violent Crime," *Newsweek*, 23 March 1981, p. 46.
2. *U.S. News and World Report*, 10 April 1989, pp. 20–21.
3. U.S. Department of Justice, *Violent Crime in the United States*, National Indicators System, Briefing Book, 1981 (Washington D.C.: U.S. Government Printing Office, 1981), p. 8.
4. Federal Bureau of Investigation, *Uniform Crime Reports*, 1982 (Washington, D.C.: U.S. Government Printing Office, 1983), p. 40.
5. Federal Bureau of Investigation, *Uniform Crime Reports*, 1984 (Washington, D.C.: U.S. Government Printing Office, 1985), p. 41.
6. Federal Bureau of Investigation, *Uniform Crime Reports*, 1985, (Washington, D.C.: U.S. Government Printing Office, 1986), p. 41.
7. Federal Bureau of Investigation, *Uniform Crime Reports*, 1988 (Washington, D.C.: U.S. Government Printing Office, 1989), p. 47.
8. "FBI Adds Violent Crime to Investigative Priorities," *Atlanta Journal*, 22 June 1989, p. A 11, col. 1.

9. Bureau of Justice Statistics, *Criminal Victimization in the United States*, 1983 (Washington, D.C.: U.S. Government Printing Office, August 1985), pp. 2–3. See also Bureau of Justice Statistics, *Households Touched by Crime*, 1988 (Washington, D.C.: U.S. Department of Justice, June 1989), pp. 1–6.

10. Gwynn Nettler, *Explaining Crime*, 3d ed. (New York: McGraw-Hill, 1984), pp. 73–74; emphasis deleted.

11. Bureau of Justice Statistics, *The Risk of Violent Crime* (Washington, D.C.: U.S. Department of Justice, May 1985).

12. Bureau of Justice Statistics, *Report to the Nation on Crime and Justice: The Data*, 2d ed. (Washington, D.C.: U.S. Department of Justice, 1988), p. 29.

13. Federal Bureau of Investigation, *Uniform Crime Reports*, 1988, pp. 23–26.

14. 2 All Eng.R. 801 (House of Lords, 1954).

15. For a discussion, see Derral Cheatwood, "Is There a Season for Homicide?" *Criminology* 26 (May 1988): 287–306.

16. See Robert M. O'Brien, "Exploring the Intersexual Nature of Violent Crimes," *Criminology* 26 (February 1988): 151–169.

17. Federal Bureau of Investigation, *Uniform Crime Reports*, 1988, pp. 8–13.

18. See Manfred Guttmacher, "The Normal and the Sociopathic Murderer," in Marvin Wolfgang, ed., *Studies in Homicide* (New York: Harper & Row, 1967), pp. 114–123. For a contrary view, see Stuart Palmer, *A Study of Murder* (New York: Thomas Y. Crowell, 1960).

19. Marvin E. Wolfgang, "A Sociological Analysis of Criminal Homicide," *Federal Probation* 23 (March 1961): 48–55 reprinted in Wolfgang, ed., *Studies in Homicide*, pp. 15–28. Quotation is on p. 15. See also Richard Block, "Homicide in Chicago: A Nine-Year Study (1965–1973)," *Journal of Criminal Law & Criminology* 66 (December 1975): 496–510.

20. For a discussion of serial murderers, see Philip Jenkins, "Myth and Murder: The Serial Killer Panic of 1983–5," *Criminal Justice Research Bulletin* 3 (Huntsville, Texas: Sam Houston State University Criminal Justice Center, 1988): 1–7, and Ronald M. Holmes and James DeBurger, *Serial Murder* (Beverly Hills, CA.: Sage Publications, 1987). For a discussion of mass murders, see Jack Levin and James Alan Fox, *Mass Murder: America's Growing Menace* (Beverly Hills, CA.: Sage Publications, 1985).

21. "Experts Peg Types of Serial Killers," *Miami Herald*, 23 June 1989, p. B3, col. 1.

22. *Ibid.*

23. Federal Bureau of Investigation, *Uniform Crime Reports*, 1988, p. 18.

24. Federal Bureau of Investigation, *Uniform Crime Reports*, 1988, pp. 16–19; 1987, pp. 8–22.

25. Caroline Wolf Harlow, Bureau of Justice Statistics, *Robbery Victims* (Washington, D.C.: U.S. Department of Justice, April, 1987): 1. For an analysis of robbery and the environment, see Stewart D'Alessio and Lisa Stolzenberg, "A Crime of Convenience: The Environment and Convenience Store Robbery," *Environment and Behavior* 22 (March 1990): 255–271.

26. Joan Petersilia et al., *Criminal Careers of Habitual Felons*, National Institute of Law Enforcement and Criminal Justice (Washington, D.C.: U.S. Government Printing Office, 1978), pp. vii and xiii.

27. Lawrence E. Cohen et al., "Robbery Victimization in the United States: An Analysis of a Nonrandom Event," *Social Science Quarterly* 62 (December 1981): 654–655. For a study of 1,266 cases of armed robbers, see Thomas Gabor et al.,

Armed Robbery: Cops, Robbers, and Victims (Springfield, IL.: Charles C. Thomas, Publisher, 1987).

28. Federal Bureau of Investigation, *Uniform Crime Reports*, 1988, p. 15.
29. See "Focusing on the Offender's Forceful Conduct: A Proposal for the Redefinition of Rape Laws," *George Washington Law Review* 56 (January 1988): 399–430.
30. Federal Bureau of Investigation, *Uniform Crime Reports*, 1987, pp. 13–15; 1988, p. 16.
31. Bureau of Justice Statistics, *The Crime of Rape* (Washington, D.C.: U.S. Department of Justice, March 1985), pp. 1–2.
32. Reported by Mike Toner, "Number of Rapes Much Higher Than Reported, Experts Say," *The Atlanta Constitution*, 17 January 1989, p. 1, col. 1.
33. See James D. Orcutt and Rebecca Faison, "Sex-Role Attitude Change and Reporting of Rape Victimization, 1973–1985," *Sociological Quarterly* 29 (no. 4, 1988): 589.
34. "Poll: Some Kids Condone Date Rape," *Dallas Morning News*, 3 May 1988, p. 6A, col. 1.
35. For a review of the literature on these findings, see R. Lance Shotland and Lynne Goodstein, "Just Because She Doesn't Want to Doesn't Mean It's Rape: An Experimentally Based Causal Model of the Perception of Rape in a Dating Situation," *Social Psychology Quarterly* 46 (September 1983): 220–232. See also Neil M. Malamuth, "Rape Proclivity Among Males," *Journal of Social Issues* 37 (Fall 1981): 138–157.
36. Andrea Parrot, Cornell University, "Comparison of Acquaintance Rape Patterns Among College Students in a Large Co-Ed University and a Small Women's College," paper presented at the 1985 National Convention for the Society for the Scientific Study of Sex, San Diego, California. For a more recent study of rape (and other campus crimes) see Michael Clay Smith, *Coping with Crime on Campus* (N.Y.: Macmillan Publishing Co., 1988).
37. Kathleen Hendrix, "Counselors Angry at Weak Response to Rise in Campus Rape," from the *Los Angeles Times*, reprinted in the *Tallahassee Democrat*, 25 August 1988, p. C5, col. 1. See also Susan Estrick, *Real Rape* (Cambridge, MA.: Harvard University Press, 1987), and Walter S. Dekeseredy, "Woman Abuse in Dating Relationships: A Critical Evaluation of Research and Theory," *International Journal of Sociology of the Family* 18 (Spring 1988): 79–95.
38. See, for example, the works of J. Bancroft, "Psychophysiology of Sexual Dysfunction," in L. Van Pragg, ed., *Handbook of Biological Psychiatry* (N.Y.: Marcel Dekker, 1980), pp. 359–392, and A. C. Kinsey et al., *Sexual Behavior in the Human Male* (Philadelphia: Saunders, 1948).
39. Ronald E. Smith et al., "Social Cognitions About Adult Male Victims of Female Sexual Assault," *Journal of Sex Research* 24 (1988): 101–112.
40. "When Boys Are Victims," *St. Petersburg Times*, 18 June 1989, p. B1, col. 6.
41. Mary Beard Deming and Ali Eppy, "The Sociology of Rape," *Sociology and Social Research* 65 (July 1981): 373.
42. Paul H. Gebhard et al., *Sex Offenders* (New York: Harper & Row, 1965), pp. 197–205.
43. See Manachem Amir, "Forcible Rape," *Federal Probation* 31 (March 1967): 51–58, and *Patterns in Forcible Rape* (Chicago: University of Chicago Press, 1971).
44. A. Nicholas Groth and H. Jean Birnbaum, *Men Who Rape: The Psychology of the Offender* (New York: Plenum, 1979), pp. 5–6.

45. *Ibid.*, pp. 13–58.

46. For a discussion of domestic violence in other countries, see David Levinson, *Family Violence in Cross Cultural Perspective* (Beverly Hills, CA.: Sage Publications, 1989).

47. Ok. Rev. Stat. Title 22, Section 60.1.

48. See Richard J. Gelles, *Family Violence* (Beverly Hills, CA.: Sage Publications, 1979), p. 11. The second edition was published in 1987.

49. Lawrence Sherman, *Domestic Violence* (Washington, D.C.: U.S. Department of Justice, 1988), p. 1. See also Susan M. Edwards, *Policing 'Domestic' Violence: Women, the Law and the State* (Beverly Hills, CA.: Sage Publications, 1989), and Kirk R. Williams and Richard Hawkins, "The Meaning of Arrest for Wife Assault," *Criminology* 27 (February 1989): 163–181.

50. In general, see Glen Kercher and Marilyn McShane, "Characterizing Child Sexual Abuse on the Basis of a Multi-Agency Sample," *Victimology* 89 (November 3–4, 1984): 364–382; David Finkelhor, "Sexual Abuse: A Sociological Perspective," *Child Abuse and Neglect* 6 (1982): 95–102. For a discussion of parental child stealing, see Michael W. Agopian, *Parental Child-Stealing* (Lexington, Mass.: D.C. Heath, 1981).

51. "Steinberg Given Maximum Term of 8⅓ to 25 Years in Child's Death," *New York Times*, 25 March 1989, p. 1, col. 3.

52. David Finkelhor, *Sexually Victimized Children* (New York: Macmillan, 1979).

53. "Reports of Child Abuse on Rise," *Justice Assistance News* 4 (May 1983): 4.

54. See Finkelhor, "Sexual Abuse."

55. "Study Says Reports of Child Abuse Are Increasing," *New York Times*, 18 February 1985, p. 11, col. 34. See also Diana E. H. Russell, *Sexual Exploitation: Rape, Child Sexual Abuse, and Workplace Harassment* (Beverly Hills, CA.: Sage Publications, 1984).

56. See "Studies Find Sexual Abuse of Children Is Widespread," *New York Times*, 13 May 1982, p. 20, col. 1, and "A Senator Recounts Her Own Experience as an Abused Child," *New York Times*, 27 April 1984, p. 1, col. 4.

57. For a brief discussion, see Sue Titus Reid, *Criminal Law* (New York: Macmillan Publishers, Inc., 1989), pp. 199–200.

58. "Molestation Trial is at 2-Year Mark," *New York Times*, 23 April 1989, p. 12, col. 6. For a discussion of sexual abuse in day care centers, see David Finkelhor and Linda Meyer, *Nursery Crimes* (Beverly Hills, CA.: Sage Publications, 1988).

59. For an analysis of a two-year nationwide study of sexual abuse in day care centers, see David Finkelhor, *Nursery Crimes: Sexual Abuse in Day Care* (Beverly Hills, CA.: Sage Publications, 1988).

60. Judith Miller and Mark Miller, "Protecting the Rights of Abused and Neglected Children," *Trial* 19 (July 1983): 69.

61. "Child Sexual Abuse: A Pioneering Study," *New York Times*, 7 February 1983, p. 15, col. 5, referring to the study by Dr. David Finkelhor of the Family Violence Research Program at the University of New Hampshire.

62. See Lois Pierce, "Father-Son Incest: Using the Literature to Guide Practice," *Social Casework* 61 (February 1987): 67–74; and Judith Halpern, "Family Therapy in Father-Son Incest: A Case Study," *Social Casework* 68 (February 1987): 88–93.

63. See Robert L. Geiser, *Hidden Victims: The Sexual Abuse of Children* (Boston: Beacon Press, 1979).

64. "The Child Victim of Incest," *New York Times*, 15 June 1982, p. 22, col. 1. For a discussion of the biosocial view of incest, see Joseph Shepher, *Incest: A Biosocial View* (New York: Academic Press, 1983).

65. Geiser, *Hidden Victims*, p. 68. For more information on incest, see D. E. H. Russell, *The Secret Trauma—Incest in the Lives of Girls and Women* (N.Y.: Basic Books, Inc., Publishers, 1986). For more information on the male victim of sexual assault, see E. Porter, *Treating the Young Male Victim of Sexual Assault— Issues and Intervention Strategies* (Syracuse, N.Y.: Safer Society Press, 1986).

66. See, for example, Gerald T. Hotaling and Murray Straus, "Violence and the Social Structure as Reflected in Children's Books from 1850–1970," in Murray Straus and Gerald T. Hotaling, eds., *The Social Causes of Husband-Wife Violence* (Minneapolis: University of Minnesota Press, 1979), and Murray Straus, "A Sociological Perspective on the Prevention and Treatment of Wife-Beating," in Maria Roy, ed., *Battered Women: A Psychosociological Study of Domestic Violence* (New York: Van Nostrand Reinhold, 1977), pp. 194–238. For a comprehensive coverage of several aspects of family violence, see the recently published volume edited by Lloyd Ohlin and Michael Tonry, *Family Violence* (Chicago: University of Chicago Press, 1989). See also Gerald T. Hotaling et al., *Coping with Family Violence: Research on Policy Perspectives* (Beverly Hills, CA.: Sage Publishers, 1988); and David Finkelhor, *Stopping Family Violence* (Beverly Hills, CA.: Sage Publications, 1988).

67. Study by psychiatrists Brant Steele and Carl Pollock, cited in Ruth Inglis, *Sins of the Fathers: A Study of the Physical and Emotional Abuse of Children* (New York: St. Martin's Press, 1978), p. 69.

68. Richard Gelles, "Child Abuse as Psychopathology: A Sociological Critique and Reformulation," *American Journal of Orthopsychiatry* 43 (1973): 611–621.

69. Gelles, *Family Violence*, pp. 32–37, 42–53.

70. Bureau of Justice Statistics, *Report to the Nation on Crime and Delinquency*, 2d ed. (Washington, D.C.: U.S. Department of Justice, 1988), p. 48.

71. "Children as Sexual Prey, and Predators," *New York Times*, 30 May 1989, p. 1, col. 2. See also Gail Elizabeth Wyatt and Gloria Johnson Powell, *Lasting Effects of Child Sexual Abuse* (Beverly Hills, CA.: Sage Publications, 1988). For an analysis of violence within generations of families, see Cathy Spatz Widom, "The Intergenerational Transmission of Violence," in Neil Alan Weiner and Marvin E. Wolfgang, eds., *Pathways to Criminal Violence* (Beverly Hills, CA.: Sage Publications, 1989), pp. 137–201. See also Gerald T. Hotaling et al., *Family Abuse and Its Consequences: New Directions in Research* (Beverly Hills, CA.: Sage Publications, 1988).

72. Candace Kruttschnitt et al., "Abuse-resistant Youth: Some Factors That May Inhibit Violent Criminal Behavior," *Social Forces* 66 (December 1987): 501.

73. See Murray Straus, Richard J. Gelles, and Suzanne Stinmetz, *Behind Closed Doors: Violence in the American Family* (New York: Doubleday, 1980).

74. Kersti Yllo and Murray A. Straus, "Interpersonal Violence Among Married and Cohabiting Couples," *Family Relations* 30 (July 1981): 345. See also R. Emerson Dobash and Russell Dobash, *Violence Against Wives: A Case Against the Patriarchy* (New York: Free Press, 1979).

75. Baily v. People, 130 P. 832, 835, 836 (Colo. Sup. Ct. 1913); footnotes and citations omitted.

76. *Justice Assistance News* 5 (February–March 1984): 2.

77. "Wife Beating: The Silent Crime," *Time*, 5 September 1983, p. 23.

78. See Gelles, *Family Violence*, p. 92. See also Straus, Gelles, and Steinmetz, *Behind Closed Doors*.

79. "Wife Beating," *Time*, pp. 23–24.

80. Donna M. Moore, ed., *Battered Women* (Beverly Hills, CA.: Sage Publications, 1979), pp. 16–19.

81. Richard Gelles, *The Violent Home* (Beverly Hills, CA.: Sage Publications, 1972).

82. Mildred Daley Pagelow, *Women-Battering: Victims and Their Experiences* (Beverly Hills, CA.: Sage Publications, 1981), p. 54. For a discussion of these myths, see pp. 54–88.

83. Moore, *Battered Women*, p. 20.

84. Gelles, *Violent Home*, pp. 95–110.

85. Warren v. State, 336 S.E.2d 221 (Ga. App. 1985).

86. Diana E. H. Russell, *The Politics of Rape: The Victim's Perspective* (Briarcliff Manor, N.Y.: Stein & Day, 1975).

87. Groth and Birnbaum, *Men Who Rape*, and Lenore Walker, *The Battered Woman* (New York: Harper & Row, 1979).

88. Report of Dr. Diana Russell, presented to the American Sociological Association and quoted in the *New York Times*, 29 November 1982, p. 20, col. 1. For a discussion of many of the issues on spousal rape, see the excellent collection of essays in Duncan Chappell, Robley Geis, and Gilbert Geis, eds., *Forcible Rape: The Crime, the Victim and the Offender* (New York: Columbia University Press, 1977).

89. David Finkelhor and Kersti Yllo, "Forced Sex in Marriage: A Preliminary Research Report," *Crime & Delinquency* 28 (July 1982): 459. See also Finkelhor and Yllo, *License to Rape: Sexual Abuse of Wives* (N.Y.: Free Press, 1987); and Richard Gelles, "Power, Sex, and Violence: The Case of Marital Rape," in Gelles, *Family Violence*, pp. 121–135.

90. State v. Rideout, *Family Law Reporter* 5 (BNA) 2164 (1979). See Or.Rev.Stat. Section 163.375.

91. Commonwealth v. James K. Chretien, Supreme Judicial Court of Massachusetts, Essex Mass. Adv.Sh. (1981) 661, 2 December 1980; 9 March 1981.

92. Gelles, "The Truth About Husband Abuse," chap. 8 in Gelles, *Family Violence*, p. 137.

93. "Striking Back," *Time*, 21 December 1987, p. 68.

94. Bureau of Justice Statistics, *Preventing Domestic Violence Against Women* (Washington, D.C.: U.S. Department of Justice, August 1986), pp. 1–2.

95. "The Plague of Violent Crime," *Newsweek*, 23 March 1981, p. 46.

96. "The Curse of Violent Crime: A Pervasive Fear of Robbery and Mayhem Threatens the Way America Lives," *Time*, 23 March 1981, p. 16. For an analysis of the fear of crime, see Steven Box et al., "Explaining Fear of Crime," *British Journal of Crimonology* 28 (Summer 1988): 340–356.

97. Bureau of Justice Statistics, *Report to the Nation on Crime and Justice*, p. 24.

98. See, for example, Kenneth Friedman et al., *Victims and Helpers: Reactions to Crime*, U.S. Department of Justice, National Institute of Justice (Washington, D.C.: U.S. Government Printing Office, 1982).

99. See Wesley G. Skogan and Michael G. Maxfield, *Coping With Crime: Individual and Neighborhood Reactions* (Beverly Hills, CA.: Sage Publications, 1981), and Mary Holland Baker et al., "The Impact of a Crime Wave: Perceptions, Fear, and Confidence in the Police," *Law & Society Review* 17 (1983): 319–335.

100. Stephanie Riger, "On Women," in Dan A. Lewis, ed., *Reactions to Crime* (Beverly Hills, Calif.: Sage Publications, 1981), pp. 47–52.

101. For a discussion of self-help as a form of crime prevention, see Donald Black, "Crime as Social Control," *American Sociological Review* 48 (1983): 34–45.

102. For a discussion, see Douglas A. Smith and Craig D. Uchida, "The Social Organization of Self-Help: A Study of Defensive Weapon Ownership," *American Sociological Review* 53 (February 1988): 94–102.

103. See Gary S. Green, "Citizen Gun Ownership and Criminal Deterrence: Theory, Research, and Policy," *Criminology* 25 (February 1987): 63–81.

104. See James D. Wright, National Institute of Justice, *The Armed Criminal in America* (Washington, D.C.: U.S. Department of Justice, 1986). See also James D. Wright and Peter H. Rossi, *Armed and Considered Dangerous: A Survey of Felons and Their Firearms* (N.Y.: Aldine de Gruyter, 1986); and Catherine F. Sproule and Deborah J. Kennett, "The Use of Firearms in Canadian Homicides 1972–1982: The Need for Gun Control," *Canadian Journal of Criminology* 30 (January 1988): 31–37.

CHAPTER 8

This chapter discusses property crimes and begins with the four serious property crimes as defined by the FBI's Uniform Crime Reports: *larceny-theft, motor vehicle theft, burglary, and arson. Because laws defining larceny-theft and burglary can only be understood in light of their historical development, brief attention is given to the history of property crimes. The second section focuses on the less serious property crimes as categorized by the UCR: forgery and counterfeiting; buying, receiving, and possessing stolen property; and embezzlement. Next is a brief look at modern thefts, some of which are discussed in more detail in the following chapter's treatment of white-collar crime. The final section explores professional and career criminals, many of whom are engaged in property crimes.*

OUTLINE

Property Crimes

KEY TERMS

arson
burglary
career criminal
cohort
computer crimes
corporate crimes
embezzlement
felony
fence
forgery
fraud
Index Offenses
larceny-theft
misdemeanor
organized crime
property crimes
white-collar crimes

"Law is never a mere abstraction. It is a very practical . . . matter. It represents the sum total of the rules by which the game of life is played . . . but this is quite a different game in different lands and in different times."[1] With those words, a noted law professor began his commentary on the development of the law of property, a development that to some extent applies to all the crimes discussed in this chapter.

The emphasis on different times is significant, for this chapter discusses crimes that are quite different from those of previous chapters. Violent and **property crimes** differ, not only in terms of the personal threat of violent crime, but also in that some of the property crimes discussed in this chapter were historically not considered criminal. Indeed, taking something from another by **fraud** or deceit or by what we would today call **embezzlement** was considered by many to be clever, not criminal.

When most business deals occurred between people who knew each other well, it was the responsibility of all parties to be sure they were being treated fairly. Thus, if you wanted to buy ten chickens from your friend, it was your responsibility to make sure that you actually got ten chickens. If your friend managed to trick you, deceive you, or mislead you, he was just smarter than you!

Times changed, however, and business relationships became more complex. The changes in social and business conditions necessitated changes in laws governing business life. The problems, statutory or otherwise, of the crimes discussed in this chapter have not yet been solved. We are just beginning to cope with some of them, such as **computer crimes.** Nor do we know how to deal with the people who are involved in the crimes discussed in this chapter. Some are occasional street criminals; others are career property offenders. Some are "just like us." That may also be true of some offenders involved in family violence, but physical violence is not condoned by most people. This chapter, however, focuses on some crimes that are similar to what, in other contexts, are considered acceptable business practices.

Property crimes are discussed by categories, beginning with the four crimes included in the FBI's list of eight serious crimes, or **Index Offenses.** The second section enumerates and discusses the crimes included in the FBI's list of Part II, or less serious, crimes. Attention is then given to such modern crimes as credit card thefts. A discussion of professional versus amateur thieves sets the stage for a look at career criminals.

SERIOUS PROPERTY CRIMES: THE OFFICIAL CATEGORIES

The official crime reports of the FBI include in the Index Offenses four property crimes: larceny-theft, motor vehicle theft, burglary, and arson

EXHIBIT 8.1

Characteristics of the Most Common Serious Property Crimes as Defined by the FBI

Crime	Definition	Facts
Burglary	Unlawful entry of any fixed structure, vehicle, or vessel used for regular residence, industry, or business, with or without force, with the intent to commit a felony or larceny.	● Residential property was targeted in 2 out of every 3 reported burglaries; nonresidential property accounted for the remaining third. ● In 1985, 42% of all residential burglaries occurred without forced entry. ● About 37% of the no-force burglaries were known to have occurred during the day between 6 a.m. and 6 p.m.
Larceny-theft	Unlawful taking or attempted taking of property other than a motor vehicle from the possession of another, by stealth, without force and without deceit, with intent to permanently deprive the owner of the property.	● Less than 5% of all personal larcenies involve contact between the victim and offender. ● Pocket picking and purse snatching most frequently occur inside nonresidential buildings or on street locations. ● Unlike most other crimes, pocket picking and purse snatching affect the elderly about as much as other age groups.
Motor vehicle theft	Unlawful taking or attempted taking of a self-propelled road vehicle owned by another, with the intent of depriving him or her of it, permanently or temporarily.	● Motor vehicle theft is relatively well reported to the police. In 1985 89% of all completed thefts were reported. ● The stolen property is more likely to be recovered in this crime than in other property crimes.
Arson	The intentional damaging or destruction or attempted damaging or destruction by means of fire or explosion of property without the consent of the owner, or of one's own property or that of another by fire or explosives with or without the intent to defraud.	● Single-family residences were the most frequent targets of arson. ● 16% of all structures where arson occurred were not in use.

SOURCE: Bureau of Justice Statistics, *Report to the Nation on Crime and Justice: The Data,* 2d ed. (Washington, D.C.: U.S. Government Printing Office, 1988), p. 3.

(see Exhibit 8.1). Each crime will be defined, the most recent data will be analyzed, and sociological research will be discussed where applicable.

Larceny-Theft

The crime of **larceny-theft,** as defined by the FBI, is a broad category that can only be understood in light of its historical development.

Historical Development of Theft

Larceny, the first theft crime in English history, was a common law crime, meaning that it was created by judges deciding cases, not by Parliament in passing statutes. Larceny was defined as a crime committed when a person misappropriated the property of another by taking that property from the possession and without the consent of the owner. The crime did not include misappropriation of property that one already had; for example, if your boss asked you to take a sheep to a customer and you decided to keep the sheep, that act was not larceny since you already had the sheep in your possession. Under that definition embezzlement and many other modern business crimes would not be larceny.

One of the reasons for requiring the property to be taken from the possession of another was that the seriousness of the stealing was not in taking possession of the property but in doing so under circumstances that might cause the owner to retaliate. Then an act of violence might occur. Also, getting possession by deceit, fraud, or embezzlement was not considered larceny because such methods indicated that the thief was smarter than the owner of the property, and that was not a crime. It was the responsibility of the owner of the property to watch business dealings more carefully.

Another feature of early English common law is very important to an understanding of how theft laws evolved. Larceny was a **felony,** or a more serious crime than a **misdemeanor,** and at one time, all felonies were punishable by death. Early statutes provided that if the amount stolen did not exceed a specified amount, the punishment might be imprisonment rather than death; but the amount was relatively small, equivalent to about the price of a sheep.

As money depreciated in value over the years and the statutes remained unchanged, the amount required for *grand larceny,* as compared to *petit larceny,* was very small. Many judges were reluctant to impose the death penalty in cases of grand larceny, and they began looking for technical ways to avoid finding the defendant guilty. One of those ways was to find something peculiar about the way in which the property had been taken. The result was that many loopholes developed in the law of theft; statutes were passed to fill the gaps in the law, resulting in a patchwork of laws on theft that "are interesting as a matter of history but embarrassing as a matter of law-enforcement."[2]

Larceny-Theft in the *Uniform Crime Reports*

The exclusion of some types of theft from larceny-theft is made clear in the following definition utilized by the *UCR*.

> Larceny-theft is the unlawful taking, carrying, leading, or riding away of property from the possession or constructive possession of another. It includes crimes such as shoplifting, pocket-picking, purse-snatching, thefts from motor vehicles, thefts of motor vehicle parts and accessories, bicycle thefts, etc., in which no use of force, violence, or fraud occurs. In the Uniform Crime Reporting Program, this crime category does not include embezzlement, "con" games, forgery, and worthless checks. Motor vehicle theft is also excluded from this category inasmuch as it is a separate Crime Index offense.[3]

Combining so many behaviors into one category of theft may solve some legal technical problems, but it creates a heterogeneous category of behavior, as Figure 8.1 indicates.

Larceny-theft is the serious crime most frequently recorded by the FBI. In 1988, over 7½ million offenses were recorded, constituting 55 percent of the Index total and 62 percent of all serious property crimes. The

FIGURE 8.1 Larceny–Theft

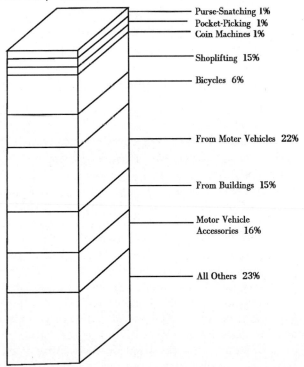

Purse-Snatching 1%
Pocket-Picking 1%
Coin Machines 1%
Shoplifting 15%
Bicycles 6%
From Moter Vehicles 22%
From Buildings 15%
Motor Vehicle Accessories 16%
All Others 23%

SOURCE: Federal Bureau of Investigation, *Uniform Crime Reports,* 1988 (Washington, D.C.: U.S. Government Printing Office, 1989), p. 37.

volume of larceny-thefts recorded by the FBI had declined between 1982 and 1984, but in 1985 there was a 5 percent increase over 1984. Despite this increase, the volume of larceny-thefts in 1985 showed a decrease of 4 percent from 1981, although it represented a 10 percent rise over the 1976 figures. By 1987 larceny-thefts were up again by 3.3 percent over 1986, and they rose another 3 percent in 1988. Larceny-thefts peak in August and drop to their lowest levels in February. The South has the highest volume; 37 percent of the total.[4]

A comparison of the volume of the major types of larceny-theft over the period 1984–1988 indicates increases in all theft crimes, including theft from motor vehicles (up 22 percent), motor vehicle accessories (up 16 percent), from buildings (up 15 percent), and shoplifting (up 15 percent). Only 20 percent of larceny-thefts were cleared by arrest in 1988. Of those arrested in 1988, 30 percent were females. Arrests for larceny-theft constituted 55 percent of the total arrests for Index crimes and 70 percent of arrests for property crimes in 1988.[5]

Caution must be used in interpreting these data. In our discussion of robbery we noted that one of the differences between theft and robbery is the use of violence or threat of violence in the latter. We used the example of purse snatching, categorized by the FBI as larceny-theft. But if sufficient force or threat of force is used, the crime will be classified as robbery. This kind of fine distinction makes it necessary for us to realize that when we compare robbers to thieves, we may not be talking about different kinds of criminals.

Analysis of Types: Focus on Shoplifting

Of the types of larceny-theft included in the *UCR* definition, sociologists have concentrated their studies on shoplifting. Shoplifting, the illegal removal of merchandise from stores by persons posing as customers, has been steadily rising in recent years, showing a 35 percent increase between 1984 and 1988.[6]

Although most shoplifters do not take large amounts of merchandise, the total cost to business is enormous. Most shoplifters are not apprehended. Those who are, are often not prosecuted. Many people who observe shoplifting are reluctant to report it, and some business managers are reluctant to insist on prosecutions when shoplifting is reported. Early sociological studies suggested that the *appearance* of the shoplifter was the variable most frequently associated with the decision to report shoplifting; hippies were more likely to be reported for shoplifting than were others.[7] Other studies found that the decision of whether or not to report shoplifting was more frequently related to the value of the goods stolen, the type of item stolen, and the method of stealing.[8] (See Highlight 8.1.)

Occasionally a well-known person will be arrested for shoplifting, although such arrests probably represent only a very small percentage of such people who actually shoplift. In 1988 former Miss America Bess Myerson was fined $100 and $48.50 in court costs after she entered a guilty

HIGHLIGHT 8.1

SHOPLIFTING: AN EASY CRIME?

High school students in Wheeling, Illinois, in cooperation with the store manager and as part of their marketing class, staged a three-hour shopping spree in which they frequently engaged in shoplifting. Numerous customers observed the commission of these crimes; no one reported any of the acts. The store manager's comment: "Nobody cares. Nobody wants to get involved. . . . It's a major problem in retail business."

SOURCE: Summarized from *San Diego Tribune,* 4 February 1982, p. 2, col. 1. Reprinted with permission.

plea to shoplifting $44 worth of merchandise from a Williamsport, Pennsylvania, store. The sixty-three-year-old Myerson told the judge that she was going out to lock her car and had then planned to pay for the merchandise, which consisted of bottles of nail polish, earrings, shoes, and flashlight batteries, all items she could no doubt afford to purchase. Myerson was already facing federal charges of fraud and bribery. She was later acquitted of those charges. In 1989 former Rep. John Jenrette was fined $2000 and sentenced to a 30-day jail term, followed by 2 years' probation and 200 hours of community service, for shoplifting a tie and shoes. Jenrette was also told to continue psychiatric and alcoholism treatment.

Gwynn Nettler has summarized research on shoplifters. The major findings are as follows:

1. Most shoplifting goes undetected and unreported when detected. . . . The proportion of shoppers who steal is small. . . .

2. Thieves, particularly young ones, continue to steal after they are apprehended if they are not otherwise punished. . . . These results run counter to an established doctrine in criminology that says that snitches desist after arrest. . . .

3. Common stories of kleptomania and of compulsive theft in menopausal women have little substance. Most shoplifting cannot be explained by Freudian ideas of the sexual significance of the objects stolen or by neurotic needs. . . .

4. Stores in university areas in the United States are particularly vulnerable to shoplifting. . . .

5. As with other unskillful thefts, there is a tendency for apprehended shoplifters to be disproportionately represented by ethnic "minorities."

6. All generalizations about the nature of shoplifters should be interpreted with caution because of the variability in law enforcement among stores, within cities, and among countries.[9]

A Classic Study: The Booster and the Snitch—In 1964 Mary Owen Cameron published what has come to be a classic in the study of shoplifting. After distinguishing the *snitch* (the pilferer) from the *booster* (commercial shoplifter), Cameron concluded that "most shoplifting, including pilfering, appears to be chronic, habitual or systematic behavior." In addition to the booster and the snitch, says Cameron, there might be a group of shoplifters who commit the offense because of an "unexpected urge to steal" or who are overcome "by an unpremeditated desire for a particular object."[10]

Cameron's data indicate that most shoplifters are not associated with a criminal subculture. Most are females, and over 90 percent have probably never been convicted of another offense. The items are usually taken for the shoplifter's personal use rather than for resale and profit. Most of the women have not thought about the possibility of being arrested, although they have considered that they might be caught. When apprehended, they often use the excuses and rationalizations characteristic of juveniles caught in a delinquent act. They do not manifest psychotic symptoms, and they are seldom repeat offenders. They probably have had childhood experiences with groups in which older children taught them the techniques of successful pilfering. Most of the women shoplifters are from families with modest budgets. They do not steal items they usually buy but luxury items that cannot come out of the family budget without sacrificing other needs of the family. The women rationalize that it is better to steal from the department store than from the family budget.

Pilferers, in contrast to other thieves, do not think of themselves as thieves and even when arrested will often resist the definition of their behavior as theft. The arrest procedure, however, forces the realization that the behavior is not just bad; it is also illegal. The pilferer at this stage will often become quite upset, even hysterical. In contrast, the professional shoplifter, upon finding it impossible to talk her way out of an arrest, will accept the inevitable. The pilferer fears the reaction of family and expects no in-group support for the behavior in question. The act of apprehension is usually sufficient to deter most pilferers from further illegal activity of this kind, but note that Nettler's summary of other studies questions this last conclusion.

Shoplifting: The International Scene—The extensive problem of shoplifting in England in recent years has led to studies indicating that shoplifting is an enduring crime, highly resistant to preventive efforts.[11] The offense gained wide publicity in England in 1980 when Lady Isobel Barnett, widow of the lord mayor of Leicester, was arrested for shoplifting a can of tuna and a carton of cream, worth about two dollars. She admitted taking the items but said it was an oversight and that the cloth bag pinned inside her coat, where the items were placed, was normally used for the flashlight she carried for protection against muggers. Lady Barnett was convicted and fined the equivalent of $650 and court costs.

Her comment was, "I have only myself to live with and I can live with myself." Four days later she was found dead, electrocuted in her bath, apparently a case of suicide. Newspapers in England carried front-page headlines of these events, one columnist reporting interviews with dozens of alleged female shoplifters who were widowed or emotionally neglected by their husbands. They felt no guilt about the crime and said that they did it for thrills and excitement. One woman indicated that shoplifting was sexually arousing: "I got an orgasm every time I slipped something into my handbag."[12]

Motor Vehicle Theft

The *UCR* tabulates motor vehicle thefts separately from other serious thefts. The crime is defined officially as "the theft or attempted theft of a motor vehicle. This definition excludes the taking of a motor vehicle for temporary use by those persons having lawful access."[13] Almost one and one-half million motor vehicle thefts are reported annually to the FBI, representing 12 percent of all Index property crimes.

Figure 8.2 graphs the trend in motor vehicle thefts from 1984 to 1988 during which time the number of offenses rose 39 percent and the rate

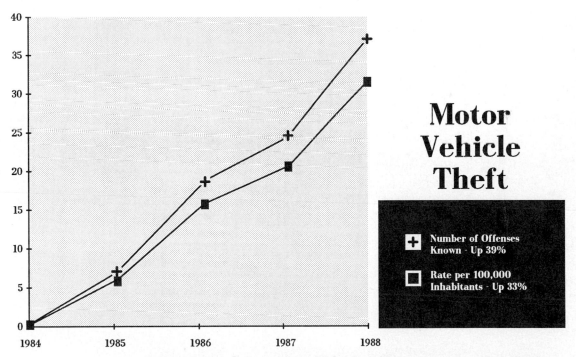

FIGURE 8.2 Trends in motor vehicle theft by percentage, 1983–1987
SOURCE: Federal Bureau of Investigation, *Uniform Crime Reports,* 1988 (Washington, D.C.: U.S. Government Printing Office, 1989), p. 40.

rose 33 percent. The estimated total loss from this crime was over $7 billion. Most of the thefts, 77 percent, involved automobiles. Only 15 percent of the reported thefts were cleared by arrest. Forty percent of the arrestees were under eighteen; 58 percent were under twenty-one. Ninety percent of the arrestees were male; 59 percent were white, and 40 percent were black.[14]

Motor vehicle theft is a crime that many of us can expect to encounter. Data from the National Automobile Theft Bureau/National Traffic Safety Administration indicate that one out of fifty registered cars will be stolen or broken into each year; 25 percent of the total reported thefts occur in New York, Los Angeles, Chicago, Detroit, and Houston; the recovery rate is less than 60 percent. Sports cars and luxury cars are the top targets. The Buick Riviera tops the list of stolen cars, followed by the Toyota Celica Supra, Cadillac Eldorado, Chevrolet Corvette, Pontiac Firebird, Chevrolet Camaro, Mazda RX-7, Porsche 911, Oldsmobile Toronado, and Pontiac Grand Prix. The state with the most thefts is California, whereas Massachusetts has the most thefts when rate per population is considered.[15]

Analysis of Motor Vehicle Theft

Despite media suggestions that motor vehicles are stolen primarily to strip the cars and sell the parts or resell the cars, the high percentage of young people arrested for these thefts may indicate joy riding. Sociologist Charles McCaghy and his colleagues found that many young people do not steal cars to resell them for a profit but to have them for a temporary period of fun and prestige. A second reason is *short-term transportation*, and a third, *long-term transportation.* This type of motor vehicle theft is committed by persons from a lower socioeconomic background who are older than the joy riders. They paint or alter the car in other ways to disguise its appearance. Others steal for *profit*, intending to sell the car rather than use it for transportation. This type of thief often operates in a highly organized business. A final reason for stealing motor vehicles is to use them in the *commission of another crime* such as robbery. This category constitutes a small portion of auto thefts.[16]

Burglary

The third serious property crime is **burglary.** The evolution of burglary statutes, like those encompassing larceny, indicates the problems the common law courts had in interpreting the elements of the crime; and some of these elements have survived in recent legislation.

Historical Development of the Crime of Burglary

Under English common law, burglary was defined as breaking and entering the dwelling of another in the night with the intent to commit a felony; however, it was punishable as a separate offense from that of the felony committed, probably in an attempt to plug legal loopholes regarding attempted crimes. Attempted crimes are difficult to prove, and the penalties are usually less severe than for completed crimes. Both situations were changed by the categorization of burglary as a separate punishable crime. The result was that if the state could not prove all the elements of the larceny or other crime that took place after the buglary, it might still be possible to convict for burglary.

Numerous problems arose with the common law definition. What was meant by breaking and entering? The cases are fascinating and in some instances absurd. Early cases held that if the owner of the home left the place unsecured, he or she was not entitled to protection. A person who entered the home through that door without permission could not be convicted of burglary. Likewise, entering through an open door did not constitute breaking and entering. If the door or window were partly opened, opening it further to enter also was not breaking and entering. It was not necessary that the door or windows be locked, only that they be closed.

The requirement of entering also presented problems. If an instrument were used to open the building and if the instrument entered the building, that action did not constitute the element of entering unless the instrument was used in the commission of the felony for which the premises were entered. However, the entry of any part of the offender could constitute an entry. The offender could also be held to have met this element of the crime by sending in a child or another person who could not be held legally responsible. In that situation the adult offender was held to have entered constructively.

The "dwelling of another" also raised interesting legal problems. A person's home was his or her castle, and it was believed that breaking and entering that dwelling was a heinous crime, punishable by death. The occupant did not have to be present; indeed, he or she could have been absent for a long time, but it had to be that person's dwelling place. An unfinished house would not count even if the workers slept there. In some circumstances, the term *dwelling* also included barns, stables, and other outhouses.

The burglary, under common law, must have been committed during the night. The difference between night and day was defined as "whether the countenance of a man could be discerned by natural light even though the sun may have set. Artificial light or moonlight, regardless of their intensity, would not suffice." Finally, to be convicted of burglary the offender had to intend to commit a felony while in the dwelling. Passing through the home to commit a felony elsewhere would not suffice.[17]

Over the years the meaning of burglary has been changed to the extent that statutes today bear little resemblance to the common law definition. Modern statutes are much broader; most do not require breaking in, and they may cover entry at any time into any kind of structure.

Burglary in the *Uniform Crime Reports*

The *UCR* defines burglary as "the unlawful entry of a structure to commit a felony or theft. The use of force to gain entry is not required. . . . Burglary . . . is categorized into three subclassifications: forcible entry, unlawful entry where no force is used, and attempted forcible entry."[18]

Over 3.2 million burglaries were reported to the FBI in 1988, representing a slight decrease over 1987 but an 8 percent increase over 1984. Burglaries constituted 23 percent of all Index Offenses and 26 percent of all Index property crimes in 1988. Two out of every three burglaries were residential; 70 percent involved forcible entry; and the estimated total loss was $3.3 billion, the average burglary resulting in a $1,014 loss for residential property.[19]

Burglary Data from Victimization Studies

Data from victimization studies are difficult to compare with *UCR* studies because of differences in the definition of burglary. Whereas the *UCR* focuses on the *intent* of the offender, the National Crime Survey (NCS) focuses on whether or not the offender had a *right to enter* the residence because of the difficulty or impossibility of establishing the concept of intent in a victimization study. The data are also difficult to compare because of the different time periods covered.

The NCS data analyzed by the Bureau of Justice Statistics (BJS) for the ten-year period 1973–1982 indicate that about 73 million households were burglarized; about 45 percent involved unlawful entry and 33 percent forcible entry. The rest were attempted entries. The percentages of both attempted and forcible entries were consistent during this period, with unlawful entry without force the only type of burglary that indicated a discernible trend. The BJS report suggests that although there is no evidence for or against the proposition that the increasing prevalence of security devices affected the trends in forcible entry burglaries, this does not mean that additional security devices are not effective in preventing burglaries. It may mean that burglars avoid houses with security devices and burglarize those without them. If that is true, improved security shifts burglaries but does not prevent their occurrence.[20] According to later BJS data, between 1975 and 1988, there was a 30 percent decrease in households victimized by burglary.[21]

Analysis of Burglary

Burglary and burglars have been studied from several approaches. Some sociologists have studied the people convicted of the burglary (often combined with those who commit larceny), trying to discover whether these types of criminals have any distinguishable characteristics.[22] Others have looked at the circumstances surrounding the crime, for example, the *type of establishment* burglarized, the *value of the loss*, the *type of entry*, and the hour of the day or night when the crime occurred.[23] Still others have looked at characteristics of the *area* in which the crime occurred. Some researchers have also concentrated on the characteristics of the victims.[24] The most extensive work, however, has been in the area of professional or career criminal studies, which may include all serious property crimes. These studies require greater analysis and will be discussed in a later section. It is not always possible to separate the burglary offenders from the studies of career criminals, but a significant number of persons convicted of burglary are habitual or professional criminals.

Most burglars are young, unskilled males. In urban areas, they are disproportionately nonwhite. Older and more talented burglars are more likely to steal alone, while young and female burglars are more likely to steal in groups. Most do not travel far from their homes to commit their crimes. "White thieves avoid black neighborhoods and blacks are wary of police patrols in white neighborhoods. Most burglars choose victims by their accessibility." Thus, well-guarded apartments and houses with adequate security are not as likely to be burglarized as those that are more vulnerable.[25]

Arson

The fourth *UCR* Index property crime is **arson.** Despite the seriousness of this crime—as the FBI bulletin says, it is a crime that "burns us all"—it has not received much attention until recently.

One senator alleges that arson for profit is "the fastest growing crime in this country." Other authorities emphasize that although "only 3 or 4 percent of those arrested for arson are suspected of doing it for profit," the actual figures are probably much higher, representing 20 to 30 percent of all arsons. Efforts are being made to identify the types of arson for hire and to take measures to reduce or eliminate the profit in these crimes. Toward this goal, increased use of federal, state, and local arson task forces, improved investigative techniques, organized strike forces, and other techniques have been utilized.[26]

In a 1982 issue of the *American Bar Association Journal*, an insurance company ran a two-page advertisement on arson for profit, alleging that although most fires are not for profit, arson has become a serious social problem and that "the largest percentage of arson fires is caused by vandals, revenge seekers, or people in need of psychiatric help."[27]

Arson in the *Uniform Crime Reports*

Arson is defined by the *UCR* as "any willful or malicious burning or attempt to burn, with or without intent to defraud, a dwelling house, public building, motor vehicle or aircraft, personal property of another, etc."[28]

TABLE 8.1 Arson, Monetary Value of Property Damaged, 1988

Property Classification	Number of Offenses	Percent Distribution
Total	81,063	100.0
Total structure	44,581	55.0
Single occupancy residential	19,290	23.8
Other residential	8,369	10.3
Storage	4,456	5.5
Industrial/manufacturing	754	.9
Other commercial	5,068	6.3
Community/public	4,141	5.1
Other structure	2,503	3.1
Total mobile	21,387	26.4
Motor vehicles	19,758	24.4
Other mobile	1,629	2.0
Other	15,095	18.6

SOURCE: Federal Bureau of Investigation, *Uniform Crime Reports,* 1988 (Washington, D.C.: U.S. Government Printing Office, 1989), p. 43.

The *UCR* includes only those fires that are found to be maliciously or willfully set. Fires of unknown or suspicious origin are excluded.

Arson was not categorized as an Index crime until recently. By congressional mandate in October 1978, to become effective in 1979, arson was moved from Part II to Part I, or Index, Offenses. Procedures were developed for reporting arson, but the *UCR* emphasizes that care must be used in interpreting data on arson, particularly trend data, which might be significantly affected by better reporting procedures rather than by increased volume and higher rates of arson.

Table 8.1 indicates that the most frequent target of arson in 1988 was single occupancy residential structures. The average damage was $12,467. Only 15 percent of the crimes were cleared by arrest, and 39 percent of those arrested were under eighteen.[29] Scholars emphasize, however, that official arson data are highly suspect and should be carefully analyzed.[30]

Analysis of Arsonists

Analysis of arson has focused on the crime, not the criminal, and some sociological theories already discussed have been utilized. For example, the sixteen fires set at dormitories at the University of Massachusetts at Amherst in 1983 were thought to be the work of copycats. Arson has also been attributed to "patterns of systematic speculation in transitional neighborhoods," racial problems, and capitalism, and the scale and complexity of this crime call into question our theories of deviance.[31] There are, however, some early studies of convicted arsonists. Most frequently cited are the works of two psychiatrists and a sociologist, who have categorized six types of arsonists.

1. *Revenge arsonists* are the most prevalent type. They are usually family members or friends who have been involved in an argument with the people against whom they seek revenge. These arsonists are often intoxicated at the time of the crime; they are potentially more dangerous than other types, and they make little attempt to conceal their actions.

2. *Vandalism arsonists* are often teenagers who think it is fun to destroy property by fire. They often work with another arsonist, in contrast to other types who usually work alone.

3. *Crime-concealment arsonists* are offenders who set fires to conceal other crimes that they have committed, for example, burglary or murder.

4. *Insurance-claim arsonists* set fires to enable them to make claims against their insurance companies. They usually commit their crimes during the day, in contrast to crime-concealment arsonists who more often work at night.

5. *Excitement arsonists* are usually intoxicated and set fire to inhabited buildings at night for the fun they find in the activity.

6. *Pyromaniacs* perhaps best fit our common stereotype of arsonists—they are the pathological firefighters who do not seem to commit the crime for financial reasons or any other practical reason but because of an irresistible impulse.[32]

A final type, identified more recently, is the person who commits *arson for hire*, or for profit. This type is rarely caught; therefore, little is known about his or her characteristics.

The main attention to the crime of arson has come from firefighters and to some extent from the police. The emphasis has been on detention, prevention, and control. "Easy to commit, hard to solve, arson poses unique problems for public safety officials. Rarely are there witnesses to the crime, and much of the evidence literally goes up in smoke."[33] Some cities have developed special arson-control task forces and other methods for combating the problem.[34]

LESS SERIOUS PROPERTY CRIMES: THE OFFICIAL CATEGORIES

The *Uniform Crime Reports* enumerates and collects data on less serious offenses, called Part II Offenses. Despite the FBI categorization of these crimes as less serious property crimes, it may be argued that they are *more* serious than arson, burglary, larceny-theft, and motor vehicle theft. The total economic loss may be greater, as in embezzlement and the erosion of society's moral fiber may be more significant. More attention is given to these issues in Chapter 9, which discusses **white-collar crimes** and **corporate crimes.** Several of these Part II Offenses are property crimes. Three of them—forgery, receiving stolen property, and embezzlement—are the subjects of sociological studies and are discussed here.

Forgery and Counterfeiting

Forgery involves falsely making or altering, with the intent to defraud, a negotiable instrument, such as a check, that is legally enforceable. The most common type of forgery is check forgery, or as it is known in prison language, paper hanging.

Many people who engage in check forgery are not professionals; they are amateurs, also called *naive check forgers.* In an earlier study of naive check forgers, Edwin Lemert applied his closure theory of analysis. According to Lemert, a person who is socially isolated and facing problems that tend to create even further isolation (such as divorce, unemployment, or alcoholism) may also encounter problems that can only be solved by money. Check forging is seen as a way to solve those problems, or as Lemert says, a way to get closure. Lemert found that check forgers did not associate with other criminals or engage in other types of crime. They were generally nonviolent and likable persons, older and more intelligent than most other criminals.[35]

Stolen Property: Buying, Receiving, Possessing

The *UCR* includes the buying, receiving, or possessing of stolen property as a Part II Offense. To make money on their acquisitions, thieves must make arrangements to exchange the goods for money or other goods. In many instances a fence is involved. A **fence** is a person who disposes of stolen goods. Many fences are professionals and connected with **organized crime,** discussed in a later chapter. The fence is an important key to the big business of property crime. The interaction of fences and thieves is diagrammed in Figure 8.3.

Recently researchers have given more attention to the role of the fence in property crimes. An example is sociologist Darrell J. Steffensmeier's *The Fence: In the Shadow of Two Worlds,* which covers all aspects of fencing, including a discussion of "The Process of Becoming and Being a Fence."[36]

In the 1970s, however, the emphasis was on developing programs for theft prevention, including antifencing programs, some of which were sponsored by the federal government. From 1974 to 1980 the government allocated approximately $30 million to cover such programs in fifty cities.

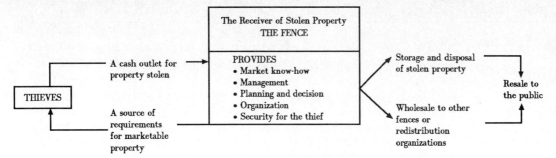

FIGURE 8.3 **Diagram of stolen property distribution system (SPDS)** *SOURCE:* Catherine A. Cotter and James W. Burrows, *Property Crime Program. A Special Report: Overview of the Sting Program and Project Summaries* (Washington, D.C.: U.S. Department of Justice, January, 1981), p. 4.

Police departments established "sting" operations—undercover agents to buy the stolen goods and then arrest the fences. An analysis of the anti-fencing program in Detroit disclosed that although the property crime rates were not cut and major fences were not apprehended, the program did have some positive results. Older offenders with prior records were arrested, the conviction rate was higher than usual, police knowledge of the stolen property market was increased, and community confidence in the criminal justice system was enhanced.[37]

Embezzlement

Under common law, if the property of another had been entrusted to you and if you had kept the property against the wishes of the owner, you would not have committed larceny-theft. Gradually it was decided that misappropriation of the property entrusted to you by another should be a crime. But larceny-theft was a felony. Since all felonies carried the death penalty, there was a reluctance to extend the crime of theft. The solution was to create a new crime, embezzlement, that carried lighter penalties.

Embezzlement refers to the misappropriation or misapplication of property or money entrusted to the care, custody, or control of the offender. The crime may involve far greater economic loss than larceny-theft but result in a less severe sentence. Over the years, however, the penalties for larceny-theft were reduced, and today many jurisdictions have a general theft statute that covers most if not all types of theft, as noted later.[38] This historical background on the law of theft aids in the understanding of the differential treatment accorded today to white-collar criminals and offenders convicted of other types of theft or burglary.

From both a sociological and a legal point of view, embezzlement and embezzlers present a problem in analysis. To analyze why the crime is committed, should embezzlement be included in the categories of theft

HIGHLIGHT 8.2

"THE CHAIRMAN" AND HIS BOARD: EMBEZZLERS NEARLY GET AWAY WITH $69 MILLION FROM FIRST CHICAGO

It took just a month to plan, and just 64 minutes to execute. On Friday, May 13—a date chosen in a spirit of mischief—an $18,000-a-year clerk at First National Bank of Chicago set in motion a simple scheme that nearly bilked his employer out of $68.7 million. Aided by a gang of accomplices and his knowledge of a few secret codes, Gabriel Taylor, 27, electronically transferred the money from accounts belonging to Merrill Lynch, United Airlines and Brown-Forman distillers to accounts that some of the conspirators had set up under assumed names at two banks in Vienna. Before the gang could collect its loot, First Chicago discovered the fraud and alerted the FBI, which last week located the money and arrested Taylor and six alleged coconspirators on charges connected with illegal wire transfers. But the embezzlers came tantalizingly close to succeeding and showed how vulnerable banks and their vast computerized cash-movement networks can be to a dishonest insider.

In this scheme, though, the apparent mastermind was an outsider: Armand Moore, 33, a burly ex-con from Detroit who called himself "the Chairman." Moore was paroled from Minnesota's Sandstone federal prison in 1986 after serving four years of an eleven-year term for fraud. In 1982 he created a Chicago "bank," actually a telephone answering service, and issued himself letters of personal credit. So convincing were these documents that ten air-charter companies leased planes to Moore, who used them to take off on cross-country shopping sprees. By the time he was caught, he owed $180,000 to the charter firms.

After his release, Moore apparently began eyeing a much bigger target: First Chicago. His contact was a cousin, Herschel Bailey, 30, who knew Otis Wilson, 30, a clerk at the bank. Wilson introduced Taylor to Moore and by last month the group included Neal Jackson, 31, Leonard Strickland, 49, and Ronald Carson, 40. They plotted their scam at meetings in a Quality Inn on Chicago's west side.

Taylor had worked for First Chicago for eight years, and was employed in its wire-transfer section, which dispatches multimillion-dollar sums around the world via computers and phone lines. The bank's biggest customers routinely call this department to transfer funds, often paying money directly into suppliers' accounts. As at most banks, transfers require that a First Chicago employee call back another executive at the customer's offices to reconfirm the order, using various code numbers. All such calls are automatically taped. Taylor had access to the codes and knew the names of the appropriate executives at various corporations. The gang's original plan called for stealing $232 million from the accounts of quite a few companies, including Hilton, but the group eventually settled on taking the $68.7 million from United, Brown-Forman and Merrill Lynch. The Chairman was able to recruit Taylor, who had no previous police record or employment problems, by offering him a cut of $28 million.

in the FBI's *UCR*, or should it be included with white-collar crime? Sociologically the crime is more like white-collar crime; legally, however, it probably belongs with other theft crimes. This is also true of modern theft crimes, discussed subsequently. The sociological analysis of embezzlement is discussed in the next chapter with white-collar crimes, but the potential impact of the crime is illustrated in Highlight 8.2.

HIGHLIGHT 8.2 (Continued)

At 8:30 a.m. on May 13, a gang member posing as a Merrill Lynch executive called First Chicago to arrange the transfer of $24 million to the account of "Lord Investments" in Vienna's Creditanstalt bank. He first heard a taped message: "This is First Chicago transfer operations. Your transaction is being recorded." Unfazed, the caller placed the order with one of Taylor's unwitting co-workers. Taylor pretended to phone another Merrill Lynch official for backup confirmation. He really called the Chicago home of Bailey, who gave an authentic-sounding "approval" as the tape rolled. The $24 million was promptly wired to New York's Citibank for later transfer to Vienna.

At 9:02 came another call, purportedly from Brown-Forman (makers of Jack Daniel's whiskey). A few code words and computer keystrokes later, and $19.7 million slid with the smoothness of sipping bourbon from Brown-Forman's account, through the New York computers of Chase Manhattan Bank and into the account of "Walter Newman" at Vienna's Focobank. At 9:34, an additional $25 million flew from the ledgers of United Airlines to Citibank for relay to the account of "GTL Industries" at Creditanstalt.

On Monday, May 16, the plan broke down—for the most banal of reasons. United and Merrill Lynch did not have enough funds in their accounts to cover outstanding checks, which started to bounce, alerting First Chicago officials that something was amiss. The bank traced the problem to Taylor and called in the FBI. Taylor named his coconspirators and agreed to make incriminating phone calls to Moore and the others that the FBI taped as evidence. Although Brown-Forman's funds were credited in Vienna, the money taken from United and Merrill Lynch was intercepted at Citibank before it left the country.

Investigators were amazed at how far the scheme proceeded before being discovered. If the gang had settled for smaller amounts or picked accounts that were less active, the crime might have gone undetected long enough for the culprits to withdraw the money from the Viennese banks. Says an investigator connected with the case: "They came a lot closer than the banks want to acknowledge."

What worries crime experts is that wire transfers, which banks use to zap some $1 trillion in funds around the globe each week, could be so susceptible to security breaches. Says a senior officer of First Chicago: "It's impossible to do something like this without the help of an insider. But once you have the insider, it's almost a childlike process."

The Chairman and his board of embezzlers made crucial mistakes, but they exposed many of the flaws in the banks' security systems. If those flaws are not fixed, copycat crooks may try new, improved versions of the scheme. Warns First Chicago spokesman Anthony Zehnder: "There are a lot of people out there taking notes."

SOURCE: Time, 30 May 1988, p. 45. Copyright 1988, Time, Inc. Reprinted by permission.

MODERN THEFT

Because of the loopholes that developed in common law, as well as the belief that other types of "taking" or "stealing" should be included in the crime of theft, modern statutes are quite different from English common law. The California statute is an example:

> Every person who shall feloniously steal, take, carry, lead, or drive away the personal property of another, or who shall fraudulently appropriate property which has been entrusted to him or who shall knowingly and designedly, by any false or fraudulent representation or pretense, defraud any other person of money, labor or real or personal property . . . is guilty of theft.[39]

A statute as broadly worded as this one includes the new kinds of theft that have come to our attention in recent years. Here are a few examples of what has occurred as technology has improved and life-styles have changed.

Modular telephones that can be plugged into almost any telephone connection are particularly susceptible to theft. These phones permit a hotel guest to dial an outside number without having to go through the hotel operator, a savings in time and cost. These phones do not have to be

Jim Bakker, former PTL chairman, shown here with his wife Tammy, was convicted of criminal fraud and sentenced to prison.

wired into the walls, a more costly procedure. Some hotel owners, after several telephone thefts, spent additional money to secure the phones by wiring through the walls, buying devices that secure the phone in place, or replacing the phones with ones that are not modular.

Credit card thefts, according to some experts, have become our fastest-growing crime. Measures to prevent these thefts include eliminating carbon paper or giving the carbons to customers to avoid the possibility that someone, such as an employee, may take the number from the carbon and use it in place of the card. People are warned not to give their credit card numbers for telephone purchases and to keep their cards in sight at all times to eliminate the possibility that the salesclerk could make out two sales slips with the imprint of the card. A further warning is not to give out the number to other people wanting identification for check cashing or other reasons. Use only a driver's license for that purpose.

In the spring of 1989, officials in the Tampa Bay area of Florida apprehended a credit card thief, Michael Massaro, whose three-week spending spree is detailed in Highlight 8.3. Massaro, thirty-seven, had credit card numbers that he had obtained from vacationers in the area. He told business persons that he was a tax deduction for his father who gave him $425,000 a year for spending money. They believed him for three weeks. When he was apprehended, Massaro pleaded guilty to grand theft and theft of a credit card. His sentence illustrates the differential treatment often granted to grand theft as compared to petty theft, where defendants may spend years in prison. Massaro was placed on four years' probation and ordered to pay back the people he had conned.[40]

Credit card thefts indicate the interrelationship between individual theft and organized crime. Muggers, prostitutes, and burglars connected with organized crime steal credit cards and then sell them to credit card rings for $15 to $50 per card. Estimated loss per year as a result of credit card theft and fraud is over $1 billion.

Cable television service has also been the target of thefts. In Oklahoma, Tulsa Cable TV spent $80,000 to advertise about theft of service and offered $10 to anyone who returned an illegal cable TV box by a certain date, no questions asked. An advertisement on television and in the papers pictured a man behind prison bars and carried the large caption "Larry hooked himself up to Tulsa Cable. He got HBO, Cinemax . . . and Six Months. Stealing cable television service is a serious crime—a crime which could lead to a fine and imprisonment in the county jail." By the deadline over 8000 illegal boxes had been returned. The project indicates that many people either see no wrong in this type of theft or think they will not get caught until pressure is put on them through the media.

A crime prevention measure in New York City's subways also indicates that at least some types of theft will decrease when punishment appears to be a probability. A study conducted in 1989 indicated that when police were not present, 31 percent of patrons did not pay subway fares. But fare evasion dropped 91 percent when police were present.

HIGHLIGHT 8.3

$30,000 SPREE AWAKENS MERCHANTS TO CREDIT-CARD CRIME

Michael Massaro's Spending Spree

● **Friday, February 23.** Takes Lear jet from Key West to Tampa, a limousine to the Don CeSar resort hotel on St. Petersburg Beach. Spends weekend cruising around in limo.

● **Monday, Feb. 26.** Takes limo to Tampa, Lear jet back to Key West.

● **Sunday, March 6.** Takes Lear jet to Tampa, then limo from airport to Hyatt Regency Westshore. Next day, rents helicopter to fly around, then returns to Clearwater Executive Airport and rides by limo back to Hyatt.

● **Tuesday, March 8.** Rents helicopter again, flies around Pinellas County with a friend, returns to the Hyatt.

● **Wednesday, March 9.** Flies by Lear jet to Miami with owner of limousine company, takes him to dinner in Miami,

charges dinner to limousine company, returns to Tampa.

● **Thursday, March 10.** Spends day with owner of limousine company and executive of promotions company, buys five bottles of expensive champagne (charged to the Hyatt), takes limo to Bennigan's restaurant in St. Petersburg, flies by Lear jet to Miami for drinks, returns to Hyatt.

● **Friday, March 11.** Back to Miami by Lear jet, spends weekend there, eating, drinking, shopping.

● **Sunday, March 13.** Returns to Tampa, checks into Holiday Inn South in St. Petersburg, same hotel where the promotion company has its headquarters, charges it to promotion company account.

● **Monday, March 14.** Tries to book charter flight that would transport two entertainers from Philadelphia to Clear-

water. Gives phony business name and address in Key West. Employee at the jet company recognizes the address as phony and starts asking questions.

● **Wednesday, March 16.** American Express catches up to Massaro and he is booked in Pinellas County Jail.

● **Wednesday, June 8.** Massaro pleads guilty to grand theft and theft of credit card. Sentenced to four years probation, told to go across street and check in with probation officer. He never does.

The Bill

● Hotel, room service: $6,300

● Limousine service: $7,900

● Chartered jets, helicopter service: $16,000

SOURCE: *St. Petersburg Times,* April 9, 1989, p. 11, col. 2, reprinted with permission from the *St. Petersburg Times.*

New York City officials estimate an annual loss of $35 to $70 million from fare evasion.[41]

PROFESSIONAL AND CAREER CRIMINALS

Some criminals work alone. They may be occasional thieves who steal for something they need; they may embezzle money from their employers;

they may steal consistently over a number of years but never develop the skills, techniques, and attitudes of professional thieves. Other criminals are considered and consider themselves trained professionals—possessing the skills, techniques, and attitudes that are common to many professional people. They usually steal for a profit. They may have long careers in crime during which they serve prison terms, one of the hazards of their occupation.

For years professional thieves have captured the interest of the public. They have been portrayed by the media, and they have provided sociologists with interesting research opportunities. This discussion will begin with an analysis of the professional thief before proceeding to the more recent approach that focuses on the career of the persistent offender.

Professional Criminal Behavior: The Early Approach

Numerous writers on professional crime have pointed out that over a long period of time there has been little change in conceptual categories of professional crime. The professional criminal, such as the professional thief, manifests highly developed career behavior patterns characterized by nonviolence, a high degree of skill, loyalty toward the loosely organized group rather than toward individuals, association with other professional as opposed to amateur criminals, long careers characterized by few arrests, and an attitude toward society in which noncriminals are seen as people who deserve to be victimized. Professional criminals have a status hierarchy that is related to a combination of skill and the expectation of high profits. They are not from the extremes of poverty. They start crime later in life than other criminals, and the peer group becomes important in terms of reinforcing their deviant self-concepts and attitudes.[42]

The classic study of professional criminals was made by Edwin Sutherland, who talked extensively with a thief who had been in the profession for more than twenty years. Sutherland had the thief write on several topics. He then submitted the manuscript to other professional thieves and talked with still others. He said none disagreed with the account.[43]

Sutherland described the profession of theft as a group way of life that has all the characteristics of other groups—techniques, codes, status, traditions, consensus, and organization. He pointed out that these characteristics are not pathological. In addition, apprenticeship and tutelage by professional thieves is a prerequisite, and an individual must be recognized by professional thieves in order to become one.

Contemporary Conceptualizations of Professional Thieves

Traditional conceptions of professional criminals have been criticized for relying mainly on anecdotes and case studies and not being systematic sociological approaches.[44] Few attempts were made to test propositions; professional crime was often confused with full-time crime, the latter characterizing individuals who did not have the skills and other characteristics of professional criminals. More recent studies have attempted to alleviate these problems.

Under the auspices of the 1967 President's Crime Commission, several investigators determined that decreased specialization characterizes the professional thief. The professional "is in business to cash in on opportunities and thus must not specialize too narrowly, for that increases the possibility of missing opportunities. Such characterizations of professional criminals indicate a radical change from the more traditional conceptualizations." They also have to be versatile because of an emphasis on hustling, which means using all available means for victimizing others to make illegal gains for oneself. Further characteristics of contemporary professional criminals, in contrast to prior ones, are an increased reliance on fences and longer careers because of increased plea bargaining, which reduces the probability of incarceration and the time spent if incarcerated. In addition, their selection of work often depends on available opportunities rather than their preferred criminal activity, the job thus becoming more important in the detemination of associations.[45]

Why is there a difference between contemporary and previous professional criminals? One explanation might be the source of data. The more recent studies are based on data collected from criminals, many of whom have been incarcerated. The previous studies may have represented the more successful, high-level, prestigious criminals who were the real professionals. Three reasons have been suggested for the change: (1) "advances in police technology and increased probabilities for the detection and recognition of known criminals . . . (2) significant shortages in the number of potential recruits . . . and (3) decreases in skill and the tendency of lessened interactional networks." It has been concluded that professional theft will decline "until its more unique qualities become only references within the history of crime."[46]

Others have argued that professional crime is increasing, and whatever changes are taking place may represent the effect of changing opportunities.[47] For example, it has been predicted that cracking safes, robbing banks, and operating confidence games will continue to decline, but that credit card and other types of fraud will increase as professionals continue to manipulate to their advantage whatever medium of exchange is used. It is also predicted that more professional criminals will become involved in drug traffic, but that it really is unreasonable to try to predict what professional crime will be like in ten years.[48]

The study of professional crime shows the intricate pattern of social interaction that develops, which is in many cases a subculture. It shows the close relationship to acceptable patterns of business relationships, emphasizing shrewdness and even condoning fraud and swindles. "The law violator is no less a product of society than the moral, upright citizen, and both of them have much more in common than they are likely to acknowledge."[49]

Career Criminals: The Modern Approach

The skills, knowledge, attitudes, and values of professional criminals that were emphasized by early researchers may not be as important to the public as **career criminals.** Today the emphasis is on the repeat offender, especially when that offender is violent. Most people are not concerned with whether the offender is professional. A very unprofessional job in violent crime is still feared. Nor is there a great concern for the attitudes and group affiliations of the person who burglarizes the home.

Semiprofessional property offenders are distinguished from professional criminals in the lack of skill and absence of a complex interactional pattern. These criminals see themselves as victims of society. They do not feel guilty about their behavior. In comparison to professional criminals, they are more hostile toward law enforcement officials and toward society, their parents, and occupational roles. Most remain in crime through middle age, at which point some change to noncriminal activities. Some studies indicate that an increasing number of amateurs are involved in bank robberies and car thefts; other studies indicate that these offenders have a rather stable criminal career. It has also been reported that semiprofessional burglars are predominantly nonwhite, male, and young, and that burglary victims are also mainly from the lower socioeconomic class. A study of black armed robbers disclosed that they are generally older than other felons, with predominantly lower-class urban backgrounds, a history of criminal activity as teenagers, and an unstable family background.[50]

Wolfgang's Studies of Delinquency Cohorts

Modern studies of chronic career offenders are usually based on the approach developed most extensively in the now classic studies of Marvin Wolfgang and his colleagues. These researchers utilized a **cohort** (a universe of persons defined by some characteristic) of 10,000 boys born in Philadelphia in 1945 who were still available for study when they became eighteen in 1963. According to official police reports, 65 percent of the boys had not been arrested before their eighteenth birthday. About one-third had had some contact with police. Forty-six percent of the delinquents stopped after the first offense, and of those who committed more than one offense, 35 percent had no more than three offenses. Less than 7 percent had five or more arrests and were defined as chronic offenders. But those offenders committed 57 percent of all crimes attributed to the cohort of 10,000.[51]

Wolfgang repeated this approach in a study of 14,000 boys born in 1958. His analyses are not complete, but he has found some similarities with the earlier study. A small percentage, around 7 percent, still commit most of the crimes; but they now commit an even higher percentage of the crimes of their cohort, including 75 percent of the reported rapes and robberies. What now exists is a chronically violent, although small, group of young males who begin their criminal careers early and continue into adult life.[52]

Rand Studies of Career Criminals

The Rand Corporation has published numerous documents on their extensive research on habitual offenders. Their research, based on data collected through the self-reports of offenders, focuses on the small percentage of offenders who commit many offenses. In analyzing this study, we should recall the earlier discussion of the pros and cons of collecting data by the SRD (Self-Report Data) method.[53]

The first Rand sample involved 49 prison inmates in California. The next study utilized a sample of 624 inmates from five California prisons, selected to represent all male prisoners in that state in terms of custody level, age, offense, and race. The study focused on the criminal activities of the inmates during the three years prior to their current incarceration.[54] A third sample was larger; jail inmates in three states—California, Michigan, and Texas.

The first Rand study found that most offenders are not specialized in their criminal activity. At any given time, they engage in a variety of criminal activities. Few criminals commit crimes at a high rate; most do so at a fairly low rate. The rate of violent crime among these inmates was very low. These findings were confirmed in the study of 624 male inmates in California. During the three years prior to their current incarceration, most of the inmates committed several other kinds of crime. Of those who reported having committed a crime other than the type for which they had been incarcerated, 49 percent listed more than four other crimes. As in the earlier study, a few inmates committed most of the reported crimes.

The Rand investigators found that neither age nor having served a prior prison term was strongly associated with offense rates. What was significant, however, was self-concept. "High-rate offenders tended to share a set of beliefs that were consistent with their criminal lifestyle— e.g., that they could beat the odds, that they were better than the average criminal, that crime was exciting, and that regular work was boring."[55]

The larger sample of 2190 prison and jail inmates was selected to check on possible problems in the first two samples and to include lesser offenses normally represented by jail populations. Analysis of data from this study confirmed that most offenders report committing few crimes; a few commit many crimes. Offenders were placed into categories, the most serious being those who reported robbery, assault, and drug deals. These were termed violent predators. They usually reported having committed these crimes at high rates and also having committed numerous other property crimes. The factors that distinguished the violent predators from other inmates were these:

- Youth
- Onset of crime (especially violent crime) before age 16

- Frequent commission of both violent and property crime before age 18
- Multiple commitments to state juvenile facilities
- Unmarried and with few family obligations
- Employed irregularly and for short times
- Frequent use of hard drugs as a juvenile
- Use of heroin at costs exceeding $50 per day
- Use of multiple combinations of drugs . . . [56]

Researchers concluded that offenders identified as career criminals see themselves as criminals; they expect to return to crime after release from prison; they began their criminal careers early in their juvenile years; they are hedonistic, viewing crime as "a safe and enjoyable way to obtain the good life"; and they view themselves as proficient criminals. They represent only 25 percent of the sample, but they committed 58 percent of all reported armed robberies, 65 percent of burglaries, 60 percent of auto thefts, and 46 percent of assaults. The investigators wisely point out that the criminal justice system might benefit by directing its incarceration efforts at these types of offenders rather than at the majority of offenders, who do not exhibit these characteristics. The study indicates that career property offenders can be identified and that some of those commit violent crimes, but "it provides no evidence of an identifiable group of career criminals who commit only violence."[57]

The Bureau of Justice Statistics Report

The Bureau of Justice Statistics has issued a Special Report on Career Criminals that utilized data on offenders from across the country. A random sample of 11,397 male and female inmates were interviewed and questioned extensively about their criminal careers. Since the major purpose of the study was to examine careers, only inmates who were at least forty at the date of last admission to prison were selected for intensive study.[58]

Data in the BJS study were analyzed by four types of offenders, all of whom were middle aged (forty or older) at the time of their last admission to prison. The typologies were concerned with three of the major stages of life: adolescence (ages seven through seventeen), young adulthood (ages eighteen through thirty-nine), middle age (age forty and over). The sample was divided as follows:

- Type 1—offenders who engaged in criminal activity in all three stages
- Type 2—offenders who engaged in criminal activity in all but young adulthood
- Type 3—offenders who engaged in criminal activity in all but adolescence
- Type 4—offenders who engaged in criminal activity in middle age only

Type 1 and 2 offenders engaged in some criminal activity during adolescence. Type 2 offenders did not engage in criminal activity during young adulthood but rather were law abiding during that time and then returned to criminal activity in middle age. They represent a small percentage of the inmate population, but it is significant that 92 percent of those offenders who reported criminal activity during adolescence continued with criminal activity during young adulthood and into middle age. These are the Type 1 offenders.

Perhaps the most surprising finding of this study is that the Type 4 offenders, those middle-age offenders who did not engage in criminal activity as adolescents or as young adults, represented almost half of all the inmates who entered prison in middle age. The BJS report explained this finding in terms of the reason for incarceration. Persons arrested for property offenses often are incarcerated for those offenses only if they have prior criminal records. But those who commit violent personal crimes are likely to be incarcerated even without a prior criminal record.

The charred facade of the Happy Land Social Club in the Bronx borough of New York, where 87 people perished in a fire. Most of the victims were Honduran and Dominican immigrants in the nations deadliest fire in 13 years. Arson is suspected.

It is therefore critical in an analysis of the crimes for which offenders are currently incarcerated to consider their prior records. Thus, the fact that 40 percent of the inmates in the BJS study were serving time for property offenses, not violent crimes, does not necessarily mean that society is incarcerating too many people for nonviolent crimes. Violence has been a part of the past record of many of these property offenders. The BJS report also suggested that although the study did not investigate the issue, it is likely that the high rates of incarceration for violent crimes of the offenders over forty represent domestic violence.

The NIJ Overview of Repeat Offenders

The National Institute of Justice (NIJ), under the authorship of Lawrence Sherman, has published an overview on repeat offenders, defining them as "people who commit serious criminal offenses at a high rate and over a long period." According to Sherman, these criminals do not specialize; they commit a variety of crime, and they differ in the extent to which they commit crimes. They commit the majority of serious, detected crimes, although they do not constitute a majority of criminals.

Sherman notes that ethical, practical, and technological problems exist when authorities track these repeat offenders. One view shared by many is that offenders are responsible for crimes they have committed but not for crimes they *may* commit at some future date. Yet, identifying repeat offenders and arresting them for crimes may significantly reduce crime. Some cities have attempted to do this, establishing ROP programs (repeat offender programs) among the police as well as prosecutors. Sherman concluded:

> Repeat offender programs seem likely to expand and proliferate. With the scarce resources of modern criminal justice confronted by growing demands, policy makers must increasingly establish priorities. The idea of focusing scarce resources on repeat offender programs—even with all the errors of prediction and ethical questions of such programs—provides an attractive basis for choosing which criminal justice course to take.[59]

The Young Criminal Years of the Violent Few

One final study of criminal careers has also gained wide attention. Donna Martin Hamparian published two major works on criminal careers. In writing an introduction to her latest work, the administrator of the Office of Juvenile Justice and Delinquency Prevention, which funded the research, explained that Hamparian's work extended that of Wolfgang and his associates and of the Rand Corporation, whose research he described "as important as anything else we have learned in recent years. Probably the most significant contribution of this study is the increased knowledge of the characteristics of those offenders who are likely to continue their criminality into adulthood."[60]

EXHIBIT 8.2

Major Findings of Hamparian's Research on the Violent Few

THE JUVENILE YEARS

1. A relatively small number of violent juvenile offenders were responsible for most of the arrests.

2. Males and blacks are overrepresented in the cohort, and they account for an even greater proportion of juvenile crime.

3. Violent juvenile offenders, as a group, do not specialize in the types of crimes they commit.

4. Relatively few violent juvenile offenders are repeat violent offenders.

5. Most violent juvenile crimes do not involve the use of weapons.

6. Fewer than one-third of the juveniles . . . had been sent to a state juvenile correctional facility, but those youths who had been incarcerated generally had a higher arrest rate after release.

THE TRANSITION TO ADULTHOOD

1. Nearly three out of every five cohort members were arrested at least once for an adult felony offense.

2. Cohort members arrested as adults were more likely to be male, index violent offenders as juveniles, first arrested at age twelve or younger, and committed at least once to a state juvenile correctional facility.

3. There is a continuity between juvenile and adult criminal careers.

THE ADULT EXPERIENCE

1. Frequency of arrests declines with age.

2. Most adult crimes committed by juvenile violent offenders are not violent.

3. Four out of ten adult offenders were arrested for at least one index violent crime.

4. Almost half of the arrested cohort members were imprisoned as adults. More than 80 percent were released, and half went back a second time.

SOURCE: Donna Martin Hamparian, *The Young Criminal Years of the Violent Few* (Washington, D.C.: U.S. Department of Justice, June 1985), pp. 7–17; emphasis and text after each conclusion deleted.

Hamparian's work was based on a cohort of 1222 people born between 1956 and 1960. She describes the juvenile arrests of these young people from 1962 to 1978 and "follows the cohort members through their early adult careers, if any, up to mid-1983." The major findings of Hamparian's studies are indicated in Exhibit 8.2. Her major conclusions are as follows:

1. Most violent juvenile offenders make the transition to adult offenders.

2. There is a continuity between juvenile and adult criminal careers.

3. A relatively few chronic offenders are responsible for a disproportionate number of crimes.

4. The frequency of arrests as adults declines with age.

5. Incarceration has not slowed the rate of arrest—in fact, the subsequent rate of arrest increases after each incarceration.[61]

CONCLUSION

This chapter has explored the most prevalent property crimes, both historically and currently. It began with a look at the Index property crimes as defined by the FBI's *Uniform Crime Reports:* larceny-theft, motor vehicle theft, burglary, and arson.

Larceny-theft was originally a felony and therefore carried the death penalty. The intricacies of the traditional laws concerning this serious crime were explored historically to see how the law has developed. Larceny-theft is still a serious crime; but it no longer carries the death penalty in this country, and some of the elements required for the crime have changed. However, larceny-theft continues to embody a variety of crimes such as shoplifting. Motor vehicle theft is a serious property crime and one that is committed quite frequently in this country, but the clearance rate is so low that it has not permitted significant sociological research on those who commit the crime.

Burglary is another common law crime with a fascinating history, which is necessary for a complete understanding of the treatment of this serious property crime today. Burglary has been studied by sociologists; but since many burglars are also repeat offenders, the analysis of this crime is often included within studies of career criminals.

Arson was only recently moved by the FBI from its list of less serious crimes to an Index Offense, now constituting one of the four Index property crimes. That means that data are not available for long-term trends; estimates are that arson is increasing, some saying it is one of the fastest growing Index property crimes.

The second section of the chapter covered some Part II property offenses as defined by the *UCR:* forgery and counterfeiting; buying, receiving, and possessing stolen property; and embezzlement. These crimes may be officially categorized as less serious, but the economic and other losses from these crimes cause some people to consider them more serious than Index property crimes.

A section on modern theft crimes was brief since many of these crimes are closely related to white-collar crimes and/or organized crime, discussed in detail in the next chapter. But since many property crimes do involve career criminals and professional thieves, the final section of the chapter was devoted to the major studies of career criminals.

Property crimes do not always receive as much popular press as violent crimes because they are less dramatic; but the effect on the American public is significant, and the volume of property crimes far exceeds the volume of violent crimes. Many of the property crimes, however, are subtle in their execution, and unlike common street crimes, are committed by people with white-collar positions. The importance of these and other crimes related to business organizations necessitates an entire chapter.

ENDNOTES

1. Rollin M. Perkins, *Criminal Law*, 3d ed. (Mineola, N.Y.: Foundation Press, 1982), p. 289.
2. *Ibid.*, p. 291. For a history of the development of the law of theft, see Jerome Hall, *Theft, Law and Society*, rev. ed. (Indianapolis: Bobbs-Merrill, 1952), chaps. 1–4; and Wayne R. LaFave and Austin W. Scott, Jr., *Criminal Law*, 2d ed. (St. Paul, Minn.: West Publishing, 1986), pp. 702–706.
3. Federal Bureau of Investigation, *Uniform Crime Reports*, 1988 (Washington, D.C.: U.S. Government Printing Office, 1989), p. 32.
4. Federal Bureau of Investigation, *Uniform Crime Reports*, 1985, p. 29; 1987, p. 29; 1988, p. 33.
5. *Ibid.*, 1988, pp. 33, 35.
6. *Ibid.*, p. 36.
7. Darrell J. Steffensmeier and Robert M. Terry, "Deviance and Respectability: An Observational Study of Reactions to Shoplifting," *Social Forces* 51 (June 1973): 417–426.
8. Michael J. Hindelang, "Decisions of Shoplifting Victims to Invoke the Criminal Justice Process," *Social Problems* 21 (April 1974): 580–593. See also Michael R. Gottfredson and Don M. Gottfredson, "Victim Decisions to Report a Crime," *Decisionmaking in Criminal Justice: Toward the Rational Exercise of Discretion* (Cambridge, Mass.: Ballinger, 1980), pp. 21–59.
9. Gwenn Nettler, *Lying, Cheating, Stealing* (Cincinnati, Ohio: Anderson Publishing Co., 1982), pp. 105–106. See also Jo Ann Ray, "Every Twelfth Shopper: Who Shoplifts and Why?" *Social Casework* 68 (April 1987): 234–239.
10. Mary Owen Cameron, "An Interpretation of Shoplifting," in Marshall B. Clinard and Richard Quinney, eds., *Criminal Behavior Systems: A Typology* (New York: Holt, Rinehart and Winston, 1967; 1986 edition published by Anderson Publishing Co.), p. 109; reprinted from Mary Owen Cameron, *The Booster and the Snitch: Department Store Shoplifting* (New York: Free Press, 1964).
11. D. P. Walsh, *Shoplifting—Controlling a Major Crime* (New York: Macmillan, 1978). See also D. J. I. Murphy, *Customers and Thieves* (Brookfield, VT.: Gower Publishing Company, 1986).

12. *Time*, 17 November 1980, p. 94.
13. *Uniform Crime Reports*, 1988, p. 38.
14. *Ibid.*, pp. 39, 41.
15. Cited in "An Almost Unstoppable Crime," *Dallas Morning News*, 10 December 1986, p. C1, col. 2.
16. Charles McCaghy et al., "Auto Theft," *Criminology* 15 (November 1977): 367–381.
17. For a discussion of the historical development of the law of burglary, see LaFave and Scott, *Criminal Law*, pp. 702–706, from which this summary has been taken.
18. *Uniform Crime Reports*, 1988, p. 27.
19. *Ibid.*, pp. 27, 28.
20. Bureau of Justice Statistics, *Household Burglary* (Washington, D.C.: U.S. Department of Justice, January 1985), pp. 1, 5.
21. Bureau of Justice Statistics, *Households Touched by Crime, 1988* (Washington, D.C.: U.S. Department of Justice, June 1989), p. 1.
22. See Don C. Gibbons, *Changing the Lawbreaker: The Treatment of Delinquents and Criminals* (Englewood Cliffs, N.J.: Prentice-Hall, 1965), pp. 106–108.
23. Chris W. Eskridge, "Prediction of Burglary: A Research Note," *Journal of Criminal Justice* 11 (no. 1, 1983): 67–75.
24. Jack L. Nasar, "Environmental Factors and Commercial Burglary," *Journal of Environmental Systems* 11 (no. 1, 1981–1982): 49–56.
25. Nettler, *Lying, Cheating, Stealing*, p. 109. For a recent analysis of juvenile burglaries, see Richard Wright and Robert H. Logie, "How Young House Burglars Choose Targets," *Howard Journal* 27 (May 1988): 92–104. See also T. Bennett and R. Wright, *Burglars on Burglary: Prevention and the Offender* (Aldershot: Gower, 1984).
26. Anthony Olen Rider, *The Firesetter: A Psychological Profile* (Washington, D.C.: U.S. Department of Justice, 1984).
27. *American Bar Association Journal* 68 (August 1982): 956.
28. *Uniform Crime Reports*, 1988, p. 42.
29. *Uniform Crime Reports*, 1988, p. 44.
30. See, for example, Walter R. Gove et al., "Are Uniform Crime Reports a Valid Indicator of the Index Crimes? An Affirmative Answer with Minor Qualifications," *Criminology* 23 (August 1985): 451–502; and Patrick G. Jackson, "Assessing the Validity of Official Data on Arson," *Criminology* 26 (February 1988): 181–195.
31. James P. Brady, "Arson, Fiscal Crisis, and Community Action: Dialectics of an Urban Crime and Popular Response," *Crime and Delinquency* 28 (April 1982): 247–270.
32. Nolan D. C. Lewis and Helen Yarnell, *Pathological Firesetting (Pyromania)* (New York: Nervous and Mental Disease Monographs, 1951), and James A. Inciardi, "The Adult Firesetter: A Typology," *Criminology* 8 (August 1970): 145–155. These works are cited and discussed in a brief but excellent essay on arson written by Inciardi and published in Sanford Kadish, ed., *Encyclopedia of Crime and Justice*, vol. 1 (New York: Free Press, 1983), pp. 76–77.
33. Henry S. Dogin, Acting Administrator, Law Enforcement Assistance Administration, in the Foreword to the Department of Justice publication, *A Survey of Arson and Arson Response Capabilities in Selected Jurisdiction* (Washington, D.C.: U.S. Government Printing Office, 1979).

34. See the government document published by the LEAA, Department of Justice, *Arson Prevention and Control* (Washington, D.C.: U.S. Government Printing Office, 1980).

35. Edwin M. Lemert, "An Isolation and Closure Theory of Naive Check Forgery," *Journal of Criminal Law, Criminology and Police Science* 44 (September-October 1953): 301–304. For a later study confirming these findings, see Maurice Gauthier, "The Psychology of the Compulsive Forger," *Canadian Journal of Corrections* 1 (July 1959): 62–69. See also Norman S. Hayner, "Characteristics of Five Offender Types," *American Sociological Review* 16 (February 1961): 96–102.

36. Darrell J. Steffensmeier, *The Fence: In the Shadow of Two Worlds* (Totowa, N.J.: Rowan & Littlefield, 1986). See also Marilyn E. Walsh, *The Fence—A New Look at the World of Property Theft* (Westport, Conn.: Greenwood Press, 1977).

37. Kenneth A. Weiner et al., "Making Inroads Into Prop-Crime: An Analysis of the Detroit Anti-Fencing Program," *Journal of Police Science and Administration* 11 (September 1983): 311–327. For information on the federal program, see Catherine A. Cotter and James W. Burrows, *Property Crime Program: A Special Report: Overview of the "Sting" Program and Project Summaries*, U.S. Department of Justice (Washington, D.C.: U.S. Government Printing Office, 1981).

38. Louis B. Schwartz, "Theft," in Kadish, *Encyclopedia of Crime and Justice*, vol. 4, p. 1544.

39. Cal. Penal Code, Section 484.

40. "$30,000 Spree Awakens Merchants to Credit-card Crime," *St. Petersburg Times*, 9 April 1988, p. I1, col. 2.

41. "New Subway Patrols Aim at Rush-Hour Criminal: The Fare Beater," *New York Times*, 28 March 1989, p. 11, col. 3.

42. For a more complete discussion of these issues, along with numerous citations of sociological works on professional criminals, see Gregory R. Staats, "Changing Conceptualizations of Professional Criminals: Implications for Criminology Theory," *Criminology* 15 (May 1977): 49–65.

43. Edwin H. Sutherland, *The Professional Thief* (Chicago: University of Chicago Press, 1937).

44. For an example of some of the earlier works, see David Maurer: *The Big Con* (New York: Signet, 1962) and *Wiz Mob: A Correlation of the Technical Argot of Pickpockets with Their Behavior Pattern* (Gainesville, Fla.: American Dialect Society, 1955).

45. Leroy Gould et al., *Crime as a Profession* (Washington, D.C.: U.S. Government Printing Office), cited in Staats, "Changing Conceptualizations of Professional Criminals," p. 60. For a study on the professional burglar, see Neal Shover, "Structures and Careers in Burglary," *Journal of Criminal Law, Criminology, and Police Science* 63 (December 1972): 540–549. See also Shover, "The Social Organization of Burglary," *Social Problems* 20 (Spring 1973): 499–514.

46. James Inciardi, "Vocational Crime," in Daniel Glaser, ed., *Handbook of Criminology* (Skokie, Ill.: Rand McNally, 1974), p. 345.

47. Clinard and Quinney, *Criminal Behavior Systems*, pp. 246–247.

48. Andrew Walker, "Sociology and Professional Crime," in Abraham Blumberg, ed., *Current Perspectives on Criminal Behavior: Original Essays on Criminology* (New York: Knopf, 1974), pp. 108–109.

49. Don C. Gibbons, *Society, Crime, and Criminal Careers; An Introduction to Criminology*, 4th ed., (Englewood Cliffs, N.J.: Prentice-Hall, 1983), p. 279.

50. For a general discussion, see Gibbons, pp. 284–288. For additional studies of

conventional criminals, see Donald MacKenzie, *Occupation: Thief* (Indianapolis: Bobbs-Merrill, 1955); Hutchins Hapgood, *Autobiography of a Thief* (New York: Fox, Duffield, 1930); John E. Conklin, *Robbery and the Criminal Justice System* (Philadelphia: Lippincott, 1972); Werner J. Einstadter, "The Social Organization of Armed Robbery," *Social Problems* 17 (Summer 1969): 64–83; Peter Letkemann, *Crime as Work* (Englewood Cliffs, N.J.: Prentice-Hall, 1973).

51. Marvin E. Wolfgang, Robert M. Figlio, and Thorsten Sellin, *Delinquency in a Birth Cohort* (Chicago: University of Chicago Press, 1972). See also Marvin Wolfgang et al., *From Boys to Man, From Delinquency to Crime* (Chicago: University of Chicago Press, 1987).

52. See Marvin E. Wolfgang, "Delinquency in a Birth Cohort II: Some Preliminary Results." Paper prepared for the Attorney General's Task Force on Violent Crime—Chicago, Illinois, June 17, 1982, and Marvin E. Wolfgang and P. E. Tracy, "The 1945 and 1958 Birth Cohorts: A Comparison of the Prevalence, Incidence, and Severity of Delinquent Behavior." Paper presented at the Conference on Public Danger, Dangerous Offenders and the Criminal Justice System, February 11–12, 1982, Harvard University, both cited in Patrick A. Langan and Lawrence A. Greenfeld, Bureau of Justice Statistics, *Career Patterns in Crime* (Washington, D.C.: U.S. Department of Justice, June 1983), p. 2.

53. For a discussion on the accuracy of such self-reports, see K. H. Marquis, *Quality of Prisoner Self-Reports: Arrest and Conviction Response Errors*, prepared for the National Institute of Justice (Santa Monica, CA.: Rand Corp., 1981).

54. See Mark A. Peterson et al., *Who Commits Crimes: A Survey of Prison Inmates* (Cambridge, Mass.: Oelgeschlager, Gunn & Hain, 1981).

55. Peter W. Greenwood with Allan Abraham, *Selective Incapacitation*, prepared for the National Institute of Justice (Santa Monica, CA.: Rand Corp., 1982), p. 19.

56. Jan Chaiken et al., *Varieties of Criminal Behavior: Summary and Policy Implications* (Santa Monica, CA.: Rand Corp., 1982), pp. v, vi, vii.

57. Mark A. Peterson et al., *Doing Crime: A Survey of California Prison Inmates* (Santa Monica, CA.: Rand Corp., 1980), pp. vii–xii.

58. Langan and Greenfeld, *Career Patterns in Crime.*

59. Lawrence Sherman, *Repeat Offenders*, National Institute of Justice (Washington, D.C.: U. S. Department of Justice, 1989), p. 3. See also Michael Gottfredson and Travis Hirschi, "Career Criminals and Selective Incapacitaton," in Joseph E. Scott and Travis Hirschi, eds., *Controversial Issues in Crime and Justice* (Beverly Hills, CA.: Sage Publications, 1988), pp. 199–209.

60. Alfred S. Regnery, quoted in the Introduction to Donna Martin Hamparian et al., *The Young Criminal Years of the Violent Few* (Washington, D.C.: U.S. Department of Justice, June 1985). Hamparian's early work, *The Violent Few*, was published in 1978.

61. Hamparian, *Young Criminal Years of the Violent Few*, p. 22. See also Arnold Barnett, and others, "Probabilistic Models of Youthful Criminal Careers," *Criminology* 25 (February 1987): 83–107.

CHAPTER 9

The history of theft, discussed in Chapter 8, provides the background for an understanding of the crimes discussed in this chapter. Many of the business activities that are technically defined as crimes are still not viewed by everyone as crimes, but rather, as shrewd business transactions, just as they were perceived historically. There is little agreement on the definitions of the crimes discussed in this chapter. There is also little agreement on how to control these illegal activities. The chapter begins with a discussion of the problem of defining white-collar crime and then proceeds to an analysis of the concept, history, types, research, and issues involved.

OUTLINE

Crimes of the Business World

KEY TERMS

administrative law
antitrust laws
blackmail
bribery
computer crime
conspiracy
corporate crimes
embezzlement
entrapment
extortion
false advertising
false pretenses
fraud
graft
insider trading
intent
white-collar crime

The analysis of types of crime, begun in Chapter 7 with crimes of violence and continued in Chapter 8 with ordinary property crimes, continues in this chapter with an analysis of white-collar crimes, or crimes of the business world. These crimes usually involve property and may involve violence, but they can be distinguished from the violent and property crimes already discussed.

The crimes included in this chapter have less obvious victims than those discussed in Chapters 7 and 8. The victim may be an individual consumer or the public in general. Even when the victim is a particular individual, the relationship between the offender and the victim is not so obvious. For example, industrial violations of safety codes may result in bodily injury (or death) to a factory worker using a defective machine, but the relationship between the worker and the person who designed and/or constructed the machine is not immediately apparent.

This separation between the victim and the offender may explain the fact that public fear of white-collar crime is usually not as severe as the fear of violent personal crime.[1] White-collar crimes also differ from ordinary serious property crimes and personal violent crimes in the violation of public trust that is often involved. On the other hand, there are also similarities between the crimes discussed in this chapter and those in Chapter 8. In many cases the same kinds of business practices are involved. In the past, as we saw in Chapter 8, some of these practices were accepted, even admired; others were considered unethical but not illegal. Today, increased technology, combined with the complexity and heterogeneity of business transactions and the inability of buyers and consumers to protect themselves, has brought about increased regulation of business transactions. Some of those regulations involve the criminal law; others are civil, or administrative.

DEFINITIONAL PROBLEMS

The most difficult problem in an analysis of white-collar crime is to define those behaviors to be included.

The Concept of White-Collar Crime

Social scientists disagree about the best way to categorize crimes associated with occupations. The most familar term, **white-collar crime,** is not uniformly defined. The term was coined by Edwin H. Sutherland in 1939 in his presidential address to the American Sociological Society and later developed in a published work.[2]

By white-collar crime, Sutherland meant "a crime committed by a person of respectability and high social status in the course of his occupation." Embezzlement by a banker, illegal sales of alcohol and narcotics, or price fixing by physicians would be examples. Excluded from this definition would be many crimes committed by upper-class people "such as most of their cases of murder, adultery, and intoxication, since these are not customarily a part of their occupational procedures. Also, it excludes the confidence games of wealthy members of the underworld, since they are not persons of respectability and high social status."[3]

Sutherland became interested in this concept of white-collar crime because most studies of crime were based on samples of institutionalized criminals that contained a high proportion of poor people. Sutherland observed that upper-class people also commit crimes but that these crimes, particularly those connected with their occupations, were often not handled by criminal courts. Rather, they were covered by **administrative law** and processed through administrative agencies; the offenders were not considered criminals and were not included in studies and theories of criminal behavior. Sutherland concluded,

> Persons of the upper socio-economic class engage in much criminal behavior; that this criminal behavior differs from the criminal behavior of the lower socio-economic class principally in the administrative procedures which are used in dealing with the offenders; and that variations in administrative procedures are not significant from the point of view of causation of crime.[4]

Sutherland was not trying to redefine white-collar crimes; nor was he saying that the law should consider offenders of such crimes as criminals and process them in the criminal courts rather than through administrative agencies. He was saying that if we want to know why crimes are committed, it is just as important to study white-collar crimes as the crimes of those who are processed through the criminal courts and incarcerated in penal institutions.

Sutherland's limitation of white-collar crimes to occupational crimes of the upper class is rejected by most authorities today. In defense of this limitation, however, August Bequai emphasizes that Sutherland was reacting to the social and economic situation of the 1930s. "In his time, and in his environment, only the wealthier classes had access to the requisite machinery necessary for the enactment of many of the crimes included in his concept of white-collar crime. . . . Technology and mass communications would ultimately open those areas of criminal endeavor to all strata of society. . . ."[5] One of the most dramatic and potentially far-reaching crimes made possible by this development of technology is computer crime, which will be discussed later in this chapter.

Bequai argues that instead of defining white-collar criminals by social class, they should be defined by the modus operandi of the crime. He points out that even though white-collar criminals may on occasion use force, what really distinguishes them from the common felon is that they commit their criminal acts by "guile, deceit, and concealment."[6]

The definition of white-collar crime adopted by the Congressional Subcommittee on Crime, Committee on the Judiciary, is as follows: "an illegal act or series of illegal acts committed by non-physical means and by concealment or guile, to obtain money or property, to avoid the payment or loss of money or property, or to obtain personal or business advantage." This definition was adopted by Congress in 1979 in The Justice System Administration Improvement Act.[7]

The crimes that might be included in this definition of white-collar crime are extensive, and categorization is difficult. Herbert Edelhertz, a noted authority on the subject, concludes that the best categorization is to classify the various crimes "by the general environment and motivation of the perpetrator," and for that purpose he suggests:

1. Crimes by persons operating on an individual, ad hoc basis, for personal gain in a nonbusiness context . . .

2. Crimes in the course of their occupations by those operating inside businesses, Government, or other establishments, or in a professional capacity, in violation of their duty of loyalty and fidelity to employer or client . . .

3. Crimes incidental to and in furtherance of business operations, but not the central purpose of such business operations . . .

4. White-collar crimes as a business, or as the central activity of the business . . .[8]

Disagreement over the definition of white-collar crime has led some to suggest that the term be replaced by *white-collar law-breaking*, which also incorporates those actions that are processed in civil courts or through administrative processes and thus technically are not crimes. The term has been defined as follows:

> White-collar violations are those violations of law to which penalties are attached and that involve the use of a violator's position of significant power, influence, or trust in the legitimate economic or political institutional order for the purpose of illegal gain, or to commit an illegal act for personal or organizational gain.[9]

Corporate Crime

Another concept that is important to an understanding of white-collar crime is **corporate crime.** Corporate crime is a form of white-collar crime, but unlike the latter, which often involves individuals or small groups of individuals acting within their professional or occupational capacity, corporate crime is organizational crime that occurs "in the context of extremely complex inter-relationships. . . . Here it is the organization, not the occupation, that is of prime importance."[10] A more precise distinction between the two is this:

If a policy making corporate executive is acting in the name of the corporation and the individual's decision to violate the law is for the benefit of the corporation, as in price-fixing violations, the violation would constitute corporate crime.

If, on the other hand, the corporate official acts against the corporation, as in the case of embezzlement, and is financing benefits in a personal way from his official connections with the corporation, his acts would constitute white collar or occupational crime.[11]

Earlier studies of white-collar crime focused on individuals who committed their crimes in secret. The lack of attention to corporate crime may have been due, first, to the complexity of the crimes and of the corporate structure. A thorough understanding of corporate crime requires expertise in areas that traditionally have not been a part of the training of social scientists. Second, the regulation of corporate crime is often carried out in administrative agencies rather than in courts. Sociologists and criminologists have generally not been as familiar with such agencies as with the judicial court process. Third, research funds have been more readily available for the study of conventional crime than for corporate crime. Fourth, the public has not been as concerned with white-collar as with conventional crime.[12]

Why change the emphasis from individual white-collar crime to a focus today on corporate crime? In the first place, in this century, the number and size of corporations have increased significantly. Today most business activities, along with many social and political activities, are influenced or controlled by corporations. Federal and state regulations have also increased dramatically.

Second, despite the fact that the media gave little publicity to the prosecution of corporate crimes during Sutherland's studies, that is not the case today. Considerable public and media attention is given to modern white-collar crimes, particularly when public officials are involved. The Watergate scandal of former President Richard M. Nixon's administration is an example. Third, the efforts of consumer advocate Ralph Nader have had a tremendous impact on public concern with corporate crime and on the increasing legislative efforts to curb such crime. Fourth, increasing concern with the environment, coupled with the realization that many corporations contribute to the pollution of that environment, led to the creation of the federal Environmental Protection Agency and to legislation in this area.

Fifth, the lack of success in curbing crime during the emphasis in the 1960s on the eradication of poverty, thought to be the best way to attack the crime problem, led to the realization that in concentrating crime control on the poor, not only was the crime problem not being solved, but also crimes committed by middle- and upper-class persons and by corporations were being ignored. Similarly, the black revolution and the prison reform movement of the 1960s and 1970s, along with the short sentences imposed on Watergate offenders, again focused attention on differential treatment in the criminal justice system. Finally, the influence of the Marxist or neo-Marxist writings in criminology have focused, among other issues, on this differential treatment.

EXTENT AND IMPACT OF WHITE-COLLAR CRIME

Estimates of the cost to society of white-collar crimes range from $40 billion to over $100 billion annually. The cost goes beyond financial losses, however. Marshall B. Clinard, in his studies of corporate crime, has emphasized the nonfinancial costs of white-collar crime. These costs consist of the "injuries and health hazards to workers and consumers . . . the incalculable costs of the damages done to the physical environment and the great social costs of the erosion of the moral base of our society. They destroy public confidence in business and our capitalist system as a whole, and they inflict serious damages on the corporations themselves and on their competitors." Indeed, the report goes further in referring to the statements of Ralph Nader that even in the matter of death, corporate crimes have a greater impact than street crimes on the American public. "Far more persons are killed through corporate criminal activities than by individual criminal homicides; even if death is an indirect result the person still died."[13]

The nature and extent of white-collar crime as well as of organized crime, along with a brief statement of the impact of both on the U.S. economy, is noted in Highlight 9.1. More recent reports attribute the failures of savings-and-loan institutions to white-collar crimes, not poor economic conditions or deregulation. Fraud and insider trading, both discussed later, were found to be pervasive. "Attorney General Dick Thornburgh . . . blamed fraud and insider abuses for 25 percent to 30 percent of the S&L failures. Industry regulators said they have found the crimes a factor in at least 70 percent of insolvent institutions."[14]

In a provocative article on white-collar crime, Robert F. Meier and James F. Short, Jr., discussed its impact on the American public, elaborating on the physical and moral costs. The physical impact of dangerous drugs and automobiles will be noted later, but the impact of white-collar crime on the moral fabric of the country is also very important. Although we do not know the extent of the relationship between these two variables, Meier and Short emphasized that "it is precisely public trust—trust in social institutions, groups, and particular persons—that may provide the social glue that is social cohesion in the community. Once that cohesiveness is weakened or broken, the social fabric itself suffers."[15]

Perhaps the actions and words of the outgoing chairman of the Securities and Exchange Commission in 1987, explaining why he donated $20 million to the Harvard Business School for a program of ethics, best emphasize the problem of white-collar crime and its impact on the moral fiber of the country.

> I've been very disturbed most recently with the large numbers of graduates of leading business and law schools who have become convicted felons. Some of those we're bringing cases against are Baker Scholars, Rhodes Scholars, Phi Beta Kappas. It's the cream of the crop, and that's what is so shocking and causes concern.[16]

WHITE-COLLAR CRIME: A SOCIOLOGICAL ANALYSIS

Committed through learning.

Despite the difficulties of defining and categorizing white-collar crimes, sociologists have identified some characteristics that distinguish white-collar offenders from other offenders. White-collar offenders differ primarily in their higher socioeconomic status and their occupational respectability and prestige. They less often perceive of themselves as criminal; many see themselves as honest people just taking advantage of a good business situation.

Even when they recognize the law-breaking aspect of their behavior, white-collar criminals rationalize that the laws are wrong or do not apply to them. Donald R. Cressey illustrated this self-concept in his study of trust violators, who were able to redefine their position and convince themselves that their behavior was essentially noncriminal. They were not stealing; they were borrowing. This they did because of unusual circumstances, a financial problem that they could not share with others, and a belief that the only way to solve that problem was through embezzling.[17]

Is white-collar crime learned? Sutherland decided that his theory of differential association, discussed earlier, was an appropriate theory for explaining the behavior. Sutherland used biographical or autobiographical descriptions as data. He examined the life history of, for example, a young businessman who engaged in illegal practices in the used-car business. He showed how that person, although never exposed to criminals, was exposed to criminal attitudes in several of his jobs and how those attitudes later enabled him to violate the law. Sutherland also noted examples of the "diffusion of criminal practices from one situation to another" as evidence that the theory of differential association is useful in explaining white-collar crime. "When one firm devises a method of increasing profits, other firms become aware of the method and adopt it."[18]

Other sociologists also point out the relevance of differential association, although Marshall Clinard has argued that differential association cannot explain all cases of white-collar crime. Personality factors are also important. Clinard enumerates some individual personality traits that he

HIGHLIGHT 9.1

WHITE-COLLAR AND ORGANIZED CRIME

White-collar and organized criminal activities have become increasingly pervasive and their effects are being felt by millions of Americans. The alarming scale and prevalence of these sophisticated crimes are just beginning to be illuminated, as recent successes in major case investigations and prosecutions have produced new sources of data to increase our current awareness and provide a basis for further research.

While they may not generate in the public the paralyzing fear elicited by such violent crimes as robbery and rape, these complex and predatory offenses have far-reaching consequences that threaten our economic security, corrupt our legitimate institutions, and undermine public trust in government and law. Moreover, their intricate and covert nature makes them especially resistant to law enforcement intervention. In an effort to address these special problems, this program announcement requests proposals for research that will improve our under-standing, prevention, and control of white-collar and organized crime.

Today, conditions exist that have caused many of these crimes to reach critical proportions, dramatically greater in frequency and scope than they were even 5 years ago. For example, the computerization of financial and investment transactions, facilitating electronic fund transfer and international stock market trading, has created opportunities and incentives for white-collar theft on a grander scale than was possible in the past. This was evident, for instance, in a 1986 Wall Street insider-trading scandal, in which speculator Ivan F. Boesky made more than $50 million on illegal stock market trades based on inside information received from former investment banker Dennis B. Levine.

Similarly, the expansion, diversification, and growing profitability of drug trafficking have provided opportunities and incentives for the emergence and growth of new organized crimi-nal groups and enterprises. Recognizing this, the President's Commission on Organized Crime stated that "This Commission has found drug trafficking to be the most widespread and lucrative organized crime activity in the United States." In fact, it could be argued that the illicit drug trade is the fastest growing and most profitable industry in the United States, if not the world. The global drug trade may bring in up to $500 billion a year and the American market—the world's biggest illegal drug market—produces annual revenues of at least $100 billion, more than twice the amount spent for all criminal and civil justice services by all levels of government. The size and pervasiveness of the illegal drug industry, and the criminality associated with it, have created new types of organized crime cartels that are so wealthy and powerful that they seem almost impervious to conventional methods of interdiction and control.

These huge profits from drugs and other organized crime enter-

---

says are relevant: "egocentricity, emotional insecurity or feelings of personal inadequacy, negative attitudes toward other persons in general, the relative importance of status symbols of money as compared with nationalism, and the relative lack of importance of one's personal, family or business reputation."[19]

Other sociologists indicate the effect of differential association by noting that even when the management of a firm changes, the firm's participation in white-collar crime often continues. But it is also possible that

HIGHLIGHT 9.1 (Continued)

prises have contributed to another major problem: that of money laundering. To finance additional drug inventories, pay their employees, and enjoy a lavish life, drug traffickers need to get their cash out of the country and convert it into a form that will disguise its illegal origin. Thus, growing amounts are sent out in bulk packages or by wire transfers from U.S. banks to foreign accounts in places with strict bank secrecy laws, such as Panama, Paraguay, and Hong Kong. Stopping this flow of illegal funds through laundering collection centers like Miami, New York City, and Los Angeles has become an increasingly critical problem for the U.S. Treasury Department and U.S. Customs Service, as well as for criminal justice officials. Although the recent suspension of banking activities in Panama, caused by the Federal indictments of General Manuel Noriega, may have temporarily suspended laundering activities in that country, few experts feel this impact will be long lasting. Some more permanent and comprehensive solutions will be necessary if drug traders and other criminals are to be deprived of the income from their illegal enterprises.

It is clear from these recent examples that insider trading, narcotics trafficking, and money laundering; and such equally serious white-collar and organized criminal activities as labor racketeering, illegal toxic waste disposal, bid rigging, and public corruption pose special challenges for criminal justice officials charged with their prevention and control. First, because of the greater profitability of many of these offenses beyond that of other types of serious crimes, many white-collar and organized crime offenders have virtually unlimited financial resources to employ in evading or corrupting law enforcement efforts to control their activities. At the same time, these greater criminal benefits require correspondingly greater risks of criminal justice detection, arrest, conviction, and sanctions for deterrence to be effective. Sec-

ond, because they often involve continuing patterns of criminal activity rather than representing merely discrete incidents of crime commission, white-collar and organized crimes may require special operational planning to develop innovative, proactive strategies for their detection, prevention, and control. And finally because of the complexity and sophistication of many of these offenses, the coordinated efforts of a wide range of technical specialists and criminal justice agencies are often essential for their effective investigation and prosecution.

For all of these reasons, then, it is essential that priority attention be given to white-collar and organized crime in order to improve our current understanding of and response to these major national problems and prevent their further escalation.

SOURCE: National Institute of Justice, *Research Program Plan: Fiscal Year 1989* (Washington, D.C.: U.S. Department of Justice, November, 1989), pp. 36–37, footnote deleted.

---

individual managers might influence their firms and that therefore personality characteristics must be considered in understanding the etiology of upper-class crime. The emphasis, however, is on sociological explanations, which may be even more important in explaining white-collar crime as opposed to other types. For example, one study of white-collar criminals disclosed that the type of reaction was closely related to the social organization of the offense. To understand white-collar criminals, therefore, it is necessary to analyze the type of white-collar crime, the mechanics of the act, and the organizational context in which it occurred.[20]

Recent Approaches to White-Collar Crime

Earlier sociological theorists tended to analyze white-collar crime and white-collar criminals as separate or distinct from other types of crime and other criminals. More recent work has challenged this approach. Travis Hirschi and Michael Gottfredson advocate that it is possible to "outline a general theory of crime capable of organizing the facts about white-collar crime at the same time it is capable of organizing the facts about all forms of crime."[21]

Rather than beginning their analysis with offenders, as many theorists do, Hirschi and Gottfredson begin with an analysis of criminal events. They look for the characteristics of criminal events that make all crime attractive to potential offenders. Money, success, or peer approval, claim these sociologists, are not the common characteristics. Rather, they are the avoidance of pain and the seeking of pleasure. "Crimes are events in which force or fraud are used to satisfy self-interest, where self-interest refers to the enhancement of pleasure and the avoidance of pain." To get maximum pleasure, the events must occur immediately, be easy to accomplish, and have a certainty of outcome. Thus, "force and fraud can provide benefit with less effort than alternative means, especially when the benefit also has the properties of rapidity and certainty." White-collar crimes, like other crimes, satisfy these characteristics for those in a position to commit them. "Crimes, including white-collar crimes, therefore require no motivation or pressure that is not present in any other form of human behavior."[22]

Hirschi and Gottfredson conclude that theories of crime that analyze crime by offender typologies, that is, comparing rapists to burglars to white-collar criminals, should be replaced by their general theory that analyzes the properties of crime. According to them, "the distinction between crime in the street and crime in the suite is an *offense* rather than an *offender* distinction, that offenders in both cases are likely to share similar characteristics."[23] Darrell Steffensmeier rejects their approach, questioning their data base (using official *Uniform Crime Reports* data on fraud and forgery) as being unrepresentative of actual white-collar crime and arguing that on the basis of sex, age, and race the offender characteristics of white-collar crime do differ from those of other criminals.[24]

Another recent analysis of white-collar crime is seen in the work of James William Coleman, who has written extensively on the subject. Coleman combines motivation and opportunity theory in his analysis of white-collar crime, concluding that white-collar crime, which he calls the nation's most serious crime problem, is caused by the coincidence of motivation and opportunity, combined with the neutralization of ethical constraints that might inhibit criminal behavior.[25]

FOCUS ON CORPORATE CRIME

In an effort to study white-collar crime in a more focused manner, recent research has examined corporate crime. In October 1979, Marshall Clinard published what he described as "the first large-scale comprehensive investigation of corporations directly related to their violations of law." This project included an explanation of the types of crime included in the category, attempted predictions of violations, and methodological problems of studying corporate crime as well as statutory efforts to control it. Two-thirds of the corporations in the study were found to have violated criminal laws, and some corporations had done so repeatedly.[26]

Since the early 1980s the popular media have supported the allegation that corporate crime is extensive, one national news magazine claiming that "of the nation's 500 largest firms, 12.2 percent were convicted of or did not contest at least one criminal offense and an additional 10.8 percent were penalized for serious noncriminal offenses." Some corporate executives had been prosecuted, but few were convicted and fewer still were sentenced. "In a few instances, almost entire industries have been caught breaking the law."[27] In 1985, *Time* concluded that the extent of "crime in the suites" would soon lead to the necessity for *Fortune* to publish a 500-Most-Wanted List.[28]

Although the results cited by the popular magazines are shocking, the two-thirds figure cited by the Clinard study is much higher. What accounts for the differences? The study by Clinard has been criticized for its methodology and its faulty conclusions, resulting from an imprecise definition of crime that encompassed any governmental act of punishment, regardless of whether it fell under administrative, civil, or criminal law. For example, Clinard considered consent decrees as indicators of corporate crime. In the context of corporate actions, consent decrees are an agreement or a contract between a federal regulatory agency and a corporation. Although a consent decree is made under the sanction of the court, it binds only the parties and not the court. Many consent decrees and other enforcement actions tabulated by Clinard do not involve criminal behavior as it is commonly understood by the general public. Clinard's study might thus be considered an analysis of the "federal administrative regulation of large corporations" and not a focused study of corporate *crime*.[29] Once again, the inclusion or exclusion of acts that fall under administrative law rather than criminal law would be a critical and determinative factor.

Other critics applaud the extension to civil and administrative law but criticize the study for its failure to consider the relationships of class, class struggle, and capitalism to corporate crime. Furthermore, the Clinard report still leaves us without answers to many of the questions that are important to a study of corporate crime, such as how well the U.S.

American corporation is policed, the extent of corporate crime, and the rates of recidivism among corporate criminals.[30]

Understanding Corporate Crime

The need to understand corporate crime was emphasized by Steven Box: "Crimes of the powerful can only be ignored at the risk of enormously increasing our chances of being victimized by them." In his analysis of corporate crime, Box begins with the premise that the long-term common goal of corporations is profit. He explains how this profit motive may be hindered by environmental uncertainties such as competitors, the state, employees, consumers, and the public.

According to Box, corporations are inherently criminogenic in that these environmental uncertainties frequently create barriers to achieving profits. Corporate managers may look for alternatives to legitimate opportunities when legitimate opportunities are limited. The five environmental uncertainties may create problems for corporations in the following ways:

- *Competitors*—technological breakthroughs; price structure; marketing techniques; mergers; new or expanding markets
- *Governments*—extending regulations to cover more corporate activities either through new laws or tougher enforcement of existing laws
- *Employees*—any collusive activity, but especially those joining trade unions pursuing "militant" wage settlements and making "radical" demands on altering conditions of work/employment
- *Consumers*—especially when demand for product is elastic and consequently fickle, or when "consumerism" is prevalent and making highly visible any dubious corporate practice
- *Public*—especially through a growing "environmentalist" sensitivity to conserving fresh air, clean countryside, and natural resources[31]

Corporate managers may see certain business crimes as rational solutions to the problems created by these five environmental uncertainties. The profit motive, combined with these proposed solutions, joins forces with three factors: the ideology of the corporate manager, problems of law enforcement, and opportunities for illegal behavior. The result, says Box, is corporate crime. His approach utilizes several of the sociological theories discussed in earlier chapters, such as subculture, opportunity structure, neutralization, and anomie. His analysis also has implications for the control of corporate crime, discussed later.

EXAMPLES OF WHITE-COLLAR CRIME

There are many types of white-collar crime. Some are committed mainly by individuals acting alone, as in the case of embezzlement; others, such as conspiracy, by definition require more than one person; still others are committed primarily by corporations. In this section a few types and examples will be discussed. Statutes defining acts as white-collar crimes will differ from jurisdiction to jurisdiction, but there are common elements.

Avoidance or Evasion of Income Taxes

Income-tax evasion is a crime in this country. The controlling federal statute is as follows:

> Any person who willfully attempts in any manner to evade or defeat any tax imposed by this title or the payment thereof shall, in addition to other penalties provided by law, be guilty of a felony and, upon conviction thereof, shall be fined not more than $100,000 ($500,000 in the case of a corporation), or imprisoned not more than 5 years, or both, together with the costs of prosecution.[32]

Some aspects of this statute and its interpretation should be noted. First, the attempt alone completes the crime; eventual success in avoiding or evading taxes adds nothing to the crime. Second, Congress intended that if willfulness, a tax deficiency, and an intent to defeat the tax are proven beyond a reasonable doubt, a felony has been committed. However, if the proof only establishes knowledge of submitting a false tax return, the crime will be prosecuted as a misdemeanor.[33] Third, the avoidance or evasion of income tax must be willful, not just accidental, to be prosecuted under this statute, and "willfulness may not be inferred solely from proof of understated taxes. A specific intent to evade or defeat the tax must be proved by independent evidence of willful affirmative acts."[34]

There are many ways to evade income tax. Two recent cases illustrate this point. Victor Posner, a Miami Beach, Florida industrialist, pleaded no contest (meaning that although he would not plead guilty he would not contest the charges against him; his plea thus cannot be used against him in a civil suit but is treated as a conviction in criminal court) to charges of federal income tax evasion. Specifically, Posner was accused of inflating the value of land he donated to a Miami Bible college. He had previously been convicted of conspiracy to evade income taxes, four counts of tax evasion, and five counts of making false statements in his federal income tax return. Those convictions had been set aside because of irregularities with the jury. Posner, because of his age (sixty-nine), did not want to face another long trial; so he entered the no contest plea.

The federal income tax fraud case that captured national attention in 1989 was that of Leona Helmsley, who was tried and convicted of income tax evasion. Her husband, Harry Helmsley, was indicted but declared incompetent to stand trial. The Helmsleys and two of their officials were charged with forty-seven counts of tax evasion, most of which asserted that they diverted money from their business to buy lavish furnishings and art objects for their personal use. Deducting such expenditures as a business expense is, of course, a violation of federal tax laws and can result in enormous tax "savings" to the alleged violator. Included are a $500,000 jade art object and a $45,000 silver clock that Leona Helmsley had made for her husband. The Helmsleys gained international attention not only because of their extensive wealth but also because of the lavish lifestyle they live. Mrs. Helmsley was convicted and sentenced to four years in prison for what the judge called "naked greed." Helmsley was also fined $7.1 million for tax fraud. She will be eligible for parole after serving sixteen months in prison. As this text went to press, her case was on appeal.

Bribery

Historically, **bribery** was narrowly defined to mean corruption in the administration of justice. The modern concept of bribery includes the voluntary gift or receipt of anything of value in corrupt payment for an official act already done or to be done, or with the corrupt intent to influence the action of a public official or any person involved with the administration of public affairs. The federal statute in this area covers bribery and **graft.**[35] Graft is narrowly defined as the offering, giving, soliciting, or receiving of anything of value in connection with the procurement of materials under a federal defense program, and there is no need to prove the intent to influence the transaction improperly.

State bribery statutes vary but may include the receiving or soliciting, as well as the giving or offering, of a bribe as a crime. Bribery statutes are not broad in scope, and courts generally limit bribery to actions within the official capacity of the public servant. Illegal campaign contributions are often at the base of bribery charges. In January 1989 three men pleaded guilty to criminal charges stemming from the Pentagon scandal. Marine official Jack A. Sherman admitted that he accepted bribes in exchange for providing confidential information about Pentagon contracts, while two other officials admitted making illegal campaign contributions to two congressmen who gave him knowledge about the defense procurement business.

Bribery in connection with inspections is also common. In 1988, officials of twenty-three companies were charged with bribery of a federal official to overlook violations of federal rules and regulations with respect to asbestos. According to the U.S. Attorney for the Eastern District of New

York, "This case involves the most deadly form of corruption because it could affect the health and safety of innocent people."[36]

Extortion

Although the two crimes are similar, bribery should be distinguished from **extortion,** or **blackmail,** which refer to obtaining property from others by wrongful use of actual or threatened force, fear, or violence, or the corrupt taking of a fee by a public officer, under color of his or her office, when that fee is not due.[37] Historically extortion was limited to the unlawful taking of money by public officials, but modern statutes have considerably broadened the crime. Some include obtaining property of another through use of force or fear that compels the victim to surrender his or her property. Some statutes have been extended to include extortion by private persons. An example of the latter is found in *Yoder v. State.* In *Yoder,* the defendant contacted his former common-law wife and threatened that unless she delivered a television set, stereo, range, refrigerator, and a promissory note to him, he would distribute lewd photographs he had taken of her during their marriage. He was arrested before she delivered any of these items and was convicted of extortion. The Court of Criminal Appeals reversed the conviction, stating that since no property was delivered with her consent, the defendant could not be guilty of extortion.[38]

Extortion and blackmail statutes were originally enacted to cover crimes not covered by robbery statutes, discussed in the previous chapter. The crime of robbery requires a threat of *immediate harm*, but property may also be obtained by threatening one of *future harm*. Thus, the crime of extortion or blackmail.

Extortion and bribery charges (as well as conspiracy, discussed below) often arise out of the same or similar transactions. A recent extortion charge that has gained national attention was the 1988 conviction of Lee Alexander, Syracuse, New York mayor, who extorted at least $1.2 million over sixteen years from contractors who were doing business with the city. An extortion attempt of international significance is featured in Highlight 9.2.

Fraud

Fraud and **false pretenses** are crimes that refer to knowingly and intentionally misrepresenting circumstances or facts to others with the intention of obtaining money or other items of value from another or of inducing another to surrender a legal right. These terms cover a variety of business practices.[39] These crimes may be committed by individuals against individuals or by businesses or corporations. Here are a few examples.

HIGHLIGHT 9.2

ARRESTS IN AN ALLEGED $10 MILLION EXTORTION PLOT

A two-month international investigation of industrial espionage ended in a Geneva parking lot yesterday when four people were arrested after trying to extort $10 million from E. I. du Pont de Nemours & Company, law-enforcement and company officials said.

The case involved some of Du Pont's most important secrets for the production of Lycra, the company's trade name for spandex fiber. Spandex is used in clothes, particularly sportswear, and Du Pont, a huge energy, chemicals and specialty-products concern, is a leading manufacturer of it.

Argentine Managers Accused

Three of the four people charged are former employees of Du Pont's Argentine subsidiary, officials said. They were arrested as they tried to escape a trap set for them, law-enforcement officials said. A warrant is out for a fifth suspect, also a former employee.

The four Argentine nationals had been with Du Pont at least 13 years, working as middle managers until they quit within the last five months. Du Pont said they were trying to sell to the company proprietary information on Lycra that they had stolen.

The arrests ended an investigation that stretched from Argentina to Wilmington, Del., to Milan, Italy. The case involved a huge cache of stolen documents, an elaborate sting operation by the Federal Bureau of Investigation and collaboration among law officials in three countries.

The F.B.I. and Du Pont gave this account of the case:

In December, one of the suspects, Bruno Skerianz, contacted Du Pont and said he had documents from the company's Argentine subsidiary on spandex technology and the production of Lycra, one of Du Pont's most important products. Mr. Skerianz, the one suspect who the F.B.I. said had not worked for Du Pont, asked for a meeting with

Du Pont officials in Wilmington, where the company has its headquarters.

Du Pont alerted the F.B.I., which assigned an agent to work undercover as a Du Pont official in the company's negotiations with Mr. Skerianz.

At the first meeting between the suspect and Du Pont, on Dec. 20, Mr. Skerianz demanded $10 million for the Lycra documents, threatening otherwise to use the information to go into business for himself or sell it to a competitor. He said that he represented several former Du Pont employees and that he did not want to bring the documents into the United States.

"He believed the documents would have been seized if he brought them into the country," said Joseph V. Corless, special agent in charge of the Maryland-Delaware F.B.I.

In a second meeting and in telephone conversations that followed, Mr. Skerianz said the documents were in Milan. Last month, Du Pont officials and the F.B.I. undercover agent went to

---

Jim Bakker, former leader of the PTL (People That Love) religious group, was charged with numerous counts of fraud, including mail fraud, wire fraud, and conspiring to defraud the public through the sale of lifetime partnerships in the ministry's Heritage Village theme park. Bakker's wife, Tammy, who participated with him in the PTL ministry, was investigated but not indicted. Bakker was convicted on all twenty-four counts, and he is currently incarcerated in a federal prison. He is the "first major television evangelist to be convicted of a felony in connection with his ministry."[40]

HIGHLIGHT 9.2 (Continued)

Milan, and the company concluded that the documents, as the suspect had contended, described exclusive Lycra information.

Du Pont contacted Mr. Skerianz and agreed to pay him $10 million. In return for the money, Du Pont was to receive a contract from the suspects stating that they would not engage in the production of spandex fibers for five years.

The Geneva meeting was scheduled for 11 A.M. yesterday in a conference room at an office building. Several Du Pont officials and the F.B.I. agent had planned to exchange a bogus $10 million check for the documents, after which the Geneva police would arrest the suspects.

Suspects Stay Away

But the suspects had apparently learned of the trap, because they stayed in their hotel room, which was under surveillance. At noon, four of the five suspects left the hotel with several huge attaché cases containing thousands of pages of documents, which they put in two cars.

"It did not appear as if they were going to the meeting," Mr. Corless said. "It looked like they were getting ready to take off."

The Geneva police arrested the four in the parking lot. Mr. Corless said the police did not know why the fifth suspect was not with the others. The documents were recovered.

Arrested with Mr. Skerianz were Raúl Armando Giordano, 36 years old, who had been an operations supervisor at Du Pont's Argentine subsidiary; Antonio Ruben Inigo, 39, a maintenance supervisor, and Maria I. Lorenzo De Bianchini, 39, a company librarian, the F.B.I. said. An arrest warrant is out for José Maria Petrosino, 44, who worked as an engineer and is thought to be still in Geneva. All five are charged with trying to affect commerce by extortion and conspiracy.

U.S. to Seek Extradition

The suspects are being held by the Swiss authorities, Mr. Corless said, and the United States will ask for extradition. William Carpenter, assistant United States attorney for Delaware, said that if convicted the suspects would face up to 20 years in prison and $250,000 fines.

A spokesman for Du Pont, John R. Malloy, said the company did not know how the suspects had gained access to the documents or when they were stolen. Nor was it clear yesterday whether the documents were originals or copies, he said.

"With copying machines today, you never know when something is taken," Mr. Malloy said.

He declined to place a value on the documents but said, "The fact that they asked $10 million gives you some idea."

SOURCE: James Hirsch, "Four Arrested in an Extortion Plot Asking $10 Million from Du Pont," *New York Times,* 28 February 1989, p. 1, c. 3; Copyright © 1988/89 by the New York Times Company. Reprinted by permission.

In 1988, Hertz Corporation pleaded guilty to defrauding 110,000 customers, motorists, and insurance companies. The company had charged inflated and sometimes fictitious collision-repair costs. Such schemes may be easy to engage in and difficult for potential victims to detect. There is no doubt, however, that the gullibility of some people facilitates the crime of fraud. For example, a man who pleaded guilty to fraud charges in Oklahoma in 1988 had no problem getting cooperation when he posed as a doctor and went door-to-door asking women to donate their breast milk. Although only one actually did so, the imposter was charged with obtain-

Lyndon H. LaRouche, Jr., former democratic presidential candidate, was sentenced to 15 years in prison upon conviction of fraud.

ing property for charity under false pretenses, soliciting for a charitable contribution under false pretenses, and fraud. He was sentenced to 200 hours of community work and ordered to undergo counseling. He was not sent to prison since the judge said he could not get proper treatment there.

Conspiracy

Conspiracy is included as a white-collar crime even though the conspiracy may involve a crime of violence against a person, such as kidnapping, or a property crime, such as distributing counterfeit money. Conspiracy is generally defined as an agreement between two or more persons to commit a criminal act or to achieve by unlawful means an act not in itself illegal. The illegal acts need not be carried out for the crime of conspiracy to be proved. Conspiracy does not exist if both the object of the plan and the methods used to achieve it are lawful.

Persons charged with other specific crimes (such as fraud) may also be charged with conspiracy if the additional elements that constitute conspiracy are believed to exist. For example, Lyndon H. LaRouche, Jr., a political extremist who has on four occasions been an independent candidate for U.S. president, was convicted of fraud and conspiracy to commit fraud against the Internal Revenue Service and supporters who loaned him millions of dollars which he had no intention of repaying. The successful prosecutor in this case said, after LaRouche was sentenced to fifteen years in prison, "I consider this an obvious conclusion to a long pattern of false statements to trusting senior citizens. . . . Their dreams for their retirement are gone. It's a sad case."[41] In 1990, La Rouche's convictions were affirmed on appeal.

Embezzlement

Embezzlement involves having rightful possession of the property of another and then wrongfully intending to deprive the owner of that property. In the upper-class context, embezzlement normally concerns corporate officers or employees and public officers. The importance of the element of rightful possession is illustrated by *Partian v. State*, in which a municipal building inspector threatened to "make it rough" for a contractor unless the contractor paid him one-half the usual inspection fee. The inspector was convicted, but the Court of Appeals reversed the conviction, stating that the inspector might be guilty of bribery or extortion but he could not be convicted of conversion or embezzlement because he did not lawfully obtain the money. This case illustrates the fact that an act might be prosecuted under any of a number of different criminal statutes, depending on their interpretation.[42]

One of the most publicized embezzlement cases of the 1980s involved famed automaker John Z. De Lorean. Two and one-half years after he was acquitted of drug charges, De Lorean was acquitted of charges that he embezzled $8.5 million from his failed sports car enterprise. But even if those acquittals ended De Lorean's criminal charges, he still faces numerous civil suits stemming from the failure of his auto company. These suits could and probably will result in years of civil litigation.

Employee Theft

Closely related to embezzlement is the crime of employee theft, in which employees who have legal access to the employer's property appropriate that property for themselves. Data on the extent of employee theft vary, but one study estimated that only 25 percent of employees were honest at all times during their employment, while 50 percent were "as honest as controls and personal motivation dictate."[43]

John P. Clark and Richard C. Hollinger, in their research on employee theft and "other forms of counterproductive deviant behavior by employees within the work setting," studied over nine thousand employees in forty-seven business corporations. Roughly one-third of the sample reported that they had taken some company property during the previous year, and over two-thirds reported counterproductive behavior such as the use of alcohol or drugs at work, abuse of sick leave, long breaks and lunches, and slow or sloppy workmanship. Business and industry losses from employee theft are estimated to be between $5 and $10 billion a year and rank along with securities theft and fraud as the top causes of business losses from nonviolent crimes. Clark and Hollinger found that the "single factor most predictive of theft involvement was the employee's perception of getting caught—the greater the perceived risks, the less the theft."[44]

More recent reports estimate that U.S. businesses lose up to $40 billion annually from employee thefts, that employee thieves have little long-term commitment to their employers, and that they are not in serious financial need when they steal. The costs to society exceed the amounts stolen, because theft results in higher prices to consumers caused by the increased need for private security and actual dollar loss as well as lost jobs.[45]

Employee theft extends beyond taking money or possessions from employers. Time stealing is also a form of theft and translates into lost production by companies. A business consultant reported that time-theft cost U.S. businesses $170 billion in 1986 and probably as much as $200 billion in 1988.[46]

False Advertising

False advertising statutes are aimed at protecting two classes of people: the consumer and the competitor. The Printer's Ink Model Statute was first passed in 1911, and by 1913, fourteen states had enacted statutes regulating false advertising. In 1914 Congress passed the Federal Trade Commission Act, proscribing methods of unfair competition in interstate commerce. This was followed by the Wheeler-Lea Amendment of 1938, which covered deceptive advertising. Under federal law, the advertising need only have the capacity to deceive; some state statutes require an actual intent to mislead. The federal statute seeks to protect the buying public from being duped into purchasing items they do not want or intend to buy; therefore, erroneous descriptions of products are illegal, as is baiting. The latter involves advertising an especially low price on a product while intending to sell a higher priced, unadvertised product.[47]

Insider Trading

In 1986 several cases of insider trading were prosecuted by the U.S. Justice Department. **Insider trading** exists when officers, directors, and stockholders who hold more than 10 percent of the stock of a corporation that is listed on a national exchange buy and sell corporate shares. Insider information is information known to these officers before it is available to

Ivan Boesky, convicted for insider trading, served a prison term and was released early in 1990.

the public. Federal law requires that such transactions be reported monthly to the Securities and Exchange Commission (SEC). This requirement is meant to ensure that insiders are not taking undue advantage of the investing public by trading information that will lead them to make large profits on their investments at the expense of other investors.

Like most areas of criminal law, the laws covering insider trading have changed rapidly and are quite complicated. There are gray areas; that is, some information may be traded without criminal liability. However, the Justice Department argued successfully in several 1986 cases that the insiders had gone too far. Most involved selling information about corporate takeovers. Ira B. Sokolow, a thirty-two-year-old investment banker, was convicted and sentenced to one year and a day in prison and three years probation after he admitted that he sold information about pending takeovers to Dennis B. Levine, the central figure in the biggest illegal insider trading scheme yet uncovered. Ilan K. Reich, thirty-one, a former partner in a top Wall Street law firm, also pleaded guilty, saying, "I pleaded guilty because I am guilty—guilty of criminal conduct, guilty of gross stupidity and guilty of betraying my family and my partners." Other young professionals were also convicted. Civil actions have also been filed, and some defendants have already agreed to pay heavy fines for their illegal activities.

One of the key defendants in the 1986 prosecutions was Ivan F. Boesky, a leading Wall Street stock market speculator who agreed to cooperate with federal officials by permitting them to record secretly his conversations with other investors. Boesky agreed to pay a $100 million fine, to plead guilty to one criminal charge (if others were dropped), and to cooperate with the government, probably in the hope of avoiding a prison sentence. Despite the large fine (which was not as large as the law permitted), Boesky is still a wealthy man, but he has been barred from the investment business for the rest of his life. The extent of Boesky's involvements are not yet uncovered; he was, however, connected with the insider ring led by Dennis B. Levine, who led the SEC to Boesky.

In April 1989 Boesky's request for early release from prison after serving one year was turned down. Boesky's attorneys based the request on the fact that Boesky's cooperation with federal prosecutors was the main reason the government had been so successful in prosecuting insider traders. The judge did not agree, stating:

> It was my expectation at the time of sentence that that degree of assistance was expected and forthcoming. . . . Accordingly, I cannot in good conscience conclude that, commendable as Boesky's behavior has been since he was sentenced, he should be given further credit.[48]

In addition to his good behavior during his year in prison, Boesky was reportedly working out on weights, jogging, and in general becoming physically fit. He complained about unfair treatment from inmates and reportedly worked out "to insure that he is able to defend himself" from inmates who attack him.[49] Boesky was released from prison in April, 1990 and has become a key government witness in cases involving Wall Street scandals.

The government's success in prosecuting insider trading cases in 1986 has continued. In December 1988, in the largest settlement ever recorded for securities law violations, Drexel Burnham Lambert, Inc., a Wall Street firm with connections to Boesky, pleaded guilty to six felony counts concerning insider trading. Drexel agreed to pay $650 million in penalties, some of which would go toward paying government prosecution expenses and over one-half of which is to be used to compensate victims. Although that might sound like a large penalty, it has been estimated that the company would have to pay $1.5 billion in fines "to deplete the company's resources enough to worry its creditors and leave it with less than the minimum capital necessary for membership in the stock exchanges."[50]

Despite the government's success, many problems have arisen in the prosecution of insider trading cases. One problem is that there were no federal statutes aimed specifically at the problem. Congress attempted to alleviate that in 1988 by passing a statute aimed specifically at insider trading and increasing penalties that could be assessed.[51] As Highlight 9.3 indicates, prosecution of these cases is also difficult for key witnesses such as Boyd Jefferies.

The extent of illegal insider trading is still not known; the government continues to investigate. Repercussions have been felt throughout the stock market in this country and in Europe. Critics claim that the SEC has gone too far in its interpretations of the law; others argue that these acts constitute white-collar crimes that should be vigorously prosecuted.

Antitrust Violations

Antitrust laws are designed to ensure fair competition and free enterprise in the private economic marketplace. Historically, common law attempted to limit restraints on trade and to control monopolies and excessive profits of middlemen. During the second half of the nineteenth century, Congress expressed concern over abusive practices of large corporations by enacting the Interstate Commerce Act of 1887 and the Sherman Antitrust Act of 1890. The latter has two main provisions:

> Sec. 1: Every contract, combination in the form of trust or otherwise, or conspiracy, in restraint of trade or commerce . . . is declared to be illegal [and is a felony punishable by fine and/or imprisonment]. . . .
> Sec. 2: Every person who shall monopolize, or attempt to monopolize or combine or conspire with any other person or persons, to monopolize any part of the trade or commerce among the several States, or with foreign nations, shall be deemed guilty of a felony [and is similarly punishable]. . . .[52]

The purpose of Section 1 is to prohibit two or more parties from joining together to fix prices. One problem with the court decisions based on this statute, however, is that there is not a clear definition of price fixing. Another difficulty is to distinguish between legal exchange of information between business people, such as trade associations that disseminate trade news and data, and illegal conduct in the exchange of information that tends to restrain trade unreasonably.[53] Section 2 of the Sherman Antitrust Act focuses on the control of monopolistic power. Troublesome issues under this section include definitions of the product market, the geographic market, and the market share. The prosecution must prove an illegal purpose and intent along with market structure and power.

The act contains criminal and civil penalties. The U.S. Department of Justice has jurisdiction to prosecute criminal actions, whereas the Federal Trade Commission is limited to administrative and civil jurisdiction. Under the Sherman and Clayton acts, privately injured parties may sue for treble damages and attorney's fees. Recently, private suits have become increasingly important in antitrust enforcement.

HIGHLIGHT 9.3

THE TRIALS OF A PROSECUTION WITNESS

Boyd L. Jefferies used to thrive on four hours of sleep a night, arriving for work at 1:30 a.m. and staying until evening to command the aggressive stock-trading desk of the brokerage that bears his name.

Now the 58-year-old ex-broker spends much of his time with defense lawyers and federal investigators, chain-smoking cigarettes, answering questions and wondering when he will get back to his passion on the 33rd floor of a downtown Los Angeles skyscraper, buying and selling big blocks of stock.

A criminal courtroom has replaced his sprawling trading desk; the tension of interrogation has replaced the thrill of stock speculation; the priority of avoiding jail time has replaced the obsession with serving clients.

Once spectacularly successful, widely admired, and courted by almost every big takeover strategist, Jefferies has been transformed over the past two years into what gangsters might call the biggest canary in his business.

He is the leading prosecution witness in at least three major fraud cases, including one against Tampa-based corporate raider Paul Bilzerian, who was named in a 12-count indictment

last month and pleaded not guilty Jan. 5.

Bilzerian is alleged to have secretly bought stock through Jefferies and Co., thus violating federal disclosure laws in two takeover attempts and two multimillion-dollar stock purchases in 1985 and 1986. His trial is scheduled for May 1.

The three cases in which Jefferies is the government's key witness arose indirectly from the man who squealed on him, Ivan F. Boesky, the stock speculator and inside trader now serving a three-year prison term.

In exchange for lenient treatment, Jefferies agreed with federal prosecutors in March 1987 to plead guilty to two violations of securities laws, cooperate in other investigations, resign from his brokerage, Jefferies & Co., and stay out of the securities business for at least five years.

"Yes, I miss it," Jefferies said, standing outside a Manhattan federal courtroom during a break in his recent witness-stand debut in the stock-manipulation case against GAF Corp. and a top company officer.

He declined to elaborate and spent much of the break in a witness waiting room, puffing Benson & Hedges 100s, chewing gum and slowly pacing the floor. He looked tan and fit in a dark-

blue business suit, but his blue eyes were slightly bloodshot and he seldom smiled.

"Here's a guy who used to get up at 1:30 in the morning to go work," said James P. Linn, Jefferies' lawyer. "It's not easy for a man who's worked like that to stand around in a federal courthouse."

Nevertheless, life isn't that bad for Jefferies. He remains fabulously wealthy and owns expensive homes in Indian Wells, Calif., and Aspen, Colo., which he shares with his wife. He spends much of his time on the telephone to keep abreast of the market, though he generally refrains from calling his colleagues at the company, Linn said.

"I suppose he's allowed to call, but the company doesn't like for him to, so he doesn't," the lawyer said.

A good golfer, Jefferies has started a scholarship program in Aspen for aspiring young golf amateurs. Although defense lawyers have tried to claim this generosity is meant to impress the judge who ultimately will sentence him, Linn denied that.

"The fact is, Boyd Jefferies had a son killed in an accident. He is passionately involved with young people, having lost his son," Linn said. "He has no ul-

HIGHLIGHT 9.3 (Continued)

terior motive in doing his golf deal."

Jefferies' punishment remains unclear, but is expected to be far less than the maximum sentence of 10 years imprisonment and $500,000 in fines he faces for pleading guilty to one count of violating stock-margin requirements and one count of aiding and abetting to keep false books.

He even suggested on the witness stand, during cross-examination by defense attorneys in the GAF trial, that he doesn't expect to serve any prison time.

To a large extent, the severity of the sentence will depend on the fruits of his cooperation, which were bruised this past week when a federal judge declared a mistrial in the GAF case because the prosecution mishandled a key piece of evidence.

Aside from his involvement with GAF and Bilzerian, Jefferies is a leading witness in the securities fraud prosecution of former client Salim B. Lewis, a New York-based securities professional.

Linn and other associates of Jefferies have tried to portray him as a man so driven to serve his customers that he crossed the bounds of legality on their behalf, not out of personal avarice.

Many big investors have expressed faith in him, such as Texas oilman T. Boone Pickens and Minneapolis takeover strategist Irwin Jacobs. But Jefferies' lawyer conceded that other clients might feel betrayed by a trusted broker who later turned state's evidence in a major criminal investigation.

"Yes, I suppose there would be some of those people," Linn said. "But Boyd still has a very loyal and large following. He did a lot of things for a lot of people."

Product of Takeover Boom

Jefferies' rapid rise, generosity and crashing downfall are part of the folklore of the 1980s takeover boom. A UCLA graduate and former ranch hand, he started in the securities business by landing an entry-level job at a small brokerage, quit six years later and founded his own firm with two employees.

By early this decade, Jefferies & Co. had swelled to more than 400 employees, with a large trading center in Los Angeles, five other offices nationwide and one in London.

It became known as the leading firm where investors could trade big blocks of stock quickly and discreetly, without going through conventional stock exchanges.

Jefferies was said to delight in making markets for high-profile stocks, and the positions he took in well-known targets sometimes determined the outcome of takeover battles.

In late 1986, for example, Jefferies helped Toronto-based Campeau Corp. acquire Allied Stores Corp. by selling the Canadian developer a large block of its Allied holdings for more than $1.7 billion.

Part of the attraction for takeover investors was Jefferies' policy of absolute confidentiality and extraordinary accommodation in doing business at their convenience, no matter when.

Despite predictions that his brokerage would falter following his plea agreement, Jefferies & Co. continues to be an aggressive trader and he intends to return there when his legal ordeal finally ends, Linn said.

"He's lost without that business. That business literally was his life," the lawyer said.

SOURCE: Rick Gladstone, "Workaholic Broker Adjusts to Life as Key Fraud Witness," *Tampa Tribune,* 15 January 1989, p. E1, col. 5. Reprinted with the permission of the Associated Press.

Crimes Committed by Government Officials

Crimes, including acts of extreme personal violence resulting in death, committed by governments in other countries, especially when committed against U.S. citizens, have been the subject of frequent discussion and analysis in this country. Some of these crimes are acts of terrorism and will be discussed in the next chapter. Until recently, however, little attention was paid to crimes committed by our government officials against private citizens. The criminal violations that occurred during Watergate in the administration of former President Nixon, leading to his resignation—the first president of this country to do so in disgrace—and the criminal convictions of many of his staff focused attention on the crimes of government officials. An example is operation ABSCAM.

Operation ABSCAM (which stands for Arab Scam) was the most extensive and probably the most controversial investigation of corruption among U.S. government officials in this country. It began in February 1978, when an informer, convicted of fraud, gave information to the FBI. This information, which led to the recovery of two very valuable paintings, also led to a decision to use the same method for investigating racketeering and influence peddling among public officials. For the next year and a half, FBI undercover agents approached public officials thought to be involved in political corruption and informed them that oil-rich Arab shieks would offer money in exchange for various political favors. The agents met the political figures in various places in Washington, D.C., and paid out considerable sums in cash. The meetings and conversations were videotaped. Several public officials were indicted and convicted.

The ABSCAM operation is important for the political corruption it has uncovered in Congress, but the actions of members of Congress have not been the only questionable activities. It has been argued that the action of the FBI amounted to **entrapment.** The FBI, in the face of strong criticism of its tactics in ABSCAM, decided to stop prematurely one of its other sting operations.[54]

Criticism of the FBI has been extensive in the days since the death of its long-time director, J. Edgar Hoover. An increasing number of violations of the civil rights of citizens have been disclosed, leading to such conclusions as follows:

> Without any legal authorization, they have tapped telephones, they have opened and read private mail, they have planted electronic bugs in offices and bedrooms, they have written anonymous and false letters to the spouses and associates and employers of people they wanted to harm, they have committed burglaries and other break-ins, they have paid informants who later lied under oath . . . they have used *agents provocateurs* to entrap others by planning and encouraging criminal conspiracies, they have incited police violence. . . . The victims were often innocent of any crime. . . . In short, the F.B.I. has long been—and perhaps still is—a secret-police force.[55]

Similar allegations have been made of the Central Intelligence Agency (CIA), which led Arthur M. Schlesinger, Jr., to "suggest an inherent danger in intelligence agencies. They form a society of their own, with purposes and standards distinct from those of the nation. Prolonged immersion in the segregated, self-contained, self-justifying world of deception and secrecy tends to erode links to reality. Intelligence operatives begin to see themselves as the appointed custodians of the national security . . . morally authorized to do things on their own as they deem in the interests of the republic."[56]

Computer Crimes

Computers have revolutionized not only the way we do business but also in many respects the way we think and act. Computers fascinate and challenge many; others are so frightened that according to some reports, they develop an intense fear of computers, called cyberphobia, and even become violent, attacking the computer. Computers have also been used to commit crimes, as Exhibit 9.1 indicates. Cracking computers has become a rite of passage of some teenagers and college students. Rather than stealing and hot-wiring cars, they steal information from computers.

The extent of **computer crimes** is unknown, but in Florida in 1989 experts estimated that 25 percent of businesses had been hit by computer crimes, that 65 percent of those crimes are not reported, and that law enforcement officials are not equipped to combat computer crimes. According to Florida Department of Law Enforcement Commissioner, James T. Moore, businesses must develop private security to combat the problems of computer crimes. Unfortunately, according to a business consultant, "Most businesses aren't aware any problem exists until it actually happens to them."[57]

In 1988, national attention was focused on computer crimes when Robert T. Morris, Jr., apparently intending no harm, made one programming error that resulted in jamming more than 6000 computers "in what has been called this country's most serious computer 'virus' attack." Morris is the son of the chief scientist at the Government's National Computer Security Center. Friends reported that young Morris, a Cornell University graduate student, was horrified at his mistake.[58] But in June 1989 Cornell officials, saying they found unauthorized passwords in Morris' computer, suspended him from school. In January 1990, Morris was convicted and faced up to five years in prison and a $250,000 fine. However, he was placed on three years' probation, fined $10,000, and ordered to perform 400 hours of community service.

Types of Computer Crimes

Computer crimes may involve the same kind of crimes already discussed in this chapter except that the computer is used in the perpetration of the

EXHIBIT 9.1

High Technology Has Provided New Opportunities for Crime

HIGH-TECHNOLOGY PROCEDURES ARE USED IN SOME TYPES OF CRIME

Over the past decade the use of computers and advanced communication techniques for business and industrial purposes has radically altered traditional means of doing business. These changes have created an environment in which white-collar abuse of fiscal trust and responsibility can result in unusually large losses. The centralized storage of individually identifiable information has also created new opportunities for white-collar crimes that involve unlawful acquisition and disclosure of data. Manipulation of computer programs can also conceal illegal transactions and prevent, or at least postpone, discovery of loss by a victim or financial institution.

PROSECUTION OF COMPUTER-RELATED CRIMES PRESENTS SPECIAL PROBLEMS

● Traditional laws are not always applicable to violations that involve automated activity.

● Evidence of computer abuse (and computer-generated evidence of other abuses) may not always be admissible in court.

● Investigators, prosecutors, and judges do not have the training needed to become familiar with computer terminology and procedures.

So far, 47 States have enacted computer crime laws that, to some degree, define illegal activites involving computerized facilities, procedures, or information. Some of the laws also refer specifically to crimes that involve credit card transactions.

GREATER USE OF HIGH TECHNOLOGY HAS INCREASED CONCERN ABOUT COMPUTER CRIME

● In 1980 about 117 trillion dollars were transferred electronically among financial institutions in roughly 60 million wire transfer transactions; this was an increase of more than 170% over the value of transactions in 1976.

● In 1983 about 262 billion dollars were processed through automated teller machines in roughly 2.7 billion transactions. This was an increase of almost 650% over the value of funds and an increase of more than 170% over the number of automated teller machine transactions in 1982.

● White-collar crime losses to banks resulting from automated teller machine fraud during 1983 were estimated at between 70 and 100 million dollars.

AUTOMATED TELLER MACHINE FRAUD IS OF SPECIAL CONCERN TO CONSUMERS

● In a sample study of 2,700 automated teller machine incidents that prompted a consumer complaint, about 45% were found to be fraud-related; of these, almost half resulted from unauthorized use of a lost or stolen automated teller machine card. Cards were lost or stolen in the home in 25% of these cases, and they were taken as part of a wallet or purse snatching in almost two-thirds of the cases.

● Average losses to accountholders were $255 per incident where loss was to the accountholder only. Where both the accountholder and the bank incurred losses, average loss to the accountholder was $74 per incident and average loss to the bank was $365 per incident.

LOST OR STOLEN CARDS ARE USED IN 49% OF ALL AUTOMATIC TELLER MACHINE FRAUDS

Type of Automated Machine Fraud	Percent of Fraudulent Incidents
Withdrawal-related incidents	
Unauthorized withdrawals:	
Card lost or stolen	49%
Card in possession of cardholder	24
Overdraft:	
Withdrawal against insufficient/bad deposit	4
Bank operations suspected to be off line or delayed	14
Deposit-related incidents	
Bad deposit:	
Stolen/fraudulent/ uncollectible check or empty envelope	3
Bad check deposited by person other than accountholder	6
Other	1
Total	100%

SOURCE: The table is from *Electronic fund transfer fraud*, BJS Special Report, March 1985.

SOURCE: Bureau of Justice Statistics, *Report to the Nation on Crime and Justice: The Data*, 2d ed. (Washington, D.C.: U.S. Department of Justice, 1988), p. 10, footnote omitted.

crime. "Computer crime may also take the form of threats of force directed against the computer itself. These crimes are usually 'sabotage' or 'ransom' cases. Computer crime cases have one commonality: the computer is either the tool or the target of the felon."[59]

A special jargon has been developed to describe computer crimes:[60]

1. *Data Diddling*, the most common, the easiest, and the safest technique, involves changing the data that will be put into the computer or that are in the computer.

2. *The Trojan Horse* method involves instructing the computer to perform unauthorized functions as well as its intended functions.

3. *The Salami Technique* refers to taking small amounts of assets from a larger source without significantly reducing the whole. For example, one might, in a bank account situation, instruct the computer to reduce specified accounts by 1 percent and place those assets in another account.

4. *Superzapping;* because computers at times malfunction, there is a need for what is sometimes called a "break glass in case of emergency" computer program. This program will "bypass all controls to modify or disclose any of the contents of the computer." In the hands of the wrong person, it can be an extremely powerful tool for crime.

5. *Data Leakage* involves removing information from the computer system or computer facility.

In May 1989 two former television executives in Tampa, Florida, facing sixteen counts of conspiracy and computer crimes, were given a break in what is believed to be the first known cases of newsroom computer tampering. Terry Cole and Mike Shapiro, both thirty-three years old and long-time friends, decided that the best way to be first in the news was to tap the computers of their competitor news stations. The judge placed Cole and Shapiro on probation, withholding conviction (meaning that if they meet all terms of probation, there will not be a record of conviction against them), fined each less than $800, and ordered them to perform 250 hours of community service work, including making one speech a year to journalists and students planning journalism careers. Said the sentencing judge, "You have taken something from your profession . . . stole it, and now it is time to give something back."[61]

Controlling Computer Crimes

Legislation regulating computer crimes reflects the varying definitions of this new type of theft. The legislation itself is relatively recent. The California statute defines computer crime as follows:

> Any person who intentionally accesses or causes to be accessed any computer system or computer network for the purpose of (1) devising or

executing any scheme or artifice to defraud or extort or (2) obtaining money, property, or services with false or fraudulent intent, representations, or promises shall be guilty of a public offense.

Any person who maliciously accesses, alters, deletes, damages, or destroys any computer system, computer network, computer program, or data shall be guilty of a public offense.[62]

Passage of a federal statute regulating computer crime did not occur until the enactment of the Comprehensive Crime Control Act of 1984. Before that time computer crimes had to be prosecuted under other statutes, such as mail fraud and wire fraud, which excluded some types of computer crimes. The penalities were also considered inadequate for computer crimes.

The 1984 federal criminal code provides penalties for anyone who "knowingly accesses a computer without authorization, or having accessed a computer with authorization," uses that opportunity to obtain information that has been declared essential for national defense or foreign relations or certain types of specified restricted data for the purpose of injuring the United States or benefiting any foreign country. The statute also includes prohibitions against using the computer to obtain illegally "information contained in a financial record of a financial institution . . . or . . . a file of a consumer reporting agency on a consumer. . . ." A third prohibition involves the illegal use of a computer to knowingly use, modify, destroy, or disclose information in, or prevent the authorized use of the computer "if such computer is operated for or on behalf of the Government of the United States and such conduct affects such operation." The statute contains some limitations on the extent to which these last two provisions will apply.

The penalties for the illegal use of a computer to secure information for the purpose of harming the United States or benefiting a foreign country range from a fine "of not more than the greater of $10,000 or twice the value obtained by the offense or imprisonment for not more than ten years, or both" for a first offense to a fine "of not more than the greater of $100,000 or twice the value obtained by the offense or imprisonment for not more than twenty years, or both" for conviction of a second offense. Attempts to commit an offense punishable under the statute are also included. Lesser penalties are provided for violation of the other provisions.[63]

It is quite possible, however, that the passing of statutes designed to prevent computer crimes will not be as effective as some would like to think. First, many establishments might not want the public to know that their employees committed crimes with the company's computers. In one case, in England, when an employee was confronted by management with his alleged use of the computer to steal money from the company over a period of years, he threatened "to expose the weaknesses of the company's computer system and ruin the company's reputation for efficient management of its affairs unless the company wrote him a letter of recommendation (so that he could get another job in the programming field). The company knuckled under, wrote him the letter, and the programmer went on to commit a similar theft against his new employer."[64]

Second, in addition to a lack of reporting and willingness to prosecute, is the difficulty of prosecution. Police do not have the technical expertise to solve computer crimes, and cases that go to trial are usually highly technical, costly, and extremely time-consuming.[65]

Ethics and the Computer

What is needed, say some authorities, is not legislation but a code of ethics concerning computer use. The Privacy Act of 1974 was a legislative beginning in protecting all people from the dissemination of information contained in computers.[66] Perhaps we should also be able to bring civil suits against companies that, through their own negligence (for example, lack of adequate computer security), allow records to be stolen.

Actually, two ethical issues are involved—the abuse of individuals by institutions, for example, when private information held in the computer is disseminated to the improper sources, and the misuse by individuals of the computers of institutions. A professor of computer science says that the ethics issues are basic: "Don't do with computers what you would consider immoral without them. An act does not gain morality because the computer has made it easy to achieve. . . . If it is immoral for someone to rummage through your desk drawers, then it is unethical for someone to make a search of your computer files." His conclusion, however, perhaps illustrates our traditional attitude toward these kinds of criminals, as compared with "real" criminals: "But because an electronic search is by definition somewhat ephemeral, many people don't see its ethical consequences."[67]

Characteristics of Computer Criminals

Few studies have been conducted on computer criminals. Bequai notes, however, that the few existing studies indicate that the criminals are usually young, very bright, and often see themselves as pitted against the computer. A National Criminal Justice Information and Statistics Service Report of the Law Enforcement Assistance Administration suggests that in attempting to detect computer criminals, researchers should keep in mind the following characteristics, which are similar to those of the "modern-day, amateur, white-collar criminal." First, their median age is twenty-five years. Such younger people may not yet be assimilated into the ethics and organization of their professions, and they have often been trained on college and university campuses where "attacking campus computer systems is not only condoned but often encouraged as an educational activity."

Second, these people are highly trained and often overtrained for the jobs they occupy. They may become bored by routine computer work.

Most will perform their criminal acts during the course of their job assignments, although that is not always the case. They are more likely than other white-collar criminals to need assistance in their criminal activity. They may have learned their acts from others in the same company; thus differential association cannot be ruled out. They demonstrate the Robin Hood syndrome—that is, they distinguish between victimizing individuals and victimizing organizations. "In addition, they rationalize that they are only harming a computer or the contents of the computer; therefore, doing no harm or causing no loss to people or organizations," a characteristic that is common to other kinds of white-collar criminals.

Some computer criminals rationalize that a computer that is not being used is fair game despite the fact that computer time is very expensive, and they are in essence stealing by not paying for that computer time. It is common for computer criminals to rationalize that because they have the technical expertise to utilize computers, they are entitled to use them for personal purposes, "for challenging intellectual exercise."[68]

Finally, as mentioned, some people try to crack computer systems just for fun and are examples of some of the theories we discussed in earlier chapters. They are succumbing to peer pressure; they are imitating television and movies, such as *War Games;* or they are just looking for new thrills and excitement.

CORPORATE BEHAVIOR AND CRIMINAL SANCTIONS

This sampling of white-collar crimes pertains to those that may be committed by individuals in a business setting or by corporative executives acting on behalf of the corporation. The major debate in analyzing corporate crime, however, arises over the issue of whether corporate managers should be held criminally liable for the actions of their employees or whether the civil law is sufficient for these cases.

In Chapter 1 we distinguished between criminal and civil law and noted that in some cases corporations (or noncorporate employers) may be held criminally liable for the acts of their employees. In this chapter we looked at Sutherland's argument that social scientists who study crime should include white-collar crimes in their research even if those violations are legally handled by administrative agencies (and are thus civil) rather than by criminal courts.

The legal argument against holding corporations criminally liable for the acts of their employees is that the criminal **intent** is not present in vicarious liability.[69] Many courts have held, however, that intent may be inferred from gross recklessness, as we will see in the following examples, but that vicarious criminal liability will not apply to crimes such as first-degree murder, which require a specific intent. Another traditional argument against holding corporations vicariously liable is that most criminal statutes begin with the words "any person," and corporations are not persons. Today that problem has been solved by statute or court decision in many jurisdictions in which the word *person* is held to include corporations. A California case explains the position taken on these issues by an appellate court that upheld a manslaughter conviction of a corporation. The court begins with the issue and facts of the case.[70]

Granite Construction Co. v. People

In this petition, we are asked to exempt corporations from prosecution for manslaughter. We refuse, holding that corporations may be prosecuted for manslaughter under existing California law.

Petitioner, a corporation, is building a power plant known as the "Helms Pumped Storage Project." On January 23, 1981, seven construction workers were killed in an accident at that project. After evidence regarding this accident was presented to the Fresno County Grand Jury, petitioner was indicted for manslaughter.

The issue is whether the California Penal Code exempts corporations from prosecution for manslaughter under Penal Code section 192. This is a question of legislative intent.

The Penal Code applies to corporations. The code defines "person" to include a corporation as well as a natural person. The Penal Code's sections on persons liable for crime, using unqualified language, make corporations proper defendants in any criminal case. . . . The California Penal Code applies to corporations, and if they commit crimes, they are liable for punishment.

Petitioner claims surprise at the prosecution of a corporation for manslaughter, asserting that the indictment was "totally unforeseeable," and that a corporation may be charged with crimes against "property," but "not against the person." This attempt to distinguish crimes against property from crimes against the person relies on the corporation's nature as an economically motivated entity. While a corporation may directly benefit from a crime against property, crimes against persons are not as directly linked to the profit motive. This argument is unsuccessful. It overlooks the substantial indirect economic benefits that may accrue to the corporation through crimes against the person. To get these economic benefits, corporate management may shortcut expensive safety precautions, respond forcibly to strikes, or engage in criminal anticompetitive behavior. If any such risk-taking is a corporate action, the corporation becomes a proper criminal defendant. . . .

[The court then distinguishes a Texas case as follows:]

This case exempts corporations from prosecution for manslaughter because Texas Penal Code Ann. Section 7.22(a) (1974) used the pronoun "he" to refer to offenders, and it accepts the argument that "soulless" corporations cannot formulate intent or, among other things, smoke tobacco. . . .

Although corporations in Texas may not be capable of forming "intent" or possess a "condition of the mind," California corporations can form intent, be reckless and commit acts through their agents. The criminal intent problem has not been squarely addressed, but corporations have been prosecuted for crimes of specific intent under the California Penal Code.

As the court in *Granite* indicates, not all states take the same position as California, but the criminal prosecutions of Ford Motor Company have focused attention on the issue of corporate criminal liability.

The Ford Pinto Case

On 13 September 1978, Ford Motor Company was indicted by a grand jury in Elkhart, Indiana, for three counts of reckless homicide stemming from the deaths of three teenagers who were killed in the fiery crash of a Ford Pinto. The victims died from burns suffered when the Pinto, upon rear-end collision at low speed, burst into flames. Ford was acquitted on 13 March 1980, but this was a precedent case concerning the criminal liability of corporations for the grossly negligent acts of their employees.

The Ford Pinto cases illustrate the interrelationship and sometimes confusion between tort and criminal law. The families of victims in these cases sued and won large judgments for wrongful death; surviving victims were compensated for their injuries. Some settled out of court; others took their cases to trial. The facts and issues involved are illustrated by the case of Richard Grimshaw. When Richard was thirteen he was a passenger in a Ford Pinto that was rear-ended. The driver of the car was injured and died a few days later. Richard suffered burns over most of his body. He "managed to survive but only through heroic medical measures." He underwent numerous surgeries for skin grafts and was facing another ten years of surgery at the time his case was appealed. He lost part of several fingers on one hand and portions of his left ear.

Richard Grimshaw sued Ford Motor Company in a civil suit and, after a six-month trial, won a judgment of $12.5 million in compensatory damages and $125 million in punitive damages. Ford's motion for a new trial was denied on the grounds that Grimshaw accept a reduction of the punitive award from $125 million to $2.5 million. Ford appealed on a number of legal issues; Grimshaw also appealed on several issues. The appellate court upheld the lower court and the judgment stood.

The Pinto represented Ford's attempt to produce a compact car that would sell for $2,000. The design, which began in 1968, and production were on a rush schedule. The reasons for considering the design of this car defective are complicated; the bottom line, however, was the location of the fuel tank. For design reasons, it was placed behind rather than over the rear axle as was the custom in other compacts at that time. This made the car less crush resistant and death by fire more probable than in other compacts. Evidence indicated that the design defects were known to Ford's corporate executives, that they were warned of the dangers, that the total cost to add additional crush space was $15.30, but that high-level officials decided to go ahead with the project for cost-saving reasons. The court concluded:[71]

Grimshaw v. Ford Motor Company

Through the results of the crash tests Ford knew that the Pinto's fuel tank and rear structure would expose consumers to serious injury or death in a 20- to 30-mile-per-hour collision. There was evidence that Ford could have corrected the hazardous design defects at minimal cost but decided to defer correction of the shortcomings by engaging in a cost-benefit analysis balancing human lives and limbs against corporate profits. Ford's institutional mentality was shown to be one of callous indifference to public safety. There was substantial evidence that Ford's conduct constituted "conscious disregard" of the probability of injury to members of the consuming public.

The *Grimshaw* case thus illustrates how gross negligence can be used in a civil suit to award punitive damages to a plaintiff. The fact that Ford was acquitted in the criminal trial does not mean that in a similar case another corporation will not be convicted. Corporations engaging in conduct that is grossly negligent or reckless may find themselves convicted of crimes.[72]

The Case of Six Flags

The Ford Motor Company indictments were followed in 1984 by indictments of the Six Flags Corporation, only the second time in our history that a state has brought an indictment against a corporation for any crime higher than negligent homicide. Two corporate executives were indicted for manslaughter and the Six Flags Corporation was indicted in New Jersey for aggravated manslaughter after eight young people died while trapped in a fire at an amusement park owned by the corporation. Aggravated manslaughter is defined in New Jersey as a form of criminal homicide committed by a person (which includes a corporation) who "purposely, knowingly, [or] recklessly . . . causes the death of another human being.''[73]

The Six Flags case raises the important issue of where we draw the line between permitting consumers to take a risk and pinning criminal (or civil) liability on corporations. In most amusement park cases, patrons assume the risk of injury from participating in the activities available at the park. This brief excerpt from *Murphy v. Steeplechase Amusement Co.*, a 1929 opinion of noted judge Benjamin Cardozo, gives the reasons. Cardozo denied civil recovery to a plaintiff who complained that he was injured on ''The Flopper,'' a ''moving belt, running upward on an inclined plane, on which passengers sit or stand'' and are thrown about during their excursion.[74]

Murphy v. Steeplechase Amusement Co.

A fall was foreseen as one of the risks of the adventure. There would have been no point to the whole thing, no adventure about it, if the risk had not been there. The very name above the gate, the Flopper, was warning to the timid. . . .

One who takes part in such a sport accepts the dangers that inhere in it so far as they are obvious and necessary. . . . The antics of the clown are not the paces of the cloistered cleric. The rough and boisterous joke, the horseplay of the crowd, evokes its own guffaws, but they are not the pleasures of tranquility. The plaintiff was not seeking a retreat for medi- tation. Visitors were tumbling about the belt to the merriment of onlook- ers when he made his choice to join them. He took the chance of a like fate, with whatever damage to his body might ensue from such a fall. The timorous may stay at home.

A different case would be here if the dangers inherent in the sport were obscure or unobserved . . . or so serious as to justify the belief that precautions of some kind must have been taken to avert them.

In denying the tort claim, Judge Cardozo, in the last paragraph of the excerpt, set the stage for other civil claims. Today those are extended to criminal prosecutions when the action or lack of action by the corporation is grossly negligent or reckless.

The deaths in the Six Flags case occurred after an unidentified youth's cigarette ignited the highly flammable foam-rubber padding in the Haunted House. The indictments are based on the argument that the corporation showed a reckless disregard for human life by using that rub- ber and by not providing adequate sprinkler systems to extinguish a fire.

Environmental Pollution

For years American industries have been faced with the problem of disposing of hazardous wastes, but in the past two decades the amount of waste has increased dramatically. With that increase has come greater understanding and appreciation of the environmental pollution that results from improper disposal. While physical scientists look for better methods of disposal, government agencies wrestle with enforcing the statutes and administrative rules developed to control the problem. Consumer advocates and political activists campaign to alert the public to the hazards of industrial waste and to place pressure on regulatory agencies charged with the responsibility of enforcing environmental protection laws.

A thorough discussion of environmental pollution is beyond the scope of this text. A 1986 *Harvard Law Review* article, for example, consumes 203 pages for an analysis of the history and current issues concerning toxic waste litigation. This section uses toxic waste as an example of the procedures and issues involved in attempting to regulate business activities through criminal law.[75]

Improper disposal of toxic waste may result in serious damage to the environment, creating hazards for all living creatures and plants. Although medical scientists do not know the extent and nature of the relationship between these hazards and human life and welfare, cancer; genetic mutation; birth defects; miscarriages; damage to the lungs, liver, kidneys, or nervous system; and death have been linked to toxic wastes. Contamination of water supplies is one of the greatest hazards of toxic wastes. "Of the 546 waste sites considered most dangerous by the Environmental Protection Agency (EPA), 410 directly threaten drinking water supplies. The EPA estimates that 90% of the 180,000 landfills, waste pits, and lagoons used to store waste liquids may threaten groundwater."[76]

Regulation of Environmental Pollution

Congress has passed statutes in an attempt to regulate the improper disposal of toxic wastes, "but Congress has not addressed the problem of compensating victims of hazardous waste releases." Courts have not solved the problem of how to prove that the improper disposal of toxic waste caused the injuries (or deaths) for which the actions are reported. "The difficulties of detecting, measuring, and assigning responsibilty for the harms of hazardous waste suggest that litigation may be an expensive and ineffective response to the problem."[77]

Most of the attempts to regulate toxic waste disposal involve administrative or civil law. In Chapter 1 we distinguished these types of law from criminal law, noting that unless the criminal law is invoked, people (and corporations) who violate regulations are technically not criminals. It may be, as Sutherland argued, that sociologists should study these violators to develop theories of why people violate regulations and laws, but it is also important to distinguish cases brought in the criminal courts from those processed through administrative agencies or civil courts. Unfortunately, this distinction is not always made, a common problem in criminology textbooks. Failure to make this distinction leads the reader to think that corporations violating administrative regulations or civil laws are violating criminal laws.

In 1980, Congress enacted CERCLA, the Comprehensive Environmental Response, Compensation, and Liability Act of 1980, described as "perhaps the most radical environmental statute in American history." This statute, along with RCRA, the Resource Conservation and Recovery Act passed in 1976 and amended in 1984, was enacted to provide the EPA with a mechanism for regulating generation, transportation, disposal, storage, and cleaning up of hazardous waste. RCRA provides both civil and criminal penalties for knowingly violating certain provisions.[78]

Implementation of these two federal regulatory statutes by EPA has been a problem, leading to slow progress and a major political scandal that "led to the firing of Rita Lavelle, the EPA's Associate Administrator for Hazardous Waste, and the resignation of EPA Administrator Anne Burford. . . . Ms. Lavelle was subsequently tried and convicted of both criminal perjury and impeding Congressional investigations of hazardous waste programs."[79]

Proper disposal of toxic wastes pointedly raises the issue of whether the civil (or administrative) law or the criminal law is the most effective regulatory measure. If people suffer property damage and personal injury when regulations and laws are violated, would they be better compensated by filing civil suits against the agency causing the pollution, getting a court order for the agency to discontinue the pollution and to pay damages to the victims, or would society (and individual victims) be better served if violators are prosecuted in the criminal courts—or should both the civil and the criminal law be utilized? No one has answered these questions to the satisfaction of most people, but one issue that is critical to an analysis of the question is deterrence. The question of deterrence is relevant to all white-collar crimes, not just corporate crimes.

The issue of how to react to corporations whose negligence results in injury or death to humans or damage to property arose again in March 1989 when Exxon's Valdez caused the great oil spill in Prince William Sound off the coast of Alaska. Nearly eleven million gallons of crude oil were dumped into the Sound. The Valdez captain, who was not on deck at the time the incident occurred, was acquitted of several serious charges and convicted of only negligent discharge of oil. Exxon will have to pay for the damages caused. But beyond that, should there be a *criminal* penalty against Exxon, and if so, what should that penalty be? Or as one commentator questioned, "Does an assault on nature make Exxon a criminal?"[80] In late 1989 Exxon sued Alaska, "Charging that the cleanup of the nation's worst oil spill was hindered because the state opposed the use of oil-dispersing chemicals."[81]

THE CONTROL OF WHITE-COLLAR CRIME

The key problem in controlling white-collar crimes is to determine which methods are most likely to deter them. In his analysis of violations within the pharmaceutical industry, John Braithwaite discusses methods of protecting consumers from the hazards of regulations designed to regulate the sale of drugs. Consider his conclusion:

> Often consumers will be better protected by a deal whereby the company agrees to dismiss certain responsible employees, immediately recall certain products from the market, institute restitutive measures and rehabilitate its organizational processes to insure that the offense will not be repeated. Legalists who opt for an absolutist principle of evenhanded enforcement of the law would cause the deaths of consumers while some cases slowly dragged through the courts.[82]

Clinard suggests that there are basically three ways to control corporate crime: improved ethics among those in corporate power; strong intervention of state and federal legal agencies, involving not only changes in corporate structure but sanctions aimed at deterring illegal behavior; and pressures from the public.[83]

With regard to corporate ethics, it might be appropriate to quote a former Lord Chancellor of England who quipped, "Did you ever expect a corporation to have a conscience, when it has no soul to be damned, and no body to be kicked?"[84] Pressures from the public have not been too great either; so that leaves criminal law.

The basic problem with using criminal law to control corporate conduct is that we really do not know how effective that approach is. Many people speculate about the deterrent effect of criminal law, but there is little empirical support for their conclusions. In fact, early studies questioned the alleged deterrent effect of criminal sanctions on white-collar criminals:

> In general, deterrence has not been realized, rehabilitation has been ignored, repeat offenders have not been removed from society, and victims have not been compensated. In large measure, these results are a product of the natural limits of the criminal justice system. As a consequence, a large number of successful white-collar crime prosecutions serve no more than a symbolic purpose.[85]

Others have argued that sanctions do have a deterrent effect on white-collar criminals; the problem has been that in the past "there appears to have been no appropriate research design for assessing the impact of sanctions applied to corporations." Using a research procedure based on the way in which corporations are organized and applying the procedure to evaluate the impact of prosecutions of corporate crime under Australia's Trade Practices Act, one investigator found that the sanctions were effective in reducing corporate recidivism for these reasons: First, in some cases, there was fear of revocation of a license to trade. Second, the fines might have been a deterrent. Third, company officials may have feared negative consumer reaction, although the evidence did not justify their unease. The evidence indicated that the main deterrent was concern about loss of reputation.[86]

This study, however, was conducted in another country and involved fines, not incarceration. It has been argued that for prison to be an effective deterrent for corporate criminals in this country, sentences would have to be lengthened and incarceration in hard-core prison facilities would have to become routine. It is doubtful, however, that Americans will go that far. Furthermore, it is quite possible that alternative forms of punishment will also be effective deterrents, particularly if they are applied consistently and fairly.[87]

Despite the disagreement over whether criminal sanctions are the best way to control white-collar crime, particularly corporate crime, it may be that criminal sanctions should be employed for symbolic reasons. It is argued that criminal sanctions serve society's need for retribution and help to preserve confidence in the system of rule by law.

It is important to keep in mind that the issue is not whether we should attempt to prevent or regulate white-collar crimes but which is the best method for doing so. Deciding that the civil law is the best response does not mean that the misconduct is considered less serious; it simply means that the civil law is perceived as the best method of control. Criminal charges are hard to prove; negligence is easier. The civil and criminal law are not mutually exclusive, but we must also consider the cost in time, attorney fees, and court personnel that are involved in an unsuccessful criminal prosecution. It is also important to understand that administrative regulation may be more effective than either the civil or the criminal law in controlling corporate conduct.

CONCLUSION

This chapter has focused on crimes of the business world. Although most of these crimes are economic, personal injury or death may also result from such white-collar crimes as mislabeling drugs, faulty design or construction of products, or environmental pollution. The crimes discussed in this chapter differ from those of the two previous chapters not so much in their impact on victims as in the way society and the legal system react to the offenders.

The discussion began with the problem of defining white-collar crime, looking at the contributions of Sutherland and those of sociologists who followed his development of the term. Particular attention was given to the term *corporate crime* and an explanation of how it differs from other white-collar crimes.

The main thrust of the chapter was an examination of a few examples of white-collar crimes. Some, like embezzlement, are usually committed by individuals in secret; others, like conspiracy, by definition involve more than one person. This discussion of white-collar crimes is illustrative, not exclusive. Greater attention was given to computer crimes and statutory attempts to curb them.

The cases of the Ford Pinto, Six Flags Amusement Park, and environmental pollution set the stage for a discussion of whether civil, administrative, or criminal law should be used to combat white-collar crime.

White-collar crimes and white-collar criminals cannot always be distinguished from organized crime and offenders involved in organized crime. The next chapter completes our discussion of types of crime and criminals by looking at organized crime and terrorism.

ENDNOTES

1. See Stanton Wheeler et al., ''White Collar Crimes and Criminals,'' *American Criminal Law Review* 25 (no. 3, 1988): 331–358.
2. Edwin H. Sutherland, *White Collar Crime* (Holt, Rinehart and Winston, 1959, 1961, paper ed.); originally published in 1949 by the Dryden Press.
3. *Ibid.*, p. 9.
4. *Ibid.*
5. August Bequai, *White-Collar Crime: A 20th-Century Crisis* (Lexington, Mass.: Heath, 1978), p. 2.
6. August Bequai, ''Wanted: The White Collar Ring,'' *Student Lawyer* 5 (May 1977): 45.
7. 42 U.S. Code, Section 3701 et seq.
8. Herbert Edelhertz, *The Nature, Impact and Prosecution of White-Collar Crime*, U.S. Department of Justice, Law Enforcement Assistance Administration (Washington, D.C.: U.S. Government Printing Office, 1970), pp. 19–20. For a recent analysis of white-collar crime, see Gary Green, *Occupational Crime* (Chicago: Nelson-Hall Publishers, 1990).
9. Albert J. Reiss, Jr., and Albert D. Biderman, *Data Sources on White-Collar Law-Breaking.* U.S. Department of Justice, National Institute of Justice (Washington, D.C.: U.S. Government Printing Office, 1980), p. xxviii.
10. Marshall B. Clinard, *Illegal Corporate Behavior* (Washington, D.C.: U.S. Government Printing Office, October 1979), Abstract.
11. *Ibid.*, p. 18.
12. See the classic study of Donald R. Cressey, *Other People's Money: A Study in the Social Psychology of Embezzlement* (New York: Free Press, 1953). See also Laura Shill Schrager and James F. Short, Jr., ''How Serious a Crime? Perceptions of Organizational and Common Crimes,'' Chapter 1 in Gilbert Geis and Ezra Stot-

land, eds., *White-Collar Crime: Theory and Research* (Beverly Hills, CA.: Sage Publications, 1980); and Peter Rossi et al., "The Seriousness of Crimes: Normative Structure and Individual Differences," *American Sociological Review* 39 (April 1974): 224–237. For more recent analyses, see Francis T. Cullen et al., "The Seriousness of Crime Revisited: Have Attitudes Toward White-Collar Crime Changed?" *Criminology* 20 (May 1982): 83–102, and Francis T. Cullen et al., "Public Support for Punishing White-Collar Crime: Blaming the Victim Revisited?" *Journal of Criminal Justice* 11 (1983): 481–493.

13. Clinard, *Illegal Corporate Behavior*, pp. xv, xvi. See also Marshall B. Clinard and Peter C. Yeager, *Corporate Crime* (New York: Free Press, 1980).

14. "GAO: Crime, Not Economic Conditions or Deregulation, Caused Thrift Crisis," *Tallahassee Democrat*, 24 March 1989, p. 7D, col. 5.

15. Robert F. Meier and James F. Short, Jr., "The Consequences of White-Collar Crime," in Herbert Edelhertz and Thomas D. Overcast, eds., *White-Collar Crime: An Agenda for Research* (Lexington, Mass.: D. C. Heath, 1982), p. 28. See also Ronald C. Kramer, "Corporate Criminality: The Development of an Idea," in Ellen Hochstedler, ed., *Corporations as Criminals* (Beverly Hills, CA.: Sage Publications, 1984), pp. 13–37.

16. John S. R. Shad, Quoted in *American Bar Association Journal* 73 (June 1, 1987).

17. Cressey, *Other People's Money*, p. 30. For a study of females who embezzle or defraud, see Dorothy Zietz, *Women Who Embezzle or Defraud: A Study of Convicted Felons* (New York: Praeger, 1981.)

18. Sutherland, *White Collar Crime*, p. 234. See also Edwin H. Sutherland, "Is 'White Collar Crime' Crime?" *American Sociological Review* 10 (April 1945): 132–139.

19. See Marshall B. Clinard and Richard Quinney, eds., *Criminal Behavior Systems: A Typology* (New York: Holt, Rinehart and Winston, 1967), p. 134. The second edition was published in 1986 by Anderson Publishing Co. See also Marshall B. Clinard, *The Black Market: A Study of White Collar Crime* (New York: Holt, Rinehart and Winston, 1952), pp. 309–310.

20. Michael L. Benson, "Denying the Guilty Mind: Accounting for Involvement in a White-Collar Crime," *Criminology* 23 (November 1985): 603.

21. Travis Hirschi and Michael Gottfredson, "Causes of White-Collar Crime," *Criminology* 25 (November 1987): 949.

22. *Ibid.*, p. 959.

23. *Ibid.*, pp. 970–971.

24. Darrell Steffensmeier, "On the Causes of 'White-Collar' Crime: An Assessment of Hirschi and Gottfredson's Claims," *Criminology* 27 (May 1989): 345–358. For a response by Hirschi and Gottfredson, see "The Significance of White-Collar Crime for a General Theory of Crime," *Criminology* 27 (May 1989): 359–371.

25. See J. W. Coleman, *Criminal Elite: The Sociology of White Collar Crime* (N.Y.: St. Martin's Press, 1985), and James William Coleman, "Toward an Integrated Theory of White-Collar Crime," *American Journal of Sociology* 93 (September 1987): 406–39. For a comment on the latter, see James Braithwaite, "White-Collar Crime, Competition, and Capitalism: Comment on Coleman," followed by Coleman's response, "Competition and the Structure of Industrial Society: Reply to Braithwaite," in *American Journal of Sociology* 94 (November 1988): 627–636. For a review of Coleman's book, see Robert F. Meier, "Review Essay," *Criminology* 24 (May 1986): 415–420.

26. Clinard, *Illegal Corporate Behavior*, Abstract.

27. "Corporate Crime: The Untold Story," *U.S. News & World Report*, 6 September 1982, p. 25.

28. "Crime in the Suites," *Time*, 10 June 1985, p. 65.

29. Leonard Orland, "Reflections on Corporate Crime: Law in Search of Theory and Scholarship," *American Criminal Law Review* 17 (Spring 1980): 508.

30. T. R. Young, "Corporate Crime: A Critique of the Clinard Report," *Contemporary Crises* 5 (July 1981): 323–326. See also Harold C. Barnett, "Corporate Capitalism, Corporate Crime," *Crime & Delinquency* 27 (January 1981): 4–23.

31. Steven Box, *Power, Crime, and Mystification* (London: Tavistock, 1983), pp. xi, 35, 36.

32. 26 U.S.C., Section 7201.

33. See United States v. Coppola, 300 F.Supp. 932 (D.C. Conn. 1969), *aff'd*, 425 F.2d 660 (2d Cir. 1969).

34. United States v. Berger, 325 F.Supp. 1297, 1303 (S.D.N.Y. 1971), *aff'd*, 456 F.2d 1349 (2d Cir. 1972), *cert. denied*, 409 U.S. 892 (1972).

35. 18 U.S.C., Section 201 et. seq. For a discussion, see "The Federal Bribery Statute and Special Interest Campaign Contributions," *Journal of Criminal Law & Criminology* 79 (Winter, 1989): 1347–1373.

36. "25 Charged in Bribery of Asbestos Inspector," *New York Times*, 8 January 1988, p. 14, col. 4.

37. See 11 U.S.C., Section 1951 (b) (2). For a discussion, see "Extortion," *American Criminal Law Review* 19 (1981–82): 396–408.

38. *Yoder v. State*, 493 P.2d 1141 (Okla. Crim. 1972).

39. See Model Penal Code, Section 224.7, Deceptive Business Practices. See also Model Penal Code, Section 223.3.

40. "Bakker is Convicted on All Counts; First Felon Among TV Evangels," *New York Times*, 6 October 1989, p. 1, col. 3.

41. "LaRouche Guilty of Fraud Conspiracy," *New York Times*, 17 December 1988, p. 9, col. 4.

42. Partian v. State, 225 S.E. 2d 736 (Ga. App. 1976).

43. Michael J. Comer, *Corporate Fraud*, 2d ed. (United Kingdom: McGraw-Hill, 1985), p. 5.

44. John P. Clark and Richard C. Hollinger, *Theft by Employees in Work Organizations* (Washington, D.C.: U.S. Department of Justice, September 1983), p. 2.

45. M. Lipman and W. R. McGraw, "Employee Theft: a $40 Billion Industry," *Annals of the American Academy of Political and Social Science* 1988: 51–59.

46. "Stealing: Long Coffee Breaks, Mental Health Days Rob Your Employer," *Miami Herald*, 22 September 1988, p. F1, col. 5.

47. See H. Blair White, "Why Did the Antitrust Division Dismiss the Case?" *American Bar Association Journal* 64 (November 1978): 1667–1671.

48. Kurt Eichenwalk, "Boesky Loses Bid To Cut Jail Term," *New York Times*, 27 April 1989, p. 29, col. 3.

49. "Inmate Boesky Is Keeping Fit," *Miami Herald*, 22 June 1989, p. 1, col. 2.

50. "Let's Make a Deal," *Time*, 2 January 1989, p. 84.

51. For discussions of legal problems with insider trading, see Helen A. Garten, "Insider Trading in the Corporate Interest," *Wisconsin Law Review* 1987 (no. 4): 573–640, and the symposium on insider trading in the *American Criminal Law Review* 26 (1988). See also James D. Cox, "Insider Trading: Regulation of Activity Is 'In Trouble,'" *Trial* 24 (September 1988): 22–28; 93–95.

52. 15 U.S. Code, Section 1–7.

53. See Symposium, "Trade Associations and the Antitrust Law," *Brooklyn Law Review* 46 (Winter 1980): 181–247.

54. For a discussion of entrapment in relation to ABSCAM, see Joseph M. Livermore, "Enforcement Workshop: ABSCAM Entrapment," *Criminal Law Bulletin* 17 (January–February 1981): 69–72.

55. Richard Harris, "Reflections: Crime in the F.B.I." *New Yorker*, 8 August 1977, p. 29.

56. Preface to Harry Rositzke, *The CIA's Secret Operations: Espionage, Counterespionage, and Covert Action* (New York: Reader's Digest Press, 1977), p. xvii.

57. Alan Goldstein, "Computer Crime Wave," *St. Petersburg Times*, 22 April 1989, p. B6, col. 2.

58. John Markoff, "How A Need for Challenge Seduced Computer Expert," *New York Times*, 6 November 1988, p. 1, col. 1.

59. August Bequai, *Computer Crime* (Lexington, Mass.: Heath, 1978), p. 4.

60. Discussed in *Computer Crime: Criminal Resource Manual*. National Criminal Justice Information and Statistics Service (Washington, D.C.: U.S. Government Printing Office, 1979), pp. 9–29. For additional bibliographic sources, see Reba A. Best and D. Cheryn Picquet, compilers, *Computer Crime, Abuse, Liability and Security: A Comprehensive Bibliography, 1970–1984* (Jefferson, N.C.: 1985).

61. Ivan J. Hathaway, "TV Newsmen Beg for a Break, Get Probation," *Tampa Tribune*, 20 May 1989, p. B1, col. 1.

62. Cal. Penal Code, Section 502 (1981 Supp).

63. Comprehensive Crime Control Act of 1984, U.S.C. 18, Section 1030(a),(c) (1984).

64. U.S. Department of Justice. *The Investigation of Computer Crime: An Operational Guide to White-Collar Crime Enforcement* (Washington, D.C.: U.S. Government Printing Office, 1980), p. 5.

65. For a discussion of computer security, see John M. Carroll, *Computer Security*, 2d ed. (Stoneham, MA.: Butterworth Publishers, 1987). See also Dorothy B. Francis, *Computer Crime* (Bergenfield, N.J.: E. P. Dutton and Company, 1987).

66. U.S.C., Section 552a (1976).

67. Dr. Joseph Weizenbaum, Professor of Computer Science at the Massachusetts Institute of Technology, quoted in "Laws to Bar Computer Misuses Remain Scarce," *New York Times*, 8 August 1983, p. 1, col. 4.

68. National Criminal Justice Information and Statistics Service, *Computer Crime* (Washington, D.C.: U.S. Government Printing Office, 1979), pp. 53–57.

69. See Nancy Frank, "Unintended Murder and Corporate Risk-taking: Defining the Concept of Justifiability," *Journal of Criminal Justice* 16 (no. 1, 1988): 17–24.

70. *Granite Construction Co. v. People*, 149 Cal. App.3d 465, 466, 467, 471, 472 (Ct. App. 5th Dist. 1983), *rehearing denied*, 26 January 1984; footnotes and citations omitted. For the implications of the intent question to the development of sociological theory, see also Donald R. Cressey, "The Poverty of Theory in Corporate Crime Research," in William S. Laufer and Freda Adler, eds., *Advances in Criminological Theory*, vol. 1 (New Brunswick, N.J.: Transaction Books, 1989).

71. *Grimshaw v. Ford Motor Company*, 174 Cal. Rptr. 348, 384 (1981).

72. For a detailed discussion of corporate crime and criminal liability, see Ellen Hochstedler, ed., *Corporations as Criminals* (Beverly Hills, CA.: Sage Publications, 1984). For a detailed discussion of the Ford Pinto case, see Francis Cullen et al., *The Ford Pinto Case and Beyond* (Cincinnati: Anderson Publishing Company, 1987).

73. N.J., Section 2C:11-4(c). For a discussion of this case, see John E. Stoner, "Cor-

porate Criminal Liability for Homicide: Can the Criminal Law Control Corporate Behavior?" *Southwestern Law Journal* 38 (1985): 1275–1296.

74. *Murphy v. Steeplechase Amusement Co.*, 250 N.Y. 479 (N.Y. 1929).

75. This symposium issue of the journal will be relied on for this discussion. See "Toxic Waste Litigation," *Harvard Law Review* 99 (1986): 1458–1661.

76. *Ibid.*, p. 1463, footnote omitted.

77. *Ibid.*, p. 1464.

78. *Ibid.*, pp. 1464–1473. RCRA is found at 42 U.S.C., Section 9601-9657 (1982), with the 1984 amendments codified at 42 U.S.C., Section 6901-6991 (1985 Supp.). CERCLA is codified at 42 U.S.C., Section 9607-9657 (1982). For a discussion, see Christopher Harris et al., "Criminal Liability for Violations of Federal Hazardous Waste Law: the 'Knowledge' of Corporations and their Executives," *Wake Forest Law Review* 23 (no. 2, 1988): 203–236.

79. See *New York Times*, 2 December 1983, p. A1, col. 1, and *New York Times*, 10 March 1983, p. A1, col. 6, cited in "Toxic Waste," 1474.

80. Stephen Labaton, *New York Times*, 23 April 1989, Section 4-1, col. 4. In general, see Donald J. Rebovich, "Policing Hazardous Waste Crime: the Importance of Regulatory/Law Enforcement Strategies and Cooperation in Offender Identification and Prosecution," *Criminal Justice Quarterly* 9 (Fall 1987): 173–184, and John DeCicco and Edward Bonanno, "A Comparative Analysis of the Criminal Environmental Laws of The Fifty States: The Need for Statutory Uniformity as a Catalyst for Effective Enforcement of Existing and Proposed Laws," *Criminal Justice Quarterly* 9 (Summer 1988): 216–220.

81. "Exxon Sues Alaska on Cleanup of Oil, Charging Hindrance," *New York Times*, 25 October 1989, p. 13, col. 6.

82. John Braithwaite, *Corporate Crime in the Pharmaceutical Industry* (London: Routledge & Kegan Paul, 1984), pp. 305–306, quoted in Gilbert Geis, "Criminological Perspectives on Corporate Regulation: A Review of Recent Research," in Brent Fisse and Peter A. French, eds., *Corrigible Corporations & Unruly Law* (San Antonio, Tex.: Trinity University Press, 1985), pp. 70–71. See this collection of excellent essays on the control of corporations.

83. Clinard, *Illegal Corporate Behavior*, p. 214. For a discussion of each approach, see pp. 214–228. See also Ralph Nader et al., *Taming the Giant Corporation* (New York: Norton, 1976); Clarence C. Walton, ed., *The Ethics of Corporate Conduct* (Englewood Cliffs, N.J.: Prentice-Hall, 1977); and Marshall Clinard, *Corporate Ethics and Crime: The Role of Middle Management* (Beverly Hills, CA.: Sage Publications, 1983).

84. Quoted in John C. Coffee, Jr., "'No Soul to Damn: No Body to Kick': An Unscandalized Inquiry Into the Problem of Corporate Punishment," *Michigan Law Review* 79 (January 1981): 386.

85. Robert W. Ogren, "The Ineffectiveness of the Criminal Sanction in Fraud and Corruption Cases: Losing the Battle Against White-Collar Crime," *The American Criminal Law Review* 11 (Summer 1973): 960. Concerning the kinds of sentences imposed on corporate offenders, see Michael L. Benson and Esteban Walker, "Sentencing the White-Collar Offender," *American Sociological Review* 53 (April 1988): 294–302.

86. Andrew Hopkins, "Controlling Corporate Deviance," *Criminology* 18 (August 1980): 198–214.

87. See Alfred S. Pelaez, "Of Crime—and Punishment: Sentencing the White-Collar Criminal," *Duquesne Law Review* 18 (Summer 1980): 823–835. For a discussion

of the philosophy of punishment and white-collar criminals, see John Braithwaite, "Challenging Just Deserts: Punishment of White-Collar Criminals," *Journal of Criminal Law & Criminology* 73 (Summer 1982): 723–763. See also John Hagan and Patricia Parker, "White-Collar Crime and Punishment: The Class Structure and Legal Sanctioning of Securities Violations," *American Sociological Review* 50 (June 1985): 302–316.

CHAPTER 10

This chapter discusses crimes that damage and destroy property and also cause injury and death. The first, organized crime, is primarily a property crime as far as the public is concerned; the second, terrorism, more frequently results in human injuries, both psychological and physical, and in death. Both organized crime and terrorism are crimes of central focus today; their impact on all people is extensive.

The first part of the chapter examines the concept of organized crime. The second half focuses on terrorism, a crime that has received considerable attention recently as terrorist acts and the extent of those acts have increased.

OUTLINE

Organized Crime and Terrorism

KEY TERMS

bribery
conspiracy
extortion
immunity (criminal)
loan sharking
Model Penal Code
organized crime
racketeering
sedition
Stockholm syndrome
syndicate
terrorism
treason
white-collar crime

The first three chapters of Part III cover violent and property crimes, but, as noted, it is often difficult to separate crimes into these two categories. Robbery is usually a violent crime; but an act of stealing, such as a purse from a person, could be theft (property crime) or robbery depending on the degree of force used. Some offenders engage in property and violent crimes and thus cannot be categorized as property or violent offenders. Despite these problems, most of the crimes discussed in Chapters 7, 8, and 9 can be categorized as essentially either violent or property crimes.

The two crime categories covered in this chapter involve both property and violent crimes. Organized crime results in extensive property losses to businesses and individuals; the hierarchy within organized crime is known for its use of violence to accomplish established goals. Likewise, terrorism, often used as a weapon to obtain political goals, encompasses vast loss and destruction of property; increases the cost of travel and other activities; and frequently results in human injury, often leading to death. Yet both organized crime and terrorism manifest some of the traits and characteristics of those who commit violent personal crimes, ordinary property crimes, and white-collar crimes.

ORGANIZED CRIME

The crimes of the underworld have for a long time provided Americans with a source of mystery and excitement and have often captured attention through movies and books. In his recently revised text on organized crime, Jay Albanese indicates that over 13,000 million copies of *The Godfather*, a novel published in 1969, have been sold. The book is "still the most popular book about crime ever published in North America." The movie, one of the most successful ever made, has grossed $166 million. According to Albanese, the difficulties of separating fact from fiction in organized crime has made scientific analysis difficult, probably accounting for the lack of social science emphasis on the study of organized crime until relatively recently.[1]

Despite the lack of scholarly work on organized crime, the successes of the underworld in eluding attempts at law enforcement are well known; in many cases, underworld activities have provided services and commodities labeled illegal by statute but considered important to the enjoyment of our daily lives. In such cases, unsuccessful law enforcement may not be viewed as a problem; indeed, the attempt of the police to enforce the laws may be seen as a nuisance. But organized crime has so infiltrated legitimate businesses that the relationship between organized crime and legitimate society is often one of cooperation.

Concept of Organized Crime

The first problem in an analysis of organized crime is to define the term. There is little agreement on the definition, as indicated in Exhibit 10.1, which also contains a listing and brief discussion of general characteristics of organized crime. In some countries the term **organized crime** is synonymous with professional crime, a concept discussed in an earlier chapter. It is true that all professional crime is to some extent organized. Early sociologists used the term *organized crime* to describe professional criminals in contrast to amateur criminals. According to Alfred Lindesmith, organized crime is "usually professional crime . . . involving a system of specifically defined relationships with mutual obligations and privileges." Edwin Sutherland and Donald Cressey defined organized crime as the "association of a small group of criminals for the execution of a certain type of crime."[2] These definitions include any small group of criminals who organize to engage in their professional work.

In recent years, however, the term *organized crime* has been used more narrowly. Many people think of organized crime as a national or international syndicate that infiltrates at the local and national level. But this view is not accepted by many social scientists; thus, it is important to distinguish the two major approaches to defining organized crime: (1) the law-enforcement perspective and (2) the social and economic perspective.

The Law Enforcement Perspective: Organized Crime and the Mafia

The view of organized crime that is most common is the law-enforcement perspective. The President's Commission on Law Enforcement and Administration of Justice, in its 1967 report, defined organized crime as "a society that seeks to operate outside the control of the American people and their working government." Organized crime, according to that report, is an organization of thousands of criminals in this country; they operate in a very complex organizational structure, and they have rules that are even more rigid and more strictly enforced than those of legitimate government. Money and power are their goals. They infiltrate legitimate as well as illegitimate businesses.[3]

The law-enforcement approach to analyzing organized crime has also been called the governmental, President's Task Force, traditional, or evolutional-centralization approach. It is most frequently associated with the work of the late criminologist, Donald Cressey, who was one of six consultants to this commission. It was Cressey, however, "who towered over the others and came to be attributed the status of major spokesperson for the Commission and its report." Donald Cressey, a prolific writer in many areas of criminology, is recognized for his outstanding contributions to the study of organized crime.[4]

EXHIBIT 10.1

Organized Crime: An Overview

What Is Organized Crime?

Although organized crime has been considered a problem throughout the century, no universally accepted definition of the term has been established. The President's Commission on Organized Crime, for example, defines the criminal group involved in organized crime as "a continuing, structured collectivity of persons who utilize criminality, violence, and a willingness to corrupt in order to gain and maintain power and profit."

Some characteristics of organized crime are generally cited:

● **Organizational continuity:** Organized crime groups ensure that they can survive the death or imprisonment of their leaders and can vary the nature of their activities to take advantage of changing criminal opportunities.

● **Hierarchical structure:** All organized crime groups are headed by a single leader and structured into a series of subordinate ranks, although they may vary in the rigidity of their hierarchy. Nationwide organizations may be composed of multiple separate chapters or "families," each unit generally headed by its own leader who is supported by the group's hierarchy of command. Intergroup disputes, joint ventures, and new membership are generally reviewed by a board composed of the leaders of the most powerful individual chapters. For example, La Cosa Nostra currently is estimated to include 24 individual "families" all under the general authority of a "National Commission" comprised of an estimated nine bosses.

● **Restricted membership:** Members must be formally accepted by the group after a demonstration of loyalty and a willingness to commit criminal acts. Membership may be limited by race or common background and generally involves a lifetime commitment to the group, which can be enforced through violent group actions.

● **Criminality/violence/power:** Power and control are key organized crime goals and may be obtained through criminal activity of one type or in multiple activities. Criminal activity may be designed directly to generate "income" or to support the group's power through bribery, violence, and intimidation. Violence is used to maintain group loyalty and to intimidate outsiders and is a threat underlying all group activity. Specific violent criminal acts include, for example, murder, kidnaping, arson, robbery, and bombings.

● **Legitimate business involvement:** Legitimate businesses are used to "launder" illegal funds or stolen merchandise. For example, illegal profits from drug sales can be claimed as legitimate profits of a noncriminal business whose accounting records have been appropriately adjusted. Legitimate business involvement also elevates the social status of organized crime figures.

● **Use of specialists:** Outside specialists, such as pilots, chemists, and arsonists, provide services under contract to organized crime groups on an intermittent or regular basis.

Organized Crime Groups Often Are Protected by Corrupt Officials in the Government and Private Sector

Such officials include inspectors who overlook violations, accountants who conceal assets, financial officers who fail to report major cash transactions, law enforcement officers who provide enforcement activity information to drug traffickers, and attorneys who have government witnesses intimidated to change their testimony. The public also supports organized crime by sometimes knowingly or unknowingly purchasing illegal goods and "hot" merchandise.

Organized Crime Groups Are Involved in Many Different Activities

In addition to its well known involvement in illegal drugs, organized crime is also involved in prostitution, gambling, and loan sharking operations and has been shown to have infiltrated legitimate industries such as construction, waste removal, wholesale and retail distribution of goods, hotel and restaurant operations, liquor sales, motor vehicle repairs, real estate, and banking.

SOURCE: Bureau of Justice Statistics, *Report to the Nation on Crime and Justice; the Data,* 2d ed. (Washington, D.C.: U. S. Department of Justice, 1988), p. 8.

EXHIBIT 10.2

Characteristics of Organized Crime

1. Organized crime is a type of conspiratorial crime, sometimes involving the hierarchical coordination of a number of persons in the planning and execution of illegal acts, or in the pursuit of a legitimate objective by unlawful means. Organized crime involves continuous commitment by key members, although some individuals with specialized skills may participate only briefly in the ongoing conspiracies. . . .

2. Organized crime has economic gain as its primary goal, though some of the participants in the conspiracy may have achievement of power or status as their objective. . . .

3. Organized crime is not limited to patently illegal enterprises or unlawful services such as gambling, prostitution, drugs, loansharking, or racketeering. It also includes such sophisticated activities as laundering of illegal money through a legitimate business, land fraud, and computer manipulation. . . .

4. Organized crime employs predatory tactics such as intimidation, violence, and corruption, and it appeals to greed to accomplish its objectives and preserve its gains. . . .

5. By experience, custom, and practice, organized crime's conspiratorial groups are usually very quick and effective in controlling and disciplining their members, associates, and victims. Therefore, organized crime participants are unlikely to disassociate themselves from the conspiracies and are in the main incorrigible. . . .

6. Organized crime is not synonymous with the Mafia or La Cosa Nostra, the most experienced, diversified, and possibly best disciplined of the conspiratorial groups. . . .

7. Organized crime does not include terrorists dedicated to political change, although organized criminals and terrorists have some characteristics in common, including types of crimes committed and strict organizational structures. . . .

SOURCE: National Advisory Commission on Criminal Justice Standards and Goals, *Organized Crime Report of the Task Force on Organized Crime* (Washington, D.C.: U.S. Government Printing Office, 1976), pp. 7–8.

When the Task Force on Organized Crime of the National Advisory Committee on Criminal Justice Standards and Goals considered the definition of organized crime, it refused to attempt a definition that would include all the criminal activities covered by all state and federal statutes. Instead, the task force chose to delineate the major characteristics of organized crime, which are enumerated in Exhibit 10.2.

Social and Economic Perspectives: Organized Crime as a Function of American Society

A second approach views organized crime as "an integral part of the nation's social, political, and economic life—as one of the major social ills, such as poverty or racism, that grew with urban living in America." Organized crime does often involve minority groups, but that involvement is seen by this second perspective as the *process* by which those groups begin to establish themselves and gain power in this society. As more acceptable avenues for this process become available, the criminals may move into legitimate enterprises while other groups move into organized crime to begin their process of integration into the society.[5]

Another version of this functional perspective comes from economists who view organized crime as operating just like other economic enterprises. Organized crime supplies goods and services to customers seeking those goods and services. Even when the supply is considered illegal by the government at a given time—for example, liquor during Prohibition—the economic process is the same as it would be if the enterprise were not defined as criminal. In organized crime, however, the *proceeds* from these illegal sales are used to engage in other illegal activities, such as corrupting public officials to provide protection from prosecution.[6]

Analysis of the Concept of Organized Crime

The two approaches to the concept of organized crime have some common elements. In both perspectives, the activity is organized and goes on beyond the life of any particular members. Both perspectives see the need for and the existence of some degree of protection, which comes from corrupting public officials. Both perspectives view organized crime as providing illegal goods and services demanded by the public. These similarities have led to this definition of organized crime:

> [It is] a persisting form of criminal activity that brings together a client-public which demands a range of goods and services defined as illegal. It is a structure or network of individuals who produce or supply those goods and services, use the capital to expand into other legitimate or illegitimate activities, and corrupt public officials with the aim of gaining their protection.[7]

Despite this attempt to articulate a definition of organized crime that is broad enough to include the two perspectives, the view of organized crime as roughly synonymous with the national (or internationl) crime syndicate characterized by Italian membership persists. This perspective has obvious implications in terms of attempts to eradicate or control crime. It leads to a focus on catching the notorious underworld criminals rather than on making changes in the social system. The lack of a generally accepted definition of organized crime also results in a variety of definitions throughout the various states.[8]

History of Organized Crime

Many scholars believe that organized crime did not exist on a large scale before this century and that its development as a large-scale operation was a result of Prohibition. The history of organized crime is thus traced back to the Volstead Act, the Eighteenth Amendment, passed in 1919, which made it illegal to sell and distribute alcohol. Others argue that although Prohibition gave organized crime "a distinctive vigor and form," the roots can be found in many American cities long before. However, our extremely puritanical approach to the suppression of vice, of which Prohibition is an example, has provided a fertile bed for the growth of organized crime. Organized crime can provide the services the public wants but are forbidden by law to enjoy.

A study of the history of organized crime must include a brief introduction to the reports of four major official studies that preceded the most recent government report. The Committee to Investigate Crime in Interstate Commerce, the Kefauver Committee, named after its chair, found widespread involvement of organized crime in gambling and other forms of racketeering.[9] The Select Committee on Improper Activities in the Labor or Management Field, the McClellan Committee, reported numerous incidents of organized criminal activity among labor unions.[10] The President's Commission on Law Enforcement and Administration of Justice found that organized crime is widespread among American cities in such activities as gambling, narcotics traffic, and **loan sharking** and that, in addition, organized criminals have invested some of their money in legitimate businesses in which they indirectly have some control.[11] Finally, the National Advisory Committee on Criminal Justice Standards and Goals, which issued its report on organized crime in 1976, concluded that organized crime had infiltrated legitimate as well as illegitimate businesses and was spreading rapidly.[12]

Organization of Organized Crime

Organized crime has a highly organized structure with the lords of the underworld at the top. These persons make all the important decisions, and since they are rarely detected, not much is known about their career patterns. At the bottom are those offenders who deal directly with the public; they frequently resemble conventional offenders in their career patterns.

Organized crime is directed by a **syndicate,** a group of persons who organize to carry out their mutual financial interests. There is disagreement about whether there is one syndicate in charge of all organized crime in this country or a number of syndicates. Some contend there is one syndicate, the *Mafia,* operating out of New York and Chicago and run by Italians from Sicily. This was the approach taken by the Kefauver Committee.[13] Others deny the existence of the Mafia.[14] According to the 1967

President's Commission, organized crime is controlled by twenty-four groups known as families. The membership of a family ranges from 20 to 700 individuals. The families operate as criminal cartels in large American cities; most cities have only one family, although New York City has five. The structure of a family is diagrammed in Figure 10.1.[15]

Each family is headed by a *boss*, who has complete authority over the family and can only be overruled by the national advisory commission. Reporting to the boss is the *underboss*, who, like the vice-president of a company, acts in the absence of the president and serves as a mediator between the boss and lower-level management. The *consigliere*, or counselor, holds a position analogous to a legal adviser in a corporation. The lieutenants, or *caporegima*, are the middlemen in the management structure. They serve as buffers between the boss or underboss and internal or external conflicts. The lower-level management comprises soldiers who "operate the illegal enterprises on a commission basis or own illicit or licit businesses under the protection of the family."[16]

Many social scientists disagree with the use of this bureaucratic analogy, which they say is too rigid to explain the social, economic, and political dynamics of the organized crime family. They describe the family in *kinship terms*, maintaining that organized crime families are called families because many are actually tied by marriage or blood and because they exhibit many of the complex ties characteristic of families.[17] Organized crime has also been analyzed in terms of an economic system and as an organization of power relationships.[18]

According to the 1967 President's Commission, the organized crime families are in frequent communication and their membership is exclusively Italian. The name of the organization has been changed from the Mafia to *La Cosa Nostra*, which means "our thing." The twenty-four groups control other groups, which may have members from other ethnic backgrounds. The ultimate authority in the organization is the *commission*, which serves primarily as a judicial body. The commission is made up of nine to twelve men, not all of equal rank and power. The respect they can command and the power they can wield seem to be related to their own wealth, their tenure on the commission, and their positions as heads of large families or groups.[19]

A subsequent presidential commission, discussed in more detail later, in its 1986 report did not define precisely the terms *Mafia* and *La Cosa Nostra* (LCN) and insisted that although the report is centered on LCN, organized crime is broader than that. LCN, however, is the "group most entrenched in labor and business," more frequently infiltrating legitimate business than any other organized crime group.[20]

Despite the focus on the Mafia and LCN, it is important to emphasize that organized crime today is much broader. As Exhibit 10.3 indicates, organized crime goes beyond the Italian influence, including other ethnic groups as well as motorcycle gangs and prison gangs. Recent reports on organized crime in some areas have focused on the growing problems

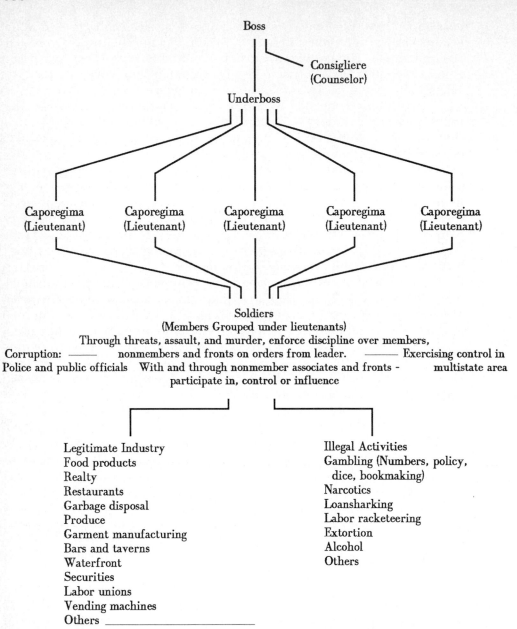

Boss
Consigliere
(Counselor)
Underboss

Caporegima
(Lieutenant)
Caporegima
(Lieutenant)
Caporegima
(Lieutenant)
Caporegima
(Lieutenant)
Caporegima
(Lieutenant)

Soldiers
(Members Grouped under lieutenants)
Through threats, assault, and murder, enforce discipline over members,
Corruption: ——— nonmembers and fronts on orders from leader. ——— Exercising control in
Police and public officials   With and through nonmember associates and fronts -   multistate area
participate in, control or influence

Legitimate Industry
Food products
Realty
Restaurants
Garbage disposal
Produce
Garment manufacturing
Bars and taverns
Waterfront
Securities
Labor unions
Vending machines
Others _____

Illegal Activities
Gambling (Numbers, policy,
   dice, bookmaking)
Narcotics
Loansharking
Labor racketeering
Extortion
Alcohol
Others

FIGURE 10.1 **Organized crime and terrorism** *SOURCE:* President's Commission on Law Enforcement and Administration of Justice, *The Challenge of Crime in a Free Society* (Washington, D.C.: U.S. Government Printing Office, 1967), p. 194.

EXHIBIT 10.3

The Impact of Organized Crime

PRESIDENT'S COMMISSION, 1967

In many ways organized crime is the most sinister kind of crime in America. The men who control it have become rich and powerful by encouraging the needy to gamble, by luring the troubled to destroy themselves with drugs, by extorting the profits of honest and hardworking businessmen . . . by maiming or murdering those who oppose them, by bribing those who are sworn to destroy them. Organized crime is not merely a few preying upon a few. In a very real sense it is dedicated to subverting not only American institutions, but the very decency and integrity that are the most cherished attributes of a free society. . . . The extraordinary thing about organized crime is that America has tolerated it for so long.[1]

PRESIDENT'S COMMISSION, 1983

Criminal cartels have existed and flourished in the Nation for decades. Although law enforcement authorities have been successful in prosecuting individuals involved in these illegal activities, the power of organized crime as an institution continues unabated. The criminal enterprise is so complex and so sophisticated that it continues to function even as literally hundreds of individual criminals are convicted. Like its legitimate corporate counterpart, the criminal organization continues its existence notwithstanding the loss of individual "executives." . . .

Organized crime has become a scourge of modern society with direct responsibility for a host of social ills. . . . Organized crime victimizes tens of thousands of working people each year by invading their pension funds and skimming the hard-earned proceeds of their labor. . . .

Organized crime in its traditional form poses a sufficient danger to justify an in-depth investigation and analysis. Today, however, we are also confronted with new forms of illegal activity. Drug rings which operate out of Latin America and have ties in the Sunbelt represent a significant new source of dangerous narcotics. Motorcycle gangs throughout the West and Southwest and prison gangs produce a reign of terror through extortion and other violent activities. In many of our urban areas, localized ethnic criminal groups prey on recent immigrants as well as small businessmen and other local community figures.

The threat of organized crime today also differs from the past by reason of its sheer size. The menace is larger and still growing.[2]

[1] President's Commission on Law Enforcement and Administration of Justice, *The Challenge of Crime in a Free Society* (Washington, D.C.: U.S. Government Printing Office, 1967), p. 209.
[2] Irving R. Kaufman, Chair, The President's Commission on Organized Crime, Public Hearing, 29 November 1983, published in President's Commission on Organized Crime, *Organized Crime: Federal Law Enforcement Perspective* (Washington, D.C.: U.S. Government Printing Office, 1983), pp. 3–5.

with Asian criminal organizations that have selected Asian businesses as their targets for armed robbery, extortion, burglary, prostitution, gambling, and murder.

The murder of two federal drug agents in Pasadena, California, in early 1988 led to the comment that "the fastest-growing force in organized crime on the West Coast" is the Chinese underworld. Authorities reported little success in dealing with this problem four years after the President's Commission on Organized Crime concluded that the involvement of Chinese in organized crime was an increasing problem. It is estimated that 80 percent of the merchants in Los Angeles' Chinatown have paid money for extortion from Chinese involved in organized crime. In addition to extortion, the Chinese are also involved in other types of crime, such as drug smuggling, racketeering, prostitution, and money laundering, most of which are discussed later in this chapter.[21]

New York City has become the hub of Chinese organized criminals, whose influence now extends to many large cities throughout the United States. According to one official, "Chinese criminals are the No. 1 emerging organized-crime group in New York—not just in drugs, but in many, many things."[22]

Ethnic gangs in organized crime are not limited to the Chinese. Other Asian groups are involved as are Jamaicans. All are difficult to detect. The Chinese and other Asian groups are "far more fluid [than the Italians]. . . . They keep very tight control of their people, too. . . . We have seen cases where people have been killed on the suspicion that they might be talking to police." Jamaican gangs "are among the hardest to track because they change names and appearance so often."[23]

Organized Crime and White-Collar Crime: A Comparison

The difference between organized crime and **white-collar crime** is not in the type of activities but in the *methods* for carrying out those activities. Violence is more frequently characteristic of organized crime. Another difference is that organized crime controls illegitimate businesses such as illegal traffic in drugs, gambling, and prostitution. Organized crime is more often associated with **racketeering,** the systematic **extortion** of money.[24]

More recent analyses by sociologists note the similarities and interrelationships between corporate crime and organized crime. Some argue that the relationship is one of mutual benefit, whereas others believe that the structure of legitimate society is necessary for the successful existence of organized crime.[25] Organized crime continues to move into new businesses. As one veteran investigator said, "These people are like cockroaches. . . . You step on them one place and they turn up somewhere else."[26]

Despite its similarity to white-collar crime, organized crime was described by the 1967 President's Commission as "the most sinister kind of crime in America." Judge Irving Kaufman, appointed by President Reagan to chair the President's Crime Commission in 1983, described the commission's study of organized crime as "cancer research." The commission reported that organized crime may be costing Americans more than $100 billion a year, cited a study "depicting organized crime as an enterprise that could rival the size of the American metal or textile industries," and indicated that the United States might be losing up to $6.5 billion in taxes each year because of organized crime.[27]

Group Support of Organized Crime

Significant support comes from the criminal groups with which the organized criminal associates. Often these are specialized groups organized around efforts to gain a monopoly over a particular kind of criminal activity, such as prostitution. They operate through threats, intimidation, **bribery,** and, when necessary, violence.

Organized crime also finds support among outside groups. The top officers are rarely caught; but when those at the lower levels are arrested, the higher-ups can often "fix" the situation and get them released. Organized crime finds protection from those outside, including, in some cases, the police, judges, and other relevant professionals. It may also gain **immunity (criminal)** through its political control in a locality. Further, the public is often tolerant of the activities of organized crime because of public demand for the services provided, as with alcohol during Prohibition. Organized criminals evade the law by infiltrating legitimate business, which cannot complain to law enforcement authorities because of their own involvement.

It has also been argued that our social structure fosters and supports organized crime. The 1986 President's Commission report concluded that although they are few in number, lawyer-criminals do exist. These are lawyers who work with organized crime. The commission called for tighter controls by bar associations to combat the problem of these unethical lawyers.

Control of Organized Crime

Efforts to eliminate organized crime have obviously been unsuccessful, and some prosecutions have been complete failures. After considerable expense in one of the longest criminal trials in United States history, all twenty defendants in New Jersey were acquitted of seventy-seven counts in August 1988. The government had argued that the twenty defendants constitute all the members of the Lucchese organized-crime family in New Jersey and that they were involved in credit-card fraud, gambling, loan sharking and illegal drug trafficking. "The acquittals are viewed as a setback in antiracketeering efforts all over the country."[28] In 1987 John Gotti, whom the Government alleged is the leader of the most powerful Mafia family, was acquitted of federal racketeering and conspiracy

In 1987, John Gotti, who helped convince law enforcement officials that he heads the nation's largest organized crime family, was acquitted of federal racketeering and conspiracy charges. In January, 1990, he was acquitted of assault and conspiracy.

charges, and in 1990 he was acquitted of assault and conspiracy charges. The government has, however, had some success, as indicated in Highlight 10.1. In 1988, Anthony (Fat Tony) Salerno, alleged boss of the Genovese crime family, along with eight other defendants, was convicted of racketeering. In 1989 Gene Gotti and John Carneglia were found guilty on drug trafficking charges, sentenced to fifty years in prison, and fined $75,000 each. Both were reputedly officers in the Gambino crime family.[29]

Statutory efforts to control organized crime include two earlier efforts: the Hobbs Anti-Racketeering Act of 1946 and the Omnibus Crime Control and Safe Streets Act of 1968. Current efforts are litigated under the Organized Crime Control Act of 1970, as amended by the 1984 Omnibus Crime Control Act.[30]

The Organized Crime Control Act of 1970

The stated purpose of this act is "to seek the eradication of organized crime in the United States by strengthening the legal tools in the evidence-gathering process, by establishing new penal prohibitions, and by providing enhanced sanctions and new remedies to deal with unlawful activities of those engaged in organized crime." Some provisions of the act are as follows:

    1. The Anti-Racketeering Act, generally called the Hobbs Act, extends federal jurisdiction over robbery, extortion, and physical

violence (including the attempt to commit these acts, the accomplished acts, or conspiracy to commit the acts) obstructing, delaying, or affecting commerce. The main thrust of the statute is a broad plan to deter professional gangsterism.

2. The act makes it a federal offense to use interstate or foreign travel or transportation in aid of racketeering enterprises. Broadly speaking, it is a federal crime to (1) distribute the proceeds of any unlawful activity, which is defined as any business enterprise involving gambling, liquor where the federal excise tax is not paid, narcotics, prostitution, extortion, bribery, and arson; (2) commit any crime of violence; or (3) otherwise promote or facilitate any unlawful activity and thereafter attempt or perform (1) or (2). This provision was intended to extend federal jurisdiction to syndicate members who profit from racketeering but who cannot be prosecuted under state statutes because they live outside the state in which the activity takes place.

3. The act proscribes illegal gambling businesses. With regard to the activities prohibited by this section of the act, Congress made the following findings, quoted in a Michigan case.[31]

United States v. Aquino

The Congress finds that (1) organized crime in the United States is a highly sophisticated, diversified, and widespread activity that annually drains billions of dollars from America's economy by unlawful conduct and the illegal use of force, fraud, and corruption; (2) organized crime derives a major portion of its power through money obtained from such illegal endeavors as syndicated gambling, loan sharking, the theft and fencing of property, the importation and distribution of narcotics and other dangerous drugs, and other forms of social exploitation; (3) this money and power are increasingly used to infiltrate and corrupt legitimate business and labor unions and to subvert and corrupt our democratic processes; (4) organized crime activities in the United States weaken the stability of the Nation's economic system, harm innocent investors, interfere with free competition, seriously burden interstate and foreign commerce, threaten the domestic security, and undermine the general welfare of the Nation and its citizens. . . .

---

4. The act makes a federal crime of any activity affecting commerce where there is a "pattern of racketeering activity" or "collection of an unlawful debt." The basic purpose of this section is to bar the investment of racketeering monies in any legitimate business.

HIGHLIGHT 10.1

ORGANIZED CRIME FIGURES CONVICTED

A man reputed to be the most powerful member of the Genovese crime family in New Jersey and two of his associates were convicted today of plotting to kill John Gotti and his brother Gene in a struggle for control of organized crime in the New York metropolitan area.

The defendants were also found guilty of arranging the 1987 murder of Irwin Schiff, a New York businessman with connections to organized crime, and of racketeering. Three other men were convicted of racketeering and illegal gambling and, in one case, conspiracy.

Federal officials said the jury verdicts would seriously damage the ability of organized crime to operate in New Jersey by removing its most experienced leaders.

Decades of Crime Cited

"Today's verdicts bring to a close criminal careers that have gone on for decades," said the United States Attorney for New Jersey, Samuel A. Alito Jr.

Louis Anthony (Bobby) Manna, 59 years old, of Jersey City, was convicted of the Gotti death plot and the Schiff murder. He was described by officials as the third-ranking member of New York's Genovese crime family and the leader of the family in New Jersey.

Also convicted were Martin (Motts) Casella, 71, of Secaucus and Richard (Bocci) DeSciscio, 42, of Bayonne, who officials said carried out the murders at the direction of Mr. Manna.

It was a significant victory for Federal prosecutors here, who last year received a stunning setback when a jury took only 14

hours to acquit 20 suspected members of the Lucchese crime family after a 21-month trial on racketeering and drug charges.

The 15-week trial included testimony describing the brutal tactics of the mob. Prosecutors made their case using scratchy tape recordings and testimony by an informer and a woman who was with Mr. Schiff the night he was shot in the back of the head at the Bravo Sergio restaurant on Second Avenue in Manhattan.

Frank (Dipsy) Daniello, 67, a former Hoboken police officer, also was convicted of conspiracy in the plan to kill John Gotti, who the authorities say heads the rival Gambino crime family.

Two others, Rocco J. Napoli, 42, of Secaucus and John Derrico, 27, of Hoboken, a cook at a restaurant owned by Mr. Casella,

---

Congress wanted to control the infiltration of legitimate businesses by organized crime; but to get a conviction under this section, government prosecutors must show a pattern of illegal acts, which is often difficult to prove.

5. The act proscribes mailing a threatening communication. The threat can be implied and need not be specific—the victim need not have been intimidated or placed in fear. In *United States v. Maisonet*, an inmate in the Lorton, Virginia prison was convicted under this statute after he sent a letter to his sentencing judge's home, stating that his sentence was illegal and that the judge was prejudiced against Puerto Ricans. The prisoner wrote, "I may have to do all my ten (10) years, but if I ever get out of here and nothing happen [sic] to me while I am in here, you will never be able to be prejudice [sic] and racist against another Puerto Rican like me."[32]

HIGHLIGHT 10.1 (Continued)

were charged in the plot on Mr. Gotti but acquitted. But they were convicted of running a gambling operation, and Mr. Napoli, a business manager of Local 21 of the Laborers Union, was found guilty of extortion.

Five Face Long Sentences

Mr. Manna, Mr. Casella and Mr. DeSciscio face minimum sentences of 75 years in prison. Mr. Napoli could get more than 75 years and Mr. Daniello 40 years. Mr. Derrico, the only defendant released on bail pending sentencing, could get five years.

Judge Maryanne Barry Trump of Federal District Court set sentencing for Aug. 3.

The central figure in the trial was Mr. Manna, who officials said has been a prominent figure in organized crime.

John C. McGinley, special agent in charge of the Federal Bureau of Investigation office in Newark, said the investigation leading to today's convictions began two and a half years ago when Mr. Manna, under scrutiny from New York officials, moved his base of operations to New Jersey.

Mr. McGinley said the F.B.I. had placed wiretaps in one of Mr. Manna's known hangouts, Casella's restaurant in Hoboken.

Mr. McGinley said that the first conversation to mention a planned murder was recorded before Mr. Schiff was killed in 1987 but that it could not be determined who the target was. The wiretaps then picked up discussions threatening the life of John Gotti.

The Government wiretaps became an issue in the trial, with defense lawyers arguing that the tapes were too unclear to be used as evidence. David Ruhnke, Mr. DeSciscio's lawyer, said he planned to appeal today's verdict because the tapes should have been thrown out. He also said that by not naming the members of the jury, the court had "sent a message that the defendants were dangerous."

After conferring with New York officials, authorities in New Jersey arrested the six defendants last July. The trial began March 7, and the court ordered the names of the jurors withheld for their protection.

SOURCE: "3 Mobsters Guilty of Plot on Gotti," New York Times, 27 June 1989, p. 24, col. 1, copyright © 1988/89 by the New York Times Company, Reprinted by permission.

The act contains numerous other provisions. For example, since its purpose is to eradicate organized crime in the United States, one section strengthens the legal tools for gathering evidence and adds new remedies, including higher damage awards. Further, to aid the prosecution in gathering information, the act gives the witness immunity in return for testifying either in court or before Congress.

Originally passed to control organized crime, the act illustrates the difficulty of separating organized crime from white-collar crime, even for purposes of analysis. The act is a very broad and flexible statute used for prosecutions against business persons; medical, legal, and other professionals; labor union leaders; government officials; and others charged with a variety of white-collar crimes. The statute has significantly expanded federal law enforcement powers.

The case of *United States v. Grzywacz* illustrates the use of this statute to prosecute successfully three former police officers of Madison, Illinois. The excerpt below describes the type of activity involved and thus the ability of the federal government to exercise legal control over an illegal activity in legitimate enterprise. Note particularly the last paragraph of the opinion, in which the court indicates its belief regarding the effect such crimes have on the moral fiber of society.[33]

United States v. Grzywacz

Appellants were alleged to have conspired to violate the . . . statute by conducting and participating in the conduct of an enterprise . . . through a pattern of racketeering activity. The indictment under which they were charged alleged as the essence of the conspiracy that the officers used their official positions as members of the police department to solicit and accept bribes and sexual favors from business establishments . . . in exchange for acquiescence in and protection of certain illegal activities by the establishments, including prostitution, and operating after closing hours. . . .

At trial the government adduced substantial evidence relating exclusively to certain acts committed jointly and separately by all three appellants. . . .This proof . . . indicated that the three officers, with the assistance of tavern owner Jenny Huey, engaged in a pattern of securing monetary payments and sexual favors from city tavern and two company operators and employees in return for "protection" of certain illegal activities by the businesses. . . .

It is appropriate to note that in its ultimate significance this case is immensely tragic not only because it involves the corruption of human beings but because the offenses found by the jury reflect a callous disregard by public servants of their moral and legal responsibilities and a sordid abuse of their public trust. Such misconduct by law enforcement officials undermines respect for the legal principles upon which the survival and growth of a free society depend.

Organized Crime Today: A View from the 1986 Commission Report

Former President Reagan indicated his concern for the need to combat organized crime in this country by naming a twenty person Organized Crime Commission in July 1983. The commission, headed by Judge Irving R. Kaufman of the U.S. Court of Appeals for the Second Circuit, issued an interim report in 1984 and in the spring of 1986 presented the President and the attorney general with its final report on labor and management racketeering.[34]

The work of the commission was not without controversy from without, but the members also disagreed on the final report. Nine members questioned the methods used for reaching final conclusions and accused the commission of mismanaging time, staff, and money. The commission spent nearly $5 million during its two-and-one-half years of work.

Five areas from the commission's reports summarized: money laundering, the meat industry, the construction industry, and drug trafficking.

Money Laundering

The commission's interim report focused on *money laundering*, defined as "the process by which one conceals the existence, illegal source, or illegal application of income, and then disguises that income to make it appear legitimate." The term is derived from the reference criminals make to dirty money that is laundered clean so that it can be used openly. For example, large sums of money obtained by selling illegal drugs must be channeled through legitimate sources to make it appear that the money has been obtained legally.

Measuring, detecting, and prosecuting illegal money laundering was done through the Bank Secrecy Act, which required banks to report any domestic transaction of more than $10,000.[35] The commission concluded that the act was not sufficient for adequate prosecutions; the penalties were too light, and the act did not permit needed government surveillance to detect money-laundering schemes. Among its recommendations and conclusions, the commission said, "If money laundering is the keystone of organized crime, these recommendations can provide the financial community and law enforcement authorities with the tools needed to dislodge that keystone, and thereby to cause irreparable damage to the operations of organized crime." The Money-Laundering Control Act of 1986 makes money laundering illegal.[36]

The Meat Industry

According to the commission's report, New York is a unique market not only because of the "myriad of goods and services it offers" but also because one-half of the members of LCN are in that state. Organized crime has gained control over a significant portion of the meat industry, one of the large industries in New York and in the country. One out of every ten dollars spent on beef in this country each year is spent by consumers in the five New York City boroughs, and it is assumed that figures are comparable for the poultry industry. Whereas the production and distribution of meat and poultry used to be done at local levels, today the industry is vast, complex, and particularly susceptible to infiltration by organized crime.

In the past, organized crime dominated many of the local unions in the meat industry; today many of the distributors are owned by organized crime members, who have several advantages over lawfully operated businesses:

1. The mob-controlled company may be able to cross-subsidize activities with funds from other illegal activities conducted by crime family members and to use cash for purchases when legitimate competitors must rely on credit.

2. The mob-controlled company can possibly bypass skilled union workers in favor of lower-paid and less-skilled nonunion employees.

3. Some organized crime figures have had far less regard than law-abiding citizens for the health and safety of the general public, thereby enabling them to reduce costs by dealing in stolen, tainted, or otherwise undesirable meat.

4. Organized crime members have repeatedly demonstrated their willingness to use threats or violence to advance their business interests.

5. Some organized crime family associates or members may exploit strategic positions in the meat distribution system to deny uncooperative meat producers access to retail markets.[37]

The Construction Industry

It is estimated that the construction industry does $227 billion in business annually, accounting for approximately 8 percent of the gross national product. It is also estimated that construction costs run about 20 percent higher because of organized crime. The commission found a substantial infiltration of organized crime in the construction industry in New York City but also found that government responses to the situation "have generally been sporadic and inconsistent. Recent developments have shown more promise," but the ability of organized crime to avoid and eliminate competition has been widespread. According to the commission, if the government is to be effective in combatting organized crime's success in eliminating competition, "it must examine the economic organization of the construction industry to determine the points at which new private and governmental initiatives can enhance competition and undermine the collusive tendencies of the industry."[38] The commission concluded that further investigation is necessary for a complete understanding of the control that organized crime has over this extremely important segment of the American economy.

In April 1988 a Senate committee was told by a former member of the Genovese organized crime family that the New York City high-rise construction business is run by the mob which controls the construction

EXHIBIT 10.4

Recommendations for a National Strategy: From the President's Commission on Organized Crime, 1986

To be successful, an attack on organized crime in our mainstream economy cannot rely solely on the enforcement of federal criminal laws. Organized crime has established economic cartels which eliminate marketplace competition by maneuvering businesses and labor officials through a kind of ownership not recognized by the law. The Commission believes that a strategy aimed at the legitimate economic base of organized crime must build upon the recent successes of law enforcement, and must be based upon intervention measures as broad-based as the nature of the threat posed by organized crime. A strategy in this area should also rely upon civil and regulatory measures tailored to the specific problems confronted in labor and management racketeering.

The Commission's central recommendations . . . address the current deficiencies of outlook and approach. . . .

1. The President, acting through the Attorney General, should adopt a national strategy to remove organized crime from the marketplace.

2. Task forces should devise and carry out a planned campaign against organized crime in each industry.

3. In support of the marketplace strategy, the Department of Justice must take on a new, more significant, and more aggressive role, and it must view organized crime's corruption of businesses as seriously as organized crime's corruption of unions.

4. The Department of Labor should consolidate criminal and civil enforcement responsibilities for oversight of labor organizations and employee benefit plans.

SOURCE: President's Commission on Organized Crime, Report to the President and the Attorney General, *The Edge: Organized Crime, Business, and Labor Unions* (Washington, D.C.: U.S. Government Printing Office, March 1986), pp. 307–314.

and concrete industries. The witness estimated that at least 50 percent of the high-rise construction business in New York was connected in some way to organized crime and that for most construction contracts "Legitimate guys ain't got a chance."[39]

Drug Trafficking

According to the latest organized crime commission, drug trafficking is the most serious problem in organized crime throughout the world today. In

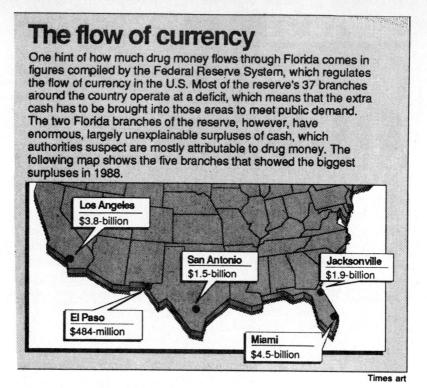

The flow of currency

One hint of how much drug money flows through Florida comes in figures compiled by the Federal Reserve System, which regulates the flow of currency in the U.S. Most of the reserve's 37 branches around the country operate at a deficit, which means that the extra cash has to be brought into those areas to meet public demand. The two Florida branches of the reserve, however, have enormous, largely unexplainable surpluses of cash, which authorities suspect are mostly attributable to drug money. The following map shows the five branches that showed the biggest surpluses in 1988.

Los Angeles
$3.8-billion

San Antonio
$1.5-billion

Jacksonville
$1.9-billion

El Paso
$484-million

Miami
$4.5-billion

Times art

FIGURE 10.2A Banks and laundering

addition to the billions of dollars in profits generated for organized crime each year through the illegal sale of drugs, the crime results in "incalculable costs on individuals, families, communities, and governments worldwide." Beyond the illegal sales are the problems of illegal use, and illegal users give organized crime its market in drugs. The commission emphasized that although the influence of organized crime is significant, the individual user of illegal drugs must also be the target of control. "The powerful, sophisticated, and thoroughly evil organized crime drug trafficking groups ... are a reflection of nothing more than our self-destructiveness."[40]

Drug trafficking is frequently tied in with the crime of money laundering, discussed above. Figure 10.2 contains information on banks and laundering and the flow of currency due to drug trafficking in U.S. cities. This provides business for banks. As federal law enforcement officials have noted, "Financial institutions in Florida, particularly banks, have long profited from the drug business. To drug traffickers, banks serve as an indispensable link in the laundering of billions of dollars each year."[41]

Banks and laundering

When they consummate a sale, drug traffickers usually have a problem— mountains of cash that can't be spent without attracting attention. That's why smugglers need banks. It is through banks that smugglers are able to "launder" their cash, blending it into the economy so that it appears legitimate. Smugglers can't just walk into a bank and deposit the money, however. By U.S. law, banks must report any cash transactions of at least $10,000 to the government. That leaves smugglers with basically two options:

1 They smuggle cash out of the country and deposit it in a foreign banking haven* where laws protect against disclosure of information about bank accounts. Then it can be transferred electronically to banks in the U.S., or it can be withdrawn in the form of cashier's checks and brought back into the U.S. for deposit. Electronic transfers and cashier's checks do not have to be reported.

2 They find ways of evading the reporting requirements so that their money can be deposited directly into U.S. banks. Sometimes they pay bribes or exorbitant service fees to compliant bank officials. More often, they go to great lengths to make numerous deposits under the $10,000 limit, using multiple accounts under different names.

*Foreign banking havens include: Cayman Islands; Panama; Netherland Antilles; the Bahamas; Luxembourg; Liechtenstein; Barbados; Bermuda.

Times art—DAVID WILLIAMS

FIGURE 10.2B

SOURCE: "Smugglers Launder Money at Bank," *St. Petersburg Times,* 17 January 1989, p. 1, col.
2. Reprinted with the permission of David Williams and the *St. Petersburg Times.*

Recommendation for the Future: The Commission Speaks

The President's Commission on Organized Crime recognized that organized crime cannot be eradicated solely by legislation and prosecution, although both are important. The recommendations of the commission for a national strategy are reproduced in Exhibit 10.4. In addition to those recommendations, scholars have emphasized the need for extensive research. The first national Conference on Organized Crime, held in November 1979, featured numerous experts on the subject, most of whom emphasized that organized crime can and should be studied scientifically. This position echoes the conclusion of the 1967 President's Commission that in organized crime "action must replace words; knowledge must replace fascination."[42]

TERRORISM

The second major focus of this chapter is **terrorism,** a crime that, compared to organized crime, more frequently involves violence. In organized crime violence is used mainly against members who violate the rules of the organization. In terrorism, innocent and unsuspecting persons often become victims of violent attacks, frequently resulting in death. Before attempting to define terrorism, however, it is important to look briefly at political crimes.

Since all laws must be interpreted, it could be argued that all law enforcement is political. The term *political crime,* however, is used here to refer to crimes that are considered criminal because they are a threat to the state or its political stability. Political crimes include any crime committed directly against the government. Examples are treason and sedition.

Treason involves assisting the enemy with information to help overthrow the government to which one owes allegiance. Treason is the only crime defined in the U.S. Constitution, which also gives Congress the authority to provide punishment for this crime. Congress has done so, providing a penalty of death (a provision that has been questioned by constitutional scholars) or imprisonment for not less than five years and a fine of not less than $10,000 for one convicted of treason. In addition, a person convicted of treason may not hold any office in the U.S. government.[43]

Sedition involves either written or oral communication aimed at overthrowing the government by defaming it or by inciting others to become involved in treason or other crimes. Sedition in the form of written expression is called *seditious libel.* The federal criminal code also pro-

An injured passenger is carried to a waiting ambulance from a Kuwaiti airliner at Tehran's airport. Iran's official Islamic Republic News Agency said he was declared dead on arrival at an airport medical center. The armed hijackers commandeered the Kuwait Airways Airbus A-300 with 161 persons aboard on a flight from Kuwait to Pakistan in December 1984.

hibits **seditious conspiracy.** A 1988 Arkansas trial of fourteen defendants for this crime, representing only the fourth time in forty years that the federal government has prosecuted for this crime, resulted in acquittals.

Actions aimed at changing the social structure may also be considered political crimes and may result from violations of statutes designed to preserve that structure or of laws with other purposes (for example, vagrancy) that may be enforced for political reasons (that is, enforced only against minorities). The student protest movements of the 1960s and 1970s, civil rights violations, and violations of draft laws are examples. In 1989, in the People's Republic of China, thousands of students demonstrated in Beijing's Tiananmen Square. When they refused to disperse, the People's Liberation Army gunned down hundreds (and some say thousands) of the unarmed students with army tanks. Many students who were not killed were subsequently arrested and executed by firing squads.

Some scholars also include in the definition of political crimes such crimes as police brutality and other acts committed by government officials against citizens. This position is emphasized by the radical approach.

As Michael J. Lynch and Graeme R. Newman suggest in their discussion of terrorism, the radical approach brings out these issues:

- terrorism is not what it appears to be on the surface,
- terrorism is defined in relation to particular economic, social and historical circumstances—or terrorism is a social construction defined by those with the power to do so in accordance with prevailing structural conditions, and
- the powerful, including the state and other economic and political elite, may, in many instances, also engage in terroristic behavior.

Lynch and Newman note, however, that we do not usually think of the government as engaging in terroristic activities. We do not perceive the state as deviant because of the ability of those in power to define deviancy in a way that avoids inclusion of their own behavior. "In a word, the political and economic elite are, by virtue of their positions and the power associated with those positions, able to structure definitions of deviance and avoid negative labels."[44]

A recent emphasis on hate groups might also illustrate a form of terrorism not traditionally included in terrorism discussions. The Department of Justice is investigating the activities of neo-Nazi skinhead groups, who are radical white supremists who terrorize nonwhites. In recent years the government has been cracking down on other hate groups, such as the Ku Klux Klan and other violent racist and anti-Jewish groups. Florida recently enacted a statute aimed at groups who engage in hate crimes against blacks, Jews, and members of any racial, religious, or ethnic groups. The lawmaker who introduced the bill was subjected to threats against his life, but he is committed to strict enforcement of the law. The law consists of two parts. The first increases the penalties of hate crimes, and the second part permits treble damages in civil suits filed by victims against individuals or organizations that coerce, intimidate, or threaten them.[45]

Definition of Terrorism

Although there is little agreement on a precise definition of terrorism, most people have a concept of what it means. A broad legal definition is one found in the American Law Institute's **Model Penal Code,** which defines terrorist threats as follows:

> A person is guilty of a felony if he threatens to commit any crime of violence with purpose to terrorize another or to cause evacuation of a building, place of assembly, or facility of public transportation, or otherwise to cause serious public inconvenience, or in reckless disregard of the risk of causing such terror or inconvenience.[46]

Applied to the political arena, terrorism has been defined simply as "[m]otivated violence for political ends."[47] The Task Force on Disorders and Terrorism of the National Advisory Committee on Criminal Justice Standards, under the direction of H. H. A. Cooper, defined terrorism as "a tactic or technique by means of which a violent act or the threat thereof is used for the prime purpose of creating overwhelming fear for coercive purposes." Terrorism is thus a political crime but may also be a violent personal crime. Acts of terrorists are planned in advance, and to be effective, terrorists must manipulate the community to which the message is addressed. The inculcation of fear is paramount and deliberate; it is the real purpose of the activity, and an audience is important. In this respect, the terror involved in an individual robbery, for example, differs from terrorism. In the latter, the immediate victim is not the important focus; the emphasis is on the larger audience.[48] It is in this respect that terrorism differs significantly from violent personal crimes.[49]

Categories of Terrorism

The task force divided terrorism into six categories:

1. *Civil disorders*—"a form of collective violence interfering with the peace, security, and normal functioning of the community."

2. *Political terrorism*—"violent criminal behavior designed primarily to generate fear in the community, or a substantial segment of it, for political purposes."

3. *Nonpolitical terrorism*—terrorism that is not aimed at political purposes but that exhibits "conscious design to create and maintain a high degree of fear for coercive purposes, but the end is individual or collective gain rather than the achievement of a political objective."

4. *Quasiterrorism*—"Those activities incidental to the commission of crimes of violence that are similar in form and method to true terrorism but which nevertheless lack its essential ingredient." It is not the main purpose of the quasiterrorists "to induce terror in the instant victim," as in the case of true terrorism. Typically, the fleeing felon who takes hostage is a quasiterrorist, whose methods are similar to those of the true terrorist but whose purposes are quite different.

5. *Limited political terrorism*—Real political terrorism is characterized by a revolutionary approach; limited political terrorism refers to "acts of terrorism which are committed for ideological or political motives but which are not part of a concerted campaign to capture control of the State."

6. *Official or state terrorism*—referring to "nations whose rule is based upon fear and oppression that reach terrorist proportions."[50]

Terrorism may consist of acts or threats or both. The task force discussed several characteristics that distinguish modern acts of terrorism from classical terrorism in its original form. First, as the result of our technological vulnerability, the potential for harm is greater today than in the past. This development has greatly increased the bargaining power of the modern terrorist, who has also been aided by the developments in intercontinental travel and mass communication. Television has carried the activities of terrorists to the entire world, and the modern terrorist thus has far more power than classical terrorists. Finally, the modern terrorist believes that through violence there is hope for his or her cause.

Objective, Strategy, and Tactics

A primary objective of terrorists is to instill fear, to terrorize, and to create violence for the sake of effect. The particular victims may not be important to the cause other than to create the fear toward which the violence is aimed. Instilling fear is, however, not the only objective of terrorists. They also seek to destroy the confidence people have in their government.

Terrorist groups have been categorized as *xenofighters*, who are fighting foreigners, or *homofighters*, who are fighting their own people. Xenofighters are often seeking removal of a foreign power or the changing of political boundaries regarding a foreign power. They have such goals as the following:

1. To attract international attention

2. To harm the relations of the target country with other nations

3. To cause insecurity and to damage the economy and public order in the target country

4. To build feelings of distrust and hostility toward the government among the target country's population

5. To cause actual damage to civilians, security forces, and property in the target country.[51]

Homofighters must win the support of their compatriots in their fight to discredit their own government; thus they must adopt policies that do not alienate the citizenry. One approach is the Robin Hood demand, in which terrorists use an acceptable cause to justify their unacceptable tactics. The kidnapping of Patricia Hearst in 1974 is an example. The Symbionese Liberation Army demanded that Hearst's family distribute free food to the needy. Some of the strategies used by homofighters are these:

1. Undermining internal security, public order, and the economy in order to create distrust of the government's ability to maintain control

2. Acquiring popular sympathy and support by positive action

3. Generating popular repulsion from extreme counterterrorist repressive measures

4. Damaging hated foreign interests

5. Harming the international position of the existing regime

6. Causing physical damage and harassing persons and institutions that represent the ruling regime.[52]

Extent of Terrorism

Top terrorism experts of the State Department reported in July 1986 that terrorist attacks can be expected to continue. The slowdown of attacks since the United States bombed Libya on April 15, 1986, should not be taken as indicative of the future. Terrorists have proved adaptable to change, indicated the report, and they can be expected to continue to attack targets designed to kill large numbers of people at a time. As airport security increases, terrorists can be expected to deploy surface-to-air missiles against commercial aircraft.

The report was referring to some of the terrorist attacks summarized in Highlight 10.2. The report also warned that although the number of attacks had decreased in the past year, the number of attacks designed to kill large numbers of people was higher in the past eighteen months than in the preceding five years.[53] The prediction was accurate, for 1987 was "the worst year in history—we had 832 reported incidents of international terrorism." The bombing of Pan American World Airways flight 103 in Scotland during the Christmas holidays in 1988 again focused attention on the extent to which some terrorists will go to make their point. In December of 1989, mail bombs sent to various offices resulted in the deaths of federal court judge Robert Vance of the Eleventh Circuit and Robert Robinson, a black lawyer and alderman from Savannah, Georgia.[54]

Terrorist attacks are not new to this or other countries although today they involve larger numbers of victims; but it was not until 1981 that the U.S. government perceived the threat of terrorism "to be serious enough to warrant classification as a major component of American foreign policy."[55] After a year of study by a joint team from the Army and Air Force, a late 1986 report indicated that the United States still does not have an effective plan for coping with terroristic attacks. The team insisted that we must develop a comprehensive civil-military strategy to defend our interests at home and abroad from terrorist attacks. However, the director of the FBI reported in August 1986 that better intelligence, effective law enforcement, increased domestic and international cooperation, and a better informed public have combined to decrease terroristic attacks in the United States from 100 incidents in 1978 to only 13 in 1984 and only 7 in 1985. He did not indicate how the FBI defined these acts, although he did claim that 23 such incidents were prevented in 1985.[56]

HIGHLIGHT 10.2

Selected Terrorist Attacks of the 1980s

Hijacking of the Achille Lauro

On October 7, 1985, the *Achille Lauro,* an Italian cruise ship in the Mediterranean, was hijacked with 400 on board. The hijackers threatened to kill their hostages unless 50 Palestinian prisoners were freed by Israel. The hostages were later released, but one passenger, Leon Klinghoffer, a tourist from New York City, was killed and his body thrown overboard. The terrorists were tried and convicted, but the Klinghoffer family and many others thought the sentences were too lenient. Only 3 defendants, all fugitives at the time of conviction, received the maximum sentence of life imprisonment. The 3 in custody were sentenced to 30, 24, and 15 years in prison.

Terrorist Attacks at Rome and Vienna Airports

During the Christmas holiday travel season in 1985, terrorists struck at the Rome and Vienna airports, throwing hand grenades into the crowds, killing seventeen and wounding one hundred or more. The attacks occurred within minutes of each other. Though the attack was appar-

ently aimed at Israelis, victims were from many countries, illustrating the possibility of death or injury because of international travel. Two defendants were convicted and sentenced to life. Another received a 30-year prison term.

Bombing of TWA Jet in Greece

In April 1986 TWA Flight 840 from Rome to Athens, carrying 115 passengers and 7 crew members, was damaged by a bomb that exploded shortly before the aircraft landed in Athens. Four passengers were killed when sucked out of the plane, a mother, her daughter, and granddaughter (three Greek Americans from Annapolis, Maryland) and a fourth passenger, also from the United States. The plane later landed safely. A bomb had been planted under one of the seats.

Hijacked Pan Am Flight 73

Four Arabic-speaking terrorists took control of Pan Am Flight 73 as passengers boarded the 747 jet bound from Karachi, Pakistan, to Frankfurt and New York in September 1986. Fifteen crew

members and 374 passengers were involved; the flight crew escaped through an escape hatch, thus eliminating the possibility that the terrorists could force the plane into the air. But before Pakistani authorities could execute an escape plan for the remaining persons on board, a power failure apparently caused the terrorists to panic and shoot. Twenty-one were killed; approximately 200 were wounded. Five Palestinians, including one who never boarded the plane, were convicted and sentenced to hang for these crimes. They were also fined the equivalent of $2,777 for each conviction. Half of the fines will go to the victims' families.

Hijacking of Kuwait Airways Flight 422

On April 5, 1988, about one hour before Kuwait Airways Flight 422 was scheduled to arrive in Kuwait on its flight from Bangkok, Thailand, the plane was hijacked by three men. The plane was held for 15 days during which all the men were searched and their personal belongings taken. A guard was beaten and killed; one hostage

Domestic Terrorism: Product Tampering

One type of terrorism that has caused great concern in the United States and for which no adequate explanation has yet been articulated is tampering with domestic products. Deaths from consumption of cyanide-tainted aspirin and cyanide-laced soup in 1986 reminded Americans that

HIGHLIGHT 10.2 (Continued)

who needed medical care was released. The women were not searched or touched in any way, and the hijackers occasionally were kind to the passengers, assuring them that they would not be harmed. After 15 days the hijackers exited the plane in the dark, after all lights illuminating the plane were turned off. They left in an Algerian jet and were flown to Damascus, Syria, from which they were driven to Lebanon.

Cruise Ship Attacked Near Athens

In July 1988 three gunmen began shooting at hundreds of tourists on board a cruise ship near Athens, Greece. Nine were killed, and 53 were wounded.

Bombing of Pan Am Flight 103

During the 1988 Christmas season, Pan Am Flight 103, bound for New York City after its flight to London, blew apart over Lockerbie, Scotland. All 259 people on board, along with 11 on the ground, were killed. Terrorism is suspected. By December 1989 police had identified a suspect, Palestinian Mohammed Abu Talb, who along with 3 oth-

ers, was convicted on the first anniversary of the Pan Am flight 103 bombing of a series of attacks in Northern Europe 4 years ago. He was sentenced to life in prison, which in Sweden, where he was convicted, usually means only 20 years in prison.

Car Bombing in San Diego, California

The wife of the captain of the Navy missile cruiser that reportedly mistakenly downed an Iranian jet in 1988, killing all passengers on board, escaped injury when her car exploded in early 1989 in what authorities have labeled a terrorist attack.

Bombing of Korea Air Jet

In April 1989 Kim Hyon Hui was sentenced to death for her role in the 1987 bombing of a South Korean airliner in which 115 people were killed. She confessed to the crime, which she said was committed as part of a plot by North Korea senior leaders to disrupt the Olympic Games, which were successfully held in Seoul. When she confessed, the defendant sobbed and said, "I don't know how to atone for my crime."

Mail Bombings

On December 16, 1989, federal appellate court Judge Robert Vance opened a package delivered to his home. He was killed and his wife was seriously injured by the bomb. Two days later police disarmed a mail bomb sent to the Court of Appeals for the Eleventh Circuit on which Vance served. On that same day Savannah, Georgia, attorney and alderman Robert E. Robinson was killed by a mail bomb. A package delivered to the local N.A.A.C.P. president in Jacksonville, Florida, was given to the sheriff's office. It contained a mail bomb. Yet another bomb injured Maryland state circuit court Judge John P. Corderman in his apartment. According to one news source,

In a nation that prides itself on the peaceful resolution of its deepest conflicts, the murder of a judge is an especially horrifying act. Vance is only the third federal judge to be murdered in this century.[1]

[1]"Murder by Mail," *Time*, 1 January 1990, p. 33.

the earlier deaths from cyanide-laced Tylenol capsules, resulting in new legislation for tamper-proof containers, had not eliminated the possibility of becoming a victim of this kind of terrorist attack.

Numerous product tampering cases have been reported, including tampering with baby food in London in 1989, but thus far only one person has been convicted of product tampering. In June 1988 Stella Nickell was sentenced to 90 years in prison for poisoning Excedrin capsules, killing her husband and one stranger. Prosecutors charged that Nickell killed her husband for insurance. It was also stated that she was tired of him. The stranger was apparently a random victim; but as the prosecutor said, "It is unnerving to think just how many people stood to die because of this woman's greed."[57]

Causes of Terrorism

Many sociological and psychological theories have been advanced to explain terrorist behavior, but the task force concluded that no single theory has been sufficient. However, it did maintain that there seems to be a correlation between the lack of social equilibrium or social cohesion and terrorism. Terroristic attacks also occur with greater frequency when conditions are improving rather than deteriorating, a phenomenon sometimes referred to as the revolution of rising expectations.

H. H. A. Cooper, in his testimony before a Senate subcommittee, pointed out that the basic questions about the characteristics of the terrorist are unanswered. Cooper argued that terroristic activity is not caused by politics or ideology; those are only rationalizations for the behavior. Cooper also emphasized the role of the mass media in terrorism. "The media can make the terrorist larger than life or cut him down to more appropriate social proportions."[58]

Victims of Terrorism

The true victim of terrorism is society. The action taken against the instant victim is coercive, designed to impress others. Terrorism can never be a victimless crime. The immediate victims are sometimes incidentally involved, as when they are killed by the randomly placed terrorist's bomb. Or they may be selected with considerable discrimination, for example, when a prominent politician is assassinated or a business person is kidnapped. Terrorism is characterized by gross indifference toward the victims, their dehumanization, and their conversion into mere elements in a deadly power play.

The ultimate objective of the terrorist, particularly the political terrorist, is the establishment of a bargaining position. Kidnapping and taking hostages are terrorist techniques par excellence for this purpose. The victims are treated largely as objects to be traded for what the terrorist wants: money, release of prisoners, publication of manifestos, or escape. These bargains are essentially extralegal and rest on a recognition of the powers of life and death that the terrorist holds over the victim. This aspect raises the most serious social, political, and humanitarian issues for those who must make these awesome decisions affecting the life and safety of the victims.

Terrorist victimization produces special individual and collective traumas. Hostages and kidnap victims often experience incongruous feelings toward their captors, and the event often constitutes a serious challenge to their own value systems. The most striking manifestation of this is the **Stockholm syndrome,** named after an incident that occurred in the Swedish capital in 1973.[59] The Stockholm syndrome is an incongruous feeling of empathy toward the hostage takers and a displacement of frustration and aggression on the part of the victims toward the authorities.

Another way in which many individuals are victimized by terrorist attacks is in the creation of fear that leads to changes in life-styles. Terrorist incidents have led many Americans to cancel their plans to travel to Europe.

Control of Terrorism

When President Reagan returned from the twelfth annual summit of industrial democracies, held in Tokyo in May 1986, he proclaimed the meeting a "triumph in Tokyo" that had produced a "strong measure of allied unity" on economic, agricultural, and antiterrorism issues. Of primary concern here is the response of the 7 summit nations to the increased terrorist acts in the year before the meeting. According to Reagan, "We agreed that the time has come to move beyond words and rhetoric. Terrorists and those who support them—especially governments—have been put on notice. It is going to be tougher from now on."

Reagan's comments followed the U.S. air raids on Libya after the Libyan government was accused of sponsoring terrorist attacks on Americans in foreign countries. The U.S. air raid had split her allies; some argued against the raid, whereas Great Britain permitted the use of her bases for launching the attack. *Time* reported that the United States "had crossed a fateful line in the intensifying battle between civilized society and terrorism, with consequences that no one could truly predict." Some who opposed the raids predicted retaliation; supporters argued that terrorist force could be met only with force. Libya's Colonel Muammar Gaddafi, whose living quarters and command center were the focus of the raid, lost an adopted daughter; two sons were injured. Gaddafi called Prime Minister Margaret Thatcher of Great Britain, who gave the United States permission to fly over her country, and President Reagan "child murderers" and vowed to get revenge. Polls taken after the raid indicated that 71 percent of Americans approved the attack, and 56 percent thought that in the long run the air raid would help stop terrorist attacks on Americans. But only 66 percent of the British respondents approved, whereas 84 percent thought the participation of Great Britain would increase the likelihood of terrorist attacks on Britain.[60]

In December 1988 just one month before he left office, President Reagan announced that the administration would pay up to $500,000 for information that leads to the "prevention, frustration, or favorable resolution" of terrorist acts against U.S. citizens or property overseas. This plan extended one announced in 1984 under which rewards had been offered in six cases but none actually paid.

What is the most effective way to respond to terrorism? If the government meets the demands of the terrorists, does that concession raise the specter of creating inconvenient or unreasonable precedents for the handling of future incidents? Ted Gurr, author of *Why Men Rebel*, says, "The most fundamental human response to the use of force is counterforce. Force threatens and angers men. Threatened, they try to defend themselves; angered, they want to retaliate."[61] What we do not know is the long-term effect of a retaliation like the U.S. air raid on Libya.

After terrorist attacks on U.S. planes, skyjacked in large numbers in the 1970s, security measures were required in all U.S. airports; skyjacking decreased. But terrorists are adaptable, as indicated by their planting of bombs *outside* the secure areas of airports. It is painfully obvious that although efforts to secure airports and aircraft have increased, they are not sufficient. The root causes of terrorism must be identified and eliminated if the threat of terrorist attacks is to be significantly reduced.

■ *CONCLUSION*

This chapter completes our analysis of types of crimes and types of criminals by looking at organized crime and terrorism, two areas of criminal behavior that are receiving increasing attention nationally and internationally. The chapter began with a brief overview of these two crimes, their similarities and differences, and a comparison with other property and violent crimes.

Organized crime is defined and explained in more than one way; the chapter examined the law enforcement perspective and the social and economic perspectives before proceeding with an analysis of the concept of organized crime. The history and organization of organized crime were examined briefly before a comparison was made between this area of criminal behavior and white-collar crime, discussed in the previous chapter.

Organized crime infiltrates legitimate as well as illegitimate businesses; it provides goods and services that the public wants despite their illegality. Consequently, there is considerable group support for the activities of organized crime, and its control is therefore made more difficult. The discussion of control focused on statutory efforts and closed with an analysis of the findings and recommendations of the President's Commission on Organized Crime, which made its final report in the spring of 1986.

National and international terrorist acts have existed for years, but only within recent years have they gained much attention. Terrorist attacks have become more frequent in number, more political in nature, and more extensive in the degree to which they inflict property damage, human injury, and death on innocent people. Fear of terrorism has inhibited many Americans from traveling abroad. The chapter examined some of the major terrorist attacks as it attempted to define and categorize this most complex, fearful, and potentially devastating form of criminal behavior.

Explanations for terrorism run the gamut of most sociological, psychological, biological, and economic theories that have already been discussed in relationship to criminal behavior. The effect of terrorism on victims was followed by a look at suggestions for control.

A study of criminal typologies makes it clear that crime is difficult to analyze by types; categories, even legal ones, are not discrete. There is considerable overlap among the activities involved in crimes of property and of violence and in the characteristics of people who engage in these activities. These four chapters may illustrate that there are more similarities than differences in criminal typologies. The difference often lies not in the behavior itself but in the reaction to it. It is therefore appropriate that attention be given to the official reaction to criminal behavior through an analysis of the criminal justice system in the United States, the focus of Part IV.

ENDNOTES

1. Jay Albanese, *Organized Crime in America*, 2d ed (Cincinnati, Ohio: Anderson Publishing Co., 1989), p. 3.
2. Quoted in Francis A. J. Ianni and Elizabeth Reuss-Ianni, "Organized Crime," in Sanford H. Kadish, ed., *Encyclopedia of Crime and Justice* (New York: Macmillan, 1983), vol. 3, p. 1095.
3. President's Commission on Law Enforcement and Administration of Justice, *The Challenge of Crime in a Free Society* (Washington, D.C.: U.S. Government Printing Office, 1967), p. 187.
4. Joseph L. Albini, "Donald Cressey's Contributions to the Study of Organized Crime: An Evaluation," *Crime & Delinquency* 34 (July 1988): 338, 339. See also Donald Cressey, *Theft of the Nation* (N.Y.: Harper & Row, 1969), and Cressey, *Criminal Organization* (N.Y.: Harper & Row, 1972).
5. Ianni and Reuss-Ianni, "Organized Crime," p. 1095.
6. *Ibid.*, p. 1097.
7. *Ibid.*, p. 1096.
8. *Ibid.* For recent accounts of organized crime, Albanese, *Organized Crime in America*, pp. 15–72. For a history, see Gus Tyler, ed., *Organized Crime in America* (Ann Arbor: University of Michigan Press, 1962), pp. 42–49.
9. Estes Kefauver, *Crime in America* (New York: Doubleday, 1951); see also Morris Ploscowe, ed., *Organized Crime and Law Enforcement* (New York: Grosby Press, 1952).
10. Robert F. Kennedy, *The Enemy Within* (New York: Harper & Row, 1960).
11. The President's Commission on Law Enforcement and Administration of Justice, *The Challenge of Crime in a Free Society* (Washington, D.C.: U.S. Gov-

ernment Printing Office, 1967). See also that commission's task force report, *Organized Crime*.

12. National Advisory Committee on Criminal Justice Standards and Goals, *Organized Crime* (Washington, D.C.: U.S. Government Printing Office, 1973). For further discussion on these commissions, see Albanese, *Organized Crime*, pp. 73–88.

13. See U.S. Senate Special Committee to Investigate Organized Crime in Interstate Commerce, *Third Interim Report*, Senate Report No. 307, 83d Cong., 1st Sess. (Washington, D.C.: U.S. Government Printing Office). The report is abridged in Kefauver, *Crime in America*.

14. Giovanni Schiavo, *The Truth about the Mafia* (New York: Vigo Press, 1962). For other accounts of the Mafia, see Frederick Sondern, Jr., *Brotherhood of Evil: The Mafia* (New York: Farrar, Straus, 1959); Ed Reid, *Mafia* (New York: Random House, 1952); Edward J. Allen, *Merchants of Menace—The Mafia* (Springfield, Ill.: Chas. C. Thomas, 1962); Norman Lewis, *The Honored Society* (New York: Putnam, 1964).

15. President's Commission, *Challenge of Crime*, pp. 192–195.

16. Ianni and Reuss-Ianni, "Organized Crime," p. 1101.

17. See Francis A. J. Ianni and Elizabeth Reuss-Ianni, eds., *A Family Business: Kinship and Social Control in Organized Crime* (New York: Russell Sage, 1972). For a discussion of these and other points of view, see Howard Abadinsky, *The Mafia in America: An Oral History* (New York: Praeger, 1981), pp. 11–20. See also Gerald E. Caiden and Herbert E. Alexander, "Introduction: Perspectives on Organized Crime," in Herbert E. Alexander and Gerald E. Caiden, eds., *The Politics and Economics of Organized Crime* (Lexington, Mass.: Heath, 1985), pp. 1–19.

18. See Joseph L. Albini, *The American Mafia: Genesis of a Legend*, Reprint (New York: Irvington, 1979).

19. President's Commission, *Challenge of Crime*, pp. 192–193. See also Robert T. Anderson, "From Mafia to Cosa Nostra," *American Journal of Sociology* 71 (November 1965): 302–310; Donald R. Cressey, *Theft of the Nation: The Structure and Operations of Organized Crime in America* (New York: Harper & Row, 1969); and Donald R. Cressey, *Criminal Organization* (New York: Harper & Row, 1972).

20. President's Commission on Organized Crime, Report to the President and the Attorney General, *The Edge: Organized Crime, Business, and Labor Unions* (Washington, D.C.: U.S. Government Printing Office, March 1986), p. xviii.

21. Paul Pringle, "Battling the Chinese Underworld," *Dallas Morning News*, 27 March 1988, p. 4A, col. 1.

22. Peter Kerr, "Chinese Criminals Move to Broaden Role in U.S.," *New York Times*, 4 January 1988, p. 1, col. 4.

23. "Ethnic Gangs & Organized Crime," *U.S. News and World Report*, 18 January 1988, pp. 29, 34.

24. See Jay S. Albanese, "What Lockheed and La Cosa Nostra Have in Common," *Crime & Delinquency* 28 (April 1982): 211–232.

25. See Andrew Szasz, "Corporations, Organized Crime, and the Disposal of Hazardous Waste: An Examination of the Making of a Criminogenic," *Criminology* 24 (February 1986): 1–28.

26. "How the Mob Really Works," *Newsweek*, 5 January 1981, p. 34.

27. "Crime Panel Issues Its Final Report," *New York Times*, 2 April 1986, p. 1, col. 2.

28. "20 Acquitted in Mob Trial," *New York Times*, 27 August 1988, p. 1, col. 6.

29. "Gotti Brother Sentenced to 50 Years," *Miami Herald*, 8 July 1989, p. 6A., col 1.

30. 18 U.S.Code, Sections 1951 et seq. (as amended 1984).

31. United States v. Aquino, 336 F.Supp. 737, 739 (D.C. Mich. 1972). For further explanation of this section of the act, see G. Robert Blakey and Harold A. Kurland, "The Development of the Federal Law of Gambling," *Cornell Law Review* 63 (August 1978): 923–1021.

32. United States v. Maisonet, 484 F.2d 1356, 1357 (4th Cir. 1973), *cert. den.*, 415 U.S. 933 (1974).

33. United States v. Grzywacz, 603 F.2d 682, 684, 685, 690 (7th Cir. 1979); footnotes and citations omitted; *cert. den.*, 446 U.S. 935 (1980).

34. The commission was established by Executive Order, No. 12435, July 28, 1983; see 96 U.S.Code, Section 1961. The interim report is *The Cash Connection: Organized Crime, Financial Institutions, and Money Laundering* (Washington, D.C.: U.S. Government Printing Office, 1984. The final report is *The Edge.*

35. 12 U.S.Code, Section 1819b, 1951-1959; 5531-5322, discussed in *The Cash Connection*, pp. 7–27.

36. *Ibid.*, p. 63. See also The Money-Laundering Control Act of 1986, U.S.Code 981, Section 1351. For a discussion see "United States v. Varbel and the Money Laundering Control Act of 1986: Money Laundering Then and Now," *Willamette Law Review* 23 (Spring 1987): 473–491.

37. President's Commission, *The Edge*, pp. 213–214.

38. *Ibid.*, pp. 217–228.

39. "Ex-mobster Ties Mafia to Half of New York's High-rise Construction," *Dallas Morning News*, 30 April 1988, p. 12A, col.1.

40. President's Commission on Organized Crime, Report to the President and the Attorney General, *America's Habit: Drug Abuse, Drug Trafficking, and Organized Crime* (Washington, D.C.: U.S. Government Printing Office, 1986), pp. 5, 13.

41. "Smugglers Launder Money at Banks," *St. Petersburg Times*, 17 January 1989, p.1, col. 2.

42. President's Commission, *The Challenge of Crime in a Free Society*, p. 209.

43. For a discussion of the history of the treason statute as well as the constitutionality of the death penalty for treason, see James G. Wilson, "Chaining the Leviathan: The Unconstitutionality of Executing Those Convicted of Treason," *University of Pittsburgh Law Review* 45 (1983): 99–179. The federal treason statute is contained in the U.S. Code, Title 18, Section 2381. For a brief discussion of the history and the legal elements of the crime, see Sue Titus Reid, *Criminal Law* (N.Y.: Macmillan Publishers, 1989), pp. 299–301.

44. Michael J. Lynch and Graeme R. Newman, "The Meaning of Terrorism: Conflicting Views From the Left," *Violence, Aggression and Terrorism* 2 (no. 4, 1988): 309, explanatory footnote omitted.

45. For a discussion of the hate movement, see Irwin Suall and David Lowe, "Special report: the Hate Movement Today: A Chronicle of Violence and Disarray," *Terrorism* 10 (no. 4, 1987): 345–364.

46. Model Penal Code, Section 211.3.

47. Brian Crozier, *Terroristic Activity, International Terrorism Part 4: Hearings Before the Subcommittee to Investigate the Administration of the Internal Security Laws of the Senate Committee on the Judiciary*, 94th Cong., 1st Sess. 180 (1975); quoted in H. H. A. Cooper, "Terrorism: New Dimensions of Violent Criminality," *Cumberland Law Review* 9 (1978): 370.

48. National Advisory Committee on Criminal Justice Standards and Goals, *Disorders and Terrorism* (Washington, D.C.: U.S. Government Printing Office, 1976), p. 3.

49. For a recent discussion of the need for a more expansive and conceptual definition of terrorism, see Jack P. Gibbs, "Conceptualization of Terrorism," *American Sociological Review* 54 (June 1989): 329–340.

50. *Ibid.*, pp. 3–7.

51. Ariel Merari, "A Classification of Terrorist Groups," *Terrorism* 1, no. 2 (1978): 332–347; as cited in Wayne A. Kerstetter, "Terrorism," in Sanford H. Kadish, ed., *Encyclopedia of Crime and Justice*, vol. 4 (Macmillan, 1983), p. 1533.

52. Merari, "Classification of Terrorist Groups," p. 339; in Kerstetter, "Terrorism," p. 1534.

53. "Terrorist Attacks Expected to Persist, U.S. Official Says," *The Dallas Morning News*, 13 July 1986, p. 26A, col. 1.

54. See "Terror in the South: Deadly Mail Bombs Claim Two Prominent Victims," *Newsweek*, 1 January 1990, p. 34.

55. Robert H. Kupperman, "Terrorism and Public Policy," in Lynn A. Curtis, ed., *American Violence and Public Policy: An Update on the National Commission on the Causes and Prevention of Violence* (New Haven, Conn.: Yale University Press, 1985), pp. 184, 188.

56. "F.B.I. Chief Hails Gains on Terror," *New York Times*, 12 August 1986, p. 12, col. 1.

57. "90 Years Imposed in two Poisonings," *New York Times*, 18 June 1988, p. 8, col. 1.

58. H. H. A. Cooper, "The Terrorist and His Victim," Hearing before the Subcommittee on Criminal Laws and Procedures of Committee on the Judiciary, U.S. Senate, 95th Cong., 1st Sess., July 21, 1977 (Washington, D.C.: U.S. Government Printing Office, 1977), pp. 2–5. See also "The Terrorist Profile," in Richard W. Kobetz and H. H. A. Cooper, *Target Terrorism: Providing Protective Services* (Gaithersburg, Md.: International Association of Chiefs of Police, 1978), pp. 119–147. For a discussion of women as terrorists, see H. H. A. Cooper, "Woman as Terrorist," in Freda Adler and Rita James Simon, eds., *The Criminology of Deviant Women* (Boston: Houghton Mifflin, 1979), pp. 150–157, and Daniel E. Georges-Abeyie, "Women as Terrorists," in Lawrence Freedman and Y. Alexander, eds., *Perspectives on Terrorism* (Wilmington, Del.: Scholarly Resources, Inc., 1983), pp. 71–84.

59. See Frederick J. Hacker, *Crusaders, Criminals, Crazies* (New York: Norton, 1976), p. 137. See also H. H. A. Cooper, "Close Encounters of an Unpleasant Kind: Preliminary Thoughts on the Stockholm Syndrome," *Legal Medical Quarterly* 2 (April 1978): 100–114.

60. "Hitting the Soruce: U.S. Bombers Strike at Libya's Author of Terrorism, Dividing Europe and Threatening a Rash of Retaliations," *Time*, 28 April 1986, pp. 16–27.

61. Ted Robert Gurr, *Why Men Rebel* (Princeton, N.J.: Princeton University Press, 1970), p. 232; quoted in Robert G. Bell, "The U.S. Response to Terrorism Against International Civil Aviation," in John D. Elliott and Leslie K. Gibson, eds., *Contemporary Terrorism: Selected Readings* (Gaithersburg, Md.: International Association of Chiefs of Police, 1978), p. 191.

PART IV

The Criminal Justice System

CHAPTER 11

This chapter begins our look into the United States criminal justice system by analyzing the philosophy on which that system rests. After examining the stages in the system, we will consider the concept of due process and then analyze four of the basic constitutional rights of defendants: the right to be free from unreasonable search and seizure, the right not to testify against oneself, the right to counsel, and the right to a trial by jury. These rights are recognized to make sure that the state, in apprehending, charging, and trying people for alleged criminal activity, follows proper procedures. But recognition of these rights at times conflicts with victims' rights, a subject we will also examine.

OUTLINE

The American System of Criminal Justice

KEY TERMS

adversary system
arraignment
arrest
bail
booking
burden of proof
contempt of court
criminal justice system
defendant
discretion
due process
equal protection
grand jury
habeas corpus
indictment
information
initial appearance
inquisitory system
jurisdiction
magistrate
Miranda warning
parole
peremptory challenges
preliminary hearing
probable cause
probation
restitution
search warrant
trial
victim's compensation program

The philosophy on which the American system of criminal justice rests is embodied in the statement of ethics of the American Bar Association: "The continued existence of a free and democratic society depends upon recognition of the new concept that justice is based upon the rule of law grounded in respect for the dignity of the individual and his capacity through reason for enlightened self-government." The American **criminal justice system** is based on the philosophy that the defendant's dignity must be recognized, that the defendant is innocent until proved guilty by the state, and that the state must follow proper procedures in proving its case against the defendant. Violation of these rules will impair the rights of defendants and threaten the foundation of the United States system of criminal justice.

STAGES IN THE CRIMINAL JUSTICE SYSTEM

4 components

The criminal justice system in the United States has four components: police, prosecution, courts, and corrections.

The *police*, responsible for the entry of most people into the system, are also involved in some pretrial procedures. The police are very important, and the next chapter will focus on their duties. The second major component is *prosecution*. The decision to prosecute in a criminal case is a crucial decision that involves the discretion of *prosecuting attorneys*, who bring the charges against the accused, and *defense attorneys*, who represent the accused, or the **defendant.**

Prosecutors and defense attorneys function within the criminal court system. *Courts*, the third major element of the criminal justice system, are presided over by *judges*. The role of judges, prosecutors, and defense attorneys will be discussed in Chapter 13 along with the structure of courts and the concepts of punishment and sentencing.

The final component of the criminal justice system is *corrections*, which includes the detainment of some defendants in jail before trial and their confinement in jails and prisons after conviction.

Figure 11.1 diagrams the specific procedures and stages of a criminal case as it flows through the four components of the system. Each stage will be described briefly.

Investigation Prior to Arrest

When a complaint is received by the police or when the police are observers at a crime scene, an investigation may be made. The police may interview witnesses and obtain information that will lead to an arrest. During the investigation, the police may briefly detain the suspect and may search for weapons.

Arrest

Most police encounters do not result in **arrest,** and the police have great discretion at this stage. When a person is officially arrested, he or she is taken into custody (usually to the police station) and charged with a crime.

Booking

When the police arrive at the police station with an arrested suspect, the suspect is booked—name of suspect and location, time, and purpose of arrest will be entered in the police arrest book, or log. The suspect may be fingerprinted, photographed, and released after **booking** if it is determined that a crime was not committed or that there is not sufficient evidence to hold the suspect for the crime.

Initial Appearance

Most states have a statutory requirement that after arrest, the suspect must be taken quickly before a magistrate for an **initial appearance.** The **magistrate,** presumed to be a neutral party, must tell the suspect his or her rights and the charge filed.

Preliminary Hearing

The defendant may waive the **preliminary hearing** in which the evidence against the accused is considered. If it is not waived, the government's evidence will be examined. The magistrate may at this stage dismiss the charges or bind the suspect over to the grand jury for an indictment or to the prosecuting attorney for an information (discussed next). The magistrate may also set **bail.**

Information

If a grand jury is not used, the prosecutor may return an **information,** an accusation by the prosecutor, based on the evidence available from police officers or private citizens. An information is a formal legal document sufficient to send a suspect to trial.

Grand Jury Indictment

In some jurisdictions the prosecutor must bring formal charges and have the approval of the grand jury, which, after examining the evidence, returns an **indictment,** or a true bill. The indictment serves the same purpose as the information; it requires the suspect to appear before a court that has **jurisdiction** to hear the charges. The **grand jury,** a specified number of private citizens chosen randomly, meets at periodic intervals to consider whether to indict suspects presented by the prosecution. The grand jury may also conduct investigations on its own.

Figure 11.1
A General View of the Criminal Justice System

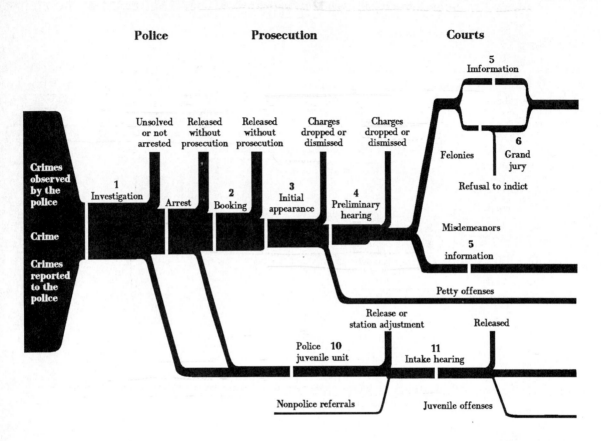

1 May continue until trial.

2 Administrative record of arrest. First step at which temporary release on bail may be avalable.

3 Before magistrate, commissioner or justice of peace. Formal notice of charge, advice of rights. Bail set. Summary trials for petty offenses usually conducted here without further processing.

4 Preliminary testing of evidence against defendant. Charge may be reduced. No separate preliminary hearing for misdemeanors in some systems.

5 Charge filed by prosecutor on basis of information submitted by police for citizens. Alternative to grand jury indictment; often used in felonies, almost always in misdemeanors.

SOURCE: President's Commission on Law Enforcement and Administration of Justice, *The Challenge of Crime in a Free Society* (Washington, D.C.: U.S. Government Printing Office, 1967), pp. 8–9.

Figure 11.1

Procedures in individual jurisdictions may vary from the pattern shown here. The differing weights of line indicate the relative volume of cases disposed of at various points in the system. But this is only suggestive since no nationwide data of this sort exist.

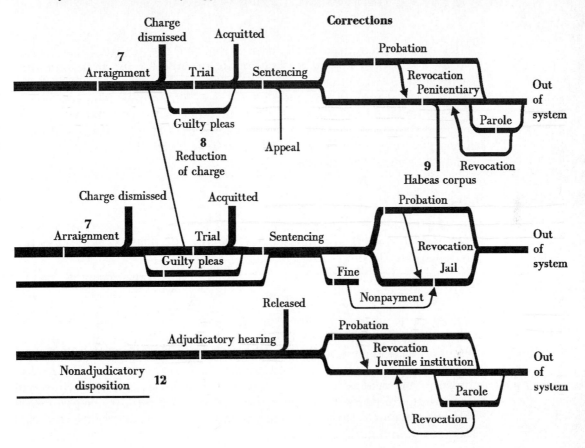

6 Reviews whether government evidence is sufficient to justify trial. Some states have no grand jury system; others seldom use it.

7 Appearance for plea: defendant elects trial by judge or jury (if available); counsel for indigent usually appointed here in felonies.

8 Charge may be reduced at any time before trial in return for plea of guilty or for other reasons.

9 Challenge on constitutional grounds to legality of detention. May be sought at any point in process.

10 Police often hold informal hearings, dismiss or adjust many cases without further processing.

11 Probation officer decides desirability of further court action.

12 Welfare agency, social services, counseling, medical care, etc., for cases where adjudicatory handling not needed.

5th Amn

The Fifth Amendment to the U.S. Constitution provides that in federal cases felonies must go through the process of indictment by a grand jury. Some state laws also require this process, but the U.S. Supreme Court has held that states are not required to use the grand jury indictment.

Arraignment

After an information or indictment is secured, the suspect must appear before a court. At this stage—the **arraignment**—for the first time after hearing the formal charges and again being informed of his or her rights, the defendant may plead. If the plea is not guilty, a trial date will be set. If the defendant has a choice of a trial by judge or by jury, that decision is made at this stage. Certain pretrial motions may also be made, such as a motion to change the place where the trial will be held or to suppress the evidence against the accused.

Reduction of Charge

For a number of reasons, the charge against the defendant may be reduced. The defendant may agree to plead guilty to lesser charges rather than stand trial on the original charge.

Trial

If the case is not dismissed and the defendant does not plead guilty, the case will go to **trial.** Most trials of minor offenses will be brief, perhaps less than an hour or two. In complex cases the trial may last for weeks or months. Witnesses will be questioned by attorneys, victims may testify, and physical evidence such as weapons allegedly used in the crime will be introduced. Rules of evidence are complex and require frequent decisions by the judge. Most defendants whose cases proceed through the trial stage are found guilty.

Sentencing

After the defendant pleads guilty or is found guilty at a trial, the judge enters a judgment of conviction and sets a date for sentencing. Sentencing in minor cases may occur immediately; but in cases involving serious offenses or defendants who have been convicted of several offenses, the judge will usually set sentencing for a future date to permit time for presentence investigations.

Appeals and Postconviction Remedies

Defendants may have legal grounds on which to appeal their convictions to an appellate court. Defendants may also challenge their confinement through various postconviction remedies such as **habeas corpus,** which, as Figure 11.1 indicates, is a "challenge on constitutional grounds to legality of detention." Through this procedure, frequently used, inmates argue that they are being confined illegally because the conditions of confinement constitute a violation of some federally guaranteed constitutional right.

Incarceration

Convicted persons may be permitted to return to the community with or without supervision while on **probation,** the most frequently imposed sentence. Others are incarcerated in jails, prisons, or work camps.

Release from the System

Upon completion of a sentence, inmates must be released. Some will be released before the end of the sentence through the process of **parole.** Inmates on parole may be returned to prison to serve the remainder of their terms if they violate parole conditions. Today many correctional systems release inmates early to reduce prison overcrowding. Many are under federal court order to keep their inmate populations at or below a specified level.

SPECIAL CHARACTERISTICS OF THE CRIMINAL JUSTICE SYSTEM

Two characteristics are important to an understanding of the criminal justice system. The first is the system effect of all elements and procedures, and the second is the element of discretion.

System Effect

The criminal justice system in the United States is both a system and a process. The system aspect is important but is often overlooked. What happens at one stage may have a significant effect on what happens at another stage or in another component.

One way in which the system interrelates may be seen in the use of probation and parole. If the judges, who grant probation, begin to do so in significantly fewer cases and substitute prison sentences, prison populations will increase, creating serious problems for financing and staffing. If parole boards significantly decrease the number of people to whom they grant parole, thus increasing the amount of time inmates will spend in prison, prison populations will increase.

This chapter points out some of the effects that changes in one part of the criminal justice system have on other parts, especially one of the most dramatic—the effect that observing defendants' rights has on enforcing the law. If we allowed police to search and seize without restrictions, and if we tortured or tricked defendants to the point that they would confess, we could have more arrests and more convictions. If we did not allow trial by jury and many of the other rights in the United States system, we could speed up the process and decrease court congestion. But these processes would also result in enlarging prison populations, many of which are already overcrowded.

A few recent examples dramatically illustrate the system effect of changing some laws or of altering the extent to which the laws are enforced. A Jacksonville, Florida, official in the sheriff's office emphasized that the crackdown on drug offenders was "bogging down the court system, crowding the jails and failing to cut down on the drug trade." A judge said that processing so many drug cases was hindering his ability to process other types of cases, such as robberies, murders, and other serious felonies.[1] Increasing the number of arrests for drug violations in New York City has led to the system effects described in Exhibit 11.1.

Discretion

In the United States criminal justice system wide discretion is permitted. It is not possible to anticipate all the facts that might be involved in all decision-making opportunities. For example, police departments do not have sufficient personnel to enforce all laws at all times. Total enforcement is probably also unwise, for there may be extenuating circumstances that justify not enforcing some laws. But if all laws are not to be enforced at all times, the police must make decisions concerning law enforcement. Police officers must also frequently decide how to allocate their time, what types of investigation to conduct, and whether a search is reasonable. There are guidelines for making these decisions, and courts, constitutions, and statutes also impose rules concerning decision making. But some discretion is inevitable.

Discretion must also be exercised by other professionals in the system, as indicated in Exhibit 11.2. Discretion is an inevitable feature of the criminal justice system. Though guidelines, laws, and constitutional amendments may be passed to regulate discretion, it cannot be eliminated. Discretion properly used is functional for the system. Many cases should not be prosecuted or tried, and a refusal to arrest may be the best approach in some cases.

One result of discretion is that the number of cases proceeding through the system is considerably smaller than the number coming to the attention of the police. Figure 11.2 pictures the funnel effect of the

EXHIBIT 11.1

System Effect of Drug Arrest "Sweeps"

New York State Chief Judge Sol Wachtler has announced plans to accelerate the processing of drug felonies in New York City this summer, saying that the Police Department's targeting of certain neighborhoods for drug arrest "sweeps" has forced a crisis upon the rest of the criminal justice system.

If drug dealers are arrested but then released because prosecutors and the courts cannot keep pace with the police department, a very dangerous disrespect for the criminal justice system results, Judge Wachtler said. "What is being lost is the certainty of punishment, which is even more important as a deterrent to crime than the severity," he said.

Currently there is a city-wide "bulge" of 2,500 cases in which drug offenders have pleaded guilty to felonies but have not been sentenced, Wachtler said, and "as fast as these 2,500 cases can be disposed of, more will be coming in." The chief judge called for creation of two temporary courtrooms at the Rikers Island jail complex in Queens, where 12,000 inmates are held. Under Wachtler's plan, judges would sentence offenders on a 24-hour basis at the jail, saving time by eliminating the need for shuttling offenders between court and the isolated jail facility.

Judge Wachtler said he planned the temporary transfer of up to 25 judges from the Civil Court of New York City to the city's Criminal Court, which handles misdemeanor cases and preliminary hearings for felony cases. Judges also will be transferred temporarily from the city's Criminal Court to state Supreme Court (the state's court of general jurisdiction). Wachtler added that he will ask judges and other court officials to defer their vacations this summer.

Wachtler emphasized that the emergency measures were not a substitute for larger budgets and staffing levels for the courts. He said court appropriations should have been increased last year when the Police Department began its Tactical Narcotics Team (TNT) program, in which squads of police officers make hundreds of street-level arrests in an effort to "clean up" neighborhoods plagued by drug dealing. "Although we represent a third and equal branch of government, we find that at budget time some branches are more equal than others," the chief judge said.

In announcing his plans, Wachtler was joined at a press conference by all five of New York City's district attorneys. The prosecutors praised the TNT units' successes in making arrests, but said the $116 million program skimped on the courts, the district attorneys, and the Legal Aid Society lawyers who represent indigent defendants. Manhattan District Attorney Robert M. Morgenthau said that many of the prosecutors in his office handled 150 felony drug cases each last year, which he called "intolerably high." TNT sweeps were expanded to include areas of Manhattan in November, and were largely responsible for a 20 percent rise in the number of drug cases filed there in the first two months of this year (6,700 cases), compared to the same period last year, according to the state Office of Court Administration.

SOURCE: "Numerous Drug Arrests Bringing Crisis to New York City Courts," *Criminal Justice Newsletter* 20 (1 May 1989), p 4.

EXHIBIT 11.2

Who Exercises Discretion in the Criminal Justice System?

These Criminal Justice Officials . . .	. . . Must Often Decide Whether or Not or How to—
Police	Enforce specific laws
	Investigate specific crimes
	Search people, vicinities, buildings
	Arrest or detain people
Prosecutors	File charges or petitions for adjudication
	Seek indictments
	Drop cases
	Reduce charges
Judges or magistrates	Set bail or conditions for release
	Accept pleas
	Determine delinquency
	Dismiss charges
	Impose sentence
	Revoke probation
Correctional officials	Assign to type of correctional facility
	Award privileges
	Punish for disciplinary infractions
Paroling authority	Determine date and conditions of parole
	Revoke parole

SOURCE: Bureau of Justice Statistics, *Report to the Nation on Crime and Justice: The Data*, 2d ed., (Washington, D.C.: U.S. Government Printing Office, 1988), p. 59.

system with a decrease in the number of cases as a defendant moves through the stages. It is estimated that of 5000 felonies that come to the attention of the police, there will be only 1500 arrests. Many of those cases will be dismissed; approximately 400 will be resolved by a plea of guilty and only 100 cases will actually go to trial. Of those who plead guilty and of those who are convicted after a trial, only about 100 will be sentenced to prison terms.[2]

There are many reasons for the decrease in cases through the various stages. In addition to the effect that the exercise of discretion by police or court officials may have, cases may also be dismissed because victims and/or witnesses refuse to testify; prosecutors do not have enough evi-

Figure 11.2
The Criminal Justice Funnel

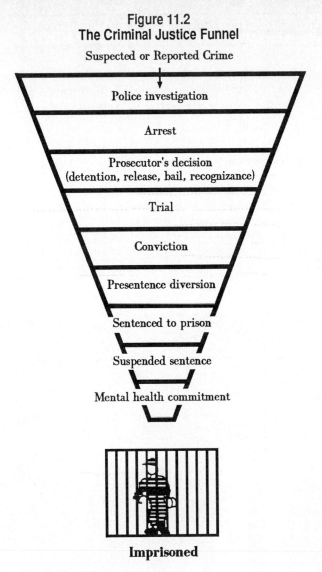

Suspected or Reported Crime

Police investigation

Arrest

Prosecutor's decision
(detention, release, bail, recognizance)

Trial

Conviction

Presentence diversion

Sentenced to prison

Suspended sentence

Mental health commitment

Imprisoned

SOURCE: Sue Titus Reid, *The Correctional System: An Introduction* (New York: Holt, Rinehart and Winston, Inc. 1981), p. 6.

dence for convictions without those testimonies. Witnesses and victims may agree to testify but fail to appear in court at the appropriate time. Time lags may result in witnesses and victims dying or moving a long distance from the jurisdiction thus making it financially unreasonable for them to appear. Improper statements by attorneys or witnesses or improper police behavior during arrest or investigation may lead the trial judge to exclude evidence that is vital to the case. Without that evidence a conviction is unlikely; so the judge dismisses the case.

CONCEPTS OF AMERICAN CRIMINAL JUSTICE

The United States system of criminal justice is based on the adversary model, characterized by the concepts of due process and equal protection, which guarantee numerous rights to defendants who are charged with crimes.

The Adversary Versus the Inquisitory System

The **adversary system** presumes that the best way to get the facts is to have a contest between the two sides—the state and the prosecuting attorney representing the side of society and the victim (in a criminal trial) versus the defense attorney and the defendant. In contrast is the **inquisitory system,** under which the accused is presumed guilty and must prove his or her innocence. The primary difference between the two systems is the

Safeguards are provided in the adversary system to attempt to prevent conviction of the innocent. Mistakes do occur, however, as evidenced in the case of Lenell Geter, wrongfully convicted in Dallas, Texas. Geter, left, served 477 days of a life sentence before being released and granted a new trial.

presumption of guilt versus the presumption of innocence which affects the **burden of proof.** Under the adversary system, the state has the burden of proving guilt; under the inquisitory system, the defendant has the burden of proving innocence. This is a major difference for in our system the burden of proof is a critical element. For example, in our criminal system the burden is that of *beyond a reasonable doubt*, as compared to the civil burden, which is *a preponderance of the evidence.* Proving that one is guilty beyond a reasonable doubt is a heavy burden, but we impose that stringent standard on the state because we believe that it is better to release a guilty person than to convict an innocent one. The issue is particularly critical when the death penalty may be imposed.

In 1989 the conviction of Randall Dale Adams was overturned after he had spent twelve years in prison and had narrowly escaped the death penalty. Adams' conviction was unanimously overturned by the highest criminal appellate court in Texas on the grounds that the prosecutor in the case had permitted perjured testimony and also had withheld evidence. The case came into public view with the release in 1988 of the movie *The Thin Blue Line*, which detailed the highlights of Adams' conviction for killing a Dallas, Texas police officer. In the wake of criticism of the District Attorney's office that was responsible for the case, two prosecutors resigned. It was later announced that Adams would not be retried since the state does not have any credible evidence that he killed the officer. This was the second time in five years that Texas prosecutors had been questioned for their overzealous efforts at "justice." Lenell Geter, a black engineer, spent sixteen months in a Texas prison on a life sentence he received upon wrongful conviction of robbery of a fast-food establishment. A 1985 study circulated by the American Civil Liberties Union concluded that in this century 345 people were wrongly convicted of capital crimes and that 25 were subsequently executed.[3] Highlight 11.1 relates the facts of another nationally publicized recent case of wrongful conviction. Although many argue that these problems are the result of "inevitable mistakes," several authorities dispute that position. C. Ronald Huff, who with others has studied 500 cases of wrongful convictions, concludes, "A substantial significant number of cases . . . are . . . attributable either to professional dishonesty and deception or to professional incompetence."[4]

Wrongful convictions may occur in either the adversary or the inquisitory systems, but in the U.S. we believe the former has greater protections against such tragedies. The adversary system has aroused considerable criticism, some of which is justified; but it is important to understand its philosophy, which is based on the concepts of due process and equal protection for all criminal defendants.

Due Process and Equal Protection

The two basic philosophies underlying the adversary system are the concepts of due process and equal protection. Both are difficult to define and have been the subjects of numerous court decisions. A former Supreme

HIGHLIGHT 11.1

WRONGFUL CONVICTION: THE CASE OF JAMES RICHARDSON

In 1989, after spending twenty-one years in prison for wrongful conviction of murdering his seven children, James Richardson was released. His words were, "I'm free at last. Thank God I'm free at last." Richardson, accompanied by former comedian Dick Gregory and others, visited his children's graves. With tears in his eyes, he said, "We ask you to look after the children all over this world. We hope that they going to escape this. . . . I never thought it was going to be like this, Oh, oh Lord."

Richardson's children died after eating poisoned food in a lunch prepared and served to them by their baby sitter while Richardson and his wife were working eight miles away in a citrus grove. Two nurses in the home where the former sitter is a patient with Alzheimer's disease testified that several years ago the sitter had confessed to murdering the children. Richardson was convicted and sentenced to death. His death sentence was overturned as the result of the Supreme Court's landmark capital punishment decision in 1972, *Furman v. Georgia*. Richardson, who came so close to execution that he was on death watch, with his head shaved, watching his coffin being made, said, "You can almost taste the sense of death on your tongue." At his release he said, "I'm still a little bit unsatisfied. It's taken so long. This should have happened twenty years ago." Richardson has filed a $35 million civil suit against the two prosecutors and the county sheriff whom he blames for his wrongful conviction, and his ex-wife plans to sue for a portion of any financial damages he receives. Negotiations are also proceeding for a movie on his life, conviction, and release.

SOURCE: Summarized by the author from media sources.

Court justice attempted to explain **due process** in this frequently quoted statement:

> "Due Process," unlike some legal rules, is not a technical conception with a fixed content unrelated to time, place and circumstances. . . . [It] cannot be imprisoned within the treacherous limits of any formula. Representing a profound attitude of fairness between man and man, and more particularly between the individual and government, "due process" is compounded of history, reason, the past course of decisions, and stout confidence in the strength of the democratic faith which we possess. Due process is not a mechanical instrument. It is not a yardstick. It is a process.[5]

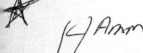

Equal Protection is also the subject of complex litigation; but simply stated, this concept, stated in the Fourteenth Amendment, prohibits treating people differently because of their membership in certain classes or groups, such as discrimination because of sex, race, or religion. The Fourteenth Amendment and other relevant amendments that pertain to some of our most precious rights are reprinted in Exhibit 11.3. Because the framers of the Constitution were concerned that the federal government might

EXHIBIT 11.3

Selected Amendments, United States Constitution

AMENDMENT IV (1791)

The right of the people to be secure in their persons, houses, papers, and effects, against unreasonable searches and seizures, shall not be violated, and no Warrants shall issue, but upon probable cause, supported by Oath or affirmation, and particularly describing the place to be searched, and the persons or things to be seized.

AMENDMENT V (1791)

capital crimes
infamous crimes

No person shall be held to answer for a capital, or otherwise infamous crime, unless on a presentment or indictment of a Grand Jury, except in cases arising in the land or naval forces, or in the Militia, when in actual service in time of War or public danger, nor shall any person be subject for the same offence to be twice put in jeopardy of life or limb; nor shall be compelled in any criminal case to be a witness against himself, nor be deprived of life, liberty, or property, without due process of law; nor shall private property be taken for public use, without just compensation.

AMENDMENT VI (1791)

In all criminal prosecutions, the accused shall enjoy the right to a speedy and public trial, by an impartial jury of the State and district wherein the crime shall have been committed, which district shall have been previously ascertained by law, and to be informed of the nature and cause of the accusation; to be confronted with the witnesses against him; to have compulsory process for obtaining witnesses in his favor, and to have the Assistance of Counsel for his defence.

AMENDMENT XIV (1868)

Most impt.

Section 1. All persons born or naturalized in the United States, and subject to the jurisdiction thereof, are citizens of the United States and of the State wherein they reside. No State shall make or enforce any law which shall abridge the privileges or immunities of citizens of the United States; nor shall any State deprive any person of life, liberty, or property, without due process of law; nor deny to any person within its jurisdiction the equal protection of the laws.

become too strong, the Bill of Rights was added to protect citizens. Some of those provisions are reprinted in Exhibit 11.3. It is clear through early Supreme Court decisions that the Bill of Rights restricts only the federal government, but gradually the Court has held that most of the provisions apply to the states through the due process clause of the Fourteenth Amendment.

SELECTED CONSTITUTIONAL RIGHTS OF DEFENDANTS

Because the battle would not be evenly matched in a criminal trial if all the powers of the government were thrown against the individual defendant, procedural safeguards have been instituted. The prosecution is required to prove its case beyond a reasonable doubt. Defendants cannot be forced to testify against themselves; their persons and possessions cannot be searched unreasonably; they are entitled to be notified of the charges against them and to have impartial and public trials by juries of their peers; they are entitled to counsel, and if they cannot afford counsel, the state must provide attorneys; defendants may be tried only once for the same offense; and they are presumed innocent until proved guilty. This section examines some of these constitutional rights. The law for these rights is very complex, however, so no attempt will be made to cover every aspect.

The Right to be Free from Unreasonable Search and Seizure

The Fourth Amendment prohibition against *unreasonable* searches and seizures has been tested in numerous cases, many of which have been decided by the U.S. Supreme Court. Unreasonable searches and seizures are prohibited because, according to the Court, the Constitution guarantees a reasonable expectation of privacy. But the protection of society also requires that at some times privacy may be invaded. In an extensive and insightful analysis of the search and seizure provision of the fourth amendment, a law professor concludes as follows:

> Fourth amendment doctrine is driven by society's attitudes and beliefs about the relative value of autonomy and security. In this continuing struggle between the individual and the collective there is only one rule: neither may utterly dominate the other—chaos and tyranny are equally to be avoided. How any society strikes the balance will reflect its history, traditions and institutions as well as the current ratio of fear and hope among its citizens. The fourth amendment embodies both the commitment of American society to "the security of one's privacy against arbitrary intrusion by the police," and the larger commitment to a written constitution as the essential guardian of that freedom.[6]

To assure that our reasonable expectation of privacy is protected, in most instances a search without a valid **search warrant** is a violation of the Fourth Amendment. The Fourth Amendment, said the Court in a 1948 decision, does not prohibit searches; but it does require that "when the right of privacy must reasonably yield to the right of search," the decision should in most cases be "drawn by a neutral and detached magistrate instead of being judged by the officer engaged in the often competitive enterprise of ferreting out crime."[7]

The search warrant is to be issued by the neutral magistrate only after a finding of **probable cause,** which means that in light of the facts of the case, a reasonable person would think that the evidence sought exists and that it exists in the place to be searched. The probable cause requirement also applies when an officer is searching without a search warrant. Probable cause has been defined by one court as follows:

> Probable cause has both a subjective and an objective component. An officer must subjectively believe that a thing is subject to seizure, and the belief must be reasonable under the circumstances. Probable cause does not require certainty.[8]

Despite its preference for warrants, the Supreme Court has allowed some exceptions, arguing, however, that these exceptions are few, specifically established, and well delineated. ‑

Automobile Searches

In *Illinois v. Gates,* the Court considered what kinds of facts the police must produce to convince a magistrate that they have probable cause to obtain a warrant to search an automobile.[9]

In *Gates,* the Police Department of Bloomingdale, Illinois, received an anonymous letter indicating that two specified people, a husband and his wife, were engaging in illegal drug sales and that on May 3 the wife would drive their car, loaded with drugs, to Florida. The husband, the letter indicated, would fly to Florida to drive the car back to Illinois with the trunk loaded with drugs. The letter also indicated that the couple currently had about $100,000 worth of drugs in their Illinois basement. After receiving this information, a police officer secured the address of the couple and found out that the husband had made a May 5 reservation to fly to Florida. Surveillance indicated that the suspect took the flight, spent the night in a motel room registered to his wife, and the next morning left the motel in a car with a woman. The license plate of the car was registered to the husband. The couple were driving north on an interstate highway frequently used for traffic to Illinois. Using these facts, the police secured a search warrant for the couple's house and automobile.

The police, with warrants, were waiting for the couple when they returned to their home in Illinois. Upon searching the house and car, the police found drugs that the state attempted to use against the couple at trial.

The Court, in upholding the issuance of the search warrant and subsequent use of the seized evidence, established a "totality of circumstances" test for determining whether probable cause to issue a search warrant exists when informers provide the information. In *Gates,* independent police verification of the allegations from the anonymous source provided sufficient information on which a magistrate could have probable cause to issue the warrants. Although neither the anonymous letter alone nor the police's conclusions concerning the reliability of the informer were sufficient for probable cause, the extensive corroborating evidence obtained by the police, coupled with the letter and the police's conclusions, provided a reliable basis for issuing the search warrant.

The Court also permits some warrantless searches of automobiles. In *U.S. v. Ross* the Court held that when police have probable cause to search a lawfully stopped automobile, they may without a warrant properly search any containers that might be used to conceal the object of the search.[10] Thus, if the car is stopped because police have probable cause to believe that it contains illegal drugs, they may search any container that is capable of concealing drugs. In *U.S. v. Johns* the Court ruled that the search of the container need not be conducted immediately, and it upheld the warrantless search of containers taken from a truck that police had probable cause to believe contained marijuana. The search of the containers was not conducted for several days.[11]

In 1987 in *Colorado v. Bertine*, the Court upheld the search of Bertine's van after Bertine was arrested for driving while intoxicated. One officer took Bertine to the police station while another took inventory of his truck which had not yet been towed. This search was conducted without a search warrant; but it was upheld because "there was no showing that the police, who were following standardized procedures, acted in bad faith or for the sole purpose of investigation." In addition, the police were responsible for the truck since they were having it towed. "Knowledge of the precise nature of the property helped guard against claims of theft, vandalism, or negligence. Such knowledge also helped to avert any danger to police or others that may have been posed by the property."[12]

Search of the Person

The law of search and seizure has also changed for persons. In *Rochin v. California* the Supreme Court stated its position on one method of searching the person for evidence of a crime.[13]

Rochin v. California

Having "some information that [petitioner here] was selling narcotics," three deputy sheriffs of the County of Los Angeles, on the morning of July 1, 1949, made for the two-story dwelling house in which Rochin lived with his mother, common-law wife, brothers and sisters. Finding the outside door open, they entered and then forced open the door to Rochin's room on the second floor. Inside they found petitioner sitting partly dressed on the side of the bed, upon which his wife was lying. On a "night stand" beside the bed the deputies spied two capsules. When asked "Whose stuff is this?" Rochin seized the capsules and put them in his mouth. A struggle ensued, in the course of which three officers "jumped upon him" and attempted to extract the capsules. The force they applied proved unavailing against Rochin's resistance. He was handcuffed and taken to a hospital. At the direction of one of the officers a doctor forced an emetic solution through a tube into Rochin's stomach against his will. This "stomach pumping" produced vomiting. In the vomited matter were found two capsules which proved to contain morphine.

Rochin was brought to trial . . . on the charge of possessing "a preparation of morphine." . . . Rochin was convicted and sentenced to sixty days' imprisonment. The chief evidence against him was the two capsules.

. . . [W]e are compelled to conclude that the proceedings by which this conviction was obtained do more than offend some fastidious squeamishness or private sentimentalism about combatting crime too energetically. This is conduct that shocks the conscience, illegally breaking into the privacy of the petitioner, the struggle to open his mouth and remove what was there, the forcible extraction of his stomach's contents—this course of proceedings by agents of government to obtain evidence is bound to offend even hardened sensibilities. They are methods too close to the rack and the screw to permit of constitutional differentiation.

The Court upheld the body search of a woman suspected of smuggling drugs at the border. A search of her rectum produced a cocaine-filled balloon. A strip search was conducted only after the authorities, with probable cause to believe the suspect was smuggling drugs, conducted a pat down search, which indicated that the suspect's abdomen was firm and that she was wearing elastic underpants lined with a paper towel. Using this evidence, authorities secured a warrant to conduct a strip search. She later excreted eighty-eight balloons containing 80 percent pure cocaine hydrochloride.

In upholding the strip search, the Court emphasized that the right to privacy is diminished at the border and frequently must give way to the government's right to enforce laws. The test established by the Court for border strip searches is whether customs officials, "considering all the facts surrounding the traveler and her trip, reasonably suspect that the traveler is smuggling contraband in her alimentary canal."[14]

Strip searches of defendants detained in jail pending trial are permitted under some circumstances. In 1979 in *Bell v. Wolfish* the Supreme Court used a reasonableness test, indicating that the strip searches of inmates after they returned from the visitor's room were necessary for security.[15] Routine strip searches of persons arrested for violating traffic ordinances are not, however, permissible, even when those persons are temporarily booked at the police station, unless the police have probable cause to believe that the suspects are hiding drugs or weapons. This issue usually arises in jurisdictions that have a policy of strip searching females but not males.

Violations of the privacy rights of an arrested person by conducting an illegal strip search may lead to successful tort (civil) actions. Thus, in April 1989 a federal appellate court held that the civil rights of a female arrested for two minor traffic offenses were violated when she was strip searched after her arrest. The court emphasized that the fact that this arrestee would come into contact with other jailed inmates was not a sufficient reason to conduct a strip search under *Bell v. Wolfish*. Violence and drugs are not normally associated with the offenses for which she was arrested. More information is therefore needed for the basis of a strip search.[16]

Search of the Home

Searches of the home are also permissible although the Supreme Court has restricted the circumstances under which such searches may be conducted and has limited the areas that may be searched. The landmark case on this issue is *Mapp v. Ohio*.[17]

Mapp v. Ohio

It appears that Miss Mapp was halfway down the stairs from the upper floor to the front door when the officers, in this highhanded manner, broke into the hall. She demanded to see the search warrant. A paper claimed to be a warrant was held up by one of the officers. She grabbed the "warrant" and placed it in her bosom. A struggle ensued in which the officers recovered the piece of paper and as a result of which they handcuffed appellant because she had been "belligerent" in resisting their official rescue of the "warrant" from her person. Running roughshod over appellant, a policeman "grabbed" her, "twisted [her] hand," and she "yelled [and] pleaded with him" because "it was hurting." Appellant, in handcuffs, was then forcibly taken upstairs to her bedroom where the officers searched a dresser, a chest of drawers, a closet and some suitcases. They also looked into a photo album and through personal papers belonging to the appellant. The search spread into the rest of the second floor including the child's bedroom, the living room, the kitchen and a dinette. The basement of the building and a trunk found therein were also searched. The obscene materials for possession of which she was ultimately convicted were discovered in the course of that widespread search.

At the trial no search warrant was produced by the prosecution, nor was the failure to produce one explained or accounted for. At best, "There is, in the record, considerable doubt as to whether there ever was any warrant for the search of the defendant's home."

The seized evidence was used against Ms. Mapp at her trial and she was convicted. The U.S. Supreme Court reversed the conviction. In 1980 the Supreme Court again emphasized the importance of protecting the privacy of the home, noting that "the Fourth Amendment has drawn a firm line at the entrance to the house. Absent exigent circumstances, that threshold may not reasonably be crossed without a warrant."[18] In 1984 the Court held that the Fourth Amendment prohibited the warrantless entry of police into a suspect's home to arrest him for a civil, nonjailable traffic offense.[19]

On the other hand, if police are properly within the home (office, or other structure), they can, without a warrant, seize some evidence under

Testing new rescue equipment for water-related emergencies one day, these same police officers may be using the aircraft for routine aerial surveillance work the next. The Supreme Court upheld the warrantless aerial surveillance of a defendant's backyard marijuana plot, ruling that no reasonable expectation of privacy exists to prohibit the surveillance.

the *plain view doctrine*. This privilege was established by the Supreme Court in 1971 in *Coolidge v. New Hampshire*.[20] In 1987, in *Arizona v. Hicks*, the Court held that probable cause is required to invoke the plain view doctrine, and in 1990 the Court permitted a warrantless "protective sweep," defined as "a quick and limited search of a premises, incident to an arrest and conducted to protect the safety of police officers or others. It is narrowly confined to a cursory visual inspection of those places in which a person might be hiding."[21]

The Supreme Court has also upheld a warrantless aerial surveillance of a defendant's fenced back yard, holding that there is no reasonable expectation of privacy to prohibit this surveillance. The search indicated that marijuana plants were being grown there.[22]

The Right Not to Testify Against Oneself

5th Amm

The Fifth Amendment states that in a criminal trial defendants cannot be compelled to testify against themselves. The idea behind the right has been expressed as follows: "We do not make even the most hardened criminal sign his own death warrant, or dig his own grave, or pull the lever that springs the trap on which he stands. We have through the course of history developed a considerable feeling of the dignity and intrinsic importance of the individual man. Even the evil man is a human being."[23]

The prohibitions against both physical and mental methods for extracting confessions are illustrated by excerpts from two cases. The first case, *Brown v. Mississippi*, gives an example of physical brutality used to elicit confessions from several black defendants. The only evidence on which the defendants could have been convicted was their involuntary confessions, secured after several whippings. The defendants were convicted and sentenced to death. The Mississippi Supreme Court upheld the convictions. The U.S. Supreme Court reversed. The Court's comments, after describing the beating of the first defendant, were as follows.[24]

Brown v. Mississippi

The other two defendants were also arrested and taken to the same jail. On Sunday night, April 1, 1934, the same deputy, accompanied by a number of white men, one of whom was also an officer, and by the jailer, came to the jail, and the two last named defendants were made to strip and they were laid over chairs and their backs were cut to pieces with a leather strap with buckles on it, and they were likewise made by the said deputy definitely to understand that the whipping would be continued unless and until they confessed, and not only confessed, but confessed in every matter of detail as demanded by those present; and in this manner the defendants confessed the crime, and as the whippings progressed and were repeated, they changed or adjusted their confession in all particulars of detail so as to conform to the demands of their torturers. When the confessions had been obtained in the exact form and contents as desired by the mob, they left with the parting admonition and warning that, if the defendants changed their story at any time in any respect from the last stated, the perpetrators of the outrage would administer the same or equally effective treatment. . . .

Because a State may dispense with a jury trial, it does not follow that it may substitute trial by ordeal. The rack and torture chamber may not be substituted for the witness stand.

. . . It would be difficult to conceive of methods more revolting to the sense of justice than those taken to procure the confessions of these petitioners, and the use of the confessions thus obtained as the basis for conviction and sentence was a clear denial of due process. . . .

Enforcement of the Right: The Miranda Warnings

Because of the prohibition against extracting confessions through physical brutality, some jurisdictions began to concentrate on psychological methods such as interrogation in a police-dominated atmosphere, where the accused would be questioned for long periods without rest and without counsel. The interrogator would pretend to have evidence of the suspect's guilt and suggest rationalizations for his or her behavior in an attempt to minimize the moral seriousness of the act. Under such pressure, many suspects would confess.

After some of these interrogation techniques were used on Miranda, he signed a confession indicating that his statement was "voluntary." On the basis of that testimony and other evidence, Miranda was convicted of kidnapping and rape and sentenced to 20 to 30 years in prison for each offense, the sentences to run concurrently.

In deciding *Miranda*, the Supreme Court emphasized the possibility that under the kinds of psychological pressures used by police in the cases before the Court, innocent defendants might confess. In our system of law, said the Court, with the tremendous powers of the state in a criminal trial, it is necessary to give defendants procedural safeguards so as to avoid conviction of the innocent as well as coerced confessions from the guilty.

The Court then interpreted the Fifth Amendment right not to have to testify against oneself as requiring that the police must tell the accused of the specifics of that right. The procedures that the police must follow in the *Miranda* **warning** are explained by the Court in the following excerpt from the case.[25]

Miranda v. Arizona

As for the procedural safeguards to be employed, unless other fully effective means are devised to inform accused persons of their right of silence
and to assure a continuous opportunity to exercise it, the following measures are required. Prior to any questioning, the person must be warned
that he has a right to remain silent, that any statement he does make may
be used as evidence against him, and that he has a right to the presence
of an attorney, either retained or appointed. The defendant may waive
effectuation of these rights, provided the waiver is made voluntarily,
knowingly and intelligently. If, however, he indicates in any manner and
at any stage of the process that he wishes to consult with an attorney
before speaking, there can be no questioning. Likewise, if the individual
is alone and indicates in any manner that he does not wish to be inter-
rogated, the police may not question him. The mere fact that he may have
answered some questions or volunteered some statements on his own
does not deprive him of the right to refrain from answering any further
inquiries until he has consulted with an attorney and thereafter consents
to be questioned.

Reaction to *Miranda*

The *Miranda* decision immediately created a controversy. Reactions have
ranged from the cry that we are licensing people to kill, rape, rob, and
steal to the argument that all the decision did was to extend to all defendants the rights that the Constitution has always guaranteed and that the
rich have always enjoyed. In evaluating these criticisms, it is important to
understand that the Court is not trying to free guilty people but, rather, to
ensure that the rights of the accused are recognized. In many retrials,
defendants are again convicted. Miranda, for example, was retried without the confession. He was again convicted and sentenced to prison. After
his release from prison, he was involved in a fight in which he was killed.

In 1986, when the *Miranda* ruling was twenty years old, the fight to
abolish it was led by former Attorney General Edwin Meese, who called
the *Miranda* case "an infamous decision."[26] However, not everyone agrees
that the decision has created problems for police and should therefore be
altered or abolished. In fact, many scholars argue that police have become
more professional as a result. According to law professor Yale Kamisar of
the University of Michigan, "most studies indicate that the prophecies of
doom have not been fulfilled." Law professor Richard Uviller, of Columbia
University, concluded on the basis of his study of New York police that
although some police violate the *Miranda rule*, most have internalized the
rules and some are even more strict than the Supreme Court requirement.
Some scholars who have studied the impact of the rule on confessions

have concluded that it has not inhibited them. Former Houston Police Chief Lee Brown (subsequently appointed Police Commissioner of New York City) says, "I don't see any detrimental impact [from *Miranda*]."[27]

A recently published study of the effect of *Miranda* on police work concluded as follows:

> It would appear . . . that the debate over the impact of Miranda v. Arizona on the ability of American police to enforce the law and protect the public amounts to little more than political rhetoric. In only .51% of criminal appeals studied over nearly a six-year period was a conviction overturned on a Miranda issue. In roughly one-half of these, police officers reinitiated questioning after the suspect had clearly invoked his right to have an attorney present during interrogation.[28]

Supreme Court Interpretations of *Miranda*

The *Miranda* decision has led to extensive litigation, many of the cases going to the Supreme Court for final review. A few decisions will show the range of questions considered by the Court in recent years.

In *Oregon v. Mathiason*, the Court considered whether the *Miranda* warnings would have to be given to a person who went to the police station and confessed after an investigator had left a card at his home. The card invited the suspect, who was on parole, to go to the police station to talk. The police alleged that the suspect voluntarily went to the station to talk, was told that he was under arrest, and then questioned without an attorney. The *Miranda* warning was not given. The police told the defendant that his fingerprints were found at the scene of the crime. That was not true, but when the defendant heard the assertion, he confessed. The Supreme Court held that the confession was not obtained in violation of the suspect's *Miranda* rights: "*Miranda* warnings are required only where there has been such a restriction on a person's freedom as to render him 'in custody.'"[29]

In 1984 in *Minnesota v. Murphy*, the Court considered whether the *Miranda* warnings would have to be given by a probation officer when talking to a client about another crime. The probationer, when questioned by his probation officer, admitted that he had raped and murdered a teen-age girl. This confession was used against the probationer at his trial, and he was convicted. His attorneys argued that his constitutional rights had been violated because his probation officer had not given him the *Miranda* warning. The Court ruled that the *Miranda* warnings were not required in such cases.[30]

If a suspect invokes the right to remain silent, the police may not legally *interrogate* that suspect until counsel has been provided, although the Court held in *Edwards v. Arizona* that the police may question a suspect who initiates the discussion.[31] In 1988, in *Arizona v. Roberson*, the Court held that the *Edwards* rule applies to bar police-initiated interrogation following a suspect's request for counsel in the context of a separate investigation. In *Edwards*, the police arrested the suspect at the scene of an alleged burglary and began to question him. They stopped the interrogation when the suspect indicated that he wanted an attorney. Three days later, while the suspect was still in custody, another officer, who did not know about the previous request for an attorney, advised the suspect of his *Miranda* rights and began to question him about another burglary. The defendant talked, but the Arizona courts later suppressed the evidence. The Supreme Court agreed, quoting the Arizona court in an earlier case, that the:

> only difference between Edwards and the appellant is that Edwards was questioned about the same offense after a request for counsel while the appellant was reinterrogated about an unrelated offense. We do not believe that this factual distinction holds any legal significance for Fifth Amendment purposes.[32]

The Court does not require that the *Miranda* warnings be given in exactly the manner described in its *Miranda* decision. In 1989 the Court upheld the conviction of a suspect who was informed, after being told of his *Miranda* right to silence and to counsel, that an attorney would be appointed for him "if and when you go to court." In *Duckworth v. Eagan*, the accused later argued that that statement "was constitutionally defective because it denies an accused indigent a clear and unequivocal warning of the right to appointed counsel before any interrogation and links an indigent's right to counsel before interrogation with a future event."[33]

The Supreme Court disagreed, saying it had "never insisted that *Miranda* warnings be given in the exact form described in that decision." In this case, said the Court, the accused was told all the basic *Miranda* rights, and the statement in question accurately described the process for obtaining an appointed attorney in the state of Indiana in which he was charged. "We think it must be relatively commonplace for a suspect, after receiving *Miranda* warnings, to ask *when* he will obtain counsel." The statement in question, indicated the court, simply anticipates that question. *Miranda* does not require that police have attorneys available at all times at the police station. It only requires that police cannot question the suspects until attorneys are provided unless the right to counsel is waived. The suspect was charged with attempted murder in the case of a woman who was stabbed nine times after refusing to have sexual relations with her assailant.

A suspect may waive the right to have counsel present prior to police questioning, but that waiver must be voluntarily, intelligently, and knowingly made. Courts must look to the facts of each case to determine whether the waiver was valid.[34]

The Right to Counsel

The Sixth Amendment, providing that in all criminal prosecutions the accused shall have "the Assistance of Counsel for his defense," became a part of the Bill of Rights in 1791. But it was not until 1963 and 1972, in two important cases, that the right to counsel became a reality for most defendants. Our discussion begins with the 1963 decision, *Gideon v. Wainwright.*

Clarence Earl Gideon was not a violent man, but he was often in trouble with the police for various violations of law. As a result, he had been in and out of prison. At his trial for breaking and entering a poolroom with the intent to commit a misdemeanor, a felony under Florida law, Gideon, acting as his own attorney, argued that he needed a lawyer. Because he had no money, he requested the court to appoint an attorney at the state's expense; but the judge replied that under Florida law, an indigent was not entitled to a court-appointed attorney except when charged with a crime that could result in a death sentence.

After telling the judge that "the United States Supreme Court says I am entitled to an attorney," Gideon conducted his own defense, "about as well as could be expected from a layman," according to the Supreme Court. Nevertheless, Gideon was convicted and sentenced to five years in prison. On January 8, 1962, the Supreme Court of the United States received a large envelope from prisoner 003826 in Florida. Mr. Gideon, who had printed his request in pencil, was asking the highest court of this country to hear his case.

The Court agreed to hear Gideon's case and appointed an attorney from a prestigious Washington, D.C., law firm to represent him. Gideon's attorney convinced the Court that it should overrule a previous case in which the Court had held that the right to counsel appointed at the government's expense if the defendant is indigent applied only to capital cases. The Court reviewed that earlier decision and other cases and then continued with an explanation of the reasons that counsel is important, as this excerpt from Gideon's case illustrates.[35]

Gideon v. Wainwright

Not only these precedents but also reason and reflection require us to recognize that in our adversary system of criminal justice, any person haled into court, who is too poor to hire a lawyer, cannot be assured a fair trial unless counsel is provided for him. . . . The right of one charged with crime to counsel may not be deemed fundamental and essential to fair trials in some countries, but it is in ours. From the very beginning, our state and national constitutions and laws have laid great emphasis on procedure and substantive safeguards designed to assure fair trials before impartial tribunals in which every defendant stands equal before the law. This noble ideal cannot be realized if the poor man charged with crime has to face his accusers without a lawyer to assist him. A defendant's need for a lawyer is nowhere better stated than in the moving words of Mr. Justice Sutherland in *Powell v. Alabama:* "The right to be heard would be, in many cases, of little avail if it did not comprehend the right to be heard by counsel. Even the intelligent and educated layman has small and sometimes no skill in the science of law. If charged with crime, he is incapable, generally, of determining for himself whether the indictment is good or bad. He is unfamiliar with the rules of evidence. Left without aid of counsel he may be put on trial without a proper charge, and convicted upon incompetent evidence irrelevant to the issue or otherwise inadmissible. He lacks both the skill and knowledge adequately to prepare his defense, even though he may have a perfect one. He requires the guiding hand of counsel at every step in the proceedings against him. Without it, though he be not guilty, he faces the danger of conviction because he does not know how to establish his innocence."

Since Gideon was convicted of a felony, the case technically applied the right to appointed counsel to felony cases only. In 1972 in *Argersinger v. Hamlin*, the Supreme Court held that the right to appointed counsel also applied to misdemeanors when conviction would result in the actual deprivation of a person's liberty.[36]

An important question not answered by *Gideon* is how soon after apprehension a suspect is entitled to appointed counsel. In *Escobedo v. Illinois*, the Court had ruled that the right to counsel begins before the trial.[37] The Court has decided numerous cases involving the right to counsel during the pretrial and trial processes. In *Brewer v. Williams*, the Court emphasized that whatever else the right to counsel may mean, it "means at least that a person is entitled to the help of a lawyer at or after the time that judicial proceedings have been initiated against him."[38] In *Maine v. Moulton*, the Court again emphasized the importance of the right to counsel prior to trial by stating that "to deprive a person of counsel during the period prior to trial may be more damaging than denial of counsel during the trial itself."[39]

The Right to Effective Counsel

The right to counsel is of little value unless the attorney who represents the defendant provides an effective defense. Thus, the right to counsel means the right to *effective* counsel. The problem, however, is that there is little consensus on the meaning of that term.

Lower federal courts have attacked this issue, but their answers have varied. A 1984 decision illustrates *ineffective* counsel. The defendant's attorney fell asleep during the trial, and the court ruled that this was inherently prejudicial. According to the court an unconscious or sleeping counsel is equivalent to no counsel at all![40]

In the spring of 1984, the Supreme Court decided two cases on effective assistance of counsel. The first case involved a defendant whose attorney specialized in real estate. He had virtually no experience in criminal law and only 25 days to prepare a defense. The second involved a death row inmate who argued that he did not have effective counsel at the non-jury sentencing stage. In announcing its decision in both cases in *Strickland v. Washington*, the Court reinstated the convictions of both defendants, thus overruling the lower federal courts' rulings. According to the Supreme Court's opinion, "The benchmark for judging any claim of ineffectiveness must be whether counsel's conduct so undermined the proper functioning of the adversarial process that the trial cannot be relied on as having produced a just result." To win on the issue of ineffective assistance of counsel, a defendant must be able to prove that his or her attorney's errors "were so serious as to deprive the defendant of a fair trial, a trial whose result is reliable."[41]

In *Strickland*, the Court gave some guidelines for determining whether a defendant has had effective counsel, and some of those guidelines are reproduced in Exhibit 11.4.

The following excerpt from *U.S. v. Cronic*, also decided in 1984, illustrates the importance of effective assistance of counsel in preserving the adversary system.[42]

U.S. v. Cronic

The right to the effective assistance of counsel is the right of the accused to require the prosecution's case to survive the crucible of meaningful adversarial testing. When a true adversarial criminal trial has been conducted— even if defense counsel may have made demonstrable errors— the kind of testing envisioned by the Sixth Amendment has occurred. But if the process loses its character as a confrontation between adversaries, the constitutional guarantee is violated.

The Right to Trial by Jury

Among other rights, the Sixth Amendment to the U.S. Constitution guarantees the right to a speedy and public trial by an impartial jury. The importance of this right was emphasized by the Supreme Court in 1968 in *Duncan v. Louisiana*. "Providing an accused with the right to be tried by a jury of his peers gave him an inestimable safeguard against the corrupt or overzealous prosecutor and against the compliant, biased, or eccentric judge."[43] This right involves the right to have a jury determine the question of guilt or innocence; it does not mean that a defendant has a right to have the jury determine sentencing, although that is permitted in some

EXHIBIT 11.4

The Supreme Court and Effective Assistance of Counsel

Until recently the Supreme Court had not given much help to lower courts in interpreting what is meant by effective assistance of counsel. In its 1984 decision in *Strickland v. Washington*, however, the Court established a two-prong test: (1) whether counsel's performance was deficient and (2) whether counsel's performance prejudiced the defendant. The Court was not very specific, however, on what those two tests mean. Here are some comments from that and other opinions, all cited by the Court in *Strickland.* Can you tell what is meant by effective assistance of counsel by reading these statements?

1. Counsel must be a reasonably competent attorney whose advice is "within the range of competence of attorneys in criminal cases."

2. To show ineffective assistance of counsel, defendants must show that "counsel's representation fell below an objective standard of reasonableness."

3. Counsel owes the client "a duty of loyalty, a duty to avoid conflicts of interest." Counsel must consult with his or her client, advocate that client's cause, and keep the client informed of the important developments in his or her case.

4. Counsel has a duty "to bring to bear such skill and knowledge as will render the trial a reliable adversarial testing process."

Are these statements too vague? According to the Court, it is not possible to articulate more specific general standards that could be applied to all cases. Each case must be analyzed individually in light of the particular facts. "More specific guidelines are not appropriate.... The proper measure of attorney performance remains simply reasonableness under prevailing professional norms."

SOURCE: *Strickland v. Washington*, 466 U.S. 668 (1984); citations omitted.

---

cases. The right to a jury trial also does not extend to the trial of some less serious offenses. The jury system is very important in the United States, which has approximately one-half of all criminal jury trials in the world, approximately 80,000 per year.[44]

Jury Selection and Impartiality

A defendant is entitled to trial by a jury that is representative of the community, but that does not mean that he or she is entitled to a jury of any particular composition. Rather, it means that the lists from which jurors are selected must not systematically exclude distinctive groups based on criteria such as sex, race, or ethnic background.[45] It also means that actual jury selection may not proceed in a discriminatory manner. But neither must juries be selected in a totally random manner. For example, during the selection process, attorneys may excuse potential jurors for *cause,* meaning that they are presumed to be biased in the case. A person may be presumed biased because of prior associations with the defendant or the judge or attorneys or for any number of other reasons. Potential jurors may also be excused through **peremptory challenges.** When attorneys use this method, they do not need a cause or a reason. The number of peremptory challenges is limited although the number varies by jurisdiction and by type of case.

In *Batson v. Kentucky*, the Court overturned part of an earlier decision and held that prosecutors may not use the peremptory challenge to exclude blacks from juries because they believe blacks will favor their own race. *Batson* is concerned primarily with issues of evidence, but its effect will be to make it easier for minority defendants to prove racial discrimination in the composition of the trial jury. Defendants must show that they are members of a defined minority group, that the prosecutor used the peremptory challenge to remove from the jury persons of that group, and that these and other facts "raise an inference that the prosecutor used the practice to exclude the [potential jurors] on account of their race." The prosecution would then have the burden of proving that the exclusion was not based on racial discrimination.[46]

The right to a jury of peers does not, however, include the right of young adults to be tried by a jury composed of other young adults. The absence of young adults on the jury does not necessarily mean that the young defendant's right to be tried by a jury of peers was violated. The defendant must show that the underrepresented group has characteristics that can be easily defined and that the group has common attitudes, experiences, or ideas in addition to a community of interest.[47] It is also permissible to exclude lawyers from jury pools.

Another issue in selecting an impartial jury concerns the attitudes and beliefs of potential jurors. These attitudes may be so prejudicial that the defendant could not possibly get a fair trial. This issue frequently arises in the context of capital cases. Should people who are opposed to the death penalty be excluded from juries in capital cases?[48]

Most states based their rules concerning jury selection on a footnote of the Supreme Court's 1968 opinion. In *Witherspoon v. Illinois* the Court said that potential jurors could be excused for cause if they made it

> unmistakably clear (1) that they would *automatically* vote against the imposition of capital punishment without regard to any evidence that might be developed at the trial of the case before them or (2) that their attitude toward the death penalty would prevent them from making an impartial decision as to the defendant's *guilt*.[49]

Persons excluded under the *Witherspoon* rule were subsequently referred to as Witherspoon excludables.

In *Wainwright v. Witt*, the Supreme Court said that it does not require a ritualistic adherence to the footnote in *Witherspoon;* the proper test for excluding a juror because of views on capital punishment does not require a conclusion that the juror would automatically vote against capital punishment or that the person's bias had to be unmistakably clear. The test established was whether the person's views on capital punishment would prevent or substantially impair him or her from performing the duties of a juror. The dissenting justices argued that:

> the inevitable result of the quest for such purity in the jury room in a capital case is not a neutral jury drawn from a fair cross-section of the community but a jury biased against the defendant, at least with respect to penalty, and a jury from which an identifiable segment of the community has been excluded.[50]

In *Lockhart v. McCree*, the Court again considered the issue of Witherspoon excludables. Before the Court were a number of social science studies that, according to the petitioners, supported the fact that if Witherspoon excludables were excluded from juries in capital cases, the remaining jurors would be more likely to convict. The Court rejected that position and held that it is permissible to single out Witherspoon excludables and exclude them from jury duty for cause. According to Justice Rehnquist, who wrote the majority opinion, Witherspoon excludables, unlike women, blacks, and Mexican Americans, are excluded for reasons they can control, their attitudes.[51]

Justice Marshall, joined by Justices Brennan and Stevens, dissented. The excerpt here from Marshall's opinion illustrates the extent of disagreement concerning the Court's decision in *Lockhart*.[52]

Lockhart v. McCree

Justice Marshall, dissenting

. . . With a glib nonchalance ill-suited to the gravity of the issue presented and the power of respondent's claims, the Court upholds a practice that allows the State a special advantage in those prosecutions where the charges are the most serious and the possible punishments, the most severe. The State's mere announcement that it intends to seek the death penalty if the defendant is found guilty of a capital offense will, under today's decision, give the prosecution license to empanel a jury especially likely to return that very verdict. Because I believe that such a blatant disregard for the rights of a capital defendant offends logic, fairness, and the Constitution, I dissent.

The Jury and the Media

The right to trial by an impartial jury means that the jurors must not be unduly influenced by the media. Defendants cannot have a fair trial if, because of pretrial publicity, the jurors have already made up their minds about the case. Therefore, the Court has issued rulings concerning when pretrial publicity is prejudicial to the defendant. Perhaps the most publicized of these rulings was *Sheppard v. Maxwell*, decided in 1966. Dr. Sam Sheppard was convicted of his wife's murder, and he served ten years in prison before his conviction was overturned. At his second trial, he was acquitted.[53]

During Sheppard's trial, private telephones were installed to allow the press to expedite their stories, and one station was permitted to set up broadcasting equipment in the room next to the jury deliberation room. With the crowd of media persons and the public, it was impossible for Sheppard to talk privately with his counsel in the courtroom during the trial. Nor was it possible inside the courtroom for counsel to approach the judge out of the jury's hearing. The jurors were also exposed to the news media.

These and many other facts were considered by the Supreme Court before overruling Sheppard's conviction. Its opinion stressed the importance of the media's First Amendment rights to free speech but also the more important right of the defendant to be tried before an unbiased jury. In conclusion, it declared, "With his life at stake, it is not requiring too much that petitioner be tried in an atmosphere undisturbed by so huge a wave of public passion. . . . The theory of our system is that the conclusions to be reached in a case will be induced only by evidence and argument in open court, and not by any outside influence, whether of private talk or public print."[54] The Court referred to the trial as having a "Roman holiday" atmosphere, complete with murder, mystery, society, and sex.

The influence of publicity on the jury was again considered in 1979 when the Court was faced with the issue of whether the press could be barred from a pretrial hearing.[55] In *Gannett Co., Inc., v. Depasquale*, the Court recognized the importance of openness but refused to recognize a constitutional right of the public to be present at pretrial hearings. The decision reopened the power struggle between the press and the Court, between the rights of the public and the rights of the defendant. Public and press reaction was predictably critical. The lead editorial in the *New York Times* was headlined "Private Justice, Public Injustice," adding, "Now the Supreme Court has endorsed secrecy in language broad enough to justify its use not only in a pre-trial context but even at a formal trial. . . . The power to make public business private is a dangerous power, far in excess of the supposed benefit."[56] *Time* magazine referred to the decision as a "stunning shock" to the press. "It is also by far the court's sharpest blow to the press in a long string of such adverse rulings."[57]

In subsequent decisions, *Gannett* has been eroded. In *Richmond*

Newspapers, Inc., v. Virginia, the Court ruled that the public and the press have a constitutional right of access to criminal trials (*Gannett* dealt with pretrial hearings), but that right is not unlimited. However, before trials could be closed, the government would have to explore other alternatives.[58] *Richmond* was criticized in the court's later decision in *Globe Newspaper Co. v. Superior Court,* which involved a Massachusetts statute that was interpreted by the Massachusetts court to require that the press be excluded during the testimony of a sexual abuse victim who is under the age of eighteen. The Supreme Court did not agree that blanket exclusion in such cases is appropriate. Each case must be analyzed in terms of its facts, and to exclude the press, the state must show a compelling reason for doing so. Although preserving the psychological welfare of the victim could be a compelling state interest, the Supreme Court said that could be done on a case-by-case analysis by looking at the age and maturity of the victim, the victim's wishes, the nature and circumstances of the crime, and other relevant variables.[59]

The Court has also held that "the qualified First Amendment right of access to criminal proceedings applies to preliminary hearings" as they were conducted in the state whose case was before the Court in a recent case. Those hearings may be closed only if 1) it can be shown that the defendant would not get a fair trial if it were open to the public and press, and 2) a fair trial cannot be provided by less drastic alternatives than closing the trial to the public.[60]

THE VICTIMS' RIGHTS

The discussion thus far has focused on some of the due process rights of criminal defendants. The right to be free of unreasonable searches and seizures, the right not to testify against oneself, the right to counsel, and the right to trial by an impartial jury are at the heart of those rights, but they are only a sample of the efforts our system has made to give defendants a fair trial. Many people feel, however, that the pendulum has swung too far, that defendants have too many rights, that society is not protected, and that victims are ignored. The decade of the 1980s has been characterized by a strong movement toward recognition of victims' rights, evidenced by the implementation of changes in the criminal justice system aimed at the needs and concerns of crime victims.[61]

Victims' Participation in the Criminal Justice System

Throughout most of our history, victims have been virtually ignored by the criminal justice system. They have been expected to testify when their alleged assailants were on trial, but they were usually not accorded minimum courtesies concerning information on where, when, why, and how. In the past few years, many jurisdictions have tried to remedy this situation. Witnesses and victims often need financial assistance as well as other kinds of assistance before they can participate in criminal proceedings. For example, they may need transportation to court, parking, babysitting, or other reasonable expenses. They may also need medical care and psychological counseling, which are provided by some jurisdictions. Some jurisdictions also permit victims to participate in negotiation proceedings with prosecutors and defense attorneys and even with offenders. Victims may also be permitted to express their concerns and opinions on issues such as sentencings.

Victims' Compensation Programs

In many cases the victims' greatest need is for financial compensation for the property losses they have incurred or for medical expenses or both. Most states have enacted **victims' compensation** legislation. The federal program will be used to illustrate some of the provisions and problems of such a system.

Congress passed the Victim and Witness Protection Act (VWPA), which applies to victims of offenders tried in federal courts. The findings and statement of purpose of the original act, passed in 1982, emphasized the importance of victims' cooperation in the criminal justice process, yet noted that victims have traditionally been either ignored by the system or "simply used as tools to identify and punish offenders." The legislation recognized that victims "suffer physical, psychological, or financial hardship first as a result of the criminal act and then as a result of contact with a criminal justice system unresponsive to the real needs of such victims." Harassment of victims and witnesses establishes guidelines for the fair treatment of crime victims and witnesses in the criminal justice system. The act then specified many other problems faced by witnesses and noted its purpose of correcting those in the federal system and of providing a model for state victim compensation legislation.[62] Highlight 11.2 contains a statement of the efforts of the Federal Bureau of Prisons to implement programs for victims and witnesses in the federal system.

Financial resources for victims may come from the federal government's compensation programs, but another source is the offender. The federal law, like many state laws, provides for **restitution** from offenders to victims. When offenders are convicted in federal courts, the sentencing judges must order them to make restitution to their victims or state reasons for not doing so.

There are some problems with victims' compensation legislation. Many programs are underfunded, and some attempts to provide adequate funding have been challenged. The restitution provision of the federal statute has been the subject of frequent litigation. Defendants argue that

HIGHLIGHT 11.2

FEDERAL PRISON SYSTEM'S VICTIM AND WITNESS PROGRAMS

The growing concern for the victims of crime in America led in the early 1980's to the passage of legislation designed to provide better compensation and protection for victims and witnesses. The Bureau of Prisons has since instituted two programs within its Correctional Programs Division that help satisfy these concerns—the Inmate Financial Responsibility Program and the Victim/Witness Notification Program.

The Victims of Crime Act and the Criminal Fine Enforcement Act, both enacted by Congress in 1984, require a diligent effort by law enforcement agencies to satisfy court-ordered financial obligations. Accordingly, the Bureau implemented the Inmate Financial Responsibility Program as a pilot project in October 1985. Results were so positive that the program was implemented Bureauwide in April 1987.

Many inmates have the resources to meet their obligations—fines, restitution, etc.—at the time they are committed. Others earn wages through UNICOR or institution work assignments. An inmate's participation in this program is closely monitored by staff and is taken into consideration when assessing his or her demonstrated level of responsible behavior. Financial responsibility is a primary factor considered in determining an inmate's custody level, housing and work assignments, and eligibility for certain programs such as furloughs.

Since full implementation of the program in April 1987, inmates have made more than $20 million in payments. As of April 1, 1989, about 10,000 inmates were participating in the program, and another 10,000 still in custody have completed their obligations. Virtually 100 percent of the funds collected by the Bureau are eventually redistributed to victims of crime through direct restitution or through the Crime Victims Fund distributed by the States.

Another Bureau program—the Victim/Witness Notification Program—was set up in 1984 following the passage of the Victim and Witness Protection Act of 1982. It established proce-

dures to be followed in notifying a victim or witness regarding a specific inmate's release or release proceedings (parole hearings, furloughs), transfers between institutions, or community corrections placement, as well as the inmate's escape or death in custody. In the case of escape, the victim or witness is notified immediately by telephone.

To further emphasize the Bureau's commitment to the rights and needs of victims and witnesses, the position of Victim/Witness Coordinator was recently created. Operating out of Central Office, the Coordinator monitors the Notification Program nationwide, provides technical assistance to Bureau staff, and acts as a liaison with other agencies and the public.

For further information on these programs, contact the Inmate Financial Responsibility Program and the Victim/Witness Notification Program at FTS 724-3081.

SOURCE: Federal Prison System, *Monday Morning Highlights,* 12 June 1989 (Washington, D.C.: U.S. Department of Justice).

judicial restitution orders without a hearing on the issues involved are unconstitutional, violating the Seventh Amendment's provision that "the right of jury trial shall be preserved" in civil cases "where the value in controversy exceeds twenty dollars." In 1983 a federal district court agreed with these arguments in an opinion that criticized Congress. The judge said, "I don't expect to be the last court to speak on this question, but it looks like I'll be the first." The written opinion of that court ended with these words: "The Court knows that it is entering where angels fear to tread, but enter it must." Part of the decision was reversed by a federal appellate court, which upheld the constitutionality of the restitution provision.[63] Other courts have declared at least a portion of the Statute unconstitutional without, for example, a judicial hearing on the extent of the victim's damages before determining the amount of restitution.[64]

THE DEFENDANTS' RIGHTS VERSUS THE VICTIMS' RIGHTS

Defendants have argued that restitution orders without a trial on that issue violate their right to a jury trial, but most federal courts have refused to accept that argument. Acceptance would increase litigation and probably decrease the successful use of restitution.

Moreover, the passage in California of Proposition 8, known as the Victim's Bill of Rights, limits the application of the exclusionary rule, which excludes from trial any evidence illegally obtained. On another issue, not relevant here, the constitutionality of Proposition 8 was upheld by a bitterly divided state supreme court in a five to four decision, but other legal challenges are expected in the near future.[65]

One of the most frequently raised issues that create conflicts between victims and defendants is whether or not a sexual abuse victim, particularly a young one, must testify in person in court or whether someone may testify as to what the victim said. Normally such information is not allowed in court because it denies the defendant the opportunity to confront and cross-examine his or her witness. On the other hand, testifying in court can be a very traumatic, even impossible task for some victims, especially young ones who have been sexually assaulted. This is particularly true when the alleged offender is a relative of the victim.

The U.S. Supreme Court considered this issue in 1988 in the case of *Coy v. Iowa*, in which the defendant was accused of sexual assault. Note the Court's resolution of the issue of whether it was proper for the alleged victims to testify behind a screen. Had you been on the Court, how would you have decided this issue?[66]

Coy v. Iowa

Appellant was convicted of two counts of lascivious acts with a child after a jury trial in which a screen placed between him and the two complaining witnesses blocked him from their sight. Appellant contends that this procedure, authorized by state statute, violated his Sixth Amendment right to confront the witnesses against him.

In August 1985, appellant was arrested and charged with sexually assaulting two 13-year-old girls earlier that month while they were camping out in the backyard of the house next door to him. According to the girls, the assailant entered their tent after they were asleep wearing a stocking over his head, shined a flashlight in their eyes, and warned them not to look at him; neither was able to describe his face. In November 1985, at the beginning of appellant's trial, the State made a motion pursuant to a recently enacted statute to allow the complaining witnesses to testify either via closed-circuit television or behind a screen. The trial court approved the use of a large screen to be placed between appellant and the witness stand during the girls' testimony. After certain lighting adjustments in the courtroom, the screen would enable appellant dimly to perceive the witnesses, but the witnesses to see him not at all.

Appellant objected strenuously to use of the screen, based first of all on his Sixth Amendment confrontation right. He argued that, although the device might succeed in its apparent aim of making the complaining witnesses feel less uneasy in giving their testimony, the Confrontation Clause directly addressed this issue by giving criminal defendants a right to face-to-face confrontation. He also argued that his right to due process was violated, since the procedure would make him appear guilty and thus erode the presumption of innocence. The trial court rejected both constitutional claims, though it instructed the jury to draw no inference of guilt from the screen.

The Iowa Supreme Court affirmed appellant's conviction. It rejected appellant's confrontation argument on the ground that, since the ability to cross-examine the witnesses was not impaired by the screen, there was no violation of the Confrontation Clause. It also rejected the due process argument, on the ground that the screening procedure was not inherently prejudicial. . . .

The Sixth Amendment gives a criminal defendant the right "to be confronted with the witnesses against him." This language. . . . [has a long historical background].

The Sixth Amendment's guarantee of face-to-face encounter between witness and accused serves ends related both to appearances and to reality. This opinion is embellished with references to and quotations from antiquity in part to convey that there is something deep in human nature that regards face-to-face confrontation between accused and accuser as "essential to a fair trial in a criminal prosecution." What was true of old is no less true in modern times. . . . The phrase still persists, "Look me in the eye and say that." Given these human feelings of what is necessary for fairness, the right of confrontation "contributes to the establishment of a system of criminal justice in which the perception as well as the reality of fairness prevails."

The perception that confrontation is essential to fairness has persisted over the centuries because there is much truth to it. A witness "May feel quite differently when he has to repeat his story looking at the man whom he will harm greatly by distorting or mistaking the facts. He can now understand what sort of human being that man is." It is always more difficult to tell a lie about a person "to his face" than "behind his back." In the former context, even if the lie is told, it will often be told less convincingly. The Confrontation Clause does not, of course, compel the witness to fix his eyes upon the defendant; he may studiously look elsewhere, but the trier of fact will draw its own conclusions. Thus the right to face-to-face confrontation serves much the same purpose as a less explicit component of the Confrontation Clause that we have had more frequent occasion to discuss—the right to cross-examine the accuser; both "ensur[e] the integrity of the fact-finding process." The State can hardly gainsay the profound effect upon a witness of standing in the presence of the person the witness accuses, since that is the very phenomenon it relies upon to establish the potential "trauma" that allegedly justified the extraordinary procedure in the present case. That face-to-face presence may, unfortunately, upset the truthful rape victim or abused child; but by the same token it may confound and undo the false accuser, or reveal the child coached by a malevolent adult. It is a truism that constitutional protections have costs.

The remaining question is whether the right to confrontation was in fact violated in this case. The screen at issue was specifically designed to enable the complaining witnesses to avoid viewing appellant as they gave their testimony, and the record indicates that it was successful in this objective. It is difficult to imagine a more obvious or damaging violation of the defendant's right to a face-to-face encounter.

The State suggests that the confrontation interest at stake here was outweighed by the necessity of protecting victims of sexual abuse. It is true that we have in the past indicated that rights conferred by the Confrontation Clause are not absolute, and may give way to other important interests. The rights referred to in those cases, however, were not the right narrowly and explicitly set forth in the Clause, but rather rights that are, or were asserted to be, reasonably implicit—namely, the right to cross-examine; the right to exclude out-of-court statements; and the asserted right to face-to-face confrontation at some point in the proceedings other than the trial itself. To hold that our determination of what implications are reasonable must take into account other important interests is not the same as holding that we can identify exceptions, in light of other important interests, to the irreducible literal meaning of the clause: "a right to *meet face to face* all those who appear and give evidence *at trial.*" We leave for another day, however, the question whether any exceptions exist. Whatever they may be, they would surely be allowed only when necessary to further an important public policy.

> . . . We find it unnecessary to reach appellant's due process claim. Since [the dependant's] constitutional right to face-to-face confrontation was violated, we reverse the judgment of the Iowa Supreme Court and remand the case.

Coy v. Iowa illustrates some of the problems that occur when attempts are made to reconcile defendants' rights with rights and needs of victims. The Court is not saying that defendants' rights will always prevail, but rather that the Court will scrutinize carefully any blanket requirements that infringe on defendants' rights. Victims may also face problems when they refuse to comply with court orders after reporting a crime. If their refusals persist, the court may hold them in **contempt of court,** as illustrated by the case described in Highlight 11.3. A question that remained after *Coy v. Iowa* was answered by the Supreme Court in *Maryland v. Craig* in late June, 1990. A 5-4 majority held that a defendant's Sixth Amendment right to confront witnesses at trial does not require all such confrontations to be face-to-face. In upholding a Maryland statute that permits a child who is the alleged victim of sexual abuse to testify outside the courtroom via television, the Court said that such is permissible provided the reliability of the child's testimony can be otherwise assured.[68]

HIGHLIGHT 11.3

MOTHER OF ALLEGED SEX VICTIM JAILED FOR CONTEMPT

Dr. Elizabeth Morgan, forty-one, served over two years in a Washington, D.C. jail for civil contempt of court for her refusal to obey court orders to make her seven-year-old child, Hilary, available for visitation with the child's father, Dr. Eric Foretich. Dr. Morgan claims that Dr. Foretich sexually molested Hilary; Dr. Foretich claims that his ex-wife is mentally ill and is trying to destroy him and his rela-tionship with his daughter, who disappeared about the time that Dr. Morgan defied the court order.

Dr. Morgan vowed to remain in jail until the year 2000, when Hilary becomes eighteen and will no longer be subject to the court's jurisdiction. Despite the pleas of many people through-out the nation, Judge Herbert B. Dixon, Jr., refused to lift the contempt citation until the child is produced or he becomes convinced that Dr. Morgan will never give in. Congress, however, decided the issue, and Dr. Morgan was released. In 1990, Hilary was located, living with her grandparents in Australia. Dr. Morgan went to Australia and began petitioning the Australian courts to give her sole custody of Hilary.

SOURCE: Summarized by the author from media sources.

CONCLUSION

This chapter introduced the U.S. system of criminal justice, looking briefly at its primary stages. The discussion emphasized the system effect, which means that changes in one element of the system affect the rest of the system. The system effect is particularly important when viewed in the context of the considerable discretion exercised within the four major divisions of the system: police, prosecution, courts, and corrections.

After distinguishing the adversari from the inquisitori system, the discussion proceeded to a brief look at the meaning of due process and equal protection, important concepts illustrated by a more detailed discussion of four constitutional rights of defendants: the right to be free of unreasonable search and seizure, the right not to testify against oneself, the right to counsel, and the right to trial by jury. The recent but widespread recognition of victims' rights was also discussed, followed by a look at the potential conflicts that arise between the rights of defendants and those of victims.

This chapter showed some of the inevitable tensions and controversies in our system of criminal justice. On the one hand, we believe in individual rights; we do not think the police or any other government officials should be able to interfere in our personal lives without just cause. But we also want to walk the streets safely; so we want adequate police protection from crime. When we are victimized, we want our property back and our medical bills paid, and we want the defendants brought to justice. But all these goals may be impossible to reach.

The tensions between the rights of the accused (or those who are thought to be likely to commit a crime) and the rights of victims and of society have been brought into focus by the FBI, which in March 1983 established new rules for domestic security investigations. These rules were in part the result of a fear of terrorism at the Los Angeles Olympic games held in the summer of 1984. These new rules no longer require that a crime be imminent before the FBI can investigate. Nor do they require an investigation into an organization to cease once its members have been prosecuted or the organization goes out of existence. Just one month after the new rules were promulgated, the FBI began setting up files on persons considered by the Secret Service to be dangerous. These persons will be watched, even though they have not committed a crime.

The advisory board of the National Crime Information Center has proposed creating files on persons who are thought to be involved with terrorism, organized crime, or narcotics, even though there is no evidence to arrest them for actual crimes. Also included would be people "known to be, believed to be, likely to be or may be associated with" a drug dealer, even if there is no evidence that the person deals in drugs or, for that matter, even knows about the drug dealer's illegal activities.

Millions of people could be included under these proposals. Furthermore, with the continued development of computerized communications, the FBI can keep tabs on people all over the country and share that information with the local police in a matter of minutes, if not seconds. Such capabilities, along with the broad scope of the tracking system proposed, leave us all open to police surveillance and the invasion of our personal privacy and other individual rights.

It is this tremendous power of the government, a power that can—in the hands of the power hungry and ruthless—violate our constitutional rights even to the point of conviction for a crime we did not commit, that requires us to provide and maintain some protection for those accused of crime. In protecting their rights, we protect the rights of us all. This need was demonstrated in *A Man for All Seasons*, a play about the life, trial, and execution of the English humanist, author, and statesman, Sir Thomas More. More, who lived from 1478 to 1535 and in 1935 was canonized by the Roman Catholic Church, stated, "Yes, I'd give the Devil benefit of law, for my own safety's sake."[67]

Yet because it is necessary to have the power of law enforcement and the power of prevention, it is essential that we have a professional police force, the focus of the next chapter.

ENDNOTES

1. "Drug Cases Overloading Court System," *Tallahassee Democrat*, 7 September 1988, p. B3, col. 1.

2. Wayne R. LaFave and Jerold H. Israel, *Criminal Procedure* (St. Paul, Minn.: West Publishing Co., 1985), pp. 19–20.

3. "25 Wrongfully Executed in U.S., Study Finds," *New York Times*, 14 November, 1985, p. 13, col. 1.

4. C. Ronald Huff, "Wrongful Conviction: Societal Tolerance of Injustice," *Social Problems and Public Policy* 4 (1987): 113. See also Huff et al., "Guilty Until Proved Innocent: Wrongful Conviction and Public Policy," *Crime & Delinquency* 32 (October 1986): 518–544.

5. Joint Anti-Fascist Refugee Committee v. McGrath, 341 U.S. 123, 162–163 (1951), Justice Felix Frankfurter concurring.

6. John M. Junker, "The Structure of the Fourth Amendment: The Scope of the Protection," *The Journal of Criminal Law & Criminology* 79 (Winter 1989): 1183, footnote reference omitted.

7. Johnson v. United States, 333 U.S. 10, 13–14 (1948). See also Katz v. United States, 389 U.S. 347 (1967).

8. State v. Massey, 750 P.2d 1192, 1193 (Or.App. 1988).

9. Illinois v. Gates, 462 U.S. 213 (1983).

10. U.S. v. Ross, 456 U.S. 798 (1982).

11. U.S. v. Johns, 469 U.S. 478 (1985).

12. Colorado v. Bertine, 479 U.S. 367 (1987). See also South Dakota v. Opperman, 428 U.S. 364 (1975), and Illinois v. Lafayette, 462 U.S. 604 (1983).

13. Rochin v. California, 342 U.S. 165, 166, 172 (1952).

14. U.S. v. Montoya de Hernandez, 473 U.S. 531 (1985).

15. Bell v. Wolfish, 441 U.S. 520 (1979).

16. Masters v. Crouch, 872 F.2d 1248 (6th. Cir. 1989), *cert. denied*, Frey v. Masters, 110 S.Ct. 503 (1989).

17. Mapp v. Ohio, 367 U.S. 643, 644 (1961).

18. Payton v. New York, 445 U.S. 573, 589–590 (1980).
19. Welsh v. Wisconsin, 466 U.S. 740 (1984).
20. Coolidge v. New Hampshire, 403 U.S. 443 (1971).
21. Arizona v. Hicks, 480 U.S. 321 (1987). For a discussion of Hicks see, "Fourth Amendment—Requiring Probable Cause for Searches and Seizures under the Plain View Doctrine," *Journal of Criminal Law & Criminology* 78 (Winter 1988): 763–791. The Court's decision on the protective sweep is Maryland v. Buie, 110 S. Ct. 1093 (1990).
22. California v. Ciraola, 476 U.S. 207 (1986).
23. Edward Bennett Williams, quoted in Alexander B. Smith and Harriet Pollack, *Crime and Justice in a Mass Society* (Waltham, Mass.: Xerox College Publishing, 1972), p. 194.
24. Brown v. Mississippi, 297 U.S. 278 (1936).
25. Miranda v. Mississippi, 384 U.S. 436 (1966).
26. "Miranda Ruling 20 Years Old, But Debate Over Its Effect Continues," *Dallas Morning News*, 8 June 1986, p. 53A, col. 1.
27. "Fighting Crime by the Rules: Why Cops Like Miranda," *Newsweek*, 18 July 1988, p. 53.
28. Karen L. Guy and Robert G. Huckabee, "Going Free on a Technicality: Another Look at the Effect of the Miranda Decision on the Criminal Justice Process," *Criminal Justice Research Bulletin* 4 (no. 1, 1988): 2–3. For a discussion of whether we should have the privilege against self-incrimination, see Donald A. Dripps, "Foreword: Against Police Interrogation—and the Privilege Against Self-Incrimination," *Journal of Criminal Law & Criminology* 78 (Winter 1988): 699–734.
29. Oregon v. Mathiason, 429 U.S. 492 (1977).
30. Minnesota v. Murphy, 465 U.S. 420 (1984).
31. See Edwards v. Arizona, 451 U.S. 477 (1981). See also Michigan v. Jackson, (1986).
32. Arizona v. Roberson, 486 U.S. 675 (1988), quoting State v. Routhier, 669 P. 2d 68, 75 (1983), *ccrt. den.*, 464 U.S. 1073 (1984).
33. Duckworth v. Eagan, 109 S.Ct. 2875 (1989).
34. On waivers of the right to counsel prior to being questioned, see North Carolina v. Butler, 441 U.S. 369 (1979); Tague v. Louisiana, 444 U.S. 469 (1979); Colorado v. Connelly, 479 U.S. 157 (1986); Colorado v. Spring, 479 U.S. 564 (1987); and Morgan v. Burbine, 475 U.S. 412 (1986).
35. Gideon v. Wainwright, 372 U.S. 335 (1963). The earlier case was Betts v. Brady, 316 U.S. 455 (1942).
36. Argersinger v. Hamlin, 407 U.S. 25, 37 (1972).
37. Escobedo v. Illinois, 378 U.S. 478 (1964).
38. Brewer v. Williams, 430 U.S. 387, 398 (1977).
39. Maine v. Moulton, 474 U.S. 159 (1985).
40. Javor v. United States, 724 F.2d 831 (9th Cir. 1984).
41. Strickland v. Washington, 466 U.S. 668 (1984).
42. U.S. v. Cronic, 466 U.S. 648 (1984).
43. Duncan v. Louisiana, 391 U.S. 145, 149 (1968).
44. For a brief history and analysis of the U.S. jury system, see Martin Howard Levin, "The Jury in a Criminal Case: Obstacles to Impartiality," *Criminal Law Bulletin* (November-December 1988): 492–520. See also John V. Singleton, "Trial by Jury: History and Preservation," *Trial* 25 (July 1989): 91–96.
45. See Taylor v. Louisiana, 419 U.S. 522 (1975).

46. Batson v. Kentucky, 476 U.S. 79 (1986). The earlier case is Swain v. Alabama, 380 U.S. 202 (1965).

47. See Barber v. Ponte, 772 F.2d 982 (1st Cir. 1985) (en banc). See also Anaya v. Hansen, 781 F.2d 1 (1st Cir. 1986), in which the same court held that young adults and blue collar workers do not constitute groups from which a cross-section of potential jurors must be drawn.

48. See, for example, Witherspoon v. Illinois, 391 U.S. 510 (1968).

49. Witherspoon v. Illinois, 391 U.S. 510, 522 (1968); emphasis in the original.

50. Wainwright v. Witt, 469 U.S. 412 (1985). See also Darden v. Wainwright, 477 U.S. 168 (1986); Gray v. Mississippi, 481 U.S. 648 (1987), and Brown v. North Carolina, 479 U.S. (1986).

51. Lockhart v. McCree, 476 U.S. 162 (1986). See also Buchanan v. Kentucky, 483 U.S. 1044 (1987).

52. Lockhart v. McCree, 476 U.S. 162 (1986), Justice Marshall, dissenting.

53. Sheppard v. Maxwell, 384 U.S. 333 (1966).

54. Sheppard v. Maxwell, 384 U.S. 333, 349 (1966), citations omitted.

55. Gannett Co., Inc. v. Depasquale, 443 U.S. 368 (1979).

56. "Private Justice, Public Injustice," *New York Times*, 5 July 1979, p. A16, col. 1.

57. "Slamming the Courtroom Doors," *Time*, 16 July 1979, p. 66.

58. Richmond Newspapers, Inc. v. Virginia, 448 U.S. 555 (1980).

59. Globe Newspaper Co. v. Superior Court, 457 U.S. 596 (1982). See also Richmond Newspapers v. Commonwealth, 281 S.E. 2d 915 (Va. 1981).

60. Press-Enterprise Co. v. Superior Court, 478 U.S. 1 (1986).

61. For a discussion of the rights of victims, see J. H. Stark and H. W. Goldstein, *Rights of Victims*, 1985. Available from the American Civil Liberties Union, 132 West 43rd Street, New York, N.Y.

62. U.S. Code, Title 18, 3663, as amended Nov. 1, 1987.

63. United States v. Welden, 568 F.Supp 516 (N.D. Ala., 1983), *affirmed in part, reversed in part*, U.S. v. Satterfield, 743 F.2d 827 (11th Cir. 1984), *cert denied sub nom*, 469 U.S. 1089 (1984). See also U.S. v. Atkinson, 788 F.2d 900 (2d Cir. 1986), and U.S. v. Brown, 744 F.2d 905 (2d Cir. 1984), *cert den.*, 469 U.S. 1089 (1984).

64. See, for example, U.S. v. Palma, 760 F.2d 475 (3d Cir. 1985), and U.S. v. Johnson, 816 F.2d 918 (3d Cir. 1987).

65. Brosnahan v. Brown, 186 Cal. Rptr. 30 (Ca. Sup. Ct. 1982). See also Cal. Const. Art. I, Section 28.

66. Coy v. Iowa, 487 U.S. 1012 (1988), footnotes, citations and case names omitted, *on remand*, State v. Coy, 433 N.W. 2d 714 (1988).

67. Maryland v. Craig, 110 S.Ct. 3157 (1990).

68. Robert Bolt, *A Man for All Seasons* (New York: Vintage Paperbacks, Random House, 1962), pp. 37–38.

CHAPTER 12

Because a formal police system is relatively new in our society, we begin this chapter with a brief history. We then discuss the levels of public police systems before taking a brief look at private security. Police personnel, the type of training and education that police officers have had historically, and recent efforts to recruit more women and minorities are noted. A section on the nature of policing focuses on its organization and three functions: law enforcement, order maintenance, and the provision of community services. We examine the way time is allocated among these three functions and the conflicts and stresses that develop as a result. Police decision making is analyzed, especially the decision whether or not to arrest or to use deadly force. That section closes with a look at police violence and corruption. Finally, we consider the control of policing.

OUTLINE

Police

KEY TERMS

arrest
constable
discretion
exclusionary rule
frankpledge
hundred
police
proactive
probable cause
reactive
sheriff
shires
subculture
tithing
watch system

Police occupy one of the most important positions in American society. To them is entrusted the right to protect the citizenry, even when the use of violence is necessary. More is expected of police than of most other professionals. They are expected to be brave, not showing fear, shock, surprise, or hurt, even in the face of the most serious tragedies. Police are expected to make decisions quickly and with the calm, cool rationality that most people exhibit only in less traumatic situations. They are expected to solve many problems that society has created but for which it has found no solutions. They are expected to treat citizens with respect, even when harassed, threatened, and verbally and physically abused.

Police also occupy one of the most controversial positions in contemporary society. At times they are hated, but they are essential when there is trouble. In short, they are indispensable in a modern complex society, but most Americans do not know how to live with them. Some police fight back with their attitudes and their weapons.

EMERGENCE OF FORMAL POLICING

Chapter 1 discusses informal social controls that characterized early, primitive societies and that exist to some extent in modern societies. As societies become more complex, formal methods of control usually become necessary; policing is an important part of that control. As laws are developed, police are needed to enforce them. A brief historical look at policing will illustrate the background of modern police systems.

Historical Police Systems

The history of policing begins with *informal policing*, in which all members of a community are responsible for maintaining order. In medieval England, policing was conducted through a system called **frankpledge**, or mutual pledge. Ten families constituted a **tithing**; within a tithing each member was responsible for the acts of all other members.

Later, a **hundred** was developed, made up of ten tithings. The hundred was under the charge of a **constable**, who can be considered the first police officer. He was apparently responsible for taking care of the weapons of the hundred. Hundreds were later combined to form **shires**, which were analogous to the present concept of counties. The shire was under the charge of an officer, appointed by the king, who was called a shire-reeve, a term that later came to be pronounced **sheriff.**

As societies became more complex, these informal methods of policing were not effective. Increased division of labor, a more heterogeneous population, and a lack of social solidarity led to a *transitional type* of policing, for example, the **watch system,** which existed in England and in Colonial America. In the watch system, bellmen regularly walked throughout the city, ringing bells and providing police services. Later they were replaced by a permanent watch of citizens and still later by paid constables.

Dissatisfaction with the watch system, because of its inability to maintain order and prevent crime, led to the emergence of the *modern type* of policing, a movement that began in London. Londoners protested the ineffectiveness of the watch system for dealing with the problems of increased industrialization, rising levels of crime, and a perceived increase and greater severity of public riots. They agitated for a formal police force. Some believed that a police force constantly patrolling the streets would reduce and eventually eliminate crime in the streets. Others, however, feared that the concentration of power that would be necessary for a formal police force would lead to abuses, especially if the force were a national one. Eventually the conflict between these two positions was resolved by the establishment of local police systems.[1]

The first modern police force, the Metropolitan Police of London, was founded in London in 1829 by Sir Robert Peel. The men employed by the force were sometimes called Peelers and sometimes Bobbies, after the founder. The officers worked full time; they wore special uniforms, and their primary function was to prevent crime. Organized by territories, they reported to a central government. Candidates had to meet high standards to qualify for a position. Until recently, Bobbies were held in high esteem by Londoners, but several incidents of corruption, incompetence, and alleged racism have tarnished the image of the once highly esteemed London Bobbies.

The rest of England slowly followed London's example. Some countries developed a centralized police system, but the United States developed a decentralized system.

PUBLIC POLICING IN THE UNITED STATES

Informal policing also came under attack in the United States. Recognition of the need for a formal police system led to the development of a professional police force in Boston in 1837. By the late 1880s, most American cities had established municipal police forces. According to the Bureau of Justice Statistics (BJS), which has issued its first report on Law Enforcement Management and Administrative Statistics (LEMAS), today there are over 15,000 state and local law enforcement agencies in the United States. Of those, approximately 3000 are sheriffs' agencies and the rest are local police agencies. Data from that report are relevant to several topics dis-

EXHIBIT 12.1

Major Findings of a Study of State and Local Law Enforcement Agencies

- Local police agencies, sheriffs' agencies, and State police agencies collectively employed 757,508 persons during fiscal year 1987 (including 555,364 sworn officers) and had operating and capital expenses totaling more than $28 billion.

- About 24% of local police employees were civilians. The percentage of civilian employees in sheriffs' agencies and State police agencies was even higher, about 32% in each.

- An estimated 12.5% of the sworn employees in sheriffs' agencies were female, compared to 7.6% in local police agencies and 4.2% in State police agencies.

- Sworn personnel in local police agencies were 85.4% white (non-Hispanic), 9.3% black, and 4.5% Hispanic; for sheriffs' agencies, the proportions were 86.6% white, 8.3% black, and 4.3% Hispanic; for State police, 88.7% white, 6.5% black, and 3.8% Hispanic.

- All State police agencies and almost all local police (99.7%) and sheriffs' agencies (97.5%) with 135 or more sworn personnel required new officer recruits to have at least a high school diploma. About 10% of State and local police agencies and about 6% of sheriffs' departments required at least some college education.

- Thirteen of the almost 12,000 local police agencies in the Nation served populations of 1 million or more, but the great majority (89%) served jurisdictions with populations under 25,000.

- Thirty-four local police agencies employed over 1,000 sworn officers each during fiscal year 1987, but more than half had fewer than 10 sworn officers and 987 employed just 1 full-time sworn officer.

- Twelve sheriffs' agencies employed over 1,000 sworn officers each, and 27 sheriffs' agencies served populations of 1 million or more.

- The main State police agency in each State had an average of 1,031 full-time sworn employees, ranging in size from slightly over 100 to nearly 6,000, and had average expenditure of over $65 million.

- Two-thirds of local police agencies authorize collective bargaining by employees.

- Approximately 88% of sworn officers in large local police agencies worked in field operations, 6% in technical support, and 5% in administration.

- The average starting salary for an entry-level officer in local police departments ranged from $13,768 in jurisdictions under 2,500 people to $22,930 in jurisdictions with populations of 1 million or more. Average starting salaries for sergeants ranged from $17,464 in the smallest jurisdictions to $35,273 in the largest. Police chiefs in cities with a population of 1 million or more had an average starting salary of $72,821 and an average maximum salary of $87,048.

SOURCE: Bureau of Justice Statistics, *Profile of State and Local Law Enforcement Agencies, 1987* (Washington, D.C.: U.S. Department of Justice, March 1989): 1–2.

cussed later in this chapter. A summary of the major findings is reprinted in Exhibit 12.1.

According to the FBI's latest official data, the public law enforcement community employs almost one-half million officers and almost 167,000 civilians. The FBI notes that the law enforcement needs of various communities differ and that one should be careful in comparing law enforcement agencies throughout the country, for they too differ in size and in the manner in which they carry out basic law enforcement functions.[2]

Decentralized Policing

The system of policing in this country is decentralized, having separate systems at the local, state, and federal levels.[3]

Local Level

Rural, county, and municipal police agencies may be found at the local level. Most studies of police focus on municipal policing, although the majority of police agencies are located in small towns, villages, or counties. Rural policing may be the responsibility of only one officer; these systems must depend on county police agencies for assistance. Officers who work in rural areas may not have had sufficient training, often work long hours without the prospect of assistance from county officers, and are paid less than their urban counterparts.

Rural policing can, however, be very rewarding for those who enjoy knowing everyone in the community and who like being involved in many activities and maintaining high visibility. Lower crime rates, particularly lower rates of violence, along with less complexity in police and community structures may also be seen as positive elements.

County policing may cover large geographical areas, creating problems for officers when they need assistance from other areas. Some county (and rural) police agencies may contract with other police agencies for services, a process that is complicated when the county system covers a large territory. The primary law enforcement officer in the county system is usually the sheriff, who may have numerous duties besides law enforcement, such as collecting county taxes, supervising some government activities, or even serving as the county coroner.

Municipal police departments are larger and more complex than rural or county departments. They have higher costs and usually deal with higher crime rates and a more diverse population, but the officers also have more training, are better paid, and usually have more education.[4]

State Level

Policing at the state level is divided into state police and state patrol. Although their duties may vary from state to state, patrol officers are primarily responsible for traffic control. They are uniformed officers, and they may be permitted to enforce some state laws; but they do not have general powers of state law enforcement. That responsibility lies with the state police, who are also uniformed officers. State police officers, in contrast to the state patrol, generally have enforcement powers over certain regulations such as those concerning fishing and gaming, gambling, horse racing, and the sale of alcoholic beverages.[5]

Federal Level

Most crimes in the United States stem from violations of state or local statutes. Although the United States does not have a national police force, there are congressional statutes that cover federal crimes. These federal statutes are enforced by more than fifty federal agencies, of which the largest and best known is the Federal Bureau of Investigation (FBI) in the

William Sessions is Director of the Federal Bureau of Investigations (FBI).

Department of Justice. The FBI is also in charge of collecting and disseminating national data on crime, published in the *Uniform Crime Reports*, discussed earlier.

The primary function of the FBI is investigative. FBI agents investigate crimes over which federal courts have jurisdiction; but they may also, when requested, investigate crimes under the jurisdiction of state and local law enforcement agencies. Today the FBI is headed by Director William S. Sessions, appointed by President Reagan to replace William H. Webster who became CIA director in 1987.

PRIVATE SECURITY

The problems that arose from decentralized policing—understaffed and underfunded public police agencies, accompanied by rising crime rates in the 1970s and early 1980s—led many people to turn to private security firms for protection. According to Albert J. Reiss, Jr., a Yale University sociologist who has published widely in many areas of policing, "Private security has outstripped the growth of the public police; more people are now working in private security than in public policing."[6]

Many of the over 1 million persons in private security have entered the field within the last decade, the greatest growth occurring during the recent and current periods of economic cutbacks in many agencies, including police departments. During this time the quality of private security has also improved, with better-trained workers available than in the past.[7]

Many types of private security services are available today; their history is traced to Allan Pinkerton, who founded Pinkerton's Security Services in 1850. Today Pinkerton's is the largest of the private security firms, with over 12,000 clients in the United States and Canada. Headquartered in New York City, Pinkerton's is responsible for the familiar term "private eye." Pinkerton's, like many other security firms, contracts to supply private security guards, investigative services, electronic surveillance devices, and private consultants.[8] Following Pinkerton's, the next largest private security companies in the United States are as follows: Burns, Wackenhut, Globe Security, and Wells Fargo.[9]

Another type of private security that is growing rapidly is private employment of public police . Reiss notes that although we do not have national data on how many police work off-hours for private security, we do know that the numbers are extensive. Three models for off-duty police employment are utilized, and Reiss' description of those is contained in Exhibit 12.2. Although one advantage of private hiring of public police is more police protection and greater visibility of public police, who are usu-

EXHIBIT 12.2

Three Models for Off-Duty Police Employment

Officer Contract model

- Each officer finds own secondary employment

- Officer independently contracts conditions of work, hours, pay

- Officer then applies for permission to accept off-duty job

- Department grants permission provided job meets minimum standards

- Employer pays officer in cash (work is called "cash detail")

Departments in Atlanta, Charlotte, Cincinnati, Minneapolis, and Omaha generally follow this model, differing on what work is permitted.

Arlington County permits uniformed employment only by permission of the police chief and only at activities funded or sponsored by the county, State, or U.S. Government. Any other work must be nonpolice in nature.

In Peoria, most secondary employment is independently contracted, but the department itself contracts for civic center jobs, lets department heads broker other work, and permits officers to broker work for other officers.

In Cincinnati, work for private parties is independently contracted, but the department contracts work for city, county, or State agencies.

Union Brokerage model

- Union, guild, or association finds paid details

- Union assigns officers who have volunteered

- Union sets assignment conditions for paid details

- Union bargains with the department over status, pay, and conditions of paid details

Most off-duty employment of Seattle police is coordinated by the Seattle Police Officers' Guild, although the officers act as independent contractors. For privately sponsored special events at the Seattle Center complex, off-duty officers are employed by the center's security officer and paid through an outside accounting firm.

Department Contract model

- Police agency contracts with employers

- Agency assigns officers and pays them from reimbursements by employers

- Agency assigns an Off-Duty Employment Coordinator to receive employer requests, issue off-duty work permits, and assign officers to paid details

- Agency negotiates with union or guild on pay, conditions, and regulations governing employment

Boston, Colorado Springs, New Haven, and St. Petersburg fit this model. Metro Dade contracts for police-related work (including, unlike most departments, work for private security firms), but lets officers contract for nonpolice jobs, each of which requires a permit.

SOURCE: Albert J. Reiss, Jr., *Private Employment of Public Police* (Washington, D.C.: National Institute of Justice, December 1988), p. 3.

ally permitted to wear their police uniforms, badges, and in some communities even drive their patrol cars, there are problems, one of which has been described by a Harvard professor of criminal justice as follows:

> At first it sounds great . . . More police out there at no more public cost. But in the long run, private financial relationships with public agencies undermines the notion of a public police force with equal protection for all.[10]

Private security should be seen as a supplement to, and not a replacement of, public policing. There have been recent efforts at cooperation between public and private security personnel in some cities.

POLICE PERSONNEL

One of the most important aspects of policing is the selection, education, and training of officers. Until recently, most police officers were young white males, with a high school education or less, who lacked sufficient training. But qualifications of police officers have been improving.

Police Education

Despite some early attempts, the major impetus for police education came with the 1967 report of the President's Commission on Law Enforcement and the Administration of Justice, which recommended that police officers have baccalaureate degrees. The government provided financial incentives and support for the development of programs of higher education, and by early 1980, it was estimated that approximately one-half of police officers in this country had received some college education under the federally funded programs.[11]

Two criticisms of police education must be considered. First, the quality of educational programs developed specifically for police has been questioned. Many of the curricula focused on technical courses and neglected the broad, liberal arts courses that might help officers develop more understanding of the people they encounter.[12] A second criticism comes from those who question whether the goal of a college education for police officers is a reasonable one. Although supporters argue that education would increase police officers' tolerance and understanding of minorities and would give some additional insights into some of the particular problems they face on duty, others contend that there is no evidence that higher education will produce more tolerant and understanding officers. In fact, a study by Robert Regoli and his colleagues found no significant difference between the level of education and most attitudes toward the police agency and its supervisors.[13]

Improved education and recruitment of minorities have become high priorities in some police departments. Lee Brown, Ph.D. and former Houston, Texas Police Chief, was recently appointed Police Commissioner of New York City.

It is also possible that the routine work of policing is less tolerable to the college-educated person. The officer may become bored with the lack of challenge and intolerant of people who have not shared the same kinds of educational experiences. After a review of the literature, two researchers concluded "that intelligence and education do not guarantee success in police force, although they are of predictive use at the training school. Higher levels of education may paradoxically give rise to more dissatisfaction and higher wastage."[14]

Despite these criticisms of police education, the emphasis on the need for educating police has recently regained momentum. In 1989 Police Executive Research Forum (PERF) published a study of police education.

After noting the increase in the average educational level of officers from 12.4 years in 1967 to nearly 14 years, the report emphasized that it appears that "the rate of increase in police education may be leveling off." Further, colleges and universities are not providing sufficient education in basic skills, such as writing and communication, that are so important to officers. The researchers emphasize that they are not suggesting that the institutions teach "police report writing," but rather, that they include basic writing and oral communication skills in the liberal arts courses that should form the basis of police education.[15]

Police Recruitment

The establishment of an effective and efficient police force requires careful recruitment and selection; yet the U.S. Commission on Civil Rights found that the standards used in policing do not accurately measure the qualities and characteristics that are necessary for performing the job. The standards also discriminate against females, racial, and ethnic minorities. The commission recommended a careful review of these procedures to be sure all measures are job related and nondiscriminatory.[16]

The commission emphasized the need for police forces to represent the composition of the populations they serve. A lack of females and minorities, said the commission, leads to increased tensions and violence in some predominantly minority neighborhoods with high crime rates. Residents of those areas may be reluctant to cooperate with crime prevention efforts if they think they will be discriminated against by police. Females, the most frequent victims of rape and other sexual assaults, may be more reluctant to report these crimes if they are not represented on police forces.

Women and Minority Officers

In recent years attempts have been made to increase the number of female and minority police officers, although the results are not sufficient. In an analysis of police departments in twenty cities, Ellen Hochstedler and her colleagues found that nonwhites were still underrepresented by about 50 percent, blacks specifically by about 67 percent, and females by about 85 percent.[17] Hochstedler concluded that it is necessary to establish hiring quotas in order to recruit and appoint sufficient women and minority officers.[18]

Some jurisdictions have established quotas or other special recruiting models in an attempt to attract more blacks and women. There has been some success, but litigation on these policies has also been extensive. The U.S. Supreme Court has recently moved in a more conservative direction in its reaction to civil rights litigation based on affirmative action hiring policies. In 1987 in *Johnson v. Transportation Agency, Santa Clara, Co., California*, the Court upheld a plan that gave preferential job treatment on the basis of sex and race. The Court also upheld an affirmative action plan that established a one-for-one racial quota for promotions. In *U.S. v. Paradise*, in a case involving Alabama state troopers, the Court held that the promotion quotas are permissible because of the long history of discriminating against racial minorities.[19]

The Court has taken a more conservative position, holding in January 1989 that Richmond, Virginia's, ordinance setting aside 30 percent of public works contracts spending for minority contractors was unconstitutional.[20] Other cases involving the burden of proof in civil rights cases may be interpreted as making it easier for employers to discriminate.[21] Still another case makes it easier for white males to challenge consent decrees that are made to settle many discrimination suits, resulting in the hiring of more women and minorities.[22]

In reacting to this last case, Benjamin L. Hooks, executive director of the National Association for the Advancement of Colored People, said:

> Night has fallen on the Court as far as civil rights are concerned. We are seeing the unraveling of gains we thought were secure. This is a bad decision, and another reminder of the Reagan legacy that will haunt this nation for years.[23]

The law suits continue, brought by whites and minorities.

Allegations of discrimination have also arisen within the FBI. In May 1988 a federal judge ordered the FBI to make changes in what the judge called an "unsystematic, excessively subjective" method of internal promotions that was shown to be discriminatory against Hispanics. The FBI was ordered to review 200 cases of Hispanic officers who had been with the department for seven years or longer in an effort to determine whether racial discrimination existed in these cases. The court also ordered that Hispanic FBI agent, Bernardo "Mat" Perez, the original plaintiff in the lawsuit, be promoted to the next level within forty-five days. Several months before the Supreme Court handed down this decision, FBI Director William S. Sessions announced sweeping internal changes in the wake of evidence that the FBI was discriminating against minorities.[24]

The problems do not end with recruitment and promotions. Women and minority officers also face problems on the job. Early studies of black police officers emphasized the role conflicts they faced. According to Nicholas Alex, black officers encountered black residents who expected a break when they violated the law; being lenient (along with many other actions by black officers), however, resulted in criticism from white peers. Black officers who want to be accepted by the community of residents they serve but also by their colleagues thus face a difficult dilemma.[25] As more blacks enter policing, they might be expected to assume some of the attitudes characteristic of white police officers, such as concern because the people they serve exhibit a basic mistrust of police. A study of black police officers in New York City has found this to be the case.[26]

Black and white officers have problems working with each other.

Black officers complain that they are not really accepted by white officers, although they generally indicate that if they need help, they believe white officers will come to their aid. But after hours, many are not accepted as friends. Women also make the same complaints. According to one professor of policing, "Police fraternity has not stretched to the point of fully embracing blacks or women. . . . It is true, in part, because black officers have segregated themselves to be a force for their own people. Self-integration interferes with the issue of solidarity, which says anyone in blue is your brother or sister."[27]

Females have also encountered problems in policing, facing rejection by some male colleagues and by some residents they serve. Critics have argued that females cannot handle the physical aspects of policing, but a careful analysis of this argument is hindered by the lack of agreement regarding the physical characteristics required. Physical differences between men and women do not in themselves mean that women do not possess sufficient physical abilities to police as well as men do, and although more women are being hired as police officers, women have not been gaining significant ground in promotions to supervisory roles in policing.[28]

Police Personality Characteristics

Police have been described as a homogeneous group who differ from other groups in various personality traits and characteristics. Early studies reported that police are emotionally maladjusted, extremely cynical and authoritarian, and impulsive risk takers. They are more rigid, punitive, physically aggressive, assertive, and lacking in self-confidence than most other people and have a preference for being supervised.[29]

It is necessary, however, to look beyond the results of these studies. For example, although some studies show that police officers are generally cynical, others indicate that they are not cynical toward all aspects of policing. Thus, more attention should be given to the variables associated with the cynical reactions of some police officers. Others have argued that cynicism is not a trait of police, but, rather, a label from society. Police are a heterogeneous, not a homogeneous, group of people who become less, not more, cynical as they grow older and as their length of service on the police force increases. Still others have contended that whatever traits police officers have, such as authoritarianism or punitiveness, they acquired them on the force, as recruits do not demonstrate these traits when they begin policing.

Some recent studies of police characteristics have focused on police chiefs. An analysis of cynicism indicates that cynicism is highest during the early years as a police officer and declines gradually with experience. The more educated chiefs from larger police departments were less likely to indicate cynical attitudes, although the study found only modest cynicism among police chiefs and not much variation in the cynicism scores.

These results may mean that the less cynical officers have the qualities thought best for administration; it may also mean that by the time they achieve the rank of chief, they have already "seen it all."[30]

In early studies of police, the emphasis was on personality, with the assumption that if we could attract different types of people, the quality of policing would improve. But the Commission on Civil Rights found that the standards used for selecting police recruits do not accurately reflect and measure the qualities needed for adequate job performance. The commission stressed the importance of psychological testing.

Analysis of some psychological test results indicate that police applicants are psychologically healthier than some other applicant groups. One analysis, which compared MMPI scores (Minnesota Multiphasic Personality Inventory, a psychological test administered to many job applicants) of police applicants with three other groups (private security guard company; male submariners; U. S. Air Force recruits), concluded as follows:

> Police . . . are somewhat more psychologically healthy than the normative population, as they are generally less depressed and anxious, and more assertive and interested in making and maintaining social contacts. . . . Second, they have a greater tendency to present a good impression of themselves than the normative population. . . . Finally, they are a more homogeneous group than the normative population.[31]

Psychological tests are important, but unless we know how they relate to the specific functions that police must perform, the results will be of little help. We need to focus on the requirements of policing and on training people to fulfill those requirements. We cannot analyze policing without looking at what police do and analyzing the conflicts and stresses they encounter. We need to know their priorities, and those priorities are not necessarily related to factors such as background or an authoritarian or nonauthoritarian personality.[32]

THE NATURE OF POLICING

Historically police have had greater responsibility for enforcing the peace than for law enforcement. It was their function to find homes and shelters for females who might be lured away from prostitution; to handle riots and other civil disturbances; to regulate refuse disposal, street sanitation, and explosives; and to inspect bars, liquor stores, and other businesses that require licensing. Police have also historically performed numerous social service functions.

Police did not initially investigate criminal activities. That was the responsibility of the victim. But once the victim had identified the guilty person, police would help apprehend him or her. Victims paid police for helping them regain stolen property. Thus, officers who became experts in finding stolen property could expect greater gain. This action led to specialization in police forces, and the practice of paying police for their services made police give careful attention to those who had the means to pay.

Today the function of policing differs from the image held by the public and preferred by police, that of the officer chasing and catching dangerous criminals. In actuality considerable time is spent in routine, boring, and nondangerous activities. But the system has developed a structure that gives the greatest awards for dangerous activities and the fewest rewards for routine functions. This situation creates problems for police, for the department, and for the community. It is therefore important to look at all police functions.

Police Functions

Law enforcement is only one of several police functions, as Exhibit 12.3 indicates. It is interesting that the source used for that exhibit lists the four functions—law enforcement, order maintenance, information gathering, and service-related duties—without the sub-categories that it used in its

---

EXHIBIT 12.3

Police Functions

The roles of police officers are—

- **Law enforcement**—applying legal sanctions (usually arrest) to behavior that violates a legal standard.
- **Order maintenance**—taking steps to control events and circumstances that disturb or threaten to disturb the peace. For example, a police officer may be called on to mediate a family dispute, to disperse an unruly crowd, or to quiet an overly boisterous party.

- **Information gathering**—asking routine questions at a crime scene, inspecting victimized premises, and filling out forms needed to register criminal complaints.
- **Service-related duties**—a broad range of activities, such as assisting injured persons, animal control, or fire calls.

SOURCE: Bureau of Justice Statistics, *Report to the Nation on Crime and Justice: The Data,* 2d ed (Washington, D.C.: U.S. Government Printing Office, 1988), p. 62.

first edition. In 1983, the Bureau of Justice Statistics categorized law enforcement and order maintenance as "two main roles of police officers" and information gathering and service-related duties as "two secondary roles of police officers." Since information gathering may and usually does occur in all three police functions, discussions generally categorize the three basic functions as law enforcement, order maintenance, and service-related functions.

Law Enforcement

Police are empowered to stop, question, detain, and arrest people who violate the law. Their law enforcement powers range from stopping traffic violators to apprehending persons suspected of committing serious felonies, and that apprehension may legally involve the use of deadly force. Police also investigate crimes and collect and preserve evidence for criminal trials.

Most of the remainder of this chapter is devoted to a discussion of the different aspects of law enforcement, but at this point it is important to understand that law enforcement powers do not give police great crime-prevention abilities. In its 1967 report, the President's Commission on Law Enforcement stressed that police are limited in their ability to prevent crime. "They did not start and cannot stop the convulsive social changes that are taking place in America. They do not enact the laws that they are required to enforce, nor do they dispose of the criminals they arrest."[33] According to the commission, the role of police in law enforcement is mainly apprehending people who commit crimes, not deterring crimes; but even in that role, they are dependent on citizens for assistance. In a provocative and often-cited work, Herbert L. Packer described what the role of police should be in the area of law enforcement: "Ideally, police should be seen as the people who keep the law of the jungle from taking over."[34]

Order Maintenance

James Q. Wilson has defined *order maintenance* as the "management of conflict situations to bring about consensual resolution." By *order* Wilson means the "absence of disorder, and by disorder is meant behavior that either disturbs or threatens to disturb the public peace or that involves face-to-face conflict among two or more persons." An example would be a domestic dispute. According to Wilson, it is crucial that police rather than some other professionals respond to such problems since they may result in violence. Wilson argues that order maintenance is the most important function of police work. Furthermore, police have wide discretion in all areas, and this discretion occurs in situations characterized by intensive conflicts and often hostile participants.[35]

Wilson's position is shared by George L. Kelling, who has studied the historical development of policing in this country. He concluded that as police work became more professional, greater emphasis was placed on law enforcement, which was more easily measured. This emphasis on law enforcement, says Kelling, reduced the emphasis on order maintenance, which led to negative effects without resulting in a decreased crime rate. Kelling, like Wilson, says the evidence indicates that when police are involved in order maintenance the relationship between police and community is improved. The result is reduced fear of crime and greater cooperation of citizens with police in crime control.[36]

Carl B. Klockars disagrees with Kelling and Wilson, taking the position that Americans have traditionally considered the primary function of policing to be law enforcement. To reduce that emphasis, says Klockars, would not reduce the crime rate and would decrease the ability of police to respond to more serious problems and violations. Klockars does not take the position that order maintenance is an unimportant police function but only that a greater emphasis should be placed on law enforcement.[37]

Service-Related Duties

Police also engage in a variety of service-related functions. People who do not know how to solve a problem might call police for help. The President's Commission on Law Enforcement advocated that although many service functions are important because of their relationship to crime control and police and community relations, we should not expect police to engage in service-related functions not related to law enforcement. Examples of service-related functions that police should perhaps retain are listed in Highlight 12.1.

HIGHLIGHT 12.1

 SUGGESTED SERVICE-RELATED FUNCTIONS OF POLICE

1. Visiting schools to educate children about law enforcement, crime prevention, the use of alcohol and other drugs, bicycle safety on the streets, and law observance.

2. Providing educational and training sessions for women, the elderly, the poor, or for that matter any group of citizens who have experienced high crime rates or who fear crimes. Rape-prevention techniques are a good example; what to do in the event of sexual assault is another.

3. Speaking to young children about the dangers of being kidnapped or sexually assaulted.

4. Meeting with residents who wish to begin neighborhood watch programs for crime prevention.

5. Fingerprinting children for identification in case of kidnapping.

6. Assisting residents with marking their valuables for easier identification and recovery in the event of theft.

7. Providing the public with information on how to decrease their chances of becoming a victim of theft or violent crime.

Police perform many service functions. Here an officer consoles a lost child.

Allocation of Time

There is obvious disagreement over which of the three functions—law enforcement, order maintenance, and service-related activities—is the most important. There is also disagreement over how time is allocated among those functions. In an early study, Wilson reported that 38 percent of police time was spent in service-related duties, followed by 30 percent in order maintenance, 22 percent in information gathering, and only 10 percent in law enforcement.[38] Those figures differed from a study in Chicago conducted two years earlier by Reiss, who found that 58 percent of calls to the police department involved requests about criminal matters and 30 percent were about noncriminal matters.[39]

Later studies, some based on observations of police on patrol rather than on analyses of calls to the police department, indicate that although police spend more time in law enforcement than in any other activity, less than one-third of police activities involve criminal activity.[40] Eric J. Scott's studies indicated that only 17 percent of calls to police were for nonviolent crimes and 2 percent for violent crimes. Among the largest percentage of calls for other reasons were as follows: a citizen wanting information (21 percent); suspicious circumstances (12 percent); public nuisances (11 percent); traffic problems (9 percent); a citizen giving information (8 percent); and interpersonal conflict (7 percent).[41]

Police say they spend more time in law enforcement than is indicated by some of the studies. So, whom do we believe? How much time do police spend in law enforcement compared to order maintenance and community services? The answer to that question may be affected by the size of the department and the size of the community as well as by the categorization of activities. For example, when police respond to a domestic dispute, some may classify that activity as law enforcement; others may classify it as order maintenance.

Regardless of how activities are categorized, it is agreed that police officers do not spend most of their time in the stereotype of police action: catching *serious* criminals. Their work is mainly **reactive,** not **proactive,** as indicated in Exhibit 12.4. That is, police depend on the assistance of victims and other citizens for crime reports. Because crime is generally nonvisible to police, they would detect very little crime without such reports.

Problem-Oriented Policing

A National Institute of Justice (NIJ) report concludes that the reactive nature of most policing is not the most efficient method. The NIJ suggests the implementation of *problem-oriented policing,* which looks at calls to police not as unique events to be processed individually but as part of a network of events. Problem-solving policing looks for patterns of events and attempts to derive solutions. For example, instead of relying on legal categories such as burglary or robbery, officers are told to group calls into problem categories. What is traditionally called a robbery might actually be part of a network of prostitution-related robberies committed in specific hotels. Alerting potential customers, hotel owners and managers, and local businesses, and talking to the prostitutes, may secure further information. With this added knowledge, police could then attempt to solve this area of criminal activity. In other words, the focus is on underlying *causes* or problems, not on the incident that precipitated an individual call.

Because of the problem-oriented approach, NIJ reports that in Newport News, Virginia, robberies in the downtown area were reduced by 39 percent, burglaries in one apartment complex were reduced by 35 percent, and thefts from vehicles parked outside a manufacturing plant were

EXHIBIT 12.4

Reactive versus Proactive Policing

The core mission of the police is to control crime. No one disputes this. Indeed, professional crime fighting enjoys wide public support as the basic strategy of policing precisely because it embodies a deep commitment to this objective. In contrast, other proposed strategies such as problem-solving or community policing appear on the surface to blur this focus. If these strategies were to leave the community more vulnerable to criminal victimization, they would be undesirable alternatives. In judging the value of alternative police strategies in controlling crime, however, one should not be misled by rhetoric or mere expressed commitment to the goal; one must keep one's eye on demonstrated effectiveness in achieving the goal.

Professional crime-fighting now relies predominantly on three tactics: (1) motorized patrol; (2) rapid response to calls for service; and (3) retrospective investigation of crimes. Over the past few decades, police responsiveness has been enhanced by connecting police to citizens by telephones, radios, and cars, and by matching police officer schedules and locations to anticipated calls for service. The police focus on serious crime has also been sharpened by screening calls for service, targeting patrol, and developing forensic technology (e.g., automated fingerprint systems, computerized criminal record files, etc.).

Although these tactics have scored their successes, they have been criticized within and outside policing for being reactive rather than proactive. They have also been criticized for failing to prevent crime.

Reactive tactics have some virtues, of course. The police go where crimes have occurred and when citizens have summoned them; otherwise, they do not intrude. The police keep their distance from the community, and thereby retain their impartiality. They do not develop the sorts of relationships with citizens that could bias their responses to crime incidents. These are virtues insofar as they protect citizens from an overly intrusive, too familiar police.

Moreover, the reactive tactics do have preventive effects—at least in theory. The prospect of the police arriving at a crime in progress as a result of a call or a chance observation is thought to deter crimes. The successful prosecution of offenders (made possible by retrospective investigation) is also thought to deter offenders. And even if it does not deter,

reduced by 53 percent.[42] Although NIJ may be exaggerating the actual effect of problem-oriented policing, considerable attention is being given today to adjusting policing to the needs of a particular neighborhood rather than assuming that policing of all areas should be the same traditional response to calls for services.[43]

a successfully prosecuted investigation incapacitates criminals who might otherwise go on to commit other crimes.

Finally, many police forces have developed proactive tactics to deal with crime problems that could not be handled through conventional reactive methods. In drug dealing, organized crime, and vice enforcement, for example, where no immediate victims exist to mobilize the police, the police have developed special units which rely on informants, covert surveillance, and undercover investigations rather than responses to calls for service. In the area of juvenile offenses where society's stake in preventing crimes seems particularly great, the police have created athletic leagues, formed partnerships with schools to deal with drug abuse and truancy, and so on. It is not strictly accurate, then, to characterize modern policing as entirely reactive.

Still, the criticism of the police as being too reactive has some force. It is possible that the police could do more to control serious crime than they now achieve. Perhaps research will yield technological breakthroughs that will dramatically improve the productivity of police investigation. For now, however, the greatest potential for improved crime control may not lie in the continued enhancement of response times, patrol tactics, and investigative techniques. Rather, improved crime control can be achieved by (1) diagnosing and managing problems in the community that produce serious crimes; (2) fostering closer relations with the community to facilitate crime solving; and (3) building self-defense capabilities within the community itself. Among the results may be increased apprehension of criminals. To the extent that problem-solving or community strategies of policing direct attention to and prepare the police to exploit local knowledge and capacity to control crime, they will be useful to the future of policing. To explore these possibilities, this paper examines what is known about serious crime: what it is, where and how it occurs, and natural points of intervention. Current and proposed police tactics are then examined in light of what is known about their effectiveness in fighting serious crime.

SOURCE: Mark H. Moore et al., National Institute of Justice, *Crime and Policing* (Washington, D.C.: U.S. Department of Justice, June 1988), pp. 1–2, footnotes omitted.

Community-Oriented Policing

George L. Kelling, noted authority on policing, has stated the current emphasis on community-oriented policing as follows: "A quiet revolution is reshaping American policing. Police in dozens of communities are returning to foot patrol." Kelling goes on to note that police are also asking citizens what they perceive as their most pressing problems as well as asking for suggestions on what might be done to solve those problems. Fear of crime is one of the most frequently mentioned concerns, and many police departments are addressing that issue.[44]

Although community policing will differ in nature among the various jurisdictions,[45] Herman Goldstein has identified the following common characteristics of this current focus in policing:

- the involvement of the community in getting police job done;
- the permanent assignment of police officers to a neighborhood in order to cultivate better relationships;
- the setting of police priorities based on the specific needs and desires of the community; and
- the meeting of these needs by the allocation of police resources and personnel otherwise assigned to responding to calls for public assistance.[46]

Community policing may increase police accountability to the community,[47] increase public cooperation with police, reduce fear of crime,[48] and assist police and the community in solving society's most crucial crime problem—drugs.[49]

One of the features of community policing is a return to foot patrol. This recent development began in Flint, Michigan, and has spread to other cities. Experiments of foot patrol in that city and in Newark, New Jersey, produced the following results:

- When foot patrol is added in neighborhoods, levels of fear decrease significantly.
- When foot patrol is withdrawn from neighborhoods, levels of fear increase significantly.
- Citizen satisfaction with police increases when foot patrol is added in neighborhoods.
- Police who patrol on foot have a greater appreciation for the values of neighborhood residents than police who patrol the same areas in automobiles.
- Police who patrol on foot have greater job satisfaction, less fear, and higher morale than officers who patrol in automobiles.[50]

The Flint study also showed a significant (40 percent) reduction in telephone calls for service when police engaged in aggressive foot patrol. A small reduction in crime also occurred.[51]

Exhibit 12.5 contains a brief contrast of traditional policing and community policing through a question-and-answer format.

Role Conflicts

The variety of police functions and the lack of consensus on how police do or should allocate their time may create a dilemma. Problem-oriented policing and community policing, or for that matter any other changes in the traditional functions of police, may create conflict. In addition, police are expected to prevent crime, which they cannot effectively do even with citizens' support, and they often do not get that support. When they do prevent crime, there is no adequate measure of what they have done. When they engage in order maintenance and service-related functions, they may face hostility in the former and unreasonable demands in the latter; that is, they are asked to solve problems for which they have no solutions.

In addition to expecting the impossible, society is often unclear about what it expects police to do in a given situation. Are they to enforce the law or ignore violations? Because a particular community expects a different type of behavior, police may not always act legally. The reaction of Chicago officers to the ambiguity of the expectations of those on patrol makes the point quite clear. Most of the officers preferred not to have patrol duty.

Among the many reasons they listed for preferring other duty assignments—more interesting work, higher pay, greater prestige, and greater freedom—the most important was "the officer has a better sense of what is expected of him."[52]

The patrol officer faces other conflicts regarding community expectations. The neighborhood may be composed of persons whose life-styles include knifings, narcotics, and domestic quarrels, and that particular neighborhood may expect the officer to ignore the laws regulating such behavior. The officer who has worked in areas where such behavior is not common may find great resistance when he or she tries to enforce these laws.

Police officers also face conflicts over human misery versus evil. When they arrive at the scene of an accident or other tragedy, they must control their emotions. An officer cannot punish the father who beat his child, nor can he or she get sick at the sight of a mangled body. Police must act with reason and perform their jobs as efficiently as possible.

There is also conflict between efficiency and the constitutional rights of citizens and between some dishonest activities of colleagues and honesty. Police officers may feel conflict between fear and courage—the desire to be courageous while realizing that they are risking their own health or lives. Maintaining order often takes the officers into a hostile environment. Those who called for help may consider the situation an emergency. But because the officers have been involved in many similar situations, they have learned by experience that the victims's version of the incident may not be reliable. Police thus may not be as sympathetic as the victim desires, and the latter may become upset at this apparent lack of understanding. Further, because only a few calls to police result in arrest, victims may think that police are not doing their jobs. The problem is that most crimes are property crimes with no clues or witnesses. Even if a suspect is found, officers must fulfill the requirements for making an arrest, and often those cannot be met.

EXHIBIT 12.5

Traditional vs. Community Policing: Questions and Answers

	Traditional	**Community policing**
Question: *Who are the police?*	A government agency principally responsible for law enforcement.	Police are the public and the public are the police: the police officers are those who are paid to give full-time attention to the duties of every citizen.
Question: *What is the relationship of the police force to other public service departments?*	Priorities often conflict.	The police are one department among many responsible for improving the quality of life.
Question: *What is the role of the police?*	Focusing on solving crimes.	A broader problem-solving approach.
Question: *How is police efficiency measured?*	By detection and arrest rates.	By the absence of crime and disorder.
Question: *What are the highest priorities?*	Crimes that are high value (e.g., bank robberies) and those involving violence.	Whatever problems disturb the community most.
Question: *What, specifically, do police deal with?*	Incidents.	Citizens' problems and concerns.
Question: *What determines the effectiveness of police?*	Response times.	Public cooperation.

Police Stress

Role conflicts have created police stress, a subject that has claimed considerable attention in recent years. Formerly considered a personal problem, stress is now seen as a corporate problem because of the effect it has on employees. Some businesses now retain a professional person to assist employees who have difficulty handling stress. Stress causes physical ill-

Traditional vs. Community Policing: Questions and Answers

	Traditional	**Community policing**
Question: *What view do police take of service calls?*	Deal with them only if there is no real police work to do.	Vital function and great opportunity.
Question: *What is police professionalism?*	Swift effective response to serious crime.	Keeping close to the community.
Question: *What kind of intelligence is most important?*	Crime intelligence (study of particular crimes or series of crimes).	Criminal intelligence (information about the activities of individuals or groups).
Question: *What is the esssential nature of police accountability?*	Highly centralized; governed by rules, regulations, and policy directives; accountable to the law.	Emphasis on local accountability to community needs.
Question: *What is the role of headquarters?*	To provide the necessary rules and policy directives.	To preach organizational values.
Question: *What is the role of the press liaison department?*	To keep the "heat" off operational officers so they can get on with the job.	To coordinate an essential channel of communication with the community.
Question: *How do the police regard prosecutions?*	As an important goal.	As one tool among many.

SOURCE: Malcolm K. Sparrow, *Implementing Community Policing*, National Institute of Justice (Washington, D.C.: U.S. Department of Justice, November 1988), pp. 8–9.

nesses, resulting in higher medical costs, lower productivity, absenteeism, and premature death, all of which may be extremely costly for business.

Although all people may encounter some stress in their jobs, there is evidence that it is particularly high among air traffic controllers, lawyers, dentists, physicians, psychiatrists, and law enforcement officers. Some argue that law enforcement is the most difficult job emotionally and psychologically because of the possibility of physical danger. The stress of

HIGHLIGHT 12.2

POLICE USE OF DEADLY FORCE: THE IMPACT

On March 31, 1983, a police officer, responding to a call from a neighbor who had not seen five-year-old Patrick and his mother for two weeks, entered their apartment with a passkey provided by the building manager. Hearing noises coming from the bedroom, the officer opened the door that the mother had tied shut. The officer saw a silhouette holding what he thought was a gun, fired, and killed the little boy who was holding a toy while he watched television.

One year later, the news media reported that the mother, who had moved from that residence in Stanton, California, to Chicago, Illinois, could barely look at another child without thinking of her little boy whose life had been taken so quickly and, at least in her mind, unnecessarily. The officer, unemployed and receiving disability retirement pay, suffers from severe stress attacks. According to his father, "The memory of that awful event has intensely affected his life. It will be with him forever." He received a $32,000 cash settlement for the psychological damage he has suffered, and he filed a $25 million claim against the city, hoping that the courts will consider the city, not the officer, liable for any lawsuits in the case. The mother filed a $20 million claim against the officer and the city. A man who claims to be the father of the deceased boy has filed claims against the city, totaling $10 million. The city has rejected those claims, but he could be successful in a civil action should he choose that course of action.

The lawsuits in this case will probably not be decided for several years, and the pain, suffering, and stress for the immediate parties will perhaps never end.

SOURCE: Summarized by the author from news media accounts.

---

policing extends beyond the police officer to his or her family. Stress may account for the high rate of divorce among police, a rate that is, according to some, higher than in most other professions (all others, according to some studies).[53]

There is one major difference between policing and most other professions. Police are trained to injure or kill; and if the situation requires, they are expected to use that ability. Indeed, they may be sanctioned for not using their weapons. However, officers who kill may be socially isolated from their colleagues. The routine procedure is to suspend officers pending investigation of a shooting. Even when the investigation indicates that the officer was justified in the killing, he or she may continue to experience stress. One officer's reactions to a killing are expressed in Highlight 12.2.

The effect of stress has led some departments to initiate stress-reduction programs, a procedure recommended by the Commission on Civil Rights. James D. Sewell, a Florida police chief with a Ph.D. in criminology, and others have emphasized that it is not sufficient, however, to institute stress management programs in police departments and assume they will be successful. Sewell and his colleagues point out that, although we started talking about police stress in 1974, we have not conducted sufficient research into the extent and causes of stress among police; nor do we know which programs are most successful.[54]

Police Subculture

One of the ways that police officers attempt to cope with stress is to isolate themselves from others, forming a **subculture** and associating only with other officers and their families. One researcher described police as a minority and found that they share many of the self-concepts characteristic of minorities. "Both suffer from a 'lack of respect'; both see the larger community as an enemy which does not understand them; both are aggressive in their response to those not in their community; both stay within their own group; and both see the other as a threat and strike out at the other."[55]

Social solidarity may be the result of the danger that police face, which necessitates the need to help one another. It may also be the result of suspiciousness, resulting in a perceptual shorthand developed to help identify people who might commit an unlawful act. It may also be the result of the conflicting demands placed on police. It is difficult for them to make friends among nonpolice.

The isolation of police is to some extent functional. It allows them to relate to the public without the undue strain that might result if they were apprehending and arresting their friends. The opposing view is that police isolation is detrimental to police and a disservice to the public. The isolation prevents police from seeing the public's views.

POLICE DECISIONS

Police are the only people most citizens will encounter in the entire system of criminal justice. Most people never go before a judge, but most at some time have contact with a police officer. Their feelings of security on the streets and in their homes may in large part be determined by their attitudes toward the effectiveness or lack thereof of the police force. Police are among the most important administrators in the United States, and they have considerable decision-making discretion in the performance of their jobs.

Initial Apprehension and Decision to Arrest

The decision to interfere with the freedom, even if momentarily, of another person is an extremely serious one. People do not like to be stopped by police; it is a frightening and confusing experience for many, and some may perceive the action of police as discriminatory. Their perceptions may be correct. Police, however, reject this conclusion, saying that they stop people only when it appears that a problem exists. The issue is even more pronounced when the possibility of an **arrest** exists.

The police officer is not only momentarily interfering with freedom but is also setting in motion a process that may result in stigmatization and incarceration. What, then, are the factors that influence the decision to stop and then to arrest?

The decision to take a suspect into custody is governed by case and statutory law. This body of law is technical and complicated. It is related to the *legal seriousness* of the suspected crime, although some studies have found that legal seriousness plays a small part in the decision. Most of the problems that police are called on to resolve are not of a legally serious nature; they are minor problems in which arrests are not usually made. Police must therefore base their decision to apprehend on criteria other than the legal seriousness of an alleged crime. The question of what these other criteria are has been relatively well researched by social scientists.

The Right to Stop and Question

Police must have **probable cause** to arrest, but probable cause is not required to stop and question in some circumstances. For instance, it is permissible for police officers to stop a person who appears suspicious or out of place in a particular place. They may stop the person and ask for identification; but they may not detain him or her unreasonably, nor may they stop *classes* of people in order to harass them.

An example of limitations on the police's stop-and-question function attracted attention in 1982 through the national media and a Supreme Court decision. White police officers had on numerous occasions stopped a thirty-six-year-old tall, black, muscular man with long hair who frequently jogged in a predominantly white neighborhood. They asked for identification on about fifteen occasions over a two-year period. When the jogger refused to identify himself or to answer other questions, police arrested him several times. He was convicted once and served several weeks in jail.

According to police, the jogger committed a misdemeanor when he violated a California statute that labeled as disorderly conduct the behavior of a person "who loiters or wanders upon the streets or from place to place without apparent reason or business or who refuses to identify himself and to account for his presence when requested by any peace officer to do so, if the surrounding circumstances are such as to indicate to a reasonable man that the public safety demands such identification."[56]

In deciding that the statute in question was void because it was vague, the U.S. Supreme Court, in *Kolender v. Lawson*, articulated the importance of individual freedoms. Recognizing that police must be able to exercise some discretion in stop-and-question situations, the Court nevertheless struck down this statute because the legislature had not, in passing it, provided sufficient guidelines on that discretion. The statute, said the Court, leaves us free to walk the streets (or jog the streets) only at the "whim of any police officer."[57]

It is important to understand, however, that the problem with this statute is not that police initially stopped a person, but that there were no standards by which to judge whether the suspect had complied with the statute. This gives police too much discretion and therefore "furnishes a convenient tool for harsh and discriminatory enforcement by local prosecuting officials, against particular groups deemed to merit their displeasure."[58]

Officers may also search vehicles under some circumstances after validly stopping a driver. But consider the following facts. Utah Highway Patrol Trooper Paul Mangelson was driving home after finishing his shift work for the day. He observed a truck going in the opposite direction following too closely behind the car in front. Trooper Mangelson made a U-turn through the median and pulled up beside the truck in an effort to determine how fast the vehicle was moving. He then noted that the drivers of the truck (which had an out-of-state tag) and of the car were Hispanic. He stopped the truck, cited the driver for "following too closely," and for driving with an expired license. He then asked the truck driver if he could search the truck, and the driver consented. The trooper found cocaine. The driver was arrested and charged with illegal possession of drugs. He moved to have the evidence suppressed. The trial court agreed; the state appealed. In the excerpt below, the appellate court considers whether the initial stop was a "pretext stop" to search the vehicle for drugs. After deciding that it was, the court then had to decide whether the consent to search removed the taint of the search and therefore the evidence seized should have been admitted.[59]

State v. Arroyo

A police officer may stop a vehicle for a traffic violation committed in his presence. Nevertheless, a police officer may not "use a misdemeanor arrest as a pretext to search for evidence of a more serious crime." Courts must look to the totality of the circumstances to determine whether a stop for a traffic violation and subsequent arrest is a pretext. This involves "an objective assessment of the officer's actions in light of the facts and circumstances confronting him at the time." The actual state of mind of the officer at the time of the challenged action is irrelevant. Thus, in this appeal, the question is whether a reasonable officer, in view of the totality of the circumstances of this case, would have stopped Arroyo for "following too closely." The proper focus is not on whether Trooper Mangelson could have validly made the stop.

[The court then reviews the facts, noting that the trooper was off duty and that few citations are given for "following too closely," that the occupants were Hispanic and the truck had an out-of-state license.]

We agree with the trial judge that the stop was an unconstitutional pretext to search for drugs. We are persuaded that a reasonable officer would not have stopped Arroyo and cited him for "following too closely" except for some unarticulated suspicion of more serious criminal activity.

[The court then considered whether the consent to search was voluntary, that is, not the result of duress or coercion, and decided that it was.]

Thus, although the original illegal stop was unconstitutional, Arroyo's subsequent voluntary consent purged the taint from the initial illegality, and the motion to suppress should not have been granted.

Accordingly, the order granting Arroyo's motion to suppress the evidence is reversed, and the case is remanded for trial.

The Sociology of Arrest

Although police are legally permitted to stop and question people and to arrest them under certain circumstances, the Supreme Court has held that "it is not the function of police to arrest, as it were, at large and to use an interrogating process at police headquarters in order to determine whom they should charge before a committing magistrate on 'probable cause.'"[60]

Police do not stop all people whom they think are violating a law. What explains the decisions to stop and subsequently to arrest? One variable is the officer's perception of community standards and attitudes and the homogeneity between police and the community.[61] A study of police activities in relation to community characteristics examined what police do after they initially apprehend a suspect. The general finding was that they do act differently in different settings. Specifically,

1. Police appear to be more active in racially mixed neighborhoods.

2. In racially heterogeneous neighborhoods, police have a greater propensity to offer assistance to residents and to initiate more contacts with suspicious persons and suspected violators. . . .

3. In high-crime areas police are less likely to stop suspicious persons, suggesting that the findings evidence a higher level of general police activity in racially mixed neighborhoods. . . .

4. Suspects confronted by police have a higher average probability of being arrested in lower-status neighborhoods than in higher-status areas. . . .

5. Police are more apt to exert coercive authority in minority and racially mixed communities.[62]

The researcher emphasized, however, that these findings do not necessarily mean that police are more prone to arrest blacks than whites. The context of the alleged criminal activity is an important factor in the decision to arrest, and it may be that those characteristics are more influential than the race of the suspect. Scholars continue to debate the issue of whether differences in arrest rates (as well as convictions, sentencing, and other decisions in the criminal justice system) reflect race (or sex) discrimination.[63]

Community expectations may also influence police decisions not to investigate or apprehend suspects in some areas. For example, police may not consider places like narrow alleys and abandoned buildings and cars to be areas that the community wishes to be investigated, even though they are known to be used for illegal purposes. After they get to know an area, the officers know what behaviors to expect, and they may permit or tolerate behavior in one area that would not be permitted in another.

Arrests may also reflect the preferences of complaining victims, as found in an earlier but extensive and classic study by Donald Black. Black also found that arrests were more likely when suspects were disrespectful and when suspects were stopped for serious crimes. Black suggested that these factors, not race per se, accounted for higher arrest rates among blacks than among whites. Others disagree, insisting that police discriminate against blacks and other minorities in arrests. The resolution of this problem is difficult; for as Black's study and many others have shown, police are lenient in their routine arrest practices. Most people who could be arrested are not arrested even when they are apprehended.[64]

The Use of Force

Laws regulating the use of force differ, but usually officers may not use lethal force unless they or other persons are threatened with serious bodily harm or death. They may, however, use as much nonlethal force as is reasonably necessary to make an arrest, control a crowd, or engage in any other legitimate police function.

Generally, a police officer cannot use deadly force to apprehend a misdemeanant, but in some states the act of fleeing is a felony. If a person flees after an arrest, the officer may be permitted to use deadly force, even if the original offense for which the arrest was made was a misdemeanor. Most jurisdictions previously permitted officers to fire at a fleeing felon, but recently these policies have changed. Today federal and many local and state law enforcement agencies prohibit the use of deadly force unless human life is threatened.

Even when a statute permits police to fire a deadly weapon at a fleeing felon, the courts may rule that under some circumstances this action violates the felon's constitutional rights. In 1983 in Tennessee, an officer fired at a fifteen-year-old who had broken into an unoccupied residence in a suburban area. The boy was killed by the police officer, who had been taught that it was legal to fire at a fleeing felon. The Tennessee statute provided that "if . . . the defendant . . . either flees or forcibly resists, the officer may use all the necessary means to effect the arrest."[65]

The boy's father brought a civil case against police for violating the civil rights of his son. The trial court held that the statute and the police officer's actions were constitutional. The Court of Appeals reversed. The Supreme Court held that the Tennessee statute "is unconstitutional insofar as it authorizes the use of deadly force against . . . an apparently unarmed, nondangerous fleeing suspect." The Court stated some of its reasons in the following excerpt.[66]

Tennessee v. Garner

The use of deadly force to prevent the escape of all felon suspects, whatever the circumstances, is constitutionally unreasonable. It is not better that all felony suspects die than that they escape. Where the suspect poses no immediate threat to the officer and no threat to others, the harm resulting from failing to apprehend him does not justify the use of deadly force to do so. It is no doubt unfortunate when a suspect who is in sight escapes, but the fact that police arrive a little late or are a little slower afoot does not always justify killing the suspect. A police officer may not seize an unarmed, nondangerous suspect by shooting him dead. The Tennessee statute is unconstitutional insofar as it authorizes the use of deadly force against such fleeing suspects.

It is not, however, unconstitutional on its face. Where the officer has probable cause to believe that the suspect poses a threat of serious physical harm, either to the officer or to others, it is not constitutionally unreasonable to prevent escape by using deadly force. Thus, if the suspect threatens the officer with a weapon or there is probable cause to believe that he has committed a crime involving the infliction or threatened infliction of serious physical harm, deadly force may be used if necessary to prevent escape, and if, where feasible, some warning has been given.

Police Violence and Brutality

Allegations of police violence and brutality are frequently featured in the media, ranging from physical abuse and harassment to illegal use of weapons that results in serious injury or death. A study of police violence in New York, thought to be the first state-wide study of police violence, found "neither systemic nor pervasive misuse" of deadly physical force, but the study did find evidence of "low-level" abuse, such as the use of racial epithets.[67] The issue of excessive force most frequently arises in civil suits brought against police who are alleged to have been unreasonable in their use of force. Civil suits are beyond the scope of this text, but it should be noted that in 1989 the U.S. Supreme Court adopted an across-the-board rule that will apply to police use of excessive force in stopping someone without an arrest as well as in arrest cases. The Court held that all such cases will be analyzed under a standard of what would have been reasonable under the Fourth Amendment in light of all the facts of each case. In *Graham v. Connor*, the Court said the test is an objective one, that is, what a reasonable person would have done under those facts, not a subjective one, what the individual officer's intentions were. In short, an officer's "good intentions" in the use of force will not excuse force that was "objectively unreasonable."[68]

Violence against police is also a critical problem today,[69] and with the escalation of such violence in some cities has come greater protective measures. In New York City, after two officers were killed on the same night in separate incidents in 1988, the Chief of Patrol issued an order that all officers must wear bullet-resistant vests on all tours of duty. In October 1989, data indicated that the number of citizens killed by police and the number of officers killed in New York City had declined from the previous year.[70]

Effects of Police Brutality

Even when police are unjustifiably charged with brutality, there may be significant impact on the whole community and not just on the individuals involved in the allegations. Approximately 50 percent of those killed by police officers are black. Studies indicate, however, that this high percentage might not necessarily represent a policy of discrimination against minorities, but, rather, a reaction to the generally higher rates of violence in the inner cities, populated mainly by minorities. Further research is needed, and there is evidence of some truth in the belief of blacks in many cities that the "police have one trigger finger for blacks and another for whites."[71]

Alleged police brutality has also led to riots. The commissions appointed to study urban riots have uniformly noted the impact of police brutality. When the public perceives an act by a police officer to be unfair, unreasonable, unnecessary, or harassing, especially when minorities are the victims, that perception may provide the impetus for urban riots. The Miami, Florida, riots that occurred in January 1989 just before the Super Bowl were sparked by the fatal shooting of a black motorcyclist by an Hispanic police officer. This is not to suggest that police actions *cause* riots, but police can reduce violent confrontations by the policies they adopt.[72] In late fall 1989, the officer was convicted of manslaughter in the deaths of two black citizens. In the spring of 1990, the officer allegedly attempted to commit suicide.

Police Corruption

Sociologist Lawrence W. Sherman has defined *corruption* as follows:

> A public official is corrupt if he accepts money or money's worth for doing something that he is under a duty to do anyway, that he is under a duty not to do, or to exercise a legitimate discretion for improper reasons.[73]

Police corruption has long been a topic of concern and study. In response to an article charging widespread corruption, the mayor of New York City established the Knapp Commission in May 1970. The commission found that police corruption was so pervasive within the New York Police Department that rookies entering the force were subjected immediately to such strong pressures that many succumbed and became corrupt; others became cynical. This attitude was attributed to the departmental belief that corruption should not be exposed and to the code of silence concerning the corrupt activities of one's peers.[74]

More recently, officials of the New York City Police Department reported that only a small percentage of the city's police officers have been corrupted. Undercover tests of integrity, whereby some officers are assigned to make secret reports on the behavior of other officers, have, they say, virtually eliminated organized corruption. The institutionalized, organized corruption found by the Knapp Commission has, however, been replaced by a new type of activity: cheating scams, such as abuse of sick leave, overtime, and military leave. Officers have also been charged with theft and drug violations, which led to a suggested rotation policy to help curb corruption. The new police officers would be shifted from precinct to precinct to help break up the networks that facilitate corruption.

Analysis of Police Corruption

From violators of traffic laws who offer an officer money not to write a ticket to organized criminals who in some cities have been able to gain extensive control over police activities, policing is rich in opportunities for corruption. Generally less corruption exists in rural police departments; more extensive corruption is found in the older, more established departments in which more opportunities exist. Sources familiar with a federal investigation in Boston say it is the largest ever conducted in a major city and that when all the evidence is in, senior police officials as well as patrol officers will be indicted. The allegations involve successful bribery of police officers to refrain from arresting, to cover up liquor license violations, and to ignore failures to appear for court appearances. Financial payoffs were allegedly involved.[75]

In late 1988, it was reported that "rampant drug trafficking and efforts to control it are posing extraordinary and increasing threats to the integrity" of the New York City Police Department. Six officers or former officers had been charged with robbing drug dealers, presumably to get drugs for their own personal use. Today's officers are recruited from a society in which drug use is far more common than in the past, and some will succumb to drug use as well as to the temptations to make enormous amounts of money from selling drugs. Whitman Knapp, who headed the Knapp Commisssion investigation in New York in 1972, commented on the situation today:

> I'm sure there's corruption . . . There cannot not be, unless you find some way of eliminating human nature. Everybody wants favors. The whole thing that I think we changed was the climate. I mean, peer pressure when we came in was *for* corruption, and I don't think that's come back. I think peer pressure is still *against* corruption.[76]

The opportunity for corruption is not the only important variable. Variation in police corruption may also depend on a police department's type of organization. James Q. Wilson analyzed police departments according to what he termed *styles* of law enforcement: the Service Style, the Legalistic Style, and the Watchman Style. These styles were found to be related to the degree of police corruption, the greatest degree being found among the Watchman Style.[77]

The *Watchman Style* emphasizes order maintenance over law enforcement. That is, the law is used to maintain order rather than to regulate conduct. In a department characterized by the Watchman Style, the police chief tries to limit the discretionary authority of the patrol officers, as one of the main concerns is that no one rocks the boat within the department. Police are recruited locally, paid low salaries, given minimum training, not rewarded for higher education, and expected to have other jobs, any of which may make them more susceptible to corruption.

The *Legalistic Style* emphasizes specialization and promotional opportunities, higher education, and attempts to recruit from the middle class. The law is seen as a means to an end; the police officer tries to be an impersonal agent of the law, uses formal rather than informal sanctions, issues traffic tickets at a high rate, and emphasizes law enforcement over order maintenance or community services.

The *Service Style* combines law enforcement and order maintenance. Emphasis is on community relations, police on patrol work out of specialized units, and decentralized command. The pace of work is more leisurely, and more promotional opportunities are stressed. Corruption is not a serious problem, and police are expected to live exemplary private lives.

Police corruption is a problem of external opportunity and response and can be explained only by a close analysis of both variables. Sherman examined the external opportunities that might be conducive to corruption. He looked at theories of community structure and anomie, indicating that the degree of anomie depends on the gap between the goals and means to achieve them. Sherman emphasized that anomie can affect the corrupters and the corruptees and that an occupational group might suffer anomie not characteristic of the entire community. Police might have an occupational anomie and therefore be more susceptible to bribes than members of other occupational groups.[78]

According to Sherman, external opportunities for corruption change recruits' frames of reference, and they begin to feel that they are outsiders in the world of nonpolice. Recruits radically redefine themselves in a relatively short period of time. Their almost exclusive contacts with other police officers emphasize and reinforce that process. The process of accepting bribes then begins. The key factor here, Sherman observed, is the extent of such corruption in the work group to which the officer is assigned. The process goes by stages, beginning with police "perks"—free coffee and meals—and moving to a free drink after work to money offered by a motorist. If the officer participates in these stages, he or she may be considered ready by colleagues to be cut in on gambling deals. That offer is hard to turn down, for it represents a chance to participate in the social solidarity of colleagues. Officers may then move on to bribes from prostitutes, pimps, or brothel operators and finally into narcotics. Police officers may stop anywhere along the ladder because of self-conception, but they will be greatly influenced in where they stop by the group definition of how far they can go.[79]

CONTROL OF POLICE ACTIVITIES

The question of controlling police is an important one; several suggestions have been made.

Control by the Courts: The Exclusionary Rule

The main method exercised by courts to control police misconduct is the **exclusionary rule.** As early as 1914, the Supreme Court held that in federal cases the prohibition against unreasonable search and seizure would not be effective unless any illegally seized evidence was excluded from the trial. In 1961 the Court held that the exclusion also applied to cases tried in state courts.[80] But it was not until the 1960s that the exclusionary rule gained much attention in the press. With the increasing recognition of defendants' rights at trial, brought about by Supreme Court decisions in the 1960s, more attention has been given to what is perhaps the most controversial aspect of the criminal justice process.

The exclusionary rule is controversial because it applies after the fact. When the illegally seized evidence is excluded from the trial, we already know who the suspect is and often believe that guilt is obvious.

Thus, when the judge rules that the knife or gun allegedly used in the murder or the confession made by the suspect cannot be used against that person in court because the evidence was obtained illegally by police, there is a strong public reaction of disbelief and outrage.

Arguments in Favor of the Exclusionary Rule

The exclusionary rule serves a symbolic purpose. If police, to obtain evidence to convict alleged criminals, violate the rights of those individuals, our government is, in a sense, supporting crime. According to the Supreme Court, when this occurs, the government becomes a lawbreaker. "It breeds contempt for law; it invites . . . anarchy."[81]

The symbolic purpose is important, but the second reason for the exclusionary rule is a practical one. It is assumed that the existence of the rule will prevent police from engaging in illegal searches and seizures. It is, of course, difficult to know whether that is true, as illegal searches may not be reported. The research on the issue reports inconclusive evidence. There is evidence, however, that the existence of the rule has led some police departments to increase the quantity and quality of police training, thus educating officers more in what they may and may not do in the area of search and seizure.[82]

Arguments for Abolishing the Exclusionary Rule

In recent years the exclusionary rule has come under severe attack, with many people calling for its abolition or at least its modification. The arguments on this side of the issue are generally the reverse of the arguments in favor. First is the argument concerning symbolism, which is based on the view that when people see obviously guilty persons going free because of a technicality, the result is to undermine respect for law and order and weaken the entire criminal justice system. It is the public's perception of letting "guilty" people go free that is crucial. The classic statement on this issue was made by Benjamin Cardozo, then a state court judge and later a justice of the Supreme Court. Cardozo wrote the 1926 opinion in which the New York Court of Appeals refused to adopt the exclusionary rule for that jurisdiction: "The criminal is to go free because the constable has blundered."[83]

Second, the abolitionists contend that the exclusionary rule should be eliminated because it results in the release of guilty people. It makes no difference how many; one is too many, argue the abolitionists. Third, the possibility of having evidence excluded from a trial because it was not properly seized leads defendants to file numerous motions to suppress evidence, which takes up a lot of court time and contributes to congestion. In criminal cases, objections to search and seizure are the most frequently raised issues.[84]

EXHIBIT 12.6

The Supreme Court Focuses on the Exclusionary Rule

In January 1984 the Supreme Court heard arguments on whether the extremely controversial exclusionary rule should be abolished or modified. The major case argued before the Court involved evidence used to convict the defendant in the murder of a woman, age twenty-nine, whose body, badly beaten, bound in wire, and burned, was found in a vacant lot in Boston on May 5, 1979. Police investigation led them to the woman's boyfriend, Osborne Sheppard. He was brought to the police station, read his *Miranda* rights, and questioned about the night of the murder. He had an alibi, but the police found that to be a lie. They began to suspect Sheppard in the murder and wanted to search his residence the next morning. Time was important, as the evidence could be destroyed.

The police officer on the case could not find a proper form for application for a search warrant; so he used the only one he could find. It was for drug cases, but he scratched out the words *controlled substances* and adapted the form to his case. On another sheet of paper, the officer described the place to be searched (the basement and second floor) and the evidence to be seized (wire, blood samples). He took the two pieces of paper to a magistrate and asked for a search warrant. The magistrate checked the forms but failed to scratch out another instance of *controlled substance*, signed the warrant, and gave it to the officer who then searched the residence and found the evidence. The blood samples matched the blood of the murdered woman, and the wire matched the wire on her body.

On the basis of this evidence, Sheppard was convicted and sentenced to life in prison. After the trial, his attorney made a motion for a new trial on the grounds that the search warrant was improper; therefore, defense argued, the evidence was not admissible. The search warrant, in addition to the changes, lack of changes, and improper form, was also not properly stapled. The Supreme Judicial Court of Massachusetts agreed with the defense and ordered a new trial. The Commonwealth of Massachusetts appealed the case to the Supreme Court. The Court praised the police search; it was proper in every respect. But, it declared, the Supreme Court of the United States had never recognized

Exceptions to the Exclusionary Rule

Several exceptions have been made to the exclusionary rule. Under the *good faith* exception, illegally obtained evidence should not be excluded from trial if it could be shown that the officers secured the evidence in good faith, that is, if they reasonably believed that they were acting in

an exception to the exclusionary rule. If the evidence, although properly taken, was taken under an improperly secured search warrant, the evidence would not be admissible.

On the last day of its 1983–1984 session, the U.S. Supreme Court reversed the Massachusetts Supreme Judicial Court and reinstated the conviction of Sheppard. In a 6–3 decision, the Court, for the first time since it adopted the exclusionary rule in 1914, narrowed the application of the rule. Writing for the majority, Justice Byron R. White said,

> The marginal or non-existent benefits produced by suppressing evidence obtained in objectively reasonable reliance on a subsequently invalidated search warrant cannot justify the substantial cost of exclusion. . . . Even assuming the rule effectively deters some police misconduct and provides incentives for the law enforcement profession as a whole to conduct itself in accord with the Fourth Amendment, it cannot be expected, and should not be applied, to deter objectively reasonable law enforcement activity.

When asked what he thought about the decision, President Ronald Reagan said, "I loved it." The Justice Department issued a statement: "Today's decision gives the American people a result we have sought for some time. . . . It gives recognition to the principle that the ascertainment of truth is a priority in our criminal justice system." Others were critical of the ruling. The Executive Director of the Civil Liberties Union of Massachusetts said he thinks the ruling sacrifices the rights of individuals by wiping out any remedy for those who are victims of governmental lawlessness. "I don't know how much of the Fourth Amendment we have left" he said.

In his dissenting opinion in the case, Supreme Court Justice William J. Brennan said, "It now appears the Court's victory over the Fourth Amendment is complete." Joined by Justice Thurgood Marshall and John Paul Stevens, Justice White's thirty-two-page dissenting opinion proclaimed that the Court was trampling on individual rights and "strangulating the exclusionary rule."

SOURCE: Information on reactions to this decision was taken from various news accounts on the day of the decision, July 5, 1984. The case is *Massachusetts v. Sheppard*, 468 U.S. 981 (1984). See also *U.S. v. Leon*, decided the same day, 468 U.S. 897 (1984).

accordance with the law. The Supreme Court's adoption of the exception in *Massachusetts v. Sheppard* is explained in Exhibit 12.6.

The Court's good faith exception to the exclusionary rule does not, however, require that all states adopt the exception. States may grant defendants greater protection in their state constitutions than is required by the federal Constitution. The Supreme Court of New Jersey rejected the good faith exception to the exclusionary rule, holding that it would not be applied in that state. While acknowledging that the exception might serve a legitimate purpose in the federal system, the court said that New Jersey's constitution "affords greater protection against unreasonable searches and seizures than does the Fourth Amendment."[85]

The Supreme Court has also adopted the *inevitable discovery* exception. In *Nix v. Williams* the Court held that illegally seized evidence is admissible if police would later have found the evidence by legal methods. And in *New York v. Quarles*, the Court recognized a *public safety* exception, holding that there are some circumstances in which police are justified in conducting a search or asking questions without first giving the *Miranda* warning. In those cases, illegally obtained evidence is admissible at trial.[86]

In subsequent cases, the Court has decided that evidence seized by officers who had a warrant to search an apartment but searched another one and found illegal drugs may be used in court because the officers acted in good faith. Furthermore, excluding the evidence would not deter officers from making such searches since they were acting in the belief that they had the right apartment.[87] The Court also ruled that evidence seized from garbage outside a person's home but without a search warrant is admissible. The Court reasoned that people who leave garbage outside their residences have no expectation of privacy that others will not go through that garbage.[88] The Court also reasoned that defendants' rights are not violated when police, acting in good faith, lose or destroy evidence that could have been used to establish innocence. In *Arizona v. Youngblood*, police failed to perform chemical tests on the victim's semen-stained clothes or to refrigerate that evidence for subsequent tests. Test results might have shown that the defendant was not the assailant in that case.[89]

Police Control of Police Activities: Professionalism

In the final analysis only police can effectively control their activities. That is, police discretion is necessary. The courts alone cannot control police activities; and even if legislation is changed and criminal codes no longer include laws that the public really does not want enforced, police retain extensive opportunities for violating individual rights. For these reasons professionalism has become the solution for police misconduct, as this statement by Jerome Skolnick suggests:

> The needed philosophy of professionalism must rest on a set of values conveying the idea that police are as much an institution dedicated to the achievement of legality in society as they are an official social organization designed to control misconduct through the invocation of punitive sanctions. . . . [W]hat must occur is a significant alteration in the ideology of police, so the "professionalization" rests on the values of a democratic legal order, rather than on technological proficiency.[90]

The importance of professionalism was dramatized by an earlier study indicating that police attitudes are not explained by the social variables of class, ethnicity, age, rank, and authoritarianism but by the impact of professionalism.[91] It is important, however, that the public is not misled; police professionalism must be real, not just illusory. One scholar of police behavior, Peter K. Manning, contends that police have adopted for themselves an impossible mandate "that claims to include the efficient, apolitical, and professional enforcement of the law." Because they cannot meet that mandate, they resort to appearances of professionalism that include creating a bureaucracy in police organization (which they see as the best and most efficient way to run the organization); using technology to indicate a scientific perspective of crime; collecting official data and using them to show how efficient they are; and devising styles of patrol that they see as part of bureaucratic efficiency. They also develop secrecy, one of their most effective sources of power, as it enables them to act without indicating what they are doing, such as cooperating with organized crime rather than fighting it. Appearances are also important, as police need convictions for their arrests. For a high rate of convictions, police may cooperate with prosecutors in persuading people to plead guilty to lesser offenses, operating on the assumption that all the people they arrest are guilty and that if they apply enough pressure, the suspects will so plead.[92]

Reorganization of Police Departments

One element of professionalism that has been suggested is the reorganization of police departments. As far back as 1967, the President's Commission on Law Enforcement and Administration of Justice asserted that professionalism would be hindered if police departments continued to refuse *lateral entry*. In many departments, police may enter the force only at the bottom and work their way up. Such policies prevent the infusion of new ideas and deny police the professional growth and development that can come through professional mobility.[93]

The Knapp Commission also recommended lateral entry, concluding that if a department is tolerant of corruption, promotions only from within could carry that tolerance to supervisory levels.[94] Rotation of officers might also decrease corruption.

Specialization

Another reform recommended for police departments is specialization, for example, an organizational pattern with specialized units such as a domestic unit, a juvenile unit, and a drunk unit with an emphasis on peace keeping, leaving most law enforcement to other officers.[95] Still other supporters of professionalism have suggested the creation of crisis intervention units because police receive so many disturbance calls involving family members and friends that might erupt into violence.[96] The aim is to prevent violence. Various methods have been tried, and the one that has received considerable attention in recent years is arrest. In the past, it was alleged that police infrequently made arrests in cases of violence involving family and friends.[97] The refusal to arrest was often related to the unwillingness of the victim to cooperate, but there were also allegations that domestic violence was viewed by police as a personal problem, not an act of violence.

An experiment in Minneapolis between 1981 and 1982 was evaluated by Lawrence W. Sherman and Richard A. Berk. Sherman and Berk compared the rates of repeat violations among three groups of offenders: those who were arrested by police, those who were advised and warned, and those who were sent away (removed from the home). Sherman and Berk found a much lower rate of repeat violations among those suspects who were arrested compared to those in the other categories.[98]

More recently, Kirk R. Williams and Richard Hawkins, in a national telephone survey using questions based on hypothetical scenarios, found that "married or cohabiting men do view arrest for wife assault as having deleterious consequences for their personal life circumstances," with personal humiliation being one of the results perceived as most likely. Williams and Hawkins suggest that further research is needed to determine just how effective a deterrent the threat of arrest might be on those who might decide to engage in wife assault.[99]

Policies Regarding the Use of Discretion

Police departments may institute policies regarding the use of discretion. **Discretion** is an inevitable part of policing. Police will always have discretion in deciding when to stop a person and whether to detain, frisk, or arrest. It is possible, however, to institute policies controlling discretion. One method is through administrative rule-making procedures.

The legislative and executive branches delegate to administrative bodies the power to make rules and policies; police may be viewed as an administrative agency. The making of rules is governed by statutes; however, administrative agencies are not free to make rules without following the specified procedures. The rules may be changed, but only according to specified procedures, and then published. In contrast, police officers are free to exercise their judgment, often even without guidelines. Therefore, it has been advocated that rules should be determined, not by police on the beat, but by higher authorities within the system. A specified rule-making procedure should be established, and the public should be allowed to participate in those procedures.[100]

The policies on discretion should include guidelines regarding selective enforcement of the law. Police cannot enforce all laws. Therefore selective enforcement is not only necessary but legal. Police may not, however, enforce certain laws only against certain groups. The adoption of proper rule-making procedures, although they refer only to general policy, would make it more difficult for police to harass certain types of individuals regarding certain laws. For example, if it is stated policy that police will not arrest those who drink in public parks unless they become disorderly, police would not be able to arrest a suspected homosexual who is drinking in an orderly manner.

Policies of discretion should also include the use of force, especially deadly force, because of its potentially harmful results. Some police departments have vague guidelines that leave too much discretion to individual police officers. Some departments have guidelines that are clear but also clearly violated; yet the police officers are rarely disciplined.

CONCLUSION

After a brief history of policing and overview of our system, we looked at a profile of police and their various functions: law enforcement, order maintenance, and community services. We examined the attitudes and the hostility police feel from the public. These and other conflicts and problems have led some police officers to withdraw into themselves, to develop a code of secrecy, and to become socially isolated from society.

Understanding the police officers' insulation from society is necessary to understand their abuse of discretion. Their decisions whether to apprehend and arrest may be made on improper grounds. That they may exceed the use of force to which they are legally entitled may lead to harassment, brutality, and sometimes violence. This discussion was followed by a consideration of police corruption, the factors influencing that corruption, and a sociological analysis of it. Finally, we discussed how the courts and police departments might exercise control over police.

Experts on police have concluded that research on policing has not been adequate because we do not know enough about the people who occupy one of the most important roles in our entire system of criminal justice. But we do know the tremendous impact their behavior can have on us as individuals and as a society. We also need to understand that the behavior that so deeply touches our lives also has a tremendous impact on the police officers themselves.

ENDNOTES

1. These methods of policing are discussed in Richard J. Lundman, *Police and Policing: An Introduction* (New York: Holt, Rinehart and Winston, 1980), pp. 15–17. For a history of policing in New York, see James F. Richardson, *The New York Police: Colonial Times to 1901* (New York: Oxford University Press, 1970). For a history of policing in England, see W. L. Melville Lee, *A History of Police in England* (London: Metheun, 1901). In general, see David H. Bayley,

"Police: History," in Sanford H. Kadish, ed., *Encyclopedia of Crime and Justice*, vol. 3 (New York: Free Press, 1983), p. 1122.

2. Federal Bureau of Investigation, *Uniform Crime Reports: Crime in the United States, 1988* (Washington, D.C.: U. S. Government Printing Office, 1989), p. 231.

3. For a brief history of views on the evolution of policing in the U.S., see Francis X. Hartmann, ed., *Debating the Evolution of American Policing* (Washington, D.C.: U. S. Department of Justice, November 1988).

4. See Egon Bittner, "Police: Urban Police," in Kadish, ed., *Encyclopedia of Crime and Justice*, pp. 1135–1139.

5. For a discussion of state police, see Robert Borkenstein, "Police: State Police," in Kadish, ed., *Encyclopedia of Crime and Justice*, pp. 1131–1135.

6. Albert J. Reiss, Jr., *Private Employment of Public Police* (Washington, D.C.: U.S. Department of Justice, December 1988): 1. See also A. J. Reiss, Jr., *Policing a City's Central District—The Oakland Story*, U.S. Department of Justice, National Institute of Justice (Washington, D.C.: U.S. Government Printing Office, 1985).

7. James S. Kakalik and Sorrel Wildhorn, *The Private Police: Security and Danger* (New York: Crane Russak & Co., 1977; copyright Rand Corp.), p. 68. For a discussion of private security in Great Britain, see Nigel South, *Policing for Profit: The Private Security Sector* (Beverly Hills, CA.: Sage Publications, 1989).

8. See William C. Cunningham and Todd H. Taylor, "Ten Years of Growth in Law Enforcement and Private Security Relationships," *The Police Chief* 1 (June 1983): 30, 31. For more detail on private security, see Daniel Ford, ed., from the report by William C. Cunningham and Todd H. Taylor, *Crime and Protection in America: A Study of Private Security and Law Enforcement Resources and Relationships* (Washington, D.C.: U.S. Government Printing Office, 1985).

9. For a discussion of the growth of private security companies, see Lloyd Klein et al., "Perceived Neighborhood Crime and the Impact of Private Security," *Crime & Delinquency* 35 (July 1989): 365–377.

10. Mark Moore, quoted in "When Private Employers Hire Public Police," *New York Times*, 26 February 1989, p. 1, col. 4. See also Marcia Chaiken and Jan Chaiken, *Public Policing—Privately Provided* (Washington, D.C.: U. S. Department of Justice, 1987).

11. U.S. Congress, House, 97th Cong., 2d sess. (daily), 24 March 1983, *Congressional Record*, vol. 128: E 1256. The 1967 report is the President's Commission on Law Enforcement and the Administration of Justice, *The Challenge of Crime in a Free Society* (Washington, D.C.: U.S. Government Printing Office, 1967), p. 109.

12. Larry T. Hoover, *Police Educational Characteristics and Curricula*, U.S. Department of Justice, LEAA, and National Institute of Law Enforcement and Criminal Justice (Washington, D.C.: U.S. Government Printing Office, July 1975), pp. 217–218.

13. Robert M. Regoli et al., "Assessing the Effect of Education on Police Officer Attitudes Toward the Police Agency and Its Supervisors," *Abstracts on Police Science* 8 (no. 6 1981): 335–341. For an earlier study, see Paul Chevigny, *Police Power* (New York: Vintage Books, 1969), pp. 272–273.

14. Elizabeth Burbeck and Adrian Furnham, "Police Officer Selection: A Critical Review of the Literature" *Journal of Police Science and Administration* 13 (March 1985): 62.

15. David L. Carter et al., *The State of Police Education: Policy Direction for the 21st Century* (Washington, D.C.: Police Executive Research Forum, 1989), pp. iii (a quote from Patrick Murphy), and 127.

16. U.S. Commission on Civil Rights, *Who Is Guarding the Guardians? A Report on Police Practices*, October 1981. For a discussion of recruitment problems, see Ellen Hochstedler, "Impediments to Hiring Minorities in Public Police Agencies," *Journal of Police Science and Administration* 12 (June 1984): 227–240.

17. Ellen Hochstedler, Robert M. Regoli, and Eric D. Poole, "Changing the Guard in American Cities: A Current Empirical Assessment of Integration in Twenty Municipal Police Departments," *Criminal Justice Review* 9, (no. 1 1984): 8–14.

18. See Ellen Hochstedler, "Impediments to Hiring Minorities in Public Police Agencies," *Journal of Police Science and Administration* 12 (June 1984): 227–240.

19. Johnson v. Transportation Agency, 480 U. S. 616 (1987). For an analysis of the decision, see "Johnson v. Transportation Agency: Are We All Equal?" *Creighton Law Review* 21 (no. 1, 1987-88): 333–358; U.S. v. Paradise, 480 U.S. 149 (1987). For an analysis of this case, see "United States v. Paradise: Another Look at Alabama's Hiring Quota," *Creighton Law Review* 21 (no. 1, 1987–88): 303–331.

20. Richmond v. Crosen, 488 U.S. 469 (January, 1989).

21. See, for example, Wards Cove v. Atonio, 110 S.Ct. 38 (1989).

22. Martin v. Wilks, 110 S.Ct. 11 (1989).

23. Quoted in "Decisions on Bias Prompt Criticism," *New York Times*, 13 June 1989, p. 9, col. 1.

24. "Judge Orders Sweeping Changes in the F.B.I.'s Promotion System," *New York Times*, 6 May 1989, p. 1, col. 2; "Director of F.B.I. Orders Changes to Erase Job Bias in the Bureau," *New York Times*, 1 March 1989, p. 12, col. 1.

25. Nicholas Alex, *Black in Blue: A Study of the Negro Policeman* (New York: Appleton-Century-Crofts, 1969).

26. Stephen Leinen, *Black Police, White Society* (New York: New York University Press, 1984).

27. Charles Bahn, professor of forensic psychology at the John Jay College of Criminal Justice, quoted in "Police Officers Tell of Strains of Living as a 'Black in Blue,'" *New York Times*, 14 February 1988, p. 1, col. 1.

28. "Women Being Hired as Officers, But Promotions Found Lagging," *Criminal Justice Newsletter* 20 (19 July 1989): p. 2.

29. See Arthur Niederhoffer, *Behind the Shield: The Police in Urban Society* (New York: Doubleday, 1969).

30. John P. Crank, Robert M. Regoli, Eric D. Poole, and Robert G. Culbertson, "Cynicism Among Police Chiefs," *Justice Quarterly* 3 (September 1986): 343–352. For a later work by the same authors, see "The Measurement of Cynicism Among Police Chiefs," *Journal of Criminal Justice* 15 (1987): 37–48.

31. Bruce N. Carpenter and Susan M. Raza, "Personality Characteristics of Police Applicants: Comparisons Across Subgroups and with Other Populations," *Journal of Police Science and Administration* 15 (March 1987): 16.

32. Michael K. Brown, *Working the Street: Police Discretion and the Dilemmas of Reform* (New York: Russell Sage, 1981), pp. xii, 7.

33. The President's Commission on Law Enforcement and Administration of Justice, *Task Force Report: The Police* (Washington, D.C.: U.S. Government Printing Office, 1967), p. 1.

Justice, *Task Force Report: The Police* (Washington, D.C.: U.S. Government Printing Office, 1967), p. 1.

34. Herbert L. Packer, *The Limits of the Criminal Sanction* (Stanford, CA.: Stanford University Press, 1968), p. 283.

35. James Q. Wilson, *Varieties of Police Behavior: The Management of Law and Order in Eight Communities* (Cambridge, Mass.: Harvard University Press, 1968), p. 21.

36. See George L. Kelling, "Order Maintenance, the Quality of Urban Life, and Police: A Line of Argument," in William A. Geller, ed., *Police Leadership in America: Crisis and Opportunity* (Chicago: American Bar Foundation, 1985), p. 297; and James Q. Wilson and George L. Kelling, "Police and Neighborhood Safety: Broken Windows," *Atlantic Monthly* 249 (March 1982): 28–38.

37. Carl B. Klockars, "Order Maintenance, the Quality of Urban Life, and Police: A Different Line of Argument," in Geller, ed., *Police Leadership*, p. 316.

38. See Wilson, *Varieties of Police Behavior*, p. 18.

39. Albert J. Reiss, Jr., *The Police and the Public* (New Haven, Conn.: Yale University Press, 1971), pp. 63, 64, 71. For a discussion of these and other studies, see Herman Goldstein, *Policing a Free Society* (Cambridge, Mass.: Ballinger, 1977), pp. 24–25.

40. Richard J. Lundman, "Police Patrol Work: A Comparative Perspective," in Richard J. Lundman, ed., *Police Behavior: A Sociological Perspective* (New York: Oxford University Press, 1980), p. 55.

41. Eric J. Scott, *Calls for Service: Citizen Demand and Initial Police Response* (Washington, D.C.: National Institute of Justice, July 1981), p. 26.

42. William Spelman and John E. Eck, *Problem-Oriented Policing* (Washington, D.C.: National Institute of Justice, October 1986).

43. See Lawrence W. Sherman, "Policing Communities: What Works?" in Albert J. Reiss, Jr., and Michael Tonry, *Communities and Crime* (Chicago: University of Chicago Press, 1986), pp. 343–386. See also Carl B. Klockars, *The Idea of Police* (Beverly Hills, CA: Sage Publications, 1985).

44. George L. Kelling, *Police and Communities: the Quiet Revolution*, National Institute of Justice (Washington, D.C.: U.S. Department of Justice, June 1988): 1. See also Mark H. Moore and Robert C. Trojanowicz, *Policing and the Fear of Crime* (Washington, D.C.: National Institute of Justice, June 1988).

45. See, for example, Roger G. Dunham and Geoffrey P. Alpert, "Neighborhood Differences in Attitudes Toward Policing: Evidence for a Mixed-Strategy Model of Policing in a Multi-Ethnic Setting," *Journal of Criminal Law & Criminology* 79 (Summer 1988): 504–523.

46. Herman Goldstein, "Toward Community-Oriented Policing: Potential, Basic Requirements, and Threshold Questions," *Crime & Delinquency* 33 (January 1977): 7. For a detailed analysis of community policing, see Robert Trojanowicz and David Carter, *The Philosophy and Role of Community Policing* (East Lansing, MI.: National Neighborhood Foot Patrol Center, School of Criminal Justice, Michigan State University, 1988).

47. See George L. Kelling et al., *Police Accountability and Community Policing*, National Institute of Justice (Washington, D.C.: U.S. Department of Justice, November 1988).

48. See Harold E. Pepinsky, "Issues of Citizen Involvement in Policing," *Crime & Delinquency* 35 (July 1989): 458–470.

49. See Robert Trojanowicz and Bonnie Bucqueroux, *Footprints. Special Issue on*

Community Policing & Drugs: What Community Policing Can Do to Help (East Lansing, MI.: National Center for Community Policing, Special issue 1989).

50. George L. Kelling, *Foot Patrol*, National Institute of Justice (Washington, D.C.: U.S. Department of Justice, 1989), p. 3.

51. See also George L. Kelling and Mark H. Moore, *The Evolving Strategy of Policing*, National Institute of Justice (Washington, D.C.: U.S. Department of Justice, November 1988). For an analysis of community policing in other countries, see D. H. Bayley, *A Model of Community Policing: The Singapore Story*, National Institute of Justice (Washington, D.C.: U.S. Department of Justice, 1988).

52. Wilson, *Varieties of Police Behavior*, p. 53.

53. See Terry Eisenberg, "Job Stress and the Police Officer: Identifying Stress Reduction Techniques," in William H. Kroes and Joseph J. Hurrell, eds., *Job Stress and the Police Officers: Identifying Stress Reduction Techniques*, Proceedings of Symposium, Cincinnati, Ohio, May 8–9, 1975 (Washington, D.C.: U.S. Government Printing Office). For a discussion of the effects of stress and how to cope with them in policing, see G. A. Goolkasian et al., *Coping with Police Stress*, National Institute of Justice (Washington, D.C.: U.S. Department of Justice, 1985).

54. James D. Sewell et al., "Stress Management in Law Enforcement: Where Do We Go From Here?" *The Police Chief* (October 1988): 98. See also Sewell, "The Boss as Victim: Stress and the Police Manager," *FBI Law Enforcement Bulletin* (February 1988): 15 19; and Sewell, "Stress in University Law Enforcement," *Journal of Higher Education* 55 (July/August 1984): 515–523.

55. Bill Sommerville, "Double Standards in Law Enforcement with Regard to Minority Status," *Issues in Criminology* 4 (Fall 1968): 39.

56. Cal. Penal Code, Section 645 (e).

57. Kolender v. Lawson, 461 U.S. 352, 358 (1983).

58. Kolender v. Lawson, 461 U.S. 352, 360 (1983).

59. State v. Arroyo, 770 P.2d 153, 155, 156 (Utah.App. 1989), footnotes and citations omitted, *review pending*, 106 Utah Adv. Rep. 63 (Utah 1989).

60. Malory v. United States, 354 U.S. 449, 456 (1957).

61. Nathan Goldman, *The Differential Selection of Juvenile Offenders for Court Appearance* (New York: National Council on Crime and Delinquency, 1963), and Irving Piliavin and Scott Briar, "Police Encounters with Juveniles," *American Journal of Sociology* 70 (September 1964): 206–214.

62. Douglas A. Smith, "The Neighborhood Context of Police Behavior," in Reiss and Tonry, *Communities and Crime*, pp. 313–341.

63. See Daniel Georges-Abeyie, *The Criminal Justice System and Blacks* (N.Y.: Clark Boardman, 1984).

64. Donald Black, "The Social Organization of Arrest," *Stanford Law Review* 23 (June 1971): 1104–1109.

65. Tenn. Code Ann., Section 40-808 (1975).

66. Tennessee v. Garner, 471 U.S. 1 (1985).

67. "Study of Police Violence Finds No Wide Abuse," *New York Times*, 19 May 1987, p. 16, col. 1.

68. Graham v. Connor, 109 S.Ct. 1865 (1989).

69. See S. G. Chapman, *Cops, Killers and Staying Alive—The Murder of Police Officers in America* (Springfield, Ill.: Charles C. Thomas, 1986.

70. "Killings by New York Police Drop, Bucking Trend," *New York Times*, 8 October 1989, p. 20, col. 3.

71. Arnold Binder and Peter Scharf, "Deadly Force in Law Enforcement," *Crime & Delinquency* 28 (January 1982): 1, 23.

72. See Catherine H. Milton et al., *Police Use of Deadly Force* (Washington, D.C.: Police Foundation, 1977), pp. 3–4, for a discussion of such findings.

73. Lawrence W. Sherman, ed., *Police Corruption: A Sociological Perspective* (New York: Doubleday, 1974), p. 6.

74. *The Knapp Commission Report on Police Corruption* (New York: Braziller, 1972), p. 260.

75. "F.B.I. Conducting Major Inquiry of Corruption in Boston's Police," *New York Times*, 23 October 1986, p. 1, col. 1.

76. "Drugs Threatening Integrity of New York Police," *New York Times*, 12 November 1988, p. 10, col. 2, emphasis in the original. See also David L. Carter and Darrel W. Stephens, eds., *Drug Abuse by Police Officers: An Analysis of Critical Policy Issues* (Springfield, Ill.: Charles C. Thomas, 1988).

77. Wilson, *Varieties of Police Behavior*, chaps. 5–7, pp. 140–226.

78. Sherman, *Police Corruption*, pp. 1–39.

79. *Ibid.*, pp. 196–201.

80. Weeks v. United States, 232 U.S. 383 (1914); Mapp v. Ohio, 367 U.S. 643 (1961).

81. Olmstead v. United States, 277 U.S. 438, 485 (1928), Justice Brandeis, dissenting. For a brief statement of the pros and cons of the rule, see Bradford P. Wilson, *Exclusionary Rule*, National Institute of Justice (Washington, D.C.: U.S. Department of Justice, 1988).

82. Stephen H. Sachs, "The Exclusionary Rule: A Prosecutor's Defense," *Criminal Justice Ethics* 1 (Summer-Fall 1982): 31, 32. This journal contains a symposium on the pros and cons of the exclusionary rule and is an excellent source on the topic.

83. People v. Defore, 150 N.E. 585, 587 (N.Y.Ct. App., 1926).

84. See Comptroller General of the United States, *Impact of the Exclusionary Rule on Federal Criminal Prosecutions* (Washington, D.C.: U.S. Government Printing Office, 19 April 1979), p. 1.

85. State v. Novembrino, 491 A.2d 37 (N.J. 1985).

86. Nix v. Williams, 467 U.S. 431 (1984); New York v. Quarles, 467 U.S. 649 (1984).

87. Maryland v. Garrison, 480 U.S. 79 (1987).

88. California v. Greenwood, 486 U.S. 35 (1988).

89. Arizona v. Youngblood, 488 U.S. 51 (1988), *rehearing den.*, 438 U.S. 1051 (1989), *remanded*, 50 Ariz. Adv. Rep. 91 (Ariz. App. 1989).

90. Jerome H. Skolnick, *Justice Without Trial*, 2d ed. (New York: John Wiley, 1975), pp. 238–239.

91. James Leo Walsh, "Professionalism and the Police: The Cop as Medical Student," *American Behavioral Scientist* 13 (May-August 1970): 705–725.

92. Peter K. Manning, "The Police: Mandate, Strategies, and Appearances," in Jack D. Douglas, ed., *Crime and Justice in America: A Critical Understanding* (Boston: Little, Brown, 1974), pp. 171, 186–191. See also Peter K. Manning, *Police Work: The Social Organization of Policing* (Cambridge, Mass.: Ballinger, 1978).

93. President's Commission on Law Enforcement and Administration of Justice, *The Challenge of Crime in a Free Society* (Washington, D.C.: U.S. Government Printing Office, 1967), p. ix.

94. *Knapp Commission Report,* p. 32.

95. Manning, "The Police," pp. 198–199.

96. Morton Bard, "Family Intervention Police Teams as a Community Mental Health Resource," *The Journal of Criminal Law, Criminology, and Police Science* 60 (1969): 247–250.

97. See Richard Langley and Roger C. Levy, *The Silent Crises* (New York: E. P. Dutton, 1977), and Maria Roy, *Battered Women* (New York: Van Nostrand Reinhold, 1977).

98. Lawrence W. Sherman and Richard A. Berk, "The Minneapolis Domestic Violence Experiment," *Police Foundation Report,* April 1984, p. 1. For the technical report see Lawrence W. Sherman and Richard A. Berk, "Deterrent Effects of Arrest for Domestic Assault," *American Sociological Review* 49 (April 1984): 261–271.

99. Kirk R. Williams and Richard Hawkins, "The Meaning of Arrest for Wife Assault," *Criminology* 27 (February 1989): 178. See also Scott L. Feld and Murray A. Straus, "Escalation and Desistance of Wife Assault in Marriage," *Criminology* 27 (February 1989): 141–161.

100. See Kenneth Culp Davis, *Police Discretion* (St. Paul, Minn.: West Publishing Co., 1975).

CHAPTER 13

This chapter analyzes the criminal court system, beginning with an overview followed by a discussion of the role of the prosecution and the defense in criminal cases. A brief look at pretrial processes precedes a more in-depth discussion of bail and plea bargaining. The trial of a criminal case features discussions on the right to a speedy trial and the role of the judge and jury. A section on sentencing begins with an overview and a discussion of corporal and capital punishment. Consideration of sentencing disparity and methods of controlling it leads into a discussion of the determinate sentence. The final section analyzes court congestion and makes suggestions concerning how it might be reduced.

OUTLINE

The Court System

KEY TERMS

appeal
appellant
appellee
bail
bail bondsman
capital punishment
charge
corporal punishment
cruel and unusual punishment
defendant
defense attorney
determinate sentence
deterrence
dual court system
fine
good-time credit
grand jury
habeas corpus
incapacitation
indeterminate sentence
indictment
information
judge
judicial review
jurisdiction
jury
just deserts
justice model
mediation
overrule
pardon
plea bargaining
presumptive sentencing
preventive detention
probation
prosecuting attorney

public defender
recidivism
rehabilitation
restitution
retribution
sentence
sentencing
sentencing council
sentencing disparity
trial
writ of certiorari

Courts may be considered the crux of the criminal justice system, for it is within the courts that the crucial pretrial, trial, and posttrial appeals and petitions either occur or are supervised. This process includes plea bargaining and sentencing. In performing some of these functions, courts involve not only the legal profession but the public as well, for private citizens constitute juries.

The importance of the courts was emphasized by the late U.S. Supreme Court Chief Justice Earl Warren when he declared in the late 1950s, "the delay and the choking congestion in federal courts . . . have created a crucial problem for constitutional government in the United States . . . it is compromising the quantity and quality of justice available to the individual citizen, and, in so doing, it leaves vulnerable throughout the world the reputation of the United States."[1]

Since the 1950s the situation has worsened both in state and federal courts, trial and appellate levels. Court congestion results in delayed trials. For the accused who are not released before trial, it may mean a long jail term in already overcrowded jail facilities. Because their court-appointed attorneys are so busy with trial cases, defendants may not see them during that period. The accused are left with many questions, no answers, and a long wait, often under inhumane conditions in local jails. Those who are incarcerated before trial face more obstacles in preparation for trial and in the reactions of the juries at trial.

The injustices created by an overworked court that must decide cases quickly and with little individualized attention are obvious, as is the lack of preparation time available to overworked prosecutors and defense attorneys. The inefficiency and injustice that the crowded court dockets and delayed trials project to the public taint the image of the entire legal system.

THE COURT SYSTEM: AN OVERVIEW

The framers of the Constitution established three branches of government—legislative, executive, and judicial. Despite some overlap, these branches are essentially separate. Courts, part of the judicial branch, are empowered to hear and decide civil disputes between and among parties and to decide criminal cases. Some courts also have the power to determine whether acts of legislatures or of Congress properly fall within constitutional provisions.

This power of **judicial review** represents the courts' great authority. The highest court of each state determines the constitutionality of that state's laws according to its own constitution. The Supreme Court is the final decision maker in the process of judicial review of the U.S. Constitution, as indicated by Chief Justice John Marshall, writing for the majority of the Supreme Court in an 1803 decision, *Marbury v. Madison.*[2]

Marbury v. Madison

It is emphatically the province and duty of the judicial department to say what the law is. . . . So if a law be in opposition to the Constitution; if both the law and the Constitution apply to a particular case, so that the court must either decide the case comformably to the law disregarding the Constitution, or conformably to the Constitution, disregarding the law; the court must determine which of these conflicting rules governs the case. This is the very essence of judicial duty.

Legal Terms and Concepts

An understanding of certain legal terms and concepts will be necessary for an analysis of how courts function. One of the most important terms is **jurisdiction,** which refers to the power of the court to hear and decide a case. If a court does not have jurisdiction over the subject matter or of the parties who are involved in the action, it may not hear the case. The jurisdiction of some courts is limited by subject matter. For example, some courts may hear only domestic dispute cases. Others may hear only civil or criminal cases; those that may hear criminal cases may be further divided by misdemeanors or felonies. Figure 13.1 will clarify this concept. Notice, for example, the three types of courts at the bottom of the figure, with the notation "All of these lower courts have limited jurisdiction in both civil and criminal cases." Figure 13.1 also indicates that the basic state trial courts have been limited to jurisdiction over probate, juvenile, and domestic relations.

Jurisdiction may be original, concurrent, exclusive, or appellate. *Original jurisdiction* refers to the court that has the power to hear the case first, that is, the court that may try the facts of the case. If more than one court has jurisdiction, the courts have *concurrent jurisdiction*. When only one court can hear a particular case, that court has *exclusive jurisdiction*. Decisions of lower courts may usually be appealed; the courts that have the power to hear and decide those appeals have *appellate jurisdiction*.

Because it is thought that the law needs stability, courts generally follow a rule of *stare decisis*, which means to abide by or adhere to cases already decided. The law, however, is also flexible, and courts may **overrule** (specifically or by implication) their previous decisions. It is always important to distinguish between the rule of the court and the dicta of the judge or justices. At times when justices or judges write opinions, they

Figure 13.1
Courts at Various Levels of Government Interact in Many Ways

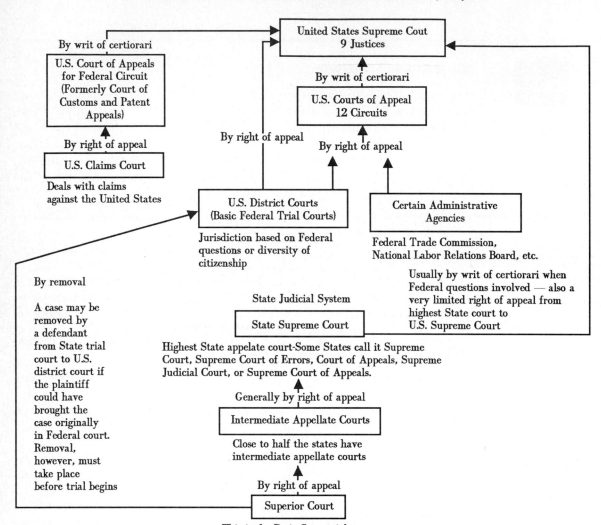

By writ of certiorari

United States Supreme Cout
9 Justices

U.S. Court of Appeals
for Federal Circuit
(Formerly Court of
Customs and Patent
Appeals)

By writ of certiorari

U.S. Courts of Appeal
12 Circuits

By right of appeal

U.S. Claims Court

Deals with claims
against the United States

By right of appeal

By right of appeal

U.S. District Courts
(Basic Federal Trial Courts)

Jurisdiction based on Federal
questions or diversity of
citizenship

Certain Administrative
Agencies

Federal Trade Commission,
National Labor Relations Board, etc.

By removal

A case may be
removed by
a defendant
from State trial
court to U.S.
district court if
the plaintiff
could have
brought the
case originally
in Federal court.
Removal,
however, must
take place
before trial begins

State Judicial System

State Supreme Court

Highest State appelate court-Some States call it Supreme
Court, Supreme Court of Errors, Court of Appeals, Supreme
Judicial Court, or Supreme Court of Appeals.

Usually by writ of certiorari when
Federal questions involved — also a
very limited right of appeal from
highest State court to
U.S. Supreme Court

Generally by right of appeal

Intermediate Appellate Courts

Close to half the states have
intermediate appellate courts

By right of appeal

Superior Court

This is the Basic State trial court.
Some states call it Circuit Court, Court of Common Pleas, and, in New York, Supreme Court.
These courts are sometimes divided into specialty areas such as probate, juvenile court, and domestic relations.

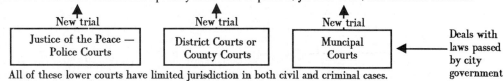

New trial

Justice of the Peace —
Police Courts

New trial

District Courts or
County Courts

New trial

Muncipal
Courts

Deals with
laws passed
by city
government

All of these lower courts have limited jurisdiction in both civil and criminal cases.

SOURCE: Reproduced with permission from William T. Schantz, *The American Legal Environment* (West Publishing Company, 1976).

expound on issues that are not part of the actual ruling of the court. These comments, called *dicta*, even if they represent the opinion of a majority of the court, must be recognized as such and not confused with the *holding* or *rule of law* of the case. For this reason, it is necessary to read cases carefully.

Legal reasoning involves a case-by-case analysis. A decided case is read and then the facts of a pending case are applied to that one. It is then argued that either the facts are similar enough so that the holding of the decided case should apply or dissimilar enough so that the holding should not apply. Since the facts differ from case to case, legal reasoning becomes a crucial part of the legal process.

In announcing decisions, U.S. appellate courts usually give written opinions often accompanied by dissenting opinions. Judges and justices who concur in the court's opinion may wish to make some comments in addition to that opinion, and they write concurring opinions. Some opinions are written by justices who concur with part of the court's decisions and dissent from the remainder.

In the United States, court decisions are recorded in official reports. Decisions of the Supreme Court are officially recorded in the *United States Reports* and will be cited, for example, as follows: *Gideon v. Wainwright*, 372 U.S. 335 (1963). However, prior to being printed in the *U.S. Reports*, which takes from one to two years, Supreme Court cases may be found in other sources, such as *U.S. Law Week* (USLW) and *The Supreme Court Reporter* (S. Ct.). Today the cases may be obtained through computer services shortly after the written opinion is released. As soon as a case is handed down, it becomes binding law; in the case of the Supreme Court, it is binding on all federal courts and on state courts where applicable— that is, where federal statutory or constitutional rights are involved. For more information on how to read a court citation, see Appendix A.

The Dual Court System

The United States has a **dual court system** made up of state and federal courts, as indicated in Figure 13.1. State crimes are prosecuted in state courts and federal crimes in federal courts. The crimes of the former are defined by state statutes and the latter by acts of Congress. Some acts may violate both federal and state statutes, though most criminal cases are tried in state courts.

State Courts

The state criminal court system differs from state to state, but all have trial courts and appellate courts. In some states the trial courts may hear the serious cases (felonies) as well as the less serious ones (misdemeanors). In other jurisdictions the level is divided, one level of courts hearing felony cases and the other hearing misdemeanors. All states have appeal courts, and some states have an intermediate appeal court. Others have only one court of appeals, which is often called the *state supreme court.*

Federal Courts

The federal court system has three levels, excluding special courts such as the U.S. Court of Military Appeals. The *district courts* are the trial courts. Cases may be appealed from those courts to the *appellate courts,* also called *circuit courts.* The highest federal court is the *Supreme Court,* basically an appellate court, although it has original jurisdiction in a few cases.

The lower federal courts and the state courts are separate systems; a state court is not bound by the decision of a lower federal court in its district. Cases may be appealed only to the U.S. Supreme Court if a federal statutory or federal constitutional right is involved.

Trial and Appellate Courts

Trial and appellate courts should be distinguished. Trial courts hear the factual evidence of a case and decide the issues of fact. These decisions may be made by a jury or by a judge if the case is tried without a jury. Appellate courts do not try the facts, such as the defendant's guilt or innocence, but in essence, they try the lower court. The **appellant**—the **defendant** at trial—alleges errors in the trial court proceeding (for example, hearsay evidence admitted, illegal confession admitted, minority groups excluded from the jury) and asks for a new trial. The **appellee**—the prosecution at a trial—argues that errors either did not exist or, if they did, did not constitute reversible errors; that is, they did not prejudice the appellant and therefore a new trial should not be granted.

When a trial court has ruled against a defendant, he or she has a right of appeal, both in the state and in the federal court system, although the defendant does not (except in a few specific types of cases) have the right to appeal to the highest court. The Supreme Court hears only a small percentage of the cases for which appeal is requested.

On appeal, the case is heard by judges, not by a jury, and the issues are confined to matters of law, not fact. The appellate court looks at the trial court record and hears oral arguments from counsel for the defense and the prosecution. It then determines whether any errors of law have been committed.

The appellate court may affirm or reverse the lower court's decision. Usually when a lower court is reversed, the case is sent back for another trial; that is, the case is *reversed and remanded.* This does not necessarily mean that the defendant is free; in fact, in most criminal cases that are reversed and remanded, the defendant is convicted when retried. A reversal and remand does not violate the Fifth Amendment prohibition against being tried twice for the same offense. But if the defendant is found not guilty at trial, he or she may not be retried for that offense,

The United States Supreme Court, consisting of nine justices, is the highest court in the country, but it hears only a small percentage of the cases appealed to the Court.

although prosecutors might appeal the case on a point of law to get a ruling that may be of benefit in future trials.

THE ROLE OF LAWYERS IN THE CRIMINAL COURT SYSTEM

In criminal cases lawyers act as defense or prosecuting attorneys, and each role is very important. They have an ethical obligation to abide by certain rules, as indicated in the American Bar Association's statement of ethics reprinted in Exhibit 13.1. Unfortunately, because lawyers do not

EXHIBIT 13.1

Preamble, American Bar Association's *Code of Professional Responsibility*

The continued existence of a free and democratic society depends upon recognition of the concept that justice is based upon the rule of law grounded in respect for the dignity of the individual and his capacity through reason for enlightened self-government. Law so grounded makes justice possible, for only through such law does the dignity of the individual attain respect and protection. Without it, individual rights become subject to unrestrained power, respect for law is destroyed, and rational self-government is impossible.

Lawyers, as guardians of the law, play a vital role in the preservation of society. The fulfillment of this role requires an understanding by lawyers of their relationship with and function in our legal system. A consequent obligation of lawyers is to maintain the highest standards of ethical conduct.

In fulfilling his professional responsibilities, a lawyer necessarily assumes various roles that require the performance of many difficult tasks. Not every situation which he may encounter can

be foreseen, but fundamental ethical principles are always present to guide him. Within the framework of these principles, a lawyer must with courage and foresight be able and ready to shape the body of the law to the ever-changing relationships of society.

The Code of Professional Responsibility points the way to the aspiring and provides standards by which to judge the transgressor. Each lawyer must find within his own conscience the touchstone against which to test the extent to which his actions should rise above minimum standards. But in the last analysis it is the desire for the respect and confidence of the members of his profession and of the society which he serves that should provide to a lawyer the incentive for the highest possible degree of ethical conduct. The possible loss of that respect and confidence is the ultimate sanction. So long as its practitioners are guided by these principles, the law will continue to be a noble profession. This is its greatness and its strength, which permit of no compromise.

always abide by ethical standards, their public image is a tarnished one. These issues cannot be explored in depth at this point, but it is important to include a brief overview of the role of attorneys in the criminal justice system.

Prosecution

The **prosecuting attorney** presents the case for the state or federal government (federal prosecutors are also called U.S. attorneys) and is therefore responsible for securing and organizing the evidence against the defendant and for arguing the case should it go to trial. Prosecutors have wide discretion. In most cases, they have the power to decide whether or not to prosecute, and these decisions are virtually unchecked. Prosecutors, after deciding to prosecute, return an **information,** an official document that initiates prosecution.

5th Amm.

The Fifth Amendment requires in some cases a grand jury indictment. A **grand jury,** composed of private citizens, hears evidence presented by the prosecution. If the grand jury believes there is sufficient evidence that the accused committed the crime or crimes in question, it returns an **indictment,** which officially begins the prosecution of the case. But even in these cases, the prosecutor usually has considerable control over the grand jury.[3]

Prosecutors also have wide discretion in determining which **charges** to bring or to present to the grand jury. For example, a person suspected of first-degree murder in a state that has a death penalty could be charged with second-degree murder, which does not carry the death penalty. Charges may also be dropped by the prosecutor. This decision does not always require the judge's permission. Once a defendant has been convicted, the prosecutor may be influential in the sentencing process. Prosecutors may differ widely in their decisions.[4]

Prosecutorial discretion is necessary in the criminal justice system. No system can state in advance all cases that should be prosecuted. Decisions must be made in light of the offense, the offender, and the resources of the system. It would be a foolish waste of resources for a prosecutor to insist on taking to trial a case in which the evidence is so weak that there is no chance of conviction. On the other hand, it would be an abuse of discretion to dismiss that case because the defendant is from a particular race, religion, or sex or because of other extralegal reasons.[5]

Defense

6th Amm

The Sixth Amendment provides that persons accused of committing a crime have a right to counsel. The attorney representing the defendant in a criminal trial is the **defense attorney.** The function of a defense attorney is to protect the legal rights of the accused. The defendant, even if guilty, is entitled to a fair trial in which the state must prove guilt beyond a reasonable doubt and in accordance with proper procedures.[6]

It is not the function of the defense attorney to decide the defendant's guilt or innocence. Attorneys are just as bound by the ethics of their profession in the defense of persons they think are guilty as in the defense of those they believe to be innocent. The function of defense attorneys is to give their clients the best advice they can within the law and ethics of the legal profession. Once this function is recognized, the defense of a person who may be guilty is understandable.

This discussion is not meant to suggest that defense attorneys do not abuse the adversary system; indeed, some do, but that abuse must be dis-

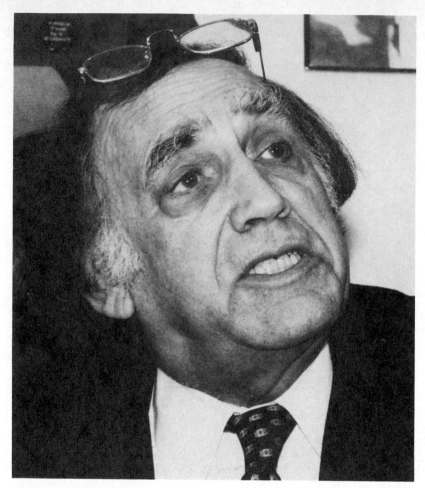

Lawyers play an important role in our criminal justice system. William M. Kunstler, pictured here, has represented many well-known defendants in criminal cases.

tinguished from the *philosophy* of the system. That philosophy is one of the strongest points of our criminal justice process—that all persons are presumed innocent until proved guilty and that they may be punished only after the government proves beyond a reasonable doubt to the satisfaction of a jury, (or a judge if the case is not tried before a jury), that the defendant is guilty. Furthermore, the government must prove its case without violating the accused's constitutional rights.[7]

The right to counsel, as discussed in an earlier chapter, has been interpreted to include the right to counsel appointed at the expense of the government if the defendant does not have the financial means to retain a private attorney. It has also been interpreted to mean the right to refuse counsel. When counsel is provided at government expense, one of three systems may be used. First attorneys may be *assigned* to particular indigent defendants. Assignments are usually made by judges from lists of attorneys who have agreed to serve in this capacity. Second some jurisdictions use a *contract* system, in which a bar association, private law firm, or individual attorney contracts with the government to provide legal assistance for indigent defendants. Third many jurisdictions use the **public defender** system, which is actually a public law firm whose mission is to provide counsel for indigent defendants. The office is usually headed by a public defender who employs assistant public defenders, all of whom are attorneys whose primary job is to represent indigent defendants.[8]

Figure 13.2 indicates the type of criminal defense system for indigents that is used in each state. Although that figure comes from a 1988 publication by the Bureau of Justice Statistics, it reflects data only through 1986. Those data indicate that almost $1 billion was spent in 1986 on legal representation for indigent defendants, representing a 60 percent increase over the amount spent in 1982. The average cost per defendant was $223, compared to an average of $196 in 1982. This figure alone would certainly raise a question of the adequacy of our provision for counsel for indigent defendants.[9]

All methods of providing attorneys for indigents have been criticized. Clearly the best efforts thus far to recruit capable and bright young attorneys into legal services for the poor have not produced the desired

FIGURE 13.2 Criminal defense systems, by type in majority of counties, 1986

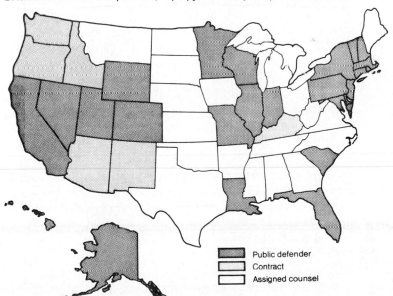

SOURCE: Bureau of Justice Statistics, *Criminal Defense for the Poor, 1986* (Washington, D.C.: U.S. Department of Justice, September 1988) p. 1.

results. A court-appointed attorney with a large caseload, low compensation, low status, and inadequate resources cannot be expected to defend his or her clients adequately. The burden of improving this situation clearly rests in two places. The legal profession should be challenged to discover ways to attract more qualified attorneys into criminal defense work, including greater prestige and rewards for such work and better preparation in law school for criminal trials. Society must also provide the money and resources necessary to make the system work as conceptualized.

PRETRIAL PROCESSES

Figure 11.1 in Chapter 11 graphed the pretrial and trial processes and briefly described each. The body of law and sociological literature on these processes is extensive and cannot be discussed briefly. This section focuses on two of the most controversial processes: pretrial release and plea bargaining.

Pretrial Release

One of the most critical periods of the criminal justice proceedings is the time between arraignment and trial. The purpose of pretrial release is to enable the defendant to prepare for trial while avoiding the harmful effects of jail detention. According to the Supreme Court, the problems faced by defendants who are incarcerated are enormous and extend beyond the most obvious one, deprivation of liberty. "The consequences of prolonged detention may be more serious than the interference occasioned by arrest. Pretrial confinement may imperil the suspect's job, interrupt his source of income, and impair his family relationships."[10]

Pretrial detainees may lose their jobs permanently and acquire the stigma attached to a jail term even though they are still *legally innocent of a crime.* They face days of loneliness and idleness, with limited opportunity to talk and visit with family and friends. They may develop psychological problems and even suffer physical problems as a result of incarceration.

The Bail System

As Exhibit 13.2 indicates, several methods are utilized for releasing defendants prior to trial, but the most controversial is the **bail** system. The bail system began in England to ensure the presence of defendants at trials, which were held infrequently because judges traveled from one jurisdiction to another. Facilities for detaining defendants before trial were ter-

EXHIBIT 13.2

Types of Pretrial Release

Both financial bonds and alternative release options are used today.

Financial bond

Fully secured bail—The defendant posts the full amount of bail with the court.

Privately secured bail—A bondsman signs a promissory note to the court for the bail amount and charges the defendant a fee for the service (usually 10% of the bail amount). If the defendant fails to appear, the bondsman must pay the court the full amount. Frequently, the bondsman requires the defendant to post collateral in addition to the fee.

Deposit bail—The courts allow the defendant to deposit a percentage (usually 10%) of the full bail with the court. The full amount of the bail is required if the defendant fails to appear. The percentage bail is returned after disposition of the case, but the court often retains 1% for administrative costs.

Unsecured bail—The defendant pays no money to the court but is liable for the full amount of bail should he or she fail to appear.

Alternative release options

Release on recognizance (ROR)—The court releases the defendant on the promise that he or she will appear in court as required.

Conditional release—The court releases the defendant subject to his or her following specific conditions set by the court, such as attendance at drug treatment therapy or staying away from the complaining witness.

Third party custody—The defendant is released into the custody of an individual or agency that promises to assure his or her appearance in court. No monetary transactions are involved in this type of release.

Citation release—Arrestees are released pending their first court appearance on a written order issued by law enforcement personnel.

SOURCE: Bureau of Justice Statistics, *Report to the Nation on Crime and Justice: The Data*, 2d ed. (Washington, D.C.: U.S. Department of Justice, 1988), p. 76.

rible, and it was expensive to maintain them. Sheriffs preferred to have someone else take care of defendants while they were awaiting trial and would often relinquish them to other people, usually friends or relatives. These people would serve as *sureties*. When the system began, if the defendants did not appear for trial after they had been placed on bail, the surety would be tried. The party furnishing bail would be reminded that he or she had the powers of a jailer and was expected to produce the accused for trial. This policy of private sureties was also followed in America but was later replaced by a system of *posting bond*.

The bail system in the United States is used to ensure the defendant's presence at trial. Early court cases made it clear that bail was not to be used to punish defendants or to protect society. Furthermore, the Supreme Court has ruled that "bail set at a figure higher than the amount reasonably calculated to [ensure that the defendant will stand trial] is 'excessive' under the Eighth Amendment."[11]

According to federal rules and some state statutes, bail may be denied in capital cases. Bail may also be denied in noncapital cases in which the defendant has a history of fleeing to avoid prosecution. The reason in both cases is consistent with the original purpose of bail—to ensure the presence of the accused at trial.

Bail and Preventive Detention

Until recently, the *only* legitimate purpose of bail was to secure the defendant's presence at trial. In 1970 with the passage of the District of Columbia Court Reform and Criminal Procedure Act, **preventive detention** was recognized as a legitimate purpose of bail. This statute permits judges to deny bail to defendants charged with dangerous crimes if the government has clear evidence, including consideration of the accused's past and present pattern of behavior, that release would endanger public safety.[12]

A few other states have similar provisions. In 1984 Congress passed a comprehensive reform of the federal criminal code, including a provision for preventive detention. Detention is authorized if no conditions of release will reasonably assure "the appearance of the person as required and the safety of any other person and the community."[13]

The act also provides that those arrested for drug offenses are presumed dangerous or likely to flee; they may therefore be detained pending trial unless they can prove that it would be reasonably safe for them to be released. The constitutionality of this provision was challenged in several federal courts, with some courts upholding its constitutionality and some declaring unconstitutional the preventive detention provision. The U.S. Supreme Court ruled in favor of the provision in *U.S. v. Salerno*, decided in 1987. The defendant in this case was Anthony "Fat Tony" Salerno, the alleged boss of the Genovese organized crime family. The twenty-nine charges against Salerno included attempted murder, racketeering, fraud, gambling, and extortion. Salerno was a good test case for the provision, for "with the possible exception of certain serial murderers, Salerno was probably the least sympathetic potential defendant to bring a test case."[14] Excerpts from the case indicate the Court's position on the constitutionality of preventive detention as well as its perceptions of why Congress passed the statute.[15]

U.S. v. Salerno

The Bail Reform Act of 1984 allows a federal court to detain an arrestee pending trial if the government demonstrates by clear and convincing evidence after an adversary hearing that no release conditions "will reasonably assure . . . the safety of any other person and the community." . . . We hold that . . . the Act fully comports with constitutional requirements.

Responding to "the alarming problem of crimes committed by persons on release, Congress formulated the Bail Reform Act of 1984 as the solution to a bail crisis in the federal courts. The Act represents the National Legislature's considered response to numerous perceived deficiencies in the federal bail process. By providing for sweeping changes in both the way federal courts consider bail applications and the circumstances under which bail is granted, Congress hoped to "give the courts adequate authority to make release decisions that give appropriate recognition to the danger a person may pose to others if released."

. . . . The Act . . . provides the arrestee with a number of procedural safeguards [and] . . . the judicial officer is not given unbridled discretion in making the detention determination. Congress has specified the considerations relevant to that decision. . . .

In our society liberty is the norm, and detention prior to trial or without trial is the carefully limited exception. We hold that the provisions for pretrial detention in the Bail Reform Act of 1984 fall within that carefully limited exception.

In 1989, while already serving a 100-year sentence for his conviction as a mob boss, "Fat Tony" Salerno sobbed as he entered his guilty plea to charges of extortion and racketeering.

Although the constitutionality of preventive detention under the specified conditions of the Bail Reform Act of 1984 has been upheld, Joseph B. Vaughn and Victor E. Kappeler note that "the jury is still out" on the issue of whether preventive detention does in fact prevent crime.[16]

Bail Bondsman

Even when bail is granted, many defendants cannot pay the full amount. Thus, a professional **bail bondsman** system evolved. In return for a fee, the bail bondsman will post bond for the accused defendant. Theoretically, if the defendant does not appear for trial, the bondsman is required to forfeit the money. In practice, forfeitures of bonds are usually not enforced. Furthermore, some bondsmen are straw men in that they do not have the necessary money to produce in cases of forfeiture. To avoid this situation, some jurisdictions require the bondsmen to prove their ability to pay in case of forfeiture.

The professional bondsman system has been criticized, and some states have placed legislative restrictions on the system or eliminated it entirely.[17]

Plea Bargaining

Another controversial pretrial process is **plea bargaining,** a negotiation between the prosecution and the defense in which the defense agrees to submit a guilty plea in exchange for a promise by the prosecutor. That promise might be to drop other charges, reduce some charges, recommend a particular sentence, or make some other promise regarding sentencing.[18]

Not all guilty pleas are the result of plea bargaining. Data indicate that most convictions are the result of guilty pleas, some of which are the result of a defense decision that pleading guilty is the best choice. Likewise, prosecutorial decisions to reduce or drop charges may be the result of prosecutorial discretion unrelated to a bargain with the defense.[19]

Plea bargaining received the recognition of the Supreme Court in 1971 when it was approved as a means of managing overloaded criminal dockets. The Court declared plea bargaining to be "an essential component" of the criminal process, which "properly administered . . . is to be encouraged."[20] Supporters of plea bargaining argue that the process is necessary because of the tremendous number of criminal cases; to try all of them would break the system. Further, plea bargaining saves the state money and time. Not all cases need to go to trial; defendants and society are better served by settling some cases out of court.

Opponents of plea bargaining argue that judges and prosecutors do not always honor the deals made between the prosecution and defense and that innocent defendants might be encouraged to plead guilty. Critics also express concern that some deals will be too good for defendants, that those charged with serious offenses will be permitted to plead guilty to less serious offenses, and that some defendants charged with violent offenses may get off too lightly.

The Supreme Court has recognized that plea bargaining must have some limitations. Specifically, it has recognized the importance of counsel at the plea-bargaining stage and the need for a public record that would indicate the defendant knowingly and voluntarily entered the guilty plea and that the promise made by the prosecuting attorney at the plea-bargaining stage was kept. But in 1978 the Court upheld the right of the prosecutor to threaten to secure a grand jury indictment against the defendant on a more serious charge if the defendant did not plead guilty to the charge already made. In *Bordenkircher v. Hayes*, the defendant was under indictment for passing a hot check for $88.30. The sentence that could have been imposed upon conviction of that offense was two to ten years.

The prosecutor told the defendant that he would recommend a five-year sentence if the defendant would plead guilty. If the defendant refused to do so, the prosecutor said he would seek an indictment under the state's Habitual Criminal Act, which provided that upon conviction of a third felony, a defendant would receive a mandatory sentence of life in prison.

The defendant refused to accept the plea-bargaining offer, went to trial, and was convicted. In a separate proceeding it was found that he had been convicted of two previous felonies. He was then sentenced to life in prison as required by the Habitual Offender Act. In a five-to-four decision, the Court emphasized that although the state may not *retaliate* against a defendant who chooses to exercise a legal right, "in the 'give-and-take' of plea bargaining, there is no such element of punishment or retaliation so long as the accused is free to accept or reject the prosecution's offer."[21]

To constitute a valid plea bargain, the defendant's plea must be knowledgeable and voluntary. In determining whether a plea is voluntary, the courts consider whether the defendant was represented by counsel; if so, the plea is less likely to be considered involuntary. The plea cannot be an irrational act based on an apparent but nonexistent advantage to the defendant. Furthermore, plea bargains leading to a guilty plea must not be induced by threats or promises to discontinue improper harassment; misrepresentation; unfulfilled promises; or promises that have no relation to proper prosecutorial business, such as a bribe.[22]

Court decisions have also placed some restrictions on plea bargaining. For example, the Arizona Court of Appeals has held invalid a guilty plea based on a prosecutor's promise not to oppose defendant's efforts to obtain conjugal visits with his wife during his incarceration. Stating that conjugal access is an "irrational basis" for entering a guilty plea, the court ruled that including this understanding within the plea bargain suggests psychological pressure that invalidates the voluntariness of the defendant's plea.[23]

Future of Plea Bargaining

States are free to abolish plea bargaining, and some have done so. A study of Alaska's abolition efforts indicated that although most bargaining had indeed been eliminated, defense attorneys were spending more time filing motions and preparing for trial, suggesting that some defendants who might have agreed to a plea bargain are insisting on a trial. Prosecutors also reported that their workloads increased; but contrary to expectations, the average processing time for felony cases had decreased, not increased.[24]

It has been argued that plea bargaining is inevitable, but a study in Philadelphia found that not to be the case. Defendants who received bench trials (trial before a judge, not a jury) without the benefit of a plea bargain still won some of the traditional advantages of plea bargaining, such as reduced charges. But the investigator argued that the reduction came after a more carefully considered application of the law to the facts than is frequently the case in plea bargains between defense and prosecution.[25]

If plea bargaining remains, its goals must be sentences close to those that would result from trial, fairness, less delay, and less disparate sentences. To achieve these goals, the parties to the negotiation must accurately perceive the conviction and sentence probabilities. The defendant should not be forced to accept higher bargained sentences because he or she is in jail, is unable to afford an attorney, or is represented by a public defender who does not have the time or resources to go to trial. Nor should prosecutors be forced to offer low bargains because of limited resources.

THE TRIAL OF A CRIMINAL CASE

The trial of a criminal case involves numerous, complicated legal procedures. This section will focus briefly only on two major issues in a criminal case: the right to a speedy trial and the roles of the judge and jury.

The Right to a Speedy Trial

The Sixth Amendment provides for the right to a speedy trial. This right does not preclude the defense or the prosecution from asking for and being granted continuances when additional time is needed to prepare. It does mean that the prosecution and defense may not delay unreasonably, but this provision has led to extensive litigation. Most of the statutes specify some circumstances under which trials may legitimately be delayed, but those provisions may also be the subject of litigation. An example is the federal provision that delays may occur when they are necessary to "serve the ends of justice."

What constitutes an unreasonable delay will, of course, have to be decided on a case-by-case basis. A 1988 decision held that even a ten-year delay between indictment and trial did not deny defendant her right to a speedy trial. Defendant, who was convicted for conspiracy to import cocaine, had, in order to avoid apprehension and prosecution, fled the jurisdiction prior to the indictment. The government had made diligent efforts to locate her for trial.[26]

The Trial Decision: Judge or Jury

Although most cases do not go to **trial,** trials are a crucial part of the criminal justice system. We have already examined some of the fundamental rights of defendants at trial, including the right to a trial by jury. But not all cases are tried before a jury, and in most instances, the defendant will be able to choose whether to be tried before a judge or a jury. Even if the defendant chooses a jury, the judge plays a significant role in the trial.

The Trial Judge

Judges are the referees in a criminal trial. Theoretically they are neither for nor against a particular position or issue but are committed to the fair implementation of the rules of evidence and law. Judges must also present the case to the jury with a **charge,** in which they explain the law applicable to the case and give the jury instructions that it must follow in arriving at a verdict. Judges may have great influence over the jury through their attitudes, their rulings, and their charges. They will also have an impact on those who testify and those who are parties to the trial. Few people experience appellate arguments, and their only contact with justice may be at a trial. Judges at trial, therefore, should be considerate and uphold the highest standards of justice in their courtrooms. The job is difficult and requires great legal expertise. It is also a powerful position; for although judges may be overruled on appeal, many cases will not be appealed. Judges also have tremendous power over defendants at sentencing.

The prestige of judges is affected by the quality of the men and women attracted to the position. Because the job has become more complex and salaries have not kept pace with inflation, it has become increasingly difficult to persuade the best-qualified persons to become judges. The result is "the specter of a judicial 'brain drain,' leading to a judiciary consisting only of the very young, the very old, and the independently wealthy."[27]

The Jury

Capital cases, or those in which the death penalty may be assessed, must be tried before a **jury;** but in other cases, defendants may elect to have a nonjury trial in which the judge decides the issue of guilt or innocence. When the case is tried before a jury, it must listen to and weigh the evidence presented by the prosecution and the defense and decide whether the defendant is guilty or not guilty. In some cases, after a finding of guilt, the same jury or another one will decide the penalty; but usually the judge determines the sentence, although many jurisdictions permit (or require) juries to make recommendations.

Some authorities believe that the jury system is among the great achievements of English and American jurisprudence, whereas others criticize the system. Sociologists have studied the jury to gather data on some of the issues; these studies have become widely recognized in the literature. Much of the information comes from the Chicago Jury Project, begun in 1954.[28] Because of opposition to that project, in which jury deliberations were taped without the knowledge of the jurors, Congress passed a statute that prohibits jury research by that method. Since that time, the studies usually use *simulated* or *mock juries.* From the jury lists, a mock jury of similar jurors is selected, presented with the case, and told to deliberate and decide the issues. Their deliberations are then recorded and analyzed. The use of mock juries has also been criticized, mostly because the jurors are not involved in a real trial; consequently, their responses may not accurately reflect how they would react in a real situation.[29]

Another technique utilized to study jury reactions is the use of *shadow juries.* This system was devised as an aid in the $300 million antitrust suit brought against the International Business Machines Corporation (IBM) in 1977. An expert was hired to select a panel of six people who were as close as possible to the actual jury in terms of backgrounds and attitudes. They were paid to sit in the courtroom every day of the trial, listen to the evidence, and report their findings each evening. The information was used by the defense in the strategy and preparation of the case. The defense won the case, and the expert went into full-time consulting, forming a company called Litigation Sciences.[30]

Although critics believe that the jury system is an ineffective method for determining facts (the results of empirical research are not clear), there is some support for the system's efficiency and accuracy.[31] The Supreme Court is convinced that juries do understand the evidence presented at trial,[32] but the research on shadow juries questions the Court's conclusion.[33]

Judge Versus Jury: An Analysis

Should criminal cases be tried before judges or juries? The debate continues, with allegations that juries are too lenient (although there is evidence that they are less lenient than judges),[34] that they do not understand the evidence, and that jury trials are too time consuming and too expensive. Still, despite the problems, the system retains great popularity, and although it may not be perfect, it does work.

SENTENCING

Sentencing is one of the most important stages in the criminal justice system. For offenders, this stage of the process determines the punishments that will be imposed and, thus, how they will spend the coming months or years. For some, sentencing determines whether they will live or die. For society it is a time of decision that necessitates not only action in particular cases but also recognition of the philosophies that underlie the punishment concept.

Sentencing and Punishment Philosophies

Throughout history many reasons have been given to justify punishment and sentencing; but they can all be categorized as either **rehabilitation, retribution, incapacitation,** or **deterrence.** Chapter 3 briefly traced the movement from rehabilitation to retribution and deterrence, but for easy reference, these philosophies are summarized in Exhibit 13.3.[35] The exhibit also mentions **just deserts,** a philosophy in vogue today, leading to the **justice model** of punishment, which embodies both the philosophies of deterrence and retribution. This model assumes that offenders will be given the penalties they deserve, in light of their crimes, and that the assessment of these deserved penalties will deter those offenders and others from committing other crimes. After a look at the types of sentences, this discussion will close with an analysis of the trends in sentencing and sentencing philosophies.

Types of Sentences: An Overview

Historically many types of **sentences** have been imposed, ranging from **corporal punishment** (much of it so painful and brutal that it resulted in death) to **probation** (the most frequently used sentence in the United States today). Probation may be a mild form of punishment with few restrictions, or it may involve severe restrictions. It is a punishment that leaves the offender in the community but usually under supervision. (It is discussed with other types of community supervision in the last chapter).

Offenders may also be required to pay a **fine,** a financial payment to the state, or **restitution,** payment to the victim. Some offenders are incarcerated in prisons or jails. These types of sentences are listed and defined in Exhibit 13.4. This section focuses on two types of punishment that have been controversial historically in this country: corporal and capital punishment.

Corporal Punishment

Historically corporal punishment was used frequently and often inflicted in public because the punishment was thought to have a deterrent effect on the offender and on the rest of society.

Corporal punishment is no longer a legally acceptable form of punishment in the criminal justice system in this country although it is used in other countries. Some scholars have recently suggested, however, that corporal punishment is more humane as well as less expensive than incarceration. Graeme Newman, who has written extensively on punishment, has suggested electric shock as a substitute for incarceration for most

EXHIBIT 13.3

Sentencing and Punishment Philosophies

Throughout history four philosophies or purposes have been used to justify punishment and sentencing.

1. *Incapacitation*—doing whatever is necessary to keep the offender from repeating the offense. Today incapacitation takes the form of incarceration, but in earlier times, it might have involved cutting off the hand of the thief, castrating the sex offender, or disfiguring the prostitute.

2. *Retribution*—taking action to get even with the offender in the same way he or she harmed victims; it is an "eye for an eye and a tooth for a tooth" approach, typical of ancient and some modern periods. Retribution is similar to *revenge*, the term used most frequently in earlier times. Retribution is once again a popular justification for sentencing and punishment, although today it is more commonly referred to as *just deserts*, which means to give the offender what he or she deserves in light of the offense committed. The modern approach is thought to be more humane than traditional retribution, although some argue nothing has changed but the name.

3. *Deterrence*—embodies the belief that punishment and sentencing will keep offenders from committing the offenses again *(individual deterrence)*, while also setting an example that will keep others from engaging in criminal activities *(general deterrence)*. Scholars frequently debate whether punishment deters, how much is needed for deterrence, and so on.

4. *Rehabilitation*—based on the belief that the offender can be changed through proper treatment. Early criminologists talked about repenting and emphasized religious training as a prerequisite. Criminals were therefore kept in solitary confinement so that they would not be corrupted by others and would have time to contemplate their actions. The more recent approach involved the establishment of treatment programs within prisons, along with diversion programs to keep juveniles and others who might be salvageable from going to prison. Rehabilitation was the dominant theory of punishment until recently, when many states rejected it and implemented a policy of retribution, or just deserts, usually coupled with an emphasis on deterrence.

offenders. Electric shock, says Newman, would inflict punishment only where it belongs—on the offender and not on the offender's family, who also suffer when the offender is incarcerated. It would remove from society the expense of incarceration and of welfare dependents whose breadwinners are in prison.

EXHIBIT 13.4

Types of Sentences

DEATH PENALTY

In some States for certain crimes such as murder, the courts may sentence an offender to death by electrocution, exposure to lethal gas, hanging, lethal injection, or other method specified by State law.

INCARCERATION

The confinement of a convicted criminal in a Federal or State prison or a local jail to serve a court-imposed sentence. Custody is usually within a jail, administered locally, or a prison, operated by the State or the Federal government. In many States, offenders sentenced to one year or less are held in a jail; those sentenced to longer terms are committed to a State prison.

PROBATION

The sentencing of an offender to community supervision by a probation agency, often as a result of suspending a sentence to confinement. Such supervision normally entails specific rules of conduct while in the community. If the rules are violated, a sentence may be imposed. Probation is the most widely used correctional disposition in the United States.

SPLIT SENTENCES, SHOCK PROBATION, AND INTERMITTENT CONFINEMENT

A penalty that explicitly requires the convicted person to serve a brief period of confinement in a local, State, or Federal facility (the "shock") followed by a period of probation. This penalty attempts to combine the use of community supervision with a short incarceration experience. Some sentences are periodic rather than continuous; for example, an offender may be required to spend a certain number of weekends in jail.

RESTITUTION AND VICTIM COMPENSATION

The offender is required to provide financial repayment, or in some jurisdictions, services in lieu of monetary restitution for the losses incurred by the victim.

COMMUNITY SERVICE

The offender is required to perform a specified amount of public service work, such as collecting trash in parks or other public facilities.

FINES

An economic penalty that requires the offender to pay a specified sum of money within limits set by law. Fines often are imposed in addition to probation or as an alternative to incarceration.

SOURCE: Bureau of Justice Statistics, *Report to the Nation on Crime and Justice: The Data* 2d ed (Washington, D.C.: U.S. Government Printing Office, 1988), p. 96.

Under Newman's proposal, all offenders would receive the same penalty for the same crime; no additional punishment would be administered because of the offender's past crimes. The punishment would, like the classical approach, fit the crime, not the criminal. Corporal punishment would be more fair for other reasons too, says Newman. Unlike prison, corporal punishment works on the offender's body, not on his or her mind.[36]

A variation on corporal punishment has also been suggested. In previous days rapists were castrated. Within the past few years, some judges have ordered chemical castration of rapists or given convicted rapists the choice of chemical castration or incarceration. This procedure is controversial, however, with some taking the position that even when it is voluntary it violates the constitutional rights of the accused.[37] Another problem is that physicians refuse to prescribe the drug used for chemical castration either because of ethical or medical reasons or fear of lawsuits.

Capital Punishment

Another form of punishment used extensively in the past and becoming more popular today is **capital punishment.** As Figure 13.3 indicates, the number of people on death row in the United States rose from 131 in 1953 to 2124 in 1989. Of those 25 are women; 58.3 percent are white; 40.2 percent are black; 6.6 percent are Hispanic, and 1 percent are American

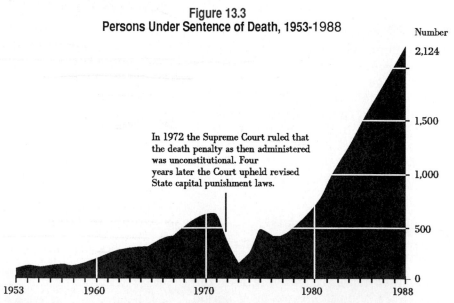

Figure 13.3
Persons Under Sentence of Death, 1953-1988

In 1972 the Supreme Court ruled that the death penalty as then administered was unconstitutional. Four years later the Court upheld revised State capital punishment laws.

SOURCE: Bureau of Justice Statistics, *Capital Punishment 1988* (Washington, D.C.: U.S. Department of Justice, July 1989), p. 2. By the end of 1990, the death row population was 2169.

there is insufficient evidence of a national consensus against exe
the retarded, and that existing procedural safeguards adequately p
the interests of mentally retarded persons such as Penry. . . .

On the record before the Court today, however, I cannot concl
that all mentally retarded people of Penry's ability—by virtue of the
mental retardation alone, and apart from any individualized considera
tion of their personal responsibility—inevitably lack the cognitive,
tional, and moral capacity to act with the degree of culpability associated
with the death penalty. Mentally retarded persons are individuals whose
abilities and experiences can vary greatly. . . .

In light of the diverse capacities and life experiences of mentally
retarded persons, it cannot be said on the record before us today that all
mentally retarded people, by definition, can never act with the level of
culpability associated with the death penalty. . . .

In sum, mental retardation is a factor that may well lessen a defendant's culpability for a capital offense. But we cannot conclude today that
the Eighth Amendment precludes the execution of any mentally retarded
person of Penry's ability convicted of a capital offense simply by virtue of
their mental retardation alone. So long as sentencers can consider and
give effect to mitigating evidence of mental retardation in imposing sentence, an individualized determination of whether "death is the appropriate punishment" can be made in each particular case. While a national
consensus against execution of the mentally retarded may someday
emerge reflecting the "evolving standards of decency that mark the progress of a maturing society," there is insufficient evidence of such a consensus today.

Methods of Capital Punishment

Historically, people have been executed in many ways: by ax, by rope, by
drawing and quartering, by boiling, by gas, by electricity, and by firearms.
Execution by firing squad is a frequently used method in other countries
today. In the United States the most popular methods have been hanging,
electrocution, and the gas chamber. More recently, death by lethal injection has been adopted.

Death Penalty Debate

Debates over the death penalty probably provoke more emotions than
reason, logic, or evidence, and the arguments have not changed much
over the years. The main arguments center on deterrence and retribution,
discussed in Chapter 3 of this book, but here we look at a few other issues
in the continuing debate.[42]

First, it has been argued that capital punishment is less expensive
than keeping a person in prison for life; and for that reason, it should be
used for serious crimes. If capital punishment were applied immediately

after a person receives sentence, the argument would be accurate. But that is never the case in the United States. The imposition of the death sentence is only the beginning of a long process of appeals. As a result, capital punishment may actually cost more than life imprisonment. The cost of incarcerating a prisoner on death row is also greater than the cost for other prisoners, as there is a need for increased security to ensure that the prisoner does not take his or her own life, is not killed by other prisoners, or is not given a chance to harm others. The cost of appeals is also high, leading some to question whether we can afford to continue executions under a system that recognizes a right to counsel and in which many death row inmates are indigent and therefore entitled to appointed counsel. In Florida, the estimated cost of an execution is closer to $3.2 million than to the total of the itemized expenses of the actual execution, which include: $150 for a funeral suit; $20 for the last meal; $150 for the executioner's fee, and $525 for the undertaker, box included. To execute a prisoner, the state of Florida spends six times as much money as it would to keep him in prison until he dies of natural causes. Figures are similar in the other thirty-six states that allow executions, studies show.[43]

Second, it is argued that capital punishment is necessary to maintain the safety of guards and inmates. Empirical evidence on the deterrence issue is inconclusive;[44] but in a recent analysis, investigators concluded that "there is no indication that our national return to capital punishment since *Furman* has had a systematic impact on police homicides."[45] On the other side is the argument that the existence of capital punishment, particularly close to a scheduled execution, enhances the chances of violence within the prison. Death row inmates fear that if one is executed by the state, others will follow. They may therefore try to kill the inmate scheduled for execution.

Third, it is argued that the use of capital punishment may hinder the rehabilitative efforts of prison personnel, especially chaplains, who work with those on death row. Further, the living conditions on death row may have a debilitating effect on those awaiting death. Fourth, it has been argued that because there is always the possibility that an innocent person might be executed, capital punishment should be abolished.

Fifth, the death penalty, it is argued, serves a symbolic purpose, indicating that life cannot be taken without severe penalty. It serves to diminish the possibility of illegal retaliation by victims' families and friends. Another argument in favor of retaining the death penalty is that most people support the penalty, and that support is growing.[46]

The Sentencing Process

The three main models of sentencing are legislative, judicial, and administrative; most systems employ one or more of these types. Some sentences may be quite innovative as Highlight 13.1 indicates.

In the *legislative model,* the legislature establishes by statute the length of the sentence for each crime. For example, a conviction of bur-

HIGHLIGHT 13.1

UNUSUAL SENTENCES RECENTLY IMPOSED

Sentencing defendants is one of the most difficult of all judicial functions. Some judges have become rather innovative in their attempts to impose sentences that might have a deterrent effect on subjects. Here are a few recent examples.

Judge John Carroll Byrnes, Baltimore City Circuit Court Judge, sentences some juveniles to "library time." They must read books as a condition of their probation. Committed to the principle that the "huge difference between good and bad in our society is education," Judge Byrnes believes that as many as fifty percent of his subjects might be improved by reading. "In the history of man, reading always does make a difference."[1]

The value of education is also emphasized by a New Orleans criminal court judge who says she is fed up with young defendants who cannot read the paperwork in their cases. These young people, many of whom have been expelled from school, are told to attend Probation Education Program (PEP) classes. If they miss one class, they must spend one weekend in jail. If they miss more, they are sent to prison. One probationer said of the judge, "It's tough; that lady doesn't let you slip up."[2]

A Michigan minister, who has frequently been cited for housing code violations, has been sentenced to spend thirty days in a roach-and-rat-infested unit which he owns and has rented to a poverty-stricken man whose daughter is in a wheelchair. "The little girl is not even physically able to knock them [the roaches and rats] off herself."[3]

The three white teenagers who overturned twenty-seven tombstones, threw rocks and broke more than twenty windows and painted racial messages on the outside walls of a black church were ordered to make public apologies to the church members and to perform a list of chores for church members. The teenagers' parents will supervise the work, and the boys, ages fourteen and fifteen, must reappear before the congregations to make certain the work is completed properly.[4]

A man who fathered his first child when he was thirteen and has subsequently had six illegitimate children has been ordered as one condition of his probation for stealing a truck not to father any more children except by his wife. Although fornication and adultery are prohibited by state law in South Carolina where the defendant was sentenced and one could therefore argue that the judge was only specifying that the defendant not violate laws while on probation, constitutional lawyers question the legitimacy of this probation condition.[5]

One final sentencing issue demonstrates the failure of an enterprising defendant to argue that he had completed his sentence. Jerry Rosenberg, who has spent twenty-five years in prison, was sentenced to life for murdering two New York police officers in 1963. Recently Rosenberg had open-heart surgery. He contends that during that surgery his heart stopped beating; therefore he died and has thus completed his sentence. The judge was amused but not convinced. "As his presence in this courtroom indicates . . . he did not die." Judge Peter Corning did not agree with Rosenberg that there are two kinds of death: reversible and irreversible.[6]

[1] Karen Klages, "Judge Sentences Library Times," *ABA Journal* (May 1989): 29.
[2] "Go to School or Go to Jail," *Tallahassee Democrat,* 17 January 1989, p. 8, col. 4.
[3] "Pastor Ordered to Live 30 Days in Infested Unit," *Miami Herald,* 23 June 1989, p. B3, col. 1.
[4] "Teens Must Work for Churches They Desecrated in S. Carolina," *Atlanta Journal and Constitution,* 25 May 1989, p. A9, col. 3.
[5] "Man Ordered to Father Kids Only With Wife," *Miami Herald,* 13 July 1989, p. 3B, col. 5.
[6] "Judge Resurrects Sentence," *Tulsa Tribune,* 24 June 1988, p. 1, col. 1.

glary carries a sentence of ten years. Under this model no discretion is allowed the judge at the time of sentencing, nor are the prison authorities or parole boards allowed discretion in determining when the inmate will be released. This type of sentence is called the **determinate, or flat-time, sentence.**

In the *judicial model*, the judge decides the length of the sentence within a legislatively established range. For example, the legislature determines that for the crime of burglary the sentence will be from five to ten years, and the judge imposes a sentence within that range.

In the *administrative* model, the legislature establishes a wide range of imprisonment for a particular crime. The judge may or must impose that sentence. For example, the legislature determines that for the crime of armed robbery, the sentence is one day to life, a sentence that is then imposed by the judge after the defendant is convicted. The decision to release the inmate is determined later by an administrative agency, usually a parole board. The type of sentence imposed in this model is called the **indeterminate sentence.**

There has always been debate over which of the three sentencing models should be used. Today the trend is away from the administrative model and indeterminate sentencing and toward the legislative model and determinate sentencing. But even this trend illustrates that most sentencing is actually a combination of the three models. For example, some of the recent legislation permits determinate sentences established by the legislature to be judicially altered if a given case has certain mitigating or aggravating circumstances. This approach is called **presumptive sentencing.**[47]

Presumptive sentencing differs from flat or determinate sentencing in that it does not remove all judicial discretion. It does, however, check the abuse of that discretion by establishing that a deviate sentence will be presumed to be improper. Thus, when the sentence is appealed, the sentencing judge has the burden of proving that there are justifiable reasons for deviating from the recommended sentence.

Various combinations of sentence types are also used. For example, a defendant may be fined and incarcerated, fined and placed on probation, or fined and ordered to pay restitution. There are also combinations of probation and incarceration, including

- *Split sentences*—where the court specifies a period of incarceration to be followed by a period of probation
- *Modification of sentence*—where the original sentencing court may reconsider an offender's prison sentence within a limited time and change it to probation
- *Shock probation*—where an offender sentenced to incarceration is released after a period of time in confinement (the shock) and resentenced to probation
- *Intermittent incarceration*—where an offender on probation may spend weekends or nights in jail[48]

Any of the sentencing models or the sentencing combinations may also be affected by other factors. Power may be given to the governor to commute a sentence of life, for example, to a specified term of years. The governor may also have the power to **pardon** an offender. (In the case of a federal crime, the President has the pardoning power.) It is also possible that sentence length may be reduced in accordance with **good-time credit,** in which sentences may be reduced because of the inmate's good behavior.

Sentencing Disparity

The current movement toward determinate sentencing is mainly the result of concern with alleged **sentencing disparity,** a concept frequently used and seldom defined. To some, sentencing disparity results when two people convicted of the same crime are given different sentences by their respective judges. Others claim that disparity exists when legislatures of different states set different penalties for the same offense; thus, robbery with a firearm may result in a twenty-five-year sentence in one state and fifteen in another. Still others say that sentencing disparity exists only when similarly situated offenders receive quite different penalties for the same offense. It is a disparity if a three-time offender in one jurisdiction receives five years for armed robbery, whereas a three-time offender in another receives fifteen years for the same offense.

The lack of agreement on the meaning of the term makes it difficult if not impossible to interpret the studies of alleged disparity. Nevertheless, numerous attempts have been made to prove or disprove sentencing disparity, ranging from allegations of racial and sexual discrimination to allegations that defendants who receive long sentences are being punished for their unpopular political views.[49]

While scholars argue over whether the criminal justice system does or does not discriminate on the basis of extra-legal characteristics (such as age or sex), many continue to believe that it does. This belief is generally based on the knowledge that a high percentage of convictions and sentencings (as well as arrests) involve blacks and other minorities as compared to whites. Despite arguments that these differentials are the result of such legal factors as prior criminal records, current offense, and other legally irrelevant variables, most minorities remain unconvinced.

The debate over whether the criminal justice system discriminates against minorities frequently arises in the context of capital punishment. Several extensive studies have been made in this area, but the U.S. Supreme Court remains unconvinced that they show unconstitutional discrimination. In its 1987 decision in *McCleskey v. Kemp*, the Court explains its reasons. McCleskey had used an empirical analysis by law professor David Baldus and others to demonstrate that capital punishment is more frequently assessed when the victim is white as compared to black, and to a lesser extent, when the offender is black rather than white.[50]

McCleskey v. Kemp

The Baldus study is actually two sophisticated statistical studies that examine over 2,000 murder cases that occurred in Georgia during the 1970s. The raw numbers collected by Professor Baldus indicate that defendants charged with killing white persons received the death penalty in 11 percent of the cases, but defendants charged with killing blacks received the death penalty in only 1 percent of the cases. The raw numbers also indicate a reverse racial disparity according to the race of the defendant: 4 percent of the black defendants received the death penalty, as opposed to 7 percent of the white defendants.

[The Court then discusses other comparisons made by the Baldus study and continues] According to this model, black defendants were 1.1 times as likely to receive a death sentence as other defendants. Thus, the Baldus study indicates that black defendants, such as McCleskey, who kill white victims have the greatest likelihood of receiving the death penalty. . . .

Finally, McCleskey's statistical proffer must be viewed in the context of his challenge. McCleskey challenges decisions at the heart of the State's criminal justice system. "[O]ne of society's most basic tasks is that of protecting the lives of its citizens and one of the most basic ways in which it achieves the task is through criminal laws against murder." Implementation of these laws necessarily requires discretionary judgments. Because discretion is essential to the criminal justice process, we would demand exceptionally clear proof before we would infer that the discretion has been abused. The unique nature of the decisions at issue in this case also counsel against adopting such an inference from the disparities indicated by the Baldus study. Accordingly, we hold that the Baldus study is clearly insufficient to support an inference that any of the decision makers in McCleskey's case acted with discriminatory purpose. . . .

At most, the Baldus study indicates a discrepancy that appears to correlate with race. Apparent disparities in sentencing are an inevitable part of our criminal justice system. The discrepancy indicated by the Baldus study is "a far cry from the major systemic defects identified in *Furman.*" As this Court has recognized, any mode for determining guilt or punishment "has its weaknesses and the potential for misuse." Specifically, "there can be 'no perfect procedure for deciding in which cases governmental authority should be used to impose death.'" . . . Where the discretion that is fundamental to our criminal process is involved, we decline to assume that what is unexplained is invidious . . . we hold that the Baldus study does not demonstrate a constitutionally significant risk of racial bias affecting the Georgia capital-sentencing process.

Control of Sentencing Disparity

Two approaches are being used to control sentencing disparity. In the first, discretion is left with the judge, but efforts are made to control the discretion. In the second, discretion is removed from the judge and placed with the legislature.

Judges have wide discretion at the sentencing stage, and various methods have been suggested for controlling it. The threat of removal or being pressured to resign is one approach, which has worked in some cases, particularly when citizens have organized court watches and publicized controversial sentencing decisions. Recently, however, considerable attention has been given to the establishment of model sentencing guidelines and **sentencing councils.**

Sentencing guidelines are seen as a way to control discretion without abolishing it while correcting the extreme disparity that can result from individualized sentencing. If a judge has an offender to sentence, the judge may consider the offender's background, the nature of the offense, or other variables without any guidelines. When sentencing guidelines are used, the difference is that the relevance of these variables may have been researched. The judge also has a benchmark of the reasonable penalty in these circumstances.

There are drawbacks, however, to sentencing guidelines. First, some are just guidelines, and there is nothing (except pressure) to prevent judges from ignoring them. In other cases judges must give written reasons for deviating from the guidelines, which may also specify general conditions under which the judge may impose a sentence outside the guidelines. Second, empirical evidence indicates that the presence of such guidelines has not significantly reduced sentencing disparity. Third, there has not been sufficient analysis of the processes used in establishing the guidelines. Finally, even if the sentencing guidelines are effective in reducing sentencing disparity among judges, the system has no effect on the prosecutor's virtually unchecked discretion in deciding which charges to file, whether to plea bargain, and, if so, how.[51]

Perhaps the most controversial sentencing guidelines have been the federal guidelines recommended by the U.S. Sentencing Commission, established as a result of the 1984 revision of the federal criminal code.[52] Those guidelines became law on November 1, 1987. They were and remain highly controversial. In the earlier months, some federal judges refused to enforce them. Others declared them unconstitutional while others held that they are constitutional.[53]

In *Mistretta v. U.S.*, the Court reviewed the history of federal sentencing, including the emphasis on rehabilitation accompanied by indeterminate sentencing, which would theoretically give judges the opportunity to impose a sentence tailored to the rehabilitative needs of an individual offender. "Serious disparities in sentences, however, were common. Rehabilitation as a sound penological theory came to be questioned and, in any event, was regarded by some as an unattainable goal for most cases." But the Sentencing Commission apparently thought that determinate sentencing would be too inflexible. Thus, the Commission recommended, and Congress accepted, guidelines that "would be successful in reducing sentence disparities while retaining the flexibility needed to adjust for unanticipated factors arising in a particular case." After discussing the constitutional issues, which are beyond the scope of this text, the Court held that the guidelines did not violate federal constitutional rights.[54]

Determinate Sentencing

The most dramatic reaction to alleged sentencing disparity has been a return to determinate sentencing. Led by Maine and California (the state that used indeterminate sentencing most extensively), most states now have some form of mandatory sentencing.[55]

Despite the warnings of advocates of determinate sentencing that a return to this method should not be a piecemeal approach, most states have not considered the total impact of their actions when legislating determinate sentences. In many states insufficient attention was given to the consequences of this movement; the results have been disastrous in some cases.

First, there is the possibility that disparity will be even greater, although of a different type. With discretion removed from judges and with stiff penalties imposed by legislatures, prosecutors might be more reluctant to prosecute; juries might be more reluctant to find defendants guilty. When either of these possibilities occurs, those defendants will receive disparate treatment compared to those who committed similar or identical crimes who are prosecuted and convicted.[56]

Second, determinate sentences may contribute to the increasingly serious problems of prison overcrowding. Third, it is doubtful whether determinate sentencing will achieve the goal of decreasing the crime rate by deterring crime. Support for this contention comes from a study concluding that although obviously those incarcerated for longer periods will not be out on the streets committing crimes, the total effect on the crime rate would be insignificant. "Our analysis indicates that for a one percent reduction in crime, prison populations must increase by 3 to 10 percent, depending on the target population to be sentenced."[57] Nor is it clear that sentencing revision will affect the rates of **recidivism** once the inmates serving those longer terms are released. Fourth, under determinate sentencing with stiffer penalties, defendants may be less likely to plead guilty and more likely to insist on trials, thus increasing the burden of the already overcrowded court system. Studies of New York's stiff drug laws and Massachusetts' mandatory and stiff penalties for illegally carrying guns indicate that many defendants began looking for ways to avoid the harsh penalties. Some fled rather than face trial. Judicial decisions showed more favor to defendants, with increased dismissals and verdicts of not guilty. Defendants were more likely to appeal their convictions. In both states, "as the stakes got higher, defendants pursued more dilatory tactics to avoid them."[58]

Finally, those who are critical of judicial discretion often take the position that the disparity created by using it will be eliminated if there are legislatively determined sentences. But this simply is not the case. Aside from the disparity that may result from the displacement of discretion to others in the criminal justice system, disparity will still exist among the states. Two persons convicted of the same offense in different states may receive different sentences because of the differences in state statutes.

APPEALS AND OTHER LEGAL CHALLENGES

Several legal challenges to a criminal conviction, sentence, and subsequent incarceration are available. Most involve complicated legal procedures and issues; but, generally, defendants who have good reason to believe that they have been unjustly treated may appeal. Immediately upon conviction a defendant may have legal grounds for the judge to grant his or her motion for a new trial or for a judgment of acquittal despite the jury verdict. This motion may be successful if the defendant can show that evidence admitted at the trial should have been excluded for some legal reason or that in some other way the defendant's constitutional rights were violated.

If the motion for a new trial or for a judgment of acquittal is not granted, as is usually the case, the defendant may appeal the conviction on points of law. An appeal of the decision of the trial court is made to a court that has appellate jurisdiction over its decisions. In effect, the appellate court looks at the actions of the trial court and decides whether the lower court committed errors that warrant a reversal of the case. Most cases are not reversed; most that are reversed are remanded for another trial, and a large percentage of defendants are again found guilty.

Defendants may also file writs. A *writ* is an order from a court for someone to do something or to give permission to do whatever has been requested. Criminal defendants frequently file a writ of **habeas corpus,** which literally means "You have the body." If the writ is granted, the court orders the jailer, sheriff, or warden to produce the person in custody who is claiming that he or she is being confined in violation of his or her rights. This writ is frequently used by inmates who are arguing that they are being confined under conditions that violate their constitutional rights.

Sentences may also be appealed, but such appeals are not usually successful. When the legislature has delegated to trial judges wide discretion in determining sentences, appellate courts will rarely overturn those decisions. The appellate court shows deference to the judge who has heard and seen the evidence, evidence that is not available on appeal. If, however, the sentence is cruel and unusual punishment, it violates the Eighth Amendment and will be declared unconstitutional. A large body of law has developed around the meaning of the phrase *cruel and unusual*, but the Court has ruled that capital punishment does not violate the Eighth Amendment unless it is applied arbitrarily or discriminatorily or unless it is disproportionate to the crime for which it is imposed. The Supreme Court has ruled that capital punishment is disproportionate to the crime of raping an adult female.[59]

The Supreme Court has also ruled that in the imposition of the death penalty, the sentencing body must consider mitigating and aggravating circumstances. Examples would be the circumstances of the crime, the prior record of the defendant, and the character and propensities of the defendant. Objective standards must be used to make future predictions concerning the likely behavior of the defendant; that is, we must inquire into the *why* of that person's behavior before a penalty as drastic as capital punishment may be imposed legally.[60]

Final Appeal: The U.S. Supreme Court

The highest court of appeal in the United States is the Supreme Court, an institution of great power that arouses considerable controversy. In recent years the Court has encountered its heaviest workload and received some of the most widespread criticism of its history. Yet after citing numerous critics of the Court, a *New York Times* editorial concluded, "The High Court, despite generations of attack and controversy, remains one of the world's most trusted institutions."[61]

Operation of the Court

The Supreme Court has almost complete control over the selection of cases that it will hear and decide. The Court does this by granting or denying a **writ of certiorari.** When the Court agrees to hear a case on appeal, it is said to have granted *certiorari*. Four of the nine justices who sit on the Court must vote in favor of the writ for it to be granted.

In an average term, the Court hears less than 5 percent of the cases filed. There are two reasons for this limitation. First, because of time, the Court must limit the number of cases heard and decided. The problem today is that the number of cases the Court is asked to hear has increased significantly, from approximately 1000 per year in 1953 to 5000 or more today. Until recently the Court had increased its work load by accepting more cases each year; but since the middle of its 1987–1988 term, the Court has been cutting back on the number of cases for which it is granting *cert.*[62]

The second reason the Court hears only some of the cases filed was stated by a former chief justice: "To remain effective, the Supreme Court must continue to decide only those cases which present questions whose resolution will have immediate importance far beyond the particular facts and parties involved."[63] An example would be the *Gideon* case, discussed earlier. The fact that Gideon did not have counsel at his trial in Florida was important only to Gideon, but his case's significance went far beyond the dispute between the prisoner and the state of Florida. The decision handed down in that case established the right of counsel for all criminal defendants in felony cases.

The Court will often hear cases when lower court decisions on the issue in question have differed. For example, before the Court decided *U.S. v. Mistretta*, 116 U.S. district judges had ruled that the federal sentencing guidelines were constitutional; 158 had ruled they were unconstitutional. Federal appellate courts had also ruled on the issue, and they too were divided.[64]

When the Supreme Court rules on an issue that has been in conflict in lower federal courts, its decision becomes the final court resolution of the issue unless or until it is overruled by a subsequent Supreme Court decision. Supreme Court decisions may also be nullified by subsequent statutes (provided they are not unconstitutional) or by constitutional amendment.

When it is in session, the Court hears arguments Monday through Wednesday for two weeks of the month. On Friday, conference day, the justices discuss the cases argued before them and decide which additional ones they will hear. A majority vote is needed for a decision in a case heard by the Court. If an even number of justices are sitting and there is a tie vote, the decision being appealed is affirmed.

The Court's decisions are handed down on opinion days, which are usually three Mondays of each month of the term. The decisions are then made public. Newspapers will pick up portions of those decisions thought to be of general interest.

The Court's Decisions

The principal function of the Supreme Court is to determine whether the litigants' federal constitutional rights have been violated. These constitutional rights must be interpreted in light of changing times and changing needs. But because we differ on our interpretation of the needs, concerns, and aspirations of our society, we also differ on the Court's interpretations; thus the Court has frequently been accused of making rather than interpreting law.

Controversial court decisions must, however, be considered in the context of constitutional law and a changing society, with its concomitant need for settling conflicts. If the Constitution is flexible and expected to change as conditions change, while at the same time maintaining some stability and dependability, it is imperative that judicial decisions reflect the changing conditions of the time. The law and the Constitution must be flexible enough to deal with different factual situations, which will require adjudication as they arise.

It is also to be expected that critics will often attack the opinions of the Court and its personnel. The publication of *The Brethren* in 1979 is an example of a publication that raised many questions about the nine justices in black robes who are charged with telling us what the law is.[65] The announced retirement of Chief Justice Warren E. Burger in early summer 1986 and President Reagan's nomination of Associate Justice William H. Rehnquist to the position of Chief Justice set off a flurry of discussion over the influence these personnel changes would have on the decisions of the Court. After long and difficult hearings, the appointment of Rehnquist was approved. Judge Antonin Scalia, the first person of Italian descent to serve on the Supreme Court, was nominated and confirmed to fill the vacancy created by Burger's retirement.

In the summer of 1987, Justice Powell, who was frequently the swing vote in the Court's five–four decision, announced his retirement. President Reagan quickly nominated Judge Robert H. Bork, a strongly conservative member of the U.S. Court of Appeals for the District of Columbia. After one of the most expensive and bitterly fought confirmation battles, the U.S. Senate, by a fifty-eight to forty-two vote, refused to confirm the appointment. Reagan, vowing to appoint a conservative justice, nominated Douglas H. Ginsburg; but after revelations that he had used marijuana first while a law student and then while on the Harvard law faculty,

"I SMELL IT, TOO... MUST BE SOMEBODY EXERCISING THEIR FIRST AMENDMENT RIGHT OF FREE SPEECH!"

SOURCE: Wayne Stayskal, *Tampa Tribune*, 23 June 1989, reprinted with permission.

public pressure forced Ginsburg to withdraw from consideration. President Reagan's third appointment, Judge Anthony McLeod Kennedy, a federal appellate judge in California, was confirmed.

As expected, the Reagan Court has become more conservative. According to the *New York Times*, in a statement made after the Court's June 1989 decision in an employment discrimination case,

> The Supreme Court's 5–4 decision in a major employment discrimination case on Monday has dispelled much of any remaining doubt about whether former President Ronald Reagan accomplished his goal of moving the Court in a more conservative direction on civil rights.[66]

This conservative movement was expected to escalate following President Bush's anticipated appointment of a justice to replace Justice William J. Brennan, who announced his retirement during the summer of 1990. In the fall of 1000, Judge David Hachett Souter was confirmed.

COURTS AND CONGESTION

There is no question that the courts are overburdened, the Supreme Court as well as the lower appellate courts and trial courts.[67] The main question, however, is whether we should reduce the amount of litigation or increase the courts' facilities and personnel to handle the increasing volume of cases.

As with most other issues, there is little consensus on this one. Former Chief Justice Burger led those who argue that the problems have been caused by lawyers and clients who are too eager to litigate. This argument is countered by a recent president of the American Trial Lawyers' Association, who contended that litigation is cost effective and that lawyers are not filing a lot of frivolous lawsuits.[68]

In addition to the argument that we litigate too much is the argument that we appeal too many cases. In the decade between 1973 and 1983, state court appeals more than doubled, a growth rate that was more than ten times the population growth, three times the appellate judgeships, and more than four times the growth rate of trial court judgeships. During that decade criminal appeals accounted for 43 to 46 percent of total appeals, compared to 10 to 15 percent of total appeals in the 1960s. Appeals in federal courts were also increasing at a rapid rate.[69]

Several methods have been suggested for alleviating court congestion. Former Chief Justice Burger suggested that frivolous litigation would be discouraged if courts fined lawyers who file such suits. In a 1986 case, Justice Burger fined an attorney $1,000, stating that the attorney "has abused his privilege to practice law by repeatedly filing frivolous papers" and "acting like a small boy who gets a loaded pistol without instruction as to when and how it is to be used."[70]

Other suggestions for decreasing court congestion include increasing the numbers of judges and other personnel. The passage of the Omnibus Judgeship Act of 1978 increased the number of federal judges.[71] In 1982 another federal circuit court was added. Reorganization of courts is another suggestion that some state systems have followed. Improving internal management of courts also relieves some congestion. Shifting judges from one court to another might, for example, ease congestion problems during the vacation of a judge in one court. Night court has been used in some cities, particularly large cities with high caseloads. Computers have been used to speed up the courts' paperwork.

Alternate dispute resolution is perhaps the most efficient way to ease court congestion. In less complicated cases, litigants may use **mediation** rather than court resolution. Mediation has been used successfully in other countries. Mediators may be lay persons with some training in dispute resolution but without the legal training of attorneys. In a less formal situation, such as a neighborhood, many disputes may be resolved successfully without the formality and cost of a court trial.[72]

CONCLUSION

This chapter has presented an overview of courts and their procedures. The chapter began with a brief explanation of legal terms necessary to understand court functions. It also examined the dual court system and explained the differences between trial and appellate courts.

The discussion then turned to the role of lawyers in the court system, looking first at the prosecution and then at the defense. Pretrial processes were discussed, with the focus on the two most controversial processes: granting or denying bail and plea bargaining. The trial of a criminal case was examined briefly, with an emphasis on the right to a speedy trial and the difference between the judge and jury as fact-finding bodies in a criminal trial.

The process of sentencing, one of the most hotly debated topics in criminal justice today, was examined. After a brief discussion of types of sentences, the discussion focused on corporal and capital punishment, two of the more controversial methods. The process of sentencing was followed by a discussion of sentencing disparity and how that might be controlled. The main control utilized today is to remove all or part of the sentencing decision from judges; the determinate sentence was therefore explained and analyzed, and attention was given to federal sentencing guidelines.

Provisions for appealing legal decisions are an important element of a criminal justice system. Procedures for appealing convictions were discussed briefly, followed by a closer look at sentencing appeals. The Supreme Court, its method of operation, and some of the controversy surrounding it were discussed. The final section focused on court congestion and suggestions for reducing it.

The importance of the court system cannot be overemphasized, for it is in the courts that the final determination is made of how many criminal justice problems will be resolved. Once a person has committed an offense for which the state can punish, even if the police's handling of the situation is above question and society has provided all the necessary resources for treatment in whatever setting that may take place, a positive resolution of the problem may easily be thwarted by the courts. The rights of due process guaranteed by the Constitution may become a farce in the hands of incompetent lawyers and judges. With long delays in trials, they can easily become meaningless. It is therefore incumbent on lawyers, judges, probation officers, and all other functionaries of the courts, as well as society, to make the improvement of courts the prime target in the war against crime.

Many of the topics discussed in this chapter underscore again the importance of discretion in the criminal justice system. Prosecutors have wide discretion in deciding whether to bring charges, which charges to bring, if and when to drop charges, whether to plea bargain, and which sentences to recommend for convicted defendants. Juries exercise discretion in deciding whether defendants are innocent or guilty. Defense attorneys exercise discretion in determining trial strategy and whether to advise their clients to plea bargain. Judges exercise discretion in their supervision of pretrial and trial procedures and in sentencing, for it is obvious that a move toward determinate sentencing does not remove all discretion.

Nor is it wise to attempt to remove all discretion in the criminal justice system. The real question is where the bounds of that discretion will lie and how discretion may be checked. It therefore seems reasonable to conclude that the control, not the abolition, of discretion is the issue. The legal profession should recognize and accept the challenge of successful control of judicial and prosecutorial discretion, especially as it relates to the sentencing decision. Some of the problems of the criminal justice system, however, cannot be solved by the legal profession alone. Society must take responsibility for offering adequate legal services for all. The whole social structure should be appraised in the realization that the criminal justice system does not exist in isolation from the rest of society. Research must be supported, and the tendency to abandon philosophies, such as treatment, before they have been given a real trial should be reexamined. As I concluded in an earlier publication,

> It is easier to put the offender out of sight than to examine the social structure for cracks. It is easier to punish than to treat. It is easier to abolish the entire system of discretionary sentencing by attacking the abuses than to correct those abuses and provide the resources needed for an adequate implementation of the philosophy of individualized sentencing. It is easier to attack the judges for "leniency" than to examine the need to decriminal-

ize the criminal code or to provide sufficient and trained facilities. It is also easier to lose than to win the war against crime.[73]

ENDNOTES

1. Earl Warren, "Delay and Congestion in the Federal Courts," quoted in Hans Zeisel, Harry Kalven, Jr., and Bernard Buckholz, eds., *Delay in Court* (Boston: Little, Brown, 1959), p. xxi.

2. Marbury v. Madison, 5 U.S. (1 Cranch) 137 (1803).

3. For more information on the grand jury, see Marvin E. Frankel and Gary P. Naftalis, *The Grand Jury: An Institution on Trial* (New York: Hill & Wang, 1977), and Sara Sun Beale and William C. Bryson, *Grand Jury Law and Practice* (Wilmette, Ill.: Callaghan and Company, 1986). For an analysis of prosecutors, see Joan E. Jacoby, *The American Prosecutor: A Search of Identity* (Lexington, Mass.: D. C. Heath, 1980). For a brief discussion of prosecutors' careers see Sue Titus Reid and Lorna Keltner, "Careers in Criminal Justice: Law," in Sanford H. Kadish, ed., *Encyclopedia of Crime and Justice*, vol. 1 (New York: Free Press, 1983).

4. Bureau of Justice Statistics, *Criminal Defense for the Poor, 1986* (Washington, D.C.: U.S. Department of Justice, September 1988): 1.

5. See Darden v. Wainwright, 477 U.S. 168 (1986), *reh. denied*, 478 U.S. 1036 (1986), *remanded*, 803 F.2d 613 (11th Cir. 1987), for an example of improper prosecutorial comments that, according to the Supreme Court, did not prejudice the defendant to the extent that a new trial was required. The defendant was executed in Florida in 1989. See also Tarpley v. Dugger, 841 F.2d 359 (11th Cir. 1988), *cert. den.*, 488 U.S. 837 (1988).

6. For a study of defense attorneys, see Paul B. Wice, *Criminal Lawyers: An Endangered Species* (Beverly Hills, CA.: Sage Publications, 1978), p. 14. See also Alan M. Dershowitz, *The Best Defense* (New York: Random House, 1982).

7. For an interesting discussion on the history and project future of the right to counsel, see William W. Greenhaigh, "The Assistance of Counsel Clause in the Year 2000," *Criminal Law Bulletin* 25 (January-February 1989): 86–112.

8. For an account of the public defender's job, based on a study of Cook County, Illinois, see Lisa J. McIntyre, *The Public Defender: The Practice of Law in the Shadows of Repute* (Chicago: University of Chicago Press, 1987).

9. Bureau of Justice Statistics, *Criminal Defense for the Poor, 1986* (Washington, D.C.: U.S. Department of Justice, September 1988): 1. See also John Rosecrance, "Accommodating Negative Client Perceptions: A Process of Neutralization," *Sociological Inquiry* 58 (Spring 1988): 194–205, and Robert L. Spangenberg, "Why We Are Not Defending the Poor Properly: What the Evidence Shows," *Criminal Justice* 2 (Spring 1987): 12–17, 40–41.

10. Gerstein v. Pugh, 420 U.S. 103, 112 (1975).

11. Stack v. Boyle, 342 U.S. 1, 5 (1951).

12. District of Columbia Court Reform Act of 1970, D.C. Code Encyl. Section 23-1321 *et. seq.*

13. 18 U.S. Code, Section 3142 (e).

14. David O. Stewart, "Pretrial Detentions Upheld," *ABA Journal* (August 1, 1987): 54.

15. U.S. v. Salerno, 481 U.S. 739 (1987), *remanded* 829 F.2d 345 (2d Cir. 1987).

16. Joseph B. Vaughn and Victor E. Kappeler, "The Denial of Bail: Pre-Trial Preventive Detention," *Criminal Justice Research Bulletin* 3 (Huntsville, Tx.: Sam

Houston State University, 1987): 4. For an analysis of recent research on pretrial release, see *Research in Corrections* 1 (October 1988), published by the Rand Corporation. This issue has several articles on pretrial release.

17. Ky. Rev. Stat. Section 431.510 *et seq.* This statute was upheld in Benboe v. Carroll, 625 F.2d 737 (6th Cir. 1980).

18. For the classic sociological study of plea bargaining, see Donald J. Newman, "Pleading Guilty for Consideration: A Study of Bargain Justice," *Journal of Criminal Law, Criminology, and Police Science* 46 (March-April 1956): 780–790. See also Donald J. Newman, *Conviction: The Determination of Guilt or Innocence Without Trial* (Boston: Little, Brown, 1966), and Arthur Rossett and Donald Cressey, *Justice by Consent* (Philadelphia: Lippincott, 1976).

19. See, for example, Barbara Boland and Elizabeth Brady, *The Prosecution of Felony Arrests, 1980* (Washington, D.C.: U.S. Department of Justice, INSLAW, Inc., 1985), p. 18. See also Dean J. Champion, "Felony Plea Bargaining and Probation: A Growing Judicial and Prosecutorial Dilemma," *Journal of Criminal Justice* 16 (1988): 201–301.

20. Santobello v. New York, 404 U.S. 257, 260-261 (1971).

21. Bordenkircher v. Hayes, 434 U.S. 357 (1978). The cases referred to in the preceding paragraph are Brady v. United States, 397 U.S. 742 (1969); Boykin v. Alabama, 395 U.S. 238 (1968); and Santobello v. New York, 404 U.S. 257 (1971).

22. Brady v. U.S., 397 U.S. 742 (1970).

23. Arizona v. Horning, Ariz. 761 P.2d 728 (Ariz.App. 1988). For other restrictions on plea bargaining, see New Jersey v. Warren, 558 A. 2d 1312 (N.J. 1989).

24. M. L. Rubinstein and T. J. White, "Plea Bargaining—Can Alaska Live Without It?" *Judicature* 62 (December-January 1979): 266–279. See also Michael L. Rubinstein and Teresa J. White, "Alaska's Ban on Plea-Bargaining," in William F. McDonald and James A. Cramer, eds., *Plea-Bargaining* (Lexington, Mass.: Lexington Books, 1980), pp. 25–56; and Michael L. Rubinstein et al., *Alaska Bans Plea Bargaining*, U.S. Department of Justice (Washington, D.C.: U.S. Government Printing Office, 1980).

25. Stephen J. Schulhofer, "Is Plea Bargaining Inevitable?" *Harvard Law Review* 97 (March 1984): 1006–1007.

26. U.S. v. Blanco, 861 F.2d 773 (2d Cir. 1988), *cert. denied*, 109 S.Ct. 1139 (1989).

27. "Courts Face Threat of 'Brain Drain' As Judges Seek Greener Pastures," *American Bar Association Journal* 66 (January 1980): 19. For a classic study of judges' attitudes, see Stuart Nagel, "Off-the-Bench Judicial Attitudes," in Glendon Schubert, ed., *Judicial Decision-Making* (New York: Free Press, 1963). Chief Justice William H. Rehnquist has urged President Bush and the U.S. Congress to increase federal judges' salaries, warning that current salaries threaten quality. See "Chief Justice Urges Increases in Federal Judges' Salaries," *New York Times*, 2 January 1989, p.7, c.5.

28. Harry Kalven and Hans Zeisel, *The American Jury* (Boston: Little, Brown, 1966).

29. See K. C. Gerbasi et al., "Justice Needs a New Blindfold: A Review of Mock Jury Research," *Psychological Bulletin* 84 (March 1977): 323–345. For a discussion of jury deliberations as a group process, see Murray Levine et al., "The Impact of Rules of Jury Deliberation on Group Development Processes," in Bruce Dennis Sales, ed., *The Trial Process* (New York: Plenum, 1981), pp. 263–304.

30. Lori B. Andrews, "Mind Control in the Courtroom," *Psychology Today* (March 1982): 66–73.

31. For an analysis, see Stuart Nagel, "Decision Theory and Juror Decision-Making," in Sales, ed., *The Trial Process*, pp. 353–386.

32. Duncan v. Louisiana, 391 U.S. 145, 156 (1968).

33. Donald E. Vinson, "The Shadow Jury: An Experiment in Litigation Science," *American Bar Association Journal* 68 (October 1982): 1246.

34. See, for example, James P. Levine, "Jury Toughness: The Impact of Conservatism on Criminal Court Verdicts," *Crime & Delinquency* 29 (January 1983): 71–87.

35. See also John M. Heineke, "Crime, Deterrence, and Choice: Testing the Rational Behavior Hypothesis," *American Sociological Review* 53 (April 1988): 303–305; Douglas A. Smith and Patrick R. Gartin, "Specifying Specific Deterrence: The Influence of Arrest on Future Criminal Activity," *American Sociological Review* 54 (February 1989): 94–105; and Raymond Paternoster, "Decisions to Participate in and Desist From Four Types of Common Delinquency: Deterrence and the Rational Choice Perspective," *Law & Society Review* 23 (no. 1 1989): 7–40.

36. Graeme Newman, *Just and Painful: A Case for the Corporal Punishment of Criminals* (New York: Macmillan, 1983).

37. See, for example, William Green, "Depo-Provera, Castration, and the Probation of Rape Offenders: Statutory and Constitutional Issues," *University of Dayton Law Review* 12 (Fall 1986): 1–26.

38. Bureau of Justice Statistics, *Capital Punishment 1988* (Washington, D.C.: U.S. Department of Justice, July 1989), p. 2, with a 1990 update.

39. Furman v. Georgia, 408 U.S. 238 (1972).

40. Stanford v. Kentucky, 109 S.Ct. 2969 (1989).

41. Penry v. Lynaugh, 109 S.Ct. 2934 (1989), *remanded,* 882 F.2d 141 (5th Cir. 1989). Case citations omitted. The Supreme Court decided several important capital punishment cases in 1990, too late to be discussed in this text, but they should be noted. See Blystone v. Pennsylvania, 110 S. Ct. 1078 (1990), Boyde v. California, 110 S. Ct. 1190 (1990), McKoy v. North Carolina, 110 S. Ct. 1227 (1990), all discussed briefly in *Criminal Justice Newsletter* 21 (15 March 1990): 5–6.

42. For arguments for and against capital punishment, see Ernest van den Haag and John P. Conrad, *The Death Penalty: A Debate* (New York: Plenum, 1983). See also Jan Gorecki, *Capital Punishment: Criminal Law and Social Evolution* (New York: Columbia University Press, 1983); David Lester, *The Death Penalty: Issues and Answers* (Springfield, Ill.: Charles C. Thomas, 1987); and Kenneth C. Haas and James A. Inciardi, eds., *Challenging Capital Punishment: Legal and Social Science Approaches* (Beverly Hills, CA.: Sage, 1988). Finally see the series of articles on the death penalty in *Justice Quarterly* 6 (June 1989): 173–218.

43. "Ending a Killer's Life Might Seem Cheap, but it Takes Millions," *Tallahassee Democrat,* 17 July 1988, reprinted from the *Miami Herald.*

44. See Richard Lempert, "The Effect of Executions on Homicide: A New Look in an Old Light," *Crime & Delinquency* 29 (January 1983): 88–115.

45. William C. Bailey and Ruth D. Peterson, "Police Killings and Capital Punishment: The Post-Furman Period," *Criminology* 25 (February 1987): 1.

46. See Frank P. Williams III et al., "The Public and the Death Penalty: Opinion As An Artifact of Question Type," *Criminal Justice Research Bulletin* 3 (Huntsville, TX.: Sam Houston State University Criminal Justice Center, 1988), for a review of the literature on public opinion on the death penalty.

47. See *Fair and Certain Punishment,* Report of the Twentieth Century Fund Task Force on Criminal Sentencing with a background paper by Alan M. Dershowitz (New York: McGraw-Hill, 1976), pp. 19–20.

48. Bureau of Justice Statistics Bulletin, *Probation and Parole* 1982 (Washington, D.C.: U.S. Government Printing Office, 1983), p. 2.

49. See, for example, Joan Petersilia, *Racial Disparities in the Criminal Justice System* (Santa Monica, CA.: The Rand Corporation, 1983); William Wilbanks, "The Myth of a Racist Criminal Justice System," and Coramae Richey Mann, "The Reality of a Racist Criminal Justice System," in *Racism in the Criminal Justice System: Two Sides of a Controversy* (Huntsville, TX.: Sam Houston State University Criminal Justice Center, 1987); Alexis M. Durham, III, "Justice in Sentencing: the Role of Prior Record of Criminal Involvement," *Journal of Criminal Law & Criminology* 78 (Fall 1987): 614–643; Daniel Georges-Abeyie, ed., *The Criminal Justice System and Blacks* (N.Y.: Clark Boardman, Ltd., 1984); and William Wilbanks, *The Myth of a Racist Criminal Justice System* (Monterey, CA.: Brooks/Cole, 1987).

50. McCleskey v. Kemp, 481 U.S. 279 (1987), footnotes and citations omitted, *reh. den.,* 482 U.S. 920 (1987).

51. For an analysis of state guidelines, see the following on Minnesota's guidelines: Terance D. Miethe and Charles A. Moore, "Officials' Reactions to Sentencing Guidelines," *Journal of Research in Crime and Delinquency* 25 (May 1988): 170–187

52. See the Sentencing Reform Act of 1984 as amended (Act), 18 U.S. Code, Section 3551 *et seq.* (1982 ed., Supp. IV), and 28 U.S. Code, Sections 991–998 (1982 ed., Supp. IV).

53. For a discussion of the constitutional issues, see Lewis J. Liman, "The Constitutional Infirmities of the United States Sentencing Commission," *Yale Law Journal* 96 (1987): 1363–1388. In January 1989 the Supreme Court upheld the constitutionality of the guidelines.

54. U.S. v. Mistretta, 488 U.S. 361 (1989). For recent discussions of state sentencing guidelines, see: John Kramer et al., "Sentencing Guidelines: A Quantitative Comparison of Sentencing Policy in Minnesota, Pennsylvania, and Washington," *Justice Quarterly* 6 (December 1989): 565–589. For a discussion of federal sentencing guidelines, see Ilene H. Nagel, "Foreword: Structuring Sentencing Discretion: The New Federal Sentencing Guidelines," *Journal of Criminal Law & Criminology* 80 (Winter 1990): 883–943; and "Separation of Powers—the Federal Sentencing Commission: Unconstitutional Delegation and Threat to Judicial Impartiality?," *Journal of Criminal Law & Criminology* 80 (Winter 1990): 944–967.

55. For a history of the trend toward determinate sentencing, see R. S. Morrelli et al., *Survey of Mandatory Sentencing in the U.S.—A Summary and Brief Analysis of Mandatory Sentencing Practices in the United States* (Harrisburg: Pennsylvania Commission on Crime and Delinquency, Division of Criminal Justice Statistics, 1981). See also Andrew von Hirsch and Kathleen J. Hanrahan, "Determinate Penalty Systems in America: An Overview," *Crime & Delinquency* 27 (July 1981): 289–316.

56. See David Brewer et al., "Determinate Sentencing in California: The First Year's Experience," *Journal of Research in Crime and Delinquency* 18 (July 1981): 200–231.

57. Joan Petersilia and Peter W. Greenwood, "Mandatory Prison Sentences: Their Projected Effects on Crime and Prison Populations," *Journal of Criminal Law & Criminology* 69 (Winter 1978): 615. See also Malcolm Davies, "Determinate Sentencing Reform in California and Its Impact on the Penal System," *British Journal of Criminology* 25 (January 1985): 1–30.

58. Kenneth Carlson, *Mandatory Sentencing: The Experience of Two States*, Police Briefs, National Institute of Justice (Washington D.C.: U.S. Government Printing Office, 1982), pp. 7, 8, 15.

59. Coker v. Georgia, 433 U.S. 584 (1977).

60. See Baldwin v. Alabama, 472 U.S. 372 (1985); Eddings v. Oklahoma, 455 U.S. 104 (1982); Lockett v. Ohio, 438 U.S. 586 (1978); Zant v. Stephens, 462 U.S. 862 (1983); Barclay v. Florida, 463 U.S. 939 (1983).

61. "Supreme Court Blues," *New York Times*, 4 October 1982, p. 18, col. 1.

62. See "As its Workload Decreases, High Court Shuns New Cases," *New York Times*, 28 November 1989, p. 1, col. 1. For a brief overview of the Court, see William H. Rehnquist, "The Supreme Court: 'The First Hundred Years Were the Hardest,'" *University of Miami Law Review* 42 (January 1988): 475–490. For more detail, see Rehnquist, *The Supreme Court: How It Was, How It is* (N.Y.: William Morrow & Company, Inc., 1987).

63. Chief Justice Fred M. Vinson, quoted in Ronald L. Carlson, *Criminal Justice Procedure*, 2d ed. (Cincinnati: W. H. Anderson, 1978), p. 243.

64. "Supreme Court Upholds Federal Sentencing Reforms," *Criminal Justice Newsletter* 20 (1 February 1989): 1.

65. Bob Woodward and Scott Armstrong, *The Brethren: Inside the Supreme Court* (New York: Simon & Schuster, 1979).

66. Linda Greenhouse, "The Court's Shift to Right," *New York Times*, 7 June 1989, p. 1, col. 1, referring to the case of Martin v. Wilks et al., 109 S. Ct. 2180 (1989), *reh. denied*, 110 S. Ct. 11 (1989). For an assessment of the Reagan years and its potential lasting impact on the Court, see Tony Platt, "U.S. Criminal Justice in the Reagan Era: An Assessment," *Crime and Social Justice* 29 (1988): 58–69.

67. For an analysis of federal courts, see Richard A. Posner, *The Federal Courts: Crisis and Reform* (Cambridge, Mass.: Harvard University Press, 1985).

68. David S. Shrager, "The Myth of the Litigious Society," *Trial* 20 (February 1984): 4. See also Jethro K. Lieberman, *The Litigious Society* (New York: Basic Books, 1981).

69. Bureau of Justice Statistics, *The Growth of Appeals* (Washington, D.C.: U.S. Department of Justice, February 1985), pp. 1–6.

70. Clark v. Florida, 475 U.S. 1134 (1986).

71. 28 U.S. Code, Section 44.133.

72. See Martin Wright and Burt Galaway, eds., *Mediation and Criminal Justice: Victims, Offenders, and Community* (Beverly Hills, CA.: Sage, 1989), and Roger Matthews, ed., *Informal Justice?* (Beverly Hills, CA.: Sage, 1988).

73. Sue Titus Reid, "A Rebuttal to the Attack on the Indeterminate Sentence," *Washington Law Review* 51 (July 1976): 606.

PART V

Social Reaction to Crime: Corrections

CHAPTER 14

This chapter focuses on the evolution of prisons and jails as punishment for offenders. It discusses the historical background of prisons in Europe and in the United States, distinguishes between prisons and jails, and then concentrates on the characteristics of United States prisons today. The central problem of overcrowding is discussed. An analysis of how inmates react to prison incorporates a discussion of the prison socialization process. Prison violence includes self-inflicted violence as well as the more familiar violence against others. This discussion concludes with an overview of prison riots. Problems of maintaining control and order within the prison are briefly discussed, and the chapter closes with an overview of the legal rights of inmates.

OUTLINE

The Confinement of Offenders

KEY TERMS

cruel and unusual punishment
deprivation model
diversion
double celling
hands-off doctrine
importation model
incarceration
jail
offender
penitentiary
prison
prisonization
reformatory
rehabilitation
social system
subculture
transportation

The confinement of offenders as a method of punishment is a relatively recent development. In a previous chapter brief attention was given to corporal and other methods of punishment used historically. Attention has also been given to the classical school of criminology in which writers argued against the harshness of punishments and the methods of ascertaining guilt and called for a more humane approach. Changes in the criminal law were the result. This chapter focuses on the evolution of **incarceration** as the punishment that accompanies the determination of guilt. The following chapter focuses on probation, parole, and community corrections.

THE EMERGENCE OF PRISONS FOR PUNISHMENT

The use of institutions for confining people against their will is ancient. **Jails** and other short-term detention facilities were used for those awaiting trials or sentencing, execution, **transportation** (deportation to other countries as punishment), whipping, or some other form of corporal punishment; but placing **offenders** in an institution for the purpose of punishment is a relatively modern development.[1]

The transition from corporal punishment to **prison** took place in the eighteenth century in many European countries. One of the most cited developments is the English use of prison hulks. The American colonies had rebelled against England's use of the new country for the transportation of criminals; the use of Australia as a penal colony had also run into difficulties. Crime rates were rising, leading to larger numbers of prisoners. Therefore, England legalized the use of hulks, which were usually broken-down war vessels. By 1828 there were 4000 prison hulks, which were characterized by overcrowding, prisoners with contagious diseases, lack of work opportunities, unsanitary conditions, lack of ventilation, and corporal punishment. England used the prison hulks until the middle of the nineteenth century. The use of ships as prisons because of overcrowding is being discussed today in some of our own prison systems.

The prison reform movement in Europe provides a lengthy and fascinating area of study far beyond the scope of this text. But mention must be made of the great prison reformer John Howard (1726–1790), an Englishman who is often credited with the beginnings of the **penitentiary** system. Howard traveled throughout Europe and brought to the attention of the world the sordid conditions under which prisoners were being confined. In 1777 he published his classic book, *State of Prisons,* which was influential in prison reform in Europe and in the United States. Among others, Howard suggested the following changes:

1. Prisons should be built in airy spots near rivers or brooks, which would alleviate the problems of sewers.

2. Every prisoner should have a small room in which to sleep alone.

3. Segregation, especially for women and young offenders, should be instituted.

4. Facilities for bathing and for killing the vermin in inmates' clothing should be provided.

5. Well-trained and honest jailkeepers should be employed and adequately salaried. The fee system, by which inmates had to pay for food and services, should be abolished, along with the custom in some prisons of permitting people to pay a fee to visit prisons for the purpose of amusement.

6. Prison rooms should be cleaned daily, and Howard specified how this was to be done to ensure sanitary conditions.[2]

AMERICAN CONTRIBUTIONS TO THE EMERGENCE OF PRISONS

Despite the existence of prisons in other countries before their emergence in the United States, the new country could claim one unique contribution, at least in theory: the substitution of prison for corporal punishment. Some claim that this idea originated in Europe. Others argue that the prison system actually began with the Newgate prison in Connecticut twenty years prior to the Walnut Street Jail in Philadelphia,[3] but it was the Pennsylvania system that became known throughout the world as the embodiment of the new philosophy.

Development of the Pennsylvania System

In the eighteenth century the Quakers of West Jersey and Pennsylvania substituted incarceration for corporal punishment. Prison was combined with hard labor rather than idleness that had characterized the English hulks. This new system was characterized by solitary confinement of inmates at hard labor.

The Walnut Street Jail

The Walnut Street Jail, which was really a prison, was typical of the institutions in the Pennsylvania system. It was remodeled to comply with the provisions of a 1790 statute that provided for solitary confinement of offenders. This statute was the beginning of the modern prison system in the United States, for it established the philosophy that was the basis for the Pennsylvania and the Auburn prison systems. Inmates worked an eight- to ten-hour day, the work was done in their cells, and they were paid. They also received religious instruction. Inmates were allowed to talk to each other only in the common rooms in the evenings. This plan was followed in some other states with variations. But by 1800 problems with the system were obvious. Crowded facilities made work within individual cells impossible, and there was not enough productive work for the large number of prisoners. The Walnut Street Jail finally failed because of lack of finances, politics, lack of personnel, and overcrowding; but it had already gained recognition throughout the world. It has been called the "birthplace of the prison system, in its present meaning, not only in the United States but throughout the world."[4]

The failure of the Walnut Street Jail and other early American prisons led some to argue for a return to corporal punishment. "By 1820, the viability of the entire prison system was in doubt, and its most dedicated supporters conceded a near total failure. Institutionalization had not only failed to pay its own way, but had also encouraged and educated the criminal to a life of crime."[5]

Prison reformers were able, however, to get Pennsylvania to enact a statute providing for solitary confinement without labor. The first prison, the Western Penitentiary, was opened in Pittsburgh in 1826. But the lack of work opportunities created problems; the law was changed to permit solitary confinement with inmates working in their cells, setting the stage for Cherry Hill and the Pennsylvania System.

Cherry Hill

In 1829 Pennsylvania established a prison named for its location in a cherry orchard. This prison was the first major attempt to implement the Pennsylvania system of solitary confinement of inmates at all times with work provided in the cells. To maintain solitary confinement without endangering the health of the inmates or permitting their escape, the architect designed a prison with seven wings, each connected to a central hub by covered passageways. The single cells had individual outside exercise yards. Inmates were not permitted to see one another even when taken to chapel. The chaplain spoke from the rotunda, with prisoners remaining in their individual cells. The Pennsylvania prison architecture was not popular in this country but became the model for most of Europe. The system that prevailed in this country was the New York plan.

The New York, or Auburn, Prison System

In contrast to the Pennsylvania system, the New York, or Auburn, plan permitted inmates to congregate; but the *silent system* was enforced. The Auburn system was much more economical than the Pennsylvania system. The architecture featured a fortresslike building with a series of tiers set in a hollow frame. The system called for strict enforcement of non-communication. The silent system was enforced by having prisoners eat face to back rather than face to face. They had to stand with arms folded and eyes down so they could not communicate with their hands; they walked in lockstep with a downward gaze. They were further isolated by rules limiting contact with the outside world. When they attended religious functions, they sat in boothlike pews that prevented them from seeing anyone other than the speaker.

Auburn's warden, Captain Elam Lynds, believed in strict discipline, taking the position that reformation could not occur until the spirit of the inmate was broken. By 1821 he was placing dangerous prisoners in solitary confinement for long periods, a practice that led to mental illness, and in some cases, death; others pleaded to be permitted to work. A commission appointed to study the prison recommended abolishing solitary confinement and putting all prisoners to work.

Evaluation of the Auburn and Pennsylvania Systems

Both the Auburn and the Pennsylvania prison systems were based on a belief that inmates would be corrupted by each other. The Pennsylvania system isolated inmates; the New York system permitted congregation but enforced the silent rule. In the Pennsylvania system, the Quaker emphasis on religious training and time for reflection was emphasized, and inmates were expected to read their Bibles and meditate. Corporal punishment was not permitted. The New York system did include corporal punishment. The prison systems also differed in architecture; that of the New York plan was less expensive to build, but the Pennsylvania system was considered more economical to administer. Both systems were quite severe, although it has been argued that both were improvements over the severe punishments that characterized this country and those in Europe before the emergence of the penitentiary. The silent system of the Auburn plan continued until relatively recently since prisons were easier to administer if contacts between inmates were not permitted.

Prison Expansion

In the late 1800s prison populations increased rapidly, and overcrowding was a problem. New prisons were built in the early 1900s, including Attica (New York) in 1931 and Stateville (Illinois) in 1925, both still in use today. Most of the prisons built in the early part of this century followed the Auburn plan of architecture. Some programs were available for inmates, and some work was provided; but the work was based on institutional rather than inmates' needs. Prison products were sold on the open market, a practice later prohibited by statute because of complaints from private industry. Attempts were made to segregate prisoners by classifications such as age, sex, and type of offense. Prison reformers argued that inmates should be treated as individuals and that communication was important. The silent system was abolished and some attempts were made to increase social activities. But by 1935, for most prisoners, "the penitentiary system had again reverted to its original status: punishment and custody."[6]

The 1800s and early 1900s were also characterized by probation and parole; those methods of reacting to offenders are discussed in the next chapter. What is of primary concern here is that the prison concept—which according to many scholars initially emerged as a substitute for corporal punishment and, according to some reformers, as a place for reformation—became a total institution for confinement with little if any emphasis on reformation. Other scholars have argued that even if prisons were initially seen as humanitarian, they evolved as institutions for the political and social manipulation of certain classes of people.[7]

The Reformatory Era

Not all early prisons were penitentiaries. In the 1800s some reformers recognized the need to separate children from adults and women from men and to classify offenders by the seriousness of their offenses. A meeting on October 12, 1870, conducted by penologist Enoch C. Wines, led to the emergence of the **reformatory** system, culminating in the establishment of the Elmira Reformatory in 1876. Elmira became the model for reformatories designed primarily for youthful offenders. Although Elmira was architecturally similar to Auburn, a greater emphasis was placed on education and vocational training. Indeterminate sentences with maximum terms, opportunity for parole, and classification of inmates according to conduct and achievement were the greatest achievements of Elmira.

It was predicted that Elmira would dominate the prison system of the United States. Headed by Superintendent Zebulon R. Brockway, proclaimed by some authorities as the "greatest warden America has ever produced," Elmira "changed the course of corrections by introducing 'scientific reform' and the 'new penology.'"[8] Modern scholars disagree on the place of Elmira in history, but it does seem clear that what was designed to be a reformatory was in fact a prison.

Beginning in 1910 the reformatory system eventually declined, mainly because of the lack of trained personnel to conduct the education and carry on the classification systems adequately. The reformatories were also characterized by some of the techniques for management and discipline characteristic of prisons. Brockway was accused of using "cruel, brutal, excessive and unusual punishment" to achieve his purpose of reforming inmates. A series of investigations led to some recommendations for change, such as the improvement of medical care, reduction of overcrowding, and the restriction of whipping to the buttocks. Serious allegations against Brockway were dropped; he continued to rule at Elmira until 1900, "and the Elmira experiment came to an end just as 'prison science' and the 'new penology' were taking hold across the country."[9] Reformatories continued, but many were really prisons, presenting only an illusion of reformation.

The Modern Era of American Prisons: An Overview

In the past few decades significant attempts have been made to change the nature of incarceration. Many of these attempts are related to the use of alternatives to incarceration, discussed in the next chapter. But changes were also made in prisons themselves. Despite the continued use of many of the fortresslike prisons built in the 1800s and early 1900s, some progressive designs were incorporated into the construction of new prisons. A greater emphasis was placed on **rehabilitation** combined with improved opportunities for education and vocational training. Treatment programs, at least in theory, were proclaimed important. Indeterminate sentences were instituted because of the claim that inmates should not be released until they were reformed; reformation would take place through counseling and training.

Despite these alleged changes, many authorities now recognize that prison reform was often illusory; few real changes occurred, and escapes and riots were increasing. As crime rates increased, rehabilitation was declared a failure. Sentences were lengthened, and prison populations strained prison capacity. As prison conditions deteriorated, federal courts became active in the prisoners' rights movement; but prisons remained. "However costly, brutal, and ineffective it may be as a cure for crime, the penitentiary endures because it has somehow come to seem inevitable."[10]

TYPES OF INSTITUTIONS FOR THE CONFINEMENT OF ADULT OFFENDERS

Adult offenders may be confined in jails, prisons, or community-based facilities. Community-based facilities will be discussed in the next chapter; jails and prisons are the focus here. Jails, prisons, and police lock-ups are distinguished in Exhibit 14.1.

Jails

The Latin root of the term *jail* is *cavea*, meaning "cavity," "cage," or "coop." It has been suggested that jails should be defined as "public cages or coops." Jails are used for short-term confinement of people awaiting trial who have either been denied bail or have been granted bail but were unable to meet its terms. Jails have an impact on far more people than do prisons. The number of people who pass through jails in this country in a given year is at least four times higher than the number of people who are incarcerated in state and federal prisons. The jail is a "major intake center not only for the entire criminal justice system, but also a place of first or last resort for a host of disguised health, welfare, and social prob-

EXHIBIT 14.1

A Comparison of Jails, Prisons, and Lockups

A Jail Is:

- a facility administered, operated, and primarily funded by a county or city;

- a place to detain people who are awaiting trial. Detention occurs after a person has been arrested and charged, but before a trial has been held to determine guilt or innocence. These people are referred to as "pre-trial detainees." They may be detained to await their first court appearance, for bail to be set and made, for trial or for release;

- used to hold people who are to be transferred to a state or federal prison;

- used to hold people who are to be transferred to a state mental hospital, alcohol or drug detoxification facility, or juvenile shelter;

- used to punish people convicted of a minor crime (usually a misdemeanor) and who have been sentenced to (usually) a year or less. The punishment in this case is deprivation of liberty by incarceration in the jail.

A jail may be known locally as a work house, stockade, house of corrections, detention center or correctional institution. In one state—Pennsylvania—jails are called prisons. Also, in six states—Delaware, Alaska, Hawaii, Rhode Island, Vermont, and Connecticut—a combined jail/prison system is operated by the state. These, however, are exceptions to the rule.

A Prison Is:

- not the same thing as a jail;

- a facility administered, operated, and funded by a state or the federal government;

- used to punish people convicted of more serious crimes (usually felonies) and in most states sentenced to more than a year.

Thus, the people in your local facility are "jailed," while those serving time in a state or federal institution have been "imprisoned."

A Lockup Is:

- a facility usually operated by police and located in police station houses or headquarters or in a separate area of the jail building;

- a temporary holding facility. Arrestees are usually held for no more than 48 hours (excluding weekends and holidays) until they are taken before a judge or released;

- used to "dry out" inebriated people;

- used to hold youths until parents can be summoned or another placement arranged.

There are more than 15,000 lockups in cities across the country. However, there has never been a national survey of lockups, and little information is available on their size, conditions or population. Many homeless people or people society cannot easily deal with are held in lockups and the suicide rate in lockups seems, from newspaper reports, to be very high.

SOURCE: *Jails in America: An Overview of Issues* (College Park, Md.: American Correctional Association, 1985), pp. 1, 2. Reprinted by permission of the American Correctional Association.

HIGHLIGHT 14.1

SOME JAIL FACTS

1. 6,200,000 commitments to jail are made each year.

2. 40 percent of the people in jail are awaiting trial—they have not been convicted of a crime.

3. 80 percent of those awaiting trial remain in jail because they are too poor to pay for bail.

4. As many as 25 to 40 percent of the people in jail in some communities are there just for being drunk in public.

5. 600,000 mentally ill people go through our jails each year.

6. 500,000 youngsters under age 18 go through adult jails and lockups each year.

The suicide rate for adults in jail is 16 times greater than for the general public.

70 percent of jail inmates are incarcerated for nonviolent crimes.

9. 45 percent of jail inmates are in 130 large jails in metropolitan areas, while the rest are housed in rural jails.

10. 35 percent of our jails are more than 50 years old.

11. 77 percent of our jails have no medical facilities.

12. 75 percent have no rehabilitation or treatment facilities.

13. 81 percent of jail inmates are housed in less than 60 square feet each (the accepted minimum standard), about the size of two regular mattresses.

14. At least 10 percent of our jails are under court order and many others have litigation pending against them for overcrowding, lack of treatment facilities and other problems.

15. Jails are expensive and you, the taxpayer, pay for them: it

costs an average of $12,000 to house one person in jail for one year, an average of $50,000 to build one new jail bed. New jail construction begun today will ultimately cost two to three times today's estimate due to spiraling user fees, interest rates and inflation.

SOURCE: National Coalition for Jail Reform, pamphlet, "Look at Your Jail," 1828 L Street, N.W., Suite 1200, Washington, D.C. 20036. The National Coalition for Jail Reform, consisting of thirty-six diverse groups, such as the National Sheriffs' Association, the American Bar Association, the National Association of Counties, the Police Foundation, the National Center for State Courts, and the American Correctional Association, is working to solve jail problems and find alternative solutions. Reprinted by permission of the National Coalition for Jail Reform.

lem cases."[11] Highlight 14.1 contains data on the variety of people who are in jails.

History of Jails

Ironically, although the jail is the oldest of the American penal institutions, less is known about it than about any of the others. Except for an occasional scathing commentary, jails have been tolerated but have received little attention. It was not until 1970 that some systematic data on jails became available. At that time the first national jail census was conducted for the Law Enforcement Assistance Administration (LEAA) by the U.S. Bureau of the Census.

Jails may be traced far back into history when they made their debut "in the form of murky dungeons, abysmal pits, unscalable precipices, strong poles or trees, and suspended cages in which hapless prisoners were kept."[12] The main purpose of those jails was to detain people awaiting trial, transportation, the death penalty, or corporal punishment. The old jails were not particularly escape-proof, and the persons in charge often received additional fees for shackling prisoners. Inmates were not separated according to any system of classification, the physical conditions were terrible, the food was inadequate, and no treatment or rehabilitation programs existed.

Although jails in this country were allegedly created as a humane replacement for corporal punishment, in reality, early jails were not humane places. The conditions in American jails worsened over the years. In 1923 Joseph Fishman, a federal prison inspector, investigator, and consultant in the United States, published a book, *Crucible of Crime*, in which he described American jails, basing his descriptions and evaluations on visits to 1500 jails. He said that some of the convicted would ask for a year in prison in preference to six months in jail because of the horrible conditions. Typical of most jails were no space, inadequate meals, no bathing facilities, no hospital, and no separate facilities for juveniles. Fishman's conclusion might be summarized by his definition of jail as

> an unbelievably filthy institution in which are confined men and women serving sentences for misdemeanors and crimes, and men and women not under sentence who are simply awaiting trial. With few exceptions, having no segregation of the unconvicted from the convicted, the well from the diseased, the youngest and most impressionable from the most degraded and hardened. Usually swarming with bedbugs, roaches, lice, and other vermin; has an odor of disinfectant and filth which is appalling; supports in complete idleness thousands of able-bodied men and women, and generally affords ample time and opportunity to assure inmates a complete course in every kind of viciousness and crime. A melting pot in which the worst elements of the raw material in the criminal world are brought forth blended and turned out in absolute perfection.[13]

In 1931, the American jail was described by the National Commission on Law Observance and Enforcement as the "most notorious correctional institution in the world."[14] More recently, the American jail has been described by noted authorities as "the worst blight in American corrections"[15] and a place where "anyone not a criminal when he goes in, will be when he comes out."[16]

Organization and Administration of Jails

The typical jail in the United States is small and was built between 1880 and 1920. There has been little renovation of its physical facilities. It is located in a small town, which is often the county seat of a predominantly rural county. These small rural jails constitute the majority of jails but house only a minority of the jail population. Some of these jails are seldom used, and most are not crowded. Most of the jail population is confined in large urban jails, which have most frequently been the targets of court suits on jail conditions.[17]

The fact that the typical jail is locally financed and administered inevitably involves the jail's administration in local politics. Historically, American jails have been under the direction and supervision of the sheriff, usually an elected official. In general, such administrators have shown little interest in jail inspections or improvements. Recently some states have assumed control of their jails, but in most jails, the standards remain low, and rehabilitative programs are virtually nonexistent.

Staffing jails is a serious problem. The workers receive low pay and usually have little or no training. Jails have low budgets because local governments have less money to spend than state or federal governments do, and jails usually have the lowest priority for local funds. Jails are generally understaffed. This absence of adequate supervision gives the inmates little protection from homosexual and other attacks. The lack of staff also increases the probability that inmates will be successful in suicide attempts. Suicide is the predominant cause of death among jail inmates and generally occurs within the first day of incarceration.[18]

Prisons

Prisons are for the long-term incarceration of offenders. Although the term is frequently used synonymously with maximum security prisons, types of prisons must be distinguished.

Types of Prisons

Maximum security, or *close-custody*, prisons are the most secure. They are usually surrounded by high fences, secured with barbed wire, and watched by armed guards in observation towers. The architecture frequently follows the Auburn plan, with large tiers of cell blocks made up of individual cells housing more than one offender each. These prisons theoretically incarcerate only serious offenders or others who might present a security risk. In reality, less serious offenders may be placed in maximum security prisons.

Medium security prisons are also usually surrounded by fences with barbed wire; armed guards may or may not be present. Housing architecture is more varied than that of the maximum security prison and may even include individual rooms or dormitories rather than cells. Inmates have greater freedom of movement and theoretically are less serious offenders.

Minimum security prisons usually do not have armed guards and many do not have fences or bars. Inmates may be housed in individual

Many prisons and jails are maximum security facilities, with inmates confined behind bars most of the time.

rooms or dormitories and will generally have greater freedom to move about within the institution than in medium or maximum security facilities.

Categories other than security levels may also differentiate prisons. Some are exclusively for women; most are exclusively for men. Some house both sexes, and although inmates in co-correctional prisons are permitted some contact, the rules do not permit sexual relations. Co-correctional prisons exist mainly in the federal system.

Prisons may also be distinguished as *state* or *federal*. It was not until the 1900s that the federal government established a separate prison system. Before that time, long-term federal prisoners were incarcerated in state prisons on a contract basis, whereas short-term federal prisoners were usually incarcerated in local jails, also on a contract basis. Today federal prisons are under the jurisdiction of the Federal Bureau of Prisons.

All states have some type of prison system, although the systems vary considerably. Most states have all levels of security, but all levels are not generally available for female offenders because of their smaller numbers. States differ significantly in the amount of money spent on prisons. In a recent study, the total spent by all states ranged between $4.28 and $4.80 billion in 1985, an average of between $49,550 to $10,700 per inmate. In contrast, that same year the federal government spent an average of $12,500 per inmate in a total operating budget of $7.9 billion.[19] Prison overcrowding exists in most but also varies in degree from state to state.

THE CRISIS OF NUMBERS

The overcrowdedness of many jails and prisons either creates or at least aggravates most of the problems that characterize penal institutions today.

Jail Populations

According to the latest available national data, in midyear 1988, our nation's jails contained 343,569 people, 5 percent more than the previous year and 54 percent more than in 1983. These figures represent 101 percent of the rated capacity of the jails, up from 85 percent in 1983. Fifty-one percent of the 1988 jail population were awaiting trial; the remainder had been convicted and were serving short terms. About 12 percent of the jails were under court orders to reduce their populations. Nine percent of jail inmates were females.[20]

Data from individual jurisdictions indicate an even bleaker picture than some of the national studies. For example, in February of 1988, 550 of the approximately 2400 inmates incarcerated in the Anna M. Kross Jail at Riker's Island, New York, (Riker's Island contains the world's largest jail complex, processing over 100,000 inmates a year) took control of the facility for over three hours in their protest of internal search procedures. Windows were broken; mattresses were burned; and minor injuries occurred although no hostages were taken. Still, as Highlight 14.2 indicates, the uprising "sounded yet another warning about the dangers of jail and prison overcrowding." In some jurisdictions jail overcrowding has led to recommendations to reduce penalties or release inmates early. In 1988 the Tennessee Sentencing Commission recommended reducing the penalties for driving while intoxicated in order to ease jail overcrowding. Drunk driving is one of the nation's most serious problems, resulting in more deaths in a two-year period (50,000) than all lives lost in ten years during the Vietnam War. DUI deaths cause $21 to $24 billion in property

HIGHLIGHT 14.2

JAIL OVERCROWDING TESTS THE INGENUITY OF CITY AND STATE

Last month's uprising in New York City's Rikers Island jail complex, in which 550 inmates seized control of 12 dormitories for three and a half hours, sounded yet another warning about the dangers of jail and prison crowding. Yet at both the city and state levels, the government response so far has amounted to chronic crisis management.

While public officials respond eagerly to demands for rigorous punishment of street criminals, few see any political benefit in support for more efficient management of prisons and other correctional programs. Taxpayers resist the fearsome cost of building secure institutions, and neighborhoods often respond in fury at the merest hint of less expensive—and less secure—work-release or drug-treatment centers.

"There is no constituency for prisons," asserted Thomas Coughlin, New York State's Commissioner of Correctional Services.

The problem afflicts the Fed-eral prison system and nearly all big urban states. Some 36 state systems operate under the supervision of Federal judges, reflecting the failure of electoral politics to manage the clash between the passion for punishment and the reluctance to provide for it. Some local jail complexes suffer the same fate. In 1983, for example, Federal Judge Morris E. Lasker ruled the crowding on Rikers Island in violation of the constitutional ban on cruel and unusual punishment and ordered 611 inmates released. Mayor Koch then found money for dormitory units to expand Rikers from 9,600 beds to 15,000.

As the dormitories filled up—today all 15,000 beds are occupied—Judge Lasker looked less kindly upon city pleas for flexibility in court-imposed crowding limits and threatened to forbid the locking up of any more prisoners.

That led to the costly refurbishing of two old Staten Island ferryboats, now moored at Rikers Island for use as jails, and the purchase of a floating barracks that the English had used to house troops during the Falklands War. The English barracks opened to inmates only recently, after a debate over its suitability for jail use and a court battle provoked by neighbors of its Lower East Side mooring near Montgomery Street.

The city now plans a major new jail on Staten Island in Rossville, adjacent to the Arthur Kill state prison. However, the acquiescence of Staten Island's Borough President, Ralph Lamberti, cost City Hall a promise that it would demand fewer shelters for the homeless in his borough.

Fancy Footwork Required

Richard Koehler, the city's Commissioner of Correction, hopes to buy yet more short-term relief with a plan to release 300 jail inmates, under the supervision of specially trained guards, to drug rehabilitation programs and jobs. The proposal failed in the Legislature last year, but Mr. Koehler

damage each year. But efforts to combat the problem through jail sentences and greater enforcement of DUI ordinances have swelled some jail populations far beyond their capacity.[21]

Prison Populations

As Figure 14.1 indicates, prison populations are much larger today than in previous decades, the sharpest increases occurring in the 1980s. The

HIGHLIGHT 14.2 (Continued)

has made an important revision: The 300 would be dispersed to existing drug programs around the city rather than housed as a group, thereby avoiding a controversy over the location of a new program.

State officials find their ingenuity similarly tested. Back in 1981, with nearly 26,000 inmates stuffing state prisons to 111 percent of capacity, state and city officials joined to promote a bond issue for $500 million to build new state penitentiaries. Despite growing public anger over crime, voters turned down the bond issue.

By the time Mario Cuomo became Governor in January 1983, crowding had increased to 118 percent of capacity. Mr.Cuomo got the Legislature's approval for a $650 million prison building plan, mostly bonded through the state's Urban Development Corporation, a maneuver that avoided the need for voter approval. But by 1987, though prison capacity had increased to more than 36,000, the convict

population had swelled to nearly 40,000.

Now the Cuomo Administration is reluctant to spend money on more prisons. The Governor instead pushed successfully last spring for other kinds of measures to relieve crowding. One resulted in upstate "boot camps" where younger convicts, supervised by "drill instructor" guards, now go through six months of physical work and rehabilitative programs instead of longer traditional prison terms. Another device was "earned eligibility"—a revision of parole practice to permit earlier release of convicts who have completed rehabilitative programs. A third was to make inmates eligible for work release two years before their parole date rather than one.

The package was pushed through the Assembly with the help of Assemblyman Dan Feldman, the Brooklyn Democrat who heads the Committee on Corrections. Mr. Feldman asserts that selective release programs "make people safer"—by insur-

ing that those released have succeeded in a rehabilitative program—"and maybe save the state some money." The Senate resisted the package, then went along when the Assembly approved five prison construction and expansion projects that would benefit communities upstate, where prisons are welcomed because each means as many as 500 recession-proof jobs.

Mr. Coughlin now permits himself to think that "we might have a pretty good handle on population." For the first time in nearly a decade, he points out, the state does not contemplate the need for massive new spending on prison construction. The effectiveness of the new release programs, however, remains to be seen.

SOURCE: David C. Anderson, "Jail Overcrowding Tests the Ingenuity of City and State," *New York Times,* 13 March 1988, p. 6E, col. 1. Copyright © by the New York Times Company. Reprinted by permission.

627,402 figure at the end of 1988 was an increase of 7.4 percent in one year and, of course, a record high prison population for the United States. During 1988, however, prison capacity, both state and federal, grew by only 5.5 percent. Joseph M. Bessette, acting director of the Bureau of Justice Statistics said, "Since 1980, the number of prisoners has grown by about 90 percent and is currently increasing by about 800 per week." Because of prison overcrowding, seventeen states had jails that were holding a

Figure 14.1
Number of Sentenced State and Federal Prisoners,
Year end, 1925-1988

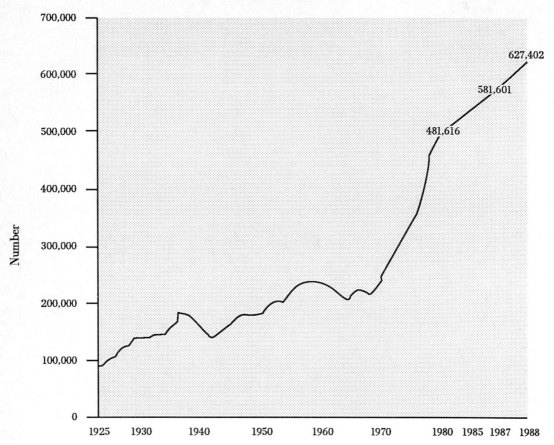

SOURCE: Bureau of Justice Statistics, *State and Federal Prisoners, 1925–1985* (Washington, D.C.: U.S. Department of Justice, October 1986), p. 1, updated from BJS, *Prisoners in 1987* (Washington, D.C.: U.S. Department of Justice, April 1988), p. 1, and *Prisoners in 1988* (April 1989), p. 1.

total of 14,314 inmates who were sentenced to prison but for whom there was no available prison space.[22]

The growth rate continues. Officials at a Washington-based organization that proposes alternatives to incarceration projected that the U.S. prison and jail populations combined (more than 900,000 by the end of 1988) would exceed one million in 1989. "The Soviet Union is the only other nation to have reached that mark."[23] Florida's projected inmate population growth is pictured in Figure 14.2.

Figure 14.2
Florida Inmate Populations and Projections, 1980-1991

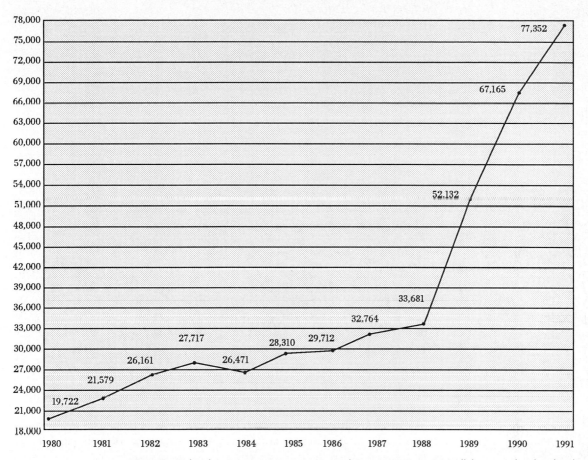

SOURCE: Richard L. Dugger, Secretary, *Annual Report: 1987–1988* (Tallahassee, Florida: Florida Department of Corrections, 1988).

The General Effect of Overcrowding

The general effect of prison overcrowding magnifies the negative aspects of prison life. Crowded prisons have more violence, deaths, and homosexual assaults, as well as more medical complaints, both physical and mental. Crowded conditions lead to more contact among inmates; one study found that inmates were more assertive and aggressive, displayed force more often, were more quick-tempered, and were more bothered by minor incidents. For example, one inmate who did not receive his medication on time stabbed another prisoner several times with a pencil.[24]

Researchers are careful to point out that hostile responses to crowded conditions cannot be attributed solely to the prison environment but that the extreme and intense nature of the reactions is caused by overcrowding. In *Ruiz v. Estelle*, a federal court analyzed the effect of the overcrowded conditions in the Texas Department of Corrections in 1980.[25]

Ruiz v. Estelle

The present extreme levels of overcrowding at TDC are harmful to inmates in a variety of ways, and the resultant injuries are legion. . . .

TDC inmates are routinely subjected to brutality, extortion, and rape at the hands of their cellmates. . . .

The overcrowding at TDC exercises a malignant effect on all aspects of inmate life. Personal living space allotted to inmates is severely restricted. Inmates are in the constant presence of others. . . . Crowded two or three to a cell or in closely packed dormitories, inmates sleep with the knowledge that they may be molested or assaulted by their fellows at any time. Their incremental exposure to disease and infection from other inmates in such narrow confinement cannot be avoided. They must urinate and defecate, unscreened, in the presence of others. Inmates in cells must live and sleep inches away from toilets; many in dormitories face the same situation. There is little respite from these conditions, for the salient fact of existence in TDC prisons is that inmates have wholly inadequate opportunities to escape the overcrowding in their living quarters.

In addition to increased violence, overcrowded prisons may induce stress in both inmates *and* staff and lead to physical and mental problems. Expert witnesses who testified in the Texas Department of Corrections case stated that the overcrowding in that system caused more physical problems among inmates. Disease spread more quickly, and living conditions were less sanitary. Some of the additional physical complaints were attributed to more mental health problems among crowded inmates.

Another contributor to stress in prison is boredom. Most inmates do not work or have access to prison programs. When facilities are overcrowded, the transportation of inmates to and from program sites becomes difficult. Many administrators merely assign inmates more time in their cells rather than cope with moving large numbers around the prison. The prison's educational, recreational, and vocational programs also have long waiting lists. Administrators do not have funds to run enough programs to keep all inmates busy; nor can they hire enough staff to manage large numbers of active inmates. Instead, inmates are expected to spend time in their cells or to do menial maintenance work. Many

One of the effects of prison overcrowding is the lack of work opportunities and vocational training. This inmate, serving a seven-year term for robbery in Massachusetts, is being provided work training and experience as part of a highly successful program that prepares inmates for release and saves the state money.

inmates in U.S. prisons, both state and federal, are confined to their cells for more than ten hours per day.

Solutions to Overcrowding

Many solutions to prison overcrowding have been suggested. Several states have passed statutes granting their governors permission to declare an emergency when prison populations reach a certain level. At that point inmates must be released to provide space for newly convicted offenders. Some jurisdictions have contracted with others to house their surplus inmates, but that is not often a viable option since an increasing number of jails and prisons are overcrowded. As mentioned earlier, some jurisdictions are planning to change or already have changed local ordinances and state statutes to decrease penalties in order to decrease jail and prison populations. Some are seeking funds for renovation and expansion of existing facilities; others are building new facilities. In 1988, 130 new facilities were under construction at an estimated cost of over $2½ billion, providing more than 53,000 additional beds.[26]

Diversion of less serious offenders from jails and prisons to other types of punishment is another solution and is discussed in more detail in the next chapter along with the increased use of home confinement with or without electronic monitoring. Prison administrators often turn to **double celling,** putting more than one inmate in a single cell, to accommodate the extra prisoners. To most of us, sharing a room may not seem a great imposition. Certainly two prisoners per cell would be reasonable. The problem, however, is that many of the cells are too small to accommodate two people under the best of circumstances. In many prisons inmates are rarely out of their cells. Nor is the double celling of inmates analogous to the sharing of dormitory rooms. As the brief excerpt from *Ruiz v. Estelle* indicates, inmates may be brutalized, even raped, by cellmates.

Double celling of inmates has been and should be looked at in the context in which it occurs. The Supreme Court approved double celling in *Rhodes v. Chapman,* involving a relatively new prison in Ohio. But the Court emphasized that in that prison inmates were frequently out of their cells. The cells were reasonably large, well heated and ventilated, many with windows that could be opened, and noise and odors were not a problem. The Supreme Court has also upheld the double celling of jail inmates; but this does not mean that in some circumstances, where inmates are brutalizing one another, where space is inadequate, and where other problems are created by overcrowding, the Court would approve double celling.[27]

Innovative Jail and Prison Financing

The cost of financing jails and prisons is such a problem today that authorities are looking for innovative ways to finance construction and maintenance of facilities as well as the cost of inmates' care. Some states levy a fee on convicted persons with the rates usually higher for serious, compared to minor, offenses. Two experts from Florida proposed the following as a solution to that state's prison overcrowding:

> Special districts established for the construction and operation of correctional facilities dedicated to the incarceration and rehabilitation of third degree felons and perhaps certain of the nonviolent second degree felony offenders who would otherwise be housed in already overcrowded state prisons. The districts we advocate would be overseen by boards appointed from a representative array of officials and citizens, managed by specialists in corrections, constrained by statewide standards adopted and monitored by the Department of Corrections and, not least important . . . financed by an ad valorem tax on taxable property within the district. . . .[28]

Other plans are in effect in Mississippi, where officials say they collect between $4 million and $5 million a year, although the individual fees of $25 and $50 are low. In Idaho all citizens pay a surcharge on their income tax which is used for prison construction. Indiana raises money for its prison capital construction fund by using a portion of the alcoholic beverage tax. Ohio has sold lease-purchase securities to finance prison construction. With the lease-purchase arrangement, the government maintains control; government officials create a nonprofit entity that acts on behalf of the government agency. Another plan is privatization.[29]

Under *privatization* of prisons and jails, a profit-making company finances, builds, and owns the jail or prison with money from private investors. The facility may then be leased to the government to operate, leaving the state (or federal government) with no responsibility for upkeep; in some cases, private industry might also manage the jail or prison.

The media has focused on privatization of jails and prisons, emphasizing some of the potential problems: quality control, accountability, security, and cost. The National Institute of Justice surveyed the situation nationally; isolated the political, administrative, and technical issues; and issued a brief report. It concluded that experimentation is needed but warned about the problem of creating an outmoded system that is run more efficiently rather than bringing some real improvements and new ideas into corrections. "If the latter can be achieved, the emerging interest of the private sector in corrections management can only be welcomed."[30] As for inmates, there is evidence that they really do not care who runs the prisons![31]

REACTIONS TO PRISON LIFE: THE INMATE'S SOCIAL WORLD

There are a variety of ways to deal with the stress created by prison life. Some inmates feel they must be active constantly in order to survive the prison experience. Their activities may include watching television or listening to the radio or stereo, obtaining and using drugs, making alcoholic beverages, lifting weights or other physical activities, cleaning the cell, scheming, or daydreaming.

Inmates must also cope with the physical, social, and psychological problems that result from the worst punishment—the deprivation of liberty. In his now classic study of male inmates, Gresham M. Sykes discussed the moral rejection by the community, (which is a constant threat to the inmate's self-concept); the deprivation of goods and services in a society that values material possessions; the deprivation of heterosexual relationships and the resulting threat to the inmate's masculinity; and the deprivation of security in an inmate population that threatens his safety and sometimes his health and life.[32]

"Rejected, impoverished, and figuratively castrated, the prisoner must face still further indignity in the extensive social control exercised by the custodians."[33] Everything the prisoners do, including the showers they can take and the hours they can sleep, is regulated by the prison staff. Inmates have no autonomy and can show no initiative. Thus they are forced to define themselves as weak, helpless, and dependent, which threatens their self-concepts as adults. The prison system rarely, if ever, permits them to function as adults.

At the same time that the inmates are adjusting to other inmates and to guards, they are also preparing for release from prison. The prison's isolated **social system,** on the one hand, stresses adaptation to the inmate **subculture** and, on the other, preparation for release.

Prisonization: Socialization into the Inmates' System

In 1940, a classic study of the prison community was published by Donald Clemmer, who proposed the concept of prisonization to explain the formation of prisoner subcultures. He defined **prisonization** as "the taking on, in greater or lesser degree, of the folkways, mores, customs, and general culture of the penitentiary." When a new inmate enters prison, he or she also begins the process of prisonization. This process is not the same for all inmates and may be affected by the inmate's personality, environment, and relationships outside prison; whether the inmate joins a primary group in prison; and the degree to which the inmate accepts the codes of prison life.[34] Prisonization may also have an effect on the inmate's adjustment after release.[35]

Clemmer's concept of prisonization was tested empirically by Stanton Wheeler in a study at the Washington State Reformatory. Although Wheeler found strong support for Clemmer's concept, he also found that the degree of prisonization varied according to the phase of an inmate's institutional career, developing along a U-shaped curve. Inmates tended to be more receptive to the institutional values of the outside world during the first period of incarceration (measured at the end of the first six months) and the last period (last six months before release) and less receptive during the middle, or prison career, period (more than six months remaining). In the last six months of incarceration, inmates are anticipating release back into society, and their main reference group shifts from the inmates within the institution to the society outside. Wheeler concluded that Clemmer's concept of prisonization should be reformulated to include the variable of the career phase.[36]

Subsequent researchers have found some support for Wheeler's U-shaped curve of attitudes.[37] In comparing prisonization among male, as compared with female, inmates, other researchers have questioned Wheeler's hypothesis. One study found that although time spent in prison was significantly related to prisonization among women inmates, this was not true among male inmates and that other variables were predictive of prisonization. Among women, attitudes toward race and the police were

Inmate social life is a problem for all, but especially for mothers. In other countries, women are often permitted to keep their babies during their incarceration, but the general practice in this country is that children are not permitted. This woman will have to give up her baby during its first year of infancy.

significant. Among men, the variables of age and attitudes toward law and the judicial system were significant.[38]

The Deprivation and Importation Models

Sociological analyses of the prisonization process and emergence of a prison subculture have followed two models: the **deprivation model** and the **importation model.**

The deprivation model is illustrated by Sykes' position that the inmate subculture is the product of an attempt to adapt to the deprivations imposed by incarceration. Inmates have few alternatives to alleviate their deprivations, loss of status, and degradation. They cannot escape psychologically or physically; they cannot eliminate the pains of imprisonment. Inmates have a choice of either uniting with fellow captives in a spirit of mutual cooperation or withdrawing to seek only the satisfaction of their own needs. In either case, their patterns of behavior are adaptations to the deprivations of their environment.

According to the deprivation model, the inmates' social system is functional in that it enables them to minimize, through cooperation, the pains of imprisonment. For example, the cooperation of inmates in exchanging favors not only removes the opportunity for some to exploit others but also enables them to accept material deprivation more easily. In addition, available goods and services are more easily distributed and shared if the inmates have a cooperative social system. This system also helps resolve the problem of personal security, alleviate the fear of further isolation, and restore the inmate's sense of self-respect and independence.[39]

The importation model is illustrated by the work of John Irwin and Donald Cressey, who maintain that too much emphasis has been placed on the impact of prison on inmates. They argue that the prison subculture is a combination of several types of subcultures that exist outside the prison and are brought by offenders when they enter.[40]

Scholars have found support for each of these models. Charles W. Thomas emphasized in his research that like the rest of us, inmates have a past, a present, and a future, and all are related to the process of prisonization. New inmates face two social systems in prison: the formal organization (resocialization) and the inmate society (prisonization). Both compete for the inmate's allegiance. The goals of the formal organization are custody and confinement: the goal of the inmates is freedom. Because these two social systems conflict, if one succeeds, the other must fail. Since the prison is not a closed system, in explaining the inmate culture, we must examine all these factors: preprison experience, both criminal and noncriminal; expectations of staff and fellow inmates; quality of contacts with persons or groups outside the walls; postprison expectations; and immediate problems of adjustment. The greater the degree of similarity between preprison activities and prison subculture values and attitudes, the more receptive the inmate will be to prisonization. Inmates from the lower, as compared with the higher, social class are more likely to become highly prisonized. Those who have the highest degree of contact with the outside world have the lowest degree of prisonization. Finally, those with a higher degree of prisonization are among those who have the bleakest postprison expectations.[41]

Leo Carroll criticized the deprivation model in his study of race relations in an eastern prison. The model "diverts attention from interrelationships between the prison and the wider society . . . and hence away from issues such as racial violence." Carroll also maintains that the models should not be seen as opposites but may in fact be complementary. According to Carroll, which form of inmate subculture prevails depends on the degree of security and deprivation in the institution. In maximum security prisons with a high degree of security, we would expect the deprivation model to prevail; but in prisons with less security and fewer deprivations, the importation model is more likely to predominate. Carroll's research generally supports the importation model, but he concluded that the model was incomplete.[42]

Other researchers have taken the position that the importation and deprivation models should be integrated, that both are important to explaining the process of prisonization. The cross-cultural studies of Ronald Akers and his colleagues are examples. The functional or adaptation model was only partially supported by their data from several countries and one U.S. jurisdiction. Their data indicated that "the inmate culture varies by whatever differences in organization environment there are from one institution to the next."[43]

This integrative approach has been summarized as follows: "The existence of collective solutions in the inmate culture and social structure is based on the common problems of adjustment to the institution, while the content of those solutions and the tendency to become prisonized are imported from the larger society."[44] It is therefore not sufficient to argue that the importation or deprivation model alone explains the inmate subculture; rather, variables of each are important.

These studies on prisonization serve to reemphasize the need to look at the total social structure, not only of the prison, but also of the preprison and postprison scenes in order to understand the effects of imprisonment on the inmate.[45]

Inmate Gangs

Gang memberships have probably existed in prisons for years, but within the past two decades the violence attributed to gangs has become a serious problem. According to the Director of the Illinois Department of Corrections, "Correctional officers today are becoming dangerously outnumbered by gang-affiliated inmates who attempt to exert their special brand of mayhem on all aspects of prison life." The gangs exist on the outside where they are involved mainly in drugs and violence. Arrests, convictions, and incarcerations of large numbers of these gangs have significantly affected inmate life within Illinois prisons. It is estimated that 80–90 percent of Illinois prison inmates are affiliated with outside street gangs. "If allowed, they influence every conceivable aspect of prison life." Within prison, gang members are involved in drug sales, gambling, sexual exploitation, extortion, and murder. "If prison administrators are not in control of their facilities, the gangs will attempt to exert their influence."[46] Prison gangs are also pervasive in other correctional systems, such as in the states of Texas and California. Gangs are also involved in prison violence.

PRISON VIOLENCE

Another reaction to prison life is violence, including violence against oneself. Prisons are a concentration of potentially violent individuals. It is not unreasonable to expect explosive and bloody behavior from them. The violence among inmates is generally underreported; many inmates are afraid to report incidents for fear of reprisals from other inmates. Administrators want to avoid the criticism that comes with the public reporting of violence in their prisons.

Some prison systems such as the one in Texas, faced with high rates of violence, have taken extra security precautions such as adding more correctional officers, conducting more searches, or instituting lockdown policies. For example, in June 1989 a federal judge declared a state of emergency at the Louisiana State Prison. The number of escapes, suicides, and murders led the judge to conclude that "these problems are so severe that the lives, safety and property of the citizens of the entire state are affected." Noting that it should not be necessary for a federal judge to have to issue such orders, Judge Frank J. Polozola indicated that should "the state fail or refuse to act, this court is again prepared to do so."[47]

Homicides and Suicides

Prison data for 1987 indicate 87 reported homicides in prisons, a 25 percent decrease from 1986, and 135 suicides, an increase of 9.8 percent over 1986.[48] The reasons for self-inflicted violence and suicides are varied. They have been linked to overcrowded institutions, the extended use of solitary confinement, and the psychological consequences of being a victim in prison. Inmates who are threatened with homosexual rape or other violence often become depressed and desperate about their physical safety. The victims may lack the interpersonal skills and resources that would help fend off would-be aggressors. They may be socially isolated. Another factor contributing to the victims' psychological state is the often repeated advice that the only options are "fight or flight." Victims know that if they submit to violence, they will be branded as weak; but if they seek help, they will be branded as snitches or rats. The psychological climate created by violence in prison therefore fosters suicide and self-mutilation.

Inmates who injure themselves are not average prisoners. They are young without histories of drug addiction, past criminal records, or past prison sentences. The inmates' reactions to suicide attempts are to downplay them. Correctional staff also downplay this type of violence because the publicity of self-mutilation, especially when a weapon is used, may reflect lax security measures at the institution. Prison administrators often segregate inmates who threaten or attempt suicide, even though psychologists recommend human contact and communication as the best prevention.[49]

Interpersonal Violence and Homosexual Attacks

Although courts have held that prison officials have a duty to provide reasonable protection of inmates against the violence of other inmates as well as of officials, the protection is not always sufficient. Even when violence is brought to their attention, officials may not take appropriate action.

In men's prisons, interpersonal violence may involve homosexual rape. It is impossible to obtain accurate data on the number of homosexual attacks in institutions and the percentage of inmates who engage in such behavior. Despite the imprecise data, there is a growing body of research on male homosexuality in prison.[50]

Accounts of initiation into prison homosexuality fall into two categories. The first are seduction games, a process that starts when a new prisoner arrives at the institution. The most common seduction game is the loan. An experienced inmate approaches the new prisoner and offers a consumer product that is generally scarce in prison, for example, candy or cigarettes. Eventually the loan is called in, and the inmate is told to pay immediately with double or more interest or become a sexual partner.[51]

The second type of prison violence is much more sudden and unexpected. New inmates may be attacked by two or more prisoners in dormitories or cells upon their arrival. An extensive study of male sexual aggression in prison found that sexual overtures might involve an actual sexual assault, other physical violence, insulting or threatening language, or mere propositions.[52] Violence can be precipitated by the aggressor or by the victim. In the first case, the aggressor plans to use violence to coerce his victim before the incident begins. In the second case, the victim reacts violently to a sexual innuendo or proposition seen as threatening. The proposition may be nothing more than a stare, a sideways glance, or any small invasion of privacy or personal space.[53]

The victim may refuse a sexual advance, and the aggressor may react violently to that refusal, interpreting it as an insult or a challenge to fight. Violence may also erupt when homosexual partners disagree. These arguments are similar to disagreements between heterosexual couples and may pertain to terminating the relationship, allocating power, rejection, or pride. Another type of sexual violence in male prisons concerns arguments between two or more rivals over the sexual favors of a third.

Homosexuality also occurs among female inmates. Although force may be used, the sexual relationship is usually consensual. It appears to develop, in most cases, out of mutual interest and for the purpose of alleviating the depersonalization of the prison and of gaining status. Women seem to be looking for love, interpersonal support, community, family, and social status.[54] For female inmates the homosexual relationship may take the place of the primary group relationships of their preprison lives. Female inmates often form "families," not primarily for sexual purposes, but to simulate the families they left behind or would like to create. For these women, the relationship with other women may not even be sexual, as in the case of male inmates, but rather one of strong emotional ties.[55]

Prison Riots

Prison violence in the extreme results in riots, the most extensive damage to prison property and to the lives of inmates and staff. Although a few

HIGHLIGHT 14.3

SELECTED PRISON VIOLENCE IN THE 1980s

Folsom, California, 1989
One inmate was killed and forty-eight were wounded during one of the most violent periods of the Folsom Prison's history. Guards were able to bring the violence, which began in the exercise yard, under control by firing ten shots into the yard. Officials said the violence was racially caused.

Coxsackie Correctional Facility, New York, 1988
Five guards were held hostage in what officials called a "15 hour reign of terror" at the Coxsackie near Albany, New York. The hostages were taken after a guard and an inmate had had an argument and presumably one had spat on the other in the disciplinary area of the prison. Inmates in that section are confined to their cells twenty-three hours a day

with one hour a day of exercise, during which the incident began. Inmates are permitted to shower only once a week. According to officials, the hostage-taking was not a planned act, and after it occurred, inmates spent fifteen hours trying to decide how to get out of the situation. The guards were assaulted, but none were seriously injured.

Pittsburgh, Pennsylvania, 1987
Rioting that led to arson and injuries to three guards, two firefighters, and twenty-four inmates occurred at the State Correctional Institution of Pittsburgh, a 105-year-old facility that was severely overcrowded at the time. The rioting started after authorities had had to evacuate some inmates from their cells to fight a

fire apparently caused by faulty wiring. Officers fired warning shots to quell the disturbance.

Moundsville, West Virginia, January 1, 1986
On January 1, 1986, inmates in the West Virginia Penitentiary, wielding homemade weapons, took guards hostage and seized control of the prison. Sixteen hostages were taken. Three inmates were killed. Inmates had control of the prison for forty-three hours, during which time they brutalized, tortured, and then killed the inmates they thought were snitches. One inmate, a convicted child molester and murderer, was dragged up and down the cellblock for other inmates to abuse. Inmates, angered by restrictions on contact visits with family and friends and

---

riots occurred in the early periods of our prisons, most riots are relatively recent. These differ from earlier ones in that although they still involve the usual complaints about food and conditions, they are more organized. They have also been quite brutal and destructive, as Highlight 14.3 indicates. In the 1960s, along with the civil rights protests and student demonstrations on campuses, prisoners' rights groups began to multiply. Criminals were viewed as normal persons except for their backgrounds of excessive discrimination and reduced opportunities. Thus, these groups focused on equalizing the legal rights and social circumstances of the prisoner and the free person.[56]

Riots during this time took a dramatic shift. Although prisoners still demanded improvements in medical care, food services, recreational opportunities, disciplinary proceedings, and educational programs, they also questioned the legitimacy of their incarceration and claimed that they were political victims of an unjust and corrupt political system. By this, prisoners meant that they were imprisoned for breaking laws enacted by

HIGHLIGHT 14.3 (Continued)

the cancellation of a Christmas open house, demanded changes in visiting regulations, better meals, better control of the temperature in their cells, better medical facilities, better living conditions, reduced population, permission to wear long hair and mustaches or beards, and an opportunity to negotiate with the governor and director of corrections. The inmates also demanded that they be treated like human beings, "not like trash and animals." The prison had been placed under court order in 1983 because of unconstitutional living conditions and overcrowding.

Santa Fe, New Mexico, 1980

On February 2, 1980, the worst prison riot in American history occurred at the state prison in Santa Fe, New Mexico. For thirty-six hours inmates rioted, burning prison facilities and torturing other inmates. At the end of the riot, thirty-three inmates were dead; the cost of replacing the penitentiary was estimated to be between $60 and $70 million. Survivors reported that inmates were tortured with blowtorches and possibly acetylene torches; some were decapitated; others were slashed and beaten.

The New Mexico riot occurred just three weeks after the completion of a special investigation of the prison. The report indicated that the prison was overcrowded, housing 1,200 persons in a prison designed for a maximum of 900. The prison was understaffed. The guards who were employed were not properly trained and their morale was low, partly because of the low salaries. The investigation was prompted by the escape in December 1979 of eleven prisoners. Management problems were illustrated by the turnover in administration; the prison had had five wardens in five years. The state director of corrections had resigned after the December escapes.

Before the riot in New Mexico, three inmates had filed suit in federal court alleging that their constitutional rights were being violated in the areas of mail and visiting privileges, food, and treatment (both psychological and medical). They also alleged that overcrowding contributed to the increase in general violence within the prison, as well as to homosexual rape.

a political system reflecting the unequal distribution of power in this country and that the sole purpose of the criminal justice system was to protect the entrenched interests of the wealthy and powerful at the expense of the poor and the weak. Prisoners asserted that their crimes were a justifiable retaliation against a society that had denied them opportunities for social and economic gains. Furthermore this denial of basic rights in prison, cruel and disproportionate punishment, racial prejudice, and other violations of the system made prisoners one of America's deprived minorities. Political protest in prisons began when prisoners, like workers and blacks, sought an effective way of expressing their demands and achieving results from the political system.

Prisoners' rights groups helped inmates focus on the expansion of their constitutional rights, better communication between prisoners and the outside world, development of meaningful work with fair wages, and restoration of their normal rights and privileges upon release. Prisoners wanted to emphasize the poor prison conditions in the hope that community sympathy and support would lead to reform. It worked in some instances, but it did not lead to substantial prison reform in most cases. For example, the riot at the Attica Correctional Facility in New York in 1971 resulted in forty-three deaths (thirty-two inmates and eleven correctional employees). This riot was described by the investigation commission as "the bloodiest one-day encounter between Americans since the Civil War." After extensive investigation and considerable litigation, reforms were ordered. But a 1985 federal court judge, hearing another case on Attica, noted that after a peaceful inmate strike about prison conditions, the only thing changed was the flavor of ice cream available for purchase. He also referred to a 1983 study of prison conditions at Attica, a report that concluded,

> The challenge now faced by state and Attica officials is to acknowledge the severity of the conditions at Attica, and to take immediate and decisive steps to correct them. It would be a tragedy of immense proportions if the administration's response is to pretend that the crisis has passed, and to walk away from the fundamental problems.[57]

Civil actions in the Attica case are almost over. In October 1989 seven former Attica inmates (or their estates) were awarded almost $1.3 million in civil damages sustained as a result of their injuries (or deaths) during the Attica uprising. Only one claim is still pending.[58]

CONTROL WITHIN PRISONS: THE ROLE OF GUARDS

In the early prisons, wardens and guards could control inmates and keep prisons secure by separating prisoners and by using brute force. Court interpretations of constitutional rights have changed the methods that may be used for maintaining internal security. But guards still play a crucial role in internal control. They have the most extensive contact and perhaps the greatest impact on inmates; but we know very little about them, as they have seldom been the subject of intensive and systematic analyses.[59]

Guards have attempted to maintain control within prisons by manipulating the inmate social-control system. Some inmates were permitted a certain degree of freedom and power over other inmates and were also permitted some infractions of the rules. In exchange, the privileged inmates used their influence in the inmate social-control system to get other inmates to behave. The system worked rather well, but federal judges have prohibited arrangements whereby inmates have control over jobs or privileges or are granted privileges by guards. These restrictions reflect judicial awareness of the corruption that may occur when guards and inmates are too cooperative.[60]

It is possible that prison reform involving the increased recognition of inmates' rights—including the prohibition of whippings and other physical brutalities and the requirement that inmates have reasonable opportunities to congregate for religious activities, for work, for educational and vocational training, for recreation, and for other social interactions—has increased the probability of physical violence. This is not to suggest that these constitutional rights should be revoked; but that if the result is a breakdown in internal security and control, other measures must be taken. Federal courts have generally required the hiring of additional guards; legislatures have been reluctant to appropriate the funds to do so.

Prison guards have thus been placed in an impossible situation. They must maintain security or lose their jobs. They cannot maintain security by traditional methods, but they are not given sufficient help and training to maintain security by constitutionally approved methods. In their frustration, some have become corrupted by inmates who, for favors, agree to help guards maintain control of other inmates, thus reverting to the older forms of control. Some have resorted to physical coercion. There is some recent evidence that prison administrators have rewarded that behavior with improved assignments and even by promotions.[61] Others have engaged in collective action, demanding better working conditions and higher pay. They have achieved some, although not enough, success in these ventures. Some have sued prison officials for failure to maintain proper working conditions to ensure the safety of guards, particularly those taken as hostages during riots.

Some guards have become cynical, although research indicates that they are less cynical when they are committed to a professional ideology and that therefore they should probably be more involved in the management of prisons.[62] Others emphasize that with the various changes in prisons, they feel "threatened by inmates, misunderstood by superiors, and unsupported by fellow officers. . . . They can no longer do their job because they feel they are no longer in control. The institution is viewed as disordered and adrift, failing to either keep or treat inmates effectively."[63]

This brief discussion of guards indicates one of the problems of changing one aspect of a system without changing another. The recognition of prisoners' rights, long overdue in this country, was done without sufficient preparation of guards and others who work with inmates on a daily basis. There is serious controversy over the resulting problems, and close attention must be given to prisoners' rights. Although many people feel that prisoners "get what they deserve," the federal courts have ruled that even prisons must maintain certain conditions to avoid violation of the Eighth Amendment ban against cruel and unusual punishment.

PRISONERS' LEGAL RIGHTS: AN OVERVIEW

In 1891 a federal court declared that the convicted felon "has as a consequence of his crime, not only forfeited his liberty, but all his personal rights except those which the law in its humanity accords to him. He is for the time being a slave of the state."[64] Thus prison officials could grant privileges to inmates as they deemed proper. Freedom of speech, freedom to worship in one's religious faith, visits from family and friends, incoming and outgoing mail, and all other important aspects of life inside prison could be regulated by officials in their discretion.

The past two decades have seen vast changes in the legal rights of inmates as federal courts have abandoned their earlier **hands-off doctrine** toward prisons. In 1974, in *Wolff v. McDonnell*, the Supreme Court declared, "But though his rights may be diminished by the needs and exigencies of the institutional environment, a prisoner is not wholly stripped of constitutional protections when he is imprisoned for crime. There is no iron curtain drawn between the Constitution and the prisons of this country."[65]

Prior to this decision lower federal courts had already begun hearing cases in which inmates alleged violations of their constitutional rights. Those and subsequent cases have covered virtually every area of life inside prison. The number of cases is immense. The law changes rapidly in this area, and lower federal courts do not always agree on how similar cases should be decided. Thus, there is usually conflict in prison legal rights until the Supreme Court decides an issue. Although the Court has decided relatively few cases in this area, some general points may be made.

It is important to understand that the Supreme Court looks at the total circumstances of a prison environment before deciding whether the alleged conditions violate the inmates' rights. This is why the case law on this subject must be read carefully. In the *Rhodes* case, discussed earlier on the issue of double celling, the Court was looking at a relatively modern prison in which inmates were permitted out of their cells frequently. Double celling might be prohibited under other circumstances, for example, when inmates are not allowed out of their cells and where there have been cases of violence, such as homosexual attacks. Mail privileges might be restricted for inmates who have been corresponding with inmates in other institutions and planning violent attacks. Visits might be restricted in individual cases when inmates have received contraband from their visitors. Freedom to move about the institution may be restricted for all inmates after a riot, particularly until order has been restored and officials have identified the instigators of the riot.

Some, but certainly not all, of the constitutional rights of defendants discussed in this text in earlier chapters have been applied to inmates. In general, inmates have been granted the right to practice their religion, to visit with family and friends, to visit with their attorneys and to address the courts, to have a limited due process hearing in discipline cases, and to be free of unreasonable searches and seizures. They must be provided reasonable medical care, be given a sufficient amount of nutritious food, and be fed and housed in sanitary conditions. They may not be physically abused by guards or other prison officials. Theoretically male and female inmates are entitled to equal protection although they need not be given identical treatment and facilities. Inmates may not be transferred arbitrarily from one institution to another, but transfers may be made when necessary for security or other recognized penal goals.

Inmate rights may be restricted when necessary for internal security. An example of proper restrictions, for example, on inmate visitation, is explained by the Supreme Court in this excerpt from a recent case, *Kentucky Department of Corrections v. Thompson*, decided on May 15, 1989.[66]

Kentucky Department of Corrections v. Thompson

Respondents do not argue—nor can it seriously be contended, in light of our prior cases—that an inmate's interest in unfettered visitation is guaranteed directly by the Due Process Clause. We have rejected the notion "that any change in the conditions of confinement having a substantial adverse impact on the prisoner involved is sufficient to invoke the protections of the Due Process Clause." This is not to say that a valid conviction extinguishes every direct due process protection; "consequences visited on the prisoner that are qualitatively different from the punishment characteristically suffered by a person convicted of crime" may invoke the protections of the Due Process Clause even in the absence of a state-created right. However, "[a]s long as the conditions or degree of confinement to which the prisoner is subjected is within the sentence imposed upon him and is not otherwise violative of the Constitution, the Due Process Clause does not in itself subject an inmate's treatment by prison authorities to judicial oversight." The denial of prison access to a particular visitor "is well within the terms of confinement ordinarily contemplated by a prison sentence," and therefore is not independently protected by the Due Process Clause.

We have held, however, that state law may create enforceable liberty interests in the prison setting. We have found, for example, that certain regulations granted inmates a protected interest in parole, in good-time credits, in freedom from involuntary transfer to a mental hospital, and in freedom from more restrictive forms of confinement within the prison. In contrast, we have found that certain state statutes and regulations did not create a protected liberty interest in transfer to another prison. The fact that certain state-created liberty interests have been found to be entitled to due process protection, while others have not, is not the result of this Court's judgment as to what interests are more significant than others; rather, our method of inquiry in these cases always has been to examine closely the language of the relevant statutes and regulations.

Stated simply, "a State creates a protected liberty interest by placing substantive limitations on official discretion." A State may do this in a number of ways. Neither the drafting of regulations nor their interpretation can be reduced to an exact science. Our past decisions suggest, however, that the most common manner in which a State creates a liberty interest is by establishing "substantive predicates" to govern official decisionmaking, and, further, by mandating the outcome to be reached upon a finding that the relevant criteria have been met. . . .

The regulations and procedures at issue in this case do provide certain "substantive predicates" to guide the decisionmaker. The state procedures provide that a visitor "may be excluded" when, *inter alia,* officials find reasonable grounds to believe that the "visitor's presence in the institution would constitute a clear and probable danger to the institution's security or interfere with [its] orderly operation." Among the more specific reasons listed for denying visitation are the visitor's connection to the inmate's criminal behavior, the visitor's past disruptive behavior or refusal to submit to a search or show proper identification, and the visitor's being under the influence of alcohol or drugs. The Reformatory Procedures are nearly identical, and include a prohibition on a visit from a former reformatory inmate, without the prior approval of the warden. These regulations and procedures contain standards to be applied by a staff member in determining whether to refer a situation to the Duty Officer for resolution, and require the staff member to notify the Duty Officer if the staff member feels that a visitor should not be allowed admittance.

The regulations at issue here, however, lack the requisite relevant mandatory language. They stop short of requiring that a particular result is to be reached upon a finding that the substantive predicates are met. The Reformatory Procedures Memorandum begins with the caveat that "administrative staff reserves the right to allow or disallow visits," and goes on to note that "it is the policy" of the Reformatory "to respect the right of inmates to have visits." This language is not mandatory. Visitors *may* be excluded if they fall within one of the described categories, but they need not be. Nor need visitors fall within one of the described categories in order to be excluded. The overall effect of the regulations is not such that an inmate can reasonably form an objective expectation that a visit would necessarily be allowed absent the occurrence of one of the listed conditions. Or, to state it differently, the regulations are not worded in such a way that an inmate could reasonably expect to enforce them against the prison officials.

The Eighth Amendment prohibition against **cruel and unusual punishment** also applies to prisons. This ruling has been interpreted to mean that inmates may not be subjected to corporal punishment such as whippings, but it does not mean that inmates may not, in appropriate circumstances, be subjected to solitary confinement or other deprivations. Again, the total circumstances must be examined to determine whether the inmate's constitutional rights have been violated. The Court has held that, to be cruel and unusual, conditions "must . . . involve the wanton and unnecessary infliction of pain, [or] be grossly disproportionate to the severity of the crime warranting imprisonment."[67] Further, the Eighth Amendment "must draw its meaning from the evolving standards of decency that mark the progress of a maturing society."[68]

ANALYSIS OF THE RECOGNITION OF PRISONERS' LEGAL RIGHTS

What has been the result of recognizing inmates' legal rights? Clearly there have been improvements in living conditions and changes in many prison rules and regulations. Prison systems have been forced into changes that should have occurred without the necessity of legal intervention. Unfortunately, this movement has been accompanied by the "get tough" sentencing policies that have led to longer sentences and reductions in prison rehabilitative programs and facilities.

Recognition of the rights of inmates has been opposed by some guards and other prison officials who claim it makes their job of maintaining security more difficult. Citizens have resented the costs involved. When inmates burned their law library in Oklahoma, it was not uncommon to hear the comment, "If they burned it, they do not get another one." But provisions must be made for access to courts.

The effects of prison reform on other parts of the criminal justice system must also be recognized. With the recognition of inmates' legal rights has come a significant increase in law suits, with prisoners, who constitute 1.5 percent of our population, filing 15 percent of the total federal law suits. This increases the problems of already overcrowded courts and lengthens the delays that all litigants face in civil courts. That does not mean, however, that we should retrench on our recognition of inmate rights, although it may suggest that some reasonable suggestions are in order for decreasing the number of frivolous lawsuits filed by prisoners and others.

We are left with the basic problem of the conflict that exists between recognizing the constitutional rights of inmates and protecting society.

This brief excerpt from a recent case, *Peterkin v. Jeffes*, summarizes the problem.[69]

Peterkin v. Jeffes

Based on the factual findings before this Court, we conclude that the totality of the conditions comprising the punishment of prisoners under sentence of death at the State Correctional Institutions at Graterford and Huntingdon does not contravene the eighth amendment. We cannot, we believe, emphasize too often that although "'confinement in a prison . . . is a form of punishment subject to scrutiny under the Eighth Amendment standards,'" courts in assessing these claims "must bear in mind that their inquiries 'spring from constitutional requirements and that judicial answers to them must reflect that fact rather than a court's idea of how best to operate a detention facility.'" The primary responsibility for operating prisons belongs to prison administrators, to other state law enforcement officials and to the state legislature. The eighth amendment does not authorize a federal court to second guess their decisions nor is it our role to express our agreement or disagreement with their overall policies or theories of prison administration, as long as we find no constitutional violation.

We recognize, as the Supreme Court has documented, that many "courts have learned from repeated investigation and bitter experience that judicial intervention is *indispensable* if constitutional dictates—not to mention considerations of basic humanity—are to be observed in the prisons." Furthermore, we are in agreement with the Court of Appeals for the Second Circuit that "lengthy segregated confinement of the type considered [in this case], after an inordinate lapse of time, may necessitate periodic review to insure that conditions once constitutional have not become cruel and unusual." For the purposes of this case, however, and carefully considering the Supreme Court's teaching that "the Eighth Amendment 'must draw its meaning from the evolving standards of decency that mark the progress of a maturing society,'" we cannot conclude that the totality of the conditions on Pennsylvania's death rows constitute punishment "grossly disproportionate to the severity of the crime[s]."

CONCLUSION

Beginning with an overview of the evolution of prison as a method of punishment, this chapter focuses on prisons and jails as institutions for confining offenders. Both European and American developments contributed to this evolution. Of particular importance today is the crush of numbers in these facilities. Overcrowding—its extent, its effects, and its potential solutions—was examined.

The chapter then turned to a discussion of the world of the inmate, beginning with the process of socialization in the prison subculture. We discussed whether inmates bring that subculture from the outside or whether it evolves as inmates attempt to adapt to the pains of imprisonment. We also discussed the impact of prison groups on inmate life. Prison violence is an aspect of prison life that receives considerable attention when riots occur, but little attention is given to the internal violence of inmates against each other or against themselves. We looked at the problem of suicide and other forms of self-violence along with homicide. Homosexual attacks were also discussed; but it was noted that among female inmates, homosexuality is usually consensual, not violent. Attention was then given to prison riots, including a brief historical background and an update on some more recent incidents.

Violence within prisons dramatically raises the question of security. How are inmates controlled? This brief discussion focused on the problems of guards, who are responsible for security. The final section contained an overview of prisoners' legal rights, an area of increasing importance and concern both to inmates and to prison officials. In the context of that discussion, areas of prison life such as visitation, mail, access to courts, education, work, physical conditions, medical care, and religion were discussed.

In conclusion, it is important to recognize that the modern prison is an institution in transition. Prison populations are soaring while budgets are being reduced. Prison administrators feel frustrated with their lack of control over prison populations. Other agencies determine how many inmates will be sent to prison and when they will be released. Many techniques used to accommodate large numbers of prisoners have been challenged in the courts, and in some cases, declared unacceptable. Administrators often find interim housing for inmates, such as tents, trailers, or other abandoned buildings.

But these may cause other problems, such as transferring inmates, maintaining proper staff supervision, and provoking lawsuits. Society has not yet made the choices that will be necessary to resolve the problems. Do we want prisons only to punish? Or do we want prisons to educate and train offenders to aid their reintegration into society? Are we going to continue to ignore the problems in prisons until riots, with their extensive destruction of property and human life, force us to look at our institutions? Are we willing to acknowledge that, as a society, we must punish criminals but that we must punish them in a way that does not wreak havoc on society at the termination of that punishment? Do we want to live in constant fear that our next-door neighbor or the person down the block is an ex-convict and that this offender's treatment in prison was so harsh that his or her cynicism and resentment are worse now than before imprisonment? Are we willing to decide to fund correctional systems that will give us back men and women who are less dangerous and better equipped to manage in the free world? It appears that "we must resign ourselves to spending more money on the people we hate most, or find creative, alternative ways to punish criminals who are not so dangerous that they have to be caged with their heads against toilets."[70]

ENDNOTES

1. For a history of the development of prisons, see Harry Elmer Barnes, *The Story of Punishment: A Record of Man's Inhumanity to Man*, 2d rev. ed. (Montclair, N.J.: Patterson Smith, 1972; originally published 1930). For a more recent version, see Herbert A. Johnson, *History of Criminal Justice* (Cincinnati, Ohio: Anderson Publishing Company, 1988).

2. John Howard, cited in George C. Killinger and Paul F. Cromwell, *Penology* (St. Paul, Minn.: West Publishing, 1973), pp. 5–11.

3. See Alexis M. Durham, III, "Newgate of Connecticut: Origins and Early Days of an Early American Prison," *Justice Quarterly* 6 (March 1989): 89–116.

4. Karl Menninger, *The Crime of Punishment* (New York: Viking Press, 1968), p. 222.

5. David J. Rothman, *The Discovery of the Asylum: Social Order in the New Republic* (Boston: Little, Brown, 1971), pp. 92–93.

6. "State Prisons in America, 1787–1937," in Killinger and Cromwell, *Penology*, p. 53.

7. See Richard Quinney, *Criminology*, 2d ed. (Boston: Little, Brown, 1979).

8. See the discussion by Alexander W. Pisciotta, "Scientific Reform: The 'New Penology' at Elmira, 1876–1900," *Crime & Delinquency* 29 (October 1983): 613–630; quotation is on page 613.

9. *Ibid.*, p. 626.

10. James Reed, "Prisons: History," in Sanford H. Kadish, ed., *Encyclopedia of Crime and Justice*, vol. 3 (New York: Free Press, 1983), pp. 1201, 1202.

11. Hans Mattick, "The Contemporary Jails of the United States: An Unknown and Neglected Area of Justice," in Daniel Glaser, ed., *Handbook of Criminology* (Skokie, Ill.: Rand McNally, 1974), pp. 777–781.

12. Edith Elisabeth Flynn, "Jails and Criminal Justice," chap. 2 in Lloyd E. Ohlin, ed., *Prisoners in America* (Englewood Cliffs, N.J.: Prentice-Hall, 1973), p. 49.

13. Joseph F. Fishman, *Crucible of Crime: The Shocking Story of the American Jail* (New York: Cosmopolis Press, 1923), pp. 13–14.

14. National Commission on Law Observance and Enforcement, *Report on Penal Institutions, Probation, and Parole*, Report of the Advisory Committee on Penal Institutions, Probation, and Parole (Washington, D.C.: U.S. Government Printing Office, 1931), p. 273.

15. Daniel Fogel, quoted in "The Scandalous U.S. Jails," *Newsweek*, 18 August 1980, p. 74.

16. Norman Carlson, quoted in the *New York Times*, 5 January 1982, p. B10.

17. For a discussion of the administration of small jails, see Larry G. Mays, "Mayberry Revisited: the Characteristics and Operations of America's Small Jails," *Justice Quarterly* 5 (no. 3, 1988): 421–440.

18. Department of Justice, National Institute of Justice, *American Prisons and Jails, Vol. III: Conditions and Costs of Confinement* (Washington, D.C.: U.S. Government Printing Office, 1980), p. 90. For a recent analysis of jail suicides, see Daniel B. Kennedy and Robert J. Homant, "Predicting Custodial Suicides: Problems with the Use of Profiles," *Justice Quarterly* 5 (no. 3, 1988): 441–456. See also Lindsay M. Hayes and Joseph R. Rowan, *National Study of Jail Suicides: Seven Years Later* (Alexandria, VA.: National Center on Institutions and Alternatives, 1988).

19. Douglas C. McDonald, *The Cost of Corrections: In Search of the Bottom Line* (Santa Monica, CA.: The Rand Corporation, February 1989): 3.

20. Bureau of Justice Statistics, *Jail Inmates 1988* (Washington, D.C.: U.S. Department of Justice, February, 1990, pp. 1, 2, 3, 4. See also Andy Hall, National Institute of Justice, *Systemwide Strategies to Alleviate Jail Crowding* (Washington, D.C.: U.S. Department of Justice, January 1987). For a study of jailed juveniles, see Ira M. Schwartz et al., "The Jailing of Juveniles in Minnesota: A Case Study," *Crime & Delinquency* 34 (April 1988): 133–149.

21. Bureau of Justice Statistics, *Jailing Drunk Drivers: Impact on the Criminal Justice System* (Washington, D.C.: U.S. Department of Justice, November 1984): 1, 2, 3. For a recent analysis of the effects of jail overcrowding, see Richard E. Wener and Christopher Keys, "The Effects of Changes in Jail Population Densities on Crowding, Sick Call, and Spatial Behavior," *Journal of Applied Social Psychology* 18 (August 1988): 852–866.

22. "Prison Population Climbed 7.4% Last Year, to 627,402," *Criminal Justice Newsletter* 20 (1 May 1989): 6.

23. "Inmate Population Predicted to Surpass 1 Million This Year," *Criminal Justice Newsletter* 20 (15 February 1989): 6. Figure 14.2 shows the prison population growth in Florida prisons, along with the projection for 1991.

24. Dale E. Smith, "Crowding and Confinement," chap. 3 in Robert Johnson and Hans Toch, eds., *The Pains of Imprisonment* (Beverly Hills, CA.: Sage Publications, 1982), pp. 45–62. An excellent review of the general problems resulting from overcrowded prisons may be found in *Overcrowded Time: Why Prisons Are So Crowded and What Can Be Done* (New York: Edna McConnell Clark Foundation, 1982).

25. Ruiz v. Estelle, 503 F.Supp. 1265, 1281–1282 (S.D. Texas 1980), *aff'd*, in part 679 F.2d. 1115 (5th cir. 1983); footnotes and citations omitted. In March 1990, the federal judge who presided over this case for a decade agreed that it was time to close the office of the special master who was charged with monitoring the Texas Prison System.

26. George M. Camp and Camille Graham Camp, *The Corrections Yearbook 1988* (South Salem, N.Y.: Criminal Justice Institute, 1988), p. 26.

27. Rhodes v. Chapman, 452 U.S. 337 (1981). See also Bell v. Wolfish, 441 U.S. 520 (1979).

28. Charles E. Miner, Jr. and Laurin A. Wollan, Jr., "Special Corrections Districts: A Solution to State Prison Overcrowding?" *Florida Bar Journal* (April 1989): 15.

29. Charles B. Dewitt, *Ohio's New Approach to Prison and Jail Financing* (Washington, D.C.: U.S. Department of Justice, July 1986), p. 1. For a history of privatization, see Alexis M. Durham III, "Rehabilitation and Correctional Privatization: Observations on the 19th Century Experience and Implications for

Modern Corrections," *Federal Probation* 53 (March 1989): 43–52, and Durham, "Origins of Interest in the Privatization of Punishment: The Nineteenth and Twentieth Century American Experience," *Criminology* 27 (February 1989): 107–140.

30. Jane Mullen, *Corrections and the Private Sector*, National Institute of Justice (Washington, D.C.: U.S. Department of Justice, March 1985), p. 7. For a discussion of financial and other problems that may arise with privatization, see "Privatization of Corrections: Is the State on a Limb When the Company Goes Bankrupt?" *Vanderbilt Law Review* 41 (March 1988): 317–341. For an overview on privatization, see Barbara J. Auerbach et al., *Work in American Prisons: the Private Sector Gets Involved* (Washington, D.C.: U.S. General Accounting Office, 1988).

31. See Samuel Jan Braker, "Prison Management, Private Enterprise Style: the Inmates' Evaluation," *New England Journal on Criminal and Civil Confinement* 14 (1988): 175–244.

32. Gresham M. Sykes, *The Society of Captives* (Princeton, N.J.: Princeton University Press, 1958), pp. 63–83.

33. Gresham M. Sykes and Sheldon L. Messinger, "The Inmate Social System," in Richard A. Cloward et al., eds., *Theoretical Studies in Social Organization of the Prison* (New York: Social Science Research Council, 1960), p. 15.

34. Donald Clemmer, *The Prison Community*, 1940 reprint ed. (New York: Holt, Rinehart and Winston, 1958), pp. 298–301.

35. See Robert J. Homant and Douglas G. Dean, "The Effect of Prisonization and Self Esteem on Inmates' Career Maturity," *Journal of Offender Counseling, Services & Rehabilitation* 12 (Spring/Summer 1988): 19–40. For a general analysis of inmate problems in coping with imprisonment, see Edward Zamble and Frank J. Porporino, *Coping, Behavior, and Adaptation in Prison Inmates* (Secaucus, N.J.: Springer–Verlag, 1988).

36. Stanton Wheeler, "Socialization in Correctional Communities," *American Sociological Review* 26 (October 1961): 697–712.

37. See, for example, Peter G. Garabedian, "Social Roles and Processes of Socialization in the Prison Community," *Social Problems* 11 (Fall 1963): 139–152; Daniel Glaser, *The Effectiveness of a Prison and Parole System*, abridged ed. (Indianapolis: Bobbs-Merrill, 1969).

38. Geoffrey P. Alpert et al., "A Comparative Look at Prisonization: Sex and Prison Culture," *Quarterly Journal of Corrections* 1 (Summer 1977): 29–34.

39. Sykes and Messinger, "The Inmate Social System," p. 17.

40. John Irwin and Donald R. Cressey, "Thieves, Convicts and the Inmate Culture," *Social Problems* 19 (Fall 1962): 142–155. For a discussion of the impact that traditional roles of women in our society have on the inmate culture, see Rose Giallombardo, *Society of Women: A Study of a Woman's Prison* (New York: John Wiley, 1966).

41. Charles W. Thomas, "Prisonization or Resocialization: A Study of External Factors Associated with the Impact of Imprisonment," *Journal of Research in Crime and Delinquency* 10 (January 1975): 13–21.

42. Leo Carroll, "Race and Three Forms of Prisoner Power: Confrontation, Censoriousness, and the Corruption of Authority," in C. Ronald Huff, ed., *Contemporary Corrections: Social Control and Conflict* (Beverly Hills, CA.: Sage Publications, 1977), p. 40. See also Leo Carroll, *Hacks, Blacks, and Cons: Race Relations in a Maximum Security Prison* (Lexington, Mass.: D. C. Heath, 1974).

43. Ronald L. Akers et al., "Prisonization in Five Countries: Type of Prison and Inmate Characteristics," *Criminology* 14 (February 1977): 538.

44. Charles W. Thomas, quoted in Akers et al., "Prisonization," p. 548. See also Charles W. Thomas et al., "Structural and Social Psychological Correlates of Prisonization," *Criminology* 16 (November 1978); 390–391; Charles W. Thomas and David M. Petersen, *Prison Organization and Inmate Structures* (Indianapolis: Bobbs-Merrill, 1977).

45. For a discussion of criticisms of prisonization, see Gordon Hawkins, *The Prison: Policy and Practice* (Chicago: University of Chicago Press, 1976), pp. 63–80. For an excellent review of the literature on prison communities or subcultures, see Lee H. Bowker, *Prisoner Subcultures* (Lexington, Mass.: D. C. Heath, 1977).

46. Michael P. Lane, "Inmate Gangs," *Corrections Today* 51 (July 1989): 98, 99. See also David K. v. Lane, 839 F.2d 1265 (7th Cir. 1988).

47. "U.S. Judge Declares State of Emergency at La. Prison," *Atlanta Journal and Constitution*, 23 June 1989, p. A4, col. 1. For a discussion on prison violence and other problems, see the recently published book by Mark S. Fleisher, *Warehousing Violence* (Beverly Hills, CA.: Sage, 1989).

48. George Camp and Camille Camp, *The Corrections Yearbook 1988* (South Salem, N.Y.: Criminal Justice Institute, 1988), p. 19. See also Daniel B. Kennedy and Robert J. Homant, "Predicting Custodial Suicides: Problems with the Use of Profiles," *Justice Quarterly* 5 (September 1988): 441–456.

49. Hans Toch, "A Psychological View of Prison Violence," chap. 4 in Albert K. Cohen et al., eds., *Prison Violence* (Lexington, Mass.: D. C. Heath, 1976), pp. 45, 49.

50. See, for example, Joseph Fishman, *Sex in Prison* (New York: National Library Press, 1934); Peter C. Buffum, *Homosexuality in Prisons* (Washington, D.C.: U.S. Government Printing Office, 1972); John Gagnon and William Simon, "The Social Meaning of Prison Homosexuality," *Federal Probation* 32 (March 1968), 23–29; Alice Propper, *Prison Homosexuality* (Lexington, Mass.: D. C. Heath, 1980); and Daniel Lockwood, *Prison Sexual Violence* (New York: Elsevier, 1980).

51. For an extended discussion of introductory homosexual rituals, see Carl Weiss and David James Friar, *Terror in the Prisons: Homosexual Rape and Why Society Condones It* (Indianapolis: Bobbs-Merrill, 1974), pp. 68–79.

52. Lockwood, *Prison Sexual Violence*, pp. 16–23.

53. Daniel Lockwood, "Reducing Prison Sexual Violence," chap. 15 in Johnson and Toch, eds., *The Pains of Imprisonment*, pp. 257–265.

54. See David A. Ward and Gene G. Kassebaum, "Women in Prison," in Robert M. Carter et al., eds., *Correctional Institutions* (Philadelphia: Lippincott, 1972), pp. 217–219.

55. See Giallombardo, *Society of Women*, and David Ward and Gene Kassebaum, "Sexual Tensions in a Women's Prison," in Leon Radzinowicz and Marvin E. Wolfgang, eds., *Crime and Justice: The Criminal in Confinement* (New York: Basic Books, 1971), pp. 146–155.

56. John Irwin, *Prisons in Turmoil* (Boston: Little, Brown, 1980), pp. 94–98.

57. Appendix A of Abdul Wali v. Coughlin, 754 F.2d 1015 (2d Cir. 1985), *disapproved by* O'Lone v. Estate of Shabazz, 482 U.S. 342 (1987), *on remand*, Appeal of Shabazz, 829 F.2d 32 (3rd Cir. 1987).

58. "Court Awards $1.3 Million to Inmates Injured at Attica," *New York Times*, 26 October 1989, p. 14, col. 1.

59. For a collection of materials on prison guards, see Ben M. Crouch, ed., *The*

Keepers: Prison Guards and Contemporary Corrections (Springfield, Ill.: Chas. C Thomas, 1980).

60. Earlier studies, such as the one by Gresham Sykes, illustrated the problem. Gresham M. Sykes, *The Society of Captives* (Princeton: Princeton University Press, 1958). For a recent test of Sykes' position, see Daniel Glaser and Lincoln J. Fry, "Corruption of Prison Staff in Inmate Discipline," *Journal of Offender Counseling, Services & Rehabilitation* 12 (Fall/Winter, 1987): 27–38.

61. See James W. Marquart, "Prison Guards and the Use of Physical Coercion on a Mechanism of Prisoner Control," *Criminology* 24 (no. 2 1986): 347–360. For a recent analysis of stress among prison guards, see Gilles Launay and Primrose J. Fielding, "Stress Among Prison Officers: Some Empirical Evidence Based on Self Report," *The Howard Journal* 28 (May 1989): 138–147.

62. See Robert M. Regoli, Eric D. Poole, and Roy Lotz, "An Empirical Assessment of the Effect of Professionalism on Cynicism Among Prison Guards," *Sociological Spectrum* 1 (1981): 53–65.

63. Eric D. Poole and Robert M. Regoli, "Alienation in Prison: An Examination of the Work Relations of Prison Guards," *Criminology* 19 (August 1981): 251–270; quotation is on p. 268. See also Stephen Walters, "Correctional Officers' Perceptions of Powerlessness," *Journal of Crime & Justice* 11 (1988): 47–59.

64. Ruffin v. Commonwealth, 62 Va. 790, 796 (1871).

65. Wolff v. McDonnell, 418 U.S. 539 (1974), *rev'd in part,* Bell v. Wolfish, 441 U.S. 520 (1979).

66. Kentucky Dept. of Corrections v. Thompson, 109 S. Ct. 1904 (1989), citations and footnotes omitted.

67. Rhodes v. Chapman, 452 U.S. 337 (1981).

68. Trop v. Dulles, 356 U.S. 86 (1958).

69. Peterkin v. Jeffes, 855 F.2d 1021 (3rd Cir. 1988), citations omitted, *on remand,* LEXIS 13828 (E.D. Pa. 1989).

70. Richard Reeves, "High Price of Punishing Criminals," *Tulsa World,* 27 June 1982, p. 13, col. 3.

CHAPTER 15

This final chapter examines the practice of handling offenders within the community rather than within closed institutions. Many offenders are not sentenced to jail or prisons; most who are incarcerated return to society, and they and society should be prepared for that event. If they are not prepared—or if we refuse to allow them to succeed upon their return—we can expect that many will return to a life of crime. Perhaps some will be criminal no matter what we do. Perhaps others can be successfully integrated into law-abiding society.

This chapter focuses on the methods for handling offenders within the community. After an overview of the problems of incarcerating offenders, the discussion proceeds to a contrast of diversion, probation, community corrections, and parole. The chapter then focuses on the two major systems under which offenders are supervised within the community: probation and parole.

OUTLINE

Corrections in the Community

Previous chapters trace the emergence of prisons and the changes in philosophies of punishment and imprisonment. Early reformers thought that offenders should be incarcerated in total institutions. Removal from home and society was seen as necessary to remove the evil influences that had led to criminal behavior. While incarcerated, offenders would have time to think and reflect on their behavior and become involved in religious services and other efforts at reformation.

Before long, however, prison reformers were declaring that incarceration in total institutions did not reduce criminal activity after the offenders were released and that it also exacerbated the existing problems of those who had served time. In 1777, reformer John Howard referred to prisons as "seats and seminaries of idleness and every vice." In prison, "by the greatest possible degree of misery, you produce the greatest possible degree of wickedness." In 1864, Jeremy Bentham declared that most prisons "include every imaginable means of infecting both body and mind . . . an ordinary prison is a school in which wickedness is taught. . . . All the inmates raise themselves to the level of the worst." In 1890 the English prison system was described as "a manufactory of lunatics and criminals." In 1922 the process of imprisonment was described as "a progressive weakening of the mental powers and of a deterioration of the character in a way which renders the prisoner less fit for useful social life, more predisposed to crime, and in consequence more liable to reconviction."

These early declarations have been described as conclusions without evidence;[1] yet as we saw in the previous chapter, there is evidence that modern prisons have also failed. The impact of incarceration in total institutions in this century has been described by sociologists as follows:

> Despite an enormous investment of time, energy, and money, no approach, treatment, or rehabilitative framework has been demonstrably successful in preventing, reducing, and controlling recidivism. So great has been our failure in altering antisocial patterns and life styles that the entire people-changing enterprise has been condemned as both ineffective and, worse, unjust. Many, if not all, seriously concerned behaviorists now firmly believe that the total institution is an historical aberration and must be eliminated with all due haste.[2]

In 1973, the National Advisory Commission on Criminal Justice Standards and Goals called for an increased emphasis on probation, already the most frequently used form of sentencing. The commission concluded, "The most hopeful move toward effective corrections is to continue and strengthen the trend away from confining people in institutions and toward supervising them in the community."[3] During the 1970s, the key word in corrections appeared to be the **reintegration** of the offender into society. Nevertheless, in the past few years we have moved away from a philosophy of **rehabilitation** and reintegration to one of **retribution** and **just deserts.** With that movement, rates of incarceration in total institutions have been increased to the point that most states are currently under court orders to reduce their prison and jail populations.

Chapter 14 discusses some of the obvious methods for solving overcrowding: building new facilities or converting others. These methods are, however, very expensive. As soon as new and larger facilities are available, they tend to be filled. Another method for handling prison overcrowding is early release of incarcerated offenders. Some states have enacted legislation that permits early release when the prison system is overcrowded. The statutes vary in required procedures, but they are all aimed at permitting administrative and executive solutions to prison emergencies.

Other solutions to overcrowding are to decrease the number of people initially incarcerated. That is usually accomplished by diverting the offender from the criminal justice system to other institutions, such as alcohol and drug treatment programs; imposing fines, restitution, or community work sentences in place of a prison term; or placing the offender on probation. All these procedures are controversial, but all also have positive features that should be addressed.

DIVERSION

When the President's Commission on Law Enforcement and the Administration of Justice issued its final reports in 1967, it emphasized the need to divert many offenders from jails and prisons. According to the commission, "For a great many offenders . . . corrections does not correct. Indeed, experts are increasingly coming to feel that the conditions under which many offenders are handled, particularly in institutions, are often a positive detriment to rehabilitation."[4] Even with the current climate, emphasizing punishment instead of rehabilitation, the possibility that incarceration is detrimental to an offender, and thus to society upon his or her release, leads many to suggest alternatives.

Technically **diversion** is meant to funnel the offender away from the criminal justice system and into community programs that might be more beneficial than incarceration. The concept is also frequently used to refer to release of the accused pending trial or pretrial diversion. Diversion has most frequently been utilized in the juvenile system, where offenders have historically been handled with less formality than is characteristic of the adult criminal court system. In the late 1960s and throughout the 1970s, diversion was a popular concept. Many diversionary programs developed; most focused on juveniles, but some provided services for adults. Adult offenders with alcohol and drug problems were typical targets. Evaluation of these programs, however, frequently indicated that instead of diversion, the programs were actually widening the net, capturing people who would not have previously been processed through the criminal court system. A foreigner who came to this country to study our diversionary programs, with the possibility of using the information in his own country, concluded that of the five programs he observed in California, "There was little actual diversion; instead, the projects were largely an extension of the justice system."[5]

To achieve real diversion, we need to

1. view prison as a finite resource,

2. reduce the number of people sent to prison, and

3. reduce the length of stay of select inmates.[6]

But since we are not doing any of the above, real diversion has not and should not be expected to occur in the near future. Thus, other alternatives are needed, and community corrections is one suggested solution.

COMMUNITY CORRECTIONS: AN ATTEMPT AT REINTEGRATION

The emphasis on diversion was accompanied by an emphasis on helping the offender who did serve time to reintegrate into the community. *Reintegration* may be defined as

> the process of preparing both the community and offender for the latter's return as a productive and accepted citizen. . . . The emphasis is on creating the circumstances around him that will enable him to lead a satisfying and law-abiding life. In the reintegration model, corrections must bring about change in the offender, within his family, among his peers, and in the institutions within which he must function successfully—that is, in his social environment.[7]

Types of Community Correctional Facilities

When we talk about **community-based corrections,** we must distinguish such facilities and programs from those that may be located in the community but are not, strictly speaking, community based. For example, the old chain gangs worked in the community, but obviously this is not what is meant by community corrections. The degree to which a correctional system is community based can be measured by the frequency, quality, and duration of community relationships as well as by the number of commitments to large state institutions, the extent to which other community services are used, and the degree of involvement by local groups and individuals.[8]

Community correctional centers comprise a wide variety of programs, from secure restraint in residential programs to nonsecure residential **halfway houses** to nonresidential programs. The distinguishing characteristics of community correctional centers generally are these:

1. The center is not located in a rural area but is in a larger community where participants live and sometimes work.

2. The correctional responsibility rests with a county or municipal political subdivision rather than with the state.

3. Offenders have considerable responsibility for working out their own treatment programs.

4. Community correctional centers are generally small and have limited budgets.

5. Most include representatives from the community who assist in the programs.

6. The emphasis is generally on establishing successful relationships in the community, with family, peers, or employers.

7. Offenders, though not in institutions, do have some degree of restraint.[9]

Exhibit 15.1 lists some types of community residential settings along with their relative degree of freedom for inmates.

The Minnesota Community Corrections Plan

The correctional system in Minnesota is an example of a joint effort between the community and the offender to reintegrate or maintain that offender in the community.

Under the Minnesota plan, counties and groups of counties are encouraged to institute local programs for all but the most serious adult offenders and for all juvenile offenders. Counties receive a state subsidy determined by a formula based on the county's correctional needs, population, and financial resources, minus the projected costs for the number of people that the county would commit to state institutions. For each eligible offender sent to a state institution, there is a charge-back from the state subsidy given to the community, which operates as a powerful incentive for the use of community corrections rather than commitment to a state institution.[10]

But the community-based corrections program in Minnesota has not been as successful as hoped. First, the extended budget savings to the Department of Corrections did not materialize. Second, there was no improvement in public protection, although the plan did not increase security risks to the community. There were also noted improvements in local correctional planning and administration along with many new community programs with expanded and high-quality services. These included delinquency prevention programs, school programs, group

EXHIBIT 15.1

Degree of Freedom in Community Residential Settings

COMMUNITY LIVING

private family placement of individuals (foster family care)

homelike setting for a small number of clients, ready access to community (group home, "mom and pop" halfway house)

homelike setting for larger number of clients, ready access to community (halfway house)

quasi-institutional setting with some degree of privacy, ready access to community (program housed in such facilities as a YMCA)

quasi-institutional setting with impersonal living arrangements, often with dormitory housing, ready access to community (prerelease center, work release center)

quasi-institutional setting with impersonal living arrangements, access to community often denied, especially to new residents (therapeutic community)

OPEN OR NONSECURE (UNLOCKED)
CLOSED (LOCKED)

institutional setting, separate from other types of incarcerated individuals (independent work release facility, separate work release dormitory in larger institution)

institutional setting, contact with other types of incarcerated individuals (work release program in smaller institution)

INCARCERATION

SOURCE: Stanley L. Stewart, "Conceptualizing Community Residential Programs—Variety in Unity," *Community Corrections* (College Park, Md.: American Correctional Association, May 1981), p. 8. Reprinted by permission of the American Correctional Association.

houses, drug and alcohol treatment centers, pretrial services, diversion programs, jail treatment programs, and victim-witness programs. There was a significant drop of 29.5 percent in the rate of commitments to juvenile institutions. There was also an increase in the severity of sentences. The use of probation declined; but probation with a condition of jail time rose, and, therefore, there were more commitments to local jails.

The Minnesota plan did not achieve one of its major goals: the reduction of the state's inmate populations. When the plan was instituted, there was a revival in public attitudes favoring incarceration for criminals. This get-tough attitude in turn affected the judges, who changed their sentencing practices to conform to community opinion. Thus, a major flaw in the plan was the control given to the judges. Any judge who continued to sentence felons to state institutions could virtually eliminate the county subsidy through the charge-back program. To remedy this problem, the Minnesota Sentencing Guidelines Commission provided guidelines for the judges on the length of sentences and whether they should be state or community sentences. The guidelines are adjusted each year to reflect the current inmate population and, in effect, set a cap on arrivals at the state's prisons.[11]

The California Plan

California voters enacted legislation that permits local governments to enter into a long-term financial plan with the state. The state will finance the construction of small, local custody centers for parole violators and other minimum-custody offenders. This financing may also include a margin of profit for the locality. After twenty years the facility is owned by the local unit and can be used for any purpose, but during the twenty-year period, it must be used as a community correctional facility. The purpose of the California statute is to help alleviate prison overcrowding. By utilizing these community facilities, the state can avoid returning many parole violators to prisons, thus leaving prison beds for more serious offenders. At the same time, the facility and its programs will provide jobs for the local economy. In his description of one facility located in Coalinga, California, one authority said:

> Providing secure housing and outstanding prerelease programs, it will help address statewide correctional needs. Adding income and jobs to the local economy, it will be a positive and beneficial force in the local community.[12]

Residential versus Nonresidential Facilities

Many of the earlier community-based treatment facilities, especially those designed for juveniles, were residential centers. Foster homes and group homes were common. A number of these treatment programs have been evaluated.[13] More recently attention has been given to the development of *nonresidential* treatment facilities.

One proposal for adult nonresidential treatment is the *nonresidential state-run work facility* (NRWF). This program entails the development of a state industrial site where offenders report for work each day while living at home. A percentage of the offenders' wages is withheld for restitution payments to victims. Nonviolent offenders are given the choice of prison or NRWF. If offenders commit crimes or violate work rules while participating in NRWF, the remainder of their sentences will be served in a prison.

Proponents of NRWF argue that it implements the basic philosophies of punishment. The restriction of freedom and the partial use of wages for fines and restitution mean that the plan has deterrent value. The plan also ensures just deserts, as the length of the sentence and the extent of the fine or restitution are proportional to the offense. Incapacitation is accomplished because the offenders are under intensive supervision. Finally, unlike many other forms of punishment, NRWF rehabilitates offenders by permitting them to continue working, remain with their families, and assume responsibility for their behavior by paying for the harm they have caused their victims and/or society. Other arguments in favor of NRWF include equity (all offenders have the same working conditions and deduction from their pay), restitution (to individual victims or to a state victim-restitution fund), flexibility (the industry can adapt to fewer or more offenders and judges are not hampered by the lack of prison space), reintegration (the offender stays in the community), cost (NRWF is self-supporting), and humaneness (NRWF avoids the overcrowding and violence of prisons).[14]

PROBATION AND PAROLE: AN OVERVIEW

Probation and parole have been the most frequently used alternatives to prison and probably the most controversial. **Probation** is a judicial determination that does not involve confinement but does involve conditions imposed by the court. In both of these characteristics, it resembles the suspended sentence. The two are distinguished, however, by a third characteristic of probation—supervision, usually by a **probation officer.** The term *probation* also refers to the status of a person placed on probation, to the subsystem of the criminal justice system that handles this disposition of offenders, and to a process that involves the activities of the probation system: preparing reports, supervising probationers, and providing or obtaining services for them.

Parole refers to the release of offenders from correctional facilities after they have served part of their sentences. It is distinguished from unconditional release in that the parolee is placed under supervision of the state, and conditions are imposed on his or her behavior. When offenders are released unconditionally from a correctional facility, the state no longer has jurisdiction to supervise their behavior. Unconditional release may occur after the entire sentence has been served or after a portion of the sentence has been served and the remainder waived because of **good-time credits** the inmate has accrued.

Data on Probation and Parole

In 1967 when the President's Commission of Law Enforcement reported its findings and recommendations on the criminal justice system, slightly more than one-half of the convicted offenders in this country were placed on probation. In 1973 the National Advisory Commission on Criminal Justice Standards and Goals claimed that probation was the most effective alternative to confinement. The commission also pointed out that parole was the most frequent form of release from prison and that it was likely to become more important in the future.

Since 1967 the percentage of offenders on probation has increased much faster than the percentage of offenders incarcerated. A National Institute of Justice (NIJ) report published in 1985 indicated that between 1974 and 1983 probation populations increased by 63 percent, prison by 48 percent, and parole by 38 percent.[15]

Data released in November 1989 indicated that by the end of 1988, 2,356,483 persons were on probation in the U.S. and 407,977 were on parole. The total number of adults under some type of correction supervision, including city and county jails, reached an all-time high of over 3.7 million, which represents an increase of 38.3 percent since 1984 and 7.3 percent since 1987. Table 15.1 indicates the break-down of offenders by type of correctional supervision in 1988.

Although probation was originally intended for nonviolent offenders, it is being used increasingly for offenders convicted of felonies, leading to the use of the term **felony probation.** In introducing a report by Joan Petersilia, the Director of the National Institute of Justice commented that her study which tracked 1600 convicted California felons who received probation in lieu of prison indicated that felony probation "is

---

TABLE 15.1   Adults Under Correctional Supervision

Of the more than 3.7 million adults under the care or custody of a correctional agency on a given day in 1988, approximately 3 out of 4 offenders were living in the community:

Supervised in the Community	74.5%
Probation	63.5
Parole	11.0
Incarcerated	25.5%
Jail	9.2
Prison	16.3
Total under Correctional Supervision	100%

The probation and parole populations increased 37.7% from 1984 to 1988.

SOURCE: Bureau of Justice Statistics, *Probation and Parole 1988* (Washington, D.C.: U.S. Department of Justice, November 1989), p. 2.

Figure 15.1
Felony Probationer Recidivism (40-Month Followup)

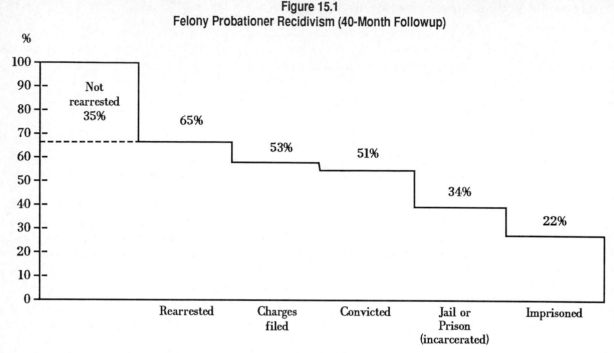

SOURCE: Joan Petersilia, National Institute of Justice, *Probation and Felony Offenders*
(Washington, D.C.: U.S. Department of Justice, March 1985), p. 3.

evolving as the sentence of choice for large numbers of convicted felons;"
and this "dramatic change has increased the risk to the public." As Figure
15.1 indicates, the **recidivism** rate for these probation felons is very high.
Petersilia concludes:

> The criminal justice system has never developed a spectrum of sanctions to
> match the spectrum of criminals. Some believe that the system overutilizes
> imprisonment because it is virtually the only severe punishment available.
> There is a critical need to establish a greater array of sentencing options.
> However, the new options must be restrictive enough to ensure public
> safety.[16]

A Bureau of Justice Statistics study of more than 2500 persons convicted of homicide in twenty-eight large court systems throughout the
country indicated that 8 percent received only probation and another 8
percent received only jail terms or jail terms combined with probation.
These data, however, must also be analyzed in the context of the definition of *homicide.* While it might at first blush appear totally unreasonable
to sentence an offender convicted of homicide to probation only, the practice might be more acceptable if it is understood that this study included
reckless homicide and vehicular homicide as well as murder and man-

slaughter. Of the 84 percent of the sample who were sentenced to prison, one-fourth received life sentences. The study also found that straight probation was the sentence for 16 percent of the convicted rapists. Sixty-five percent of the convicted rapists were sentenced to prison; 18 percent received either a jail term only or jail plus probation.[17]

FOCUS ON PROBATION

Scholars do not agree on the origin of probation, but like many other aspects of our criminal justice system, it is often traced to English common law. Probation in the United States is usually traced to a prosperous shoemaker in Boston, John Augustus, often called the "Father of Probation." As early as 1841 Augustus introduced into the Boston courts the concept of friendly supervision in the community. He personally paid the fines for many people who were jailed; he then worked on rehabilitation.

> His method was to bail the offender after conviction, to utilize this favor as an entering wedge to the convict's confidence and friendship, and through such evidence of friendliness as helping the offender to obtain a job and aiding his family in various ways, to drive a wedge home. When the defendant was later brought into court for sentence, Augustus would report on his progress toward reformation, and the judge would usually fine the convict one cent and costs, instead of committing him to an institution.[18]

Massachusetts passed the first statute, enacting probation officially in 1878. By 1900 only five states had probation statutes; but the establishment of the juvenile court in 1899 in Chicago gave impetus to the probation movement. By 1915, thirty-three states had probation statutes; by 1957 all states had such statutes. In 1925 a statute authorizing probation in federal courts was enacted.

Probation comes from the Latin word *probare* which means "to test" or "to prove." Over the years, however, there has been considerable debate and little consensus on whether probation can bring about rehabilitation. More recently, the concept of **Intensive Probation Supervision (IPS)** has gained prominence and has focused on another purpose of probation—the diversion of defendants from incarceration. In enacting legislation providing for IPS, the Texas legislature specifically stated a goal of diverting at least 1000 persons from incarceration in the Texas Department of Corrections.[19] Diversion is seen as one way to attack the massive problem of prison overcrowding.[20]

In addition to diversion, IPS has other objectives. First, in many jurisdictions, probation case loads are so high and probation is considered so ineffective, both in helping the offender and in protecting society, that judges may see no alternative to the incarceration of convicted offenders but IPS. Second, despite the increased cost of IPS compared with traditional forms of probation, a difference that results from smaller case loads, IPS is still considerably less costly than incarceration. For example, in Texas regular probation costs about 92 cents a day (of which 58 cents is paid by the state, the rest by the probationer), incarceration costs about $14.57 per day per inmate, and IPS costs about $5.00 per day. Third, there is some evidence that IPS has eliminated some of the negative public attitude toward probation in that it may be viewed as more punitive because of the increased supervision. There is also evidence that IPS is more effective than traditional probation in decreasing recidivism.

Evaluation of IPS has not been as extensive as would be necessary for conclusions on its success or failure at this time, but there are some reports. In an analysis of juveniles involved in IPS programs, investigators in Michigan concluded that in many cases IPS "can serve as a less expensive alternative to incarceration with no appreciably greater risk of harm to the community."[21] Studies also indicate that IPS has been successful in New Jersey, resulting in some cost savings without increasing the risk to society.[22]

Decision to Grant Probation

Probation, which may be granted only by the court, is technically a form of sentencing. In reality, however, it is usually considered to be a disposition in lieu of sentencing. In some cases the court will sentence a defendant to a term of incarceration but suspend that sentence for a specified period of time during which the offender will be on probation. If the offender does not violate the terms of probation for that period of time, the sentence will never be imposed; but if the offender does violate probation, he or she will be incarcerated. Because probation is a form of sentencing, which the Supreme Court considers to be a critical stage in the criminal justice system, the defendant is entitled to due process at the probation hearing. Under the U.S. Constitution due process requires that a person may not be deprived of life, liberty, or property without reasonable and lawful procedures. This means, among other things, that the judge may not be unreasonable, arbitrary, or capricious in the decision to grant probation. The defendant is entitled to an attorney at this stage as well as when probation is revoked and the suspended sentence is imposed.[23]

Probation Supervision

Authorities have not agreed on important issues in probation, such as whether the size of a probation officer's case load is significantly related to the success or failure of the officer's probationers. But it is clear that traditional probation has problems. Supervision practices and the conditions of probation vary from jurisdiction to jurisdiction with little supervision in many cases. For example, in the current nationwide crackdown on driving while intoxicated, many jurisdictions are, in addition to other punishments, placing offenders on probation. But probation often entails no more than mailing a card once a month to the probation officer, indicating that the probationer has not violated the terms of probation.

In today's IPS programs, on the other hand, intensive supervision is required. In Georgia, for example, IPS is conducted by teams made up of a probation officer and a surveillance officer who together have a maximum case load of twenty-five. They see their probationers at least five times a week and may even check on them twice in one evening. The terms of probation are stiff. The probationer is required to get and keep a job, pay both a fine and restitution, fulfill community service requirements, and meet a 7:00 P.M. curfew. The only eligible offenders are those who are sentenced to prison; thus, the probationer can look at the terms of probation in light of the alternative—incarceration.[24]

House Arrest and Electronic Monitoring

Prison overcrowding in the past decade has led to yet another proposed solution—**house arrest,** with or without electronic monitoring. Offenders are placed on probation in their own homes; they must follow specified regulations, including restrictions on when they may leave the premises and for what purposes. House arrest is used extensively in some states, such as Florida, to alleviate prison overcrowding. Exhibit 15.2 summarizes the Florida program. The advantages and disadvantages of house arrest have been summarized by Joan Petersilia, researcher at the Rand Corporation. The advantages include cost effectiveness, social benefits (such as permitting the offender to keep a job and continue interacting with his/her family), flexibility that enables adaptation of the plan to the individual needs of the offender and of the community, and the implementation ease and timeliness.

> Because house arrest sentencing requires no new facilties and can use existing probation personnel, it is one of the easier programs to implement (particularly if no electronic monitoring devices are used). House arrest programs, for the most part, do not require legislative changes and can be set up by administrative decisions. The conditions of house arrest are usually easy to communicate, facilitating implementation.[25]

Petersilia also lists the disadvantages of house arrest:

1. House arrest may widen the net of social control.

2. House arrest may narrow the net of social control.

3. House arrest focuses primarily on offender surveillance.

4. House arrest is intrusive and possibly illegal.

Electronic monitoring and house arrest are being used to keep offenders in the community but under surveillance.

5. Race and class bias may enter into participant selection.

6. House arrest compromises public safety.[26]

It is probably that last disadvantage that most concerns the public. Despite the widespread use and reported success of house arrest in Florida, for example, a July 18, 1989, report indicated that a man who had confessed to twenty rapes may have been on house arrest and even wearing an electronic monitor when he committed some of those rapes.[27]

Offenders under house arrest may be electronically monitored. Devices are attached to the offender's ankle or wrist and monitored by a probation officer, who can then determine whether the offender violates

EXHIBIT 15.2

Florida's Community Control Program

Florida's house arrest program, known as "Community Control," was established in 1983 to help alleviate prison crowding in the State. It is the most ambitious program of its type in the country, with about 5,000 offenders "locked up" in their homes on any one day. Leonard Flynn, a panelist on this Crime File segment, oversees the program's operations for the Florida Department of Corrections.

Florida's program targets "incarceration-bound" offenders, including misdemeanants and felons. Each offender is supervised by a community control officer, whose primary function is to ensure that the offender is adhering to court-ordered house arrest restrictions. The community control officer works nights and weekends to monitor compliance. For the more serious offenders, an electronic monitoring system is used. This system operates by having a central computer randomly telephone the offender during designated hours. The offender responds to the telephone call by placing a receiving module (contained in a watch-like wristband) into a modem. The computer verifies the action via a remote printer.

Offenders are permitted to leave their residences only for court-approved employment, rehabilitation, or community service activities. Participants must pay monthly supervision fees of $30 to $50 to offset the costs of supervision, pay restitution to victims, and provide for their own and their family's support.

Officials in Florida consider the house arrest program to be a resounding success. Since 70 percent of those 10,000 persons were believed likely to have been sent to prison otherwise, real cost savings have been realized. In Florida, it costs about $3 per day to supervise a house arrest offender, compared with $28 per day for imprisonment.

Florida's success, coupled with the intense pressure that nearly every State is feeling to reduce prison commitments, ensures that interest in house arrest will continue to grow. An additional impetus is provided by manufacturers of electronic monitoring equipment, who promote their products as a means to achieve public safety without incurring exorbitant costs. Consequently, it is important to consider the major advantages and disadvantages of house arrest programs as well as the larger conceptual issues that such sentencing practices raise.

SOURCE: Joan Petersilia, *House Arrest* (Washington, D.C.: National Institute of Justice, U.S. Department of Justice, 1988), pp. 1–2.

Figure 15-2
Number of offenders being electronically monitored on February 14, 1988.

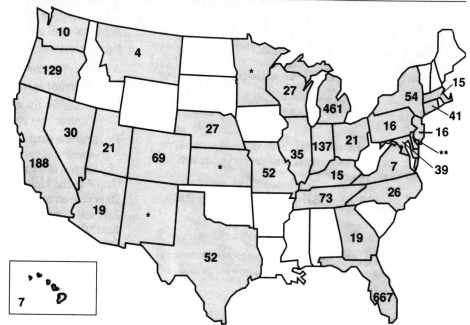

* Programs exist, but no offenders were being monitored on this date.
** No response.
Note: There are no programs in Alaska.

SOURCE: Annesley K. Schmidt, "Electronic Monitoring of Offenders Increases," *National Institute of Justice Reports* (January/February 1989), p. 2.

curfew. The use of electronic monitoring began in 1964, but only recently has the practice gained significant attention.[28] Preliminary reports indicate success but emphasize that further research is needed. According to the National Institute of Justice study, electronic monitoring results in substantial savings to the criminal justice system, is acceptable to the local community, does not appear to pose legal problems when used as an alternative to detention, and has few equipment failures.[29] Not all agree, however, on the question of the legality of electronic monitoring. Authorities disagree on the extent of the legal issues; but some have taken the position that when they are litigated, the constitutionality of electronic devices will be upheld.[30] Clearly the use of electronic monitoring is increasing. Figure 15.2 indicates the extent of use in the United States in 1988, while Figure 15.3 indicates the type of offenses committed by offenders who were on electronic monitoring.[31]

Figure 15-3
Electronically monitored offenders categorized by offense

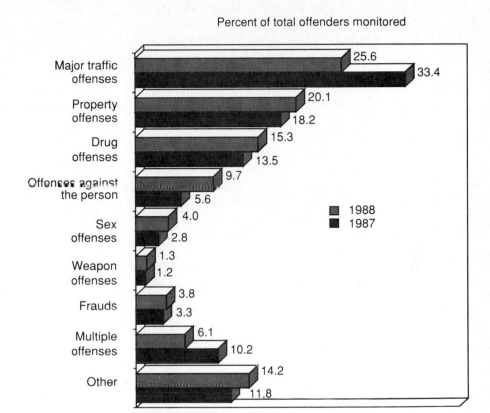

Percent of total offenders monitored

	1988	1987
Major traffic offenses	25.6	33.4
Property offenses	20.1	18.2
Drug offenses	15.3	13.5
Offenses against the person	9.7	5.6
Sex offenses	4.0	2.8
Weapon offenses	1.3	1.2
Frauds	3.8	3.3
Multiple offenses	6.1	10.2
Other	14.2	11.8

SOURCE: Annesley K. Schmidt, "Electronic Monitoring of Offenders Increases," *National Institute of Justice Reports* (January/February 1989), p. 3.

FOCUS ON PAROLE

Authorities do not agree on the origin of parole. Some trace it to the English system of sending criminals to the American colonies. Criminals were pardoned by the English government after being sold to the highest bidder in America. The buyer then became the master of the individual, whose new status was that of indentured servant. The system is similar to parole in that the individual, to receive the change in status, would agree to certain conditions similar to the ones currently imposed by parole boards.[32]

Others claim that the concept of conditioned liberty was first introduced in France around 1830. It was an intermediary step of freedom, with supervision between prison confinement and complete freedom in the community. Still others trace the history of parole to the reform efforts of Captain Alexander Maconochie, who began the reformatory movement in 1840 in Australia where he was in charge of the worst of England's penal colonies—Norfolk Island. Maconochie eliminated the flat sentence and instituted a system of *marks* which inmates could earn for good behavior and work—marks were used to reduce the amount of time served in the prison colony. Maconochie evaluated his term at Norfolk in these words: "I found Norfolk Island a hell, but left it an orderly and well-regulated community." His work was not appreciated by the English, however, and he was recalled. His reform efforts did have a later effect in England and in America.[33]

Maconochie's system was taken to Ireland by Sir Walter Crofton, who added supervision to the early release program. In 1870 Crofton spoke to the American Prison Association, which then adopted a "Declaration of Principles" that included a parole release program. The actual use of formal parole in the United States is traced to 1876 in the Elmira Reformatory in New York State. Although the plans differed, all states and the federal government eventually adopted parole. It was used extensively although in recent years it has been seriously questioned, and as already noted, abolished in some jurisdictions.[34]

PURPOSE OF PAROLE

Inmates face many problems upon release from prison. Releasing them on parole theoretically provides some assistance in coping with those problems. Highlight 15.1 illustrates some of the problems of releasees.

Inmates' Problems Upon Release

Most releasees have limited or no financial resources. Many do not have employment and some do not even have established residences and families to whom they may return. Most receive indifferent and, in many cases, hostile reactions from the community. Those who have been incarcerated for long periods of time have the additional problem of catching up on how contemporary society does things. All encounter emotional problems in reacting to the new environment, and many feel depressed, estranged, lonely, and rejected. Some institutions offer training sessions to

HIGHLIGHT 15.1

Release From Prison is Traumatic for Some Offenders

After spending thirty years in prison in Indiana, Ralph Lobaugh was released. The freedom for which he had fought during fourteen years, however, was too much for him. After two months outside the walls Lobaugh decided he could not cope and went back to prison. Lobaugh "just wanted to live in a cell again and be with his old friends." His case is unusual, but the problems of readjusting to life outside walls are significant. If inmates are not prepared for their return to life outside the walls, if they cannot find jobs, and if they face continued discrimination and harassment, their chances of returning to the institution on additional charges will be greatly enhanced.

SOURCE: Summarized by the author from news media.

William Singleton, released after a prison term served for brutally battering a young woman, had to spend his parole term on the grounds of a California prison because no community wanted him among its people. After his unconditional release he moved to Florida, where he was charged with theft in 1990. He decided not to contest the charge, saying he did not think he could get a fair trial.

assist inmates in preparing for release; others offer halfway programs for a gradual reentry into society. Most make some attempt to deal with the two most immediate problems—money and jobs.

Institutions react to the financial problems of released prisoners in several ways. The most frequent method of assistance is clothing. Most institutions require that prisoners send their personal clothing home when they enter prison; thus, at the time of release, it is necessary for the institutions to replace the clothing.

The next most common type of assistance is gate money, a financial grant given to each inmate at departure, although some institutions give the money only if the inmate has not acquired a savings account from work assignments during incarceration. Others give very small amounts. For most inmates these funds must pay for transportation, food, clothing, shelter, and other expenses until their first paycheck arrives.

The second major problem of ex-offenders is employment. The importance of having a job on release is dramatically illustrated by an early study of a job placement program for ex-offenders in Seattle. The data indicated that those who were employed full time had an 87 percent chance of successfully completing their parole, compared with only 55 percent for those who were employed half time, and 27 percent for those who worked only occasionally.[35]

Several types of programs have been developed to aid ex-offenders in job hunting. One of the most successful, the Alston Wilkes Society, is this country's largest private, statewide, nonprofit organization offering services to present and former inmates and their families. Many inmates move from institutions to an Alston Wilkes home, where they must find jobs within three weeks, pay rent, and save 20 percent of their income. The program offers classes in filling out job applications and role-playing interview sessions. Donations of clothing and tools are collected and made available to needy clients.[36]

A national assessment and evaluation of community-based programs that assist ex-offenders in finding and retaining employment concluded that because there was such great variation in the types of employment services offered and the delivery methods, we do not know which services are the most effective. Furthermore, most programs reported that the majority of their clients were successfully placed in jobs. Clients also have lower rates of recidivism than do comparison groups although outcomes are not consistent, and there is reason to question the methodological adequacy of most evaluations.[37]

Preparation for Release

Some institutions help prepare inmates for release, but the availability of **prerelease programs** is limited. They differ from institution to institution, ranging from information on etiquette and changing social mores to practical details of how to tie a tie and interview for a job. Some prisons hold prerelease classes, and others have prerelease centers or halfway houses. The reports of success vary. It is clear that more research into the effectiveness of prerelease programs is needed before definite conclusions can be drawn. Prerelease programs do, however, appear to be a positive step toward helping inmates make the difficult adjustments from the restrictive prison environment to the free world.

Work release and furloughs are also used to prepare inmates for release. The extensive use of these programs in the United States is very recent, stemming from their provision in the federal system by the Prisoner Rehabilitation Act of 1965; however, most of the programs in existence today were established by state laws after the 1965 federal law had been passed.

Furloughs are brief absences from the institution, usually for a specified purpose other than work or study. Furloughs may be granted to allow inmates to visit sick relatives, attend family funerals, secure employment, obtain a driver's license, meet with future parole officers, arrange for housing, or visit family members. Furloughs may last from several hours to several days. The main advantage of furloughs is that the offenders are placed in contact with their families and the outside world. Inmates have a chance to make decisions on their own, away from the closely monitored prison routine, and the community also is given time to adjust to the offender.

In **work release** programs the inmate is released from incarceration to work or attend school. Inmates may participate in vocational study, take courses at an educational institution, or work at a job in the community. An earlier study of work release in North Carolina found that work releasees had more stable employment records after release, significantly lower unemployment rates, and higher wages than releasees who had not participated in work release programs. Subjectively, they did not report greater family stability, but they did say that their ability to send support payments to their families while they were incarcerated was one major positive aspect of the program. Psychological testing indicated that those who participated in work release had attitudes that were significantly less amoral and antisocial and demonstrated less hyperactivity than those who did not participate. This study found that the benefits of work release outweigh any disadvantages and that such programs should be encouraged because they reduce postrelease criminal activity.[38]

One of the advantages of furlough and work release is that they give offenders an opportunity for close contacts with their families. Close family ties may ease the problems of adjusting to society. In addition, work release enables offenders to provide some financial support for their families and also helps improve the inmates' attitudes toward socially responsible work. Self-esteem, self-image, and self-respect all are frequently mentioned as benefits of work release.

Another possible advantage is the lowered cost compared to incarceration. Inmates on work release may be required to reimburse the state for part of the cost of their incarceration. They also pay taxes and contribute to victim restitution funds. Some research, however, has demonstrated that the hidden costs of work release programs lead to longer sentences actually being served before the inmates are released unconditionally. The cost of prison staff time for supervision may override any economic benefit.[39]

Additional problems with work release pertain to the participants in the programs. The releasees may have problems in adjusting to the community during the day and then to the institution at night. Indeed, it might be easier to make a complete break with the institution and attempt to readjust to society without having to return to prison. Also, release during the day may eliminate or interrupt participation in some prison programs that are beneficial to the offender. In addition, problems may arise over the use of money earned. Transportation is often a problem because many correctional institutions are not located in urban areas where inmates are most likely to find jobs.

A final problem with work release and furlough is the possibility that participants may commit additional crimes or escape from supervision. For these reasons, the use of furloughs became a critical issue in the 1988 presidential campaign. Then Vice President George Bush reminded his opponent, Massachusetts Governor Michael Dukakis, and society that Willie Horton, while on furlough from a Massachusetts prison, broke into a Maryland home. He terrorized the occupants for twelve hours and stabbed Clifford Barnes and twice raped Barnes' fiancee. Horton, who was serving a term of life without possibility of parole for a 1974 murder, had been on nine weekend passes with no known problems. On his tenth pass he escaped, and one year later he committed these violent crimes. Willie Horton's name and picture became almost as well-known as those of the presidential candidates. The judge who sentenced Horton for the Maryland crimes refused to send him back to Massachusetts. In his sentencing report he said, "This man should never draw a breath of free air again. He is devoid of conscience and should die in prison."[40]

Most states permit furloughs, although Massachusetts was the only one that permitted furloughs for those sentenced to life without parole. Governor Dukakis tightened that provision under the pressure of the Willie Horton case. Donna Comeau, whose teenage brother was fatally stabbed by Horton, helped start Citizens Against an Unsafe Society (CAUS), which is fighting for the abolition of furloughs. But a study released in 1988 indicated that almost 10 percent of all state and federal inmates were granted furloughs. An advocate proclaimed that the system is "widespread, successful and relatively problem free. Although some officials indicated that restrictions had been placed on furloughs in their state programs, Indiana officials were the only ones to report serious difficulties with their furlough program."[41]

The Parole System

The organization of parole is complex. In general, it consists of two main divisions: the **parole board,** responsible for release decisions, and the **parole officers,** who supervise parolees. These divisions carry out the four main functions of parole: releasing and placing prisoners on parole, supervising personnel, releasing parolees from supervision upon completion of their sentences or proof that they are no longer a risk to the community, and revoking parole when the parolees have violated its conditions.

The Parole Hearing and Decision-Making Process

The most important stage in the administration of parole is the parole hearing. Until recently the legal requirements at this stage were unclear and the nature of the hearing differed from state to state. Most allowed the inmate to be present; some, however, only reviewed the files. The parole board might have heard cases with all members present or have divided into panels, each panel hearing and deciding different cases. The hearings were usually private, attended only by the inmate, members of the board, and a representative of the institution in which the inmate was incarcerated. Reports from family members, from psychology or other treatment personnel, or from institutional staff members might have been included. The board might have wanted information concerning the inmate's plans upon release. Reasons for denial might or might not have been given to the inmates considered for parole.

The federal courts were divided over the requirements of due process at the parole hearing; but in 1979, in *Greenholtz v. Inmates of Nebraska Penal and Correctional Complex*, the Supreme Court held that due process requirements were met by the Nebraska statute that allowed an inmate, at the time of the first parole decision in his or her case, an opportunity to be heard and a statement of the reasons for denial. The Nebraska statute, said the Court, did create an expectation of parole that must be protected by due process. Whether that expectation exists in other state statutes would have to be determined by examining the statutes. The Court did not agree, however, that the Constitution requires a parole hearing to involve all the elements of due process required at trial. The Court also held that due process at the parole hearing does not require the parole board to specify the particular evidence that influenced its denial.[42]

In *Board of Pardons v. Allen*, decided in 1987, the Court reaffirmed its decision in *Greenholtz*, holding that the Montana statute created an expectation of parole provided certain conditions are met by the inmate. Thus, if the inmate meets those conditions, parole must be granted. Once again, it is the wording of the statute, not the possibility of parole per se, that creates the expectation of liberty that must be protected. The use of *shall* rather then *may* in the statutes in question creates this expectation. According to one legal scholar, "These procedural protections could increase inmate confidence in the fairness of the system: a confidence many inmates give up while trying to survive in a hostile, overcrowded prison."[43]

Prior to these decisions, John Irwin emphasized the problems that arbitrary decisions by parole boards could create for inmates. In his classic book, *The Felon*, Irwin said arbitrariness by parole boards created a sense of injustice, and this sense of injustice further increases the loss of commitment to conventional society.[44]

Perhaps Justice Hugo Black best summarized the view of many inmates toward the parole board:

> In the course of my reading—by no means confined to law—I have reviewed many of the world's religions. The tenets of many faiths hold the deity to be a trinity. Seemingly, the parole boards, by whatever names designated in the various states, have in too many instances sought to enlarge this to include themselves as members.[45]

What criteria should be used in the decision-making process? Two approaches have been used to predict which applicants for parole would be successful if released. The first type is *statistical* prediction based on **prediction scales.** Criminological research on the use of statistics to predict future criminal behavior began in the 1920s with a study that attempted to relate factors such as age, education, and past criminal record to parole violations. The resulting table was then used to predict whether other, similar offenders would be suitable candidates for parole.[46]

A review of statistical prediction studies yields mixed results, but there are problems in comparing these studies. Some are based on reconviction data, and others are based on arrest data; the latter, of course, include those who are arrested but not convicted of the crime. The only general conclusion from statistical prediction studies is that it may be easier to predict nonviolent than violent crimes.[47]

The second and most common approach is *clinical* prediction. In this method, an expert examines an inmate and gives a subjective opinion about the likelihood of future crime. Clinical prediction studies also have yielded mixed results. Generally, the studies have shown an overprediction of dangerousness; that is, many offenders who are not violent are predicted to be dangerous and are thus retained in institutions.[48]

Today prediction is generally based on parole guidelines. In the federal parole system, for example, guidelines were adopted in an attempt to standardize decision making. Those guidelines were hotly debated and widely discussed. The 1984 revision of the federal criminal code provided for a five-year phase out of the use of parole as early release from prison. But according to the chair of the U.S. Parole Commission,

> I think there will always be the function of parole. When you talk about parole, you're talking about two things: first, discretionary release

and second, supervision. There's always going to be a need for supervision, and I think discretionary release by a parole board is better than determinate sentencing . . . The word "parole" may change in the future, because politicians seem to feel that it is a bad word. . . . Parole will be around even if we call it something else because it's rational and it's protective of the public interest and the security of the community.[49]

What happens when parole is abolished as a method of release from prison? Most states with flat-term or determinate sentencing laws still allow early release based on good-time credits earned in the institution. The most obvious result of abolishing release by parole boards has been an increase in time served in institutions, but there have been repercussions in other areas also. Parole boards with limited discretion can no longer act to reduce acute overcrowding in prisons. Where good-time provisions still exist, the control of sentence length has moved from the parole board to prison officials. Individual prison guards make the basic decisions about inmate conduct and behavior and therefore control their good-time credits. Prosecutors and judges who adjust their charging and sentencing practices also have more discretionary power. Thus, abolition of parole may only relocate, not remove, discretion.

In earlier discussions we have noted that discretion exists in all areas of the criminal justice system. The exercise of that discretion involves predictions. Police, judges, probation and parole officers, and correctional personnel all make decisions on the basis of predictions of what will be the result of those decisions. Clearly our ability to predict accurately is limited; as Exhibit 15.3 indicates, it may not improve in the near future. But the point is that predictions will be made and discretion will be exercised. After an analysis of the literature on prediction, Todd Clear concluded:

> It is difficult to imagine a corrections process devoid of prediction. Therefore, the decision maker is left with two questions: First, to what degree and in what manner should correctional policy allow for predictions as a consideration in dealing with individual offenders? And second, what must be done to ensure that the correctional policy is carried out in the highest quality manner possible?[50]

PROBATION AND PAROLE REVOCATION

Historically the granting of parole and the revocation of probation or parole were conducted with little if any due process. The Supreme Court has ruled that certain due process requirements must be observed at revocation proceedings. In 1967 in *Mempa v. Rhay*, the Court ruled that a probationer is entitled to be represented by counsel (state appointed for indigents) at a combined revocation and sentencing hearing because

EXHIBIT 15.3

How Well Can We Predict?

Our current ability to predict long-term violent behavior is no better than one accurate prediction of violence out of every three. Furthermore, few prospective studies of future violence have been completed (Monahan 1981). Prospective studies have a much higher validity than retrospective studies because they can help determine causal relationships rather than just identifying correlations of specific factors and violent behavior.

These limits on the current ability to predict are widely recognized in the legal and psychiatric professions and in the courts. All members of the Supreme Court have recognized the current limits on our capacity to predict violent behavior (*Barefoot v. Estelle*, 463 U.S. 880 [1983]).

We assume that this one-in-three accuracy rate is the best social scientists will be able to achieve for several decades. New and alternative approaches to prediction have been suggested. In particular, predictions may be improved by focusing on situational and environmental factors, random elements in behavior, and other factors which look to the places and people with whom the targeted individuals interact. The absolute limit on the ability to predict dangerousness may well have been approached given the exceptional nature of the behavior being predicted and the role of chance and circumstance in generating specific instances of violent conduct.

Given the paucity of adequate data, the judge, police officer, prosecutor, or prison administrator must determine the point at which data become adequate to use as a guide to decisionmaking.

SOURCE: Norval Morris and Marc Miller, *Predictions of Dangerousness in the Criminal Law*, National Institute of Justice (Washington, D.C.: U.S. Department of Justice, March 1987), p. 3.

sentencing is a stage of the actual criminal proceeding, "where substantial rights of a criminal accused may be affected."[51]

In 1972 the Court looked at parole revocation. In *Morrissey v. Brewer*, it held that before parole may be revoked, the parolee is entitled to two hearings. The first is a hearing to determine whether there is probable cause to believe that the individual has violated any of the terms of parole. The second and more extensive hearing is to consider the evidence and determine whether parole should be revoked.

In *Morrissey*, the Court stated that (1) the purpose of parole is rehabilitation; (2) until the rules are violated, an individual may remain on parole; (3) full due process rights used in criminal trials do not apply to parole revocation; (4) the termination of liberty by revocation results in "grievous loss," mandating some due process protection; (5) informal parole revocation hearings are proper; (6) parole should not be revoked unless the rules are violated; and (7) the requirements of due process will change with particular cases.[52]

The Supreme Court requires the following elements of due process at the actual parole revocation proceedings:

1. Written notice of the alleged violations of parole

2. Disclosure to the parolee of the evidence of violation

3. Opportunity to be heard in person and to present evidence as well as witnesses

4. Right to confront and cross-examine adverse witnesses unless good cause can be shown for not allowing this confrontation

5. Right to judgment by a detached and neutral hearing body

6. Written statement of reasons for revoking parole as well as of the evidence used in arriving at that decision

The importance of fairness in the revocation of parole is emphasized by the Supreme Court in this brief excerpt:[53]

Morrissey v. Brewer

The parolee is not the only one who has a stake in his conditional liberty. Society has a stake in whatever may be the chance of restoring him to normal and useful life within the law. Society thus has an interest in not having parole revoked because of erroneous information or because of an erroneous evaluation of the need to revoke parole, given the breach of parole conditions. And society has a further interest in treating the parolee with basic fairness: fair treatment in parole revocations will enhance the chance of rehabilitation by avoiding reactions to arbitrariness.

In 1973 in *Gagnon v. Scarpelli,* the Court held that the minimum due process requirements of *Morrissey* apply to probation revocation hearings. The Court also considered whether counsel is required at all revocation hearings, deciding that this should be determined on a case-by-case basis. The Court held that counsel should be required when it is necessary for fundamental fairness. For example, an inmate who had serious communication problems might need counsel at revocation hearings in order for those hearings to be fair.[54]

The Court also decided two important revocation cases in recent years. In 1983, in *Bearden v. Georgia*, it held that probation cannot be revoked because an indigent cannot pay a fine and restitution unless there is a determination that the probationer has not made a bona fide effort or that there were not adequate alternative methods of punishment.[55] In 1985 in *Black v. Romano*, the Court held that generally when a court revokes probation and a suspended prison sentence is imposed, the court does not have to indicate that it considered alternatives to prison. This case did not involve the indigency issue regarding failure to pay a fine and restitution as in the *Bearden* case.[56]

Even when following the Supreme Court guidelines, it is important to remember that revocation of probation or parole is a serious matter. It is possible to grant fair hearings and still revoke probation or parole because of some minor infraction of the rules. For example, in some jurisdictions, any violation of parole terms will result in revocation and return to prison. In deciding what actions are serious enough to warrant parole revocation, we should keep in mind the potentially harmful effects of incarceration as well as its increased cost compared to parole. As budget problems continue to plague the corrections system and prisons continue to be overcrowded, we must consider costs when deciding how to punish. Violent offenders are one issue; but violation of a minor parole condition, such as driving a car without permission of the parole officer, is quite another.

AIDS IN PROBATION AND PAROLE

The prevalance of Acquired Immune Deficiency Syndrome, or AIDS, with its lethal results has created medical, social, and legal problems for society and community corrections, including probation and parole. In June of 1989, the National Institute of Justice released a report on the problem of AIDS in probation and parole. This brief summary is based on that report.[57]

AIDS was first diagnosed among previously healthy male homosexual or bisexual men in New York and San Francisco in 1981, although as early as 1978 the condition, which results in an inability of the body to fight infections, was found in blood that had been donated to blood banks. AIDS is caused by a virus known as the Human Immunodeficiency Virus (HIV), which attacks certain white blood cells and renders them unable to combat infections. The virus may, after entering a host cell, remain dormant for a long period; thus, AIDS symptoms may not show up immediately after the virus is contracted. But once the virus is stimulated into action, and scientists do not know what causes that to happen, it reproduces rapidly. Thus far, there is no known cure for AIDS. The virus is transmitted through inoculation with blood or blood products, sexual contact, and perinatal transmission. Sexual contact is the most frequent method of transmission, accounting for approximately 64 percent of AIDS cases. The virus may be transmitted through heterosexual as well as homosexual contacts.[58]

In 1984 only 4000 cases of AIDS were reported, but by May of 1988 the number had grown to almost 60,000. "The comment heard often early in the epidemic that the early cases were only the 'tip of the iceberg' has proven tragically to be accurate. Of the cases diagnosed as of this report, 56 percent have died."[59] AIDS becomes a special problem for probation and parole because the age group that is at the greatest risk, ages twenty to thirty-nine, is the age group in which most probationers and parolees fall. Secondly, this population has a high rate of intravenous drug users, another critical method of transmitting the disease. It could thus be predicted that numerous inmates as well as offenders on probation and parole will be at high risk for HIV or already have contracted AIDS. Initial studies indicate the prediction is accurate.

It thus becomes extremely important for probation and parole agencies to develop policies and practices concerning testing for the AIDS virus as well as for protecting the community (and other offenders) to the greatest extent possible from contact with the disease. Legal issues regarding testing and treatment, isolation, and other problems must also be considered. These and other issues are part of the American Probation and Parole Association Position Statement on AIDS, reprinted in Exhibit 15.4. But policy statements are only a beginning. Continued research on a cure must be accompanied by intensive education of the general public as well as by targeted education of high-risk groups and AIDS testing to minimize the spread of the deadly disease.[60]

EVALUATION OF PROBATION AND PAROLE

Evaluation of probation and parole usually involves a study of recidivism, which may include new law violations or violation of the terms of probation or parole. Researchers do not agree on the meaning of the term; nor do they agree on how it should be measured. The result is that data on recidivism vary. Early studies indicated that up to two-thirds of those released from prison became recidivists; these figures were questioned in an extensive analysis of federal data by Daniel Glaser, who argued that the best way to study recidivism is to follow a cohort of offenders for a specified period after their release.[61]

Marvin E. Wolfgang and his colleagues have done so with juveniles.

EXHIBIT 15.4

American Probation and Parole Association Position Statement on AIDS

Introduction

Acquired Immune Deficiency Syndrome (AIDS) has emerged as a significant concern and challenge to correctional administrators. As the numbers of HIV positives, persons with ARC, and persons with AIDS continue to multiply, probation and parole personnel must be aware of the implications of various actions and non-actions, confidentiality issues, and medical facts. Policies and procedures governing all facets of AIDS prevention and education must reflect best current medical and ethical practices.

Discussion

The American Probation and Parole Association supports the findings and recommendations of the National Institute of Justice in "AIDS and the Law Enforcement Officer" and "AIDS in Correc-

tional Facilities." While neither of these publications specifically addresses the unique issues faced by probation and parole officers, the detailed analysis assesses many of the major areas of concern expressed by staff.

Education of all citizens about the dangers and means of transmission of the human immunodeficiency virus is a primary social objective. Offenders demonstrating high risk behaviors should be targeted for intensive educational efforts. Drug-abusers, in particular, should receive special attention and services. Other offenders should also be provided with information about preventive measures and testing options.

Disclosure of offender medical information presents difficult ethical, legal and professional dilemmas. As a general rule, such information is confidential. When staff become aware that a specific offender is HIV-positive, disclosure to

In their earlier analysis they found that 46 percent of the delinquents stopped after the first offense, and of those who committed more than one offense, 35 percent had no more than three offenses. Those who committed many offenses, the chronic offenders, were most likely to be nonwhite and from low socioeconomic backgrounds. The authors suggest that it might be wasteful to launch a treatment program to involve all delinquents after their first official contact with the police, that it might even be wise to wait until after the third offense and concentrate efforts on chronic offenders, who, according to this study, had a 70 percent chance of being arrested again.[62]

Glaser's work preceded that of Wolfgang and his colleagues, who are

other parties without the subject's informed consent is a violation of his/her right to privacy. In special cases where there is evidence suggesting on-going high-risk behavior that might result in the infection of a third party, the right to privacy may be outweighed by a duty to warn possible victims. In such cases, staff should be encouraged to seek supervisory and legal assistance on a case by case basis.

In the daily performance of their duties, probation and parole officers are rarely exposed to situations where viral transmission is possible. The only recognized means of contracting the AIDS virus is through blood to blood contact or semen to blood contact. Neither is likely to occur in the context of the probation/parole officer's job. Common hygienic procedures and recognition of high-risk behaviors and situations should be sufficient to prevent exposure. Officers may wish to carry rubber or surgical protective wear. The AIDS virus is not easily transmitted, and there is no evidence that professionals employed in law enforcement fields are at risk of contracting it, if standard procedures are followed.

Position

All jurisdictions should develop policies and procedures which stress regular training, utilizing the latest medical research; provision of appropriate safety and hygienic materials, equipment, and information; consideration of prevailing confidentiality statutes; and opportunities for staff to discuss issues of concern.

SOURCE: Reprinted in Dana Eser Hunt, *Aids in Probation and Parole*, National Institute of Justice (Washington, D.C.: U.S. Department of Justice, June 1989), p. 50.

currently updating their cohort study.[63] Glaser argued that the recidivist figure was not more than one-third and that it would be affected by several variables, such as probation and parole. Where use of probation is high, and thus only the worst risks are sent to prison, a higher recidivist rate can be expected. When parole is used extensively, resulting in the release of high-risk persons early, higher recidivist rates are also likely. Glaser found a recidivist rate of 35 percent in his study of federal prisons.

In an early and often-cited study of the recidivist rates of probationers, Ralph England found that 17.7 percent of his sample of 500 probationers were convicted of another crime after release from probation. Of those convictions, 27.6 percent occurred within the first year. The 87 failures had a total of 166 separate reconvictions, nearly one-third of which involved violations of liquor and gambling statutes. Few of the convictions were for serious crimes. England found that the variables most associated with failure on probation were "youthfulness, a history of previous trouble with the law, an urban background in socially and economically disadvantaged segments of society, and some element of personal *anomie*."[64]

Recent studies of recidivism have focused on felony probation and parole. We have noted that more felony offenders are being placed on probation, mainly because of prison overcrowding. Joan Petersilia, a senior researcher in the Rand Corporation's criminal justice program, directed the Rand study of felony probation, sponsored by the National Institute of Justice. Petersilia reports that nearly two-thirds of all convicted offenders are placed on probation. Using data from 16,000 offenders convicted of felonies in 1980 in California, Petersilia studied recidivism data of 1600 offenders who received probation rather than a prison sentence.

The Rand study found that two-thirds of the offenders were rearrested, 51 percent were convicted of a new crime, and 34 percent were given a jail or prison sentence. The recidivists committed the crimes of burglary, theft, and robbery. The study did indicate that certain variables are significantly related to recidivism:

> *Type of conviction crime*—Property offenders had the highest rates of recidivism.

> *Number of prior juvenile and adult convictions*—The greater the number, the higher the probability of recidivism.

> *Income at arrest*—Regardless of source or amount, the presence of income was associated with lower recidivism.

> *Household composition*—If the offender was living with spouse and/or children, recidivism was lower.[65]

Despite the association of these variables with recidivism, as Figure 15.3 indicates, information derived from them permits only a 69 percent chance of accurately predicting recidivism, compared to a 54 percent chance of successful prediction by chance alone.

Petersilia acknowledged that felony probation presents great risks. But she warned against premature conclusions based on the reported data: "Rather than castigate probation, critics should realize these findings actually indict the attitudes and policies that placed unrealistic and overwhelming demands on probation agencies."[66] Petersilia suggests a more extensive use of IPS, Intensive Probation Supervision, discussed earlier.

Petersilia is not the only researcher to warn about the danger of abandoning probation (or parole). A New York City judge bluntly declared that critics of the New York parole system "should consider the fact that we do not measure the success rate of an operating room in a hospital by the number of bodies in the morgue. We measure the success rate by indicating how many individuals, after the operation, are well and able to function and are able to contribute."[67]

CONCLUSION

This chapter focuses on handling offenders within the community by putting them in community correction facilities, placing them on probation without a prison term, or releasing them early from prison on parole. It began with a brief discussion of the diversion of offenders from the correctional system and then looked at community corrections and the concept of reintegration of offenders into the community after they have served time in prison. In response to claims that treatment in prison did not work and that incarceration is too expensive, community programs were proposed as the answer to both problems.

After an overview of probation and parole, the chapter turned to a more intensive analysis of probation. The purpose of probation was discussed briefly, followed by the probation decision, probation supervision, and a closer look at the newest focus in probation: house arrest, with or without electronic monitoring.

Next came a discussion of parole, including its purpose, the problems inmates face when they are released from prison, the parole hearing, and the parole decision. Supervision, revocation, and evaluation of probation and parole have many common features; a section was devoted to each of these topics. The legal issues of revocation were noted with reference to Supreme Court decisions. The most recent and most critical problem of AIDS was discussed, followed by an evaluation of probation and parole, including a look at recidivism and how it relates to these measures.

Prisons have been declared failures although they may be necessary for many offenders. Clearly we cannot continue increasing the incarceration rates without massive expense or the increased use of probation and parole. There are indications that despite their unpopularity, probation and parole will continue to be used for large numbers of offenders. It seems wise, therefore, to study the problems and attempt to improve both systems.

ENDNOTES

1. Gordon Hawkins, *The Prison: Policy and Practice* (Chicago: University of Chicago Press, 1976), pp. 56–59.
2. Harry E. Allen et al., "Sociopathy: An Experiment on Internal Environmental Control," *American Behavioral Scientist* 20 (November–December 1976): 215.

3. National Advisory Commission on Criminal Justice Standards and Goals, *A National Strategy to Reduce Crime* (Washington, D.C.: U.S. Government Printing Office, 1973), p. 121.

4. President's Commission on Law Enforcement and Administration of Justice, *The Challenge of Crime in a Free Society* (Washington D.C.: U.S. Government Printing Office, 1967), p. 159.

5. Margo Andriessen, "A Foreigner's View of American Diversion," *Crime & Delinquency* 26 (January 1980): 70.

6. Roger L. Lauen, *Community-Managed Corrections and Other Solutions to America's Prison Crisis* (Laurel, Md.: American Correctional Association, 1988), p. 117.

7. Robert M. Carter et al., *Program Models: Community Correctional Centers* (Washington, D.C.: U.S. Government Printing Office, 1980), p. 3.

8. E. K. Nelson et al., *Program Models: Unification of Community Corrections* (Washington, D.C.: U.S. Government Printing Office, 1980), p. 13. See also Andrew Rutherford and Osman Bengur, *Community Based Alternatives to Juvenile Incarceration*, National Evaluation Program, Phase I, Summary Report, National Institute of Law Enforcement and Criminal Justice, LEAA (Washington, D.C.: U.S. Government Printing Office, 1976).

9. See James McSparron, "Community Correction and Diversion: Costs and Benefits, Subsidy Modes, and Start-up Recommendation," *Crime & Delinquency* 26 (April 1980): 226–247. See also S. Christopher Baird and Dennis Wagner, "Measuring Diversion: The Florida Community Control Program," *Crime & Delinquency* 36 (January 1990): 112–125.

10. Minn. Stat. Ann. Section 401.01 *et seq.* The law was later amended so that charge-back applied only to juveniles and those adults sentenced before 1980.

11. For a discussion of the Minnesota Plan, see Kenneth F. Schoen, "The Community Corrections Act," *Crime & Delinquency* 24 (October 1978): 458–464.

12. Povl Boesen, "California Law Encourages Community Corrections," *Corrections Today* 51 (April 1989): 38.

13. For information on some of these programs, see Lloyd W. McCorkle et al., *The Highfields Story: An Experimental Treatment Project for Youthful Offenders* (New York: Holt, Rinehart and Winston, 1968), and H. Ashley Weeks, *Youthful Offenders at Highfields* (Ann Arbor: University of Michigan Press, 1958).

14. See Steven Balkin, "Prisoners by Day: A Proposal to Sentence Non-Violent Offenders to Non-Residential Work Facilities." *Judicature* 64 (October 1980): 154–164.

15. Joan Petersilia, National Institute of Justice, *Probation and Felony Offenders* (Washington, D.C.: U.S. Department of Justice, March 1985): 1–2. See also Petersilia et al., *Granting Felons Probation: Public Risks and Alternatives* (Santa Monica, CA.: Rand Corporation, 1985), and Dean J. Champion, *Felony Probation: Problems and Prospects* (Westport, C.T.: Greenwood Press, 1988).

16. Bureau of Justice Statistics, *Probation and Parole 1988* (Washington, D.C.: U.S. Department of Justice, November 1989), p. 1.

17. Bureau of Justice Statistics, *Sentencing Outcomes in 28 Felony Courts* (Washington, D.C.: U.S. Department of Justice, 1987), p. 1.

18. Sheldon Glueck, quoted in Harry Elmer Barnes and Negley K. Teeters, *New Horizons in Criminology*, 3d ed. (Englewood Cliffs, N.J.: Prentice-Hall, 1959), p. 554.

19. Tex. Code Crim. Pro. 42.121, Section 1.01. For a discussion of the IPS movement, see Todd R. Clear and Patricia L. Hardyman, "The New Intensive Supervision

Movement," *Crime & Delinquency* 36 (January 1990): 42–90. For an analysis of the program's future, see James M. Byrne, "The Future of Intensive Probation Supervision and the New Intermediate Sanctions," *Crime & Delinquency* 36 (January 1990): 6–41.

20. For a brief but excellent description and analysis, along with empirical data of the Texas probation and practice laws, see Rolando V. del Carmen, *Probation Law and Practice in Texas* (Huntsville, TX.: Criminal Justice Center, Sam Houston State University, 1989).

21. Study by William H. Barton and Jeffrey A. Butts of the Center for the Study of Youth Policy at the University of Michigan, cited in *Criminal Justice Newsletter*, (1 May 1989): p. 3.

22. See Frank S. Pearson, "Evaluation of New Jersey's Intensive Supervision Program," *Federal Probation* 34 (October 1988): 437–438. For a report on attitudes toward IPS, see Joan K. Hall et al., "A Comparison of Program Administrator Attitudes About Florida Community Control: An Adult Intensive Probation Supervision Program," *Crime & Delinquency* 35 (April 1989): 303–308. See also Edward J. Latessa and Gennaro F. Vita, "The Effects of Intensive Supervision on Shock Probationers," *Journal of Criminal Justice* 16 (no. 4, 1988): 319–330; Frank S. Pearson and Alice Glasel Harper, "Contingent Intermediate Sentences: New Jersey's Intensive Supervision Program," *Crime & Delinquency* 36 (January 1990): 75–86; Joan Petersilia, "Conditions that Permit Intensive Supervision Programs to Survive," *Crime & Delinquency* 36 (January 1990): 126–145; and Joan Petersilia and Susan Turner, "Comparing Intensive and Regular Supervision for High-Risk Probationers: Early Results from an Experiment in California," *Crime & Delinquency* 36 (January 1990): 87–111, and *Supervision Outcomes—a Caseload Comparison.* (Richmond, VA.: Virginia Department of Corrections, 1988).

23. Mempa v. Rhay, 389 U.S. 128 (1967).

24. Stephen Gettinger, "Intensive Supervision: Can It Rehabilitate Probation?" *Corrections Magazine* 9 (April 1983): 7–8.

25. Joan Petersilia, National Institute of Justice, *House Arrest* (Washington, D.C.: U.S. Department of Justice, 1988), p. 2.

26. *Ibid.*, pp. 3–4.

27. "Man on House Arrest Confesses to 10 Rapes," *St. Petersburg Times,* 19 July 1989, p. 4B., col. 1.

28. See Ralph Kirkland Gable, "Application of Personal Telemonitoring to Current Problems in Corrections," *Journal of Criminal Justice* 14 (1986): 167–176. See also Joseph B. Vaughn, "Planning for Change: The Use of Electronic Monitoring as a Correctional Alternative," in Belinda R. McCarthy, ed., *Intermediate Punishments: Intensive Supervision, Home Confinement, and Electronic Surveillance* (Monsey, N.Y.: Criminal Justice Press, 1987), pp. 153–168. This source contains other pertinent and recent articles on house arrest and electronic monitoring.

29. Daniel Ford and Annesley K. Schmidt, "Electronically Monitored Home Confinement," *National Institute of Justice Reports* (November 1985): 2.

30. Rolando V. del Carmen and Joseph B. Vaughn, "Legal Issues in the Use of Electronic Surveillance in Probation," *Federal Probation* 50 (no. 2 1986): 60–69.

31. For recent information on electronic monitoring, see Mike Goss, "Electronic Monitoring: The Missing Link for Successful House Arrest," *Corrections Today* 51 (July 1989): 106–108, and Jerry Silvia, "Home Detention: New Technology Enhances Program," *Corrections Today* 51 (July 1989): 130–132.

32. "The Origins of Parole," in George G. Killinger and Paul F. Cromwell, Jr., eds.,

Corrections in the Community: Alternatives to Imprisonment (St. Paul, Minn.: West Publishing, 1974), p. 400. For information about the history and development of parole, see Michael R. Gottfredson and Don M. Gottfredson, *Decision-making in Criminal Justice: Toward the Rational Exercise of Discretion* (Cambridge, Mass.: Ballinger, 1980), pp. 281–372, and Neil Morgan, "The Shaping of Parole in England and Wales," *Criminal Law Review*, March 1983, pp. 137–151.

33. Barnes and Teeters, eds., *New Horizons*, pp. 417–422.

34. For an analysis of public opinion on parole in California, see Walter L. Barkdull, "Parole and the Public: a Look at Attitudes in California," *Federal Probation* 52 (no. 3, 1988): 15–20.

35. Richard J. Simmons, "M-2 (Man-to-Man) Job Therapy," chap. 9 in Calvert R. Dodge, ed., *A Nation Without Prisons: Alternatives to Incarceration* (Lexington, Mass.: D. C. Heath, 1975), p. 175.

36. Marc R. Levinson, "In South Carolina, Community Corrections Means the Alston Wilkes Society," *Corrections Magazine* 9 (June 1983): 41–46.

37. See Mary A. Toborg et al., *The Transition from Prison to Employment: An Assessment of Community-Based Assistance Programs*, National Institute of Law Enforcement and Criminal Justice, LEAA (Washington, D.C.: U.S. Government Printing Office, 1978), p. iii.

38. Ann D. Witte, "Work Release in North Carolina—A Program That Works!" *Law and Contemporary Problems* 41 (Winter 1977): 230–251.

39. For a review of the research on this subject, see Jonathan F. Katz and Scott H. Decker, "An Analysis of Work Release: The Institutionalization of Unsubstantiated Reforms," *Criminal Justice and Behavior* 9 (June 1982): 229–250.

40. Prince George's County Circuit Court Judge Vincent Femia, quoted in "Campaign Focus on Furloughs Prompts Review of Programs," *Criminal Justice Newsletter* 19 (1 December 1988), p. 3.

41. "Study of 53,000 Inmates on Furlough in '87 Finds Few Did Harm," *New York Times*, 12 October 1988, p. 12, col. 1.

42. Greenholtz v. Inmates of Nebraska Penal and Correctional Complex, 442 U.S. 1 (1979). See also Board of Pardons v. Allen, 482 U.S. 369 (1987).

43. Linda M. Trueb, "The Expectancy of Parole in Montana: A Right Entitled to Some Due Process," *Montana Law Review* 48 (Summer 1987): 390.

44. John Irwin, *The Felon* (Englewood Cliffs, N.J.: Prentice-Hall, 1970), p. 173.

45. Quoted in Jessica Mitford, *Kind and Usual Punishment: The Prison Business* (New York: Knopf, 1973), p. 216.

46. U.S. Department of Justice, *Sentencing and Parole Release, Classification Instruments for Criminal Justice Decisions*, vol. 4 (Washington, D.C.: U.S. Government Printing Office, 1979), p. 7.

47. See, for example, John S. Carroll, "Judgments of Recidivism Risk: The Use of Base-rate Information on Parole Decisions," in Paul D. Lipsitt and Bruce D. Sales, eds., *New Directions in Psycholegal Research* (New York: Van Nostrand Reinhold, 1980), pp. 66–86, and Don M. Gottfredson et al., *Guidelines for Parole and Sentencing: A Policy Control Method* (Lexington, Mass.: D. C. Heath, 1978).

48. See, for example, Harry L. Kozol et al., "The Diagnosis and Treatment of Dangerousness," *Crime and Delinquency* 18 (October 1972): 371–392, and Mark David Albertson, "Can Violence Be Predicted?" *Criminal Justice* 3 and 4 (Winter 1989): 18–21.

49. "The Future of Federal Parole: Interview with Benjamin F. Baer," *Corrections Today* 50 (October 1988): 36. For a brief account of the parole system in Mary-

land, see Paul J. Davis, "Parole in Maryland: Heading into a New Era," *Corrections Today* 51 (June 1989): 88.

50. Todd Clear, *Statistical Prediction in Corrections* (Washington, D.C.: National Institute of Corrections, March 1988), p. 35.

51. Mempa v. Rhay, 389 U.S. 128 (1967).

52. Morrissey v. Brewer, 408 U.S. 471 (1972).

53. Morrissey v. Brewer, 408 U.S. 471, 484 (1972).

54. Gagnon v. Scarpelli, 411 U.S. 778 (1973).

55. Bearden v. Georgia, 461 U.S. 660 (1983).

56. Black v. Romano, 471 U.S. 606 (1985), *reh. den.*, 473 U.S. 921 (1985).

57. Dana Eser Hunt, *Aids in Probation and Parole*, National Institute of Justice (Washington, D.C.: U.S. Department of Justice, June 1989).

58. *Ibid.*, pp. 3–10.

59. *Ibid.*, p. 15.

60. For an analysis of AIDS in New York, the state with the greatest problem, see Cathy Potler, *AIDS in Prison: A Crisis in New York State Corrections* (N.Y.: Correctional Association of New York, 1988).

61. Daniel Glaser, *The Effectiveness of a Prison and Parole System* (Indianapolis: Bobbs-Merrill, 1964).

62. Marvin E. Wolfgang et al., *Delinquency in a Birth Cohort* (Chicago: The University of Chicago Press, 1972).

63. See Marvin E. Wolfgang et al., *From Boy to Man, from Delinquency to Crime* (Chicago: University of Chicago Press, 1987).

64. Ralph W. England, "A Study of Postprobation Recidivism Among Five Hundred Federal Offenders," *Federal Probation* 19 (September 1955): 10–16; quotation is on p. 15, with emphasis in the original.

65. Joan Petersilia, *Probation and Felony Offenders*, Research in Brief, National Institute of Justice (Washington, D.C.: U.S. Department of Justice, March 1985), p. 4; emphasis deleted.

66. Joan Petersilia, "Rand's Research: A Closer Look," *Corrections Today* 47 (June 1985): 37.

67. Burton B. Roberts, Justice of the Bronx Supreme Court in New York City, quoted in *Criminal Justice Newsletter* 19 (1 March 1984): 1.

Glossary

administrative law regulations governing public administrative agencies, which affect private persons as the agencies make rules, investigate problems, and decide cases.

adultery sexual intercourse between two people when one is married to someone else or when both are married to other people.

adversary system a legal system involving a contest between two opponents, a prosecuting attorney and a defense attorney, both attempting to convince the judge and/or jury of their version of the case.

aggravated assault the unlawful use of force with a deadly weapon by one person against another with the intent to commit a violent personal crime such as murder or rape, or, in some states, with a hood or mask to conceal one's identity.

anomie a state of normlessness in society, which may be caused by decreased homogeneity and which provides a setting conducive to crimes and other antisocial acts.

antitrust laws state and federal governments have antitrust statutes to protect trade and commerce from unlawful restraints, such as price fixing, price discrimination, and monopolies.

appeal a step in a judicial proceeding, petitioning a higher court to review a lower court's decision. A case that has been so transferred is "on appeal."

appellant the losing party in a lower court who appeals to a higher court for review of the lower court's decision.

appellee the winning party in a lower court who argues on appeal that the lower court's decision was correctly made.

arraignment in criminal practice, the stage in the criminal justice system when the defendant appears before the court, hears the indictment, and pleads guilty or not guilty to the charges.

arrest depriving a person of his or her liberty; taking a person into custody for the purpose of formally charging him or her with a crime.

arrest warrant see **warrant**.

arson the willful and malicious burning of structures. Modern statutes often have a more severe penalty for the burning of a dwelling than of other real property.

bail a system of posting bond to guarantee a defendant's presence at trial while allowing the accused to be released until that time.

bail bondsman one who in return for a fee posts the bond for the accused and theoretically forfeits the money to the state if the defendant does not appear in court.

battered woman syndrome psychological, emotional, and physiological reactions suffered by a wife who has been battered by her spouse; recognized now by some courts as a defense when the victim murders her husband.

behavior theory theory based on the belief that all behavior is learned and can be unlearned. It is the basis for behavior modification, the approach used for changing behavior in both institutionalized and non-institutionalized settings.

biocriminology introduction of biological variables into the study of modern criminology

blackmail see extortion.

booking the process of officially recording an arrest and entering the suspect's name, offense charged, place, time, arresting officer, and reason for arrest; usually done at a police station by the arresting officer.

bribery offering money, goods, services, information, or anything else of value for the purpose of influencing public officials to act in a particular way.

burden of proof in a legal sense, the duty or necessity of proving a disputed fact as a case progresses. For example, in a criminal case the state has the burden of proving the defendant's guilt beyond a reasonable doubt.

Bureau of Justice Statistics (BJS) agency authorized by Congress in 1981 to furnish an objective, independent, and competent source of crime data to the government. The agency also analyzes data and issues reports on the amount and characteristics of crime.

burglary breaking and entering any type of enclosed structure without consent and with the intent to commit a felony.

capital punishment the imposition of the death penalty for an offender convicted of a capital offense.

career criminal a person who commits a variety of offenses over an extended period of time; also refers to offenders who specialize in particular types of crime, for example, burglary.

cartographic school an approach to criminology that uses population data to ascertain the influence of geographical phenomena, such as climate, location, and topography, and social conditions on criminal behavior.

case law the aggregate of reported judicial decisions, which are legally binding court interpretations of written statutes and previous court decisions or rules made by courts in the absence of written statutes or other sources of law. See also **common law.**

causation the idea that the occurrence of events is determined by cause-and-effect relationships. Causation assumes a relationship between two phenomena in which the occurrence of the former brings about changes in the latter. A *necessary cause* is one without which a given effect cannot occur; a *sufficient cause* is always followed or accompanied by a given effect and may or may not be a necessary cause. Indirect causation involves a chain of events leading to a final effect. In the legal sense, causation is the element of a crime that requires the existence of a causal relationship between the offender's conduct and the particular harmful consequences.

charge the formal allegation that a suspect has committed a specific offense. The term also means instructions on matters of law given by a judge to the jury.

chemical castration the use of female hormones to alter the chemical balance of a particular male's hormones, to reduce his sex drive and potency; has been used as a sentence on some sex offenders, but when appealed, courts have declared this punishment to be unconstitutional when imposed on an unwilling male.

child abuse physical and emotional abuse of children, including sexual abuse and child pornography.

civil law that part of the law concerned with the rules and enforcement of private or civil rights as distinguished from criminal law. In a civil suit, an individual who has been harmed seeks personal compensation in court rather than criminal punishment through state prosecution.

classical theorists writers and philosophers who argued that the punishment should fit the crime. The popularization of this school of thought led to the abolition of the death penalty and torture in some countries and generally to more humane treatment of criminals.

cognitive development psychological theory of behavior based on the belief that people organize their thoughts into rules and laws and that the way in which those thoughts are organized results in either criminal or noncriminal behavior. This organization of thoughts is called *moral reasoning*, and when applied to law, *legal reasoning*.

cohort the total universe of people defined by an event or events. For example, all children living in Minneapolis in 1990 and enrolled in the eighth grade constitute a cohort. This cohort might be interviewed or given questionnaires to gather data on delinquent behavior. At specified intervals, for example, every five years in the future, the cohort might again be tested to discover the existence of delinquent behavior.

common law broadly defined, common law is the body of law and legal theory that originated in England and was adopted in the United States; it is distinguished from Roman law, civil law, and canon law by its emphasis on the binding nature of interpretative court decisions. In a narrower sense, common law refers to the customs, traditions, judicial decisions, and other materials that guide courts in decision making, as opposed to the courts' use of written statutes or the Constitution. See also **case law**.

community-based corrections an approach to punishment that stresses reintegration of the offender into the community through the use of local facilities. As an alternative to incarceration, the offender may be placed in the community on probation or, in conjunction with imprisonment, in programs such as parole, furlough, work release, foster homes, or halfway houses.

computer crime commission of any crime involving the use of a computer.

concentric circle an ecological theory that divides cities into zones based on environmental qualities and attempts to find a relationship with crime and delinquency rates.

conflict approach in contrast with the consensus approach, the conflict approach views values, norms, and laws as creating dissension and conflict. Conflict thinkers do not agree on the nature or the source of the conflict; nor do they agree on what to call this perspective. The *pluralistic* approach sees conflict emerging from multiple sources, and the *critical* approach assumes that the conflict reflects the political power of the society's elite groups. Also called *Marxist, new conflict approach, New Criminology, materialist criminology,* and *socialist criminology*.

consensus approach an explanation of the evolution of law that considers law to be the formalized views and values of the people, arising from the aggregate of social values and developing through social interaction. Criminal law, then, is a reflection of societal values broader than the values of special interest groups and individuals.

conspiracy agreeing with another to join together for the purpose of committing an unlawful act, or agreeing to use unlawful means to commit an act that would otherwise be lawful. The unlawful act does not have to be committed; the crime of conspiracy involves the agreement to do the unlawful act.

constable term referring to the first police officers who presided over the hundreds in the frankpledge system. Today, the term refers to a municipal court officer whose duties include keeping the peace, executing court papers, transporting prisoners, and maintaining the custody of juries.

constitutional approach a theory of criminal behavior that assumes that behavior is influenced by the structure or physical characteristics of a person's body.

containment theory an explanation of criminal behavior that focuses on two insulating factors: first, the individual's favorable self-concept (definition of self) and commitment to long-range legitimate goals and, second, the pressure of the external social structure against criminal activity.

contempt of court an act done to embarrass, humiliate, or undermine the power of the court; may be civil or criminal; often is declared by a judge whose order has been violated.

control group in an experiment with two or more groups, the control group is used as a standard and is not introduced to the experimental variable. The control group is similar to the experimental group in all other relevant factors. Investigators can then measure the differences between the control and experimental groups before and after the variable is used with the experimental group.

corporal punishment infliction of penalties on the physical body.

corporate crime an intentional act or omission of an act that violates criminal statutory or case law and that is committed by individuals in a corporate organization for its benefit.

crime an intentional act or omission of an act that violates criminal statutory or case law and for which the state provides a specified punishment.

Crime Classification System (CCS) collection of crime data based on the severity of crimes and the effect of the crimes on victims.

crime rate in the *Uniform Crime Reports*, the number of offenses recorded per 100,000 population.

crimes known to the police the record of those serious offenses for which the police find evidence that the crime actually occurred.

criminal justice system the agencies responsible for enforcing criminal laws, including legislatures, police, courts, and corrections. Their decisions pertain to the prevention, detection, and investigation of crime; the apprehension, accusation, detention, and trial of suspects; and the conviction, sentencing, incarceration, or official supervision of adjudicated defendants.

criminal law the statutes and norms whose violation will subject the accused person to government prosecution. In general, criminal laws encompass those wrongs considered to be so serious as to threaten the welfare of the entire state.

criminologists those professionals who study crime, criminals, and criminal behavior.

cruel and unusual punishment punishment prohibited by the Eighth Amendment of the U.S. Constitution. The interpretation rests with the courts. Some examples are excessive lengths or conditions in sentences and the death penalty for rape without murder.

culture conflict theory an analysis of crime resting on clash-of-conduct norms, both of which are partially accepted and lead to contradictory standards and opposing loyalties. *Primary conflict* refers to the clash-of-conduct norms between two different cultures, and *secondary conflict* refers to the clash-of-conduct norms between groups in a single culture.

date rape   see rape.

defendant   in criminal law, the party charged with a crime and against whom a criminal proceeding is pending or has commenced.

defense attorney   the attorney who represents the accused in criminal proceedings before, during, and after trial and whose main function is to protect the legal rights of the accused.

demonology   a belief that persons are possessed by evil spirits that cause crime and other evil behavior and that this behavior can be eliminated only when the spirits are eliminated.

deprivation model   a theory of prisonization based on the belief that the inmate subculture arises from prisoners' adaptation to the severe physical and psychological losses imposed by incarceration.

determinate sentence   the length of the sentence is determined by the legislature, and no variation is allowed by the judge, the correctional institution, or the parole board.

determinism   a doctrine holding that one's options, decisions, and actions are decided by inherited or evironmental causes acting on one's character.

deterrence   a justification for punishment based on the prevention or discouragement of crime through fear or danger, as by punishing offenders to serve as examples to potential criminals or by incarcerating offenders to prevent them from committing further criminal acts.

differential anticipation theory   explains criminal behavior by postulating that when people consider the available legiti-

mate and illegitimate behaviors, they select the alternative that is perceived or anticipated to be the best. It makes no difference which actually is the best; it is the anticipation or perception of it that determines the choice.

differential association-reinforcement theory   a crime-causation theory based on the belief that criminal behavior is learned through associations with criminal behaviors and attitudes combined with a social-learning theory of operant conditioning. Criminal behavior, then, is learned through associations and is continued or discontinued as a result of the positive or negative reinforcement received.

differential association theory   denotes a person's associations that differ from those of other persons; a theory of crime causation resting on the belief that criminal behavior is learned through associations with criminal behavior and attitudes. A person who engages in criminal behavior can be differentiated by the quality or quantity of his or her learning through associations with those who define criminal activity favorably and the relative isolation from lawful social norms.

differential identification theory   explains criminal behavior by using the perspectives of others in determining one's own choices of behaviors. Those others may be real or imaginary people.

differential opportunity   a theory that attempts to combine the concepts of anomie and differential association by analyzing both the legitimate and the illegitimate opportunity structures available to individuals. Criminal behavior is possible because the environment has models of crime as well as opportunities to interact with those models.

discretion   in the criminal justice system, the authority to make decisions and choose among options according to one's own judgment rather than according to specific legal rules and facts. Discretionary decision making may result in actions tailored to individual circumstances and in inconsistent handling of offenders at several stages.

diversion correctly used, diversion removes the offender from the criminal justice system and channels him or her into, for example, a social welfare agency. Diversion has also been used to describe the handling of juveniles in a system separate from the adult criminal justice system and the sentencing of offenders to community-based correctional facilities rather than to prison.

double celling the practice of housing two (or more) inmates in a room designed for one.

dual court system the separate judicial structure of various levels of courts within each state in addition to the national structure of federal courts. The origin of the laws violated usually dictates whether the state or federal court is an appropriate forum for the case. The state system generally comprises lower and higher trial courts, appellate courts, and a state supreme court that governs the interpretation of laws within a state. The federal system comprises district trial courts, circuit appellate courts, and the U.S. Supreme Court. Trial courts hear factual evidence, and the issues are decided by a judge or a jury. Appellate court judges review the decisions of lower courts.

dualistic fallacy in criminological studies, the assumption that a population has two mutually exclusive subclasses, such as criminals and noncriminals.

due process a fundamental idea under the U.S. Constitution that a person should not be deprived of life, liberty, or property without reasonable and lawful procedures. The exact interpretation of what is required by due process rests with the courts.

Durham rule a test of insanity (also known as the product rule) that states that "an accused is not criminally responsible if his unlawful act was the product of mental disease or mental defect."

ecological school an approach to criminology that studies the quantitative relationship between geographic phenomena and crime.

embezzlement obtaining rightful possession of property with the owner's consent and subsequently wrongfully depriving the owner of that property.

entrapment a defense alleging that a government agent instigated a crime by making false representations, appealing to the defendant's sympathy or friendship, or offering an inducement to the defendant to commit a crime.

equal protection the constitutional principle that guarantees all people the same treatment in the criminal justice system regardless of their race, religion, or sex.

exclusionary rule the Fourth Amendment of the U.S. Constitution provides that "the right of the people to be secure in their persons, houses, papers and effects, against unreasonable searches and seizures shall not be violated and no warrants shall issue, but upon probable cause. . . ." Evidence seized in violation of the Fourth Amendment may be excluded from criminal trials; the most common examples of excluded evidence are statements made or property seized during an illegal arrest, search, or line-up. In recent cases, the Supreme Court has ruled that some illegally seized evidence may be used at trial.

ex post facto a law that provides punishment for an act that was not defined as a crime when the act was committed. It may also increase the penalty for a crime.

extortion obtaining property from another by wrongful use of actual or threatened force, fear, or violence, or the corrupt taking of a fee by a public officer, under color of his or her office, when that fee is not due.

false advertising the use of untrue statements or other forms of notice to solicit business from the public.

false pretenses representation of some fact or circumstance that is not true and that is meant to mislead the other party.

felony a serious type of offense, such as murder, armed robbery, or rape. Punishments for felonies range from imprisonment for one year to death.

felony-murder doctrine used to hold a defendant liable for murder if a human life is taken during the commission of another felony, such as armed robbery, kidnapping, or arson.

felony probation placing on probation an offender convicted of a felony.

fence a person who disposes of stolen goods.

fine a type of punishment in which the offender is ordered to pay a sum of money to the state in lieu of or in addition to other forms of punishment.

folkways norms of acting that arise from unconscious habits or routine ways of doing things. Folkways are the "correct" way of doing things because they are the traditional customs, habits, and behavior of a given group, tribe, or nation. Mild ridicule or ostracism follows the infringement of a folkway, whereas severe disapproval results from the infringement of mores.

forcible rape see rape.

forgery falsely making or altering, with the intent to defraud, a negotiable and legally enforceable instrument, such as a check.

fornication from the Latin word for brothel (*fornix*), meaning unlawful sexual intercourse between two unmarried persons.

frankpledge mutual pledge system in old English law, in which ten families, constituting a **tithing**, were responsible for the acts of all other members. Ten tithings constituted a **hundred**, which was under the charge of a **constable**, considered to be the first police officer. Hundreds were later combined to form **shires**, similar to counties, over which a **sheriff** had jurisdiction.

fraud falsely representing a fact, either by conduct or by words or writing, in order to induce a person to rely on the misrepresentation and surrender something of value.

free will a philosphy advocating punishment severe enough for people to choose to avoid criminal acts. It includes the belief that a certain criminal act warrants a certain punishment without any variation.

functional consequences a social system's beneficial and harmonious results from changes in one part of the system that have positive effects on another part.

furlough an authorized, temporary leave from prison, during which the inmate may be attending a funeral, visiting his or her family, or attempting to secure a job.

general deterrence the philosophy of punishment resting on the belief that punishment in an individual case will inhibit others from committing the same offense.

good-time credit credit resulting in a reduction of prison time; awarded for satisfactory behavior in prison.

graft popularly refers to the corruption of public officials to fraudulently obtain public money or position; the federal statute narrowly defines graft as the offering, giving, soliciting, or receiving of anything of value in connection with the procurement of materials under a federal defense program.

grand jury a group of citizens convened by legal authority to conduct secret investigations of evidence, evaluate accusations against suspects for trial, and issue indictments.

granny bashing physical abuse of elderly parents.

habeas corpus a written court order to bring the accused before the court to determine whether the defendant's custody and confinement are lawful under constitutional due process of law.

halfway house a prerelease center used to help the inmate in changing from prison life to community life or a facility that focuses on special adjustment problems of offenders, such as a drug or alcohol treatment center. The term is also used to describe a residential facility used as an alternative to prison for high-risk offenders considered unsuitable for probation.

hands-off doctrine a doctrine used by federal courts to justify nonintervention in the daily administration of correctional facilities; has been abandoned recently, but only when federal constitutional rights are at issue.

hedonism the belief that people choose pleasure and avoid pain. In law, its proponents advocate clearly written laws and certainty of punishment without any departure from the prescribed penalty.

house arrest a type of probation that permits the offender to remain at home under supervision. In some cases electronic monitoring of the offender's activities is used.

hundred see frankpledge.

immunity (criminal) exemption from criminal liability for acts that would otherwise be criminal.

importation model a theory of prisonization based on the idea that the inmate subculture arises not only from internal prison experiences but also from external patterns of behavior that the inmate brings to the prison.

incapacitation a theory of punishment and a goal of sentencing, generally implemented by incarcerating an offender to prevent him or her from committing any other crimes.

incarceration to confine in a jail or a prison as a form of punishment for a criminal act.

incest sexual relations between members of the immediate family, other than husband and wife.

indeterminate sentence the length of the sentence is determined not by the legislature or the court but by professionals at the institution or by parole boards that decide when an offender is ready to return to society. The actual sentence given by the judge may range from one day to life.

Index Offenses the serious crimes as reported by the FBI's *Uniform Crime Reports:* murder and nonnegligent manslaughter, forcible rape, robbery, aggravated assault, burglary, larceny-theft, motor vehicle theft, and arson.

indictment the grand jury's written accusation formally charging the named suspect with a criminal offense. An indictment arises from matters placed before the grand jury by the prosecutor.

individual (or specific) deterrence a philosophy of punishment based on the idea that the threat of punishment may prevent an individual from committing any crimes. The use of incarceration is an example.

information the most common formal document used to charge a person with a specific offense. The prosecutor, acting on evidence from police or citizens, files this document with the court, and it is tested at the preliminary hearing. Unlike the indictment, this procedure does not require participation by the grand jury.

initial appearance the defendant's first appearance before a magistrate; this process must take place quickly if the accused has been detained in jail after arrest. At the initial appearance the magistrate will decide whether probable cause exists to detain the suspect and, if so, tell the suspect of the charges and of his or her constitutional rights, including the right to an attorney.

inquisitory system a system in which the accused is presumed to be guilty and must prove his or her innocence.

insanity defense a defense that enables the defendant to be found not guilty because he or she does not have the mental ability required for legal responsibility for criminal behavior.

insider trading exists when officers, directors, and stockholders who own more than 10 percent of a corporation's stock that is listed on a national exchange buy and sell corporate shares based on information known to the officers before it is available to the public. Federal law requires that such transactions must be reported monthly to the Securities and Exchange Commission.

Intensive Probation Supervision (IPS) close supervision of probationers by probation officers who have smaller than average case loads.

intent in the legal sense, intent is the design, determination, or purpose with which a person uses a particular means to effect a certain result; it shows the presence of will in the act that consummates a crime.

irresistible impulse test a test for insanity stating that an accused cannot be found guilty for a criminal act if he or she is unable to control the actions leading to a crime even though the accused may have known the act was wrong. See also **M'Naghten rule** and **Substantial Capacity Test.**

jail a locally administered confinement facility used to detain persons awaiting a trial or those serving sentences of less than one year.

judge a judicial officer, elected or appointed to preside over a court of law. Judges are to be neutral and final arbiters of law and have primary responsibility for all court activities, ranging from monitoring the attorneys and instructing the jury to deciding cases and sentencing those found guilty.

judicial review the courts' power to determine whether legislative and executive acts infringe on the rights guaranteed by state constitutions and the U.S. Constitution. This power may be limited by statutes, case holdings, the U.S. Constitution itself, or by restrictions placed on federal courts with regard to interference in state matters.

jurisdiction the lawful right to exercise official authority, whether executive, judicial, or legislative; the territory of authority within which such power may be exercised. For the police, it refers to the geographical boundaries of power; for the courts, it refers to the power to hear and decide cases.

jury in a criminal case, a number of persons summoned to court and sworn to hear the trial, to determine certain facts, and to render a verdict of guilty or not guilty. In some jurisdictions, juries recommend or determine sentences.

just deserts the idea that an individual who commits a crime deserves to suffer for it; also called *retribution.*

justice model a philosophy holding that justice is achieved when offenders receive punishments based on what is deserved by their offenses as written in the law; the crime determines the punishment. In sentencing, this model presumes that prison should be used only as a last resort. Flat-time sentences are set for each offense. Parole is abolished, and early release can be achieved only through good-time credit.

labeling theory an attempt to explain deviance as a social process by which some people who commit deviant acts come to be known as deviants and others do not. Deviance is seen as a consequence of society's decision to apply that term to a person, and deviant behavior is behavior that society labels as deviant.

larceny see larceny-theft.

larceny-theft the taking of personal property without the owner's consent and with the intent to deprive the owner of it permanently. Historically, *petit larceny* involved small amounts, with imprisonment as punishment, and *grand larceny* involved larger amounts and the death penalty. Most modern theft statutes abolish the common law distinctions, and courts have ruled that the death penalty may not be imposed for larceny alone.

loan sharking lending money at very high interest rates and later using extortionate means to force the borrower to repay the loan.

magistrate a lower judicial officer in the state or federal court system.

mala in se acts morally wrong in themselves, such as rape, murder, or robbery.

mala prohibita acts that are wrong because they are prohibited by positive law, that is, legislation.

marital rape see rape.

mediation the act of attempting to settle claims between parties outside the courtroom; programs for noncourt settlement of disputes were instituted to help reduce the backlog of cases in the court systems.

mens rea criminal intent; the guilty or wrongful purpose of the defendant at the time he or she committed a criminal act.

Miranda **warning** the rule from *Miranda v. Arizona*, which mandates that before the interrogation of persons in custody, they must be told of their right to remain silent and that anything they say may be used as evidence against them and of their right to an attorney, who will be appointed if they cannot afford to hire one.

misdemeanor an offense less serious than a felony, such as disorderly conduct, prostitution or public drunkenness, and generally having a penalty of short-term incarceration in a local facility, a fine, or probation.

M'Naghten Rule frequently used as a test of insanity in American courts. For the insanity defense to be effective, the defendant at the time of the crime must have suffered from a defect of reason and consequently not have known the nature and quality of the act or that the act was wrong. In some jurisdictions, knowing the difference between right and wrong is still a defense if defendants can show that they had an "irresistible impulse" and therefore could not control their behavior. See also **substantial capacity test** and **irresistible impulse test.**

Model Penal Code the American Law Institute's codification of basic and general criminal law; often used as the basis for drafting new criminal laws.

mores the social norms that give a group or society its moral standards of behavior and that are considered essential to its preservation and welfare. Nonconformity to mores is severely sanctioned by the group, even though the term generally refers to those standards that have not been enacted as part of the formal criminal law.

murder the unlawful and unjustified killing of a human being with malice aforethought: the intent to kill, the intent to do great bodily harm, an act done in willful disregard of the strong likelihood that death or great injury would result, or a killing done during the commission of another felony.

National Crime Survey (NCS) victimization data collected and published annually by the Bureau of Justice Statistics (BJS).

National Incident-Based Reporting System (NABRS) a new method of collecting crime data which views crimes as involving numerous elements. Twenty-two crimes will be categorized when this system is implemented in the near future.

National Youth Survey (NYS) program for gathering data on crime by interviewing adolescents over a five-year period. The program has been structured to overcome many of the criticisms of other self-report studies.

neoclassical school those who argued that situations or circumstances that made it impossible to exercise free will were reasons to exempt the accused from conviction.

nonnegligent manslaughter see voluntary manslaughter.

norms the rules or standards of behavior shared by members of a group or society and defined by the common expectations of the group with regard to the types of appropriate behaviors.

offender a person who commits an offense; used in statutes to describe a person implicated in the commission of a crime.

organized crime the highly structured association of people who bind together to make large profits through illegal and legal means while utilizing graft and corruption in the criminal justice arena to protect their activities from criminal prosecution.

overrule because the courts are flexible they may reverse a previous decision.

pardon an act by the head of state that exempts an individual from punishment for a crime he or she committed and removes the legal consequences of the conviction. Pardons may be absolute or have conditions attached; may be individual or granted to a group or class of offenders; or may be partial, in which case the pardon remits only part of the punishment or removes some of the legal disabilities resulting from conviction.

parole the continued custody and supervision in the community by federal or state authorities after an offender is released from an institution before expiration of the sentenced term. Parolees who violate the conditions of parole may be returned to the institution.

parole boards the panels at the state and federal levels that decide how much of a sentence an offender will serve in the institution and whether he or she is ready to return to society with continued supervision in the community.

parole officer the government employee responsible for counselling and supervising inmates released on parole in the community.

penitentiary state or federal prison or place of punishment used for the confinement of offenders convicted of serious crimes and sentenced for a term of more than one year.

peremptory challenges challenges by prosecution or defense attorneys to excuse a potential juror from the jury panel. No reason is required. Each side is entitled to a specified number of peremptory challenges.

phrenology a theory of behavior based on the idea that the exterior of the skull corresponds to the interior and to the brain's conformation; thus a propensity toward certain types of behavior may be discovered by examining the "bumps" on the head.

plea bargaining the negotiation between the prosecution and the defense for reduction of the punishment. Normally, the charge is reduced in return for the defendant's plea of guilty to a lesser charge or a promise of cooperation with the prosecutor in providing evidence or testimony in other cases.

police local law enforcement officials within the department of government that maintains and enforces law and order throughout a geographical area.

positive school a belief that the study of crime should emphasize the individual, scientific treatment of the criminal, not the postconviction punishment. Adherents believed that the punishment should fit the criminal, not the crime.

postraumatic stress disorder (PTSD) legally recognized defense to criminal behavior in some countries; refers to severe trances or flashbacks characteristic of some men who fought in Vietnam.

prediction scales statistical measurements of antecedent factors used to identify those variables that make more probable the occurrence of a future event or behavior. The scales are then used to predict the success or failure of persons, based on the presence or absence of these variables. These scales or tables have been used to predict results in such areas as marriage, parole, and delinquent or criminal behavior.

preliminary hearing an open court proceeding before a judge, used to determine if there is probable cause to believe that the defendant committed a crime and should be held for trial.

premenstrual tension syndrome (PMS) tension suffered by some women before and during menstruation; in some countries, a legally recognized defense to criminal bchavior.

prerelease programs a system of programs within institutions that assist inmates in adjusting to life in normal society. The programs cover subjects such as money management, interviewing for jobs, and basic social skills.

presumptive sentencing a method for determining punishment in which the legislature sets a standard sentence in the statute, but the judge may vary that sentence if the case has mitigating or aggravating circumstances.

preventive detention a practice of holding the accused in jail before trial to ensure that he or she will not commit further crimes and will be present at trial. This may be done illegitimately by setting the bail so high that the accused cannot raise the money or legitimately by statutory provision.

prison a state or federal custodial facility for the confinement of adults sentenced to more than one year.

prisonization the process by which a prison inmate assimilates the customs, norms, values, and culture of prison life.

proactive the response of the police to criminal behavior in which they actively detect crimes and seek offenders rather than rely on citizens' reports of crimes.

probable cause an evidentiary standard; a set of facts and circumstances that justifies a reasonably intelligent and prudent person's belief that an accused person has committed a specific crime.

probation a judicial determination in which the offender is allowed to remain in the community under conditioned supervision. The term also refers to the component of the criminal justice system that administers all phases of probation.

probation officer the official employed by a probation agency who is responsible for preparing presentence reports, supervising offenders placed on probation, and helping them integrate into society as lawful citizens.

property crimes those crimes not directed toward the person, such as burglary, larceny-theft, motor vehicle theft, or arson.

prosecuting attorney a government official whose duty is to initiate and maintain criminal proceedings on behalf of the government against persons accused of committing crimes.

psychiatry a field of medicine that specializes in the understanding, diagnosis, treatment, and prevention of mental problems.

psychoanalysis a special branch of psychiatry based on the theories of Sigmund Freud and employing a particular personality theory and method of treatment; the approach concentrates on individual case study.

public defender an attorney (a government officer) whose function is to represent defendants who cannot afford to hire private lawyers.

rape unlawful sexual intercourse; called **forcible rape** if committed against the victim's will by the use of threats or force. **Statutory rape** refers to consensual sexual intercourse with a consenting person who is below the legal age of consent. In **date rape,** the victim has voluntarily chosen to be with the offender and may have agreed to some intimacy but has not agreed to sexual intercourse which occurs by force. **Marital rape** occurs when the victim of forced intercourse is the spouse. See also **rape by instrumentation.**

rape by instrumentation any intrusion by the male penis of any part of a person's body that could be interpreted for the purpose of sexual arousal or gratification or as an act of violence, or the forced intrusion of any object into the genital or anal openings of another person's body. See also **rape.**

reactive the response of police to criminal behavior in which they rely on notification by citizens that a crime has been committed instead of actively detecting crimes and seeking offenders.

recidivism may mean further violations of the law by released inmates, or it may denote noncriminal violations of conditions by probationers and parolees.

reformatory correctional facility that is less secure and that at least in theory has as its primary goal the rehabilitation of offenders.

rehabilitation the rationale for reformation of offenders, based on the premise that human behavior is the result of antecedent causes that may be known by objective analysis and permit scientific control of human behavior. The focus is on treatment, not punishment, of the offender.

reintegration a philosophy of punishment that focuses on returning the offender to the community with restored education, employment, and family ties.

restitution a type of punishment in which the offender must reimburse the victim financially or with services. It may be required in lieu of or in addition to a fine or other punishment or as a condition of probation.

retribution a theory of punishment that contends that an offender should be punished for the crimes committed because he or she deserves it.

revenge a doctrine under which a person who violates the law should be punished in the same way the victim suffered.

robbery taking personal property from the possession of another against his or her will by the use of force or fear.

routine activity theory a theory explaining crime by means of three elements: (1) likely offenders (people who are motivated to commit crimes), (2) suitable targets (presence of things that are valuable and that can be transported fairly easily), and (3) absence of capable guardians (people who can prevent the criminal activity).

search warrant see **warrant.**

sedition communications, either written or oral, that are aimed at overthrowing the government by stirring up treason or other crimes or by defaming the government.

self-concept see **containment theory.**

self-defense a legal defense for using whatever force or reasonable means is necessary to protect oneself from violence or threatened violence.

self-report data (SRD) method of collecting data by asking people to give information about their prior involvement in crime; based on selected samples of the total population or a subset such as juveniles or incarcerated criminals. Data may be obtained in several ways, such as by anonymous questionnaires or interviews.

sentence the decision of the judge or jury, according to statutory law, fixing the punishment for an offender after conviction.

sentencing the postconviction stage in the criminal justice system that includes all those decisions the court makes with regard to the official handling of a person who pleads guilty or is convicted of a crime.

sentencing disparity a term used to describe the variations and inequities that result when defendants convicted of the same crime receive sentences of different lengths.

serial murderers persons who commit more than one murder but at different times, in contrast with mass murderers, who murder a number of people at one time.

sheriff a county's chief law enforcement officer, usually elected by popular vote, who performs such varied functions as collecting county taxes, supervising some government activities, and serving as the county coroner in some jurisdictions.

shires see **frankpledge.**

social-control theory an explanation of criminal behavior that focuses on the control mechanisms, techniques, and strategies for regulating human behavior, leading to conformity or obedience to the society's rules, and that argues that deviance results when social controls are weakened or break down so that individuals are not motivated to conform to them.

socialization the basic lifelong social process by which an individual is integrated into a social group by learning its culture, values, and social roles.

social-learning theory based on the assumption that although human aggression may be influenced by physiological characteristics, their activation depends on learning and is subject to the person's control. Social learning thus determines whether aggressive behavior will occur and, if so, the nature of that behavior.

social system the interrelationship of acts, roles, and statuses of the various people who make up the social structure; a social group or set of interacting persons or groups considered a unitary whole because it reflects the common values, social norms, and objectives of the individuals who comprise it, even though it is considered distinct from those individuals.

sociobiology the application of principles of biology to the study of social behavior.

sociopath modern term for psychopathy; referring to a person who is antisocial, highly impulsive, aggressive, and appears to have little or no concern for society's values. The person has difficulty establishing meaningful relationships with others.

sodomy   historically, a term that referred to both bestiality (intercourse between a human and an animal) and buggery (anal intercourse by a man with another man or with a woman) and that was called a *crime against nature*. In more modern statutes, the term is often used to refer to any type of sexual relations considered to be "unnatural," including buggery and bestiality as well as oral sex.

status offense   a class of crime that does not consist of proscribed action or inaction, but of the personal condition or characteristic of the accused, for example, being a vagrant. In juvenile law, may refer to a variety of acts that would not be considered criminal if committed by an adult. Examples are being insubordinate, truant, or a runaway.

statutory law   law created or defined in a written enactment by the legislature, as opposed to case law.

statutory rape   see rape.

Stockholm syndrome   incongruous feeling of empathy by hostages toward the hostage takers and a displacement of frustration and aggression on the part of the victims against the authorities.

subculture   an identifiable segment of society or group having specific patterns of behavior, folkways, and mores that set that group apart from the other groups within a culture or society.

substantial capacity test or ALI Rule   a test of insanity that states that a person cannot be held accountable for a criminal act if he or she is unable to appreciate the wrongfulness of that act because of a mental disease or defect. See also **M'Naghten rule** and **irresistible impulse test.**

syndicate   group of persons who organize for the purpose of carrying out matters (usually financial) of mutual interest, not illegal by definition, but often associated with illegal activities such as organized crime.

terrorism   violent acts or the use of the threat of violence to create fear, alarm, dread, or coercion, usually against governments.

tithing   see frankpledge.

tort   the area of law referring to civil wrongs such as slander and libel and automobile, industrial, or another type of accident caused by negligence, medical malpractice, and trespassing on property. Some actions, such as trespassing on property and assault and battery, are crimes as well as torts.

transportation   the historical practice of deporting criminals to other countries as punishment.

treason   the act of betraying or otherwise attempting to overthrow the government to which one owes allegiance.

trial   the formal fact-finding process in court in which all evidence in a case is presented and a decision is made by the judge or jury about whether the defendant is guilty, beyond a reasonable doubt, of criminal charges.

Uniform Crime Reports (UCR)   the official government source of national crime data; collected, compiled, and published by the Federal Bureau of Investigation.

utilitarianism   the ethical theory that makes the happiness of the individual or society the end and the criterion of the morally good and right. In politics, this means that the greatest happiness of the greatest number is the sole end and criterion of all public action.

victimless crimes   offenses that interfere with the normative order of society; also called public order crimes. Examples are vagrancy, disorderly conduct, gambling, narcotics offenses, public drunkenness, and some types of sexual behavior.

victims' compensation programs plans for providing a variety of services to victims to help them face the emotional, social, and economic consequences of crime.

violent crimes serious crimes against the person (as contrasted to serious crimes against property): forcible rape, robbery, murder and nonnegligent manslaughter, and aggravated assault, as defined by the FBI and published in its *Uniform Crime Reports* in its Index Offenses.

voluntary manslaughter an intentional killing under mitigating circumstances of adequate provocation, mistaken justification, or diminished capacity, which reduce the offense from murder to manslaughter; also called *nonnegligent manslaughter.*

warrant a writ issued by a court authorizing specific acts by law enforcement officials, for example, the arrest of a person or the search of a specific place.

watch system system of policing that existed in early England and in Colonial America. Bellmen regularly walked throughout the city, ringing bells and pro-viding police services. Later they were replaced by a permanent watch of citizens and still later by paid constables.

white-collar crimes the term used to describe violations of the law by persons with higher status; it usually refers to corporate or individual crimes in connection with businesses or occupations regarded as a legitimate part of society.

work release an authorized absence that allows the inmate to hold a job or attend school but that requires him or her to return to the institution during nonworking hours.

writ of certiorari a document issued to a lower court directing that the record of a case be transferred to the superior court for review.

XYY chromosome theory a constitutional theory of criminal behavior based on the premise that there is a relationship between the extra Y chromosome found in some males and a propensity toward criminal activity.

Appendix A: Guide to Legal Citations of Reported Decisions

Furman v. Georgia   408 U.S. 238, 308 (1972).

The name of the case [*Furman v. Georgia*] is followed by the volume number [408] and the abbreviated title of the reporter [U.S.]; next is the page number on which the case begins [238]; the second number [308] denotes the page on which the cited material or quotation appears; the date follows in parentheses [(1972)]. This basic format is used for all case citations. Following is a list of reporter abbreviations, later case history, and explanatory abbreviations:

At., At.2d; Atlantic Reporter, Atlantic Reporter Second Series

Cal. Rptr: California Reporter

F.2d: Federal Reporter Second Series

F.Supp: Federal Supplement

N.Y.S.2d: New York Supplement Second

N.W., N.W.2d: North Western Reporter, North Western Reporter Second Series

N.E., N.E.2d: North Eastern Reporter, North Eastern Reporter Second Series

P.,P.2d: Pacific Reporter, Pacific Reporter Second Series

S.E., S.E.2d: South Eastern Reporter, South Eastern Reporter Second Series

S.Ct.: Supreme Court Reporter

U.S.: United States Reports

Wis.: Wisconsin Reporter

Aff'd: affirmed; the appellate court confirms and ratifies the decision of the lower court. *Aff'd sub nom* means that the name of the case is not the same at the appellate court as it was in the lower court. *Aff'd per curiam* means that the opinion was written by the court as opposed to being written by a single judge.

cert. denied: certiorari denied; the U.S. Supreme Court refused to grant the writ of certiorari thereby refusing to hear and decide the case.

concurring opinion: an opinion of a judge that agrees with the result but disagrees with the reasoning of the majority opinion.

dissenting opinion: an opinion of a judge that disagrees with the result and the reasoning of the majority opinion.

reh. denied: rehearing denied; the court refuses to consider the case a second time.

remanded: sent back to the lower court for another decision.

rev'd: reversed; overthrown, set aside, made void, changed to the contrary or to a former decision. The court on appeal may reverse the lower court decision *and* remand the case for the lower court to give another decision.

vacated: annulled, set aside, rendered void.

Index of Cases

Index of Names

Subjects

CREDITS AND PERMISSIONS

13, Wide World Photos. 14, Wide World Photos. 44, Wide World Photos. 52, Wide World Photos. 91, Bettmann Archives. 93, Bettmann Archives. 98, Wide World Photos. 103, Wide World Photos. 142, Wide World Photos. 165, Wide World Photos. 195, Wide World Photos. 227, Wide World Photos. 238, Wide World Photos. 264, Wide World Photos. 283, Wide World Photos. 326, Wide World Photos. 334, Wide World Photos. 360, Wide World Photos. 363, Wide World Photos. 404, Wide World Photos. 415, Wide World Photos. 442, Wide World Photos. 451, Wide World Photos. 482, Wide World Press. 486, Wide World Photos. 494, Sue Titus Reid. 533, Wide World Photos. 536, Wide World Photos. 586, Sue Titus Reid. 593, Wide World Photos. 597, Wide World Photos. 637, Wide World Photos.

27, Cartoon, "The Media is Asking . . . Beefed up War on Drugs!" by Wayne Stayskal, from *The Tampa Tribune-Times*, August 20, 1989. Copyright © 1989 by and reprinted by permission of Wayne Stayskal/The Tampa Tribune-Times.